Lecture Notes in Computer Science 13511

More information about this series at https://link.springer.com/bookseries/558

Alex Orailoglu · Marc Reichenbach ·
Matthias Jung (Eds.)

Embedded Computer Systems: Architectures, Modeling, and Simulation

22nd International Conference, SAMOS 2022
Samos, Greece, July 3–7, 2022
Proceedings

 Springer

Editors
Alex Orailoglu
University of California
La Jolla, CA, USA

Marc Reichenbach
BTU-Cottbus Senftenberg
Cottbus, Germany

Matthias Jung
Fraunhofer IESE
Kaiserslautern, Germany

ISSN 0302-9743   ISSN 1611-3349 (electronic)
Lecture Notes in Computer Science
ISBN 978-3-031-15073-9   ISBN 978-3-031-15074-6 (eBook)
https://doi.org/10.1007/978-3-031-15074-6

This Springer imprint is published by the registered company Springer Nature Switzerland AG
The registered company address is: Gewerbestrasse 11, 6330 Cham, Switzerland

Preface

SAMOS is a conference with a unique format. It brings together every year researchers from both academia and industry on the topic of embedded systems in the perfect setting of the island of Samos. Last year the conference was held virtually due to the COVID-19 pandemic, but this year SAMOS took place in person during July 3–7, 2022.

The SAMOS 2022 keynotes covered a wide range of embedded systems design aspects, including talks on future microprocessors by Yale Patt, University of Texas at Austin, extreme-scale virtual screening by Cristina Silvano, Polimi, and power monitors by William Fornaciari, Polimi. A specific focus was also put on machine learning and memory systems through tutorials by Michele Saad, Adobe, and Onur Mutlu, ETH Zurich.

The SAMOS 2022 proceedings comprise a selection of publications targeting either systems themselves - through their applications, architectures, and underlying processors - or methods created to automate their design. A total of 44 papers were submitted to the conference and 21 papers were selected by the Program Committee to be presented at SAMOS 2022 (48% acceptance rate). Two special sessions were included in the program to gather novel work on security and to report recent results of European projects.

The SAMOS 2022 committee would like to acknowledge the generous support of the many reviewers who contributed to the quality of these proceedings. We hope that you enjoy reading them!

July 2022

Alex Orailoglu
Marc Reichenbach
Matthias Jung

Organization

General Chair

Alex Orailoglu   University of California, San Diego, USA

Program Chairs

Marc Reichenbach   Brandenburg University of Technology
Cottbus-Senftenberg, Germany

Matthias Jung   Fraunhofer IESE, Germany

Special Session Chairs

Innovative Architectures and Tools for Security

Francesco Regazzoni   Università della Svizzera italiana, Switzerland,
and University of Amsterdam, The Netherlands

European Research Projects on Digital Systems, Services, and Platforms

Giovanni Agosta   Politecnico di Milano, Italy
Jasmin Jahic   University of Cambridge, UK
Dimitrios Soudris   National Technical University of Athens, Greece

Tutorial Chairs

Michele Saad   Adobe, USA
Onur Mutlu   ETH Zurich, Switzerland

Web Chair

Jasmin Jahic   University of Cambridge, UK

Proceedings and Finance Chair

Carlo Galuzzi   Delft University of Technology, The Netherlands

Submission and Publicity Chair

Andy D. Pimentel   University of Amsterdam, The Netherlands

Steering Committee

Shuvra Bhattacharyya	University of Maryland, College Park, USA, and IETR, France
Holger Blume	Leibniz Universität Hannover, Germany
Ed F. Deprettere	Leiden University, The Netherlands
Nikitas Dimopoulos	University of Victoria, Canada
Carlo Galuzzi	Delft University of Technology, The Netherlands
Georgi N. Gaydadjiev	Maxeler Technologies, UK
John Glossner	Optimum Semiconductor Technologies, USA
Walid Najjar	University of California, Riverside, USA
Andy D. Pimentel	University of Amsterdam, The Netherlands
Olli Silvén	University of Oulu, Finland
Dimitrios Soudris	National Technical University of Athens, Greece
Jarmo Takala	Tampere University, Finland
Stephan Wong	TU Delft, The Netherlands

Program Committee

Giovanni Agosta	Politecnico di Milano, Italy
Shuvra Bhattacharyya	University of Maryland, College Park, USA
Holger Blume	Leibniz Universität Hannover, Germany
Luigi Carro	UFRGS, Brazil
Jeronimo Castrillon	TU Dresden, Germany
Ricardo Chaves	INESC-ID, Portugal
Francesco Conti	UniBo, Italy
Karol Desnos	INSA Rennes, France
Vassilios V. Dimakopoulos	University of Ioannina, Greece
Giorgos Dimitrakopoulos	Democritus University of Thrace, Greece
Nikitas Dimopoulos	University of Victoria, Canada
Lide Duan	University of Texas at San Antonio, USA
Holger Flatt	Fraunhofer IOSB, Germany
Carlo Galuzzi	Delft University of Technology, The Netherlands
Georgi N. Gaydadjiev	Maxeler Technologies, UK
Andreas Gerstlauer	University of Texas at Austin, USA
John Glossner	Optimum Semiconductor Technologies Inc., USA
Diana Goehringer	TU Dresden, Germany
Xinfei Guo	University of Virginia, USA
Soonhoi Ha	Seoul National University, South Korea
Frank Hannig	University of Erlangen-Nuremberg, Germany
Christian Haubelt	University of Rostock, Germany
Jasmin Jahić	University of Cambridge, UK
Pekka Jääskeläinen	Tampere University, Finland

Theo Ungerer	University of Augsburg, Germany
Carlos Valderrama	University of Mons, Belgium
Norbert Wehn	TU Kaiserslautern, Germany
Stephan Wong	Delft University of Technology, The Netherlands
Roger Woods	Queen's University Belfast, UK

Additional Reviewers

Muhammad Ali
Lilas Alrahis
J. L. F. Betting
Viralii Burtsev
Alessio Colucci
Rafael Fao de Moura
Fernando Fernandes dos Santos
Conrad Foik
Davide Gadioli
Bagus Hanindhito
Veronia Iskandar
Mihir Kekkar
Nesrine Khouzami
Troya Kyl
Christos Lamprakos

Alberto Marchisio
Ricardo Nobre
Elbruz Ozen
Sotirios Panagiotou
Daniele Passaretti
Christodoulos Peltekis
Patrick Plagwitz
Bastian Schulte
Matteo Scrugli
Kyuhong Shim
Dennis Sprute
Qinzhe Wu
Hanzhi Xun
Sicong Yuan

Contents

High Level Synthesis

High-Level Synthesis of Digital Circuits from Template Haskell and SDF-AP

H. H. Folmer[1]([⊠]) [iD], R. de Groote[2], and M. J. G. Bekooij[1]

[1] CAES: Computer Architectures for Embedded Systems, University of Twente, Enschede, Netherlands
{h.h.folmer,m.j.g.bekooij}@utwente.nl
[2] Saxion Hogeschool, Enschede, Netherlands
e.degroote@saxion.nl

Abstract. Functional languages as input specifications for HLS-tools allow to specify data dependencies but do not contain a notion of time nor execution order. In this paper, we propose a method to add this notion to the functional description using the dataflow model SDF-AP. SDF-AP consists of patterns that express consumption and production that we can use to enforce resource usage. We created an HLS-tool that can synthesize parallel hardware, both data and control path, based on the repetition, expressed in Higher-Order Functions, combined with specified SDF-AP patterns.

Our HLS-tool, based on Template Haskell, generates an Abstract Syntax Tree based on the given patterns and the functional description uses the Clash-compiler to generate VHDL/Verilog.

Case studies show consistent resource consumption and temporal behavior for our HLS-tool. A comparison with a commercially available HLS-tool shows that our tool outperforms in terms of latency and sometimes in resource consumption.

The method and tool presented in this paper offer more transparency to the developer and allow to specify more accurately the synthesized hardware compared to what is possible with pragmas of the Vitis HLS-tool.

1 Introduction

A functional program describes a set of functions and their composition. Referential transparency/side-effect free, a key feature of functional languages, not only makes formal reasoning easier but also prevents unwanted so-called false dependencies in the specification. Because of this, functional specifications are inherently parallel, and as a consequence, there is no need for parallelism extraction [8]. In the approach taken in this paper, we use a functional input language for hardware development. Functional specifications can neither specify resource consumption nor temporal behavior, only data dependencies and (basic)operations. To synthesize FPGA logic, the notion of both time and resource usage have to be introduced. Due to a limited resource budget, one

A. Orailoglu et al. (Eds.): SAMOS 2022, LNCS 13511, pp. 3–27, 2022.
https://doi.org/10.1007/978-3-031-15074-6_1

often has to perform a time-area trade-off. Modelling time and resource consumption during the development stage could speed up the design process and indicate whether a certain design will meet the time and resource requirements. Temporal modelling can also be used for latency and throughput analysis, and buffer size optimizations.

In this paper, we introduce a method to combine a functional description with consumption and production patterns according to the Static Data-Flow with Access Patterns (SDF-AP) model [31]. Given this specification, we generate a hardware design that is *correct by construction*. We have created an High-Level Synthesis (HLS) tool that implements the methods proposed in this paper. The tool uses the Clash-compiler and is part of the Haskell ecosystem [2]. The Clash language is a subset of Haskell functional language and can be converted to VHDL or Verilog using the Clash-compiler. The input specification is a purely functional description that only describes data dependencies. This input description can be automatically converted to a *fully combinational circuit* in VHDL or Verilog using the Clash-compiler. The input description does not contain any clocked behavior and can be simulated and checked using the Haskell/Clash Interactive environment. Often, due to resource constraints, the fully parallel description can not be synthesized as one combinational circuit because it does not fit on the FPGA or is too slow due to the length of the combinational path. Our tool uses Template Haskell to convert the combinational Clash description into a clocked Clash description where hardware resources are shared over time, and registers and blockRAMs are introduced for (intermediate) storage. This clocked description can also be simulated and checked in the Haskell/Clash Interactive environment. This method allows for an *iterative design* style because one can make a change to an individual node in the SDF-AP graph and test the functional and temporal behavior in the same environment without entering the entire synthesis pipeline.

The proposed method uses access patterns from SDF-AP to provide the engineer with a transparent way of performing the time-area trade-off. The architecture generated is consistent with the given functional input description in combination with access patterns from the SDF-AP graph. The validity of these patterns can be checked by the compiler. Invalid patterns will terminate the compilation process. Changes to the access patterns consistently scale the resulting hardware architecture. This consistency is required to provide an engineer with transparency on the consequences of his design choices. Another advantage of the usage of the SDF-AP model is that it allows for the usage of the analysis methods available [10].

Many of the current state-of-the-art HLS-tools have C/C++ as input specification. These languages are well known, have a large codebase, and a standard compiler already exists that can parse and check the code. Imperative languages may allow direct control over storage, which was desirable for programming small embedded Von-Neumann devices but this could also apply to the synthesis of hardware architectures. However, deriving true data dependencies and parallelism from sequential C++ code proves to be difficult [17]. To find only true data dependencies for a language that has pointers, one encounters the pointer aliasing problem which is undecidable [18,24]. Therefore, the dependencies derived from the imperative input specification could contain false dependencies which limit the scheduling. The current state-of-the-art HLS-tools like Vitis have introduced pragmas to allow the engineer to annotate the input specification to prevent false dependencies and influence the time-area trade-off [32]. However, as opposed to the access patterns in our method, these pragmas can be ignored by the compiler, which makes the design process not transparent. Our case studies show that sometimes the Vitis compiler ignores pragmas and generated inefficient designs.

In Sect. 2 we discuss several temporal modelling and design techniques. In Sect. 3 we explain the SDF-AP model and in Sect. 4 we explain the basic idea of how we combined this model with a functional description. The further workings of the HLS tool and design flow are described in Sect. 4.1. An example of code and some limitations of the tool are discussed in Sect. 5. Section 6 contains three case studies, where we demonstrate the capabilities of our tool on a dot-product, Center of Mass (CoM) computations on images, and a 2D DCT. The case studies demonstrate the effects of different access patterns and node decomposition on latency, throughput, and resource usage. We also compare different versions in each case study with results from the Vitis HLS tool. The input specification for Vitis is C++ code with pragmas to introduce parallelism.

2   Related Work

2.1   High-Level Synthesis Tools

HLS is an active research topic and many major contributions have been made towards it. Cong et al. give an overview of early HLS-tool developments [4]. They summarize the purpose and goals of HLS and indicate that there are many opportunities for further improvement. Traditional HLS-tools use an imperative language as a behavioral input description and usually generate a Control Data Flow Graph (CDFG) [5]. The next step is to, given constraints, generate a structural Register-Transfer Level (RTL) description. AutoPilot (a predecessor of the Vivado HLS-tool) is used to demonstrate the effectiveness of HLS, given a specification in C/C++. They conclude that for C/C++ programs it remains difficult to capture parallelism which complicates both design and verification.

Sun et al. point out that resource sharing and scheduling are two major features in HLS techniques that the current HLS-tools still struggle with [29]. An important point that they make is that the HLS-tool obfuscates the relationship between the source code and the generated hardware, which in turn makes it hard to identify suboptimal parts of the code. This non-transparency in the design flow is one of the aspects that this paper addresses. Sun et al. also claim that for effective usage of HLS-tools, a rigorous understanding of the expected hardware is required.

Schafer et al. give a summary of multiple techniques used in the HLS process [25]. Controlling the process is typically done by setting different synthesis options, also called knobs. The authors classify these knobs into three families: The first knob is synthesis directives added to the source code in the form of comments or pragmas. The second exploration knob is global synthesis options that apply to the entire behavioral description to be synthesized. The last exploration knob allows users to control the number and type of Functional Unit (FU)s. Reducing the number of FUs forces the HLS process to share resources, which might lead to smaller designs, albeit increasing the designs latency.

Lahti et al. present a survey of the scientific literature published since 2010 about the Quality of Results (QoR) and productivity differences between the HLS and RTL design flows [17]. The survey indicates that even the newest generation of HLS-tools do not provide as good performance and resource usage as manual RTL does. Using an HLS-tool increases productivity by a factor of six, but iterative design is required.

Huang et al. present a survey paper of the scientific literature published since 2014 on performance improvements of HLS-tools [13]. The survey contains a summary of both commercial and academic tools of which 13 of the 16 tools use C/C++ (subset) as input language. In their conclusion, they state that the main work of optimization of HLS-tools is on improving the QoR but insufficient attention has been paid to improve the ease of use of the HLS-tools.

In our method, we use a functional language as input specification. Whereas traditional HLS-tools need to generate structure from a behavioral description, our functional input specification already contains structure. We are not required to obtain parallelism or derive only true dependencies because parallelism is implicit and the functional specification only contains true data dependencies [8]. To find only true data dependencies for a language that has pointers, one encounters the pointer aliasing problem which is undecidable [18,24]. Functional languages offer concepts like function composition, referential transparency, Higher-order function (HOF)s, and types, that provide a high level of abstraction [1,2].

2.2 Temporal Models for Hardware Design

There are several models available to analyze temporal behavior for hardware. Lee and Messerschmitt introduced the Static Data-Flow (SDF) model and it consists of nodes, edges and tokens, where edges have consumption and production values that specify the number of data elements (tokens) to be produced and consumed [21]. A node can fire when it has sufficient tokens, according to the consumption rates, on all of its input edges, and will produce tokens, according to the production rate, on all of its output edges at the end of its firing.

Horstmannshoff et al. glue high-level components together, usually from a library, by mapping SDF to an RTL communication architecture [11,12]. Multirate specifications are implemented as sequential components. They present SDF without a notion of time in the model and the presumption that every component, after an initialization, performs its calculation periodically. Every component is slowed down to the period of the entire system using clock gating or adding registers (re-timing). They use SDF analysis techniques such as the repetition vector and topology matrix to determine how much every node (component) should be delayed. A central control unit is introduced to provide the correct control signals to the datapath.

The GRAPE-II framework provides a sequential implementation of multi-rate dataflow graphs (SDF, Cyclo-Static Data-Flow (CSDF)) with a distributed block control [19,20]. As input for hardware synthesis, it requires a VHDL description, then an engineer has to supply the tool with target-specific information, for example; clock frequency, resources. Then it uses a set of different tools to do resource estimation, re-timing, assignment, routing, buffer minimization and scheduling. Every tool bases its decisions on a comparison of performance estimates of various alternatives. These estimates are obtained by calling the next tool in the script in estimate mode, in which a tool returns an estimate of the performance in an extremely short amount of time.

Ptolemy II is an open-source framework with an actor-oriented design that also supports VHDL code generation from dataflow specifications [9,22,33,34]. It implements a parallel structure for a multi-rate input graph. From an SDF graph, a Directed Acyclic Graph (DAG) is constructed using a valid sequential schedule. The DAG shows all the individual units of computation and the flow of data between them, and the hardware structure can be generated. Sen and Bhattacharyya extend this technique providing an algorithm and framework to find the optimal application of data-parallel hardware implementations from SDF graphs [26].

Chandrachoodan et al. provide a method for a hierarchical view of Homogeneous Synchronous Data-Flow (HSDF) graphs for Digital Signal Processor (DSP) applications [3]. The new hierarchical node (block) has a delay of the worst case of all the paths from input to output inside. The model uses *timing pairs* that can be used to compute a *constraint time*, which can be used to describe the "execution time" of a block.

SDF is used in Jungs work to generate RTL codes for a hardware system including buffers and muxes [15]. They aim to generate a *correct-by-construction* VHDL design from SDF to accelerate both design and verification. A node in their model corresponds to a coarse grain functional block such as an FIR filter and DCT. It uses a centralized control structure and multi-rate specifications can be implemented parallel as well as sequentially or a hybrid.

Other approaches are based on the CAL language for HW/SW co-design [14,30]. Actors are described in an XML format and transformed into a sequential program in Static Single Assignment (SSA) from which hardware synthesis is performed. Siret et al. use CAL in their HLS two-step approach in which they compile dataflow programs into hardware while keeping as many similarities as possible from the source and then letting the synthesis tool perform optimizations [28].

Kondratyev et al. propose an HLS scheduling approach in which they split the SystemC input specification into a Control Flow Graph (CFG) and a Data Flow Graph (DFG) [16]. The CFG is constructed using conditionals, loops, and waits in the input specification. The DFG represents the operations with their data dependencies. By using different scheduling methods they construct a mapping between both graphs and use a commercial HLS tool to synthesize hardware.

The methods mentioned above use dataflow to generate glue logic between components or analyze the throughput, latency, and the required buffer sizes of the application. However, information from the model does not affect the implementation of the node itself. In our approach, information from the model influences the hardware that is synthesized for the nodes, because we generate control and datapath from it, with the desired resource sharing and parallelism.

3   SDF-AP

SDF and CSDF have the same underlying firing rule, which states that an actor can fire when there are enough tokens available on all its inputs. Many hardware IP blocks, on the other hand, require that data arrive at specific clock cycles from the start of execution. Suppose an actor requires 3 tokens to be delivered in 3 consecutive clock cycles, this cannot be expressed in SDF or CSDF because the firing rule states that an actor waits until specified tokens arrive for this phase, not subsequent phases. Therefore, designing hardware using these models can lead to inefficient or incorrect designs. In [31] this problem is further explained and an extension of SDF is introduced called SDF-AP is introduced. This extension is elaborated in [10] and states that introducing actor stalling for example by disabling the clock to freeze the execution of a node is not a satisfactory solution due to the overhead.

SDF-AP consists of a set of nodes and edges/channels with consumption and production patterns called *access patterns*. These patterns describe the number of tokens consumed or produced in each clock cycle of the node firing. The execution time of a node denotes the number of clock cycles it takes to complete one firing. SDF-AP relies on strict pattern matching, which means that a node can only fire if it can be guaranteed that it will be able to complete all the phases. The key difference between CSDF and SDF-AP is that in CSDF it is allowed to have (stalling) time between phases of the firing, and in SDF-AP this is not allowed. An example of an SDF-AP graph with a schedule is shown in Fig. 1. The actor p produces, according to the production pattern $pp = [0, 1]$, data after every second clock cycle of its firing. The schedule (Fig. 1b) shows 3 consecutive firings of p, starting at $t = 0, 2, 4$. The actor c requires that it can read 3 tokens in 3 consecutive clock cycles of its firing ($cp = [1, 1, 1]$). At $t = 4$ c can fire because it is known upfront that it can complete its firing since the last token that is required will arrive at $t = 6$.

SDF-AP also has its shortcomings, which are explained in [6,7] and a solution is introduced, called Static Data-Flow with Actors with Stretchable Access Patterns (SDF-ASAP), in which consumption patterns do not form a minimum requirement, but rather a maximum consumption pattern from which the real execution may be a stretched version. Additional computation patterns are introduced to further specify the relation between tokens on the production and the consumption of a node. This information can be used to stretch the patterns

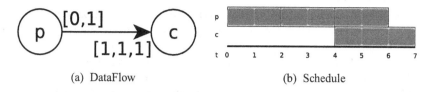

(a) DataFlow   (b) Schedule

Fig. 1. SDF-AP example

to allow for earlier execution of nodes and hence reduce the FIFO sizes for the edges. For now, we focused on SDF-AP, because even if earlier firings lead to smaller FIFO sizes, data has to be stored somewhere, and since we are generating both the entire control- and datapath those values will be stored inside a node. Therefore it will increase the complexity of the controllers of both the FIFOs and nodes, it will increase the resource consumption of a node, but, it will decrease the FIFO sizes. SDF-ASAP remains an interesting candidate for our solution because stretchable patterns can prevent the actor from stalling, especially for computations that require sliding windows. Therefore, further implementation is future work.

4   From Functional Description to SDF-AP

In this section, we explore the key idea of combining SDF-AP and the functional description for both design and analysability of hardware. First, we show the general toolflow, after which we discuss the conformance relation between the model and hardware and what our tool will generate for each element in SDF-AP. After that, we discuss the basic idea of combining SDF-AP patterns with a functional description to automatically generate a hardware architecture. In Sect. 4.4 we describe the advantages of this approach.

4.1   Template Haskell: The Toolflow

As mentioned in the introduction we use Template Haskell, an extension of the Haskell compiler, to transform the functional input description to a clocked clash description. Template Haskell is the standard framework for doing type-safe, at compile-time metaprogramming in the Glasgow Haskell Compiler (GHC). It allows writing Haskell meta programs, which are evaluated at compile-time, and which produce Haskell programs as the results of their execution [27]. The Template Haskell extension allows us to analyze and change the Abstract Syntax Tree (AST) of a given description, through a process in which the AST is extracted, modified, and afterward inserted back into the compilation process. As an input for our tool, we have the functional specification combined with the specific access patterns for each input and output. Invalid access patterns can be detected in the early stages of compilation and the engineer will be notified about the inconsistency in his specification. Based on the patterns, our tool first generates a structure with partially predefined components. The partially predefined components are for example a FIFO with a length that can be defined at compile-time or an input selector with a width that can be defined at compile-time. Those components are now completed and linked together using the information from the patterns. Then the tool generates an AST from these now fully predefined components and inserts the AST of the input description into it. The new AST now contains the control structure and the datapath from the functional description. If there is repetition in the given AST, using higher-order functions, then the tool can reuse the hardware of the repeating function according to the production and consumption patterns. The amount of parallel hardware synthesized for the higher-order functions matches the patterns, this concept is further explained in Sect. 4.3. The new "clocked" AST is inserted back into the compilation process and VHDL or Verilog is generated. An overview of this process is shown in Fig. 2. Both the clash code and Verilog/VHDL are generated, they can be tested and simulated, but in practice, one would mainly test the input description, because the generated code is *correct-by-construction*.

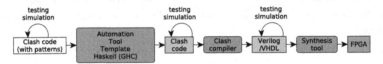

Fig. 2. Toolflow

4.2   Conformance Relation

This section provides the conformance relation between the SDF-AP model and the hardware that is generated from it. First, an example is presented to give an intuition of the conformance relation.

Example: An example is shown in Fig. 3 where the blue controller belongs to the p node and controls when the node starts, when the result must be placed on the output, and signals the FIFO controller in what phase the node p is in. This node controller requires knowing the production pattern from the SDF-AP model. The FIFO controller controls when data must be placed in the FIFO and signals the controller of node c (green/red) whether it can fire. It needs the production (blue) pattern and the consumption (red) pattern from the model. The node controller of c (green/red) only knows the production (green) and consumption (red) pattern.

Edges: For every edge in the dataflow graph, a FIFO is generated. Alongside the FIFO, a small controller is generated that checks whether, according to that specific edge, a node can fire. This check is comparing the number of elements in the FIFO with the minimum number of elements required. This minimum number required varies for each phase of the producing node. Therefore, a list

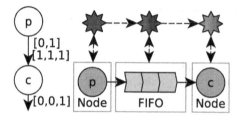

Fig. 3. Conformance between model and hardware architecture (Color figure online)

containing these minimums is calculated at compile-time using Algorithm 1. A list for an edge between node A and B with PP = $[0, 1, 1]$ and CP = $[1, 1, 1, 1, 1]$ would be as follows: If A is in its first phase of firing, then B can start if there are 2 or more elements in the FIFO because in the future A will produce 2 elements and B needs 4 elements in 4 clock cycles. If A is in the second phase, then B can start if there are 2 or more elements in the FIFO because A will produce 1 element in this phase, and 1 in the next phase. If A is in the third phase, then B can start if there are 3 or more elements in the FIFO because A will produce 1 element in this third phase. So the list that keeps track of the minimum number of elements required in the FIFO before a node can fire according to that edge is [2,2,3] in this example. Algorithm 1 calculates such a list for a given production and consumption pattern. For every firing (j) the PPJ is the remaining firing pattern. For example, for the phase $j = 1$ firing this PPJ = $[1, 1]$. 0's are added to make the patterns equal, so $[1, 1, 0, 0]$. SPP is a list that contains how many elements the node is going to produce in the future, so that is $[1, 2, 2, 2]$ in our example for phase $j = 1$. SCP contains the number of elements in total thus far required for every phase of the consumer, so for a CP of $[1, 1, 1, 1]$ that is $[1, 2, 3, 4]$. FC_j is the maximum difference between SPP and SCP, for the phase $j = 1$, is 2, hence 2 elements are required in the FIFO if B can start its execution. The above calculating is performed for every phase j of the producing node.

In hardware, a FIFO can either be a blockRAM or a group of registers. For now, the choice between blockRAM or registers depends on the size of the input. The SDF-AP model allows for varying integers as consumption and production, in our case we restrict the consumption and production patterns to only exist of 0's and n, where n is the size of the incoming data. All the patterns that belong to the same node have to have the same length.

Nodes: A node represents a piece of hardware that can perform some task. Data consumed and produced by the node are stored in the FIFOs that are generated from the edges. However, a node can have its internal state stored inside. Alongside the hardware of the node, there is a small controller generated that controls the operation. It keeps track of the node phase counter and controls when the input and output are enabled, this is based on the consumption and production patterns. The FIFO controllers signal whether, according to that specific edge, a node can fire. The node controller receives these signals from

---

Algorithm 1: Algorithm to compute the minimum number of elements required in a FIFO before a node can fire.

Input : PP, CP
Output : FC, a list of minimum number of elements required in the FIFO for every phase of the producing node

for $j = 0$ to *length(PP)* **do**
  PPJ = *drop j* PP
  add 0's to shortest pattern, so that *length*(CP) == *length*(PPJ)
  for $i = 1$ to *length(CP)* **do**
    $\text{SPP}_i = \sum_0^i \text{PPJ}_i$
    $\text{SCP}_i = \sum_0^i \text{CP}_i$
  end
  $\text{FC}_j = \max_i (\text{SPP}_i - \text{SCP}_i)$
end

---

the FIFO controllers and starts or continues the firing of the node. It controls multiplexers for input and output values.

4.3 The Basic Idea of Combining SDF-AP with a Functional Language

In a functional description, repetition is expressed using recursion or higher-order functions. We currently focus on higher-order functions due to their expressiveness of structure. The basic idea is that we combine consumption and production patterns from SDF-AP with functions from the specification. Combining the repetition, expressed using higher-order functions, with patterns from SDF-AP, we can generate a hardware architecture with a time-area trade-off automatically. This principle is explained in the following example using a dot-product specification in Haskell (Listing 1.1), with two higher-order functions (*foldl1* and *zipWith*). *foldl1* is called a foldable function because it combines all input values to a single output. According to the type definition (line 1-3), the *dotp* function receives 2 vectors of 6 values and produces a single value.

Listing 1.1. *dotp* function

```
1  dotp :: Vec 6 (Unsigned 8)
2        -> Vec 6 (Unsigned 8)
3        -> Unsigned 8
4  dotp xs ys = o
5    where o  = foldl1 (+) 0 ws
6          ws = zipWith (*) xs ys
```

In the first design iteration, we can have a single SDF-AP actor representing the *dotp* function with both consumption patterns $cp = [6]$ and the production pattern $pp = [1]$ (Fig. 4a). The schedule in Fig. 4b shows that the system takes

1 clock cycle to complete its computation. Our tool receives both the *dotp* function (Listing 1.1) and the consumption and production patterns (as shown in Listing 1.2) and generates the hardware architecture as shown in Fig. 4c. The patterns are given in a list of tuples containing production and consumption pattern of every edge (pp,cp). In Listing 1.2 the tuple for both incoming edges is ([6],[6]), so the production pattern for both edges is the same as the consumption pattern. The hardware consists of, as described in the conformance relation, two FIFOs for incoming data, 6 multipliers, 6 adders, and controllers for both FIFOs and a controller for the *dotp* node. The resource consumption is consistent with the access patterns.

Listing 1.2. *dotp* in the Template Haskell function

```
1  $( tool  'dotp  [([6],[6]),([6],[6])]  [1])
```

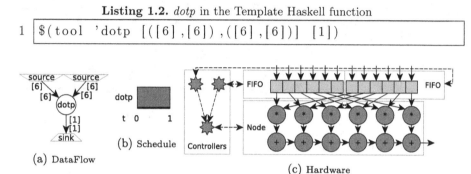

(a) DataFlow   (b) Schedule   Controllers   (c) Hardware

Fig. 4. Function *dotp* with $cps = [6]$ and $pp = [1]$

In the second design iteration, we can examine the *dotp* function and model both higher-order functions (*foldl1* and *zipWith*) as separate SDF-AP actors (Fig. 5a). The consumption and production patterns of the *zw* node are $cp_{zw} = [6]$, and $pp_{zw} = [6]$. The consumption and production patterns of the *fl* node are $cp_{fl} = [6]$, and $pp_{fl} = [1]$. The hardware (Fig. 5c) that is generated from these patterns and the function description of both higher-order functions consists of 6 multipliers, 6 adders, and FIFOs on the input edges of both nodes. According to the schedule (Fig. 5b), the entire system takes 2 clock cycles before producing the result. Introducing an additional edge results in an additional FIFO, this is fully transparent for the engineer and the resource consumption shows consistent behavior.

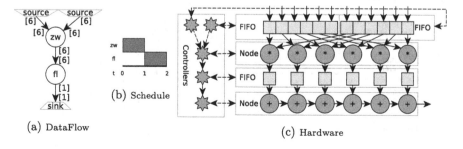

(a) DataFlow   (b) Schedule   Controllers   (c) Hardware

Fig. 5. Function *dotp* with separate nodes for *zipWith* and *foldl1*

In the third design iteration, we can change the consumption and production patterns of the *zw* actor to $cp_{zw} = pp_{zw} = [2, 2, 2]$ (Fig. 6a). There are a couple of different permutations possible on the patterns that would result in a feasible architecture, those permutations are $[1, 1, 1, 1, 1, 1], [2, 2, 2], [3, 3]$. These are the divisors of the original pattern. For now, we discard all the remaining permutations because in hardware it introduces control-overhead if we allow different integers in the same pattern. The resulting hardware (Fig. 6c) consists of 2 multipliers, 6 adders, and FIFOs on the input edges of both nodes. According to the schedule (Fig. 6b), the entire system takes 4 clock cycles.

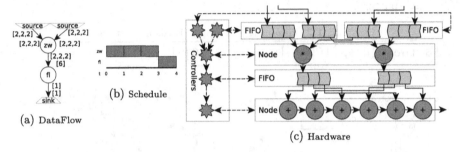

Fig. 6. Function *dotp* with modified patterns for *zw*

In the previous scenario, it can be seen that it is very inefficient to leave the *fl* function untouched. The 6 adders in the *foldl1* part of the system are idle in 3 of the 4 clock cycles. Therefore, bundling the production pattern of the *zw* node to the *fl* node results in a much more efficient architecture. The consumption pattern of the *fl* node then becomes $cp_{fl} = [2, 2, 2]$ and the production pattern $pp_{fl} = [0, 0, 1]$. Changing these patterns results in an architecture that consists of 2 multipliers, 2 adders, and FIFOs on input edges (Fig. 7a and 7c). The schedule (Fig. 7b) now shows that the entire system also takes 4 clock cycles. This is because the *fl* node can start as soon as the *zw* node has finished its first firing phase. The control logic generated by the tool facilitates this schedule automatically. We also introduced the first optimization; if an edge has the same production pattern as the consumption pattern we remove the FIFO controller and introduce a pipeline register. Both resource consumption and the schedule of the architecture match the expectations of the graph with access patterns, making the design process transparent. The resource consumption in DSPs scales consistently with the change in patterns.

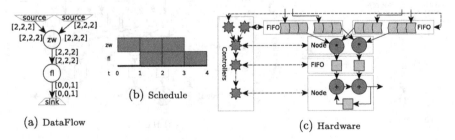

Fig. 7. Function *dotp* with modified patterns for both *zw* and *fl*

4.4   The Advantages

There are several advantages of method and tool to combine a functional description with SDF-AP:

– The generation of control and datapath is automated, and therefore lifts the burden of the engineer.
– The time-area trade-off is transparent. By tuning the consumption and production patterns including the functional description, the engineer steers both the timing and the structure of the generated architecture.
– The engineer can steer the time-area trade-off by describing the functionality using specific higher-order functions. Often, functionality can be expressed using different higher-order functions. If an engineer knows beforehand that these higher-order functions are the first place where a time-area trade-off can be made, he can choose to use specific higher-order functions to steer the direction of this trade-off.
– The typechecker of functional languages can be used to check and verify the input specification with access patterns. This typechecker is also part of the Haskell ecosystem.
– Iterative design is possible due to the analysis and simulation techniques of dataflow and functional languages. Haskell comes with an interactive Read-Evaluate-Print-Loop (REPL) that allows simulation of functional behavior. An engineer can use several analysis techniques from the SDF-AP model to determine throughput, latency, buffer sizes, and bottlenecks and change the input specification before entering the remaining design flow.
– The possibility to introduce hierarchy. Production and consumption patterns can be bundled, multiple nodes with bundled patterns can be modelled as one node, which will reduce the search space for automation in the future. Bundling not only allows for hierarchy but also excludes irrational design pattern combinations that lead to inefficient hardware architectures. Besides bundling it is also possible to check how local changes to the design influence the design as a whole.

4.5   The Current Limitations

There are several limitations of the proposed method and tool:

– Due to the choice for distributed local controllers, there is hardware control overhead introduced at every edge and node of the SDF-AP model. The overhead introduced by the node controllers is smaller than the FIFO controllers, since they only switch multiplexers on the input and output of the node based on signals received from FIFO controllers, and count phases. The FIFO controllers have to count the number of elements in the FIFO and if enough elements are presents, signals the node controller. Since production and consumption patterns are known at compile-time, many calculations can be performed at compile-time and therefore reducing the size of the circuitry. Still, if the nodes are very small components, for example, one adder, then the controller overhead is relatively large.

– Only the repetition expressed in higher-order functions allows for an automatic time-area trade-off based on patterns.
– There is no algorithm yet that sets production and consumption patterns, the selection of these patterns is still completely up to the engineer. Future work remains to search the design space automatically and find access patterns that result in an architecture that both satisfies area and time constraints.
– If the tool receives a folding function at the root of the AST, it will automatically determine the state variables if the hardware needs to share its resources over time. However, if there is a folding function somewhere inside the AST, and not at the root, the tool is unable to determine the internal state required and generate an architecture. For example, if the *dotp* function from Listing 1.1 is given to our tool, then it is unable to determine that there is a *foldl1* function inside it. Hence our tool is not able to determine the internal state required for an architecture. This limitation is further demonstrated in the Lloyds case study (See Sect. 5) and is planned to be resolved in the future.
– Resources between different higher-order functions will not be shared by this method alone. For example, the function *foo* from Listing 1.3 uses two times the higher-order function *zipWith*, but the tool is currently unable to share the resources between those two higher-order functions. This means that the minimum number of multipliers required is 2 (one for each zipWith).

Listing 1.3. Function with multiple HOFs

```
1   foo xs ys zs = (o1, o2) where
2     o1  = zipWith (*) xs ys
3     o2  = zipWith (*) xs zs
```

5   Node Decomposition

In the section, we demonstrate the effects of decomposing a single node into multiple nodes on resource usage and show the code necessary to specify the SDF-AP graph in our HLS tool. Decomposing a single node means introducing extra edges, and hence extra FIFOs in the architecture. To demonstrate this we use Lloyds algorithm [23] that finds the center of each set of Euclidean spaces and re-partitions the input to the closest center. It consists of iterating through these two steps: assigning data points to a cluster and then centering the cluster point. For demonstration purposes, the input is 18 different points that the hardware needs to cluster using Lloyds algorithm. The synthesis results of all the different versions are shown in Table 1.

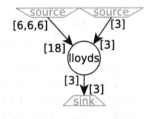

Fig. 8. Lloyds 1 node

In the graphs, the input is provided in chunks of 6 to limit the number of inputs bits on the FPGA. Figure 8 shows one node containing the entire

Table 1. Resources usage for different versions of the Lloyds algorithm

Nodes	1 (Fig. 8)	3 (Fig. 9a)	4 (Fig. 9b)	5 (Fig. 9c)	5 (Fig. 9d)
LUT	8935	10522	12136	14427	5034
Registers	185	296	333	382	553
Memory bits	648	648	648	648	540
RAMB36E1	10	33	37	104	41
RAMB18E1	1	2	2	3	3
DSPs	108	108	108	108	12
FMAX (MHz)	25	37	37	42	75
Latency (cycles)	1	3	3	4	7
Latency (ns)	40	81	81	95	93

algorithm, it consumes 18 coordinates and 3 initial cluster center coordinates in one clock cycle. The SDF-AP graphs in this paper contain source and sink nodes that provide or consume data but those are not synthesized. The next clock cycle it delivers the 3 updated cluster center points. To perform one iteration of the Lloyds algorithm in 1 clock cycle for 18 input points and 3 cluster points requires the resources shown in the second column of Table 1. One input edge has the same production and consumption pattern, hence there is no need to initialize a complete FIFO and controller, only some registers. The input and output values are vectors of tuples containing coordinates as 18-bit values, therefore the amount of memory bits required is $18 \times (18 + 18) = 648$.

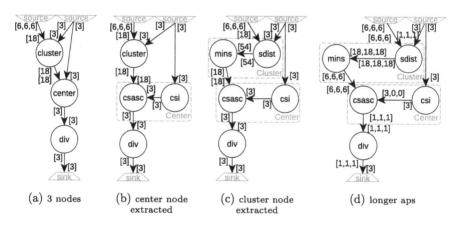

(a) 3 nodes   (b) center node extracted   (c) cluster node extracted   (d) longer aps

Fig. 9. SDF-AP graphs of Lloyds algorithm

Suppose we want to reduce the resource usage, then the straightforward solution would be to just adjust the patterns of the lloyds node. However, there are foldable functions inside the lloyds node. The HLS tool is currently unable to determine what the internal state must be if these foldable functions are somewhere inside the AST. Therefore, we need to decompose the nodes first, so that our tool can recognize the foldable functions, and hence determine what the internal state of that specific foldable function should be. This limitation should be solved in the future by introducing a hierarchy on both clocked and unclocked input specifications. For now, to reduce the resource usage, we need to decompose the nodes into smaller ones, until we have singled out all the foldable nodes. Figure 9a shows the Lloyds algorithm in SDF-AP but now split into 3 nodes, which results in a pipelined version of the algorithm. The input from the source nodes provides the same data to the `cluster` node as well as to the `center` node. The amount of LUTs increased due to the extra registers required for the additional edges. Only registers are required because the production and consumption patterns for these edges are the same. The splitting of nodes also results in a 48% higher maximum clock frequency. The throughput is still 1 point every clock cycle, but the latency is increased to 3 clock cycles.

In Fig. 9b the node that calculates the new center points is split into two nodes; `csasc` and `csi`. Due to the additional edges, additional registers are required and hence the increase of LUTs (See Table 1). The `csasc` node is a foldable node that contains the *foldl* function (See line 5). The amount of DSP blocks remains 108.

Figure 9c shows the node `cluster` also decomposed into 2 separate nodes. Again, introducing register consumption, increasing latency, but the throughput stays the same (Column 5 of Table 1). In this case, the `mins` node contains the foldable function *foldl* (See Listing 1.4 line 3). Now that all the foldable functions are in separate nodes we can start the time-area trade-off by changing the patterns.

Listing 1.4. Node definitions of Fig. 9d

```
1  tSdist=$(tool  'sdist  [(([6,6,6],[6,6,6]),([3],[1,1,1]))]
2                          [18,18,18])
3  tMins =$(tool  'mins   [([18,18,18],[18,18,18])]
4                          [6,6,6])
5  tCsi  =$(tool  'csi    [([3],[3])]
6                          [3])
7  tCsasc=$(tool  'foldl  [([3],[3,0,0]),([6,6,6],[6,6,6])]
8                          [1,1,1])
9  tDiv  =$(tool  'div    [([1,1,1], [1,1,1])]
10                         [1,1,1])
```

Listing 1.5. Nodes composed of Fig. 9d

```
1  tCluster  ps  cs  =  mns  where
2      dys  =  tSdist  ps  cs
3      mns  =  tMins  dys
4
5  tCenter  pscs  cs  =  csast  where
6      cst  =  tCsi  g  cs
```

```
 7 │    csast = tCsasc f cst pscs
 8 │
 9 │ lloyds ps cs = cs' where
10 │    pscs  = tCluster ps cs
11 │    csast = tCenter pscs cs
12 │    cs'   = tDiv csast
```

In Fig. 9d the consumption and production patterns are changed so that the computations per node are divided over 3 clock cycles. As expected, the number of DSP blocks required is lowered to 12, also the logic utilization is roughly a third. The foldable nodes now require an internal state, this state is stored in registers, hence the increase in the number of registers. Due to the reuse of hardware over time the total amount of LUTs is also one-third of the LUTs used in the previous version. The amount of blockRAM required is slightly lower compared to the previous version due to the changed consumption pattern on the *sdist* node. The code for the entire SDF-AP graph is shown in Listing 1.4. Lines 1–10 show the timed node definitions using the Template Haskell tool, for example, the *mins* function is purely combinational that calculates the minimum value over a set of vectors.

Listing 1.5 shows the composition of the nodes. The *tMins* is the generated clocked version of *mins* with the desired input and output patterns. Lines 1–3 are the functional description of the SDF-AP actor `cluster`, which is decomposed into 2 nodes. Lines 5–7 are the description of the actor `center` and lines 9–12 describe the composition of the SDF-AP graph. This section demonstrates the change in resource usage when nodes are decomposed and which introduces new edges. It also highlights that support for hierarchy in the design specification can be desirable.

6 Case Studies

For evaluation and comparison, we implemented several algorithms using our proposed HLS method as well as the commercially available Vitis HLS, provided by Xilinx, currently the largest FPGA vendor. For the dot-product case study, we also have a comparison with the HLS-tool provided by Intel. We kept the input description for our tool and the Vitis tool as similar as possible to enable a fair comparison in terms of transparency, consistency, and performance of the resulting architecture. As a consequence, we did not perform code transformations by hand, such as combining nested loops into a single loop. All repetition in the C++ specification is expressed using for-loops and in the functional specification using HOFs. One major difference between both approaches is that Vitis generates without pragmas a hardware architecture in which all computations are performed sequentially, whereas our HLS-tool generates without patterns a fully parallel combinational architecture. For Vitis, we used pragmas, like unrolling and partitioning of data, to steer the tool. For our HLS-tool, we used the access patterns. For the synthesis of the generated Verilog code, we used Vivado v2020.2 and a Virtex 7 as target FPGA.

The algorithms we used for the case study are the dot-product, Center of Mass (CoM) computations on images, and a 2D Discrete Cosine Transform (DCT). The dot-product serves as a simple starting point and allows easy comparison of different versions. The CoM case study is slightly more complex but has dependencies that are straightforward to derive and has a lot of potential parallelism. The 2D DCT has nodes that have fixed patterns because it has predefined IP blocks and hence those are modelled with fixed patterns.

The SDF-AP graphs in these studies contain **source** and **sink** nodes that provide or consume data but those are not synthesized. For a single node with patterns of length 1, the overhead is in the range of 11 LUTs with 11 registers. We also measured the time it took to generate Verilog from the input description with the HLS-tools. Our HLS-tool took 48 s to generate Verilog for all the designs, Vitis took 66 min and 17 s.

6.1   Dot Product Case Study

The SDF-AP graph of the dot-product is shown in Fig. 10. As mentioned in Sect. 4.2, for every edge our tool synthesizes a FIFO, except the edges to the **sink** nodes. A FIFO in our tool can either be a collection of registers or blockRAM.

Table 2. Resources usage of our HLS-tool in comparison with Intel HLS synthesized in Quartus 18.1

Dotproduct	Our HLS-tool				Intel HLS			
ap	[1,1,...,1]	[5,5,5,5]	[10,10]	[20]	No unroll	Unroll 5	Unroll 10	Unroll 20
ALMs	94	198	289	459	1701	4128	7731	–
Registers	67	73	77	84	2759	5901	10763	–
Memory bits	720	720	720	720	0	10240	20480	–
DSPs	1	3	6	10	1	3	5	–
FMAX (MHz)	199	174	170	170	206	197	168	–
Latency (cycles)	21	5	3	2	40	40	40	–
Latency (ns)	106	29	18	12	194	203	238	–

For the Dot product case study we also made a comparison between our tool and the Intel HLS. The nodes are described in the Intel C++ input as two for-loops and for our HLS-tool as two HOFs. The synthesized results from Quartus 18.1 are shown in Table 2. From the analysis of the results, we can conclude that in general the architecture produced by Intel HLS consumes significantly more resources. This was because it generates a processor architecture using an Avalon bus system for all the communication. Intel was unable to generate an architecture that showed correct behavior for the *unroll 20* version. For both tools, an increase in Adaptive Logic Module (ALM)s

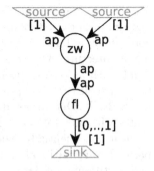

Fig. 10. SDF-AP graph for dot product

can be seen as we increase the parallelism. In our HLS the register and block-RAM usage stay roughly the same. The amount of blockRAM can be calculated for the two input edges that need to both store 20×18-bit values $= 720$. The edge between the zw and fl have the same production and consumption pattern and registers are introduced instead of a FIFO with a controller. For Intel HLS both registers and blockRAM usage increases with a larger unroll. The number of DSPs increases also as more parallelism is introduced and Quartus can synthesize 1 DSPs for 2 multiplications. As parallelism increases in our HLS, we see a slightly lower FMAX due to the increased combinational path for the adders in the fl node. With Intel HLS we see the opposite and the FMAX increases as more parallelism is introduced. The latency in nanoseconds that our tool can achieve is lower for all cases compared to Intel.

On average our tool uses 22 times fewer resources and has a 7.5 times lower latency both in clock cycles and in nanoseconds. From a resource consumption, both in ALMs and blockRAM and latency perspective, our HLS-tool is more consistent compared to Intel HLS. This case study also demonstrates that pragmas steering parallelism does not always predictably affect latency. Since the Intel HLS tends to introduce a large bus and overhead, we decided to use Vitis HLS and Vivado for all the case studies. For a comparison with Vitis, we used the same input specification for our HLS as we used for the comparison with Intel. Vitis generates multiple input buffers in a sequence before streaming the values to the multipliers and adders. It also creates pipelined adders to sum the results of the multiplications. Both of these decisions result in an increased latency in nanoseconds, but allow for a higher clock frequency. Table 3 shows the comparison of resource conpsumption between our HLS and Vitis. The amount of LUTs and registers increases with introducing more parallelism. When the FIFO depth is below a certain threshold Vivado introduces registers instead of blockRAM for storage. The register usage for our HLS increases with more parallelism. DSP usage scales according to the parallelism introduced using patterns or pragmas. The FMAX decreases as more parallelism is introduced but a steeper decrease is shown for Vitis. Latency in cycles shows unpredictable behavior for Vitis. Somehow the tool is unable to find a shorter schedule for the extra parallelism

Table 3. Resources usage of our HLS-tool in comparison with Vitis HLS synthesized in Vivado

Dotproduct	Our HLS-tool				Vitis HLS			
ap	[1,1,...,1]	[5,5,5,5]	[10,10]	[20]	No unroll	Unroll 5	Unroll 10	Unroll 20
LUTs	126	329	582	595	277	381	471	707
Registers	66	261	449	1530	425	529	643	640
RAMB18E1	1	0	0	0	0	0	0	0
DSPs	1	5	10	20	1	5	10	20
FMAX (MHz)	150	162	146	131	283	189	148	107
Latency (cycles)	21	5	3	2	29	42	57	49
Latency (ns)	140	31	21	15	103	222	386	459

that is introduced. This results in much longer latency in nanoseconds compared to our HLS-tool. The architectures produced by Vitis achieve a higher FMAX, except the *unroll 20* variant, but combined with the latency in cycles the latency in nanoseconds is significantly longer compared to our HLS-tool, except the *no unroll* variant.

On average Vitis requires 30% more LUTs and has a 14 times higher latency in nanoseconds compared to the architectures produced by our HLS-tool. From a resource consumption and latency perspective, our HLS-tool is more consistent compared to Vitis. This case study also demonstrates that pragmas steering parallelism does not always predictably affect latency.

6.2   Center of Mass Case Study

For this case study, we use a center of mass computation on gray-scale images to demonstrate the effect of parallelization through patterns or pragmas. An image is chopped into blocks of 8 × 8 pixels and the center of mass of those blocks is computed. Vitis synthesizes a large input buffer where the pixels are streamed into. From this buffer the data is fed through a pipelined version of the algorithm consisting of adders and multipliers. The computation for the center of mass of an 8 × 8 image does not require many DSPs. As shown in the first column of Table 4, calculations for an 8 × 8 image do not require many resources and hence we can parallelize to decrease latency in nanoseconds. In this column, we set the ap to [1] to reflect a single CoM calculation for an 8 × 8 image. For our HLS the number of logic cells and DSPs is consistent with the parallelism specified by the pattern. For a single computation, 20 DSPs are required, when we use the access pattern $ap = [16, 16, ..., 16]$, we need $16 \times 20 = 320$ DSP. For the access pattern $ap = [64, 64, 64, 64]$ we need $64 \times 20 = 1280$ DSPs. For the access patterns $[16, 16, ..., 16]$ and $[64, 64, 64, 64]$ Vivado introduces blockRAM to store data. The FMAX stays roughly constant because the longest combinational path is not increased, only extra parallelism is introduced. Since there is a single node in Fig. 11, the latency in clock cycles is the length of the pattern.

With Vitis, we also see an increase in LUTs when more parallelism is introduced using pragmas. From the *unroll 16* variant to the *unroll 64* variant no extra blockRAMs or DSPs are introduced, but many more registers. The latency in cycles also stays at 700, meaning that Vitis is unable to find a better schedule compared to the *unroll 16* variant.

The patterns show a consistent and predictable behavior in terms of resource consumption and latency. The Vitis tool is not able to generate a schedule that efficiently utilizes the extra parallelism introduced using pragmas. On average the Vitis architecture consumed 40% fewer LUTs and 15 times more registers. Vitis can achieve a higher clock frequency but a large number of clock

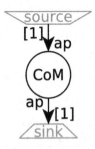

Fig. 11. SDF-AP graph for CoM

cycles results in an on average 18 times higher latency in nanoseconds compared to our HLS.

Table 4. Resources usage for different versions of the CoM algorithm

CoM	Our HLS			Vitis HLS		
ap	[1]	[16, 16.., 16]	[64, 64, 64, 64]	No unroll	Unroll 16	Unroll 64
LUTs	1577	31744	125017	2035	11513	29476
Registers	681	355	1026	2438	8309	19783
RAMB36E1	0	144	576	0	0	0
RAMB18E1	0	0	0	66	132	132
DSPs	20	320	1280	12	24	24
FMAX (MHz)	33	28	27	157	115	110
Latency (cycles)	256	16	4	825	700	700
Latency (ns)	7724	565	151	5265	6096	6366

6.3 DCT2D Case Study

The DCT is implemented using an 8×8 input matrix with 18-bit values. The SDF-AP graph is shown in Fig. 12 where the access pattern ap is shown as a variable. The numbers in the patterns represent the number of vectors containing 8 18-bit values, so $[4, 4]$ means an input width of a 4×8 matrix. The patterns for the **transpose** nodes remain fixed to demonstrate the case when the engineer is not able to change the behavior of certain nodes (which is the case for external IPs). An overview of the hardware synthesis of different access patterns for the three different FIFO types is shown in Table 5.

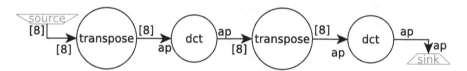

Fig. 12. SDF-AP graph for a 2D DCT

Table 5. Resources usage for different versions of the DCT2D algorithm

DCT2D	Our HLS-tool				Vitis HLS			
ap	[1,1,...,1]	[2,2,2,2]	[4,4]	[8]	No unroll	Unroll 2	Unroll 4	Unroll 8
LUTs	2569	4224	7786	17442	3370	2622	3507	4558
Registers	5308	5311	5311	5311	4577	5108	5091	6083
RAMB18E1	0	0	0	0	5	19	21	8
DSPs	56	112	224	448	56	4	16	28
FMAX (MHz)	91	92	98	102	171	205	189	148
Latency (cycles)	18	10	6	4	213	2322	2162	269
Latency (ns)	199	109	61	39	1246	11327	11439	1818

The number of logic cells used roughly doubles when we double the parallelism using patterns. This amount of registers stays roughly the same through all the patterns since we do not introduce new edges. The number of DSPs is consistent with the specified access patterns, scaling the pattern with the factor 2 also doubles the DSP consumption. The longest combinational path is not changed by parallelization and hence the FMAX remains almost the same. The latency in cycles is deduced from the SDF-AP graph and the latency in nanoseconds shows a predictable decrease when more parallelism is introduced.

Vitis is somehow able to utilize more parallelism if no pragmas are given, the tool does not tell us how and why this is the case. This parallelization effect is especially visible in the DSP consumption and the latency in cycles. However, when we signal the compiler that some of the loops can be unrolled, it introduces more LUTs for the *unroll 4* and *unroll 8* variant. The latency in cycles shows very inconsistent behavior since the *unroll 2* and *unroll 4* variants have a latency that is 10 times higher than the *no unroll* variant.

From the results of Table 5, we conclude that the usage of logic cells for our HLS-tool on average is 30% higher and that the DSP usage scale predictable according to the specified input patterns. The speed-up for our tool varies between 6.3 and 188 times and is 86 on average.

7   Conclusion

We combined the SDF-AP temporal analysis model with a functional input language to automatically generate both control and datapath in hardware. Access patterns are used to specify resource usage and temporal behavior, providing the engineer with a transparent way of performing the time-area trade-off. From the schedules of these SDF-AP graphs follow the latency and throughput of the generated hardware.

Our HLS-tool uses the metaprogramming capabilities of Template Haskell to modify the AST during the compilation process. The existing Clash-compiler is then used to generate VHDL or Verilog. Invalid patterns can be detected in the early stages of compilation and the process can be stopped and the engineer notified. The amount of control hardware overhead depends on the chosen design granularity but is overall small. For a single node with patterns of length 1, the overhead is in the range of 40 ALMs and 50 registers.

Access patterns in our HLS-tool offer much more control over the resulting architecture compared to the pragmas of Vitis. Doubling pattern length while halving the consumption, results in half the DSP and logic cell consumption, but double the latency. Using SDF-AP opens up the possiblity of empolying dataflow analysis techniques. Case studies show consistent resource consumption and temporal behavior for our HLS.

Resource consumption in the Dot product case study is 30% lower compared to Vitis and the average speedup in latency in nanoseconds is 14 times. For the 2D DCT, our HLS-tool utilizes 30% more LUTs but is 86 times faster on average. For the CoM case study our tool consumed on average 40% more logic cells but can achieve a speedup of 18 times. For both the 2D DCT and the CoM case study Vitis is unable to utilize the extra parallelism introduced with pragmas and resulting in an inefficient schedule that leads to high latency in nanoseconds.

References

1. Baaij, C.P.R.: Digital circuit in CλaSH: functional specifications and type-directed synthesis. Ph.D. thesis, University of Twente (2015). https://doi.org/10.3990/1. 9789036538039
2. Baaij, C., Kooijman, M., Kuper, J., Boeijink, W., Gerards, M.: Clash: structural descriptions of synchronous hardware using Haskell. In: Proceedings of the 13th EUROMICRO Conference on Digital System Design: Architectures, Methods and Tools, pp. 714–721. IEEE Computer Society, September 2010. https://doi.org/10. 1109/DSD.2010.21, eemcs-eprint-18376
3. Chandrachoodan, N., Bhattacharyya, S.S., Liu, K.J.R.: The hierarchical timing pair model for multirate DSP applications. IEEE Trans. Sig. Process. **52**(5), 1209–1217 (2004). https://doi.org/10.1109/TSP.2004.826178
4. Cong, J., Liu, B., Neuendorffer, S., Noguera, J., Vissers, K., Zhang, Z.: High-level synthesis for FPGAs: from prototyping to deployment. IEEE Trans. Comput. Aided Des. Integr. Circuits Syst. **30**(4), 473–491 (2011). https://doi.org/10.1109/ TCAD.2011.2110592
5. Cong, J., Zhang, Z.: An efficient and versatile scheduling algorithm based on SDC formulation. In: 2006 43rd ACM/IEEE Design Automation Conference. pp. 433–438 (2006). https://doi.org/10.1145/1146909.1147025
6. Du, K., Domas, S., Lenczner, M.: A solution to overcome some limitations of SDF based models. In: 2018 IEEE International Conference on Industrial Technology (ICIT), pp. 1395–1400, February 2018. https://doi.org/10.1109/ICIT.2018. 8352384
7. Du, K., Domas, S., Lenczner, M.: Actors with stretchable access patterns. Integration (2019). https://doi.org/10.1016/j.vlsi.2019.01.001
8. Edwards, S.A.: The challenges of synthesizing hardware from C-like languages. IEEE Des. Test Comput. **23**(5), 375–386 (2006)
9. Eker, J., et al.: Taming heterogeneity - the Ptolemy approach. Proc. IEEE **91**(1), 127–144 (2003). https://doi.org/10.1109/JPROC.2002.805829
10. Ghosal, A., et al.: Static dataflow with access patterns: semantics and analysis. In: Proceedings - Design Automation Conference (2012). https://doi.org/10.1145/ 2228360.2228479
11. Horstmannshoff, J., Grotker, T., Meyr, H.: Mapping multirate dataflow to complex RT level hardware models, pp. 283–292 (1997). https://doi.org/10.1109/ASAP. 1997.606834
12. Horstmannshoff, J., Meyr, H.: Optimized system synthesis of complex RT level building blocks from multirate dataflow graphs. In: Proceedings 12th International Symposium on System Synthesis, pp. 38–43, November 1999. https://doi.org/10. 1109/ISSS.1999.814258
13. Huang, L., Li, D.-L., Wang, K.-P., Gao, T., Tavares, A.: A survey on performance optimization of high-level synthesis tools. J. Comput. Sci. Technol. **35**(3), 697–720 (2020). https://doi.org/10.1007/s11390-020-9414-8

14. Janneck, J.W., Miller, I.D., Parlour, D.B., Roquier, G., Wipliez, M., Raulet, M.: Synthesizing hardware from dataflow programs: an MPEG-4 simple profile decoder case study. In: 2008 IEEE Workshop on Signal Processing Systems, pp. 287–292. IEEE (2008)
15. Jung, H., Yang, H., Ha, S.: Optimized RTL code generation from coarse-grain dataflow specification for fast HW/SW cosynthesis. J. Sig. Process. Syst. **52**(1), 13–34 (2008)
16. Kondratyev, A., Lavagno, L., Meyer, M., Watanabe, Y.: Exploiting area/delay tradeoffs in high-level synthesis. In: 2012 Design, Automation and Test in Europe Conference and Exhibition (DATE), pp. 1024–1029. IEEE (2012)
17. Lahti, S., Sjövall, P., Vanne, J., Hämäläinen, T.D.: Are we there yet? A study on the state of high-level synthesis. IEEE Trans. Comput. Aided Des. Integr. Circuits Syst. **38**(5), 898–911 (2019). https://doi.org/10.1109/TCAD.2018.2834439
18. Landi, W.: Undecidability of static analysis. ACM Lett. Program. Lang. Syst. **1**(4), 323–337 (1992). https://doi.org/10.1145/161494.161501, http://portal.acm.org/citation.cfm?doid=161494.161501
19. Lauwereins, R., Engels, M., Ad, M., Peperstraete, J.: Rapid Prototyping of Digital Signal Processing Systems with GRAPE-II (1994)
20. Lauwereins, R., Engels, M., Adé, M., Peperstraete, J.A.: Grape-II: a system-level prototyping environment for DSP applications. Computer **28**(2), 35–43 (1995)
21. Lee, E.A., Messerschmitt, D.G.: Synchronous data flow. Proc. IEEE **75**(9), 1235–1245 (1987). https://doi.org/10.1109/PROC.1987.13876
22. Leung, M.K., Filiba, T.E., Nagpal, V.: VHDL code generation in the Ptolemy II environment. Technical report UCB/EECS-2008-140, EECS Department, University of Berkeley (2008)
23. Lloyd, S.: Least squares quantization in PCM. IEEE Trans. Inf. Theory **28**(2), 129–137 (1982). https://doi.org/10.1109/TIT.1982.1056489
24. Ramalingam, G.: The undecidability of aliasing. ACM Trans. Program. Lang. Syst. (TOPLAS) **16**(5), 1467–1471 (1994)
25. Schafer, B.C., Wang, Z.: High-level synthesis design space exploration: past, present, and future. IEEE Trans. Comput. Aided Des. Integr. Circuits Syst. **39**(10), 2628–2639 (2020). https://doi.org/10.1109/TCAD.2019.2943570, https://ieeexplore.ieee.org/document/8847448/
26. Sen, M., Bhattacharyya, S.: Systematic exploitation of data parallelism in hardware synthesis of DSP applications. In: International Conference on Acoustics, Speech, and Signal Processing. ICASSP 2004, vol. 5, pp. 229–232 (2004). https://doi.org/10.1109/ICASSP.2004.1327089
27. Sheard, T., Peyton Jones, S.: Template meta-programming for Haskell. In: Proceedings of the 2002 Haskell Workshop, Pittsburgh, pp. 1–16, October 2002. https://www.microsoft.com/en-us/research/publication/template-meta-programming-for-haskell/
28. Siret, N., Wipliez, M., Nezan, J.F., Palumbo, F.: Generation of efficient high-level hardware code from dataflow programs. In: Design, Automation and Test in Europe (DATE), p. NC. Dresden, Germany (2012). https://hal.archives-ouvertes.fr/hal-00763804
29. Sun, Z., et al.: Designing high-quality hardware on a development effort budget: a study of the current state of high-level synthesis. In: 2016 21st Asia and South Pacific Design Automation Conference (ASP-DAC), pp. 218–225, January 2016. https://doi.org/10.1109/ASPDAC.2016.7428014
30. Thavot, R., et al.: Dataflow design of a co-processor architecture for image processing, January 2008

31. Tripakis, S., et al.: Correct and non-defensive glue design using abstract models. In: 2011 Proceedings of the Ninth IEEE/ACM/IFIP International Conference on Hardware/Software Codesign and System Synthesis (CODES+ISSS), pp. 59–68 (2011). https://doi.org/10.1145/2039370.2039382
32. Vivado: Vitis High-Level Synthesis. https://www.xilinx.com/products/design-tools/vivado/integration/esl-design.html
33. Williamson, M.C., Lee, E.A.: Synthesis of parallel hardware implementations from synchronous dataflow graph specifications. In: Conference Record of The Thirtieth Asilomar Conference on Signals, Systems and Computers, vol. 2, pp. 1340–1343, November 1996. https://doi.org/10.1109/ACSSC.1996.599166
34. Williamson, M.C.: Synthesis of parallel hardware implementations from synchronous dataflow graph specifications. Ph.D. thesis, EECS Department, University of California, Berkeley, June 1998. http://www2.eecs.berkeley.edu/Pubs/TechRpts/1998/3474.html

Implementing Synthetic Aperture Radar Backprojection in Chisel – A Field Report

Niklas Rother[✉][iD], Christian Fahnemann[iD], and Holger Blume[iD]

Institute of Microelectronic Systems, Leibniz University Hannover,
Hannover, Germany
{rother,fahnemann,blume}@ims.uni-hannover.de

Abstract. Chisel is an emerging hardware description language which is especially popular in the RISC-V community. In this report, we evaluate its application in the field of general digital hardware design. A dedicated hardware implementation of a Synthetic Aperture Radar (SAR) processing algorithm is used as an example case for a real-world application. It is targeting a modern high performance FPGA platform. We analyze the difference in code size compared to a VHDL implementation. In contrast to related publications, we classify the code lines into several categories, providing a more detailed view. Overall, the number of lines was reduced by 74% while the amount of boilerplate code was reduced by 83%. Additionally, we report on our experience using Chisel in this practical application. We found the generative concept and the flexibility introduced by modern software paradigms superior to traditional hardware description languages. This increased productivity, especially during timing closure. However, additional programming skills not associated with classic hardware design are required to fully leverage its advantages. We recommend Chisel as a language for all hardware design tasks and expect its popularity to increase in the future.

Keywords: Hardware description languages · Chisel · SAR · VHDL

1 Introduction

Following Moore's law, the complexity of digital designs has continuously increased in the last years. Today, most designs are not created from scratch, but rather are modifications or combinations of existing blocks (IP cores). In this context, the hardware description languages that are traditionally used in this field—Verilog and VHDL—have begun to show their limitations. One attempt to create a more modern hardware design language is *Chisel* [3], developed at the University of California, Berkeley.

While Chisel has found adoption in the RISC-V community, its use as a general language for digital design is limited up to now. In this paper we report on the use of Chisel for an FPGA implementation of the Backprojection algorithm used in Synthetic Aperture Radar (SAR). Our existing implementation

A. Orailoglu et al. (Eds.): SAMOS 2022, LNCS 13511, pp. 28–42, 2022.
https://doi.org/10.1007/978-3-031-15074-6_2

Input Files ⟶ Scala Compiler ⟶ Java Runtime ⟶ Output File

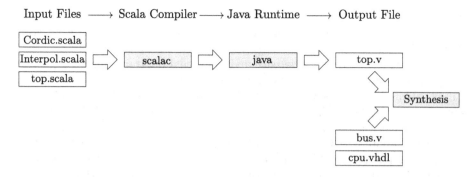

Fig. 1. Chisel synthesis process. The input files are compiled using the Scala compiler and the result is executed on the Java Runtime. This results in a single Verilog file, containing the generated code. This is used together with (optional) additional files in the conventional synthesis workflow.

[4] was implemented in VHDL. To explore the possibilities of a more modern language, the design was re-implemented from scratch in Chisel. This paper provides an extensive comparison of both implementations in terms of code size. Additionally, we describe our experience working with Chisel and list strengths and weaknesses we discovered.

Chisel is described by its authors as a *hardware construction language*, compared to Verilog and VHDL, which are *hardware description languages* [3]. The latter were originally developed to describe and simulate existing hardware designs. Only later, they have been repurposed for hardware synthesis. Current digital designs often are a collection of pre-existing modules (IP cores) that are parametrized and interconnected using a bus interface (e.g. AXI, Avalon, etc.) to form larger systems (System-on-Chip, SoC). Highly configurable structures were not envisioned during the design of Verilog and VHDL and are therefore notoriously hard to describe with them.

Chisel is built around the idea of *hardware generators*, i.e. executable design descriptions that can flexibly adapt themselves based on parameters. From a technical point of view, Chisel is an extension of the Scala programming language, which itself is build atop the Java Virtual Machine. The output of the Chisel build flow is a Verilog file which can be processed by conventional tools. A visual overview of this flow is shown in Fig. 1. The input files are compiled using the Scala compiler, and the resulting program is executed using the Java Runtime. This program then generates a single Verilog file as the output, containing a description of the generated hardware. This file can then be processed by conventional synthesis tools, optionally together with other source files written in VHDL, Verilog, etc. From a user perspective, the complete process from the input to the output files is usually orchestrated using the *sbt* tool and is executed using sbt run.

One important aspect of Chisel is, that the hardware generators are runnable programs that are *executed* during the elaboration phase to assemble the final circuit. Since the generators are implemented in Scala, arbitrary code can be executed in this stage to e.g. generate lookup tables or adapt the generated design to the chosen parameterization. Chisel inherits most aspects of Scala, like object-oriented design, type inference and functional programming. This allows complex hardware generators to be expressed in a few lines of code. Besides this, Chisel can also be used as a mere replacement for Verilog or VHDL. In this case, some features of Chisel, like the bulk-connect operator (<>), can help to reduce the verbosity of the code.

One shall note that Chisel is not a *high level synthesis* (HLS) language. The hardware design must still be carried out at the register level, Chisel can not e.g. extract a datapath design from a algorithmic description. Area and timing results are therefore expected to be a close match to a Verilog or VHDL description of the same circuit (cf. [9]).

Part of the Chisel ecosystem is *ChiselTest* [11], a testing library integrated with *ScalaTest*. It allows to write unit-tests for hardware described in Chisel. The tests can be either executed in a simulator implemented in Scala, or delegated to *Verilator*, an open-source Verilog simulator. As the tests are implemented in Scala, arbitrary Scala code can be executed during the test to generate test stimuli or check the expected results against a software implementation, in comparison to classic workflows where stimuli and expected results are often generated outside the testbench.

Comparable studies on the relation of Verilog and Chisel have previously been reported [2,3,7,9]. The original paper on Chisel [3] reports a 65% decrease in lines of code (LoC) for a 3-stage 32-bit RISC processor converted from Verilog to Chisel. Im et al. [7] also found a 53% decrease in LoC for a 64-bit RISC-V processor. Both performed physical layout for an ASIC process and found comparable area requirements for the Chisel and Verilog version.

Lennon et al. [9] performed an extensive evaluation of a Chisel implementation compared to a workflow where Verilog code is generated using a Tcl script. Typical building blocks of FPGA-designs, like arbiters and FIFOs were used for evaluation. They found the synthesis time, FPGA resource requirements, and maximum reachable frequency to be comparable, but noted that Chisel did not support asynchronous resets[1], which reduced the maximum frequency for FPGAs not supporting synchronous resets. The LoC were reduced by 0% to 37%, depending on the design. Compared to the Tcl+Verilog workflow, the authors experienced an increase in coding speed by a factor of 3, which they attribute to the more helpful error messages of Chisel and the fact that Tcl is not aware of Verilog syntax. In their conclusion, Lennon et al. mention the steep learning curve of Chisel and the need to understand the software aspects: "Although Chisel designers require a foundation in software design to allow them to utilize Chisel's power, constructing circuits with Chisel requires an identical appreciation of the hardware being described to that held by Verilog designers." [9].

---

[1] Support for asynchronous resets has since then been added to Chisel in version 3.2.0.

Arcas et al. [2] compared hardware implementations of algorithms commonly found in database applications. Verilog, Bluespec SystemVerilog, Altera OpenCL, LegUp, and Chisel were used for the comparison. Resource requirements and maximum frequency are reported to be on par between the Verilog and Chisel implementation. The LoC of the Chisel implementation are reduced by 11% to 16%, aside the "hash probe" design, where the LoC are increased by 25%. They likewise conclude that "some Scala knowledge" [2] is needed to efficiently work with Chisel.

The cited studies either focus on processors designs, or use very small examples to evaluate Chisel. While the reported results look promising, it remains open whether Chisel is also beneficial for general data processing applications, besides processor design. To the best of the authors knowledge, this is the first report evaluating the use of Chisel for a sophisticated real-world application involving a dedicated hardware architecture.

The rest of this work is structured as follows: Sect. 2 describes the system architecture and the underlying algorithm used for this evaluation. A quantitative comparison of the Chisel and VHDL implementation are given in Sect. 3, followed by a report on our experience while using Chisel in Sect. 4. A conclusion is drawn in Sect. 5.

2   System Description

In the following sections we briefly describe the principle and application of Synthetic Aperture Radar (SAR), the image formation algorithm Backprojection (BP), and give an architectural overview of our implementation. Both, the VHDL and the Chisel implementation, are fully working on an FPGA platform and produce identical results.

2.1   Synthetic Aperture Radar (SAR)

Acquiring near-live images of remote locations has many applications ranging from surveillance to disaster control. Often, electro-optic sensors (cameras) are used for this. While these provide a good solution for aerial imaging in decent environmental conditions, they cannot provide usable images without daylight or when clouds or smoke block the cameras' view.

An alternative imaging technique is synthetic aperture radar (SAR). Radar pulses are transmitted continuously and the received echoes are captured and stored while flying alongside the area of interest [5]. By merging the captured echo signals using a SAR processor, an aerial image of the scene is generated which shows the reflectiveness per ground area. Since radar waves have a much lower frequency than visible light and actively illuminate the scene with their signal, these systems can operate independent of daylight and penetrate most weather phenomena and air pollution.

2.2 Backprojection (BP)

To generate a usable image from the acquired raw data, an image formation step is necessary. The main part of this is called azimuth compression (AC) and essentially synthesizes a huge virtual antenna which, in turn, has a high spatial resolution. Historically, algorithms used in digital SAR processors have been optimized using frequency domain operations. While these enable a computationally efficient image formation, they are sensitive to deviations in the flight path, which need to be compensated separately. In face of current technology, especially in the field of FPGAs, time-domain-based image processing was shown to be feasible. This enables ideal correction of known flight errors or even deliberately chosen nonlinear flight trajectories [6].

One straightforward AC algorithm for SAR is Backprojection (BP). This time domain based technique can be summarized as follows: The output image is defined as a pixel grid of size $X \times Y$ encompassing the secene. For each of these pixels $g_{x,y}$, BP takes the echo captures d_m of all radar pulses into account. Based on the real-world locations of the image pixel and the antenna while capturing the echo, their geometric distance Δr is calculated. This information indicates, where echo data from this image position is stored. It is then used to interpolate a sample $d_m[\Delta r]$ from the echo data. These complex-valued samples from all radar pulses are then added per pixel. Also, a phase-correction factor k is used to enable coherent processing. After this process, areas with strong reflectors will have a high absolute pixel value while the coherent sum for non-reflective pixels will dissolve into noise. Equation (1) summarizes the BP computation per pixel.

$$g_{x,y} = \sum d_m[\Delta r] \cdot e^{i2k\Delta r} \tag{1}$$

Since there is no interdependence between the pixels, the image dimensions $x \in [0, (X-1)]$ and $y \in [0, (Y-1)]$ yield two straight-forward parallelization domains.

2.3 Architecture Overview

This section gives an overview of our architecture for the SAR Backprojection algorithm, so that the extent and complexity of the implementation can be estimated. A more detailed description of the VHDL implementation has been published earlier [4].

For our design we chose the aforementioned parallelization strategy in the pixel domain: The basic processing element is called a "submodule"; a block diagram of it is shown in Fig. 2. A submodule is capable of storing a number of neighboring pixels in an output buffer, called the line accumulator. The required part of the echo data from one pulse is fed into an input buffer. The input buffer and accumulating output buffer both consist of two Block-RAM-based memories each. These are swapped back and forth using multiplexers in order to allow filling and flushing the buffers while the projection of the next/previous line is ongoing.

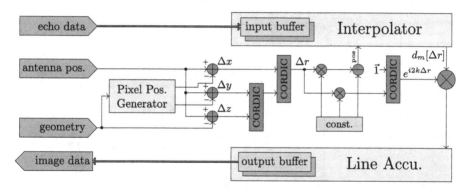

Fig. 2. GBP submodule core architecture. Two CORDICs are used to calculate the distance Δr for each pixel, which is sent to the interpolator. The result $d_m[\Delta r]$ is multiplied by a phase correction factor $e^{i2k\Delta r}$ and stored in the accumulator. Arrow types denote data types: $\rightarrow$ for normal busses and $\Rightarrow$ for AXI Stream connections.

The beginning of the processing chain is marked by the "Pixel Position Generator", that successively generates the real-world coordinate of the pixels on the current image region. The generated position is subtracted from the antenna position, and two CORDIC instances [12] are used to calculate the 3D vector length, which is the distance Δr from the antenna to the pixel. The result is given to the interpolator, which fetches the required samples from the input buffer. Additionally, a phase correction $e^{i2k\Delta r}$ is calculated using another CORDIC instance. The phase correction is applied before the sample is transferred to the accumulator and is stored in the output buffer. After all input data has been processed, the output buffer is flushed to main memory and a new set of pixels is computed.

An arbitrary number of these submodules can be used in parallel, each computing different subsets of the final image. As all submodules operate on the same echo data, this data can be broadcasted, keeping memory read accesses constant. The outer interface of these submodules consists of the echo data input stream, the image data output stream, control signals, and ports for the geometric parameters (cf. Fig. 2).

While the older VHDL implementation manages the coordination of the submodules using a central finite state machine (FSM), the newer Chisel implementation uses a miniature control processor called PacoBlaze [8]. This has the advantage of providing more flexibility and reprogrammability compared to a hardcoded FSM while still not taking up as much area as a full-featured microcontroller.

The interpolator implements a sinc interpolation to generate a sample at a fractional position, using a structure similar to a FIR filter. A block diagram of the interpolator is shown in Fig. 3. The incoming position is split into an integer and a fraction part. The integral part is used to select samples from the input buffer. The buffer memory is organized in a way that t samples are

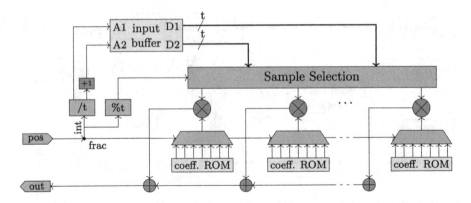

Fig. 3. Interpolator architecture. The incoming position is split into an integer and a fractional part. The integral part is used to fetch t samples from the dual-port memory, centered around the requested position. The samples are multiplied by coefficients selected by the fractional part, and summed up to form the interpolation result.

stored in a single memory word. It is implemented with dual port access so that two locations can be accessed at the same time. To perform the interpolation, two adjacent words—containing $2t$ samples in total—are fetched. From them, t samples, centered around the integer position, are extracted. The fractional part is used to select a set of coefficients which a pre-calculated and stored in a ROM. Every sample is multiplied with one of the coefficients; and the sum of these forms the interpolation result.

Outside of the submodules, apart from the control unit, there are only memory interfaces and other bus infrastructure. This is highly dependent on the platform and not in the scope of this paper. Although both implementations are proven to work on the system level, comparisons will focus on the internals of the submodule (including the interpolator), since they are closely matched among both implementations.

3   Measurements

In order to assess the expressivity of Chisel we performed measurements of the code size (number of lines of code) and the readability of the generated Verilog code. Both investigation considered only the backprojection submodule described above, which is implemented similar in the VHDL and Chisel version of the code. The remaining parts of the systems, namely the control logic and bus infrastructure was realized differently between both versions and would therefore be meaningless to compare. While the Chisel implementation describes the same hardware design, it was created independently of the existing VHDL code, as opposed to a mere transcription between languages. Both designs have been carried out by experienced hardware designers.

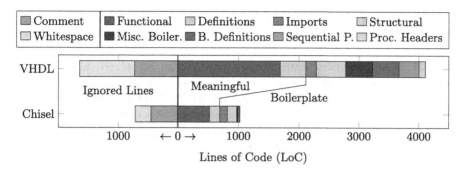

Fig. 4. Bar chart of the code size analysis result, divided into ignored lines, meaningful code and boilerplate code.

3.1 Code Size

The Chisel implementation of the Backprojection submodule consists of 19 files with 1736 LoC in total, whereas the VHDL description consists of 25 files and 5755 LoC. To further investigate the differences of the two languages, we classified every line of code into one of the following categories:

Whitespace (WS). Empty lines

Comment (COM). Lines containing only source code comments

Structural (STR). Lines containing only structural syntax elements, such as opening or closing braces ({/}) or begin/end

Imports (IMP). Import statements for other namespaces/packages

Boilerplate Definitions (BD). Lines consisting only of a declaration of a signal (VHDL) or Wire (Chisel), without any value assignment

Sequential Process (SQ). *(VHDL only)* Lines attributed to the sequential process of the Two Process design methodology [10] which separates the register description from combinatorial logic

Process Headers (PH). *(VHDL only)* Lines containing process headers, including sensitivity lists

Misc. Boilerplate (MB). Miscellaneous statements required for syntax, but containing no actual information; i.a. component declarations in VHDL

Definitions (DEF). Definitions of types, entities, Bundles and functions

Functional code (FUN). Everything else, i.e. code that describes the system's actual function, including module instantiations and signal connections

Examples for every category, as well as the distributions of the lines over the categories can be found in Table 1. A graphical overview of the line counts per category is shown in Fig. 4. Additionally, Appendix A contains a code example with classifications in VHDL and Chisel. The code examples are stylistically similar to the real implementations.

For all further analyses, lines from the *Whitespace* and *Comment* categories will be excluded. Furthermore, the categories *Structural*, *Imports*, *Boilerplate Definitions*, *Sequential Process*, *Process Headers*, and *Misc. Boilerplate* can be summed up as *Boilerplate code*; *Definitions* and *Functional code* as *Meaningful code*. With this high-level separation, it can be seen that the amount of *Meaningful* code is reduced by 67% comparing the VHDL and Chisel implementation, while the amount of *Boilerplate* code decreased by 83%. This gives a first indication that Chisel generally allows for more compact and expressive code, while especially verbose and redundant code is reduced.

Table 1. Code categories with examples, line count and their prevalence in the two implementations. Examples annotated using the markers can be found in Appendix A.

Category	Marker	Examples	LoC	Frac. [%]
		Chisel		
Whitespace	WS		264	15.2
Comment	COM	`// single line comment` `/* multi line comment ...`	450	25.9
Functional	FUN	`val reg_b = RegNext(c);` `inst_d.io.x <> inst_e.io.y;`	524	30.2
Definitions	DEF	`class X (...) extends Module` `val in_a = Input(SInt(n.W));`	166	9.6
Imports	IMP	`import chisel3._`	125	7.2
Structural	STR	`)};`	155	8.9
Misc. Boilerplate	MB	`val io = IO(new Bundle {`	19	1.1
Boilerplate Def.	BD	`val wire_a = Wire(Bool());`	33	1.9
		VHDL		
Whitespace	WS		921	16.0
Comment	COM	`-- single line comment`	724	12.6
Functional	FUN	`constant B : integer := C+1;` `sig_b <= not sig_c;`	1689	29.3
Definitions	DEF	`in_a : in std_logic;` `entity X is`	426	7.4
Imports	IMP	`use ieee.std_logic.all;`	172	3.0
Structural	STR	`begin` `end if;`	490	8.5

Misc. Boilerplate	MB	`architecture Y of X is`
		`port map (`
		`component Z ...`
			449	7.8

Boilerplate Def.	BD	`signal sig_b : std_logic;` `variable var_k : real;`	443	7.7
Sequential Process	SQ	`process (clk)` `if rising_edge(clk) then`	333	5.8
Process Headers	PH	`process (a, b, c, d)`	108	1.9

Table 2. Number of signal names in the Verilog code generated by Chisel, split by readability.

Category	Example	Count	Fraction [%]
Clear	`resetAccu`	6650	86.0
Derived	`dmaIndex_T_5`	478	6.2
Opaque	`GEN_47`	607	7.8

Concerning the meaningful code, most of the surplus lines in the VHDL implementation can be attributed to individual signal connections among entities. Chisel allows complete bi-directional `Bundles` to be connected using the bulk-connect operator (`<>`), which significantly reduces the number of lines required. Another cause for the reduced code size in Chisel is the implicit connection of clock and reset signals, as well as the implementation of the lookup table generation for the CORDICs and the interpolator, which is very verbose in VHDL.

The additional boilerplate code in VHDL is twofold. First, in the VHDL code a `component` declaration exists for every entity referenced; in Chisel this is not required. Second, register definitions are much more verbose in VHDL than in Chisel. In VHDL, following the Two Process methodology, a typical register definition consists of the declaration of two signals, an entry in the sequential process and the sensitivity list of the combinatorial process, and a reset definition. In Chisel, a register, together with its reset value, can be declared in one line of code; the clock and reset connections are implicit. Generally, Chisel allows signals to be declared inline with their driving logic, while in VHDL declaration and assignment have to be split up.

3.2 Transparency of Generated Code

Generally, the Verilog code files generated by Chisel are not intended to be human-readable and should be considered an opaque artifact. On the other hand, the warnings reported in the synthesis process and messages from timing analysis always refer to this generated code. It is therefore important to be able to find the Chisel source code location which is related to a certain Verilog line. A classic example is timing closure, where a failing path may be reported, consisting of Verilog signal names. To measure how easy it will be to find the root cause of a timing violation, we counted the number of signal definitions in the generated Verilog code and divided them into three categories: *Clear* names, having exactly the name of a Chisel signal; *derived* names, starting with a Chisel name but having a suffix in the form of "_T_1"; and *opaque* names, which are purely artificial and have the form like "GEN_57".

Numerous wires from the latter category are used to describe the content of read-only memories (e.g. the instruction memory of the microcontroller). This memory is inferred as Block-RAM by the synthesis tool, the wires therefore were excluded from the counting. We performed this measurements using Chisel 3.5.0. The results are reported in Table 2. Only 7.8% of the signal names were found to be opaque; most of them occurred in more abstract code like an AXI register file generator.

4 Experience Using Chisel

In this section we summarize our own experience while working with Chisel. The author had no prior knowledge in Chisel and used the re-implementation of the described Backprojection module as an opportunity to learn Chisel.

We found working with Chisel to be highly productive. As shown in Sect. 3.1 VHDL is overly verbose when it comes to declaring registers or connecting large busses. Also the fact that only synthesizable hardware can be described in Chisel made the coding experience more pleasant; the feeling of "fighting the tool" to reach a certain implementation was removed.

As described above, our design includes the *PacoBlaze* softcore [8], which is only available as Verilog code. We used a Chisel BlackBox to include it in the design. This generally worked well, although simulation with *ChiselTest* and Verilator was only possible after combining all source files of the PacoBlaze into a single file. Generally, the workflow of writing small modules and thoroughly testing them using unit tests with ChiselTest has proven to be very successful. In many cases, the expected test results and stimuli could be generated using a software implementation of the algorithm in Scala, so that all code was implemented in the same language. Compared to the typical workflow, where test vectors are generated in MATLAB or Python and then executed using a Verilog/VHDL testbench, this approach turned out to have less overhead, encouraging the designer to actually include tests for every single module.

Timing closure for the design was easy to achieve. The mapping from reported timing violations in the synthesis tool (*Xilinx Vivado* in our case) to the corresponding Chisel source code location was generally easy. As shown above, only about 8% of the wires in the generated Verilog code used generic names, therefore the reported paths always included enough information to find their context. To insert a register in a problematic path, it often was enough to wrap the expression with RegNext(). When the failing path was inside an AXI-Stream, a more complex register slice needed to be inserted. The object-oriented approach of Chisel allowed us to define a concise generator function to insert an arbitrary number of these register slices. Combined with the bulk-connect operator of Chisel, this could be applied with a single line of code, similar to a simple register. We generally found the iteration speed in timing closure very high.

While implementing the CORDIC algorithm we found the possibility to execute arbitrary Scala code during elaboration time very useful. Using this, we could calculate the CORDIC gain constant and the angular lookup tables for arbitrary iteration counts on the fly, without falling back to hard-coded constants in the source code.

One downside of Chisel is its steep learning curve. This is partly due to Chisel being a relatively young language, so not much learning material being available yet. Also the documentation of Chisel is sparse in some parts. In line with the findings of Lennon et al. and Alon et al. [1, 9], we also see a requirement to have some experience in modern programming languages—something not necessarily found among hardware designers—to fully harness the power of Chisel. Since the full knowledge of digital design is still required, this raises the bar for new designers. On the other hand we would not consider that a shortcoming of Chisel, but as an effect coming from the situation the field of digital design is in: Chisel can be used on a very similar level as Verilog or VHDL, and then mainly helps to reduce the verbosity. For complex and parametrizable designs, as today's IP cores, a certain complexity in the hardware description will always be required. Chisel here allows for highly sophisticated hardware generators which enable a flexibility that might be unreachable using a classic Tcl+Verilog design flow.

5   Conclusion

In this field report, we analyzed the practical use of the Chisel hardware description language. As an example design, we used an implementation of the Backprojection algorithm for Synthetic Aperture Radar (SAR). To assess the advantages over traditional languages, we examined the differences to a VHDL implementation by classifying every line of code into one of several categories. The analysis showed that the number of code lines was reduced by about 74% from the VHDL to the Chisel implementation; boilerplate code was reduced by 83%. This indicates that Chisel is more expressive and allows to describe the same design in fewer lines of code. Especially, the amount of boilerplate code was reduces significantly.

Furthermore, we analyzed the Verilog code generated by Chisel and found only 7.8% of the signals to have generic, meaningless names. Thus, few problems are to be expected when trying to find the Chisel code corresponding to a signal in the generated code.

Finally, we gave a personal impression of our experience with Chisel. We generally found Chisel to be very productive and powerful, but also saw the need of some programming knowledge to fully unleash the power of the language. It allows for higher productivity and flexible reuse of designs.

In our opinion, Chisel is an exciting new technology that has the power to free the field of digital design from the corset of traditional hardware description languages. It is by far not limited to processor design and thus should be considered for all fields of digital hardware design.

A   Code Examples

This appendix provides the code of an example design in Chisel and VHDL to make our methodology more clear. Every line of the source code has been classified according to Table 1. The code presented here is not part of the original source used for this study, but is written in a similar style. In can be seen, that especially the amount of boilerplate code (categories MB, BD, and SQ) is reduced, but the Chisel code is also less verbose in general.

A.1   Chisel Code

```
DEF     package example
WS
IMP     import chisel3._
        import chisel3.util._
WS
DEF     class Example(n : Int) extends Module
STR     {
BD        val io = IO(new Bundle {
DEF         val in_val = Input(UInt(n.W))
            val out_val = Output(UInt(n.W))
STR       })
WS
FUN       val bypass = RegNext(io.in_val, init = 0.U)
          val in_masked = io.in_val & "b111".U
WS
FUN       val exampleInst = Module(new Example2())
          exampleInst.io.data_in := in_masked
WS
FUN       io.out_val := Mux(io.in_val > 5.U, exampleInst.io.data_out, bypass)
STR     }
```

A.2   VHDL Code

```
IMP    library IEEE;
       use IEEE.std_logic_1164.all;
       use IEEE.numeric_std.all;
WS
DEF    entity example is
STR      generic (
DEF        N : integer := 8
STR      );
         port (
DEF        clk     : in  std_logic;
           reset   : in  std_logic;
           in_val  : in  std_logic_vector(N-1 downto 0);
           out_val : out std_logic_vector(N-1 downto 0)
STR      );
       end entity;
WS
MB     architecture rtl of example is
BD       component example2
           generic ( N : integer );
STR        port (
BD           clk      : in  std_logic;
             reset    : in  std_logic;
             data_in  : in  std_logic_vector(N-1 downto 0);
             data_out : out std_logic_vector(N-1 downto 0)
STR        );
         end component;
DEF      signal c_bypass, n_bypass : std_logic_vector(N-1 downto 0);
         signal in_masked : std_logic_vector(N-1 downto 0);
         signal comp_out : std_logic_vector(N-1 downto 0);
STR    begin
FUN      in_masked <= in_val and std_logic_vector(to_unsigned(2#111#, N));
         n_bypass <= in_val;
WS
FUN      example_inst : example2
STR        generic map (
FUN          N  => N
STR        ) port map (
FUN          clk      => clk,
             reset    => reset,
             data_in  => in_masked,
             data_out => comp_out
STR        );
WS
SQ       SEQ : process(clk)
         begin
           if rising_edge(clk) then
             if reset = '1' then
               c_bypass <= (others => '0');
             else
               c_bypass <= n_bypass;
             end if;
           end if;
         end process;
WS
PH       MUX : process (c_bypass, in_val, comp_out)
STR      begin
FUN        out_val <= c_bypass;
           if unsigned(in_val) > 5 then
             out_val <= comp_out;
STR        end if;
         end process;
       end rtl;
```

References

1. Alon, E., Asanović, K., Bachrach, J., Nikolić, B.: Open-source EDA tools and IP, a view from the trenches. In: Proceedings of the 56th Annual Design Automation Conference 2019. ACM, June 2019. https://doi.org/10.1145/3316781.3323481
2. Arcas-Abella, O., Ndu, G., Sonmez, N., et al.: An empirical evaluation of high-level synthesis languages and tools for database acceleration. In: 2014 24th International Conference on Field Programmable Logic and Applications (FPL), pp. 1–8. IEEE (2014). https://doi.org/10.1109/FPL.2014.6927484
3. Bachrach, J., Vo, H., Richards, B., et al.: Chisel: constructing hardware in a Scala embedded language. In: DAC Design Automation Conference 2012, pp. 1212–1221. IEEE (2012). https://doi.org/10.1145/2228360.2228584
4. Cholewa, F., Pfitzner, M., Fahnemann, C., Pirsch, P., Blume, H.: Synthetic aperture radar with backprojection: a scalable, platform independent architecture for exhaustive FPGA resource utilization. In: 2014 International Radar Conference, pp. 1–5. IEEE (2014). https://doi.org/10.1109/RADAR.2014.7060455
5. Curlander, J.C., McDonough, R.N.: Synthetic Aperture Radar, vol. 11. Wiley, New York (1991)
6. Duersch, M.I.: Backprojection for synthetic aperture radar. Ph.D. thesis, Brigham Young University (2013)
7. Im, J., Kang, S.: Comparative analysis between verilog and chisel in Risc-V core design and verification. In: 2021 18th International SoC Design Conference (ISOCC), pp. 59–60. IEEE (2021). https://doi.org/10.1109/ISOCC53507.2021.9614007
8. Kocik, P.B.: Pacoblaze - a synthesizable behavioral verilog picoblaze clone. https://bleyer.org/pacoblaze/. Accessed 31 Jan 2022
9. Lennon, P., Gahan, R.: A comparative study of chisel for FPGA design. In: 2018 29th Irish Signals and Systems Conference (ISSC), pp. 1–6. IEEE (2018). https://doi.org/10.1109/ISSC.2018.8585292
10. Pedroni, V.A.: Finite State Machines in Hardware: Theory and Design (with VHDL and SystemVerilog). MIT Press, Cambridge (2013)
11. Lin, R., Kevin Laeufer, C.M., et al.: ChiselTest: the official testing library for chisel circuits. https://github.com/ucb-bar/chiseltest. Accessed 31 Jan 2022
12. Volder, J.E.: The cordic trigonometric computing technique. IRE Trans. Electron. Comput. **EC-8**(3), 330–334 (1959). https://doi.org/10.1109/TEC.1959.5222693

EasyHBM: Simple and Fast HBM Access for FPGAs Using High-Level-Synthesis

Lars Schwenger[1]([⊠]), Philipp Holzinger[1], Dietmar Fey[1],
Hector Gerardo Munoz Hernandez[2], and Marc Reichenbach[2]

[1] Chair of Computer Architecture, Friedrich-Alexander Universität
Erlangen-Nürnberg, 91058 Erlangen, Germany
{lars.schwenger,philipp.holzinger,dietmar.fey}@fau.de

[2] Chair of Computer Engineering, Brandenburg University of Technology
Cottbus-Senftenberg, 03046 Cottbus, Germany
{hector.munozhernandez,marc.reichenbach}@b-tu.de

Abstract. High-Level Synthesis (HLS) has become increasingly popular for FPGA accelerators. Its main benefit is the considerably simpler development and faster time-to-market than traditional RTL designs. HLS also allows developers with less in-depth hardware design knowledge to employ FPGA accelerators for their applications. However, like traditional CPUs, these designs often suffer from an insufficient memory bandwidth to provide data to all computational units. High-Bandwidth Memory (HBM) has been developed and recently added to commercial FPGAs to overcome the limited bandwidth. As stacked DRAM, it achieves a substantially higher bandwidth than traditional DRAM through its high number of independent memory channels. However, current HLS tools do not fully take this characteristic into account. They generate accelerators that either do not automatically use all available channels for HBM access and thus lose performance or require more complex manual data partitioning and replication schemes between the channels. That leads to failure to meet the expected gains of application developers. Therefore, in this paper, we propose an utterly application-independent way to efficiently handle HBM as a unified pool of memory in an HLS tool in a generic manner. It keeps the advantage of high bandwidth for many applications while hiding the multi-channel complexity from the developer's HLS accelerator description. That enables the design of HLS cores that run efficiently on FPGAs without deep consideration of the available memory.

1 Introduction

As technology advances, modern FPGA accelerators are more restricted by available memory bandwidth rather than compute resources. Processing Elements (PE) often process data faster than can be provided by traditional DRAM. This challenge has been known in academia and industry for two decades [1,2]. In recent years, several technologies have been proposed to address this problem.

© The Author(s), under exclusive license to Springer Nature Switzerland AG 2022
A. Orailoglu et al. (Eds.): SAMOS 2022, LNCS 13511, pp. 43–57, 2022.
https://doi.org/10.1007/978-3-031-15074-6_3

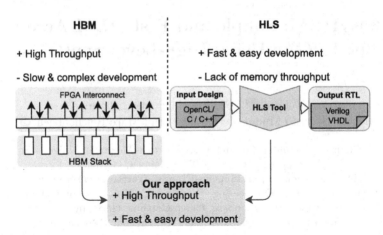

Fig. 1. Our approach combines the high throughput offered by HBM with the fast and easy development offered by HLS while eliminating the complex handling of HBM.

One of those is High Bandwidth Memory (HBM), which is now also present in several commercial devices [3]. HBM, which consists of stacked DRAM, increases the number of parallel (pseudo) memory channels (PCH) and thus the bandwidth.

At the same time application-specific accelerator designer use more often High-Level Synthesis (HLS). Here, developers can describe *PE* with more expressive high-level languages like C/C++ and OpenCL. The widespread use of these languages in the software industry gives easier access to FPGA based technologies. Especially for developers with less in-depth hardware design knowledge.

Despite these benefits, current HLS tools still have limitations. One issue is the system-level integration of accelerators with HBM [4]. Its high number of independent memory channels requires memory parallelization. Also *PCH* show difference in access latencies and the memory controllers are complex [5–7]. As a result, this leads to a higher design effort despite using HLS.

This paper presents an HLS design approach shown in Fig. 1 to overcome this challenge. It automates the parallelization of memory access for HBM while keeping the high-level source code simple. To this end, we integrate memory structure information into the HLS flow. The memory accesses are statically and dynamically scheduled and additionally buffered. That leads to parallel usage of all available *PCH* with minimal redundant load and store operations. The number of instantiated *PE* depends on the expected bandwidth. The main contributions of our work can be summarized as:

1. Efficient utilization of HBM throughput, which increases accelerator performance.
2. Simplifying HBM access in particular for less experienced users.
3. Reducing host software overhead for data management compared to traditional methods.

The paper is structured as follows: Sect. 2 summarizes existing research. Section 3 evaluates the existing design approaches compared to our one. The architecture is explained in Sect. 4. Finally, we evaluate our approach compared to the traditional methods in Sect. 5.

2 Related Work

Many architectures explicitly designed for HBM achieve excellent results due to the increased memory bandwidth [8–10]. This performance boost is the result of the simultaneous use of many *PCH* that HBM provides. Each individual *PCH* is slower than traditional DRAM channels, but they have a higher total throughput [3]. Nevertheless, this parallelization requires a sophisticated hardware design in combination with application-specific data partitioning. Therefore, these applications are primarily hand-tailored solutions for a specific HBM configuration. Thus, they lack portability for other HBM and regular DRAM setups. In contrast, our approach simplifies memory usage, especially of complex HBM interfaces. This allows developers with less knowledge of HBM to access most of its potential.

Xilinx offers an ASIC crossbar to streamline the accelerator design for HBM. It creates a unified global address space and allows access to any *PCH* from any AXI port in the FPGA. However, research showed that its restricted number of lateral connections could decrease the performance of many access patterns under heavy load [6]. Moreover, its structure and address mapping scheme can cause easily unfavorable data distributions. In this case, bus contention when multiple AXI ports access the same channel severely decreases the HBM throughput [5,6]. Therefore, the AISC crossbar does not achieve its original goal of optimizing the design process.

Current state-of-the-art HLS tools like Xilinx Vitis [11] and Intel HLS [12] reflect this in their integration of HBM. They treat HBM only as a set of independent channels that can be connected by the developer rather than as a holistic memory resource. With such tools, there are currently two main approaches to integrate HBM. First, the replication of *PEs*, where each *PE* is exclusively connected to its own *PCH*. Second, a hand-tailored design via modification of the source code. For example, by an expansion of the number of kernel arguments to map these to distinct memory ports. Section 3 features a more detailed comparison of these approaches. In summary, both methods leave most of the difficulties with HBM to the developers. They are therefore not well suited for simple and fast usage.

Several interconnects on top of HBM have been developed to overcome these design problems. HBM-Connect minimizes the conflicts on the lateral connections via a butterfly crossbar [7]. It uses buffer structures to enable accessing HBM with full bursts and offers integration into Vitis HLS via a library. While this mitigates HBM throughput degradation, the *PCH* are still treated as independent. Consequently, developers must distribute data by themselves to ensure parallel usage of all *PCH*. That poses a significant disadvantage if a developer ports an HLS kernel from a non-HBM FPGA or even GPU to an HBM FPGA. It would require considerate development time to find a correct memory placement in combination with the correct usage of these buffers.

At the same time, the Memory Access Optimizer (MAO) has been presented as a replacement for the Xilinx ASIC [6]. Like HBM-Connect, MAO omits the lateral connections of the Xilinx Interconnect through a hierarchical distribution network that routes the memory requests of the Bus Masters (BM) to the correct *PCH*. Unlike HBM-Connect, MAO also handles the data distribution along *PCH* via an address mapping scheme. The MAO maps consecutive addresses of the BM to different *PCH*. Therefore, reducing the contention and increasing the parallelization without explicitly placing the data. As a third feature, MAO implements transaction reorder buffers near the BM. These free the bus fabric from outstanding requests by accepting and storing out-of-order transactions caused by varying *PCH* access and routing delays. This reduces the bus contention and backpressure on the bus fabric for both BM and PCH. These feature of MAO enables developers to overcome many problems of designing an accelerator for HBM.

However, the MAO currently lacks support for HLS. While simple HLS *PEs* or multi-accelerator-systems can use the MAO as an advanced interconnect, it does not use the potential of HBM to its fullest. A more complex HLS accelerator needs to implement many AXI buses, handle possible dependencies of requests, and automatically cache data locally. Furthermore, it must also be capable of processing the high amount of data provided by the HBM. Current HLS tools cannot provide this without significant guidance from the developer. Our approach solves this challenge by coordinating MAO with customized HLS cores over several layers. This also allows developers with minimal hardware design knowledge to create accelerated applications using HBM.

As a basis for this close integration of HLS accelerators and HBM, we use the HERA framework [13]. It was developed to simplify the use of reconfigurable logic in general-purpose systems by allowing application developers and users to work completely independently without knowledge about the concrete hardware setup. For this purpose, HERA provides the FPGA hardware, driver, user-space libraries for language support like OpenCL, and a system daemon with an own HLS tool for synthesis. This close feedback between system setup and application HLS can e.g. guarantee the alignment of memory or automatically provide information about the system to the HLS tool. However, it currently does not support multi-channel memory like HBM at all. Nevertheless, these features make it perfectly suited as a basis for extentions with the novel methodology presented in this paper in the following.

Table 1. Comparison of HBM integration approaches into HLS: The top row shows a schematic of each approach. *Replication* assigns each PE one PCH. Then the PE is copied X times to match the number of PCH. The *Handcrafted* approach modifies the source code to create a single PE with X BM connected to the X PCH of the HBM. Our method introduces an intermediate layer consisting of a scheduler, buffer, and the MAO. That enables the number of PEs (Y) to be independent of the number of PCHs (X). Each following row shows how well the implementation performs in each category.

Architecture	⬜ ··X HLS PEs·· ⬜ HBM ⬜ ··· X PCHs ··· ⬜	HLS PE ··· X BMs ··· HBM ⬜ ··· X PCHs ··· ⬜	⬜ ··Y HLS PEs·· ⬜ SCHEDULER BUFFER MAO ··· X BMs ··· HBM ⬜ ··· X PCHs ··· ⬜
Expected Memory	–	–	+
Expected Performance	0*	+	+
Host Complexity	–	–	+
Accel Complexity	+	–	+

* + for embarrassingly parallel problems

3 Methodology

While the works from Sect. 2 address some of the challenges of using HBM with HLS, they are not sufficient. In this section, we examine the problems of current approaches on the example of a general matrix-matrix-multiplication (GEMM). Based on that, we derive a methodology that we present in detail in Sect. 4.

Listing 1.1 shows a basic memory-bound GEMM kernel. This implementation suffers from a lack of bandwidth. Memory access to the second matrix do not reuse loaded DRAM pages and are not suited for AXI bursts. The first traditional approach, called *Replication*, generates an IP block of an HLS kernel description. Then the HLS tool replicates the individual PE to match the number of *PCH* of the HBM. Therefore, each *PE* can use the total bandwidth of one *PCH*. This approach has three potential downsides.

Each *PE* has access to a limited part of the entire HBM as it only utilizes one *PCH*. The cited Xilinx crossbar tries to facilitate this problem such that each *PE* can access each PCH. However, suppose the developer does not prepare the data carefully. Many access patterns will lead to situations where each *PE* accesses the same *PCH*. As explained earlier, this diminishes any performance gains due to several reasons. HBM-Connect reduces this loss by eliminating the lateral connections, but the performance will still drop if all *PE* access the same *PCH* [7].

```
__kernel void matrix_multiplication(__global const int *a,
        __global const int *b,__global int *c,
        const unsigned int a_cols,const unsigned int b_cols){
    unsigned int col_c = get_global_id(0);
    unsigned int row_c = get_global_id(1);
    int acc = 0;
    for(unsigned int j=0; j<a_cols; j=j+1){
        acc += a[row_c*a_cols+j] * b[j*b_cols+col_c];
    }
    c[row_c*b_cols+col_c] = acc;
}
```

Listing 1.1. Basic GEMM kernel: Two loads have to be performed to execute an operation. Matrix A can be loaded via burst access but for matrix B the data of each consecutive item is at a different place.

The second downside, the distribution of data, is a result of that problem. The host system must partition or copy the data to the respective *PCH*s to avoid performance losses or allow a single connection between *PE* and *PCH*. After the computation, it must also collect the results from each *PCH*. Dependent on the kernel's access pattern, this can expand the overhead of the host prior to the start of the accelerator. In addition, it increases the development time of the host software. The address mapping scheme of the MAO explained in Sect. 2 circumvents this [6]. As a result, the developer can work with a continuous address space. That is especially good for developers accustomed to designing for GPUs and CPUs.

However, if the different *PEs* access the same address through the MAO or the MAO maps different data to the same *PCH*, the *PEs* still access the same *PCH*. That limits the throughput. Cases like that show that the MAO does not simply make everything easier but adds its own design consideration. Therefore it is better to omit the MAO for these cases and distribute the data instead.

The last problem involves the actual HLS design of the *PE*. For example, the GEMM in Listing 1.1 cannot use the entire bandwidth due to its access pattern. In the best case, replicating the *PE* leads to a linear execution speed-up. If the *PE* is not optimal, this does not lead to overall good performance despite using HBM. Nevertheless, embarrassingly parallel problems optimized for a single AXI port often do not suffer from this downside. Here, a single PE does not need more bandwidth. In these cases *Replication* is the best way to gain speed-up.

A solution to this problem is a more widespread method: *Handcrafted* designs. These relate precisely to the available number of *PCH*. In this case, the engineer modifies the HLS source code to achieve an access pattern and data flow that profits more from the HBM. For example, a *PE* uses more ports to allow a better parallel loading of the data for its computation. A handcrafted design is, in most cases, performance-wise, the best solution. As earlier mentioned, much research showed excellent solutions using HBM for a broad number of problems. However, this increases the development complexity and time. Listing 1.2 shows an example of the GEMM with four input ports. In Vitis HLS in- and output ports are created from the number of kernel arguments. These must then be

```
__kernel void matrix_multiplication(__global const int *a0,
        __global const int *b0,__global const int *a1,
        __global const int *b1,__global int *c0,__global int *c1,
        const unsigned int a_cols,const unsigned int b_cols){
    unsigned int col_c = get_global_id(0);
    unsigned int row_c = get_global_id(1);
    int acc[4] = {0,0,0,0};
    for(unsigned int j=0; j<a_cols; j=j+2){
        for(unsigned int i=0; i<2; i=i+1){
            acc[i]+= a0[row_c*a_cols+j]*b0[j*b_cols+col_c+i];
            acc[2+i]+= a1[(row_c+1)*a_cols+j]*b0[j*b_cols+col_c+i];
            acc[i]+= a0[row_c*a_cols+j+1]*b1[(j+1)*b_cols+col_c+i];
            acc[2+i]+= a1[(row_c+1)*a_cols+j+1]*b1[(j+1)*b_cols+col_c+i
                ];
        }
    }
    for(unsigned int i=0; i<4; i=i+1){
        c0[row_c*b_cols+col_c+i] = acc[i];
        c1[(row_c+1)*b_cols+col_c+i] = acc[2+i];
    }
}
```

Listing 1.2. GEMM Kernel with four input arguments: Each port can perform burst access of at least two. All ports access a different place in memory. In contrast to the basic kernel, this reduces access latencies.

used in a clever way to increase the performance. The shown kernel is not the best implementation for a GEMM with four ports, but it serves to illustrate the increase in complexity. A comparison with a State-Of-The-Art accelerator has no benefit because this work tries to simplify the general HLS design process with HBM and not compete with particular implementations.

In Summary, four potential design problems are shown in Table 1: Memory size reduction, data partitioning, performance bottleneck, and design complexity. The MAO addresses the first two problems but leaves the actual handling of such an increased bandwidth to the developer. Therefore, we use the MAO to eliminate the reduction of memory size and data partitioning and combine it with scheduling, buffering, and replication of *PE*. That enables more efficient processing and thus higher performance. Also, it prevents simultaneous access to the same PCH. The original kernel shown in Listing 1.1 requires no modification. Instead, we add the various layers around the *PE* to match the required bandwidth. Moreover, this keeps a low design complexity for the developer.

4 Architecture

One of the main challenges of HLS is the currently insufficient simplicity. Although it has been developed to speed up the design of hardware and thus shorten the time from application concept to an accelerated implementation, current HLS tools still often rely on an FPGA platform-specific code style. This is in particular true for modern devices with HBM. As one of the core concepts of die-stacked HBM, it incorporates a large amount (usually ≥ 16) of disjunct, independent memory channels. However, this architecture characteristic should primarily not be of concern for application developers as its handling

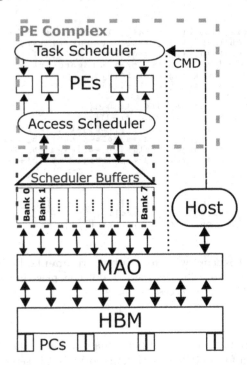

Fig. 2. The architecture of our approach: The MAO connects to the HBM through N (e.g., 8) AXI-Ports. It links the Buffer and the host with the HBM. The Buffer has N banks that enable parallel access on each PCH. The Access Scheduler allows a variable number of PEs in the PE Complex.

is not intuitive for developers with a background in CPU and GPU programming. Therefore, an HLS tool should, in contrast to existing solutions, be able to exploit memory access parallelism, without resorting to developer intervention. A schematic for such an architecture is depicted in Fig. 2. It processes tasks of a grid-like structure as used in many parallelization paradigms like OpenCL and OpenMP, in a pipelined fashion on its dedicated *PE* cores. Hereby, optimization considerations regarding the memory interface of HBM have to be taken into account by HLS tools on multiple levels.

4.1   PE High-Level Synthesis

First of all, the *PEs* themselves need to be generated from the high-level source code and prepared for many wide data buses. For this purpose we extended the HLS compiler of the HERA framework [13] that extracts control and data flow, and instantiates an equivalent hardware FSM. Their overall structure can be seen in Fig. 3. Core of an *PE* is the *pipeline logic* that calculates the actual kernel. Hereby, a new work-item of the grid is dispatched every cycle by the *Task Scheduler* such that every stage processes a different one at a time. To use the

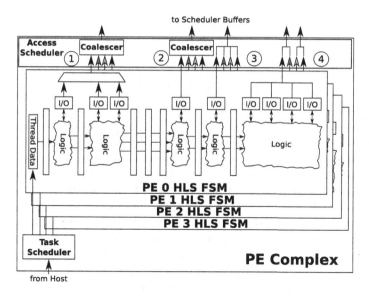

Fig. 3. Structure of the HLS generated PEs and schematic of different memory access optimization techniques.

high-level source code independently on various platforms we presume that it does not contain any accommodations for HBM. This means, the appropriate data widths and number of memory channels are not implemented, such that all memory access optimizations have to be performed by the HLS tool. Therefore, we extended the HERA compiler with the four following measures that form the I/O patterns (1)–(4) seen in Fig. 3.

First, we **vectorize** and pack all successive memory accesses within a kernel work-items e.g. generated by unrolled loops inside a *PE* ((4)). This allows fetching and storing more data at once with every request and thus a more effectively use of the HBM.

Second, the HLS tool **assigns priorities** to every load and store of the kernel depending on its relative usage. This is estimated by their location in hot loops or divergent branches and their addresses. For instance, a memory location that always needs to be accessed every cycle is the most important while constants that are static for all work-items in the grid are the least. These are then sorted and assigned to local memory ports such that high priority accesses work in parallel and low priority ones are grouped to save hardware resources. This can be seen in Fig. 3 where pattern (1) groups multiple internal I/O ports with a multiplexer to minimize the resources needed. In contrast, patterns (2)–(4) are determined to be performance critical and therefore instantiated as exclusive concurrent accesses.

Third, the thus generated *PE* itself is **duplicated** until the predicted *PE* throughput matches the total available bandwidth of the memory. This forms a *PE Complex* whose number of *PEs* is not equivalent to the number of *PCHs* since less *PEs* are needed when they are highly internally vectorized and more if this was not possible for the kernel. Nevertheless, the shared *Task Scheduler* ensures that the *PE Complex* behaves like a single accelerator for the user. As the grid-like execution paradigm fosters linearly increasing addresses of memory accesses over consecutive work-items, the *Task Scheduler* also distributes their IDs in round-roubing fashion over consecutive *PEs*.

Fourth, the memory buses are **coalesced** over all *PEs* in the *PE Complex*. This is either done statically at compile time ((3)-(4)) or dynamically with additional *Coalescer* hardware ((1)-(2)). To make a decision the HLS tool analyzes the address paths of loads and stores in a kernel regarding their alignment and divergence. It is then combined with the dispatch of consecutive work-items to consecutive *PEs* by the *Task Scheduler* and memory allocation alignment guarantees ensured by the HERA framework. If consecutive addresses are requested by the *PEs*, a static bus packing can be instantiated ((3)-(4)). For the statically determined constants a special resource reduced *Coalescer* is used to fetch and buffer them once for all work-items (1). Finally, in case the memory access patterns are too complex or not predictable, a full *Coalescer* is used to combine as many requests as possible at runtime ((2)). These four measures combined make the overall HLS memory ports wider, reduce the total number of memory requests, and therefore lowers the pressure on the upstream memory interface to the *Scheduler Buffers* in the following.

4.2   HBM Connection

These *Scheduler Buffers* are the interface between the HBM via the MAO and the HLS PE Complex as seen in Fig. 4. They serve two purposes. On the one hand, caching HBM requests increases the possible bandwidth of a kernel [14]. More minor redundant memory accesses cause this. On the other hand, the buffers minimize the chance that BMs access the same *PCH* via the MAO. In other words, they generate requests which use the available *PCH* fully parallel.

We constructed the *Scheduler Buffers* as banked memory, which is the core design idea of this buffer. Each one connects to one AXI port of the MAO. Each buffer performs a burst access, taking the first item after the complete burst of the previous one. That allows parallel access to all *PCH* because the address mapping scheme of the MAO described in Sect. 2 selects the next *PCH* after all addresses belonging to one burst. That ensures the optimal usage of the MAO. The implementation of the buffers can happen in various forms. We opted for a full cache because most developers, only experienced in CPU and GPU design, are familiar with caches. The used cache is not entirely optimized and lacks the ability of latency hiding. Better optimized caches or other banked buffers might exceed the performance of our implementation without changing the overall method as we can swap the buffer layer easily. The overall downsides of the buffers is the resource consumption, as each bank is implemented as BRAM-blocks.

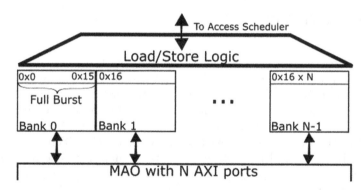

Fig. 4. The architecture of the Scheduler Buffers: Each of the N memory banks connects to one AXI port of the MAO. The banks perform simultaneous burst access. Due to the address mapping scheme of the MAO, all PCH of the HBM are used. The Buffers are connected to the Access Scheduler that performs load and stores.

5   Evaluation

Table 1 shows four potential issues of the system integration with HBM. Based on these, we derive three evaluation factors: Setup overhead, hardware design complexity, and the actual performance of the accelerator. We combine the setup overhead with the memory reduction because these are closely linked. The starting point of each design approach is a source code written in OpenCL like in Listing 1.1. The VHDL IP cores are generated with Vitis HLS 2019.2 for the traditional approaches and with HERA for ours [13]. We connect the accelerator to the HBM and build the design with Vivado 2019.2 at 300 MHz. Finally, we execute the design on a Virtex Ultrascale+ XCVU37P FPGA.

We selected two common applications for the evaluation: GEMM and 4×4 convolution with fixed weights. We picked those because they are both used in many fields accelerated via FPGAs like machine learning and image processing. Furthermore, the GEMM has a suboptimal but simpler to develop memory access pattern in OpenCL, which makes it more susceptible to HBM related memory throughput problems. In contrast, the convolution features a relatively straightforward one. As established, a heavily customized HLS design for a specific architecture usually outperforms a more generic HLS implementation for all tool chains. However, this comes with enormously increased design complexity and development time. In contrast, our approach targets developers with less hardware design and HBM experience, and those with little time budgets. Therefore, we focus on simpler, more generic kernels like those seen in Listing 1.1 without much optimization. Nevertheless, we still implemented some optimizations in the direction of a more *handcrafted* approach for comparison Here, added more ports to better utilize memory bursts and data reuse like in Listing 1.2.

5.1 Design Complexity

In general, the *Replication* approach and ours have the same complexity, while the *Handcrafted* one has a much higher one. It is hard to distinctly separate a regular design and a handcrafted one since there is some overlap in practice. However, especially FPGA specific code annotations strongly depend on the developer's experience and can generate vastly different results. As this diverges the stated goals in this work, we omit them in the following.

We chose the Halstead complexity metric to assess the differences in design complexity [15]. The Halstead Metric is a static analysis that determines the effort to develop a program based on the source code's unique (n_1) and total number of operators (N_1) and unique (n_2) and total operands (N_2). The *Program Length* $N_1 + N_2 = N$ and *Vocabulary* $n_1 + n_2 = n$ are calculated based on these variables. Additional metrics are *Volume V* (Eq. (1a)), an indicator of the information contained in the source code. The *Difficulty D* (Eq. (1b)) and the *Effort E* (Eq. (1c)) measure the time to understand, respectively, to write the code. Table 2 shows our and the *Replication* results compared to the *Handcrafted* approach with four and eight *PCH*. We limit ourselves to a maximal of eight *PCHs* for simplicity. Our tool supports more *PCHs* but the design comparison would be more challenging. In the case of the 4×4 convolution, we only use four ports for the *Handcrafted* approach as more ports would alter the source code significantly.

$$V = N * log_2(n) \tag{1a}$$
$$D = n_1/2 * N_2/n_2 \tag{1b}$$
$$E = D * V \tag{1c}$$

It is evident that the Volume, Difficulty, and Effort increase with more *PCH*. The primary reason for this is the increase in the *Program Length* and the Halstead *Volume* because the developer needs to handle more kernel arguments. That is especially true for the GEMM. Its more complicated access pattern increases the *Effort* strongly. Instead, adding more ports to the 4×4 convolution kernel does not increase the *Effort* that much because we can omit one loop, and therefore the *Difficulty* does not increase much. That showcases that applications with simpler access patterns can be handcrafted easier but difficult ones are not well supported, which is a problem for especially inexperienced developers.

5.2 Setup Overhead

As mentioned in Sect. 3, the MAO can reduce the setup overhead. However, as the *Replication* and the *Handcrafted* approach do not consider its address mapping, it can lead to worse performance than distributing the data. As a consequence, we distribute the data by both methods by hand. Our approach integrates the address mapping into the architecture and can therefore eliminate additional setup overhead through the MAO.

Table 2. The difference in design complexity between the replication/our approach and handcrafted using Halstead metrics.

	GEMM			Convolution	
	Replication/Ours	Handcrafted four ports	Handcrafted eight ports	Replication/Ours	Handcrafted four ports
n_1	17	17	17	19	19
n_2	11	17	26	12	16
N_1	57	145	367	57	97
N_2	32	107	294	40	63
N	89	252	661	97	160
n	28	34	43	31	35
V	427.85	1282.04	3586.76	480.56	820.69
D	24.73	53.50	96.12	31.67	37.40
E	10580.73	68589.14	344759.37	10580.73	30693.81

The convolution with *Replication* does not increase the overhead because the image can be partitioned near-perfectly between all *PCHs*. However, each *PCH* must hold a copy in the *Handcrafted* approach as each input port must access the whole image. For the GEMM, both approaches need to replicate data between the *PCH*. In the case of *Replication*, if the result matrix is evenly divided, at least two *PEs* share the same input. The Handcrafted kernel again needs a complete copy of the input matrices in each *PCH*. Additional to this setup overhead, *Replication* and *Handcrafted* need a host design to perform this distribution. That increases development complexity.

5.3 Performance

We measured the runtime and the hardware utilization as a metric for the accelerator's performance. Again, it is essential to note that a highly optimized HLS code for this specific chip and configuration will outperform all solutions described here. However, it is not the comparison we aim for. It has a much higher design complexity.

Table 3 shows the performance result of the convolution on a 4096 × 4096 image. *Replication* shows the expected linear increase in performance and hardware resources. Initially, the performance increase is better than *Handcrafted* with two ports, but with four ports, this turns around. It also shows a much better utilization to runtime ratio. The *Handcrafted* approach with two *PEs* also shows less hardware utilization if it reaches a similar runtime to ours with four *PEs*. However, this is its limit for this number of *PCHs*. Our approach can increase the performance by using more *PE* with the same number of *PCH*. Simply adding more ports to a kernel is insufficient, and our approach can match the increased bandwidth by adding more *PEs*. That can happen without additional design overhead. The downside of our approach is the increased hardware

Table 3. Performance comparison of Convolution Kernels

	Replication		Handcrafted		Ours			
#PCHs	1	8	8	8	1	8	8	8
#PEs	1	8	4	2	1	4	8	16
Runtime (s)	6.642	0.883	0.832	0.223	2.043	0.257	0.095	0.043
LUTs	9868	78732	34683	27833	6197	54732	61763	101770
FF	13907	111021	44320	38766	9223	62830	77829	114081
BRAM	9.5	48	32.5	22.5	19.5	76	148.5	148.5
DSPs	28	224	62	36	12	48	96	192

Table 4. Performance comparison of Matrix-Matrix-Multiplication

	Replication		Handcrafted			Ours			
#PCHs	1	8	8	8	8	1	8	8	8
#PEs	1	8	4	2	1	1	4	8	16
Runtime (s)	23.856	2.982	1.640	2.798	0.779	2.679	0.551	0.208	0.105
LUTs	9296	74025	344388	30406	35141	9149	25709	30832	41835
FF	12675	101523	44260	41614	52127	11866	46893	55036	68229
BRAM	3	52	11.5	17.5	23.5	26	76	148.5	148.5
DSPs	15	120	60	108	85	12	36	72	144

utilization, especially BRAM blocks for the buffer. However, this is not a strong constraint, as most HBM FPGAs feature enough resources to host such designs.

The GEMM shows a similar picture, albeit with generally worse performance. Table 4 shows the performance results for 512×512 matrices. None of the approaches can handle the more complex access pattern very well. It shows well the limit of the Replication approach. The initial performance with one *PCH* is not good, and therefore, the linear increase does not improve much. On the other side, the *Handcrafted* displays that simple modifications are not enough to increase the used bandwidth and therefore increase the runtime. The *PE* with four *PCH* utilizes more DSPs but shows worse performance than the one with two *PCH*. That changes with eight *PCHs*, but the performance is still not good. Except for the BRAM blocks, our approach has a similar hardware utilization with 8 *PEs* as the *Handcrafted* approach with 8 *PCH*. However, the performance of our approach is four times better. Improving the buffer layer could increase the performance to even better levels.

In summary, our approach achieves an overall better compute performance by using the HBM compared to traditional methods. It is also important to note that the performance of the traditional approaches would be even worse because the runtime measurements omit the setup overhead through the data distribution.

6   Conclusion

We have shown that it is possible to abstract the HBM architecture from the high-level source code in HLS. With this method, even inexperienced developers can benefit from the high HBM throughput without changing their host or accelerator code. That is in contrast to traditional methods, where a higher bandwidth can often only be attained by modifying the HL code significantly. In the future, a better buffering layer than the used cache needs to be incorporated as the current bottleneck of our application is due to missing latency hiding. Additionally, we want to provide a far more extensive evaluation for more different kinds of applications.

Acknowledgment. This work has been supported by the Xilinx University Program (XUP) with the Virtex UltraScale+ HBM FPGA chip.

References

1. Wilkes, M.V.: The memory gap and the future of high performance memories. SIGARCH Comput. Archit. News **29**(1), 2–7 (2001)
2. Carvalho, C.: The gap between processor and memory speeds, January 2002
3. Jun, H., et al.: HBM (high bandwidth Memory) DRAM technology and architecture. In: IEEE International Memory Workshop, pp. 1–4 (2017)
4. Choi, Y., Chi, Y., Wang, J., Guo, L., Cong, J.: When HLS Meets FPGA HBM: Benchmarking and Bandwidth Optimization (2020)
5. Kara, K., Hagleitner, C., Diamantopoulos, D., Syrivelis, D., Alonso, G.: High bandwidth memory on FPGAs: a data analytics perspective. In: 30th International Conference on Field-Programmable Logic and Applications (2020)
6. Holzinger, P., Reiser, D., Hahn, T., Reichenbach, M.: Fast HBM access with FPGAs: analysis, architectures, and applications. In: IEEE International Parallel Distributed Processing Symposium Workshops, pp. 152–159 (2021)
7. Choi, Y., Chi, Y., Qiao, W., Samardzic, N., Cong, J.: HBM connect: high-performance HLS interconnect for FPGA HBM. In: ACM/SIGDA International Symposium on Field-Programmable Gate Arrays, FPGA 2021, pp. 116–126. Association for Computing Machinery, New York (2021)
8. Singh, G., et al.: FPGA-based near-memory acceleration of modern data-intensive applications. IEEE Micro **41**(4), 39–48 (2021)
9. Yang, Y., Kuppannagari, S.R., Prasanna, V.K.: A high throughput parallel hash table accelerator on HBM-enabled FPGAs. In: International Conference on Field-Programmable Technology, pp. 148–153 (2020)
10. Du, C., Yamaguchi, Y.: High-level synthesis design for stencil computations on FPGA with high bandwidth memory. Electronics **9**(8) (2020)
11. Xilinx, Inc.: Vitis Unified Software Platform, November 2019
12. Intel, Inc.: Intel High Level Synthesis Compiler Best Practices Guide, October 2021
13. Holzinger, P., Reichenbach, M.: The HERA methodology: reconfigurable logic in general-purpose computing. IEEE Access **9**, 147212–147236 (2021)
14. Fujita, N., Kobayashi, R., Yamaguchi, Y., Boku, T.: HBM2 memory system for hpc applications on an FPGA. In: IEEE International Conference on Cluster Computing, pp. 783–786 (2021)
15. Halstead, M.H.: Elements of Software Science. (Operating and Programming Systems Series), Elsevier Science Inc., Amsterdam (1977)

Memory Systems

TREAM: A Tool for Evaluating Error Resilience of <u>Tree</u>-Based Models Using <u>A</u>pproximate <u>M</u>emory

Mikail Yayla[(✉)] [iD], Zahra Valipour Dehnoo[iD], Mojtaba Masoudinejad[iD], and Jian-Jia Chen[iD]

Department of Computer Science, TU Dortmund University, Dortmund, Germany
{mikail.yayla,zahra.valipour,mojtaba.masoudinejad,
jian-jia.chen}@tu-dortmund.de

Abstract. Approximate memories reduce the resource demand of machine learning (ML) systems at the cost of bit errors. ML models have an intrinsic error resilience and are therefore suitable candidates to use with approximate memories. Although the error resilience of neural networks has been considered in many studies, tree-based applications have received less attention. In addition, there is no tool available to specifically evaluate the error resilience of tree-based models. In this work, we present TREAM, a general tool built upon the sklearn framework for injecting bit flips during the inference of tree-based models. TREAM is capable of injecting bit flips into the tree and input parameters, i.e. feature and split values, in addition to feature and children indices. It can also be used for both floating point and integer values.

Furthermore, we provide an abstract assessment of bit flip injection into the aforementioned parameters. Based on this, we construct a set of experiments using TREAM for different random forest structures and datasets over a set of bit error rates, where the relation between accuracy and bit error rate is considered for error resilience. The results demonstrate that child indices have the highest deviations in accuracy under bit errors. Moreover, the results give us insights into how varying numbers of trees, depth and different datasets affect the resilience.

Keywords: Random forest · Decision tree · Approximate memory · Error resilience · Bit errors

1 Introduction

Over the past decade, machine learning (ML) algorithms have become ubiquitous on various hardware platforms. For instance, by integrating ML into embedded devices, data can be processed directly at the edge instead of being sent over the network [4,7]. Among ML algorithms, decision trees (DTs) are one of the most widely used [3]. This popularity is due to their interpretability, simplicity and excellent results, specifically in the form of random forests (RFs) [16]. DTs/RFs

© The Author(s), under exclusive license to Springer Nature Switzerland AG 2022
A. Orailoglu et al. (Eds.): SAMOS 2022, LNCS 13511, pp. 61–73, 2022.
https://doi.org/10.1007/978-3-031-15074-6_4

can be successfully applied to complex problems, such as high-dimensional data [17] and can even outperform other ML models, such as neural networks for structured data [4]. Therefore, they are suitable candidates for ML application in resource-constrained embedded systems [7].

To achieve competitive inference accuracy, high depths and a large number of trees are recommended, which requires storing large amount of data in the memory. Hence, the memory subsystem is the main resource used in tree-based models [2], which makes it a challenge to apply them on conventional memories.

Recent studies have explored the use of approximate memory realized by reducing the memory supply voltage and tuning latency parameters. Although an approximate memory can achieve lower power consumption and faster access, it can cause high bit error rates (BERs). This has been explored for a variety of state-of-the-art and emerging memory technologies, e.g. for volatile memories (SRAM [19], DRAM [11]), and approximate non-volatile memories (RRAM [9], MRAM or STT-RAM [10], FeFET [20]). Furthermore, various studies have investigated the error resilience of ML models by creating a bit flip (i.e. faults) injector tool. Most of these studies focus on deep neural networks and propose several tools. The framework in [12] enables the modeling of bit flips into various parts of the hardware. Similarly, [5,13,15] propose tools and techniques to quantify the error resilience and accuracy trade-offs of neural networks. Although TensorFI [6] injects bit flips into any generic ML program written using TensorFlow, faults are only injected into the TensorFlow operators and not into the memory used by the program. In addition, it is not designed specifically for RFs or other tree-based models.

Hence, a tool for evaluating the accuracy of tree-based models under errors from approximate memory would allow us to conduct design space exploration in this domain. To the best of our knowledge, this work is the first study that investigates the error resilience of DTs/RFs with bit-flip injection into the DT/RF data. Specifically, we assess tree-based models with approximate memory, for which there are also no corresponding studies in the literature. This makes it possible to explore the future low-power systems employing tree-based models with approximate memory.

Ultimately, this tool allows users to inject the bit flips into DT/RF data for all the above-mentioned memory types. In this manner, after selecting the injection site or node data type, the injection into the integer or floating point data values can be performed in the form of multiple bit flips. All intended configurations are first recorded and then executed during the inference phase. Therefore, it enables the investigation of the impact of errors on tree-based models in approximate memory.

Our Contributions Are as Follows:

- We present TREAM, which makes possible to evaluate the accuracy under errors from approximate memories or other sources of bit errors for tree-based ML-models. It is based on the popular machine learning library sklearn. We plan to publish the tool along with the paper.

- We provide an abstract assessment of the effects of bit flips into the different error sites, i.e. split and feature values, and feature and child indices.
- Using our tool, we conduct a series of experiments on different datasets for evaluating the inference accuracy degradation of the tree-based models due to errors. In the analyses, we identify the most susceptible parts of trees to errors, and determine the influence of the number of trees and depth on the accuracy.

The rest of this paper is organized as follows. In Sect. 2, we present the system model along with the posed research questions. TREAM and its implementation as the bit flip injector tool is shown in Sect. 3. In Sect. 4, we address the effect of bit flips in tree-based models. The experimental results and answers to the research questions are presented in Sect. 5. The tool TREAM is available at https://github.com/myay/TREAM.

2   System Model

Let us consider a supervised learning problem to build a prediction model M from a labeled training dataset $\mathcal{D} = \{(\vec{x}_i, y_i) | i = 1, \ldots, N\}$. The model's input is a vector $\vec{x}_i = (x_i^1, \ldots, x_i^d)^\top \in \mathcal{X} \subseteq \mathbb{R}^d$, and a prediction $y_i \in \mathcal{Y}$ is a class index $c \in \mathbb{N}_0$. Note that the indices $1 \ldots d$ in the components of $\vec{x}_i$ represent the dimension and not exponents. The model $M : \vec{x} \to c$ is applied to predict the class for an input $\vec{x}$, where it may be an unseen input $(\vec{x} \notin \mathcal{D})$.

A decision tree (DT) is a flow-like process used as a model for predicting unseen data, based on the learned information from the training data. Suppose that $\mathbf{G} = (\mathbf{V}, \mathbf{E})$ is a DT composed of $|\mathbf{V}|$ vertices (typically called *nodes* in this context) and $|\mathbf{E}|$ directed edges, in which $|\mathbf{E}| = |\mathbf{V}| - 1$. There is one *root* in $\mathbf{V}$, which has no incoming edge. We consider *binary DTs*, in which a node $v \in \mathbf{V}$ is either a *leaf* without any outgoing edge or an *internal node* with exactly two outgoing edges. In a binary DT, a leaf provides a classification label and an internal node $v \in \mathbf{V}$ is a split decision based on a comparison of a certain *feature* (f_v) from the input data with the *split value* (s_v), also called *threshold*, learned during the training to further classify the input using either the left or the right child.

The *depth* (K) of a DT is the longest path from the root to one of the leaves. An example of a binary DT is presented in Fig. 1a. Each comparison divides the possible feature space into subsections with hyperplanes at the thresholds, such as in Fig. 1b, which operates with five classes using four thresholds.

A DT's inference process from the root to a leaf can be implemented either in the *if-else* or in the *native* form [2]. Sklearn uses the *native* realization with a high level structure similar to Listing 1.1 written in Cython. The type SIZE_t in the node is an unsigned integer and DOUBLE_t is a floating point value with double precision. The data used on the node for **feature**, **split**, **leftchild**, and **rightchild** are shown in Listing 1.1. There are also other data, e.g. a binary value to mark a node as leaf (not shown here).

A RF is an ensemble made of multiple DTs, predicting by majority votes. For brevity, the term *tree-based models* is used hereafter as an RF with T decision trees with $T \geq 1$.

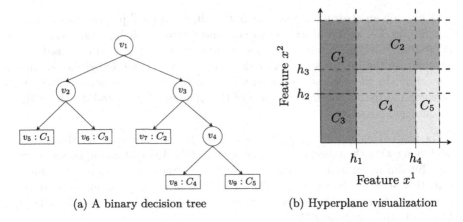

(a) A binary decision tree   (b) Hyperplane visualization

Fig. 1. Left: A DT with 4 internal nodes (in circle) and 5 leafs (in rectangular). Right: Partitions of space by the nodes (hyperplanes) of a DT into five classes.

```
cdef struct node:
    SIZE_t feature # targeted feature
    DOUBLE_t split # threshold
    SIZE_t leftchild
    SIZE_t rightchild
    ...
# all nodes and leafs of a tree are stored in this array
Node tree = [[350,143.5,1,2,...],[1,7.5,3,4],...]
# high-level description of predict function
def predict(X):
    i = 0
    while node is not leaf:
        if X[tree[i].feature] <= tree[i].split:
            i = node.leftchild
        else:
            i = node.rightchild
    return tree[i].prediction
```

Listing 1.1. Native realization of a DT in Cython

2.1 Memory and Error Model

Using the native realization of the DTs from Listing 1.1, the node data for making decisions includes the split value, feature value, feature index and two child indices. We suppose that they are stored in a one-dimensional array data structure in the memory with possible bit flips. In this study, we assume that the hardware (i.e. memory) may suffer from *transient faults* captured in a bit error model. Application of this model on the bit representation of the data is realized by injecting bit flips into the memory. Specifically, we consider that the bit errors are manifested as *multiple-bit flips*, and that they are *symmetric*, i.e., the probability for flipping $0 \rightarrow 1$ is the same as $1 \rightarrow 0$. This assumption characterizes the probability of bit flips every time when a bit is read from the unreliable memory, also referred to as *approximate memory*.

We consider that errors occur during the inference phase of tree-based models with the probability of error, referred to as bit error rate (BER). This can occur in the bit representation of the mentioned node data read from the unreliable memory. Consequently, bit flips are injected into the binary representations of split and feature values, and the indices for features and children, according to the bit error model of the hardware. This model matches the assumptions in recent studies about approximate volatile memories (SRAM [18], DRAM [11]), and non-volatile memories (RRAM [9], MRAM or STT-RAM [10], and FeFET [20]). Errors stemming from other types of faults may also be applied using this model.

2.2 Definitions for Error Resilience

Let us use A_β to quantify the accuracy of models (M) under bit flip injection with BER (β). When this accuracy is measured using a set of experiments with $\beta \in \mathcal{B}$, we define the error resilience as:

$$R_M(\mathcal{B}) = \frac{100}{|\mathcal{B}| \times A_0} \sum_{\forall \beta \in \mathcal{B}} A_\beta \quad [\%] \tag{1}$$

In this formulation A_0 represents the accuracy of the original model without any bit flip injection and is used as the reference. Higher drops in the accuracy will reduce the nominator and result in smaller resilience factors.

2.3 Research Questions

Considering a tree-based model with approximate memory storing the node's data, the main goal is to analyze the impact of bit errors on the inference accuracy. To this end, the following research questions will be evaluated:

- **RQ1:** Which data in the tree-based model is more sensitive to the errors?
- **RQ2:** What is the influence of depth and the number of trees in the ensemble on the error resilience?
- **RQ3:** Are there differences concerning error resilience among different datasets?

3 TREAM: An Extension to Sklearn

TREAM is an extension for the well-known machine learning library sklearn [14]. Sklearn provides implementations of common supervised and unsupervised ML algorithms with a Python-based interface. It is one of the most efficient ML-tools available due to its use of Numpy and Cython in the back-end [14].

3.1 High-Level Overview of TREAM

According to the structure of DT in Listing 1.1, the bit flip injection into the following data sites are considered: 1) Split value, 2) feature value, 3) feature index, and 4) child indices. These sites can be selected individually or in any combination to perform the error resilience and accuracy evaluation.

Algorithm 1 shows the high-level overview of how TREAM works. It first initializes the experiment parameters and then activates bit flip injection into the aforementioned sites depending on the flags. From Line 11 on, the program iterates over the specified BERs in the experiment parameters. The bit flip injection takes place during the model inference and are only injected into the accessed data for efficiency. The accuracy estimation is repeated for the specified number in *REPs* (i.e. repetitions, specified in the experiment parameters). When the execution of the loop is finished, a list of accuracies is returned.

Algorithm 1: TREAM high-level overview

Input: Trained Model M, Input $\vec{X}$, Set of BERs ($\mathcal{B}$)
Output: Accuracy $\vec{A}$ over $\mathcal{B}$
1 Initialize experiment parameters
2 Initialize list of accuracies $\vec{A}$
3 **if** *BitFlipSplitValue* **then**
4 | activate SplitValueInjection
5 **if** *BitFlipFeatureValue* **then**
6 | activate FeatureValueInjection
7 **if** *BitFlipFeatureIdx* **then**
8 | activate FeatureIndexInjection
9 **if** *BitFlipChildIdx* **then**
10 | activate ChildIndexInjection
11 **for** β *in* $\mathcal{B}$ **do**
12 | **for** *rep in REPs* **do**
13 | | Apply model $M(\vec{X})$ under β
14 | | Append A_β to $\vec{A}$
15 **return** $\vec{A}$

The process of bit flip injections into tree-based models can be configured through an external configuration file (ECF) to enable fast design space exploration for error resilient systems. It provides the required parameters and configurations to train a model (or load a pre-trained model) and inject bit flips in the specified sites during inference. This workflow is shown in Fig. 2.

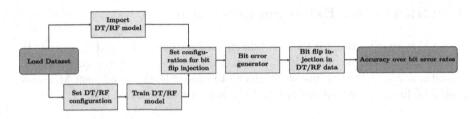

Fig. 2. TREAM operational steps.

3.2   Implementation

The back-end of the tree computations in sklearn is implemented in the programming language Cython [1]. Cython code uses Python-based syntax, with optional syntax inspired by the programming language C (such as specifying data types). When the implementation is complete and the code should be executed, it is compiled to C/C++ code first, and then processed further. This not only produces efficient machine code, it also allows direct bit-level access to the DT's data, enabling the iteration through the binary representation of values and their manipulation. Hence, this is used to implement the bit flip injection during the inference. In the following, we explain how we extended the sklearn codebase to support bit flip injection into the DT data.

New Files are files that were not part of sklearn and are added for the implementation of TREAM.

`sklearn/tree/_bfi.pdx`: This file includes type and function definitions for bit flip injections, for floating point and integer representations with any number of bits. For example, the function for the floating point format is cdef DTYPE_t bfi_float (DTYPE_t x, DTYPE_t ber). Input (x) and bit error rate (BER, in decimal) need to be specified.

`sklearn/tree/_bfi.pyx`: This file provides the implementation of the bit flip injection. We note that floating-point numbers are represented by the IEEE 754 binary format in modern computing systems. Therefore, bit flip injection can be directly applied onto the binary representation of floating points or integers. To achieve this in Cython, the corresponding bits, denoted as $\vec{a}$, of a floating point number or an integer are copied using the memcpy function (to work around the strict-aliasing rule). Then, a loop iterates over each bit that can flip, and if the corresponding random value is smaller than the BER, the bit is marked as '1', i.e., to be flipped; otherwise, marked as '0', i.e., kept as it is. Suppose that $\vec{m}$ is the resulting bit vector of the above operation. Then, $\vec{m}$ is considered as a mask and the bit flips are performed using the $\vec{a} := \vec{m}$ xor $\vec{a}$, in which xor is a bit-wise xor operation. In the end, the bit vector $\vec{a}$ containing the original input (with flips, if bits have been flipped) are copied to the original value, again using memcpy.

Modified Files are files that have been part of the original sklearn but are modified for the TREAM implementation.

`sklearn/tree/_tree.pxd` and `sklearn/tree/_tree.pyx`: with values to turn on and off bit flip injection into different types of DT data during inference. BERs can also be specified for each type of data. In the function `apply_dense`, the bit flip injection function calls are performed (the case sparse application is not supported, but can easily be added).

`sklearn/tree/setup.py`: To compile sklearn with the changes, this installation file has been extended with the new files related to `_bfi.pyx`.

4   The Effect of Bit Flips in Tree-Based Models

In this section we give an overview of the effects of bit flips in the different bit flip sites in tree-based models and how bit flips are related to the model structure.

By this we intend to give context for the research questions, before conducting the bit flip injection experiments.

4.1   Bit Flips in Split and Feature Value

Let us denote the nodes' comparison using $x \leq s$, where x is an input feature and s the split value. When bit flips occur in the bit representation of s (independent of the data type), the representation with bit flips (s^*) encodes either a larger or a smaller value. Depending on the values of x and s, i.e. whether $x > s$ or $x \leq s$, the magnitude of s^* determines whether the node chooses the wrong child. For the wrong child to be chosen, the magnitude of s^* has to be small or large enough to *invert* the result of the comparison $x \leq s$. The same principle holds for bit flips in the bit representation of the feature value x.

We now explain how a wrong child (by bit flips in s and/or x) can affect the prediction. Consider a DT with only two features, splitting the space with hyperplanes h_i as shown in Fig. 1. For h_1 and h_4, the split to the left child corresponds to splitting the feature space such that the space on the left remains. For s_2 and s_3, a split to the left child corresponds to splitting the feature space such that the space above remains. For right children, the space is partitioned the other way around. As an example, consider a two-dimensional input $\vec{x} = (x^1, x^2)$ belonging to the class C_2. The model has to predict this class from the five classes denoted as C_1–C_5. A wrong child selection in v_1 will fall either in C_1 or C_3, which are the wrong classes. The same principle applies to all the other nodes. In each case, one wrong split leads to a wrong classification.

4.2   Bit Flips in Child Indices

Child indices are unsigned integers, one pointing to the index for the left and one for the right child. Considering that only the child indices have bit flips in their bit representation, following cases can occur:

1. The index under bit flips gets out of array bounds. In this case, a memory address which is not inside the memory region reserved for the nodes will be accessed which may store any other data. This memory address could also be protected by the operating system, and an access attempt could cause a segmentation fault, leading to a termination of the program.
2. The index under bit flips stays inside the array bounds reserved for the node. In this case, the wrong index will be used, though it is a valid node in the tree. If the execution jumps to a parent node, the execution is repeated. If this happens repeatedly, the execution time may become longer.

4.3   Bit Flips in Feature Index

Bit flips in the bit representation of the feature index (also an unsigned integer) can have the following outcomes:

1. The feature index under bit flips gets out of bounds. This case is the same as case 1 for the child index.
2. The feature index under bit flips stays inside the array bounds reserved for the feature values. In this case, a wrong feature will be chosen which may have a value different to the correct one. This is similar to the case in Sect. 4.1.

5 Evaluation

To demonstrate the TREAM tool, we introduce bit flips into tree-based ML models. We focus on RFs with depths and number of trees in $\{5, 10\}$. As datasets, we use MNIST, sensorless-drive, wine-quality, and adult, from the UCI machine learning repository [8].

For training RFs, the standard sklean libraries, without any error tolerance or correction methods are used. After training an RF, the accuracy under errors is evaluated using TREAM with BERs between $10^{-5}\%$ and 50%. To acquire precise estimates of the accuracy, the inference under each BER is repeated five times for each RF. All experiments are run on a machine with Intel Core i7-8700K 3.70 GHz, 32 GB RAM.

We inject bit flips into the bit representations of the floating point format of the split and feature values. TREAM also supports bit flip injection into integer representations. The feature index is an unsigned integer, into which bit flips are also injected. A check finds out-of-bounds errors in the index of the feature value (explained in Sect. 4.1) and sets it to zero which retrieves the first feature. If it is within the bounds, the feature at the wrong index is retrieved by the node. The child indices are unsigned integers as well. If bit flips cause the child indices to get out of bounds, the execution of the tree is terminated and the class with index zero is returned as the prediction. If the indices are within the bounds, a wrong node is retrieved as the next child node.

Using TREAM, the effect of bit flip injection on all data sites on the RF accuracy of two example datasets are presented in Fig. 3. The value K refers to the maximum depth of the trees, and T refers to the number of trees in the RFs.

The extracted accuracies after bit flip injections can be used to quantify the error resilience of each data site for each dataset using Eq. (1). From collected data this value is presented for all datasets in Table 1. Using accuracy drops and extracted resilience factors we refer to the research questions posed in Sect. 2.3.

RQ1: According to Fig. 3 (fourth column), we observe that the child indices are most sensitive to errors. This leads to wrong decisions with one bit flip, which causes a high accuracy drop despite small BERs. Bit flips in the split value, feature value, and feature index (columns one to three in Fig. 3) are less sensitive to errors compared to the child index. In these three cases, bit flips may not always lead to a wrong decision. The bit flips may be tolerated without a change of the nodes traversed to reach a leaf. The resilience values in Table 1 also support this. The values for the CI are the lowest among one dataset.

RQ2: In Table 1 we observe for all datasets and for the first three bit flip injection sites (split value, feature value and feature index), that inclusion of more trees

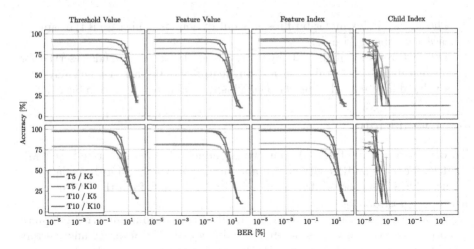

Fig. 3. Accuracy over BERs for different RFs, varying bit flip sites, datasets, and RF architectures. Row 1: MNIST, Row 2: sensorless-drive.

Table 1. Error resilience (in percent) of different experiments with bit flip injection on Feature Value (FV), Threshold Value (TV), Feature Index (FI) and Child Index (CI)

Model	MNIST				Sensorless-drive				Wine quality				Adult			
	FV	TV	FI	CI	FV	TV	FI	CI	FV	TV	FI	CI	FV	TV	FI	CI
T5/K5	87.9	93.3	88.3	31.9	88.5	87.9	89.7	28.1	93.4	95.0	96.9	86.1	98.1	97.8	98.6	91.5
T5/K10	87.9	91.6	88.6	24.3	86.8	87.5	90.3	22.0	90.6	90.8	94.1	80.9	97.5	96.0	97.8	89.3
T10/K5	89.2	94.6	89.3	32.4	88.7	88.9	91.3	30.0	95.9	96.9	97.4	85.9	98.5	97.8	98.4	90.6
T10/K10	89.0	93.4	89.9	27.2	88.4	88.8	91.7	24.9	92.0	92.2	94.3	78.2	98.1	97.1	98.1	89.2

in the RF can enable a slightly better resilience. However, in some cases this is a weak improvement or may not hold (e.g. CI in wine-quality, and FI and CI in adult). Furthermore, the variance of the accuracy for child index plots is high, which makes observations challenging. Regarding the influence of the tree depth on resilience, no consistent observations can be made from Fig. 3 and Table 1.

RQ3: Among the datasets, a certain amount of bit flips are tolerated without significant accuracy degradation, for small BERs. We also observe that a higher BER directly increases the accuracy drop. Furthermore, the BERs at which the accuracy drops drastically is similar (between 10^{-1} and 10^1) for the threshold value, feature value, and feature index. For the child index this region is between 10^{-5} and 10^{-4}. However, we observe that the resilience values vary largely in Table 1. MNIST and sensorless-drive have CI resilience around 20–30%, while wine-quality and adult have values around 78–90%. The high resilience values for CI for adult and wine-quality are due to the inherent imbalance in these datasets.

To provide a sense on the effect of bit flip injection on the execution time, latency evaluations are provided in Table 2. Each set of values is averaged from five repetitions on the test set performed for eight different BERs, each for 10 000

Table 2. Execution times (in seconds) for the MNIST dataset averaged from 40 times on the test set sized 10 000 elements.

Model	TREAM [s]			sklearn [s]		
	Average	Avg.-min.	Max.-avg.	Average	Avg.-min.	Max.-avg.
T5/K5	3.64	$9 \cdot 10^{-2}$	0.16	$6.5 \cdot 10^{-2}$	$5 \cdot 10^{-3}$	$4 \cdot 10^{-3}$
T5/K10	7.15	0.22	0.63	$7.5 \cdot 10^{-2}$	0	$3 \cdot 10^{-3}$
T10/K5	7.29	0.19	0.71	$8.4 \cdot 10^{-2}$	0	0
T10/K10	13.71	1.64	0.5	0.11	0	$1 \cdot 10^{-3}$

samples. We observe that TREAM has additional timing overheads compared to the sklearn. This overhead is to be expected, since bit flips are injected into the parameters during the inference phase.

6 Conclusion

We present TREAM, an extension of sklearn, for error resilience analysis of tree-based models (DT/RF). TREAM can be configured to inject bit flips into the node data and input data, i.e. split and feature value, and feature and child indices, during the inference phase. The evaluations demonstrate that the child index is the most sensitive parameter of the node to the bit flips. Moreover, more trees in an RF can tolerate more errors and the accuracy of various datasets under bit flip injections can vary. We believe that this tool will help the research community explore the design of efficient systems using ML on the resource-constrained edge.

As a future work, we plan to find solutions for the timing overhead in the TREAM tool, which occurs due to the fact that the bit flip injections are performed every time the data is fetched from the memory. Furthermore, we plan to use TREAM to evaluate tree-based models under specific approximate memories, with the goal of quantifying the efficiency benefits.

Acknowledgements. This paper has been supported by Deutsche Forschungsgemeinshaft (DFG) as part of the Collaborative Research Center SFB 876 "Providing Information by Resource-Constrained Analysis" (project number 124020371) and project OneMemory (project number 405422836).

References

1. Behnel, S., Bradshaw, R., Citro, C., Dalcin, L., Seljebotn, D.S., Smith, K.: Cython: the best of both worlds. Comput. Sci. Eng. **13**(2), 31–39 (2011). https://doi.org/10.1109/MCSE.2010.118
2. Buschjager, S., Chen, K.H., Chen, J.J., Morik, K.: Realization of random forest for real-time evaluation through tree framing. In: 2018 IEEE International Conference on Data Mining (ICDM), pp. 19–28. IEEE (2018). https://doi.org/10.1109/ICDM.2018.00017

3. Charbuty, B., Abdulazeez, A.: Classification based on decision tree algorithm for machine learning. J. Appl. Sci. Technol. Trends **2**(01), 20–28 (2021). https://doi.org/10.38094/jastt20165

4. Chen, K.H., et al.: Efficient realization of decision trees for real-time inference. ACM Trans. Embed. Comput. Syst. (TECS) (2022). https://doi.org/10.1145/3508019

5. Chen, Z., Li, G., Pattabiraman, K., DeBardeleben, N.: BinFi: an efficient fault injector for safety-critical machine learning systems. In: Proceedings of the International Conference for High Performance Computing, Networking, Storage and Analysis, pp. 1–23 (2019). https://doi.org/10.1145/3295500.3356177

6. Chen, Z., Narayanan, N., Fang, B., Li, G., Pattabiraman, K., DeBardeleben, N.: TensorFi: a flexible fault injection framework for tensorflow applications. In: 2020 IEEE 31st International Symposium on Software Reliability Engineering (ISSRE), pp. 426–435. IEEE (2020). https://doi.org/10.1109/ISSRE5003.2020.00047

7. Cornetta, G., Touhafi, A.: Design and evaluation of a new machine learning framework for IoT and embedded devices. Electronics **10**(5), 600 (2021). https://doi.org/10.3390/electronics10050600

8. Dua, D., Graff, C.: UCI machine learning repository (2017). https://archive.ics.uci.edu/ml

9. Hirtzlin, T., et al.: Outstanding bit error tolerance of resistive ram-based binarized neural networks. In: 2019 IEEE International Conference on Artificial Intelligence Circuits and Systems (AICAS), pp. 288–292. IEEE (2019). https://doi.org/10.1109/AICAS.2019.8771544

10. Hirtzlin, T., et al.: Implementing binarized neural networks with magnetoresistive ram without error correction. In: 2019 IEEE/ACM International Symposium on Nanoscale Architectures (NANOARCH), pp. 1–5. IEEE (2019). https://doi.org/10.1109/NANOARCH47378.2019.181300

11. Koppula, S., et al.: Eden: enabling energy-efficient, high-performance deep neural network inference using approximate dram. In: Proceedings of the 52nd Annual IEEE/ACM International Symposium on Microarchitecture, pp. 166–181 (2019). https://doi.org/10.1145/3352460.3358280

12. Li, G., et al.: Understanding error propagation in deep learning neural network (DNN) accelerators and applications. In: Proceedings of the International Conference for High Performance Computing, Networking, Storage and Analysis, pp. 1–12 (2017). https://doi.org/10.1145/3126908.3126964

13. Mahmoud, A., et al.: PytorchFi: a runtime perturbation tool for DNNs. In: 2020 50th Annual IEEE/IFIP International Conference on Dependable Systems and Networks Workshops (DSN-W), pp. 25–31. IEEE (2020). https://doi.org/10.1109/DSN-W50199.2020.00014

14. Pedregosa, F., et al.: Scikit-learn: machine learning in python. J. Mach. Learn. Res. **12**, 2825–2830 (2011)

15. Reagen, B., et al.: Ares: a framework for quantifying the resilience of deep neural networks. In: 2018 55th ACM/ESDA/IEEE Design Automation Conference (DAC), pp. 1–6. IEEE (2018). https://doi.org/10.1109/DAC.2018.8465834

16. Rodriguez-Galiano, V., Sanchez-Castillo, M., Chica-Olmo, M., Chica-Rivas, M.: Machine learning predictive models for mineral prospectivity: an evaluation of neural networks, random forest, regression trees and support vector machines. Ore Geol. Rev. **71**, 804–818 (2015). https://doi.org/10.1016/j.oregeorev.2015.01.001

17. Shaik, A.B., Srinivasan, S.: A brief survey on random forest ensembles in classification model. In: Bhattacharyya, S., Hassanien, A.E., Gupta, D., Khanna, A., Pan, I. (eds.) International Conference on Innovative Computing and Communications. LNNS, vol. 56, pp. 253–260. Springer, Singapore (2019). https://doi.org/10.1007/978-981-13-2354-6_27

18. Sun, X., et al.: Low-VDD operation of SRAM synaptic array for implementing ternary neural network. IEEE Trans. Very Large Scale Integr. (VLSI) Syst. **25**(10), 2962–2965 (2017). https://doi.org/10.1109/TVLSI.2017.2727528

19. Yang, L., Bankman, D., Moons, B., Verhelst, M., Murmann, B.: Bit error tolerance of a CIFAR-10 binarized convolutional neural network processor. In: 2018 IEEE International Symposium on Circuits and Systems (ISCAS), pp. 1–5. IEEE (2018). https://doi.org/10.1109/ISCAS.2018.8351255

20. Yayla, M., et al.: FEFET-based binarized neural networks under temperature-dependent bit errors. IEEE Trans. Comput. (2021). https://doi.org/10.1109/TC.2021.3104736

Split'n'Cover: ISO 26262 Hardware Safety Analysis with SystemC

Denis Uecker and Matthias Jung[(⊠)]

Fraunhofer IESE, Kaiserslautern, Germany
{denis.uecker,matthias.jung}@iese.fraunhofer.de

Abstract. The development of safe hardware is a major concern in automotive applications. The parts 5 and 11 of the ISO 26262 define procedures and methods for the development of hardware to achieve a specific automotive safety integrity level. In this paper, we present a novel methodology that combines the hardware metrics analysis of ISO 26262 with SystemC-based virtual prototyping. To show the applicability of our methodology, we modeled the LPDDR4 memory system of a current state-of-the-art ADAS system and estimated the ASIL level of this system. The new methodology is implemented in SystemC and is provided as open-source.

Keywords: ISO 26262 · SystemC · DRAM · LPDDR4 · Safety

1 Introduction

Functional safety is a major concern in the development of automotive applications because the lives of drivers, passengers, and other road users must be protected to the highest degree. Therefore, the development of automotive components requires the usage of specific quality and safety standards, such as ISO 26262 [5]. The implementation of this standard is intended to ensure the functional safety of a system with electrical/electronic components in road vehicles. Especially Parts 5 and 11 of the standard deal with the development processes at the hardware level and define procedures and methods for achieving a specific *Automotive Safety Integrity Level* (ASIL). For the development of a product, it is therefore very important to address safety concerns already from the beginning. However, the approaches for estimating hardware metrics are based on spreadsheets, which hardly scale for large hardware systems.

Virtual prototypes based on SystemC are high-speed, fully functional software models of physical hardware systems that can model complex hardware/software systems with reasonable simulation speed. These virtual prototypes are used in industry to reduce time to market and improve the quality of the product [4].

In this paper, we present a novel methodology for combining the advantages of SystemC-based virtual prototypes with the safety analysis required by the ISO 26262 standards. Compared to previous works, our approach does not focus

© The Author(s), under exclusive license to Springer Nature Switzerland AG 2022
A. Orailoglu et al. (Eds.): SAMOS 2022, LNCS 13511, pp. 74–89, 2022.
https://doi.org/10.1007/978-3-031-15074-6_5

on the simulation of the system and on error injections; rather, we focus on the specific methodology required by ISO 26262 regarding the evaluation of the hardware architectural metrics and how this can be implemented in the SystemC standard as an extension. Failure modeling can be seen as a type of modeling that is orthogonal to the modeling of the functionality. However, with our approach, both aspects can be integrated in the same simulation models, which provides the opportunity to analyze structure, functionality, and safety aspects simultaneously. Due to the power of the SystemC framework, we have a high level of interoperability, and functional legacy models could be enhanced by our safety amendments. The presented method receives failure rates in *Failure in Time* (FIT) and directly calculates the achievable ASIL as well as the hardware metrics as output.

In summary, we make the following contributions:

- We present a set of basic blocks that represent the operations required by ISO 26262.
- We present, for the first time, a methodology, called Split'n'Cover, that uses these basic blocks to model and evaluate hardware systems regarding ASIL.
- We provide an open-source reference implementation as a SystemC library software[1].
- We show the application of this methodology for an example DRAM memory system in the automotive context.

This paper is structured as follows: Sect. 2 provides some background on ISO 26262 and the required hardware metrics. Related work is discussed in Sect. 3. The actual methodology is presented in Sect. 4, whereas the actual implementation in SystemC is explained in Sect. 5. Section 6 presents an actual case study for an LPDDR4 DRAM memory system. Finally, Sect. 7 concludes the paper.

2   Background

In this section, we present the basic requirements on safety in order to understand the hardware metric analysis of ISO 26262. For the safety analysis of hardware, we follow the definitions of Laprie et al. [2]:

Fault: Is a defect within the system and the root cause of the violation of a safety goal, e.g., a stuck-at 0 or single event upset due to a cosmic ray.

Error: Is an erroneous internal state e.g., in the memory or the CPU, where the fault becomes visible.

Failure: Is when the error is observed and the system's behavior deviates from the specification. This might lead to the violation of a safety goal.

As shown in Fig. 1, hardware failure rates $\lambda(t)$ usually follow the so-called *Bathtub Curve*. In phase **I**, we can observe early failures called *Infant Mortality*. In phase **II**, there exists a constant failure rate, known as random failures. This phase is also called *Useful Lifetime*. Therefore, a burn-in process of the product is used to artificially age the product. The third phase **III** shows the *Wear-Out* of the product, where the failure rate increases due to wear-out, i. e., aging effects.

---

[1] https://github.com/myzinsky/ISO26262SystemC.

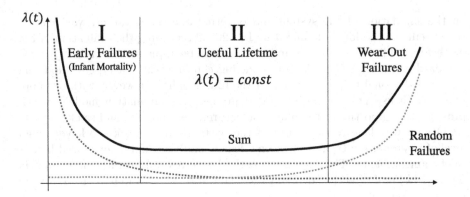

Fig. 1. Hardware failure bathtub curve [5]

For the analysis of hardware failures the ISO 26262 assumes that the hardware is used during its useful lifetime and that the failure rate $\lambda(t)$ is constant (c. f. ISO 26262-11 [5]). For constant failure rates, we can assume the exponential failure distribution

$$F(t) = 1 - e^{-\lambda \cdot t}$$

The constant failure rate of this distribution λ is measured in *Failure in Time* (FIT), where 1 FIT represents one failure in 10^9 hours, which is approximately one failure in 114,080 years. For the hardware metrics, ISO 26262 distinguishes several different failure rates, among them:

- λ_{SPF} *Single-Point Fault Failure Rate*: Considers faults that are not covered by any safety mechanism and immediately leads to the violation of a safety goal.
- λ_{RF} *Residual Fault Failure Rate*: Considers faults where a safety mechanism is implemented, but is not controlled by the safety mechanism and leads to the violation of a safety goal.
- λ_{MPF} *Multi-Point Fault Failure Rate*: Considers several independent faults, which in combination lead to the violation of a safety goal. For this paper, especially the latent faults $\lambda_{\text{MPF,L}}$ are important, whose presence is neither detected by a safety mechanism nor perceived by the driver.
- λ_{S} *Safe Fault Failure Rate*: Considers faults that do not have any significant influence on the violation of a safety goal.

The total failure rate is the sum of the above failure rates:

$$\lambda = \lambda_{\text{SPF}} + \lambda_{\text{RF}} + \lambda_{\text{MPF}} + \lambda_{\text{S}}$$

Table 1. Requirements according to ISO 26262 [5]

ASIL	SPFM	LFM	Residual FIT
A	-	-	<1000
B	>90%	>60%	<100
C	>97%	>80%	<100
D	>99%	>90%	<10

The ISO 26262 furthermore specifies the hardware metrics used to evaluate the risk posed by hardware elements:

Single-Point Fault Metric (SPFM): This metric reflects the coverage of a hardware element with respect to single-point faults either by design or by coverage via safety mechanisms.

$$\text{SPFM} = 1 - \frac{\sum (\lambda_{\text{SPF}} + \lambda_{\text{RF}})}{\sum \lambda}$$

Latent Fault Metric (LFM): This metric reflects the coverage of an hardware element with respect to latent faults either by design (primarily safe faults), fault coverage via safety mechanisms, or by the driver's recognition of a fault's existence within the fault-tolerant time interval of a safety goal.

$$\text{LFM} = 1 - \frac{\sum \lambda_{\text{MPF,L}}}{\sum (\lambda - \lambda_{\text{SPF}} - \lambda_{\text{RF}})}$$

Table 1 shows the required target values for λ_{RF}, SPFM, and LFM to reach a specific ASIL. For example, the highest level ASIL D can only be reached if the SPFM is greater than 99%, the LFM is greater than 90%, and the residual failure rate is below 10.

3   Related Work

This section discusses related work and the state of the art. Today's safety standards, such as ISO 26262, usually recommend a *Failure Mode and Effect Analysis* (FMEA) or Fault Tree Analysis (FTA). The FMEA is performed by creating spreadsheets. In complex systems, these spreadsheets will grow extensively; multi-levels are traditionally not supported; and for safety engineers, it is really hard to handle this and adapt it during change management. A much more structured approach is the so-called *Fault Tree Analysis* (FTA). Especially the *Component Fault Trees* (CFT) introduced by Adler et al. [1] provide several structural advantages compared to spreadsheet approaches. These fault trees allow a clear structuring of the model and fully capture the hardware's complexity all at once. However, with these CFTs, it is not easy to derive the actual metrics required by the ISO 26262 for the ASIL rating because a *Minimal Cut*

Set (MCS) analysis has to be performed, which is a complicated additional step that has to be solved. Furthermore, the optimization of the ASIL level resulting from the introduction of new safety measures is not visible directly due to this additional step. Another shortcoming is the necessary translation of failure rates into failure probabilities, which are used in the FTA, and back again into failure rates to calculate the hardware metrics. Adler et al. [1] already introduced the modeling element *Measure*, which allows making a distinction between faults and failing safety measures and, in principle, makes it possible to retrieve the hardware metrics from the MCS analysis. However, the authors leave open whether the *Measure* element shall be used to express classical failures of the mechanism (expressed by a failure rate) or insufficiencies by design (expressed as diagnostic coverage in percent). The distinction issue that the authors observed for modeling measures also applies to splits in the failure propagation due to the system structure. To model this with CFTs, *basic events* with constant probability combined with an *AND-gate* could be used, but the split is then treated as a failure. Another option would be to separate the initial fault into several basic events for every split during the failure propagation through the system, which leads to high modeling effort in complex systems. Our method overcomes these disadvantages because the metrics can be derived directly and a clear one-to-one mapping between metrics and the hardware exists, which enables easy optimization by introducing new safety measures.

The usage of SystemC-based virtual prototypes for safety analysis is already well established. However, all these approaches focus on simulation of the functionality and injection of errors. For example, in [7], the authors present how virtual prototypes can support the FMEA process. There also exist other works whose main focus is on fault injection during functional simulations [8, 12–14]. As mentioned above, all of these previous works focus on functional simulation and error injection for ISO 26262 support. The focus of our work lies on the static hardware metrics analysis of ISO 26262 and how it can be realized within SystemC.

4   Methodology

In the following, we will describe our new methodology for estimating the hardware metrics required by ISO 26262. Similar to CFTs, our methodology is object-oriented; i.e., it models the system with the hardware components that also exist in reality. The safety behavior of each component is modeled in the component itself by using five central building blocks, which are shown in Fig. 2 and explained below.

The *Basic Event* block represents internal faults, with a specific failure rate λ_{BE}. The *Sum* block receives the failure rates λ_0 to λ_n and computes the sum of these failure rates.

The *Coverage* block can be used to model the *Diagnostic Coverage* (DC) of a specific safety measure. The input failure rate λ_{in} is reduced by the DC rate c of this safety measure:

$$\lambda_{RF} = \lambda_{in} \cdot (1 - c)$$

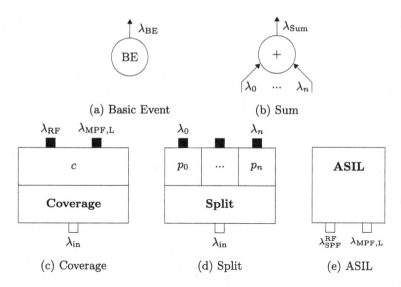

Fig. 2. Calculation blocks for the safety methodology

For instance, if $\lambda = 100\,\mathrm{FIT}$ and $c = 0.95$, only 5% of the failures, i.e., $5\,\mathrm{FIT}$, are propagated. According to the ISO 26262, the covered FITs must be added to the latent failures $\lambda_{\mathrm{MPF,L}}$ to consider the scenario where the safety measure is defect:

$$\lambda_{\mathrm{MPF,L}} = \lambda_{\mathrm{in}} \cdot c$$

In our example, $95\,\mathrm{FIT}$ are propagated to the latent fault metrics if no other measure reduces these failures.

The *Split* block distributes the incoming failure rate to an arbitrary number of output ports according to specific rates p_i, where the condition

$$\sum_{i=0}^{n} p_i \leq 1$$

must hold; otherwise, new failures will be created out of nowhere. It is possible for some parts of the incoming failure rate to completely vanish because of the split; i.e., they are not propagated. These faults are called *Safe Faults* because they will never lead to a safety goal violation. The safe fault failure rate can therefore be described as:

$$\lambda_S = \lambda_{\mathrm{in}} \cdot \left(1 - \sum_{i=0}^{n} p_i\right)$$

In summary, the *Split* block is used to model failure distributions caused by the system structure; e.g., when a data stream is divided, or when the safety mechanism adds additional errors during the correction of unsupported faults, such as double-bit errors in a single-error correction mechanism.

The last required block is the *ASIL* block, which calculates the ASIL from the λ_{SPF}, λ_{RF}, and $\lambda_{\mathrm{MPF,L}}$ within the entire system. This block implements the logic of Table 1.

With these five blocks, it is possible to model the safety behavior of hardware in compliance with the ISO 26262. We would like to mention here that it is only necessary to consider faults of safety-related components. Components that are not safety related do not have to be modeled at all, or their errors do not need to be modeled or connected (and thus not considered in the sum of all errors). In Sect. 6, we will present the modeling of a real-world automotive memory system in order to understand the interaction of these blocks.

5 Implementation

In this section, we will describe the implementation of the building blocks in SystemC, which is well established and a de-facto industry standard. Therefore, there already exist a lot of functional simulation models that can be enhanced with our safety methodology. SystemC offers the right infrastructure by providing the concept of modules, ports, and signals that are required for our basic blocks. Unlike graphical safety tools, it also offers programmability, and repetitions can be handled by loops. Furthermore, SystemC's port check is really helpful in the development phase of the safety model since it will complain about unbound ports at the beginning of a simulation. The failure rates are propagated by using a classical `sc_signal<double>`. For all blocks, we use the dynamic binding of SystemC for the sake of convenience. All blocks contain classical `SC_METHODs`; i.e., during the first delta cycles of the SystemC simulation, all hardware safety measures are already computed and are printed out at the end of a simulation.

The first block is the *Basic Event* block shown in Listing 1, which receives the failure rate (`rate`) as a constructor parameter and propagates this value to its output port.

The *Sum* block has a dynamic input port array and a single output port. In its computation method, it calculates the summation of the incoming failure rates on all input ports, as shown in Listing 2.

The *Coverage* block, shown in Listing 3, receives the DC as a constructor parameter and calculates λ_{RF} (`output`) and $\lambda_{\mathrm{MPF,L}}$ (`latent`) according to the formulas presented in Sect. 4.

Compared to the other blocks, the implementation of the *Split* block is more complicated. Since we want to support dynamic binding and direct assignment of the failure distribution rate, we derived a custom `sc_split_port` from `sc_port` that overwrites the `bind` methods in order to allow specifying the split rate directly with the dynamic binding, as shown in Listing 4.

The actual implementation of the *Split* component is shown in Listing 5. It receives a failure rate as input and distributes it to the output ports according to the assigned split rates.

The last building block is the *ASIL* block, which estimates the ASIL rate of the system according to Table 1. It receives the single point and residual failure

```
1   SC_MODULE(basic_event) {
2       sc_out<double> output;
3       double rate;
4
5       SC_HAS_PROCESS(basic_event);
6       basic_event(sc_module_name name, double rate) : output("output"),
7                                                       rate(rate)
8       {
9           SC_METHOD(compute_fit);
10      }
11
12      void compute_fit() {
13          output.write(rate);
14      }
15  };
```

Listing 1: Implementation of the Basic Event Block in SystemC

```
1   SC_MODULE(sum) {
2       sc_port<sc_signal_in_if<double>, 0, SC_ONE_OR_MORE_BOUND> inputs;
3       sc_out<double> output;
4
5       SC_CTOR(sum) : output("output") {
6           SC_METHOD(compute_fit);
7           sensitive << inputs;
8       }
9
10      void compute_fit() {
11          double sum = 0.0;
12          for(int i=0; i < inputs.size(); i++) {
13              sum += inputs[i]->read();
14          }
15          output.write(sum);
16      }
17  };
```

Listing 2: Implementation of the Sum Block in SystemC

rates $\lambda_{\mathrm{SPF}} + \lambda_{\mathrm{RF}}$ and the latent failure rates $\lambda_{\mathrm{MPF,L}}$ as input. Furthermore, it receives the total failure rate λ as input, calculates the ASIL level, and prints it from the destructor call at the end of the simulation, as shown in Listing 6.

6   Experimental Case Study and Results

In order to verify the validity of our new methodology, we modeled the automotive LPDDR4 DRAM architecture presented in [11] (*Scenario 1*). The authors used CFTs [1] for their analysis, which has the disadvantage that the analysis of

```
1   SC_MODULE(coverage) {
2       sc_in<double> input;
3       sc_out<double> output;
4       sc_port<sc_signal_inout_if<double>,0,SC_ZERO_OR_MORE_BOUND> latent;
5
6       double dc;
7
8       SC_HAS_PROCESS(coverage);
9       coverage(sc_module_name name, double dc) : input("input"),
10                                                 output("output"),
11                                                 dc(dc)
12      {
13          SC_METHOD(compute_fit);
14          sensitive << input;
15      }
16
17      void compute_fit() {
18          output.write(input.read()*(1-dc));
19          if(latent.bind_count() != 0) {
20              latent->write(input.read()*dc);
21          }
22      }
23  };
```

Listing 3: Implementation of the Coverage Block in SystemC

```
1   template <class T>
2   class sc_split_out :
3       public sc_port<sc_signal_inout_if<T>,0,SC_ONE_OR_MORE_BOUND>
4   {
5   public:
6       std::vector<double> split_rates;
7
8       void bind(sc_interface& interface , double rate) {
9           sc_port_base::bind(interface);
10          split_rates.push_back(rate);
11      }
12
13      void bind(sc_out<double>& parent, double rate) {
14          sc_port_base::bind(parent);
15          split_rates.push_back(rate);
16      }
17  };
```

Listing 4: Implementation of the Custom Split Port in SystemC

the system is hampered since the Boolean equations do not relate directly to the required ISO 26262 metrics and can therefore not be calculated directly. Figure 3 shows a safety model of this architecture realized with our new methodology.

```
1   SC_MODULE(split) {
2       sc_in<double> input;
3       sc_split_out<double> outputs;
4
5       SC_CTOR(split) : input("input") {
6           SC_METHOD(compute_fit);
7           sensitive << input;
8       }
9
10      void compute_fit() {
11          for(int i=0; i < outputs.size(); i++) {
12              double rate = outputs.split_rates.at(i);
13              outputs[i]->write(input.read()*rate);
14          }
15      }
16  };
```

Listing 5: Implementation of the Split Block in SystemC

With this example, the power of the newly introduced blocks can be explained. The source code of this example is available on GitHub[2]. Most of the errors in the model originate in the DRAM array itself. According to [3,9,11], we modeled the four main errors that may occur in the DRAM array: *Single-Bit Errors* (SBE), *Double-Bit Errors* (DBE), *Multi-Bit Errors* (MBE), and *Wrong Data* (WD). The exact distribution of these errors and failure rates was obtained from *Scenario 1* in [11]. As shown in Fig. 3, these errors are propagating upwards in the system to the next component, which is the internal LPDDR4 *Single Error Correction* (SEC), which uses a $(136, 128)$ Hamming *Error Correction Code* (ECC).

This SEC ECC is a safety mechanism that can correct 100% of all single-bit errors. Therefore, all SBEs are fully covered, such that the residual failure rate λ_{RF} for SBEs is reduced to zero, which is modeled by using the *Coverage* block. However, if this SEC ECC safety mechanism is defective, the covered failure rate must be added to the latent SBE failure rate $\lambda_{MPF,L}$ which propagates to the next component. Additionally, the failure rate of the SEC ECC itself must be added to the latent failure rate. Therefore, we modeled an additional *Basic Event* called *SEC ECC Broken* (SB).

In the case of an incoming DBE, two cases have to be differentiated. First, if there is a defect in the SEC engine, the DBE will stay a DBE. Second, if there is no defect in the SEC engine, the SEC will either detect that there is an uncorrectable error or attempt to correct the data, resulting in the introduction of a third error. The probability of introducing a third error largely depends on the specific code that is used. According to [11], 83% of the DBEs stay DBEs,

---

[2] https://github.com/myzinsky/ISO26262SystemC/blob/master/examples/dram-metrics-example.cpp.

```
1   SC_MODULE(asil) {
2       sc_in<double> residual;
3       sc_in<double> latent;
4
5       double spfm;
6       double lfm;
7       std::string asil_level;
8       double total;
9
10      SC_HAS_PROCESS(asil);
11      asil(sc_module_name name, double total) : total(total) {
12          SC_METHOD(compute);
13          sensitive << residual << latent;
14      }
15
16      void compute() {
17          spfm = 100*(1-(residual/(total)));
18          lfm = 100*(1-(latent/(total-residual)));
19          asil_level = "QM";
20
21          if(residual < 1000.0) {
22              asil_level = "ASIL A";
23          }
24          if(spfm > 90.0 && lfm > 60.0 && residual < 100.0) {
25              asil_level = "ASIL B";
26          }
27          if(spfm > 97.0 && lfm > 80.0 && residual < 100.0) {
28              asil_level = "ASIL C";
29          }
30          if(spfm > 99.0 && lfm > 90.0 && residual < 10.0) {
31              asil_level = "ASIL D";
32          }
33      }
34
35      ~asil() {
36          // Print out of the estimated ASIL level ...
37      }
38  };
```

Listing 6: Implementation of the ASIL Block in SystemC

while a third error (TBE) is introduced for 17%. In order to model this behavior, a *Split* component is used, which distributes the incoming DBE failure rate to DBE and TBE failure rates, respectively. In the case of an incoming MBE and WD, the SEC engine will not be able to correct any bit errors. Thus, these failure rates are always propagated.

In this model, there exist further components in the DRAM, the DRAM bus, and the DRAM controller in the *System on Chip* (SoC). For instance, in the DRAM-TRIM component, the redundancy of the code is removed. Thus, the

Table 2. Comparison with Fault Tree Analysis

	SPFM	LFM	Residual FIT
[11]	87.5%	94.3%	529.35
This work	87.45%	94.2%	529.63

number of data errors might also be reduced. For further explanations of these components, we refer to the paper [11].

By using the same input parameters, we can reproduce the results of [11], as shown in Table 2. Thus, our methodology is valid and can be used instead of the more complex CFTs. The small deviation of the results is due to some rounding effects.

However, unlike in the state of the art, where only a single DRAM failure rate is analyzed, we went one step further with our analysis. Because we are using SystemC, we can easily compute many different scenarios in parallel. In order to analyze the safety behavior of the provided DRAM system and the ECC safety measures, we sweep the DRAM's failure rate λ_{DRAM} from 1 FIT to 2500 FIT in several simulations. For this simulation, we assume that only the DRAM related hardware components influence the safety goal under consideration, and leave out other hardware elements on the SoC, which were considered in [11]. In practice, failure rate budgets are distributed to the involved hardware elements. In this case, as shown in Fig. 4, we could reach the requirement for ASIL D (<10 FIT) if the DRAM's failure rate stays below 53 FIT. However, if we take a look at the relative metrics shown in Fig. 5, we can see that, with a value of 81%, the SPFM is far away from the ASIL D threshold of 99%. We cannot even reach ASIL B, which has a SPFM threshold of 90%. From the LFM perspective, we could easily reach ASIL B and even ASIL C for higher λ_{DRAM} rates. Since for any ASIL classification, both the relative and absolute metrics must be fulfilled, we can observe that, independent of the DRAM's failure rate λ_{DRAM}, we cannot achieve a higher level than ASIL A. Thus, it does not help to improve the failure rates of the DRAM technology itself. Moreover, it is necessary to introduce more robust and holistic safety measures within the DRAM and the memory controller, as well as on software level.

This confirms the results presented by [9,11] for single scenarios. They also conclude that with the current ECC safety measures, no higher safety level than ASIL A can be achieved. Since it is not likely that future DRAM technologies will lead to a decrease in the failure rates, it is highly important to introduce further safety measures to make the DRAM system ready for higher ASIL levels.

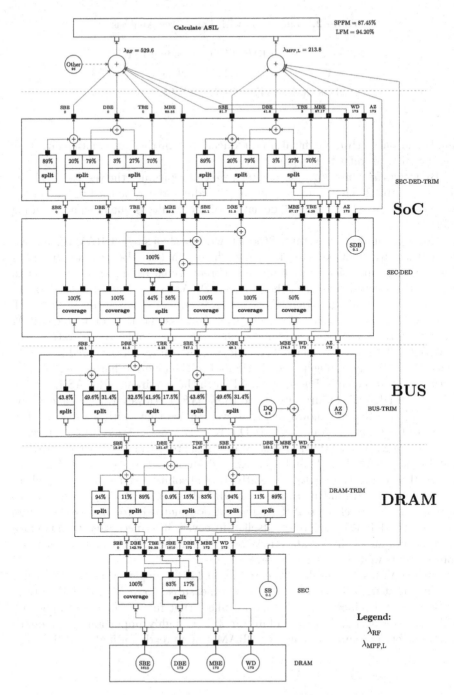

Fig. 3. Safety model of an LPDDR4 system according to the architecture of [11]

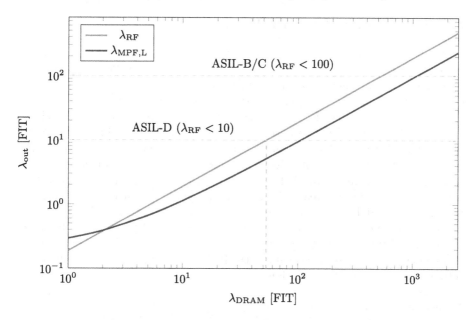

Fig. 4. Absolute

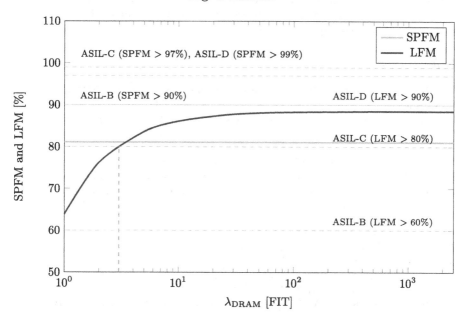

Fig. 5. Relative

7   Conclusion and Future Work

In this paper, we presented a new methodology for modeling the safety behavior of modern hardware systems in compliance with the ISO 26262 automotive standard. The implementation of this new methodology is provided as an open-source SystemC library and can be used to enhance legacy models with safety and quality analysis. In order to demonstrate the power of this new methodology, we modeled a state-of-the-art automotive DRAM memory architecture. Based on this model, we simulated a continuous space of failure rates of the DRAM system. We conclude that with the current safety measures, it is not possible to achieve a rating higher than ASIL A. In the future, we will analyze new safety measures that could help reach the goal of an ASIL D certification by using the presented methodology. Furthermore, we plan to integrate this methodology into the open-source design space exploration framework DRAMSys [6,10]. Depending on the configuration of the DRAM architecture with different numbers of ranks, channels, and safety mechanism the ISO 26262 metrics could be calculated automatically with each simulation.

Acknowledgments. This work was supported by the Fraunhofer and DFG cooperation program (grant no. 248750294) and by the Fraunhofer High Performance Center for Simulation- and Software-based Innovation. We thank Micron and Mercedes-Benz for the vivid discussions on this topic. Furthermore, we thank Sonnhild Namingha for proofreading this manuscript.

References

1. Adler, R., et al.: Integration of component fault trees into the UML. In: Dingel, J., Solberg, A. (eds.) MODELS 2010. LNCS, vol. 6627, pp. 312–327. Springer, Heidelberg (2011). https://doi.org/10.1007/978-3-642-21210-9_30
2. Avizienis, A., Laprie, J.C., Randell, B., Landwehr, C.: Basic concepts and taxonomy of dependable and secure computing. IEEE Trans. Depend. Secur. Comput. **1**(1), 11–33 (2004). https://doi.org/10.1109/TDSC.2004.2
3. Boehm, A.: DRAM - more important than you think for achieving automotive functional safety (2021). https://www.designnews.com/electronics/dram-more-important-you-think-achieving-automotive-functional-safety. Accessed 16 July 2021
4. De Schutter, T.: Better Software. Faster!: Best Practices in Virtual Prototyping. Synopsys Press, USA (2014)
5. ISO: Road Vehicles - Functional safety (2011)
6. Jung, M., Weis, C., Wehn, N.: DRAMSys: a flexible DRAM subsystem design space exploration framework. IPSJ Trans. Syst. LSI Des. Methodol. (T-SLDM) (2015). https://doi.org/10.2197/ipsjtsldm.8.63
7. Reiter, S., Pressler, M., Viehl, A., Bringmann, O., Rosenstiel, W.: Reliability assessment of safety-relevant automotive systems in a model-based design flow. In: 2013 18th Asia and South Pacific Design Automation Conference (ASP-DAC), pp. 417–422 (2013). https://doi.org/10.1109/ASPDAC.2013.6509632
8. Silva, A.d., Parra, P., Polo, O.R., Sánchez, S.: Runtime instrumentation of SystemC/TLM2 interfaces for fault tolerance requirements verification in software cosimulation. Model. Simul. Eng. **2014** (2014). https://doi.org/10.1155/2014/105051

9. Buch, S.: Micron Technology: Questions to Ask Your Memory Supplier About Functional Safety for DRAM (2020). https://www.youtube.com/watch?v=mzcbt XdWDcg. Accessed 16 July 2021

10. Steiner, L., Jung, M., Prado, F.S., Bykov, K., Wehn, N.: DRAMSys4.0: a fast and cycle-accurate SystemC/TLM-based DRAM simulator. In: Orailoglu, A., Jung, M., Reichenbach, M. (eds.) SAMOS 2020. LNCS, vol. 12471, pp. 110–126. Springer, Cham (2020). https://doi.org/10.1007/978-3-030-60939-9_8

11. Steiner, L., Kraft, K., Uecker, D., Jung, M., Huonker, M., Wehn, N.: An LPDDR4 safety model for automotive applications. In: ACM/IEEE International Symposium on Memory Systems (MEMSYS 2021), October 2021

12. Tabacaru, B.A.: On fault-effect analysis at the virtual-prototype abstraction level. TU München (2019)

13. Tabacaru, B.A., Chaari, M., Ecker, W., Kruse, T., Novello, C.: Fault-effect analysis on system-level hardware modeling using virtual prototypes. In: 2016 Forum on Specification and Design Languages (FDL), pp. 1–7 (2016). https://doi.org/10.1109/FDL.2016.7880368

14. Weissnegger, R., Schuss, M., Kreiner, C., Pistauer, M., Römer, K., Steger, C.: Simulation-based verification of automotive safety-critical systems based on east-ADL. Procedia Comput. Sci. **83**, 245–252 (2016). https://doi.org/10.1016/j.procs.2016.04.122, https://www.sciencedirect.com/science/article/pii/S1877050916301454, The 7th International Conference on Ambient Systems, Networks and Technologies (ANT 2016)/The 6th International Conference on Sustainable Energy Information Technology (SEIT-2016)/Affiliated Workshops

Tagged Geometric History Length Access Interval Prediction for Tightly Coupled Memory Systems

Viktor Razilov[✉], Robert Wittig, Emil Matúš, and Gerhard Fettweis

Vodafone Chair Mobile Communications Systems, Technische Universität Dresden,
01062 Dresden, Germany
{viktor.razilov,robert.wittig,emil.matus,gerhard.fettweis}@tu-dresden.de

Abstract. In embedded systems, tightly coupled memories (TCMs) are usually shared between multiple masters for the purpose of performance scalability, hardware efficiency and software flexibility. On the one hand, memory sharing improves area utilization, but on the other hand, this can lead to a performance degradation due to an increase in access conflicts. To mitigate the associated performance penalty, access interval prediction (AIP) has been proposed. In a similar fashion to branch prediction, AIP exploits program flow regularity to predict the cycle of the next memory access. We show that this structural similarity allows for adaption of state-of-the-art branch predictors, such as the TAgged GEometric history length (TAGE) branch predictor. Our analysis on memory access traces reveals that the obtained TAGE access interval predictor predicts over 97% of memory accesses outperforming all previously presented AIP schemes.

Keywords: Memory prediction · Access interval · Shared memory · MPSoC

1 Introduction

Since the end of Dennard scaling, computer architects have shifted to exploiting thread-level parallelism by integrating multiple processing elements (PE) as a system on chip. In area- and energy-constrained embedded systems, PEs may communicate via a shared scratchpad tightly coupled memory (TCM) to increase area utilization.

A drawback of this approach is the introduction of access conflicts. Since the access latency of TCMs is usually limited to a single clock cycle, on-line conflict resolution and arbitration logic may degrade the clock frequency, and thus the system performance. The degradation becomes more severe when different run-time priorities have to be considered, as is the case in mobile communication platforms [1], for example.

Access interval prediction (AIP) has been proposed to resolve TCM access conflicts in advance [2,3]. Memory accesses of PEs are predicted in the time

© The Author(s), under exclusive license to Springer Nature Switzerland AG 2022
A. Orailoglu et al. (Eds.): SAMOS 2022, LNCS 13511, pp. 90–100, 2022.
https://doi.org/10.1007/978-3-031-15074-6_6

domain so that an off-line arbiter speculatively allocates memory access time slots to one of the them. Logic on the path between the PEs and the TCM is kept to a minimum while priorities can be accounted for.

In an AIP system, mispredictions lead to misallocations. Therefore, a high prediction accuracy is crucial. AIP schemes such as the access look-ahead buffer (ALB) [2] or the maximum a-posteriori (MAP) estimator [3] achieve average hit rates of 50% (c.f., Sect. 5) or have not been designed with hardware implementation in mind, respectively.

To find better-performing predictors, we turn to branch prediction for inspiration because it is a well-researched problem that is similar to AIP. In the former, the outcomes of conditional branches are predicted and instructions are executed speculatively based on the prediction. A plethora of high-precision branch predictors have been proposed [4]. Of these, the TAGE predictor [5] is widely considered to be state of the art [4]. It works by recording branch outcome sequences of multiple history lengths.

In this paper, we leverage the maturity of the TAGE branch predictor (TAGE-BP) for AIP. We adapt TAGE to work on sequences of interval lengths and evaluate the performance of the TAGE access interval predictor (TAGE-AIP) on access traces of MiBench [6] on a RISC-V core.

The rest of the paper is structured as follows: Sect. 2 provides an overview of the background and related work on memory sharing and arbitration. Afterwards, in Sect. 3, we review AIP and introduce the system model and the notation used throughout this paper. In Sect. 4, the TAGE-BP is adapted for AIP. We analyze the main modifications and show the trade-offs involved. A comparison to other predictors is made in Sect. 5. We finish with conclusions in Sect. 6.

2   Background and Related Work

Shared memory systems are designed such that memory can be used by each master as seamlessly as if it had its own. A master is any entity that uses the shared memory, e.g., a central processing unit (CPU) or a dedicated accelerator. The memory system has to grant memory access to masters upon their request. As multi-ported static random access memory (SRAM) is prohibitively area-expensive, it also has to resolve conflicts when multiple masters request access concurrently.

Architectures such as the T-CREST [7] or MERASA [8] are able to arbitrate between masters with different priorities and ensure an upper bound for the transaction latency. However, their additional delay of several cycles renders them unsuitable for TCMs.

On-chip memory arbiters for TCMs [9–13] have instead been optimized for low latency omitting additional prioritization logic. They achieve a good average performance but the performance of high-priority tasks is degraded.

The number of conflicts may be reduced by banking SRAM cells [2,12–14]: If simultaneous requests target different memory banks they are not conflicting. This approach works especially well with compile-time information available.

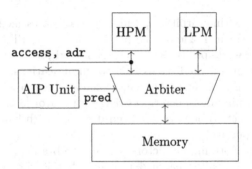

Fig. 1. AIP system model.

AIP on the other hand is able to consider priorities utilizing only run-time information. High-priority tasks are sped up without degrading the clock frequency. Simple prediction schemes, such as the ALB [2], predict up to 50% of accesses on data memory. The work in [3] showed that more sophisticated statistical methods may be able to reach accuracies over 90%.

3   Access Interval Prediction

3.1   System Overview

Figure 1 depicts the model of a system employing AIP. Two masters, a high-priority master (HPM) and a low-priority master (LPM), share a TCM. The HPM is the data port of a RISC-V core, the LPM a data movement engine accessing the memory every cycle. When the HPM requests the memory, it should always be granted unhindered access by the arbiter.

To achieve this without elongating the path between TCM and masters, we add the AIP unit. It monitors the memory interface of the HPM which is made up of `access` and `adr`. `access` is set whenever an access (read or write) on the address `adr` takes place. The AIP unit predicts the next access and sets `pred` whenever it determines that the HPM will request the memory in the next cycle. When this happens, the arbiter pre-allocates the memory to the HPM, and to the LPM otherwise.

This simple model allows performance comparison of different prediction schemes. AIP can also be scaled to more complex priority hierarchies, since it is possible to do predictions for multiple masters and the priority logic is placed offline.

3.2   Theory and Notation

We regard the program flow as a sequence of n_{access} access blocks. Each access block $B_i = (A_i, I_i)$ contains the address A_i accessed at cycle K_i and the length of the interval until the next access is determined by $I_i = K_{i+1} - K_i$. The program stops with the last access at K_{end}.

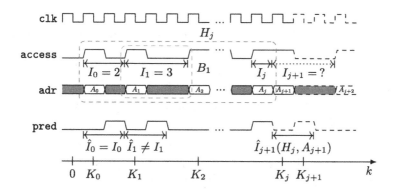

Fig. 2. Example waveform of access and prediction signals. At cycle $k = K_j$, the AIP unit tries to predict the length of the interval I_{j+1} until the next access at K_{j+1}. The prediction $\hat{I}_{j+1}$ may be subject to the access history H_j and the current address A_{j+1}. The dashed signals are not known at prediction time.

An excerpt of an example program is shown in Fig. 2. $j + 1$ access intervals were completed and can be summarized as history $H_j = (B_i)_{i=0}^{j}$. After each access on an address A_i, the predictor makes a prediction of the next interval $\hat{I}_i$ based on H_{i-1} and A_i. Subsequently, pred is set at cycle $k = K_i + \hat{I}_i - 1$.

If $\text{access}(k) = \text{pred}(k - 1) = 1$, an access has been predicted correctly. We denote n_{hit} the number of correctly predicted accesses, $P_{\text{hit}} = \frac{n_{\text{hit}}}{n_{\text{access}}}$ the hit rate, and $P_{\text{miss}} = 1 - P_{\text{hit}}$ the miss rate.

When $\text{pred}(k - 1) = 1 \neq \text{access}(k)$, a false positive prediction occurs. The memory is mistakenly reserved for the HPM and memory utilization is impaired. The interval utilization, the percentage of idle cycles where the memory is not blocked because of false predictions, is determined from the number of false positives n_{fp} by

$$U_{\text{I}} = 1 - \frac{n_{\text{fp}}}{K_{\text{end}} + 1 - n_{\text{access}}}. \tag{1}$$

4   TAGE Access Interval Predictor

A detailed description and analysis of the original TAGE-BP can be found in [5]. TAGE prediction is based on prediction by partial matching (PPM) [15]. PPM works by tracking the frequency of events after subsequences in H_i. For each H_i, PPM searches the longest subsequence of H_{i-1} which is a suffix of H_i. The prediction is then given by the most frequent successor of the matching subsequence.

PPM can be implemented in software by traversing a suffix-tree-like structure. TAGE is a hardware approximation of PPM: Instead of matching sequences of any length, only a few lengths are selected after a geometric series. And instead of iterating through the different history lengths, a hash map is used for each selected length.

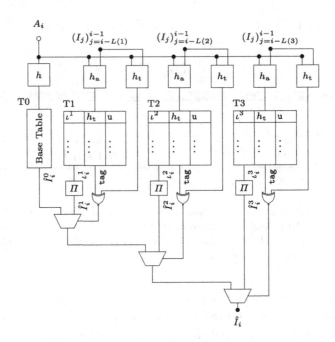

Fig. 3. TAGE-AIP with 4 components, each of which provides a subprediction based on the information indexed with the access address and the last intervals. For each subprediction, a tag check is performed and among the matches the one with the longest interval history is selected as the final prediction.

4.1 Design

The TAGE-AIP's basic structure, as shown in Fig. 3, is similar to the TAGE-BP. It is made out of n_T components, of which every component t utilizes a different history length

$$L(t) = \begin{cases} \lceil \alpha^{t-1} L(1) - 0.5 \rceil & \text{if } 1 \le t < n_T \\ 0 & \text{if } t = 0. \end{cases} \quad (2)$$

The spacing α and the first length $L(1)$ are chosen at design-time. For example, $\alpha = 2.88$ and $L(1) = 1$ lead to $L(t) = (0, 1, 3, 8, 24, \ldots)$.

The base table with n_I entries provides the fallback prediction when no tag matches. As can be seen from Eq. (2), the base table employs only the address and no past intervals. Each interval I_i is stored at the address generated with a simple hash $h(A_i)$ (e.g., bit slicing) of the accessed address. When the address $A_j = A_i$ (or another address for which $h(A_j) = h(A_i)$) is accessed again, the base table emits $\hat{I}_j^0 = I_i$.

The other tables consist of a memory bank with n_I entries from which the prediction information ι_i^t, a tag and the useful counter u of bit-widths w_ι, w_t and w_u, respectively, are read. The subprediction $\hat{I}_i^t$ of width w_I is computed from

ι_i^t by means of the subpredictor Π. In contrast to the TAGE-BP, we consider a variety of subpredictors (c.f. Sect. 4.3).

The table is addressed with a $\log_2 n_\mathrm{I}$-bit wide hash h_a of the context

$$C_i^t = \left(I_{i-L(t)}, \ldots, I_{i-2}, I_{i-1}, A_i\right) \tag{3}$$

containing the last $L(t)$ intervals and the currently accessed address. A different hash function $h_\mathrm{t} \neq h_\mathrm{a}$ yields a tag from the same input C_i^t to detect hash collisions of h_a. Both, h_a and h_t, are based on circular shift registers similar to [16]. Only subpredictions for which the tag matches are considered. Of these, the component with the highest $L(t)$ provides the final prediction $\hat{I}_i$. The useful counter u is used as in [5] to keep track of entries that can be overwritten because they provide the same prediction as another entry with a shorter context.

$\hat{I}_i$ is finally compared with a cycle counter which is reset at every access. The predictor sets **pred** when the next cycle is $\hat{I}_i$ cycles after the last access.

4.2   Interval Representation

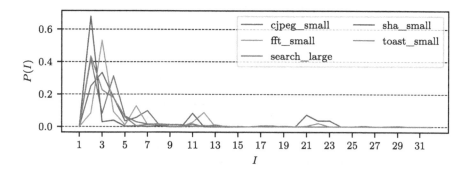

Fig. 4. Probability mass function of recorded access intervals.

In the case of branch prediction, the event to be predicted, branch outcome, has only two possible values. A single bit suffices for representation. More bits need to be allocated for interval representation. In theory, the set of possible intervals $\mathbb{N}^+$ is infinite. However, large intervals occur rarely as can be seen in Fig. 4, which shows the probability $P(I)$ of different intervals during the execution of selected MiBench programs. For example, only 4% or 0.1% of intervals exceed $I = 16$ or $I = 32$, respectively.

When w_I bits are used, intervals up to length $I_{\max} = 2^{w_\mathrm{I}}$ are encoded correctly, whereas overflowing intervals $I > I_{\max}$ are aliased to $I \bmod I_{\max}$. On the other hand, larger w_I generally lead to higher w_ι and thus impose higher memory requirements. The storage requirements in bits of prediction information, tags and useful counters is

$$M = n_\mathrm{T} n_\mathrm{I} w_\iota + (n_\mathrm{T} - 1) n_\mathrm{I}(w_\mathrm{u} + w_\mathrm{t}). \tag{4}$$

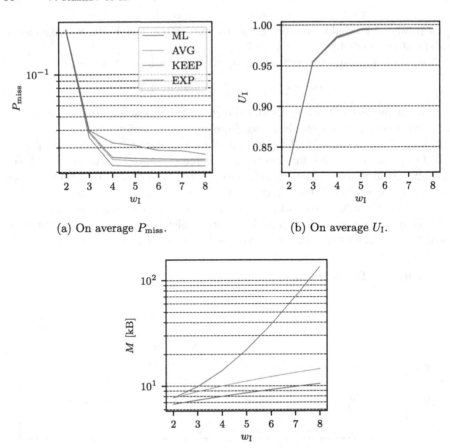

(a) On average P_miss.

(b) On average U_I.

(c) On memory size of prediction tables.

Fig. 5. Performance impact of different w_I and subprediction methods. All other predictor parameters are as listed in Table 1.

4.3   Subprediction and Update Method

Once an entry is allocated in a table at the address determined by $h_\text{a}(C_k^t)$, it is possible to save arbitrary information ι^t about the outcomes of the corresponding context. Based on this information, a subprediction $\hat{I}_i^t = \Pi(\iota^t)$ is computed whenever the current context matches $C_i^t = C_k^t$. When the subprediction was used as the final prediction, the entry will be updated.

The TAGE-BP stores a saturating counter that is incremented when the branch is taken and decremented otherwise. This method effectively tracks which of the two possible outcomes happened the most often and selects it.

An equivalent for AIP is the maximum-likelihood (ML) subprediction method which is similar to [3]. It can be realized by storing a counter for each possible interval and selecting the interval with the highest counter. The associated memory complexity is in the order of $\mathcal{O}(2^{w_I})$. With the help of hashes and truncation, the memory requirement might be reduced at the cost of degraded performance.

Instead, we evaluate three approaches with linear memory complexity:

1. AVG, where the prediction is the moving average of the last $n = 2$ outcomes of C_i^t.
2. EXP, where exponential smoothing is used. The new prediction is the average of the last prediction $\hat{I}_i^t$ and the actual interval I_i.
3. KEEP, where a prediction is kept for the entire existence of an entry until it is overwritten. If a new entry is allocated for C_l^t with the outcome I_l, then the table predicts $\hat{I}_i = I_l$ whenever $h_a(C_i^t) = h_a(C_l^t)$.

5 Performance Evaluation

For performance evaluation, we executed selected programs (c.f. Fig. 4) of the MiBench [6] embedded benchmark suite on the simple RISC-V processor model from gem5 [17] (TimingSimpleCPU) and traced `access` and `adr` during execution. Technical limitations prevented the use of the entire MiBench suite. Figure 5 illustrates the average prediction accuracy and interval utilization of different TAGE-AIP configurations for these traces, as well as the associated memory requirements.

5.1 Interval Representation

If w_I is too small, too many collisions occur and the predictor is unable to properly record and recall interval histories. Prediction performance, in terms of P_{miss} and U_I, increases with w_I until a saturation point is hit at $w_I = 5$ as almost none of the recorded traces exhibit intervals $I > 2^5 = 32$.

5.2 Subprediction and Update Method

There is a noticeable trade-off between prediction accuracy and memory requirements. The method with the lowest P_{miss}, ML, needs the most memory. AVG requires less memory but prediction accuracy is slightly impaired. Finally, EXP and KEEP are the most inaccurate but also the least complex. U_I is nearly the same for all methods.

We choose $w_I = 4$ and EXP as this combination yields the lowest product MP_{miss}. Other parameters were determined as in Table 1 by random search within the specified ranges. More sophisticated design space exploration (DSE) for the other parameters is outside the scope of this paper. This resulting combination achieves $P_{\text{hit}} = 97.5\%$ and $U_I = 98.5\%$ with $M = 8\,\text{kB}$ of memory.

Table 1. Parameters of the TAGE access interval predictor

Parameter	n_T	$L(1)$	α	w_t	w_u	n_I	w_I	Π
Value	5	1	2.88	9	2	1024	4	EXP
Range	1–15	1–50	0.5–50	4–20	1–5	2–4096	2–8	ML,AVG,KEEP,EXP

Table 2. Comparison of different access interval predictors.

Predictor	P_{hit} [%]	U_I [%]	M [kB]
CBE	51.5	90.2	–
ALB (1024 entries)	52.3	91.0	0.63
ALB (16384 entries)	56.9	92.0	10.00
TAGE-AIP	97.5	98.5	8.00

5.3 Comparison

A comparison between different access interval predictors is drawn in Table 2. TAGE-AIP predicts more accurately than the ALB and the simple counter based estimator (CBE) [2] which does not rely on SRAM blocks. The improved hit rate comes at a price of higher memory complexity. Therefore, TAGE may be used where a high prediction accuracy is more important than a low predictor overhead.

6   Conclusion and Outlook

In this paper, we derived the TAGE-AIP from the TAGE-BP and explored the adjustments that are needed to predict intervals instead of branch outcomes. Multiple bits are needed for representation of the former. This raises memory requirements but does not hinder sufficiently accurate prediction. We showed that 4–5 bits are enough for interval representation as interval exceeding 16 or 32 cycles are rare.

Furthermore, different methods of storing interval information and computing a prediction from it were discussed. Keeping track of the frequency of each possible outcome, as is done in branch prediction with means of saturating up-down counters, is too memory-expensive in the case of AIP. Therefore we investigated alternatives of which a moving average of the last outcomes and exponential smoothing proved to be efficient. The resulting TAGE-AIP reaches a hit rate over 97% while being implementable with moderate hardware requirements of 8 kB of SRAM.

Finally, we made a comparison to other access interval predictors found in literature. Our proposed predictor achieves higher prediction accuracy than any other implementable predictor at the price of higher memory complexity.

It should be noted that while TAGE is known to be precise it also has a high update cost. Therefore, further research will address register transfer logic design of the proposed TAGE-AIP and investigate the timing overhead. Another open topic is the performance of adaptations of other state-of-the-art branch predictors, such as gshare, GEHL, or Perceptron [4].

Acknowledgment. This work was funded in part by the German Federal Ministry of Education and Research (BMBF) in the project "E4C" (project number 16ME0426K). We thank the Center for Information Services and High Performance Computing (ZIH) at TU Dresden for generous allocation of compute resources.

References

1. Haas, S., et al.: A heterogenous SDR MPSoC in 28 nm CMOS for low-latency wireless applications. In: DAC. ACM Press, New York (2017). https://doi.org/10.1145/3061639.3062188
2. Wittig, R., Pauls, F., Matus, E., Fettweis, G.: Access interval prediction for tightly coupled memory systems. In: Pnevmatikatos, D.N., Pelcat, M., Jung, M. (eds.) SAMOS 2019. LNCS, vol. 11733, pp. 229–240. Springer, Cham (2019). https://doi.org/10.1007/978-3-030-27562-4_16
3. Wittig, R., Hasler, M., Matus, E., Fettweis, G.: Statistical access interval prediction for tightly coupled memory systems. In: COOL CHIPS. IEEE (2019). https://doi.org/10.1109/CoolChips.2019.8721304
4. Mittal, S.: A survey of techniques for dynamic branch prediction. Concurr. Comput. Pract. Exp. **31**(1), 1–36 (2018)
5. Seznec, A., Michaud, P.: A case for (partially) TAgged GEometric history length branch prediction. J. Instruct. Level Parall. **8** (2006). https://www.jilp.org/vol8
6. Guthaus, M.R., Ringenberg, J.S., Ernst, D., Austin, T.M., Mudge, T., Brown, R.B.: MiBench: a free, commercially representative embedded benchmark suite. In: 4th Annual Workshop on Workload Characterization. IEEE (2001)
7. Schoeberl, M., et al.: T-CREST: time-predictable multi-core architecture for embedded systems. J. Syst. Archit. **61**(9), 449–471 (2015). https://doi.org/10.1016/j.sysarc.2015.04.002
8. Paolieri, M., Quiñones, E., Carzola, F.J., Bernat, G., Valero, M.: Hardware support for WCET analysis of hard real-time multicore systems. In: ISCA. ACM Press, New York (2009). https://doi.org/10.1145/1555754.1555764
9. Ax, J., et al.: CoreVA-MPSoC: a many-core architecture with tightly coupled shared and local data memories. IEEE Trans. Parallel Distrib. Syst. **29**(5), 1030–1043 (2018). https://doi.org/10.1109/TPDS.2017.2785799
10. Gelado, I., Cabezas, J., Stone, J.E., Patel, S., Navarro, N., Hwu, W.-M.W.: An asymmetric distributed shared memory model for heterogeneous parallel systems. In: ASPLOS. ACM Press, New York (2010). https://doi.org/10.1145/1736020.1736059
11. Wittig, R., Hasler, M., Matus, E., Fettweis, G.: Queue based memory management unit for heterogeneous MPSoCs. In: DATE. IEEE (2019). https://doi.org/10.23919/DATE.2019.8715129
12. Bates, D., Bradbury, A., Koltes, A., Mullins, R.: Exploiting tightly-coupled cores. In: SAMOS. IEEE (2013). https://doi.org/10.1109/SAMOS.2013.6621138
13. Rahimi, A., Loi, I., Kakoee, M.R., Benini, L.: A fully-synthesizable single-cycle interconnection network for shared-L1 processor clusters. In: DATE. IEEE (2011). https://doi.org/10.1109/DATE.2011.5763085

14. Gautschi, M., Rossi, D., Benini, L.: Customizing an open source processor to fit in an ultra-low power cluster with a shared L1 memory. In: GLSVLSI. IEEE (2014). https://doi.org/10.1145/2591513.2591569
15. Cleary, J., Witten, I.: Data compression using adaptive coding and partial string matching. IEEE Trans. Commun. **32**(4), 396–402 (1984)
16. Michaud, P.: A PPM-like, tag-based branch predictor. J. Instruct. Level Parall. **7**, (2005). https://www.jilp.org/vol7
17. Lowe-Power, J., et al. The gem5 simulator: version 20.0+. (2020). https://arxiv.org/abs/2007.03152

Processor Architecture

NanoController: A Minimal and Flexible Processor Architecture for Ultra-Low-Power Always-On System State Controllers

Moritz Weißbrich[(✉)] and Guillermo Payá-Vayá

Chair for Chip Design for Embedded Computing, Technische Universität Braunschweig, Mühlenpfordtstraße 22-23, 38106 Braunschweig, Germany
{m.weissbrich,g.paya-vaya}@tu-braunschweig.de

Abstract. Distributed nodes in IoT and wireless sensor networks, which are powered by small batteries or energy harvesting, are constrained to very limited energy budgets. By intelligent power management and power gating strategies for the main microcontroller of the system, the energy efficiency can be significantly increased. However, timer-based, periodical power-up sequences are too inflexible to implement these strategies, and the use of a programmable power management controller demands minimum area and ultra-low power consumption from this system part itself. In this paper, the NanoController processor architecture is proposed, which is intended to be used as a flexible system state controller in the always-on domain of smart devices. The NanoController features a compact ISA, minimal silicon area and power consumption, and enables the implementation of efficient power management strategies in comparison to much simpler and constrained always-on timer circuits. For a power management control application of an electronic door lock, the NanoController is compared to small state-of-the-art controller architectures and has up to 86% smaller code size and up to 92% less silicon area and power consumption for 65 nm standard cell ASIC implementations.

Keywords: Instruction-set architecture · Processor architecture · Ultra-low-power microcontroller

1 Introduction

During recent years, the demand for very energy-efficient embedded systems is increasing. Examples are distributed wireless sensor networks [1] or IoT devices in building automation, including intelligent room sensors, electronic door locks [15], etc. Such devices may be installed in locations without a wired power supply, and battery-powered operation or self-powering via energy harvesting (EH) are the only feasible solutions [19]. In order to maximize battery life, or to enable operation on a very limited budget of harvested energy, the

© The Author(s), under exclusive license to Springer Nature Switzerland AG 2022
A. Orailoglu et al. (Eds.): SAMOS 2022, LNCS 13511, pp. 103–119, 2022.
https://doi.org/10.1007/978-3-031-15074-6_7

power consumption of the system needs to be minimized, including the micro-controller. For example, for electronic door locks, continuous operation at less than 1µW average power consumption is desired for an estimated solar and RF indoor EH profile in an office building [15].

In the above-mentioned devices, there are typically relatively simple events with frequent execution, e.g., updating sensor data values, or continuously check-ing for proximity of a key card in electronic door locks. Only in significantly less frequent cases, a more complex system reaction is required, e.g., processing encrypted RFID communication with an actual key card few times per day. The state-of-the-art approach is to use *sleep modes* in order to reduce the energy con-sumption of microcontroller devices when no processing is required. Typically, a single, general-purpose microcontroller is used to process all frequent and infre-quent events, triggered in a periodical fashion [19]. On each event, the complete core wakes up, independent of whether full processing performance is required for the event or not. This behavior can cause peak energy consumption that might empty the energy storage of systems powered by EH only. Furthermore, the microcontroller is always supplied with power and held ready for wake-up, which causes continuous leakage power consumption.

By introducing power domains and *power gating*, leakage can be further decreased. The basic idea is to eliminate leakage completely during inactivity of the microcontroller. A state-of-the-art approach is an always-on timer device like the NanoTimer IC [19], which is connected to power management circuitry and periodically controls power-down and power-up cycles of the microcontroller. However, this concept does not address the issue of possibly unnecessary peri-odical power-up cycles. For wireless sensor network nodes powered by EH, it has been identified that *conditional* power-up, based on received packet headers and the current energy budget, can increase the energy efficiency compared to always periodical power-up [1]. However, this approach requires an additional, intelligent power management controller instead of just a timer device in order to implement the strategy for conditional power gating of the main microcon-troller. This *system state controller* should be able to replace a small and simple periodical timer circuit in the always-on domain of a system-on-chip. Therefore, *ultra-low* silicon area and power consumption on the one hand, but also sufficient programming flexibility and moderate processing performance for implementing intelligent power management strategies on the other hand are required.

In this paper, the *NanoController* data path architecture and ISA are pro-posed. The NanoController is a minimal and energy-efficient controller architec-ture intended for always-on system state and power management control tasks, and for simple events with frequent execution. Yet, the architecture is extend-able and programmable in order to adapt to various application requirements. It should be noted that an embedded system using the NanoController typically still contains a general-purpose microcontroller. However, this core will only be required for infrequent tasks and can be power-gated most of the time under program control of the NanoController, which minimizes the total power con-sumption of the system. The main contributions of this paper are:

Table 1. Classification of selected commercial microprocessor architectures and ISAs

Class	Overview	Instruction set features
0-address (Stack) [2, 8]	*Inmos Transputer* - 8/16/32-bit data path - 8-bit instr. (4-bit opcode)	*Variable Length Encoding:* Extension Opcode for longer opcode fields, Prefix Operand to form larger addresses
	Atmel MARC-4 - 4-bit data path - 8/16-bit instructions	*Variable Length Encoding* for longer addressing modes, *Forth-inspired instructions*
1-address (Accumulator) [10, 14, 21]	*Microchip PIC16* - 8-bit data path - 14-bit instructions	*Control-oriented Conditional Skips* (skip next instruction on bit set/cleared)
	NEC μCOM-75X - 4-bit data path - 8/16/24-bit instructions	*Variable Instr. Length* (multi-cycle execution), *Control-oriented Compare & Skip, GETI instr.* to shorten encoding of frequent instructions
	TI TMS1000 - 4-bit data path - 8-bit instructions	Dedicated *Memory Address Offset* register, automatically incremented
2-address [5, 13]	*Atmel AVR* (RISC/CISC) - 8-bit data path - 16-bit instructions	Optimized for C compiler, *single-cycle* *execution* (overlapping fetch/execute cycles), register *post-increment* addr. mode
	TI MSP430 (RISC/CISC) - 16-bit data path - 16/32/48-bit instructions	Optimized for C compiler, *Variable Instr.* *Length* (multi-cycle execution), *post-* *increment & special constants* addr. modes
3-address [18]	*MIPS* (RISC) - 32-bit data path - 32-bit instructions	Optimized for C compiler 5-stage *pipeline execution*

1. Proposal and detailed description of the minimal *NanoController* data path architecture and ISA for programmable system state controllers,
2. application of variable-length ISA encoding mechanisms to increase the code density and to reduce the instruction memory size and leakage power,
3. and the hardware evaluation of a 65 nm standard cell ASIC implementation in terms of silicon area and power consumption. The proposed architecture is compared to state-of-the-art microcontroller architectures for an exemplary power management control application of an electronic door lock.

This paper is organized as follows: In Sect. 2, related work regarding processor architecture, ISA organization and encoding is presented and classified. Inspired by the observed features, the minimal NanoController architecture and ISA are proposed in Sect. 3. In Sect. 4, a gate-level ASIC implementation of the proposed architecture is evaluated and compared with reference microcontroller implementations. Also, a chip design using the NanoController in a silicon-proven system is demonstrated. Section 5 concludes the paper.

2   Related Work

This section focuses on a classification of ISA and architecture concepts that are used in small microcontrollers and can serve as an inspiration for a tiny system state and power management controller. According to the organization classification scheme used in [17], the number of operand addresses normally encoded in an instruction is used. In Table 1, a selection of commercial 0-, 1-, 2-, and 3-address machine architectures is presented. The selected examples have specific features that reduce either the silicon area of the logic, or reduce the program code size and, consequently, the silicon area of the instruction memory.

The class of *0-address machines*, also called *stack architectures*, is characterized by operating on an ordered stack of data. Therefore, no explicit operand encoding is required within the instruction, which minimizes the individual instruction size. The MARC-4 architecture [2] has 8-bit wide instructions, however, for branch target addresses, instructions are extended to 16 bits by using a *variable-length encoding* technique. In the Transputer architecture [8], variable-length instruction encoding is applied to both opcodes and immediate operands. The Transputer ISA is remarkable because frequently used instructions are compacted to only 4-bit wide opcodes, which increases the code density. There are other non-commercial stack architectures with short Forth-inspired instructions found in the literature, namely the EP32 [7] and the MSL16 [12]. The former architecture features 35 different 6-bit wide instructions. The latter architecture has 17 instructions, where 16 regular instructions are encoded in 4 bits and the GOTO instruction is encoded with 16 bits. Each fourth instruction is reduced to only 3 bits by a *special position encoding* trade-off (only a subset of the ISA can be used here), with the freed bit indicating if GOTO is following.

Accumulator architectures form the class of *1-address machines*. Here, one explicit source operand address is provided with the operations, while a dedicated accumulator register is implicitly used as the second operand and is overwritten by the new result. The accumulator architectures shown in Table 1 include features to compact the program code size, like automatically incrementing memory address offsets [21], or replacing frequently used operations by shorter instruction aliases [14]. *Variable-length instruction encoding* is also an important technique in these architectures. Mostly, it is combined with *multi-cycle instruction execution*, where additional clock cycles are used in order to fetch further instruction parts from the memory. Another compaction technique are instructions that *conditionally skip* a single instruction in order to avoid branches in simple control decisions, which are found, e.g., in PIC controllers [10].

Architectures with *2- or 3-address* instructions are the most general-purpose implementations for microcontrollers and provide large programming flexibility. However, due to the encoding of multiple operands and addressing modes, the instructions are longer than for the other classes, typically with a minimum of 16 or 32 bits. The MSP430 architecture [5] even has instruction lengths of up to 48 bits. Although AVR [13] and MSP430 have simple RISC ISAs designed for code generation by C compilers, there are a few features for compact code that can be associated with *Complex Instruction Set Computer* (CISC) operations, e.g., *post-increment* and *special constants* encoding for loop structures.

Besides RISC and CISC classification, the *Minimal Instruction Set Computer* (MISC) term appeared for special architectures that provide very few instructions and, thus, require only a minimal opcode length. The architecture presented in [6] is intended as a soft-controller for small FPGA devices and

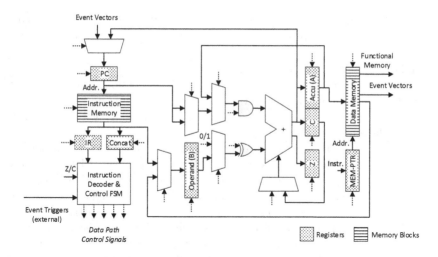

Fig. 1. Schematic block diagram of the NanoController architecture.

only has jump and move instructions, performing operations by moving data between *functional memory* cells, which are memory-mapped functional units. Application-specific operations can be added by placing custom functional units in the functional memory address space.

The scope for the work in this paper is a compact control-oriented ISA, which needs to be clearly distinguished from *code compression*. In the literature, code compression techniques are studied extensively in order to reduce the memory footprint of long instruction words. For this purpose, code is compacted at compile time, and a decompressor circuit is inserted between instruction memory and instruction decoder. Well-known approaches are, e.g., fixed decompressor hardware or programmable translation tables for more flexibility [11]. Moreover, there are bitmask- and pattern-aware compression approaches [3]. While these techniques are effective in compressing instructions wider than 32 or even 64 bits, they do not have a direct correlation with the actual processor ISA and are out of scope of this paper. In order to reduce memory power consumption, however, selected techniques to further compress the NanoController code size may be applied in future work. Since this paper focuses on architectural aspects, approaches like, e.g., *near- and sub-threshold computing*, are also out of scope, but may later be combined with the presented architecture as well.

3   NanoController Architecture

3.1   Data Path

In Fig. 1, the schematic blocks of the NanoController architecture are depicted. The data path follows the concept of a 1-address machine, i.e., it contains an adder circuit and an *accumulator register* (A). A is used to provide the first addition operand and to store the result, e.g., an updated system state variable. To exchange the contents of A, a *data memory* is included. The second *operand* (B) and the *data memory address pointer* (MEM-PTR) are maintained in special registers. Therefore, these values may be reused in subsequent instructions, which is one of the implemented ISA concepts to reduce the program code size (cf. Sect. 3.2). *Zero* (Z) and *Carry* (C) flag registers are updated implicitly in order to omit explicit condition encoding in branch instructions. Finally, the data path contains several multiplexers, AND masking for the first and XOR masking for the second operand, which are used to extend the adder with subtraction, increment, decrement and clearing functionality.

Several data path mechanisms are implemented in order to reduce the amount of logic components and required code size for control flow tasks. The use of variable *multi-cycle* instruction execution and resource sharing allows to use the adder in the data path for updating the *program counter* (PC). Due to that, each instruction requires at least 3 cycles, i.e., one cycle to fetch the instruction to the *instruction register* (IR), one cycle to decode the instruction and to increment the PC, and one cycle for execution. More complex operations with multiple steps are stretched to further execution cycles. If the PC value overflows the data path width, an additional cycle is inserted to correct the carry. These mechanisms prioritize a small logic size at the expense of increased execution cycles, however, these are not considered to be a limiting factor in system and power management control. Furthermore, in order to reduce the code size, parts of the data memory address space are used as functional memory and for event vectors. Here, the term *functional memory* is used for a memory location that triggers implicit actions or calculates specific functions when updated, e.g., starts a timer or toggles output pins [6]. By that, no dedicated I/O instructions are necessary. In the program code, only the actual system state variables are updated, and external control actions are performed implicitly. A similar concept is applied with *event vector* addresses, which are initialized by the programmer and are used to set the PC to different program code sections for internal and external events, e.g., timer countdown or toggling an input pin. This way, a direct mapping table between events and executed code is established, eliminating the instruction overhead of interrupt handlers in software.

3.2   Control Path and ISA

In Table 2, the instruction set is described. There are 16 4-bit wide instruction opcodes, including basic arithmetic (ADDI, SUBI, CMPI) and load/store operations for accumulator and data memory (LDI, LD, ST). Furthermore, data memory contents can be incremented, decremented or cleared with a single instruction (LIS, LDS, CST) for more compact code. A flag-based branch (BNE) is available, as well as a decrementing branch (DBNE) to implement loop iterations with a single instruction. The selection of these operations has been driven by the idea of a general *programmable finite state machine* (FSM), which is characterized by sequences of linear state transitions (variable increment/decrement) and value-dependent state branches. In Sect. 4.1, it is shown how an FSM-like control flow is mapped using this instruction set. A SLEEP instruction is provided to pause program execution when the handling of an event is finished. When a new event is

Table 2. Instruction set of the NanoController architecture.

Class	Mnemonic	Description
Arithmetic	ADDI	ADD Immediate to accumulator
	SUBI	SUBtract Immediate from accumulator
	CMPI	CoMPare Immediate with accumulator, set flags
Load/Store	LDI	LoaD Immediate into accumulator
	LD	LoaD from data memory
	ST	STore to data memory
	STL	STore to data memory at Last used address
Single Instr. Memory Modify	LIS	Load-Increment-Store data memory
	LISL	Load-Increment-Store data memory at Last used address
	LDS	Load-Decrement-Store data memory
	LDSL	Load-Decrement-Store data memory at Last used address
	CST	Clear accumulator, STore to data memory
	CSTL	Clear accumulator, STore to data memory at Last used address
Branch	BNE	read flags, Branch if Not Equal zero
	DBNE	Decrement accumulator, Branch if Not Equal zero
Sleep	SLEEP	SLEEP until next wake-up trigger

triggered, execution continues at the code positions defined by the event vectors (cf. Sect. 3.1). If other events are triggered while still processing a previous one, these events will be queued and executed sequentially, following a pre-designed event prioritization scheme.

Furthermore, *variable-length instruction encoding* is applied in order to compact the program code. Each instruction, i.e., an opcode and one operand, can span multiple addresses in the instruction memory, with the 4-bit opcode being the minimum addressable unit (word). Due to the multi-cycle execution paradigm, a variable number of words can be loaded in multiple, subsequent clock cycles. The information not encoded in the instruction is reused from previous register contents. In the extreme case (STL, LISL, LDSL, CSTL), the instruction is formed by the 4-bit opcode only and the required address operand is provided entirely by the contents of the MEM-PTR register (last used address). The SLEEP instruction does not have any operands and only requires the opcode. For other instructions, the immediate operand (for ADDI, SUBI, CMPI, LDI) or address operand (for LD, ST, LIS, LDS, CST, BNE, DBNE) is provided as a chain of 4-bit words following the opcode, starting from the LSB. In these cases, 3 bits of the word are used for the data value and one bit is indicating that at least one more word from the instruction memory should be concatenated to the data value (Concat bit in Fig. 1). If the chain of concatenated words should reach the data path width, the 4 bits of the last word may be fully used for data, because another word cannot follow. The use of this variable-length instruction encoding technique is a design trade-off. On the one hand, it compacts the code in cases of, e.g., small initialization values, accesses to nearby memory addresses and short loops. On the other hand, the Concat bit presents additional overhead if many long values need to be encoded and the data path is wide compared to the instruction memory width. For the exemplary control application in Sect. 4.1, there is a benefit from this technique (7-bit data path parameterization, a maximum of two concatenated data words, many short address values).

Finally, it should be mentioned that a particular binary encoding of the opcodes is not presented in Table 2, because it has no influence on the operation of the architecture itself. However, for a specific hardware implementation of the NanoController, the encoding has an impact on the circuit area and power consumption of the instruction decoder. The designer may therefore choose to deliberately change the opcode encoding in order to optimize the hardware implementation for certain applications. A design space exploration tool for instruction set encoding optimization has been proposed recently [23].

3.3   Program Code Generation

Since the program code length is expected to be short (considerably less than 50 instructions), NanoController applications are currently written by hand in assembly language. In order to generate binary machine code from the mnemonics in Table 2, a table assembler tool [24] has been adapted to the NanoController ISA. The use of assembly language allows the programmer to explicitly exploit variable-length operand encoding (cf. Sect. 3.2) and manually optimize the code length. Automatic target address calculation is included, so labels may be used in the code to simplify branch instructions.

For verification and debugging of the implemented application code, behavioral simulation is applied. The NanoController architecture has been described at the system level as a cycle-accurate SystemC model, which executes application code within a simulation testbench. Due to the very small logic complexity of the architecture, SystemC simulation is reasonably fast and a separate instruction set simulator tool is not required. Moreover, this approach has the advantage that the simulation testbench can be extended with a cycle-accurate model of the later system environment. Additionally, the model may be accompanied by RTL or gate-level HDL implementations of the NanoController without effort, which directly enables functional and pre-silicon hardware verification techniques.

4   Evaluation

The proposed NanoController architecture is evaluated for programmable *system state control* in always-on operation, i.e., only application code of the power management control part of an exemplary application is considered in this paper. For comparison of the results to other state-of-the-art programmable controllers, four processor architectures used in small microcontrollers have been selected, i.e., MIPS [18], AVR [13], the MSP430-compatible NEO430 architecture [16],

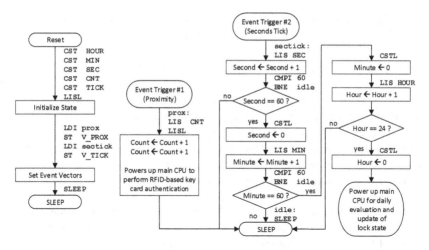

Fig. 2. Flowchart of evaluation code (Electronic Door Lock). Corresponding NanoController instruction sequences are denoted at the upper right-hand side of each element.

and a PIC16F84-compatible architecture [4]. The NanoController[1], MIPS and AVR architectures have been implemented by the authors at RTL using VHDL, while NEO430 and PIC16F84 are obtained from opencores.org projects as a VHDL or Verilog description at RTL, respectively [4,16]. Architectural performance is compared in terms of code size, executed instructions and cycles in RTL simulation. In order to evaluate silicon area and energy consumption of instruction memory and core logic, standard cell ASIC synthesis using the UMC 65 nm low-leakage technology is performed using Synopsys Design Compiler S-2021.06. Switching activity is obtained in gate-level simulation using Mentor QuestaSim 2021.3 and analyzed using Synopsys PrimePower S-2021.06. Beforehand, all source RTL codes have been manually prepared for standard cell mapping, e.g., with respect to set and reset capabilities of available flip-flop cells. Fully relaxed clock frequency constraints were given to the synthesis tool in order to favor optimization for small silicon area. The obtained performance is sufficient for the always-on control application described in the following.

4.1 Exemplary Control Application

A flow chart of the exemplary system state control application is shown in Fig. 2. It resembles the always-on system state machine and power management strategy of an electronic door lock, which has been a case study for a processing platform powered by energy harvesting in a previous project [15]. The required operations include incrementing and resetting system state variables as well as control flow decisions, i.e., branches. Corresponding NanoController assembler code is denoted next to the operations, using the mnemonics from the ISA in

---

[1] Repository: https://github.com/tubs-eis/NanoController.

Table 2. Functionally equivalent assembler code has also been manually implemented for the reference processor architectures.

The application consists of three parts, i.e., initialization after reset, reacting to the proximity of a transponder key, and triggering daily lock state updates by maintaining a real-time clock (RTC). The initialization part is shown on the left side of Fig. 2. Here, the RTC variables HOUR, MIN, SEC and the proximity counter CNT are cleared. Furthermore, an oscillator generating a tick every second is reset via CST TICK and the compact LISL instruction, incrementing the last used functional memory address. Before setting program execution to sleep, vector addresses for event handling are set.

A capacitive sensor triggers a proximity event in case the door lock is approached with an RFID key card, shown as trigger #1 in the center of Fig. 2. Here, the state of the CNT variable is incremented twice, using the compact LISL instruction again for the second increment. It should be mentioned that this is a showcase of the *functional memory* concept implemented in the NanoController. Only two instructions are required to maintain a counter of proximity events in the MSBs, while the LSB is used as a direct enable trigger for power management circuitry. Based on this, the main microcontroller in the on/off domain of the system is powered up in order to process the encrypted RFID communication with the key card. All compared reference architectures require additional IO instructions for the same functionality.

Finally, the right side of Fig. 2 shows the RTC part of the control application. Based on a digital tick generator (event trigger #2), the state variables for seconds, minutes and hours of a day are incremented in order to trigger regular lock state updates, i.e., powering up the larger main microcontroller to receive new lock permissions and access schedules. For this, comparisons with a maximum numeric value of 60 are performed. In order to fully exploit the immediate value range provided by the variable-length instruction encoding (cf. Sect. 3.2), a data path width of 7 bit is selected for the NanoController. This parameterization is comparable to the minimum data path width of 8 bit for the reference architectures. In total, the control and data path of the NanoController require *only 219 gates* in its 65 nm standard cell ASIC implementation (815 μm^2), emphasizing the very small footprint.

The scope of the presented basic application is system state and power management control in the always-on power domain of a larger system. By using a very small and energy-efficient processor architecture, the power management strategy can be flexibly re-programmed and extended after fabrication, which has been the initial motivation behind the minimal ISA and data path design of the NanoController. Nonetheless, there is no general restriction to control-oriented operation by design, and for specialized systems, additional functional units or co-processors can be added by using the functional memory concept. Therefore, it can be interesting to also apply the proposed NanoController architecture as a tiny ASIP, e.g., in applications requiring continuous, always-on pre-filtering and threshold detection in digital audio samples, which is subject of our current research.

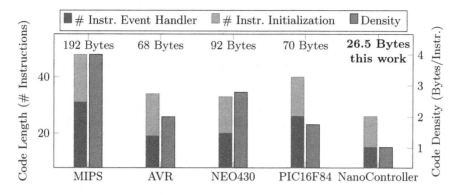

Fig. 3. Comparison of the code length and density for implementations of the exemplary control application. The code size in bytes is denoted above the bars.

4.2 Code Size Comparison

In the bar plot in Fig. 3, the code length (number of instructions) is compared for the application described in Sect. 4.1. Furthermore, the code density (average instruction width) and absolute total code size are shown. For all metrics, smaller values are better. It can be seen that the event handler routines have considerable differences in code length. The NanoController requires the least instructions due to the functional memory concept, because all other architectures require separate instructions to update state variables and to set IO pins. The code lengths of the 2-operand architectures AVR and NEO430 are comparable. Due to the 1-operand accumulator architecture of the PIC, additional move instructions to the accumulator are required to prepare comparison operations. Although the NanoController also is a 1-operand accumulator machine, additional move instructions are not required due to the availability of the combined load-increment-store instruction LIS. This instruction is useful for updating both the accumulator register and the state variable in memory with a single instruction. Therefore, the instruction count of AVR and NEO430 can also be reached with the 1-address NanoController architecture. The MIPS generally requires more instructions because event source arbitration needs to be handled in software. All other architectures have hardware support for multiple interrupt or event vectors and, therefore, require less instructions.

Regarding the code density and size, MIPS, AVR and PIC are using fixed-size 32, 16 and 14 bit wide instructions, respectively. Therefore, the density is constant and the total code size is proportional to the instruction amount. The NEO430 uses variable instruction-length encoding, however, the minimum instruction width is 16 bits. Complex memory-memory addressing modes increase the instruction width up to 48 bits, therefore, the code size in bytes is larger than for AVR and PIC. The NanoController exploits variable-length encoding with compact instruction widths between 4 and 12 bits in total. Therefore, it features the smallest code size and average instruction width. For the given application, the NanoController requires between 21% and 46% less instructions at a 42% to 75% higher code density. This results in 61% to 86% smaller total code size in bytes, which reduces silicon area and power consumption of the instruction memory for the always-on system state controller.

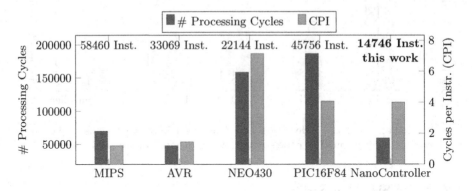

Fig. 4. Comparison of processing cycles and CPI. The total number of executed instructions is denoted above the bars.

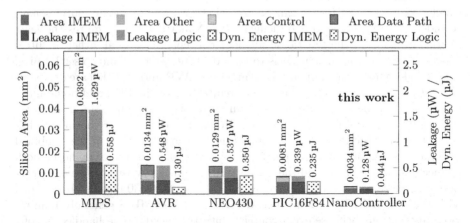

Fig. 5. Comparison of required silicon area, leakage power and dynamic energy consumption for processing the exemplary control application (UMC 65 nm low-leakage standard cell ASIC technology).

4.3 Performance Comparison

The application from Sect. 4.1 is simulated for a workload of 42 triggers of event #1 and 3600 triggers of event #2, which corresponds to heavy door lock use within one hour of a day. For all architectures, the number of required processing cycles, executed effective instructions and the resulting average cycles per instruction (CPI) are obtained, which are shown in Fig. 4. For all metrics, smaller values are better. The architectures can be divided into two groups. At first, there are pipeline and single-cycle architectures (MIPS, AVR), which achieve a CPI value close to 1 (1.19 and 1.44, respectively). The CPI is reduced due to handling the interrupt events, either due to pipeline flushes and bubbles on the MIPS or due to hardware stack operations on the AVR for entry and returning from the event handlers. Second, there are the architectures with multi-cycle execution paradigm (NEO430, PIC, NanoController), which execute each instructions in multiple cycles with CPI values between 4 and 7.15. The NanoController has a CPI comparable to the PIC architecture. However, due to the compact, control-oriented ISA, the least number of executed instructions is required. For the given workload, the NanoController effectively processes 15% to 68% less cycles than MIPS, NEO430 and PIC, and only 24% more than the single-cycle AVR. It has to be mentioned that the achieved performance is not the primary design goal of an always-on system state controller. All compared architectures are easily capable of operating with sufficient performance for event handling in the exemplary application. However, the number of required cycles heavily influences the energy requirements for processing, which is crucial in the always-on domain of a platform powered by energy harvesting. The presented results show that, despite its minimal resources, the NanoController does not perform worse than the reference architectures in terms of processing performance for control flow.

4.4   Silicon Area and Power/Energy Consumption

The silicon area after synthesis is compared in Fig. 5 for the required instruction memory (IMEM), other logic (input and output signals, digital tick generator), control and data path. Also, the leakage power consumption in µW and the required dynamic energy in µJ for the workload described in Sect. 4.3 are shown. Leakage behaves proportionally to the required area, as IMEM and logic are continuously powered in the always-on domain of the system. Due to the small size, each IMEM has been implemented as *standard cell memory* (SCM) with a flip-flop array [20], which achieved improved leakage and dynamic power consumption compared to available SRAM macro IP for the UMC 65 nm technology for the targeted relaxed clock constraints. Each IMEM size corresponds to the required code size in bytes evaluated in Sect. 4.2.

For 2- and 3-operand architectures, the data path area is dominated by the register file size. MIPS uses a 32-bit wide data path and 31 general-purpose registers, resulting in 992 bits of register space. Despite different data path widths of 8 and 16 bit for AVR and NEO430, respectively, the data path area is comparable due to the identical register file space of 256 bits (32 registers for AVR, 16 registers for NEO430). The PIC and NanoController do not use a general-purpose register file due to the 1-address accumulator architecture and, therefore, both have a very small data path implementation.

In the evaluated application, the compared architectures are used as a system state controller in the always-on power domain, which controls the power management for the rest of the system. Therefore, continuous leakage will be

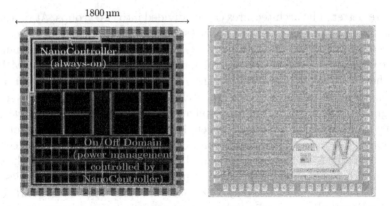

Fig. 6. Layout view (left) and microscope photograph (right) of the manufactured ASIC with integrated NanoController

the dominant component of power consumption. Figure 5 shows that continuous leakage (in µW) is proportional to the silicon area. Therefore, the smallest architectures also have the smallest power consumption. Quantitatively, the NanoController core including IMEM requires between 58% and 92% less silicon area and leakage power than the reference implementations.

Compared to leakage, the dynamic energy required to process the exemplary application is absolutely negligible. In Fig. 5, the combined power-energy scale on the right side shows leakage power in µW, equivalent to µJ when considering one second of elapsed time. The length of the bars illustrates that *already within one second*, more leakage energy is consumed than the dynamic energy required for *one hour of system control workload* given in µJ. This is the case for all compared architectures. To put it into numbers, dynamic energy only accounts for 0.007% to 0.019% of the total energy consumption within one hour, which emphasizes the importance of minimum area and leakage power for an always-on system state and power management controller, while still providing sufficient programming flexibility. These design goals have been targeted with the NanoController.

For demonstration purposes, the presented NanoController has been manufactured as a digital standard cell ASIC design using the UMC 65 nm low-leakage technology. Recently, the ASIC has been successfully tested and evaluated for the electronic door lock application [15,22]. Figure 6 shows the CAD layout view and the microscope die shot of one of the samples. The ASIC design follows the intended system concept with the programmable NanoController in a tiny always-on domain for system state control and frequent event handling. Only 0.3% of the total die area are required for the logic and instruction memory cells of the NanoController, which have been placed in the upper left corner. The NanoController controls the power management strategy for the remaining part of the chip, which is a switched on/off domain. In this ASIC, the on/off domain contains a 32-bit general-purpose microcontroller based on transport-triggered architectural principles, which has been designed with the open-source *TTA Co-*

Design Environment (TCE) [9]. Implementation details of this domain are out of scope of this paper and are presented separately in [22]. The on/off domain is *normally in power shut-off* and will only be activated for infrequent complex processing, minimizing the total average power consumption of the system. In real measurements, the average power consumption of the ASIC, dominated by leakage of the always-on NanoController domain, is found to be in the range below 200 nW, which is in good agreement with the power simulation results for the post-synthesis gate-level netlist presented in this paper (128.3 nW leakage power). Furthermore, it is also competitive with the much simpler NanoTimer IC [19] for periodical power management control (<400 nW average power consumption), which does not allow programmable power management strategies.

5   Conclusion

With intelligent power management strategies, the average total power consumption of an embedded system can be significantly reduced. For the overall energy efficiency, it is important that the always-on system state and power management controller *itself* requires *minimum silicon area and leakage power consumption*, while still providing sufficient programming flexibility for implementing these strategies. In this paper, the very small and ultra-low-power *NanoController* architecture for system state and power management controllers has been proposed and described in detail, focusing on the data path architecture and ISA. The NanoController is flexible and programmable, e.g., for applying updates and extensions to the power management strategy in intelligent sensor and control nodes powered by energy harvesting. Variable-length ISA encoding and functional memory techniques are applied to increase the program code density in order to reduce the instruction memory size and leakage power. Despite its simplicity, the architecture is prepared to be easily extended with additional functional units in order to adapt to different application requirements. Therefore, it can also be interesting to use the NanoController as a tiny ASIP in applications requiring continuous processing at moderate performance requirements, e.g., always-on audio sample pre-filtering and threshold-based detection of acoustic events, which is subject of current research.

When compared to reference implementations for MIPS, AVR, MSP430 and PIC microcontrollers used as an always-on *system state controller*, the NanoController ISA provides between 61% and 86% smaller total code size for an exemplary application, i.e., power management control of an electronic door lock [15]. Therefore, the capacity, silicon area and leakage power consumption of the instruction memory (IMEM) in the always-on domain are reduced. In a 65 nm standard cell ASIC implementation, the NanoController data path and control logic require *only 219 cells*. Taking both core logic and IMEM into account, the silicon area and leakage power consumption of the NanoController are between 58% and 92% smaller than for the reference architectures. In future work, it is planned to investigate code compaction and compression techniques in order to further optimize the required memory size, which still has significant contributions in relation to the very small NanoController logic.

References

1. Aoudia, F.A., Gautier, M., Magno, M., Berder, O., Benini, L.: Leveraging energy harvesting and wake-up receivers for long-term wireless sensor networks. Sensors **18**(5), 1578 (2018)
2. Atmel Corporation: MARC4 4-bit Microcontrollers: Programmer's Guide (2004)
3. Chen, P.Y., Wu, C.C., Jiang, Y.J.: Bitmask-based code compression methods for balancing power consumption and code size for hard real-time embedded systems. Microprocess. Microsyst. **36**(3), 267–279 (2012)
4. Clayton, J.: OpenCores.org project risc16f84. https://opencores.org/projects/risc16f84. Accessed 9 June 2022
5. Davies, J.H.: MSP430 microcontroller basics. Elsevier (2008)
6. Halverson Jr., R., Lew, A.: An FPGA-based minimal instruction set computer. Technical report (1995)
7. Hjrtland, E., Chen, L.: EP32 - a 32-bit Foth micorprocessor. In: 2007 Canadian Conference on Electrical and Computer Engineering, pp. 518–521 (2007)
8. INMOS Ltd.: Transputer reference manual. Prentice Hall Intl. (UK) Ltd. (1988)
9. Jääskeläinen, P., Viitanen, T., Takala, J., Berg, H.: HW/SW co-design toolset for customization of exposed datapath processors. In: Computing Platforms for Software-Defined Radio, pp. 147–164. Springer International Publishing (2017). https://doi.org/10.1007/978-3-319-49679-5_8
10. Katzen, S.: The Quintessential PIC® Microcontroller. Springer Science & Business Media (2006)
11. Lefurgy, C., Mudge, T.: Code compression for DSP. Michigan Univ ANN Arbor Dept of Electrical Engineering and Computer Science, Technical report (1998)
12. Leong, P.H.W., Tsang, P.K., Lee, T.K.: A FPGA based Forth microprocessor. In: Proceedings of the IEEE Symposium on FPGAs for Custom Computing Machines, pp. 254–255 (1998)
13. Mazidi, M.A., Naimi, S., Naimi, S.: The AVR Microcontroller and Embedded Systems: Using Assembly and C. Prentice Hall, Upper Saddle River, NJ (2011)
14. NEC Electronics (Europe) GmbH (Düsseldorf): μCOM-75X Family 4-bit CMOS Microcomputer. User's manual
15. Neujahr, M., Möller, S., Passoke, J., Blume, H.: Flexible Plattform für Energiesammelsysteme für die Gebäudeautomation - MEH (project report in German language). Technical report (2021), in acquisition, accessible via tib.eu
16. Nolting, S.: The NEO430 processor. https://github.com/stnolting/neo430. Accessed 09 June 2022
17. Nurmi, J.: Processor design: system-on-chip computing for ASICs and FPGAs. Springer Science & Business Media (2007)
18. Patterson, D.A., Hennessy, J.L.: Computer Organization and Design MIPS Edition: The Hardware/Software Interface. Morgan Kaufmann (2020)
19. Pickering, P.: Designing ultra-low-power sensor nodes for IoT applications. https://www.electronicdesign.com/power-management/article/21802213/designing-ultralowpower-sensor-nodes-for-iot-applications (2016). Accessed 09 June 2022
20. Teman, A., Rossi, D., Meinerzhagen, P., Benini, L., Burg, A.: Power, area, and performance optimization of standard cell memory arrays through controlled placement. ACM Trans. Des. Autom. Electron. Syst. **21**(4), 1–25 (2016)
21. Texas Instruments Inc.: TMS 1000 Series Data Manual (1975)
22. Weißbrich, M., Blume, H., Payá-Vayá, G.: A silicon-proof controller system for flexible ultra-low-power energy harvesting platforms. In: 2022 11th International Conference on Modern Circuits and Systems Technologies (MOCAST) (2022)

23. Weißbrich, M., Moreno-Medina, J.A., Payá-Vayá, G.: Using genetic algorithms to optimize the instruction-set encoding on processor cores. In: 2021 10th International Conference on Modern Circuits and Systems Technologies (MOCAST) (2021)
24. Williams, A.: Universal cross assembler. https://github.com/wd5gnr/axasm (2015). Accessed 9 June 2022

ControlPULP: A RISC-V Power Controller for HPC Processors with Parallel Control-Law Computation Acceleration

Alessandro Ottaviano[1(✉)], Robert Balas[1], Giovanni Bambini[2],
Corrado Bonfanti[2], Simone Benatti[2], Davide Rossi[2], Luca Benini[1,2],
and Andrea Bartolini[2]

[1] ETH Zurich, Zürich, Switzerland
aottaviano@iis.ee.ethz.ch
[2] University of Bologna, Bologna, Italy

Abstract. High-Performance Computing (HPC) processors are nowadays integrated Cyber-Physical Systems requiring complex and high-performance closed-loop control strategies for efficient power and thermal management. To satisfy high-bandwidth, real-time multi-input multi-output (MIMO) optimal power control requirements, high-end processors integrate on-die Power Controller Systems (PCS). Traditional PCS is based on a simple microcontroller core supported by dedicated interface logic and sequencers. More scalable and flexible PCS architectures are required to support advanced MIMO control algorithms required for managing the ever-increasing number of cores, power states, and process, voltage, temperature (PVT) variability.

In this paper, we present ControlPULP, a complete, open-source HW/SW RISC-V parallel PCS platform consisting of a single-core microcontroller coupled with a scalable multi-core cluster system with a specialized DMA engine and a fast multi-core interrupt controller for parallel acceleration of real-time power management policies. ControlPULP relies on a real-time OS (FreeRTOS) to schedule a Power Control Firmware (PCF) software layer. We evaluate ControlPULP design choices in a cycle-accurate, event-based simulation environment and show the benefits of the proposed multi-core acceleration solution. We demonstrate ControlPULP in a PCS use-case targeting a next-generation 72-cores HPC processor. We show that the multi-core cluster accelerates the PCF achieving 4.9x speedup with respect to single-core execution.

Keywords: RISC-V · HPC processor · Power and thermal control · Scalable · Parallel microcontroller

1 Introduction

After the end of Dennard's scaling, the increase in power density has become an undesired but unavoidable collateral effect of the performance gain obtained with

A. Orailoglu et al. (Eds.): SAMOS 2022, LNCS 13511, pp. 120–135, 2022.
https://doi.org/10.1007/978-3-031-15074-6_8

technological scaling. This trend has made the processing elements at the heart of computing nodes energy, power, and thermally constrained [10]. Modern high-performance processors feature a large number of cores. The most notable examples are AWS Graviton 2 (64 ARM Neoverse N1 cores) [9], Intel Alder Lake-S Xeon (16 cores, 24 threads) [8], AMD Epyc 7003 Milan (up to 64 Zen 3 cores) [1], SiPearl Rhea Processor (72 ARM Neoverse V1 Zeus cores) [6] and the NVIDIA Grace CPU Superchip (144 ARM Neoverse N2 cores). Their application workload requires a dynamic trade-off between maximum performance (fastest operating point [5]) in CPU-bound execution phases and energy efficiency in memory-bound execution phases (energy-aware CPU [21]). Hence, all modern processors integrate on-die Power Controller Subsystems as dedicated hardware resources co-designed with a Power Control Firmware (PCF) implementing complex MIMO power management policies. Advanced power management involves embedding and interleaving a plurality of activities in the PCS, namely (i) dynamic control of the CPU power consumption with short time constants [16] to prevent thermal hazards and to meet the TDP limit (power capping [11]), (ii) real-time interaction with inputs provided by on-die (Operating System - OS - power management interfaces and on-chip sensors) and off-die (Baseboard Management Controller - BMC -, Voltage Regulator Modules - VRMs -) units and (iii) dynamic power budget allocation between general-purpose (CPUs) and other integrated subsystems, such as graphics processors (GPUs) [21].

Existing on-die PCSs share a common design structure with an integrated single-core microcontroller[1] supported by dedicated hardware state machines [21] or more generic accelerators [18] (Sect. 2). The hardware typically takes advantage of specific software libraries[2](See footnote 1) to implement the real-time execution environment required to run power management policies under tight timing constraints.

Many-core power management requires fine-grained control of the operating points of the processing elements [12] to meet a given processor power consumption setpoint while minimizing performance penalties. Moreover, the control policy has to provide fast, reactive, and predictable responses to promptly handle the incoming requests from the OS or BMC and prevent thermal hazards. A flexible and scalable way to manage these computationally intensive operations is required to provide a high-quality level of control performance per core and to support more advanced experimental control policies. This scenario suggests the need for a performant and capable PCS architecture optimized for handling a fine-grained, per-core performance state control strategy on a large number of controlled cores within the required timing deadlines. In this work, we address the requirement mentioned above and make the following contributions:

1. We design an end-to-end RISC-V parallel PCS architecture named ControlPULP, based on open RISC-V cores and hardware IPs [19]. To the best of our knowledge, ControlPULP is the first fully open-source[3] (hardware and

---

[1] https://github.com/ARM-software/SCP-firmware.

[2] https://github.com/open-power.

[3] https://github.com/pulp-platform/control-pulp.

software) PCS with a configurable number of cores and hardware resources to track the computational requirements of the increasingly complex power management policies of current and future high-performance processors (Sect. 3). ControlPULP integrates a multi-core cluster with per-core FPUs for reactive control policy step computation, without the additional complexity of floating-point to fixed-point conversion.

2. The cluster integrates a specialized DMA to accelerate the data transfers from on-chip sensors and off-chip peripherals. It allows data acquisition from 2D strided data access patterns, a crucial capability when reading from private, per-core sensors with equally spaced address mapping (Sect. 4.3).

3. We tailor ControlPULP to meet real-time power management requirements. The architecture achieves low interrupt latency thanks to a platform-level interrupt controller (RISC-V PLIC [17]) tasked to process the global interrupts associated with OS- and BMC- driven commands and a low latency predictable interconnect infrastructure (Sect. 4.3).

4. We demonstrate the end-to-end capabilities of ControlPULP with a case study on the control quality of the PCF, that achieves 6% more precise setpoint tracking than the only openly documented SoA control policy implemented by the IBM on-chip controller (Sect. 4.5).

2 Related Work

There is little publicly available information on commercial state-of-the-art (SoA) PCS architectures. To the best of the authors' knowledge, the main four market-standard PCS are: Intel Power Control Unit (PCU) introduced with Nehalem microprocessor [7], the ARM System Control Processor (SCP) [13], the System Management Units (SMU) integrated with AMD Zeppelin, and the IBM On-Chip Controller (OCC) introduced with Power8 microprocessor.

Intel's PCU is a combination of dedicated hardware state machines and an integrated microcontroller [21]. It provides power management functionalities such as Dynamic Voltage Frequency Scaling (DVFS) through voltage-frequency control states (P-states and C-states), selected by the HW (Hardware-Managed P-States, HWP). The PCU communicates with the processing elements with a specialized link through Power Management Agents (PMAs). Intel's main control loop runs at 500 µs [22].

AMD adopts a multiple power controller design, with one SMU for each CPU tile (group of cores). All SMUs act as slave components, monitoring local conditions and capturing data. One of the SMUs also acts as a master, gathering all information from the slave components and then choosing the operating point for each core [4].

ARM implements two independent PCSs based on the ARM Cortex-M7 microcontroller, SCP and MCP (System and Manageability Control Processor, respectively). The SCP provides power management functionality, while the MCP supports communications functionality. In ARM based SoCs the interaction with the OS is handled by the System Control and Management Interface

(SCMI) protocol [2]. SCMI provides a set of OS-agnostic standard SW and HW interfaces for power domain, voltage, clock and sensor management through a shared, interrupt-driven mailbox system with the PCS.

The IBM power controller, called OCC, is composed of 5 units: a central PowerPC 405 processor with 768 KiB of dedicated SRAM and four general-purpose engines for data collection from PVT sensors (GPEs) and performance state and CPU stop functions control (PGPE and SGPE) respectively. IBM's main control loop runs on PowerPC 405 at 250 µs [18]. It uses a Frequency Voting Box to select a frequency for each core conservatively based on the minimum input - highest Pstate - from several independent power-control (Control Vote) and temperature-capping (Thermal Control Vote) features. The Thermal Control Vote consists of one PID with a periodicity of 16 ms that reduces the frequency of each core based on the temperature of the hottest element. Furthermore, similarly to ARM's SCMI standard, IBM's OCC uses a Command Write Attention/Interrupt mechanism to notify the PGPE of an incoming asynchronous command/request to be processed(See footnote 2), for instance, the desired PState. PGPE arbitrates this information with the Voting Box output from the PowerPC 405 according to a minimum PState policy.

Last, it has been shown [3] that a single-core, RISC-V based microcontroller can execute similar control algorithms with a control loop of 500 µs. Nevertheless, the underlying PCS architecture did not support an adequate I/O system infrastructure with on-die and off-die actors, global interrupt lines for OS-based commands dispatching, and a floating-point unit for the PCF's workload routine.

All the SoA power controllers lack the flexibility and scalability of a multicore architecture supported by adequate IO bandwidth and fast interrupt handling hardware, which is the critical innovation provided by ControlPULP.

3   The ControlPULP Platform

ControlPULP extends commercial controllers' single-core microcontroller structure, providing the first multi-core RISC-V PCS architecture. In the following, we detail ControlPULP's hardware architecture (Sect. 3.1) and its design trade-offs. To further analyze the benefits of ControlPULP's design choices with a control algorithm use-case (Sect. 4), we also describe the PCF software structure and the surrounding controlled ecosystem in Sect. 3.2.

3.1   System Architecture

Figure 1 provides a block diagram overview of ControlPULP. The top-level subsystem of the design is the Manager Core, a CV32E40P open-source[4] industry-grade processor core and a set of System I/O interfaces to interact with peripherals and memory-mapped devices (Sect. 3.1). The primary micro-controller-like subsystem is also present in a similar form in the SoA designs surveyed in Sect. 2

---

[4] https://github.com/openhwgroup/cv32e40p.

Real-Time and Predictability. The following architectural design decisions were taken concerning RAM banking and interrupt processing to make the design more suitable for real-time workloads.

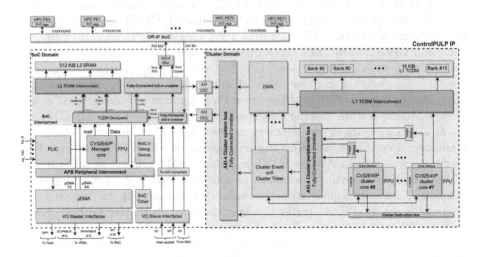

Fig. 1. ControlPULP architecture.

L2 Memory Banks Constant Access Time. The L2 RAM, which is the RAM block connected to the Manager Core and System I/O interfaces, is sized to 512 KiB, enough to fit the whole firmware binary and data so that no swapping is required. The L2 RAM comprises six banks. The access time to each bank is constant when there are no access conflicts. Two of these banks are marked private to prevent DMA transfers from peripherals and other components from disturbing the Manager Core's instruction and data fetching. The Manager Core has exclusive access to those.

Low Constant Latency PLIC Interrupt Controller. We integrate a low and constant latency RISC-V interrupt controller (Platform Level Interrupt Controller, PLIC) [17] capable of entering the interrupt handler within 46 cycles (Sect. 4.3). The PLIC can handle up to 144 secure and non-secure global interrupt lines fed to ControlPULP from the mailbox infrastructure. The PLIC multiplexes them in the SoC domain Manager Core as external interrupts. The PLIC is paired with the existing Core Local Interrupt (CLINT) unit in the CV32E40P core, managing software and timer interrupts. The PLIC/CLINT configuration performs hardware-based priority arbitration with vectored interrupts that helps reduce the interrupt response latency (Sect. 4), a crucial property to increase responsiveness on external, agents-driven requests.

Cluster Accelerator. To meet the computational demands of the control algorithms, especially when scaling to a large number of controlled high-performance cores and improving the control performance, we opt for a flexible programmable accelerator, namely a cluster of RISC-V processors. The cluster consists of a team of CV32E40P cores (workers) tightly coupled to 128 KiB RAM (L1) and a DMA engine.

Multi-core Computing System. Control algorithms (Sect. 3.2) can be parallelized on the cluster (Sect. 4.2), with a high level of flexibility on the RISC-V cores to improve and update control algorithms. This is in sharp contrast with hard-wired control logic featured in SoA controllers (Sect. 2) which lack flexibility. The Manager Core offloads the control algorithm to the team of workers in the cluster. Each worker has a private instruction cache that copies the instructions to be fetched from L2 and accesses L1 through a single-cycle latency logarithmic interconnect.

In the most straightforward parallelization scheme, a worker computes the control action (Sect. 3.2) for a subset of the controlled cores. The number of workers in the cluster is parametric. In the following, we assume it equals 8, a pretty large configuration, to demonstrate scalability. Each core in the cluster features an FPU with a configurable number of pipeline stages. In our instantiation, we use one internal pipeline stage, which is sufficient to meet our frequency target. Furthermore, Montagna et al. [15] show that this configuration achieves high performance and reasonable area/energy efficiency on a large number of benchmarks.

2-D DMA Transfer Engine. The cluster domain integrates a multi-channel DMA with direct access to L1 RAM and low-programming-latency (62 clock cycles, Sect. 4.3). The DMA's main task is to provide direct communication between L2 and L1 memories in parallel and without intervention from the Manager or cluster cores [20].

We tailored the DMA's capabilities to suit the control policy use case by (i) directly routing the cluster DMA to the PVT sensors registers through the outgoing AXI master interface, which guarantees flexibility by decoupling data transfers and computation phases, (ii) exploiting 2-D transfers for equally spaced PVT registers accesses and (iii) increasing the number of outstanding transactions (up to 128) to hide the latency of regular transfers.

Commercial PCS also separate the actual computation from data acquisition. For instance, IBM OCC employs general-purpose cores (GPEs) tasked to read the processing elements data and temperatures instead of a data mover engine with a micro-coded programming interface [18]. Our DMA-based solution achieves higher performance than data-mover cores and reduces hardware cost.

System I/O Interfaces

Low Latency AXI4 External Interfaces. ControlPULP features two AXI4 ports, one Master and one Slave, with 64-bit W/R, 32-bit AW/AR wide channels. They play a crucial role in the ControlPULP design and guarantee low-latency communication with the controlled system. The AXI slave maps to a region of the SoC domain's L2 SRAM drives the PCS's booting process, and loads the PCF binary into L2 SRAM. The AXI master is the transport layer over which the PCS collects PVT sensors data and power policy target requirements. It dispatches the optimal frequency operating point during the control policy (Sect. 3.2). We internally routed this channel to initiate data transfers from both the SoC and Cluster domains through the arbitration of fully-connected AXI4 crossbars.

SCMI. ControlPULP adopts and implements the ARM standard SCMI protocol to handle external power, performance, and system management requests. SCMI allows an OS kernel that supports SCMI to interact with ControlPULP without needing a bespoke driver directly. Furthermore, the design of the SCMI protocol reflects the industry trend of delegating power and performance to a dedicated subsystem [14]. SCMI involves an interface channel for secure and non-secure communication between a caller (agent, i.e. an HPC processing element) and a callee (platform, i.e. ControlPULP). The latter interprets the messages delivered by the former in a shared memory area (mailbox region, Fig. 2a) and responds according to a specific protocol. The proposed PCS implements a doorbell-based (interrupt-driven) transport mechanism through the PLIC. In our use case with 72 controlled cores, the platform can process up to 144 secure and non-secure interrupt notifications.

High Latency Peripherals. ControlPULP integrates a peripheral subsystem in the SoC domain inherited from the PULP design, where an I/O data engine unit (μDMA) allows autonomous communication between off-die elements and the L2 SRAM. In this work, we upgrade the peripheral subsystem to handle off-die communication services through industry-standard power management interfaces. The PCS integrates 6 AVSBUS and PMBUS interfaces to VRMs and 1 QSPI to external non-volatile memory, while 5 I2C master/slave interfaces manage the communication with the BMC. The Power Management Bus (PMBUS) and Advanced Voltage Bus (AVSBUS) bus protocols extend I2C and SPI respectively to provide digital monitoring of voltage and power rails, preserving optimal speed/power consumption trade-off.

3.2 Power Control Firmware

The PCF executes the thermal and power control functions and manages on-die and off-die communications and data transfers. FreeRTOS, an industry-grade, lightweight, and open-source operating system for microcontrollers, serves as the basis for real-time priority-driven scheduling with static tasks priorities and preemption.

The control routine consists of two periodic tasks characterized by multiple harmonic frequencies: the **Fast Power Control Task (FPCT)** (8 kHz) and the **Periodic Control Task (PCT)** (2 kHz). Splitting the control routine into two tasks grants more fine-grained scheduling and helps meet different performance requirements and sensors-update frequencies. Power has faster changes due to instruction-level variation of the effective capacitance of the computing unit, while temperature variations are slower. The control has to handle these widely split time scales. Furthermore, power sensors (VRMs) generally update more frequently than temperature sensors.

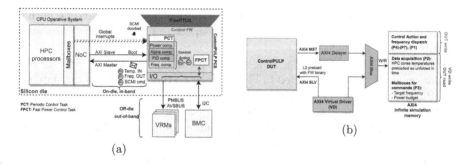

Fig. 2. (a) PCF inputs and outputs interactions. **(b)** ControlPULP RTL testbench simulation environment.

The PCT is the main control task. It receives the desired operating point (clock frequency) for each processing element and controls it to meet the physical and imposed constraints of the system. It executes a two-layer control strategy [3] consisting of a Power Dispatching Layer and a Thermal Regulator Layer. The PCT control step n consists of 7 phases: **(P1)** Allocate the controlled clock frequency computed at step $n - 1$ to each core; **(P2)** Read the PVT sensor's registers and the workload characteristics from each core for step $n + 1$; **(P3)** Obtain commands and information on the constraints (target frequency, power budget) from the OS and BMC; **(P4)** Compute the estimated power for each core and the total consumed power of the system; **(P5)** Apply a power capping algorithm, such as Alpha [3] when the total power exceeds the power budget constraint; **(P6)** Further reduce the power of each core through PIDs computation when the temperature at phase (P2) from step $n - 1$ exceeds the threshold; **(P7)** Compute and dispatch a frequency to apply at (P1) in step $n + 1$. The transient data computed in these phases are saved for telemetry purposes.

The FPCT tackles the changes in the power consumption of the system. It periodically reads the power consumption of the voltage rails from the VRMs, programs micro-architectural power/instruction throughput capping interfaces (if supported by the processing element), and modifies the power budget threshold of the PCT as requested by the BMC.

Figure 2a depicts the real-time inputs and outputs the PCF has to interact with. 'on-die' designates any element of the HPC CPU that resides on the chip die, such as PVT sensors and registers, frequency actuators, and mailboxes. In-band services refer to SCMI-based interaction and PVT registers data acquisition. 'Off-die' indicates VRMs communication and BMC requests through out-of-band services. Last, we name 'Control Action' the computational body of the PCF execution (P4)–(P7).

4   Experimental Results

In this section, we analyze and characterize both hardware (the ControlPULP platform) and software (the PCF) layers:

- We assess and break down ControlPULP's post-synthesis area and determine the minimum area overhead (<1%) with respect to a modern HPC processor chip (Sect. 4.1).
- We evaluate ControlPULP with a testbench running in a cycle-accurate simulation environment, depicted in Fig. 2b. The testbench does not emulate the HPC processor at the RTL level. Instead, we model the closed-loop with a shared memory region between the PCS platform—the device under test—and the system under control. The real-time temperature and telemetry information from the HPC processor are computed beforehand in software (MATLAB Simulink) and stored in the simulation memory as unfolded in time. Furthermore, we model the interconnect network (Fig. 2a) latency by introducing a programmable latency into the AXI4 ports.
- In the described test scenario, we first study the parallelization of the Control Action (P4)-(P7) on the cluster (Sect. 4.2). We then characterize in-band transfers, namely strided DMA accesses for data acquisition from PVT registers and low interrupt latency with SCMI command processing (Sect. 4.3). Finally, we show the overall performance improvement when accelerating control tasks in the cluster compared to single-core (Sect. 4.4).
- We evaluate the PCF control policy quality in a pure software-based simulation using MATLAB Simulink. We show that the PCF compares favorably against the most well documented and open SoA industrial solution on the market, the IBM OCC (Sect. 4.5).

4.1   Area Evaluation

We synthesize ControlPULP in GlobalFoundries 22FDX FD-SOI technology using Synopsys Design Compiler 2019.12. For this technology, one gate equivalent (GE) equals 0.199 μm^2. The design has an overall area of 9.1 MGE when imposing a system clock frequency of 500 MHz. As from the area breakdown shown in Table 1, the cluster accelerator accounts for about 32% of the design.

The target controlled system die area is assumed comparable to other commercials, multi-core (>64) server-class processors, such as [9] (about 457 mm^2). By scaling the gate-equivalent count of the HPC CPU die in the same technology node of this work, ControlPULP would still represent less than 1% of the available die area[5]. This first-order estimation makes the design choice of a parallel PCS valuable since its capabilities are much increased, while the silicon area cost remains negligible within a high-performance processor die.

4.2   Firmware Control Action

In the following, we analyze the execution of the PCF phases (P4)-(P7) on the multi-core cluster accelerator. We enforce power capping (Alpha reduction [3])

---

[5] This has to be considered a first approximation, since it compares post-synthesis results with publicly available data of a modern HPC die, nowadays manufactured in a more advanced technology node.

Table 1. ControlPULP post-synthesis area breakdown on GF22FDX technology.

Unit	Area [mm^2]	Area [kGE]	Percentage [%]
Cluster unit	0.467	2336.7	25.5
SoC unit	0.135	675.9	7.39
L1 SRAM	0.119	595.7	6.51
L2 SRAM	1.108	5542.1	60.6
Total	**1.830**	**9150.3**	**100**

to evaluate each computational phase fairly. Each cluster core is responsible for a subset of the controlled processing elements. The parallelisation is implemented as a fork-join process where the workload is statically distributed among the workers. In ControlPULP, the construct is implemented by means of a per-worker `thread_id` $\in [0 : N_{workers} - 1]$, and an equally distributed `chunk_size` where `chunk_size` $= \dfrac{N_{ctrl\_cores}}{N_{workers}}$. We are interested in extracting performance figures for the Control Action in a single periodic step n. We execute the PCF for S steps to amortize the effect of the initially cold instruction cache. Finally, we perform the arithmetic mean over S to get the mean absolute execution time for each (P4)-(P7) phase.

We report the execution time τ_0 and the multi-core speedup $\left(\frac{\tau_{0,single}}{\tau_{0,multi}}\right)$ at varying number of controlled cores N_{cc} for each PCF phase in Figs. 3a and 3b respectively. The total speedup of the full Control Action at fixed N_{cc} is the geometric mean over the speedups of each phase. In our use case of 72 controlled processing elements, ControlPULP executes the Control Action 5.5× faster than in single-core configuration, reaching 6.5x with 296 controlled cores.

We make the following observations. First, multi-core speedup scales with the number of controlled cores due to the increased workload and is affected by the workload characteristics of each phase. Second, the Control Action is not a fully computational step. In fact, instruction branching associated with power and frequency bounds checks per-core introduces additional load/store stalls due to data access contention in multi-core configuration. Finally, the computational body of (P6) and (P7) can be separated into independent parallel tasks, and is thus an embarrassingly parallel problem. Instead, (P4) and (P5) show dependency across the values computed by the workers in the form of reduction sums, i.e., in (P4) to calculate the total power of the CPU and (P5) to calculate a normalization base for Alpha power capping [3] and again the total CPU power. When a reduction sum is needed, we use a hardware barrier to synchronize the threads and join the concurrent execution on the cluster master core (core 0), which carries out the reduction. The overhead from synchronization and single-core reduction accounts for 112 and 24 clock cycles, respectively.

As it can be seen from the above analysis, the increased parallel compute capability to handle the workload of the control routine, paired with the general purpose nature of the accelerator, enable us to (i) improve the control perfor-

Table 2. Interrupt latency from interrupt edge to the first instruction in the interrupt handler in number of cycles.

Location	Increment [cycles]	Sum [cycles]
PLIC input to output	2	2
CLINT input to core	7	9
Jump in vector table to PLIC handler	2	11
Save caller save regs (addi + 15 regs)	17	28
Claim PLIC interrupt (read id)	8	36
Compute and load PLIC handler address	8	44
Jump to PLIC handler address	2	46
Summary	–	**46**

mances paving the way to more advanced algorithms and (ii) be fully flexible when designing the control algorithm.

4.3   In-band Services

PVT Sensors. To assess in-band services involving PVT physical sensors—phases (P1) and (P2)—, we measure the transfer time required for reading data bursts on the AXI master bus with the SoC timer. The exploration is three-fold: (i) direct data gathering from the ControlPULP cluster's cores, (ii) data gathering by offloading the transfers to the DMA in 1-D configuration, and (iii) DMA offload in 2-D configuration [20]. For (i) and (ii), we investigate the data collection on either 1-core or 8-cores configurations. The address range is equally distributed among the issuing cores in the latter scenario. In (iii), one core performs the read operation to highlight the advantages of offloading a single, large transfer with non-contiguous but uniformly spaced addresses to the DMA, which increases the addresses by the selected stride. This configuration becomes important when atomically gathering PVT information from equally spaced address locations (HPC PEs) with only one transfer request. As in Sect. 4.2, we use synchronization barriers to coordinate the eight cores. Figure 3c reports the execution time τ_1 required for data movement when reading from up to 1000 PVT registers (4B each), an estimate bound given the number of processing elements and the information needed from them (P, V, T, i.e. $\geq$ 3 lower bound). Figure 3c shows that the best DMA-based transfers assuming 1000 PVT registers (2-D) are 5.3× faster than single-core direct data gathering.

SCMI. An interrupt-driven (doorbell) transport regulates the communication in the agent-platform direction—phase (P3) of the Periodic Control Task. Table 2 gives an overview of the overall PLIC interrupt latency measured as the number of cycles from the triggering edge in the PLIC to the ISR Handler's first instruction. The RTL testbench environment (Fig. 2b) emulates the shared mailboxes.

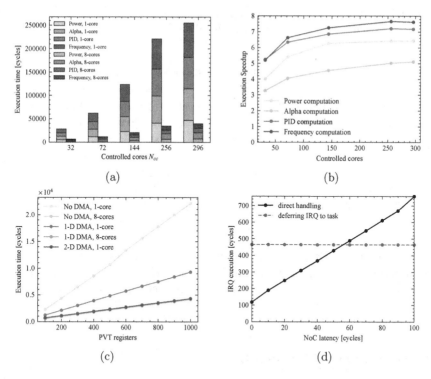

Fig. 3. (a)–(b) Firmware Control Action, execution time, and speedup comparison between single-core (SoC domain) and 8-cores (Cluster domain). **(c)** In-band data acquisition from simulated PVT registers, execution time without and with DMA in 1-D and 2-D configurations. **(d)** Execution time in the interrupt handler from the interrupt edge to its completion with a basic SCMI message at varying interconnect network access latency to the mailbox.

Each global interrupt line is paired with a mailbox that can host one command message and is associated with a unique agent over an SCMI channel. The minimum size of an SCMI message (header and payload) is 32B when employing a 4B payload for platform response according to standard specifications [2]. Figure 3d shows the execution time of an SCMI command decoding and response (Base Protocol, `protocol_id = 0x10`, `message_id = 0x0` [2]) when an external simulated driver rings a doorbell to the PCS. In the experiment, we emulate the latency of the interconnect network between ControlPULP and the mailbox location in the die (Figs. 2a) as described in Fig. 2b. The latency has a large impact on the load/store access times, thus the time spent in the ISR, which grows with the interconnect delay size. We address the issue using the FreeRTOS timer API `xTimerPendFunctionCallFromISR()` to defer pending interrupts and keep the ISR time short and insensitive to the CPU interconnect network delay (Fig. 3d). From Fig. 3d, we see that deferring interrupt handling to a task is preferable over direct handling, as it is network-latency insensitive and faster for realistic

Table 3. Execution time T of a PCT step, single-core and cluster configurations. SCMI commands exchange and off-die transfers, handled by the SoC Manager core, are not included in the comparison since they are a shared overhead.

Firmware phase	Time step	Execution time [cycles]		Speedup
		1-core	Multi-core	
Control action (P4)–(P7)	τ_0	61867	11372	5.5×
In-band transfers (P1),(P2)	τ_1	5463	3523 (DMA)	1.6×
Offload to the cluster	τ_2	–	389	–
L2 - L1 transfers	τ_3	–	434 (DMA)	–
L1 - L2 transfers	τ_4	–	872 (DMA)	–
Return from cluster	τ_5	–	574	–
Step total time	T	67330	13641	**4.9×**

NoC latencies larger than 50 cycles. Other existing solutions, such as ARM SCP firmware, propose a bespoke Deferred Response Architecture (See footnote 1) to mark selected requests coming from an agent as pending and defer the platform response. We instead rely on a trusted scheduler that decouples OS and PCF driver APIs improving flexibility and portability.

4.4   System-Level PCF Step Evaluation

The standalone evaluations of ControlPULP's architectural features from the previous sections need to be finalized with the overall Periodic Control Task step cycle count comparison between accelerator enhanced and single-core configurations, reported in Table 3 in the case of 72 controlled cores. Table 3 shows a breakdown of the required actions. The total execution time computation differs in the two domains. In the single-core case, we execute sequentially with less overhead ($T_{single} = \tau_0 + \tau_1$). In the multi-core case, ($T_{multi} = max(\tau_0, \tau_1) + \sum_{i=2}^{5} \tau_i$) we (i) execute the computation τ_0 and data acquisition τ_1 at step n concurrently, (ii) rely on $\tau_{0,multi} \ll \tau_{0,single}$, and (iii) introduce an overhead due to additional data movement involving L1 and L2, which is essential to keep data telemetry between SoC and cluster domains during the PCT.

Overall, multi-core execution achieves a 4.9× speedup over a single-core configuration. This helps reduce the PCF periodic control policy hyper-period (the least common multiple of the control tasks periods) [16] and increase the available computation time within the hyper-period, respectively.

4.5   Control-Level PCF Step Evaluation

Control Comparison with SoA Solutions. The control quality of the PCF step is tightly coupled with the architecture of the system to be controlled. Benchmarks comparisons concern the overall HPC chip performance and are not focused on the controller alone. The only commercial solution available for cross-benchmarking is the IBM OCC (Sect. 2). To enable a meaningful comparison, we use MATLAB Simulink to model (i) the HPC die as control target and (ii) the IBM's control action excluding few architecture-specific features, and the two-layer PCF control [3] executed by ControlPULP. The PID-like coefficients of the IBM control are adapted for the HPC chip model. We assume a constant voltage of 0.75 V and neither overhead nor delays in the PLLs and VRMs operating point transitions. The simulation runs for 2 s. The HPC chip model consists of a 9-cores tile. Each core executes diverse synthetic[6] workloads: Core 1/Core 3 and Core2/Core 4 execute maximum power (MAX) and low power (LOW) instructions, respectively. Core 5, 6, and 9 execute heterogeneous mixed instruction (MIX), while Core 7 and Core 8 are exposed to sharp instruction types switching (FAST) to stress the power limiter and the shorter timing constants of the temperature response. The DVFS target frequency for each core is kept constant at the maximum frequency, while the power budget is changed five times during the simulation to stress all the elements of the control action.

First, we show that a controller with a multi-core cluster able to deliver higher computational power is beneficial for the performances of the HPC chip. We compare the IBM control and a version of it with a per-core temperature PID for frequency reduction. The comparison highlights the positive effect of having fine-grained control made possible by the cluster. The performance, measured as the number of retired instructions, is shown in Fig. 4. Using only one temperature for the whole tile results in an average performance reduction per core of 5.55%, while Cores executing high-power instructions (Core 1 and Core 3) receive a performance increase of 4% and 5% respectively. In fact, being the frequency reduction based on the hotter cores and thus a shared penalty, neighboring cores get colder, and other cores consume less power during power capping phases, leaving more power available to boost performances of Core 1 and Core 3. As from Sect. 2, the IBM control policy considers the maximum temperature among the processing elements when applying frequency reduction. We conjecture that this limitation is enforced by the limited control policy complexity that can be handled by IBM's OCC. On the other end, ControlPULP enables fine-grained frequency reduction on a per-core temperature granularity.

Last, we compare the PCF control and the IBM control version with per-core temperature PIDs. The comparison is used to show the validity of the considered PCF control as well as how the accelerator allows fine-grain control decisions by favoring the more demanding workloads. In the latter scenario, the PCF shows a performance increase in executed instructions that ranges from +2.75% to +4.97%. This holds true for cores with mixed instructions (+0.1% to +6.08%) as well, while cores involved in less demanding workloads witness a decrease between −2.72% and −3.76%. Thus, the modified policy with per-core temperature PID calculation, enabled by the parallel cluster, can selectively boost the instructions retired by the critical cores, achieving a higher application performance on the HPC chip while still meeting the thermal cap.

---

[6] In order to assess the controller, the evaluation of a real workload is out of scope for this work as it requires more complex co-simulation setup. We refer to synthetic workloads that cover relevant corner cases for the ControlPULP.

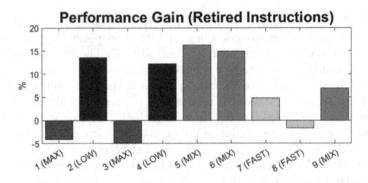

Fig. 4. Performance analysis. Comparison between the original IBM OCC firmware and modified IBM OCC firmware with per-core temperature PID for frequency reduction.

5   Conclusion

In this paper, we presented ControlPULP, a complete RISC-V Power Control System for HPC processors that exploits multi-core capabilities to accelerate control algorithms and features specialized DMA and fast interrupt handling and synchronization. This allows us to apply more fine-grained control policies resulting in better control performance. With the proposed architecture, a control policy step executes 4.9x faster than in single-core configuration. ControlPULP enables the implementation of more complex control algorithms capable of dispatching fine-grained frequency targets with better accuracy.

Acknowledgment. The study has been conducted in the context of EU H2020-JTI-EuroHPC-2019-1 project REGALE (g.n. 956560), EuroHPC EU PILOT project (g.a. 101034126), EU Pilot for exascale EuroHPC EUPEX (g. a. 101033975), and European Processor Initiative (EPI) SGA2 (g.a. 101036168).

References

1. AMD: Epyc 7003 Milan (2021). https://en.wikichip.org/wiki/amd/epyc
2. ARM Ltd.: Arm System Control and Management Interface v3.0. https://developer.arm.com/documentation/den0056/latest
3. Bambini, G., et al.: An open-source scalable thermal and power controller for HPC processors. In: 2020 IEEE 38th International Conference on Computer Design (ICCD), pp. 364–367 (2020)
4. Burd, T., et al.: "zeppelin": an soc for multichip architectures. IEEE J. Solid-State Circ. **54**(1), 133–143 (2019). https://doi.org/10.1109/JSSC.2018.2873584
5. Cesarini, D., Bartolini, A., Bonfa, P., Cavazzoni, C., Benini, L.: Countdown: a run-time library for performance-neutral energy saving in MPI applications. IEEE Trans. Comput. **70**, 682–695 (2020)
6. Group, T.L.: Sipearl develops arm hpc chip (2020). https://www.linleygroup.com/newsletters/newsletter_detail.php?num=6227&year=2020&tag=3

7. Gunther, S., Deval, A., Burton, T., Kumar, R.: Energy-efficient computing: power management system on the nehalem family of processors. Intel Technol. J. **14**(3), 50–66 (2010)
8. Intel: Alder Lake (2021). https://en.wikichip.org/wiki/intel/microarchitectures/alder_lake#Codenames
9. Labs, A.: AWS Graviton 2 (2020). https://en.wikichip.org/wiki/annapurna_labs/alpine/alc12b00
10. Leiserson, C.E., et al.: There's plenty of room at the top: what will drive computer performance after Moore's law? Science **368**(6495) (2020)
11. Liu, Z., Zhu, H.: A survey of the research on power management techniques for high-performance systems. Softw. Pract. Expert **40**, 943–964 (2010). https://doi.org/10.1002/spe.v40:11
12. LLC, G.: Power management for multiple processor cores (US Patent US8402290B2) (2020)
13. Ltd., A.: System control processor firmware. https://developer.arm.com/tools-and-software/open-source-software/firmware/scp-firmware
14. Ltd., A.: Power and Performance Management using Arm SCMI Specification. Technical report (2019)
15. Montagna, F., et al.: A low-power transprecision floating-point cluster for efficient near-sensor data analytics. IEEE Trans. Parallel Distrib. Syst. **33**(5), 1038–1053 (2022). https://doi.org/10.1109/TPDS.2021.3101764
16. Ripoll, I., Ballester, R.: Period selection for minimal hyper-period in real-time systems (2014)
17. RISC-V: RISC-V Platform Level Interrupt Controller. https://github.com/riscv/riscv-plic-spec/blob/master/riscv-plic.adoc
18. Rosedahl, T., Broyles, M., Lefurgy, C., Christensen, B., Feng, W.: Power/performance controlling techniques in OpenPOWER. In: Kunkel, J.M., Yokota, R., Taufer, M., Shalf, J. (eds.) ISC High Performance 2017. LNCS, vol. 10524, pp. 275–289. Springer, Cham (2017). https://doi.org/10.1007/978-3-319-67630-2_21
19. Rossi, D., et al.: PULP: a parallel ultra low power platform for next generation IoT applications. In: 2015 IEEE Hot Chips 27 Symposium (HCS), pp. 1–39 (2015)
20. Rossi, D., Loi, I., Haugou, G., Benini, L.: Ultra-low-latency lightweight DMA for tightly coupled multi-core clusters. In: Proceedings of the 11th ACM Conference on Computing Frontiers, CF 2014. Association for Computing Machinery, New York (2014)
21. Rotem, E., Naveh, A., Ananthakrishnan, A., Weissmann, E., Rajwan, D.: Power-management architecture of the intel microarchitecture code-named sandy bridge. IEEE Micro **32**(2), 20–27 (2012). https://doi.org/10.1109/MM.2012.12
22. Schöne, R., Ilsche, T., Bielert, M., Gocht, A., Hackenberg, D.: Energy efficiency features of the intel skylake-sp processor and their impact on performance. In: 2019 International Conference on High Performance Computing Simulation (HPCS), pp. 399–406 (2019)

Embedded Software Systems
and Beyond

CASA: An Approach for Exposing and Documenting Concurrency-Related Software Properties

Jasmin Jahić[1]([✉]) [iD], Volkan Doganci[2]([✉]), and Hubert Gehring[2]([✉])

[1] University of Cambridge, Cambridge, UK
jj542@cam.ac.uk
[2] Siemens AG, Fuerth, Germany
{volkan.doganci,hubert.gehring}@siemens.com

Abstract. Finding concurrency bugs is hard because of two reasons. Reconstruction of concurrency-specific software properties from source code or binary is an NP-hard problem, and some information might not be present in the software implementation at all (e.g., intentions of synchronisation). Existing approaches for finding concurrency bugs use over-approximating analyses and testing, but these respectively often lead to potential false warnings or fail to report some concurrency bugs. Without knowledge of concurrency properties (memory locations shared between threads and used synchronisation mechanisms), it is hard to complement existing analyses and make their output more precise. Furthermore, choosing a testing tool without knowledge of concurrency-specific software properties is also a challenge and can result in big overhead.

Therefore, in this paper we present a light-weight approach that forces developers to plan and document decisions about used synchronisation mechanisms during development. The approach is implemented as part of Agile SCRUM framework. Documented concurrency-related decisions are used to choose adequate testing tools and improve their precision.

Keywords: Concurrency · Synchronisation · Architectural decisions · Agile · Reverse engineering · Concurrency bugs · SCRUM

1 Introduction

Finding concurrency bugs is a well researched area. Various algorithms exist for finding concurrency bugs [6,28] based on static analysis [17,23], dynamic analysis [12,13], or combination of these two [30]. Static analysis can be complete (i.e., it can find all concurrency bugs), but often produces too many false warnings. Dynamic analysis is more precise, but is limited by executed test cases.

This work was supported by the Engineering and Physical Sciences Research Council (EPSRC) through grant reference EP/P020011/1.

Regardless of the type of used technique or algorithm for finding concurrency bugs, these always need to perform the following operations [11]: i) identify memory shared between threads, ii) recognise synchronisation mechanisms used by developers, iii) understand synchronisation intentions that developers have, and iv) recognise different patterns of concurrency bugs (e.g., data races, deadlocks).

However, for n threads and their i instructions, there is 2^{n*i} possible interleaving of instruction executions. Analysis of these execution paths and the identification of shared memory between threads is an NP-hard problem [26]. Furthermore, although programming languages define possible synchronisation primitives, developers can also introduce user-defined synchronisation mechanisms (e.g., based on scheduling or spinning loops) [13,15]. These two challenges often lead to analysis imprecision. Over-approximation of shared memory locations can lead to false warnings, while not recognising some of them can lead to a failure to detect concurrency bugs. If an approach is not able to recognise a synchronisation mechanism, then it will falsely report accesses to shared memory synchronised by that mechanism as bugs.

Further motivation for this problem are challenges that testers in industry face when choosing tools for finding concurrency bugs. In practice, each tool is able to recognise only a certain set of synchronisation mechanisms, and is able to find only certain types of concurrency bugs (e.g., data races and deadlocks). Choosing an inappropriate tool for finding concurrency bugs has two major negative effects. First, the tool might report too many false warnings or might fail to report some concurrency bugs. Second, the time required for integration of these tools into industrial engineering environments might be significant, as we show in this paper. Most of the existing tools for finding concurrency bugs are not professional, out-of-the-shelf tools. Instead, they have certain requirements and operate under certain assumptions. In industry, especially in embedded systems, engineers often have pre-defined development environments (e.g., a version of operating system common for all teams, limited set of allowed libraries). In the worst case scenario, engineers spend too much time integrating a tool for finding concurrency bugs into their environment, only to discover that such tool is not appropriate considering synchronisation mechanisms and types of concurrency bugs they have in their system (of which they are not fully aware upfront).

In summary, it is not possible, with high precision, to reverse-engineer software concurrency properties needed for finding concurrency bugs (used shared memory, synchronisation intentions) from source code/binary alone. Existing analyses have theoretical limitations (NP-hard problem) and the information might not be present in the software implementation at all (e.g., user-defined synchronisation and intentions). Therefore, it is necessary to obtain these information elsewhere to improve precision of the existing approaches (i.e., filter out false warnings). Furthermore, in practice, testers need these (hard to get) information to choose adequate tools for finding concurrency bugs.

Therefore, instead of trying to reverse-engineer synchronisation-related software properties or rely on developers' good memory and their long-term commitment to their companies, we suggest to document synchronisation-related decisions as they are being made. For this purpose, we have developed our Continuous engineering Approach for exposing and documenting concurrency-related SoftwAre properties during development (*CASA*). We defined a process for capturing architectural decisions during development, making them transparent, and creating a communication medium between developers and architects to agree and align synchronisation. *CASA* includes guidelines to identify concurrency-related software components and initiate a discussion about their concurrency-related properties, focusing on used synchronisation mechanisms. This is particularly important for embedded systems, in which synchronisation mechanisms should not compromise real-time constraints nor cause deadlocks that can lead to safety-critical situations. We suggest a template to document synchronisation mechanisms and dependencies between components, and finally we discuss how to use this information when creating testing strategies for concurrent software. We have implemented our approach within Agile development methodology, using *SCRUM*, and tested it in a multinational company. The results show that this light-weight approach is able to capture synchronisation-relevant decisions of concurrent software. We have evaluated how much time developers spend for actions prescribed by *CASA* to expose and document shared memory and synchronisation mechanisms in multithreaded software. The results show that the overhead introduced by our approach is insignificant compared to the potential overhead caused by choosing an inappropriate tools for finding concurrency bugs in industry.

This paper is organised as follows. In Sect. 2, we briefly discuss related work. In Sect. 3, we present components of our approach for exposing concurrency software properties, and in Sect. 4 we present integration of the approach within Agile *SCRUM*. Section 5 presents the results of the evaluation, including quantitative evaluation through a use case in a multinational company, and qualitative results of a survey with software professionals. Finally, we conclude in Sect. 6.

2   Related Work

Common synchronisation mechanisms in concurrent software include locks, barriers, inter-thread synchronisation, monitors and conditional variables, scheduling, and a variety of non-blocking synchronisation [10] (e.g., ring and buffer). Besides these, developers can create their own implementations of synchronisation, or combine some of these mechanisms. If developers use synchronisation in an improper way, concurrency bugs can appear. The most common ones are data races, atomicity violations, order violations, priority inversions, deadlocks, livelocks, and starvation. These lists are not complete, because a concurrency bug originates whenever there is a difference between expected and manifested behavior of software, which involves concurrency. Because there is a huge space for such opportunity, it is hard to design tools based on patterns that are able to recognise [15], without any further assistance, if some piece of code is in fact a synchronisation mechanism, leading to testing imprecision [11].

Despite these limitations, there exists a number of approaches that try to identify shared memory and used synchronisation mechanisms in software (e.g., Astrée [23], Eraser Lockset [28], Happens-before based [6], atomicity violation [20]), and try to visualise the results of such analysis [16,22,32,33] to enable developers and architects to manage concurrency. However, the problem is NP-hard [25,26]. Furthermore, the concurrency model we choose for threads is nontrivial, not comprehensible to humans [19], and the lack of properly defined interfaces for accessing shared memory [14] make the challenge complex to reason about. It is often the case that engineers spend more time trying to understand if a reported bug is the real bug, then fixing real bugs [7].

3   Exposing and Documenting Concurrency-Related Software Architecture Decisions

Our Continuous engineering Approach for exposing and documenting concurrency related SoftwAre properties (*CASA*) works as a bottom-up approach that prescribes collaboration of developers on common software components to identify concurrency-critical dependencies between them and within them (Fig. 1). To determine if software components and development performed on them are concurrency critical, *CASA* prescribes a Guideline for Identification of Concurrency-Critical Components (*GICCS*, Sect. 3.1). The purpose of the guideline is to "force" developers to align synchronisation mechanisms used in concurrency-critical component(s). For the purpose of documenting and discussing synchronisation, *CASA* introduces the concept of synchronisation tables (Sect. 3.2). *CASA* prescribes these activities to properly expose and deal with synchronisation-related architectural decisions, and integrate gathered architecture knowledge into a testing strategy.

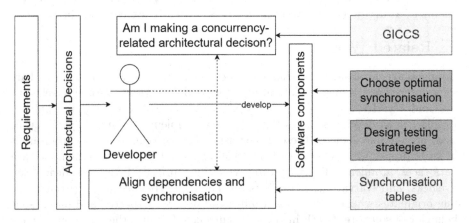

Fig. 1. CASA conceptual solution (full arrows: information flow; dotted arrows: research questions addressed by CASA). Highlighted parts represent CASA components and contributions.

3.1 Guideline for Identification of Concurrency-Critical Components (GICCS)

A developer starts their work with a task or a requirement about a new feature or a change request. The first step in initiating a discussion about concurrency-relevant architecturally-significant properties of software components is to identify concurrency-critical components. In order to identify them, the question is, what are the aspects that are associated with concurrency. Therefore, we have analysed systematic state-of-the-art literature reviews in this domain, focusing on types of concurrency, synchronisation mechanisms, and types of concurrency bugs [1–5,8,9,21,31]. Our focus was predominantly on multithreaded software, where threads communicate using shared memory, but considering equivalence between shared memory systems and message passing systems [4], our approach is also applicable to message passing systems.

Identified concurrency aspects include use of concurrent execution flows (e.g., threads), existence of associated shared states (e.g., shared memory locations), and use of synchronisation mechanisms. Based on the identified concurrency aspects from the literature, we have concluded a simple Guideline for Identification of Concurrency Critical componentS (*GICCS*), with questions that guide developers and help them to identify if a component has anything to do with concurrency. According to *GICCS*, a component is concurrency-critical if it can be associated with at least one concurrency aspect, meaning that there is at least one *positive* answer to these questions:

1. Does a component run in a separate execution flow, or are there multiple execution flows within a component (are there multiple threads)?
2. Does a component require or update some shared/global state?
3. Does a component use any sort of synchronisation (either explicit or adhoc synchronisation)?

3.2 Documentation of Synchronisation Mechanisms

There are two main goals of *GICCS*: i) identification of concurrency-critical components and ii) initiation of a discussion between developers in terms of concurrent execution flows, shared states, and synchronisation. If, at any point during discussion guided by *GICCS* it becomes obvious that more than one component is accessing the same shared state or if synchronisation mechanisms are used in the context of component's functionality, there is a need for documenting these concurrency aspects. When shared states are identified (the schedule of this activity depends on the development practice), developers need to align synchronisation mechanisms. Furthermore, if synchronisation mechanisms between components are identified, it is necessary to reason if those components share any state, and if yes, again align synchronisation mechanisms.

In order to conclude this activity, it is necessary to document dependencies between components and used synchronisation mechanisms. For this purpose, *CASA* introduces a concept of "synchronisation table" (Fig. 2). In order to show concurrency dependencies between components and their threads, this table uses the intersections of its columns and rows. Each input in the table (dependency between components), consists of a shared variable name, associated thread function, and thread ID, along with associated list of synchronisation mechanisms that the thread is using to access the variable (because, it could be that a thread uses more than one synchronisation mechanism for accessing the same variable, which already indicates a potential problem). Each shared variable has a dedicated cell in the context of the intersection.

In the context of industrial software systems, we differentiate between components, applications and modules. A *component* is the smallest software part, developed as either a static or dynamic library in the system. It can have its own threads or can be accessed by other threads. An *application* is a program that performs specific tasks and it may consist of several components and their threads. A *module* consists of several applications with a focus on only one area of system's functionality (i.e. transfer, communication, visualization etc.), and it may consist of several processes.

Each of these abstraction levels may have one synchronisation table. For example, if a component has many threads, developers can create and maintain a synchronisation table per component, where axes are labeled by thread IDs and functions (e.g., t_1f_1), and intersections between them contain shared variables and used synchronisation mechanisms. In addition, synchronisation mechanisms between modules may require an additional synchronisation table. If threads from different components in an application depend on each other via synchronisation mechanisms or share variables, developers will create a synchronisation table on the application level. In that case, as we have visualized, in Fig. 2, when a component has more than one thread, developers will use the synchronisation table on the application level to specify synchronisation mechanisms between threads of that component (i.e., the same component on both axes). On the level of modules and on the level of inter-module dependencies, developers would record synchronisation and shared states between processes, because it is common that applications execute as separate processes (their threads do not directly share common memory space), and often rely on inter-process communication mechanisms. Before this activity, developers need to agree with architects on which level they need to document concurrency-related dependencies.

3.3   Testing of Concurrent Software with CASA's Support

During software development, *GICCS* initiates a discussion about concurrency aspects of software. When concurrency-relevant components are recognised, developers use synchronisation tables to document synchronisation mechanisms used in software and dependencies between threads of the same component, between components, applications and modules of software. Resulting synchronisation tables contain information about synchronisation decisions. These tables are input to testers. They use them to reason if the existing testing process and set of tools for testing are able to recognize all synchronisation mechanisms used in software. If not, the tables drive them to select tools that are able to detect

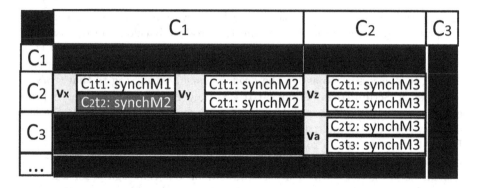

Fig. 2. Synchronisation table: Component (C) to component overview of synchronisation mechanisms for accessing shared variables (v).

types of synchronisation mechanisms present in the software, and complement those tools with additional analyses to improve their precision (e.g., scripts to remove false warnings).

4   Integration of CASA in Agile SCRUM

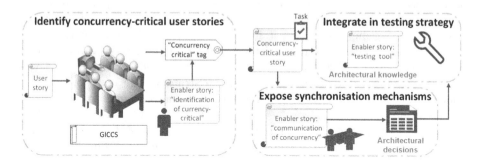

Fig. 3. CASA and SCRUM: Activities of Continuous Engineering Approach for exposing Concurrency-related Software Architecture Decisions.

SCRUM [29] is a light-weight Agile framework [27] for developing, delivering, and sustaining software products. *User story* is a brief, informal explanation of some aspect of a software system written from the perspective of the end user or customer. *Enabler stories* bring visibility to the work items needed to support exploration, architecture, infrastructure, and compliance.

CASA complements *SCRUM* with several activities and artifacts (Fig. 3). To enable these additional activities, before discussing/planning user stories for a new sprint, one of developers creates an "*identification of concurrency-critical user stories*" enabler story (Table 1). Developers working in the same team start the process by taking user stories from the product backlog and discuss them to identify "*concurrency-critical*" user stories by using *GICCS* (Sect. 3.1). If developers identify that a user story involves components that are concurrency-critical, it is necessary to assign the "*concurrency critical*" tag to that story.

When a Scrum Team applies *GICCS*, they might not be able to properly answer its suggested questions for several reasons. These include the lack of knowledge about multithreading, uncertainties about the implementation, Rough Upfront Design (a rough design for the user story), and the lack of information from other teams. The last point is critical, because if a user story has dependencies on the work of other teams or on external legacy software, the Scrum Team that discusses such user story may not be able to properly reason about used shared states or used synchronisation mechanisms. If any of these situations arises, one developer needs to conclude the enabler story "*identification of concurrency-critical user story*" before developers can proceed with regular *SCRUM* activities of potential concurrency-critical stories. For example, when a team lacks information about potential concurrency, it is necessary to escalate the enabler story to a higher inter-team level.

If the conclusion is that a user story is not concurrency-critical, the process regarding concurrency checks ends here. Otherwise, it is necessary to proceed by discussing synchronisation mechanisms. For this activity, it is necessary that one of the developers creates "*communication of concurrency*" enabler story (Table 2). For every user story tagged with "*concurrency-critical*", for which there exists a "*communication of concurrency*" enabler story, the process of development is as follows. After the enabler story is created, one of the developers of the Scrum Team takes it from the backlog and works on this story before the team starts working on the associated concurrency-critical user story. The developer responsible for this enabler story communicates with other developers to agree on an optimal synchronisation strategy. The main task of this enabler story is to expose used synchronisation mechanisms and force alignment of synchronisation mechanisms between developers. To complete this enabler story, it is necessary to create/update the documentation of discussed synchronisation mechanisms for concurrent software parts using synchronisation tables (Sect. 3.2).

In order to test concurrency-critical user stories, it is essential to find appropriate testing tools and integrate them into testing process. Testers take, one-by-one, *concurrency-critical* user stories. They ensure that a testing tool for finding concurrency bugs is available in the Scrum Team *AND* is able to handle reported synchronisation mechanisms. If not, they create a "*testing tool*" enabler story (Table 3) and find additional testing tools with the help of synchronisation tables (this is a solution and market space exploration, and we do not discuss it as we consider that testers, provided that they have all information about used synchronisation mechanisms, can complete this task). In order to select appropriate testing tools, testers need to observe what kind of synchronisation mechanisms these tools can detect. A tool that they select must be able to detect synchronisation mechanisms present in synchronisation tables. An additional important aspect, when selecting adequate testing tools, is the ability of these tools to enable configuration of their analysis algorithms. Besides standard synchronisation mechanisms (e.g., mutex), developers tend to implement their own, user-defined adhoc synchronisation mechanisms. This can be done for various reasons (e.g., ensure liveness properties, reduce memory consumption). If a tool is not flexible in this regard, it might not be possible to further configure it to filter out common false warnings. Running testing tools and handling reports of concurrency bugs is a challenging task. For every reported concurrency bug, testers compare it with synchronisation tables and inspect the source code. In this way, they are able to conclude if reported concurrency bugs are indeed bugs, or if the reported bugs are false warnings because of the tools imprecision. If the reported bugs do not match synchronisation tables, a tester reports them to developers for a further analysis. The final step of the testing process is elimination of false warnings. If testers can recognise a pattern of false warnings (e.g., poor handling of some synchronisation mechanisms), they can either configure the testing tools (if possible), or write scripts that filter out the testing results to eliminate these false warnings. After resolving reported concurrency bugs, the team can conclude the "*testing tool*" enabler story.

Table 1. Enabler story template: identification of concurrency-critical user stories

Title	Identify concurrency-critical aspects of the user stories
As a	developer
I want to	know concurrency-critical aspects in my software
So that	team can test it with appropriate tools
Acceptance criteria	Identify concurrency-critical user stories; If a user story is concurrency-critical, it is tagged as such, and the necessary tasks are created

Table 2. Enabler story template: communication of concurrency

Title	Need to align about synchronisation mechanisms
As a	developer
I want to	align synchronisation mechanisms for shared variables
So that	we can prevent improper use of synchronisation
Acceptance criteria	Synchronisation mechanisms are aligned and documented

When developers work on a concurrency-critical user story in a sprint, the coding of this story should be consistent with the associated synchronisation tables. Therefore, during the code review phase, the participants check any inconsistencies or missing entries in synchronisation tables. When the synchronisation

Table 3. Enabler story template: testing tool

Title	Integrate a testing tool for finding concurrency bugs
As a	tester
I want to	test the concurrency-critical user stories
So that	I can find concurrency bugs.
Acceptance criteria	Understand possible concurrency bugs; Collect affected user stories. Collect used synchronisation mechanisms; Choose a testing tool. Eliminate false warnings by configuring the tool; Create test reports

tables and the source code reflect the same state in terms of synchronisation mechanisms and shared variables, developers conclude the concurrency-critical user story, which ensures that documentation matches implementation.

5   Evaluation

In order to evaluate our approach, we have applied it in an industrial use case (Sect. 5.1) and conducted a survey among software engineering professionals to understand how they perceive it (Sect. 5.2).

5.1   Setup I: Reverse Engineering of Synchronisation Decisions in Industrial Environment

The evaluation was performed in a multinational company, which counts thousands of employees. We focused on teams that are developing an industrial embedded systems for human-machine interfaces. This project is running since 2015, it was first released in 2020, and is currently in its third major revision. It is developed using C/C++ and Qt Framework. Around 300 engineers and architects are working on this project, and they integrate some software components from other teams in other business lines. There are 13 teams, with each team consisting of 8 people. The teams are organised in Agile manner, and use *SCRUM* with 2 weeks long sprints.

There are some information about how the message passing works via threads (e.g. enqueue/dequeue), and some sequence diagrams visualize asynchronous function calls. However, architectural documents do not contain any information about synchronisation intentions nor used mechanisms. As the consequence of challenges with concurrency and synchronisation, the teams face issues with availability, performance (due to shared memory between different project layers), and reliability of their software. There was an attempt to visualize the threads model, but the effort was not completed and it was abandoned.

We organised the evaluation activities in two parts. In the first part, we evaluated potential organisational constraints and the time needed to adopt tools for finding concurrency bugs. In the second part, we evaluated the main activity related to gathering information that existing analysis cannot reverse-engineer: how much time on average a Scrum Team spends on discussing if a user story is concurrency-critical and documenting its findings when using our approach (application of *GICCS*).

Adopting Tools for Finding Concurrency Bugs in Industrial Environments. We have evaluated three approaches for finding concurrency bugs: two established tools (Helgrind [24] and ThreadSanitizer [30]), and one state-of-the-art research approach (BOSMI [13]). To find concurrency bugs, these tools aim to detect (improper) synchronisation between threads.

We first report our experiences in terms of a pure compatibility of the tools (*Helgrind, ThreadSanitizer,* and *BOSMI*) and the tested industrial system (Debian 9 64-bit, gcc 6.3.0). *Helgrind* was working well with the original project setup, without any required changes (it takes binary as an input). On the other hand, *ThreadSanitizer* required to switch from gcc to clang compiler, and to add certain macros and flags to CMake and Make files. In the original setup, it reported an error, which we were able to fix only with an upgrade of the operating system. Clang had issues with compiling class members with static variables and non-void functions without a return value. In general, clang seems to be more strict in type checking and would report bugs on pieces of code that gcc would report as warnings. *BOSMI* is based on LLVM [18], and it requires a specific clang version. Because it uses clang (like *ThreadSanitizer*), the same clang-related changes were required to enable *BOSMI* to work. In summary, Helgrind and BOSMI support 32-bit and 64-bit applications, but ThreadSanitizer supports only 64-bit applications.

Dealing with these issues was somewhat time consuming. Setting up Helgrind with the existing environment was straightforward and took less than one day. However, ThreadSanitizer was more demanding and setting it up took around one working week. BOSMI took two weeks to integrate in the existing development environment. One could fairly argue that it is necessary to perform these actions once per project (or a group of projects). However, there is a fundamental issue with these changes. There existed architectural decisions regarding the platform and development environment for all teams (common in embedded systems). If engineers were to use different settings (e.g., Linux packages and compiler versions), these could result in incompatible setups, overheads, and issues with quality properties. Therefore, changing compilers or versions of operating systems is (often) not allowed during a project.

In terms of what these tools are capable of to provide, we inspected what kind of synchronisation mechanisms they are able to detect. *Helgrind* and *ThreadSanitizer* can recognise POSIX pthread primitives (locks, barriers, semaphore, condition variables, fork/join). *BOSMI* is limited to locks and non-blocking synchronisation related to synchronisation and scheduling. None of these tools supports ad-hoc synchronisation, which leads to false warnings. There are other important differences between these tools, such is specification of annotations, code coverage, test generation, and level of details in reports about bugs. BOSMI generates test cases and quantifies code coverage, but needs LLVM infrastructure. ThreadSanitizer and Helgrind do not offer these features.

Therefore, we conclude that using testing tools for reconstructing synchronisation decisions in industrial environments is not straightforward. It can be a time consuming task, especially because a tool needs to be compatible with pre-defined development environment. If testers choose a tool that is not covering all synchronisation mechanisms present in software, then there is a limited gain. The worst part is that testers might not even understand that they are missing something until there are issues with concurrency bugs or other quality properties of software (e.g., performance issues due to improper use of synchronisation). That is why it is absolutely necessary to understand concurrency-related architectural decisions.

Identification of Concurrency-Critical User Stories. In the second part, we have evaluated how our Guideline for Identification of Concurrency Critical componentS (*GICCS*) performs in practice. The focus of the evaluation was on time needed for discussion and identification of concurrency-critical user stories. We observed the discussion and collected the feedback regarding benefits and potential issues of *GICCS*. For this purpose, we organized the evaluation with one team working in the fore-mentioned setup. The team members that participated in evaluation included seven participants (Scrum Master, Product Owner, and five Scrum Engineers), and they did not have any process for dealing with concurrency issues.

It took less than 30 min to explain the approach to all team members, and for them to understand the goals of the evaluation. The team discussed 7 user stories as part of their sprint planning. On average, they needed 2 min and 10 s to identify if a user story is concurrency critical. Out of 7, they identified 2 user stories as concurrency critical.

The team agreed that *GICCS* is compatible with their *SCRUM* activities due to short discussion time. The team also agreed that no additional questions are necessary to identify concurrency-critical user stories. The team communicated that questions of *GICCS* offer a systematic way for discussing concurrency, and that these questions could be a checklist. In the opinion of this team, the checklist would increase the awareness of concurrency issues and make them transparent.

5.2   Setup II: Survey with Software Engineering Professionals

To understand how industry professionals perceive suitability of our approach for solving their concurrency issues, we have surveyed 11 individuals[1] selected from our personal network (10 from the fore-mentioned company, and 1 from a research institute). There were 2 product owners with more than 6 years of experience each, 1 architect with more than 10 years of experience, 2 Scrum Masters

---

[1] According to ACM template for Questionnaire Surveys - www.acmsigsoft.github.io/EmpiricalStandards/docs/?standard=QuestionnaireSurveys.

with more than 6 years of experience each, and 6 developers of whom 3 had more than 10 years of experience and only the youngest developer had less than 3 years of experience. The survey comprised a questionnaire with three types of questions. The first type aimed to understand does *CASA* cover the most important issues regarding concurrency and how adequate are *GICCS* and synchronisation tables for identifying and capturing concurrency aspects of software. The second type of questions aimed to investigate if our approach is compatible with development approaches and methodologies used by survey's participants. Finally, we asked for demographic information. We first presented *CASA* and discussed it with participants, after which they filled in the questionnaire.

Table 4. Summary of the results of the survey on suitability of CASA to deal with concurrency issues and compatibility of CASA with the existing development approaches. Strongly agree (SA), Agree (A), Neutral (N), Disagree (D), Strongly disagree (SD), and Not Answered (NA)

Question	SA	A	N	D	SD	NA
CASA covers the most important concurrency issues	3	5	3	0	0	0
GICCS covers the most important aspects for identification of concurrency critical components	3	7	1	0	0	0
Synchronisation tables capture the most Important details regarding synchronisation	5	2	3	0	1	0
Synchronisation tables enable to remove false bug warnings	5	5	1	0	0	0
Testing tool enabler story contains enough details For integration of testing tools	8	2	1	0	0	0
CASA enabler stories are compatible with your dev. process	1	6	3	0	0	1
GICCS is compatible with your development process	3	6	1	1	0	0
Synch. tables are compatible with your development process	0	8	1	0	1	1

The survey results (Table 4) show that 3 out of 11 survey's participants *strongly agree* that *CASA* covers the most important concurrency issues, while 5 of ouf 11 *agree* with the same statement. Three out of 11 of them *strongly agree* and 7 of out of 11 *agree* that *GICCS* covers the most important aspects for identification of concurrency-critical software components and user stories. The survey participants also have the positive view regarding the level of details captured by synchronisation tables and the usefulness of those details to help and remove false warnings when trying to find concurrency bugs. There is an overwhelmingly positive perception that the *"testing tool"* enabler story provides enough details required for integration of adequate testing tools - the information that the survey participants concluded that they were often missing.

Most of the survey participants consider *CASA* and its artifacts compatible with their existing development processes. However, from one of the survey participants, we received negative feedback regarding the integration of *CASA* and its artifacts in their existing process. After the clarification, we have established that the participant uses Waterfall in their organisation, where we presented *CASA* as being implemented using Agile *SCRUM*. However, even this participant *agreed* that the enabler story for the testing tool contains enough details for the integration of the testing tools, and that our approach helps to eliminate false positives.

5.3 Threats to Validity

During the use case evaluation in the industrial environment we focused on dynamic tools, and avoided purely static analysis tools. We did this because dynamic tools, being based on execution of test cases, have a better reputation in industry. False warnings that static approaches often produce can result in huge overhead, often forcing developers to dedicate more time reasoning if reported bugs are false warnings than to fix them.

Our focus was on measuring the time necessary for identification of concurrency critical user stories (*GICCS*) and discussion about related concurrency aspects (e.g., synchronisation mechanisms). Choosing testing tools based on these results is outside of our scope, and it is the job of testers. Thanks to *GICCS*, their job is easier considering that *GICCS* provides them with the information about implemented synchronisation mechanisms, and even helps them to remove false warnings. The survey results confirm this conclusion.

There exists a potential challenge with the scalability of the synchronisation tables, for recording of used synchronisation mechanisms. However, we consider that this depends on the concrete implementation of the tables. Our focus was on evaluating if information captured by these tables contain the level of details that engineers need in order to manage their concurrent software systems. It is up to engineers to tailor their implementation.

6 Conclusion

In this paper, we have presented our Continuous engineering Approach for exposing and documenting concurrency-related SoftwAre properties (*CASA*) that captures concurrency-related architecturally-significant decisions just in time when developers decide about them. The alternative to our approach are existing reverse-engineering tools, which are imprecise (due to theoretical limitations of static and dynamic analysis, and the fact that developers keep finding new ways to use concurrency making these tools easily outdated), and for which we have shown that they require a significant effort for integration in industrial development environments. Future work will explore integration of our approach with other development methodologies.

References

1. Abbaspour Asadollah, S., Sundmark, D., Eldh, S., Hansson, H.: Concurrency bugs in open source software: a case study. J. Internet Serv. Appl. **8**(1), 4 (2017)
2. Arora, V., Bhatia, R., Singh, M.: A systematic review of approaches for testing concurrent programs. Concurr. Comput. Pract. Exp. **28**(5), 1572–1611 (2016)
3. Balakrishnan, G., et al.: Scalable and precise program analysis at NEC. In: Formal Methods in Computer Aided Design, pp. 273–274 (2010)
4. Bianchi, F., Margara, A., Pezze, M.: A survey of recent trends in testing concurrent software systems. IEEE Trans. Softw. Eng. **44**, 747–783 (2017)
5. Choi, S.E., Lewis, E.C.: A study of common pitfalls in simple multi-threaded programs. SIGCSE Bull. **32**(1), 325–329 (2000). https://doi.org/10.1145/331795. 331879
6. Dinning, A., Schonberg, E.: Detecting access anomalies in programs with critical sections. SIGPLAN Not. **26**(12), 85–96 (1991). https://doi.org/10.1145/127695. 122767
7. Durkin, T.: What the media couldn't tell you about the mars pathfinder. Robot Sci. Technol. **1**(1), 3 (1998)
8. Havelund, K., Goldberg, A.: Verify Your Runs. Springer, Heidelberg (2008). https://doi.org/10.1007/978-3-540-69149-5_40
9. Hong, S., Kim, M.: A survey of race bug detection techniques for multithreaded programmes. Softw. Test. Verif. Reliabil. **25**(3), 191–217. https://doi.org/10.1002/ stvr.1564, https://onlinelibrary.wiley.com/doi/abs/10.1002/stvr.1564
10. Jahić, J., Ali, K., Chatrangoon, M., Jahani, N.: (dis)advantages of lock-free synchronization mechanisms for multicore embedded systems. In: Proceedings of the 48th International Conference on Parallel Processing: Workshops, ICPP 2019. Association for Computing Machinery, New York (2019)
11. Jahić, J., Bauer, T., Kuhn, T., Wehn, N., Antonino, P.O.: FERA: a framework for critical assessment of execution monitoring based approaches for finding concurrency bugs. In: Arai, K., Kapoor, S., Bhatia, R. (eds.) SAI 2020. AISC, vol. 1228, pp. 54–74. Springer, Cham (2020). https://doi.org/10.1007/978-3-030-52249-0_5
12. Jahic, J., Jung, M., Kuhn, T., Kestel, C., Wehn, N.: A framework for non-intrusive trace-driven simulation of manycore architectures with dynamic tracing configuration. In: Colombo, C., Leucker, M. (eds.) RV 2018. LNCS, vol. 11237, pp. 458–468. Springer, Cham (2018). https://doi.org/10.1007/978-3-030-03769-7_28
13. Jahić, J., Kuhn, T., Jung, M., Wehn, N.: Bosmi: a framework for non-intrusive monitoring and testing of embedded multithreaded software on the logical level. In: Proceedings of the 18th International Conference on Embedded Computer Systems: Architectures, Modeling, and Simulation, SAMOS 2018, pp. 131–138. Association for Computing Machinery, New York (2018)
14. Jahić, J., Kumar, V., Antonino, P.O., Wirrer, G.: Testing the implementation of concurrent autosar drivers against architecture decisions. In: 2019 IEEE International Conference on Software Architecture (ICSA), pp. 171–180 (2019)
15. Jannesari, A., Tichy, W.F.: Identifying ad-hoc synchronization for enhanced race detection. In: 2010 IEEE International Symposium on Parallel Distributed Processing (IPDPS), pp. 1–10 (2010). https://doi.org/10.1109/IPDPS.2010.5470343
16. Karran, B., Trümper, J., Döllner, J.: Synctrace: visual thread-interplay analysis. In: First IEEE Working Conference on Software Visualization (VISSOFT), pp. 1–10. IEEE, Eindhoven (2013)

17. Keul, S.: Tuning static data race analysis for automotive control software. In: 2011 IEEE 11th International Working Conference on Source Code Analysis and Manipulation, pp. 45–54 (2011)
18. Lattner, C., Adve, V.: Llvm: a compilation framework for lifelong program analysis amp; transformation. In: International Symposium on Code Generation and Optimization, 2004, CGO 2004, pp. 75–86 (2004). https://doi.org/10.1109/CGO.2004.1281665
19. Lee, E.A.: The problem with threads. Computer 39(5), 33–42 (2006)
20. Lu, S., Tucek, J., Qin, F., Zhou, Y.: Avio: detecting atomicity violations via access-interleaving invariants. IEEE Micro 27(1), 26–35 (2007)
21. Lu, S., Park, S., Seo, E., Zhou, Y.: Learning from mistakes: a comprehensive study on real world concurrency bug characteristics. SIGOPS Oper. Syst. Rev. 42(2), 329–339 (2008)
22. May, J., Berman, F.: Creating views for debugging parallel programs. In: IEEE Scalable High Performance Computing Conference (SHPCC), pp. 833–840. IEEE, Knoxville (1994)
23. Miné, A., et al.: Taking static analysis to the next level: proving the absence of run-time errors and data races with astrée. In: 8th European Congress on Embedded Real Time Software and Systems (ERTS 2016), Toulouse, France (2016). https://hal.archives-ouvertes.fr/hal-01271552
24. Nethercote, N., Seward, J.: Valgrind: A framework for heavyweight dynamic binary instrumentation. In: Proceedings of the 28th ACM SIGPLAN Conference on Programming Language Design and Implementation, PLDI 2007, pp. 89–100. Association for Computing Machinery, New York (2007). https://doi.org/10.1145/1250734.1250746, https://doi.org/10.1145/1250734.1250746
25. Netzer, R.H.B., Miller, B.P.: What are race conditions?: some issues and formalizations. ACM Lett. Program. Lang. Syst. 1(1), 74–88 (1992)
26. Netzer, R.H., Miller, B.P.: On the complexity of event ordering for shared-memory parallel program executions. In: In Proceedings of the 1990 International Conference on Parallel Processing, pp. 93–97 (1990)
27. Rubin, K.S.: Essential Scrum: A Practical Guide to the Most Popular Agile Process, 1st edn. Addison-Wesley Professional, Boston (2012)
28. Savage, S., Burrows, M., Nelson, G., Sobalvarro, P., Anderson, T.: Eraser: a dynamic data race detector for multithreaded programs. ACM Trans. Comput. Syst. 15(4), 391–411 (1997)
29. Schwaber, K., Sutherland, J.: The scrum guide (2020). https://scrumguides.org/scrum-guide.html. Accessed 19 Apr 2021
30. Serebryany, K., Iskhodzhanov, T.: Threadsanitizer: data race detection in practice. In: Proceedings of the Workshop on Binary Instrumentation and Applications, WBIA, pp. 62–71. Association for Computing Machinery, New York (2009)
31. Souza, S.R.S., Brito, M.A.S., Silva, R.A., Souza, P.S.L., Zaluska, E.: Research in concurrent software testing: a systematic review. In: Proceedings of the Workshop on Parallel and Distributed Systems: Testing, Analysis, and Debugging, PADTAD 2011, pp. 1–5. ACM, New York (2011)
32. Stasko, J.T., Kraemer, E.: A methodology for building application-specific visualizations of parallel programs. J. Para. Distrib. Comput. 18(2), 258–264 (1993)
33. Wilhelm, A., Čakarić, F., Gerndt, M., Schuele, T.: Tool-based interactive software parallelization: a case study. In: The 40th International Conference on Software Engineering: Software Engineering in Practice, pp. 115–123. Association for Computing Machinery (ACM), Gothenburg (2018)

High-Level Simulation of Embedded Software Vulnerabilities to EM Side-Channel Attacks

Aditya Thimmaiah[✉], Vishnuvardhan V. Iyer, Andreas Gerstlauer, and Michael Orshansky

Department of Electrical and Computer Engineering, The University of Texas at Austin, Austin, TX 78712, USA
{auditt,vishnuv.iyer,gerstl,orshansky}@utexas.edu

Abstract. Attacks on embedded devices using the electromagnetic (EM) side channel have proliferated. Predicting software vulnerability to such attacks requires an ability to simulate EM fields during software development rather than relying on expensive lab-based measurements. We propose a modeling approach capable of synthesizing instruction-level EM traces for arbitrary software, using a one-time pre-characterization of a processor. Reducing the cost of dictionary construction is a major contribution of this paper. Results on a set of benchmarks show that synthesized traces are accurate in estimating EM emanations with less than 5% mean absolute percentage error (MAPE) compared to measurements. Furthermore, synthesized traces predict control flow leakage with an accuracy of 87% or more based on the side-channel vulnerability factor (SVF) metric.

Keywords: Embedded security · EM side-channel · EM simulation

1 Introduction

Evaluating the security risks of software running on embedded and IoT systems has become essential. Attacks through the electromagnetic (EM) side-channel are an especially pernicious threat due to their non-invasive nature [5]. EM fields emanating from a chip during program execution can be used for recovery of cryptographic keys [4] and tracking program control flow [6]. Analysis of EM vulnerabilities are typically performed using lab-based measurements. However, lab-based EM measurement setups can be costly, time-consuming and require expertise not available to typical software developers. Therefore, an EM simulator capable of synthesizing EM traces corresponding to on-chip activity with accuracy that is sufficient for security assessment is highly desirable.

A security-focused EM simulator needs to represent information pertinent to leakage analysis. Prior work has approached the construction of such simulators specifically for application-specific integrated circuits (ASICs) concerned with implementation of cryptographic algorithms [8,9,16]. However, they require

© The Author(s), under exclusive license to Springer Nature Switzerland AG 2022
A. Orailoglu et al. (Eds.): SAMOS 2022, LNCS 13511, pp. 155–170, 2022.
https://doi.org/10.1007/978-3-031-15074-6_10

detailed layout simulation or rely on the working of the cryptographic algorithm to simplify simulator complexity thus limiting generality. Most of the literature on side-channel analysis of software running on general purpose micro-controllers has been in the power domain [10,13,15]. These works construct a dictionary by modeling power consumption of the micro-controller as a function of switching activity in selected architectural blocks, and then using the pre-characterized dictionary to synthesize traces for arbitrary programs running on the micro-controller. However, construction of such dictionaries may become infeasible as the number of selected blocks and their interactions and dependencies increases. Current approaches therefore compromise between complexity in dictionary construction and accuracy of synthesized traces. Moreover, the additional spatial component increases complexity in the EM versus power domain.

In this paper, we seek to develop an EM simulator that is capable of synthesizing instruction-level EM traces to assess the vulnerability of arbitrary software running on embedded micro-controllers against EM side channel attacks (EMSCAs). We present a methodology that significantly reduces the cost of dictionary construction without compromising EM trace synthesis accuracy. We achieve this by hypothesizing that in a class of non-pipelined micro-controllers possessing a single bus architecture, a condensed set of architectural blocks can be identified to characterize the EM emanation during different cycles of each instruction's execution. We identify these dominant architectural blocks to model for every cycle of all instructions in the instruction set architecture (ISA) using a statistical feature selection algorithm. By constructing dictionaries at the cycle level for dominant blocks and dependencies, only the switching activity of a small subset of architectural blocks is required to be modeled, thereby combating combinatorial explosion. We demonstrate that dominant blocks and dependencies identified at one spatial location remain consistent across others, thereby simplifying feature selection overhead. We also observe that instructions accessing the same micro-architectural components may share similarities in their EM traces and hence can be clustered during a post-processing step. This allows to share cycle dictionaries across instructions and further reduce the cost of dictionary construction. In summary, the contributions of the paper are as follows:

- We propose a simulation platform that is capable of synthesizing EM traces corresponding to arbitrary software running on embedded micro-controllers, enabling testing of software against EMSCAs at development stage;
- We propose novel feature selection and redundancy removal algorithms to identify the dominant architectural blocks for each cycle and cluster cycles of different instructions with similar EM signatures to reduce the cost of dictionary construction;
- We demonstrate our synthesis approach by implementing it on an AT89S51 micro-controller belonging to the 8051-family, where synthesized traces are evaluated on five benchmark programs and shown to be in agreement with measurements with better than 95% accuracy; and

– We use the simulator to predict the side-channel vulnerability factor (SVF) of a benchmark program. We validate the result against the SVF extracted from measured traces and show that they agree with >87% accuracy.

The rest of the paper is organized as follows: Sect. 2 discusses the related work. Section 3 details the proposed synthesis flow including the feature selection and redundancy removal algorithms for dictionary construction and synthesis. Section 4 presents an accuracy evaluation of our synthesis flow and a case study of utilizing the proposed EM trace simulator for control-flow prediction. Finally, Sect. 5 concludes the paper with a summary and an outlook on future work.

2   Related Work

EM trace simulators specifically for ASICs concerned with cryptographic algorithms have been studied in [16] and [8]. The authors investigated a pre-silicon approach by using 3D full-wave EM field solvers on a given chip layout to simulate the EM fields. Although these approaches enable prediction of susceptibility to EMSCAs during the hardware design stage, they are limited by the large overhead of simulating the entire chip layout [11]. Moreover, the study in [16] dealing with ASICs for the advanced encryption standard (AES) simplifies the simulation complexity by only considering the circuit state corresponding to the final round of AES targeted by key recovery attacks. This dependency of the simulation on the working of the target algorithm limits their applicability. An extension of this approach to a 16-bit general purpose micro-controller was presented in [9]. However, they were only able to show that the differential traces between simulation and measurement at the instruction level (difference between the traces of an instruction for its extreme values) share a similar trend. Furthermore, all such approaches require-layout related information, which may not always be available.

In the power domain, a post-silicon approach to modeling security-related power consumption of a general purpose micro-controller was presented in [13]. Power consumption at the instruction level was modeled via the switching activity of specific architectural blocks, which were assumed to be sufficient for capturing the power consumed by the micro-controller as a whole. However, the presented approach may become computationally infeasible as the number of considered architectural blocks increases, since the traces required to simulate the power consumption would need to be modeled under all combinations of the considered blocks and their dependencies. An attempt to address these issues was made in [15]. Rather than model the power consumption at the assembly language instruction level as in [13], they modeled power consumption only during assignment, arithmetic, relational and bitwise operations of a higher-level programming language (C++) used to program the micro-controller. Dictionaries for synthesizing traces corresponding to these operations were then constructed by identifying the most suitable leakage model (Hamming Weight or Hamming distance between old and new value of the variable manipulated by these operations) through correlation with the measured power trace. Therefore, accuracy

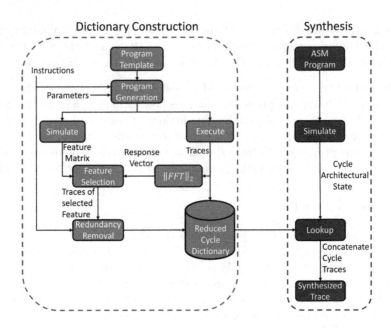

Fig. 1. Overview of our proposed EM trace synthesis approach.

in simulation of power consumed was traded off for simplicity of dictionary construction (since only a change in a single software variable as opposed to changes in several different hardware architectural blocks is considered). Our approach combats combinatorial explosion of [13] by refining the initially selected architectural blocks using feature selection to identify the dominant blocks to model for each cycle. Moreover, since we construct the dictionary at a lower level of abstraction than [15], the degradation in accuracy of synthesis is not significant.

An EM trace simulator was presented in [10] that uses a grey box modeling approach (combining hardware implementation knowledge and statistical analysis of leakage traces) similar to ours. They introduce a post-processing step to cluster dictionary entries sharing a similar leakage profile, which we similarly utilize in our work to reduce the cost of dictionary construction. However, their investigation of synthesis of EM traces is limited to one spatial location, specifically the one closest to the power pins. Moreover, only results documenting correlation between locations (in cycles) of peaks of measured and simulated EM traces is presented. By contrast, we demonstrate that our approach is capable of synthesizing EM traces across multiple spatial locations and document correlation between synthesized and measured traces for benchmarks at arbitrary cycle-level granularity.

3   EM Synthesis Flow

Figure 1 presents an overview of our proposed synthesis flow. Our approach consists of two stages, *Dictionary Construction* and *Synthesis*. In the dictionary construction stage, the micro-controller is pre-characterized to construct a dictionary capable of synthesizing EM traces. First, micro-benchmarks that execute the instruction being characterized in different contexts are generated from program templates under varying values of the parameters assumed to define the architectural state of the micro-controller, such as contents of the internal RAM (data memory), the internal ROM (program memory), the program counter, etc. The micro-benchmarks are then executed on a cycle-level simulator and a physical chip instance of the selected micro-controller to collect prediction features and EM trace measurements, respectively.

EM emanations of the real chip during micro-benchmark executions are sensed using an H-field probe and acquired. The acquired EM traces are subsequently partitioned into sub-traces of cycle length. We apply a transform (L^2-norm of the Fast Fourier Transform (FFT)) to the cycle-length traces to obtain a response variable. This transform allows us to combat any jitter in the acquired traces that may affect the feature selection process. In parallel, a cycle-level simulator is used to identify the architectural state of the CPU before and after the execution of every instruction appearing in the micro-benchmarks. The architectural state for a given cycle forms a *Feature Vector* (vector containing values of the considered parameters), and the *Feature Vectors* and their corresponding response variables are concatenated across cycles to obtain the *Feature Matrix* and the *Response Vector*, respectively.

In the final step of dictionary construction, we apply feature selection to identify the most important features in the *Feature Matrix* that best describe the *Response Vector*. Based on the results of feature selection, the collected cycle-length traces corresponding to the distinct combinations of the identified most important features are stored in the dictionary as individual entries. Finally, a post-processing step is performed to cluster the dictionary entries with similar leakage profiles to allow sharing of cycle dictionaries across instructions. The identification of such similarities allows further reduction of dictionary construction time across spatial locations.

The synthesis stage is then concerned with the synthesis of the EM trace corresponding to a given arbitrary assembly program using the dictionary constructed during pre-characterization. A given program is executed on the cycle-level simulator and the values of the dominant parameters are collected for every cycle based on the instruction appearing at that cycle. These dominant parameters are then used to lookup the dictionary entry for the corresponding stored EM trace. This process is repeated for every instruction in the program and the retrieved traces are concatenated to produce the synthesized trace.

3.1 Dictionary Construction

The power consumption and hence EM emanations of a micro-controller are generally highly correlated with the switching activity of its architectural blocks, which are in turn correlated with the switching activity at the block inputs. The architectural state at a given instant may be defined as a collection of values at the inputs of these architectural blocks at that instant. The architectural state is generally composed of the internal RAM, program memory (ROM), program counter (PC) and other registers, etc. Although each of their switching activity may contribute to the total power consumed during the execution of an instruction, some may be more dominant than others during different cycles. The dependency of power consumption on switching activity is generally described using *Hamming Weight* (HW) and *Hamming Distance* (HD) models [7]. In the following, we use the word *parameter* to refer to the HW or HD of the inputs of architectural blocks.

A *Baseline* approach to constructing a dictionary would involve collecting traces for all possible combinations of the values assumed by these parameters for all instructions and blocks active in any given cycle. However, as the number of parameters considered increases, the number of traces required to cover all possible combinations may become infeasible to measure experimentally. Instead, we propose using feature selection to identify the dominant parameters during the different cycles of an instruction and hence collect traces corresponding to these cycles. In this paper, we target EM trace synthesis for embedded micro-controllers. In non-pipelined micro-controllers, only one instruction is active in any cycle. Furthermore, in a single-bus architecture, each instruction executes in multiple cycles and only a limited number of blocks is active in each cycle. We propose a feature selection algorithm to identify the dominant blocks and parameters for each instruction and cycle. With this, the number of traces required to characterize a cycle of an instruction is proportional to the number of values assumed by its dominant parameters.

In addition, if these dominant parameters identified for different cycles of an instruction remain consistent spatially, then the cost of feature selection is incurred only for a single spatial location. Smaller dictionaries for other spatial locations can be constructed making use of this dominant feature information.

Feature Selection. In this section, we demonstrate the application of feature selection to identify the dominant parameters and show that the results obtained at one spatial location remain consistent across other locations.

In this paper, we use *RReliefF* [12] as the feature selection method. To apply feature selection to identify the dominant parameters for different cycles of an instruction, we need the *Response Vector* and the *Feature Matrix*. The feature matrix contains all the values assumed by the considered parameters during the execution of this instruction, while the response vector contains the L^2-norm of the FFT of cycles in the corresponding measured EM trace. The feature matrix and the response vector are then fed to *RReliefF*, which assigns weights to each parameter/feature considered in the feature matrix based on its relevance in predicting the response vector. Features assigned with close to zero or negative weights are considered to be statistically irrelevant and hence can be disregarded from further analysis. To select important features amongst those with positive weights, *RReliefF* employs a threshold τ [14] known as the relevance level. The features/parameters whose weights exceed the relevance level are the dominant parameters. Since we apply feature selection to each cycle separately, the dom-

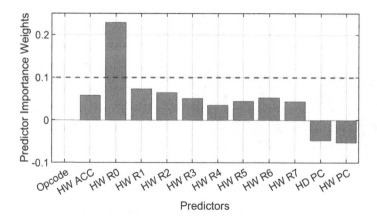

Fig. 2. Ranking of features for the third cycle of *NOP*.

inant parameters are identified for each cycle of each instruction. Therefore, a dictionary required to synthesize the EM traces for the cycles of an instruction can be constructed by collecting EM traces for distinct values assumed by the dominant parameters in each cycle as opposed to collecting EM traces for all possible values assumed by combinations of all considered parameters.

We now demonstrate the application of feature selection in identifying the dominant parameters for the third cycle of the *NOP* instruction of the microcontroller used in our experiments (see Sect. 4). The parameters considered for feature selection are the HW of the Accumulator (ACC), the HWs of General Purpose Registers (GPRs) R0-R7, the HW and the HD of the PC, and the HW of instruction-specific operands. The training set required to construct the feature matrix and the response vector are obtained by collecting the EM traces during the execution of the *NOP* instruction under varying values for the considered parameters (encompassing all possible HWs and HDs). The response vector is computed by applying the L^2 norm to the Fast Fourier Transform (FFT) of the sections of acquired traces corresponding to the third cycle, whereas the HW of ACC, HW of GPRs, and HW and HD of the PC in the third cycle form the feature matrix. Figure 2 shows the weights assigned by *RReliefF* to the considered features and for a chosen relevance level (τ) of 0.1. It is evident that the HW of R0 is the most important feature/dominant parameter, while all other features/parameters can be discarded.

To validate the sufficiency of using a single dominant parameter to build a dictionary for the third cycle of *NOP*, we compare the performances of models trained with

1. Only the highest ranked feature
2. Only the second highest ranked feature
3. A combination of the highest and second highest ranked features
4. No feature, i.e. only using an averaged trace

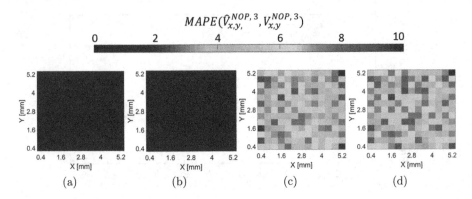

Fig. 3. Spatial variation of MAPE between true and model forecast traces for the third cycle of *NOP* for models trained with different features. The MAPE here has been averaged over 500 traces for each spatial location. (a) HW of R0, (b) HW of R0 and R1, (c) HW of R1, and (d) no feature/averaged, models.

The performance of a model in this paper is evaluated by computing the mean absolute percentage error (MAPE) between the model forecast trace and the true trace as,

$$MAPE(\hat{V}_{x,y}^{i,k}, V_{x,y}^{i,k}) = \frac{100}{n} \times \sum_{t=1}^{n} \frac{|v_{x,y,t}^{i,k} - \hat{v}_{x,y,t}^{i,k}|}{|v_{t,x,y}^{i,k}|}, \tag{1}$$

where $\hat{V}_{x,y}^{i,k}$ and $V_{x,y}^{i,k}$ are the model forecast and true measured test trace respectively, for the kth cycle of instruction i at the spatial location (x, y) containing n samples $\hat{v}_{x,y,t}^{i,k}$ and $v_{x,y,t}^{i,k}, t = 1 \ldots n$. From Fig. 3 we see that the model trained with the highest ranked feature (Fig. 3(a)) is comparable in performance to that of a two feature model (Fig. 3(b)). Therefore, since the degradation in accuracy in using a single feature model for the third cycle of *NOP* relative to the true trace is not significant, we can considerably reduce the cost of dictionary construction by using a single feature model. By contrast, models using no feature (Fig. 3(d)) or only the second highest ranked feature (Fig. 3(c)) show poor accuracy. This confirms the need for proper feature selection.

Furthermore, based on the observation that these results hold true across spatial locations, we can offset the cost of feature selection by utilizing the important feature identified at one spatial location to build dictionaries at others.

Redundancy Removal. We can further reduce the complexity of dictionary construction by identifying similarities in cycle dictionaries across instructions. If two or more instructions share the same dominant parameters for a particular cycle and their EM traces are similar, then the dictionary for that cycle can be shared. We identify such potential redundancies in cycle dictionaries of two instructions by comparing their respective cycle models after *Feature Selection*. The models for cycles at a specific spatial location, sharing the same dominant

Table 1. MAPE between model forecast traces for instruction-cycles of *NOP* and *MOV A, R0* instructions at spatial location (5 mm, 5 mm).

Instruction cycle (k)	Dominant parameters		Maximum MAPE($\hat{V}^{NOP,k}$, $\hat{V}^{MOV,k}$)
	NOP	MOV A, R0	
1	HD of PC	HD of PC	15.8%
2	HW of ACC	HW of ACC	0.3%
3	HW of R0	HW of R0	1.2%
4	*N/A**	*N/A**	*N/A**
5	*N/A**	HW of R0	*N/A**
6	HW of ACC	HW of ACC	0.5%

* Dominant parameters of cycles for which variation in traces are statistically insignificant with considered parameters are designated as *N/A*.

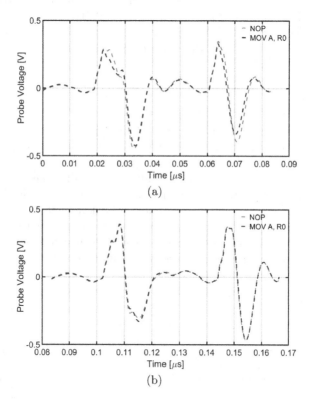

Fig. 4. EM traces for the first and second cycles of *NOP* and *MOV A, R0* at the spatial location (x,y) = (5 mm,5 mm): (a) EM traces for the first cycle show a MAPE($\hat{V}^{NOP,1}$, $\hat{V}^{MOV,1}$) of 10.6% for a HD value of the PC of 2, (b) EM traces for the second cycle show a MAPE($\hat{V}^{NOP,2}$, $\hat{V}^{MOV,2}$) of 0.01% for a HW value of the ACC of 0.

parameters are compared using the MAPE metric. A low maximum MAPE across all values of all dominant parameters implies that the models are similar and hence can be used as an indicator for potential sharing.

We demonstrate this optimization on the instructions *NOP* and *MOV A, R0* in our micro-controller. The dominant parameters for different cycles of *NOP* and *MOV A, R0* are given in Table 1. We see that the first, second, third and sixth cycles share the same dominant parameters between the two instructions. Therefore, the dictionaries for these cycles can potentially be shared. From the computed maximum MAPE metric between cycle models of *NOP* and *MOV A, R0* across all possible HWs and/or HDs of all dominant parameters, it is evident that dictionaries for the second, third and sixth cycles can be shared between the two instructions. By contrast, since the first cycle shows a large MAPE, separate dictionaries have to be built for this cycle for the two instructions. This result is visualized in Fig. 4, where the traces for the first cycle of the two instructions show a large difference as shown in Fig. 4(a), while traces for the second cycle agree with each other (Fig. 4(b)). Therefore, for this example, we can reduce the dictionary cost for one of the instructions by 50% provided we have the dictionary for the other.

3.2   Synthesis

We finally discuss the procedure for using this dictionary to synthesize complete traces of an assembly program. Given an assembly program, we execute it using a cycle-level simulator. During the execution of an instruction, we collect the values assumed by the dominant parameters (identified during the feature selection process) for all the cycles of that instruction. We then look up the dictionary for the EM traces corresponding to these values of the dominant parameters for each cycle of the instruction. These EM traces are then concatenated to synthesize the EM trace for that instruction. This procedure is repeated till the end of execution of the program to synthesize the complete trace.

4   Experiments

We evaluate our approach using an AT89S51 belonging to the 8051 family of micro-controllers built around the Intel C-51 ISA. The device operates at a clock frequency of 2 MHz and is programmed serially via an ISP programmer. The EM field emanated from the device is measured using a 1mm radius H-field probe RF-U 2.5-2 from Langer. Riscure's EM Probe Station is used to vary the spatial location of the probe over the micro-controller's area (10 mm × 10 mm). A PA303 30dB pre-amplifier is used to amplify the measured EM traces. We sample traces at 5 GS/s using a Keysight DSOS054A oscilloscope with a bandwidth of 500 MHz. Each acquired trace is averaged 200 times before being processed. Our experimental setup is shown in Fig. 5.

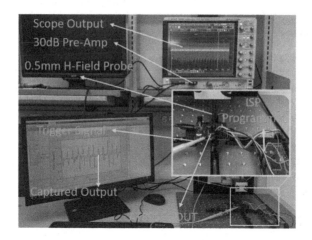

Fig. 5. Measurement setup used for acquisition of traces.

The 8051 micro-controller architecture includes a register file with 8 GPRs numbered R0-R7 and an Accumulator register ACC. Each of these registers are 8 bits wide. The GPRs along with ACC are addressed as part of the internal RAM, which is 128 bytes in size. An assembly instruction in the C-51 ISA can take any of the GPRs, the ACC or any RAM address as an operand. Consequently, their values can be manipulated by the execution of an instruction hence contributing to switching activity. Therefore, we consider these as the parameters during the micro-benchmark generation sub-stage. As stated before, the micro-benchmarks are used for collecting training data for the feature selection sub-stage. They are generated from a standard template and consist of two sections, an initialization section where random values are assigned to the considered parameters and the execution section that contains the instruction being characterized. Listing 1 shows an example micro-benchmark for collecting training data to identify the dominant parameters for the cycles of the *NOP* instruction. Traces of the instruction being characterized for varying values of the HWs and the HDs of the PC are collected by including multiple executions of the instruction in the template (for brevity, only two such *NOP* instructions are shown in Listing 1).

The accuracy of our EM simulator is evaluated by comparing the synthesized and measured traces for a set of standard benchmark programs from the Dalton benchmark suite [2]. The Dalton benchmarks were originally developed to optimize the power consumption of 8051 cores.

4.1   Accuracy and Dictionary Cost

We first evaluate the degradation in accuracy and the reduction in cost of dictionary construction due to the *Feature Selection* optimization alone. Dictionaries capable of synthesizing traces for all cycles of all the instructions in the ISA were constructed using just the feature selection optimization, where we applied *RReliefF* with 10 nearest neighbors and a relevance factor of $\tau = 0.1$.

```
PRECHAR:    CPL P1.3            ; For Triggering the Oscilloscope
            CPL P1.3

            MOV A , #1d         ; Random Values for considered parameters
            MOV R0, #40d
            MOV R1, #15d
            CLR C
            MOV R2, #159d
            MOV R3, #255d
            MOV R4, #0d
            MOV R5, #119d
            MOV R6, #64d
            MOV R7, #50d

            NOP                 ; Instruction being characterized
            NOP
            . . .
```

Listing 1: Micro-benchmark to collect training data for the *NOP* instruction.

To evaluate accuracy at instruction and cycle granularity, we generate 100 assembly programs, each containing all the instructions in the ISA in random order and with random values for all the considered parameters. EM traces for each program were synthesized using our flow and measured on the device in our lab setup. Each of the 100 synthesized and test traces corresponding to the same assembly programs are then divided into instruction- and cycle-level traces indexed using the i, k scheme described earlier. Finally, the synthesized and measured traces are compared at the instruction and cycle level using MAPE to compute accuracy. The MAPE results corresponding to the same instruction-cycle are then averaged across cycles of the same type in the 100 assembly programs. A maximum MAPE is similarly computed. Table 2 summarizes the average and maximum MAPE results for the first six instruction-cycles of all instructions. We see from the tabulated results that the average number of dominant parameters for any given cycle across all instructions is a small subset of the total considered parameters, which is consistent with our argument for feature selection. Furthermore, the degradation in accuracy between the synthesized and measured test traces is not substantial. However, compared to a baseline dictionary that would require 10^{12} entries, the total number of traces required to construct a dictionary for the whole ISA is reduced by eight orders of magnitude.

We next perform a similar evaluation of our approach when the *Redundancy Removal* optimization is used in addition to *Feature Selection*. Table 3 summarizes the result for the first six instruction-cycles of all instructions in the ISA. The table shows the number of distinct instructions along with accuracy and dictionary size results. Results show that dictionaries created for a small subset of instructions are sufficient to synthesize traces for all the other instructions in the ISA. We observe that the degradation in accuracy is slightly higher than when using the *Feature Selection* optimization alone, but is still not significant.

Table 2. Feature selection summary.

Instruction cycle	Average no. dominant param.	MAPE		No. of dict. entries
		Avg	Max	
1	2	1.0%	3.4%	2,560
2	1	1.1%	3.9%	2,304
3	1	1.1%	3.8%	2,304
4	0.9	1.6%	3.6%	8,820
5	0.7	0.3%	2.6%	2,187
6	1.1	1.6%	3.3%	3,278

Table 3. Redundancy removal summary.

Instruction cycle	No. of instructions	MAPE		No. of dict. entries	Reduction rel. to feature sel.
		Avg	Max		
1	9	1.1%	4%	90	96.5%
2	1	2.3%	4.9%	9	99.6%
3	1	1.3%	4.2%	9	99.6%
4	7	1.2%	3.8%	541	92.9%
5	6	1.7%	4.2%	54	97.5%
6	24	2.6%	4.8%	353	89.2%

However, the reduction in the number of dictionary entries is substantial. We only need to measure and record on the order of 10^3 traces to construct the entire dictionary using this optimization. This represents an over 90% reduction in dictionary size compared to feature selection alone, and a nine order of magnitude reduction compared to the baseline approach.

With the effect on accuracy and cost due to the optimizations studied, we now proceed to validate our synthesis approach on real-world benchmark programs. Accuracy is computed using the MAPE between the synthesized trace and test trace across all samples in each benchmark. Table 4 shows that the synthesized traces agree well with the test traces across the benchmark programs. Overall, synthesized traces agree with measurements with less than 5% MAPE.

Table 5 compares the computational resources required by each of the considered approaches. To ensure a fair comparison, only one trace required for building the dictionary is recorded for each micro-benchmark. All traces are stored as double precision arrays with each trace stored in the dictionaries requiring ≈ 3 KB of disk space. As discussed above, the total number of traces required to build a dictionary for the entire ISA using the *Redundancy Removal* optimization is 9 orders of magnitude lower than the *Baseline* approach. Consequently the improvement in memory and time required is substantial.

Table 4. MAPE between test and synthesized traces for benchmark programs.

Benchmarks	Size (Bytes)	MAPE
GCD	55	3%
FIB	303	3%
SORT	572	4.2%
SQRT	1167	2.8%
MATRIX	490	2.7%

Table 5. Resources for a single spatial location (5 GHz sampling frequency).

Construction method	Traces	Memory	Time
Baseline	10^{12}*	3 PB*	$\approx 5 \times 10^9$ h*
Feature selection	10^4	40 MB	60 h
Redundancy removal	10^3	4 MB	6 h

* Projected

4.2   Case Study: Compile-Time Control Flow Prediction

We further performed a case study to show the applicability of the synthesis flow in predicting the vulnerability/information leakage of a software program. We use the side-channel vulnerability factor (SVF) metric from [3] to measure the control flow leakage of the *GCD* benchmark program from [2], a snippet of which is shown in Listing 2. Control-flow leakage here refers to the certainty with which the *If-Else* block executions can be predicted using the information available through the EM side-channel. Computation of SVF requires two inputs, the *Oracle Distance Vector* and the *Side-Channel Distance Vector*. An *oracle* trace is the ground-truth pattern of *If-Else* block executions. Corresponding synthesized or measured EM traces are the *side-channel* traces. The *Oracle Distance Vector* is computed by applying a distance function to the elements of the oracle trace in a pairwise manner [1], where we choose XOR as the distance function in this work. The *Side-Channel Distance Vector* is computed in a similar manner from the side-channel trace elements, where we use the Euclidean distance between the L^2-norm of the FFT of elements as the distance function. Finally, the information leakage is estimated by computing the Pearson Correlation between the oracle and side-channel distance vectors. We computed cycle-level SVF using both synthesized and measured EM traces for six variations of the GCD benchmark using register or direct addressing and replacing the instruction at the *IF* label in Listing 2 with variants with different leakage. Results in Table 6 show that for both register and direct addressing, the measured and synthesized SVF agree with at least 87% accuracy.

```
LOOP:    MOV   A, R6
         . . .
         SETB  C
         SUBB  A, R7
         JC    ELSE
IF:      CLR   C        ;;;If-Block;;;
         MOV   A, R6
         SUBB  A, R7
         MOV   R6, A
         SJMP  LOOP
ELSE:    CLR   C        ;;;Else-Block;;;
         MOV   A, R7
         SUBB  A, R6
         MOV   R7, A
         SJMP  LOOP
```

Listing 2: Disassembled GCD program.

Table 6. Correlation of cycle-level SVF between measured and synthesized traces.

Addressing mode	IF-Instruction	SVF correlation
Register	CLR C	87%
Register	NOP	87%
Register	MOV A, R6	87%
Direct	CLR C	93%
Direct	NOP	92%
Direct	MOV A, 0×08	90%

5   Summary and Conclusions

In this paper, we presented a methodology to allow synthesis of security-relevant EM traces at instruction and cycle granularity for the class of micro-controllers possessing a single bus architecture. Different EMSCAs require varying levels of granularity in the EM traces to pose a threat to the running software. Our proposed synthesis flow allows EM traces to be synthesized at a granularity similar to that observed using measurement. Thus, we can equip software design environment with EM side-channel awareness to predict and hence fortify the software against EMSCAs during the design cycle of the software. The cost of pre-characterization was reduced through the application of feature selection to identify dominant features and redundancy removal to share dictionaries across instructions. The cost associated with collecting the training data set for feature selection was justified by demonstrating that the identified dominant features remain consistent spatially and hence the information obtained at one spatial location can be utilized to construct dictionaries at others. Traces synthesized using the proposed approach were shown to be accurate with less than 5% MAPE compared to measurements, and a case study of control-flow leakage prediction showed an agreement with measured test traces with better than 87% accuracy. In future work, we plan on extending our approach to pipelined micro-controllers.

Acknowledgments. This work was supported in part by NSF grant CCF-1901446.

References

1. Arsath, K.F.M., Ganesan, V., Bodduna, R., Rebeiro, C.: PARAM: a microprocessor hardened for power side-channel attack resistance. In: HOST (2020)
2. Dalton-Project: Benchmark Applications for Synthesizeable VHDL Model, University of California Riverside. http://www.ann.ece.ufl.edu/i8051/i8051benchmarks/index.html
3. Demme, J., Martin, R., Waksman, A., Sethumadhavan, S.: Side-channel vulnerability factor: a metric for measuring information leakage. In: ISCA (2012)
4. Genkin, D., Pachmanov, L., Pipman, I., Tromer, E.: ECDH key-extraction via low-bandwidth electromagnetic attacks on PCs. In: CT-RSA (2016)
5. Getz, R., Moeckel, B.: Understanding and eliminating EMI in microcontroller applications (1996)
6. Han, Y., Etigowni, S., Liu, H., Zonouz, S., Petropulu, A.: Watch me, but don't touch me! contactless control flow monitoring via electromagnetic emanations. In: CCCS (2017)
7. Iyer, V.V., Yilmaz, A.E.: Using the ANOVA F-statistic to isolate information-revealing near-field measurement configurations for embedded systems. In: EMC+SIPI (2021)
8. Kumar, A., Scarborough, C., Yilmaz, A., Orshansky, M.: Efficient simulation of EM side-channel attack resilience. In: ICCAD (2017)
9. Li, H., Markettos, A., Moore, S.: Security evaluation against electromagnetic analysis at design time. In: HLDVT (2005)
10. McCann, D., Oswald, E., Whitnall, C.: Towards practical tools for side channel aware software engineering: 'Grey Box' modelling for instruction leakages. In: USENIX Security (2017)
11. Menichelli, F., Menicocci, R., Olivieri, M., Trifiletti, A.: High-level side-channel attack modeling and simulation for security-critical systems on chips. IEEE TDSC **5**(3), 164–176 (2008)
12. Robnik-Sikonja, M., Kononenko, I.: An adaptation of relief for attribute estimation in regression. In: ICML (1997)
13. Thuillet, C., Andouard, P., Ly, O.: A smart card power analysis simulator. In: CSE (2009)
14. Urbanowicz, R.J., Meeker, M., La Cava, W., Olson, R.S., Moore, J.H.: Relief-based feature selection: introduction and review. J. Biomed. Inf. **85**, 189–203 (2018)
15. Veshchikov, N.: SILK: high level of abstraction leakage simulator for side channel analysis. In: PPREW (2014)
16. Yoshikawa, M., Asai, T.: Platform for verification of electromagnetic analysis attacks against cryptographic circuits. In: ITNG (2013)

Deep Learning Optimization I

A Design Space Exploration Methodology for Enabling Tensor Train Decomposition in Edge Devices

Milad Kokhazadeh[1], Georgios Keramidas[1,2(✉)], Vasilios Kelefouras[3], and Iakovos Stamoulis[2]

[1] School of Informatics, Aristotle University of Thessaloniki, Thessaloniki, Greece
{kokhazad,gkeramidas}@csd.auth.gr
[2] Think Silicon, S.A. An Applied Materials Company, Patras, Greece
{g.keramidas,i.stamoulis}@think-silicon.com
[3] School of Engineering, Computing and Mathematics, University of Plymouth, Plymouth, UK
vasilios.kelefouras@plymouth.ac.uk

Abstract. Deep Neural Networks (DNN) have made significant advances in various fields, including speech recognition and image processing. Typically, modern DNNs are both compute and memory intensive and as a consequence their deployment on edge devices is a challenging problem. A well-known technique to address this issue is Low-Rank Factorization (LRF), where a weight tensor is approximated with one or more lower-rank tensors, reducing the number of executed instructions and memory footprint. However, finding an efficient solution is a complex and time-consuming process as LRF includes a huge design space and different solutions provide different trade-offs in terms of FLOPs, memory size, and prediction accuracy. In this work a methodology is presented that formulates the LRF problem as a (FLOPs vs. memory vs. prediction accuracy) Design Space Exploration (DSE) problem. Then, the DSE space is drastically pruned by removing inefficient solutions. Our experimental results prove that it is possible to output a limited set of solutions with better accuracy, memory, and FLOPs compared to the original (non-factorized) model. Our methodology has been developed as a standalone, parameterized module integrated into T3F library of TensorFlow 2.X.

Keywords: Deep neural networks · Network compression · Low-rank factorization · Tensor train · Design space exploration

1 Introduction

In recent years, the world has witnessed the era of Artificial Intelligence (AI) revolution, especially in the fields of Machine Learning (ML) and Deep Learning (DL), attracting the attention of many researchers in various applications fields [1]. Such an example is the Internet-of-Things (IoT) ML-based applications, where DNNs are employed on embedded devices with limited compute and memory capabilities [2].

© The Author(s), under exclusive license to Springer Nature Switzerland AG 2022
A. Orailoglu et al. (Eds.): SAMOS 2022, LNCS 13511, pp. 173–186, 2022.
https://doi.org/10.1007/978-3-031-15074-6_11

State-of-the-art DNN models consist of a vast number of parameters (hundreds of billions) and require trillions of computational operations not only during the training, but also at the inference phase [3]. Therefore, executing these models on Resource-Constrained Devices (RCD), e.g., edge and IoT devices, is a challenging task. The problem becomes even more challenging when the target applications are characterized by specific real-time constraints [4]. As a result, many techniques have been recently proposed to compress and accelerate DNN models [5, 6]. DNN compression methods reduce the model's memory size and computational requirements without significantly impacting its accuracy. In general, DNN compression techniques are classified into five main categories [6]: pruning [7], quantization [8], compact convolutional filters [9], knowledge distillation [10], and low-rank factorization [11].

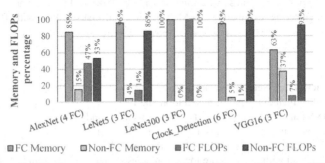

Fig. 1. Memory and FLOPs percentages of FC and Non-FC layers for the five different models considered in this work. FC layers take up a large portion of a DNN model's memory (from 63% up to 100%)

Pruning techniques reduce the complexity of DNN models by removing unnecessary elements [7] (e.g., neurons or filters [12–14]). Quantization is a well-studied technique targeting to transform the 32-bit Floating-Point (FP32) weights and/or activations into less-accurate data types e.g., INT8 or FP16 [8]. In the compact convolutional filter techniques, special structural convolutional filters are designed to reduce the parameter space and save storage/computations [9]. Finally, knowledge distillation is the process of transferring the knowledge from a large model to a smaller one by following a student-teacher learning model [15]. The two latter techniques can be applied only to the convolutional layers [6]. On the contrary, Low-Rank Factorization (LRF) can be used to reduce both the number of Floating Point Operations (FLOPs) as well as the memory size in both convolutional and Fully Connected (FC) layers by transforming the original tensors into smaller ones [11]. However, employing LRF in a neural network model is not trivial: it includes a huge design space and different solutions provide different trade-offs among FLOPs, memory size, and prediction accuracy; therefore, finding an efficient solution is not a trivial task.

In this paper, we provide a methodology to guide the LRF process focusing on the FC layers of typical DNN models, as the FC memory arrays typically account for the largest percentage of overall memory size of DNN models. Figure 1 indicates that the memory size of FC layers' ranges from 63% up to 100% of the total DNN memory size.

The steps of the proposed methodology are as follows. First, all the FC layers' parameters are extracted from a given DNN model. Second, all possible LRF solutions are generated using the T3F library [16]. Then, the vast design space is pruned in two phases and a (limited) set of solutions is selected for re-evaluation/calibration according to specific target metrics (FLOPs, memory size, and accuracy) that are provided as inputs to our methodology.

The main contributions of this work are:

- A method that formulates the LRF problem as a (FLOPs, memory size, accuracy) DSE problem
- A step-by-step methodology that effectively prunes the design space
- A fully parameterized and standalone DSE tool integrated into T3F library (part of TensorFlow 2.X [17])
- An evaluation of the proposed DSE approach on five popular DNN models

The Rest of This Paper is Organized as Follows: In Sect. 2, we put this work in the context of related work and present the relevant background information. The proposed methodology is presented in a step-by-step basis in Sect. 3, while the experimental results are discussed in Sect. 4. Finally, Sect. 5 is dedicated to conclusions and future work.

2 Background and Related Works

2.1 Low-Rank Factorization

LRF refers to the process of approximating and decomposing a matrix or a tensor by using smaller matrices or tensors [18]. Suppose $M \in \mathbb{R}^{m \times n}$ is a matrix with m rows and n columns. Given a rank r, M can be approximated by $M' \in \mathbb{R}^{m \times n}$; M' has a lower rank k and it can be represented by the product of two (or more) thinner matrices $U \in \mathbb{R}^{m \times k}$ and $V \in \mathbb{R}^{k \times n}$ with m rows/k columns and k rows/n columns, respectively (as shown in Fig. 2). The element (i,j) from M is retrieved by multiplying the $i\text{-}th$ row of U by the $j\text{-}th$ column of V. The original matrix M needs to store $m \times n$ elements, while the approximated matrix M' needs to store $(m \times k) + (k \times n)$ elements [18].

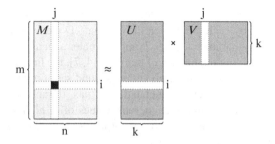

Fig. 2. Low-Rank Factorization (LRF)

To decompose the input matrices, different methods exist, such as Singular Value Decomposition (SVD) [19–21], QR decomposition [22, 23], interpolative decomposition [24], and none-negative factorization [25]. Given that tensors are multidimensional generalizations of matrices, they need different methods to be decomposed e.g., Tucker Decomposition [26, 27] or Canonical Polyadic Decomposition (CPD) [28, 29]. Another way to decompose tensors is to transform the input tensor into a two-dimensional (2D) matrix and then perform the decomposition process using one of the abovementioned matrix decomposition techniques [30, 31].

2.2 Tensor-Train (TT) Format and T3F Library

A popular method to decompose the multidimensional tensors is the TT format, proposed in [32]. This is a stable method and does not suffer from curse of dimensionality [32]; furthermore, the number of parameters needed is similar to that in CPD [32]. A Tensor $A(j_1, j_2, ..., j_d)$ with d dimensions can be represented in TT format if for each element with index $j_k = 1, 2, ..., n_k$ and each dimension $k = 1, 2, ..., d$ there is a collection of matrices $G_k[j_k]$ such that all the elements of A can be computed by the following product [33]:

$$A(j_1, j_2, ..., j_d) = G_1[j_1]G_2[j_2]...G_d[j_d] \qquad (1)$$

All the matrices $G_k[j_k]$ related to the same dimension k are restricted to be of the same size $r_{k-1} \times r_k$. The values r_0 and r_d are equal to 1 in order to keep the matrix product (Eq. 1) of size 1×1.

As noted, the proposed DSE methodology is built on top of the T3F library as a fully parameterized, stand-alone module. T3F is a library [16] for TT-Decomposition and currently is only available for FC layers (however our methodology is general enough and can be applied also in convolution layers; however, extending the proposed methodology in convolution layers is left for future work). In the current version, our target is the FC layers, because as depicted in Fig. 1, the FC layers occupy the largest memory size in typical DNN architectures. The main primitive of T3F library is *TT-Matrix*, a generalization of the Kronecker product [34]. By using the *TT-format*, T3F library compresses the 2D array of a FC layer by using a small set of parameters.

The inputs to the modified T3F module are: i) the weight matrix of the original FC layer (2D array), ii) the max_tt_rank value, and iii) a set of tensor configuration parameters. The latter set of parameters is related to the shape of the output tensors; if these tensors are multiplied by each other, then the original 2D matrix can be approximated e.g., the following set of parameters [4, 5, 7] approximates a matrix of size 784×625. In other words, by multiplying the first set of numbers [4, 7], the first dimension of weight matrix (784) is produced and by multiplying the second set of numbers [5], the second dimension of weight matrix (625) is generated. The max_tt_rank parameter defines the density of the compression; small max_tt_rank values offer higher compression rate. After the decomposition is done, T3F library outputs a set of 4D tensors (called cores) with the following shapes/parameters sizes:

Core #1 dim: $(1, s_1, o_1, \max\_tt\_rank)$.

Core #2 dim: $(\max\_tt\_rank, s_2, o_2, \max\_tt\_rank)$.

Core #3 dim: (max _tt_rank, s_3, o_3, max _tt_rank).

Core #4 dim: (max _tt_rank, s_4, o_4, 1).

where s_1, s_2, s_3, s_4 and o_1, o_2, o_3, o_4 are related to the set of tensor configuration parameters ($[[s_1, s_2, s_3, s_4], [o_1, o_2, o_3, o_4]]$). As noted, if the above tensors are multiplied by each other, the original 2D matrix is approximated. The overall memory size needed is given by the following formula (2):

$$(1 \times s_1 \times o_1 \times \max\_tt\_rank) + (\max\_tt\_rank \times s_2 \times o_2 \times \max\_tt\_rank)$$
$$+ (\max\_tt\_rank \times s_3 \times o_3 \times \max\_tt\_rank) + (\max\_tt\_rank \times s_4 \times o_4 \times 1) \quad (2)$$

2.3 Motivation

The main challenge in employing LRF for a specific DNN model is to select a suitable rank parameter [31]. Given a predefined rank value, the process of extracting the decomposed matrices or tensors is a well-defined and straightforward process. For example, for an input matrix M and for a given rank value r, the (output) low rank matrix with the minimal or target approximation error can be generated by employing the SVD algorithm [35].

While many researchers devised techniques targeting to find the best rank value [31, 36–38], it has been proven that this is an NP-hard problem [31]. For example, assuming a max rank value of 10 in LeNet5 model [39] (LeNet5 consists of three FC layers with dimensions 400 × 120, 120 × 84, and 84 × 10, respectively), the entire design space contains about 252 million possible ways to configure the decomposed matrices. Given that a model calibration phase (typically for more than three epochs) must be employed for each extracted solution, this means that 252M × 3 × 1 s (approximately 8750 days assuming that each epoch takes about 1 s) are needed to cover the whole design space. To the best our knowledge there is no similar work that formulates the LRF problem as a DSE problem.

3 Methodology

To address the above problem, a DSE methodology and a fully parameterized tool are proposed in this work. The target is to ease and guide the LRF process in FC layers. The

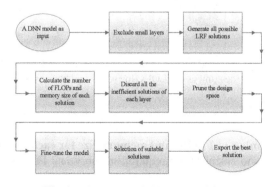

Fig. 3. The proposed DSE methodology

main steps of the proposed methodology are shown in Fig. 3. In the rest of this section, a detailed description of each step in Fig. 3 is provided.

1. Exclude small layers: As noted, the first step of our approach is to extract and analyze all FC layers of a given DNN model. Among all the extracted FC layers, the layers with small memory sizes with respect to the overall memory footprint of the model (based on a threshold) are discarded. The aim of LFR is to reduce the memory size and computations required, thus applying LRF to layers with meager sizes does not provide significant memory/FLOP gains. As part of this work, a threshold with value equal to 10% (found experimentally) is used i.e., the layers of which the memory size is less than 10% of the overall DNN size are not considered in our methodology. Further quantifying this threshold is left for future work.

2. Generate all possible LRF solutions: In this step, all different LRF solutions are extracted using our methodology and generated by using the T3F library. For all remaining cases, the weight matrices are converted to smaller size tensors according to TT format. Note that in our approach, each solution (related to a weight matrix) is extracted as a set of configuration parameters. The first one is the length (based on the numbers participating in the composition e.g., for $100 = 2 * 5 * 5 * 2$, the combination length is equal to 4). The second number is the maximum rank. The maximum rank defines how dense the compression will be. In this step, all possible solutions are extracted for each layer individually.

Let us give an example by using the well-known AlexNet model [40]. There are four FC layers in the AlexNet model; two of which are excluded by step 1. The remaining layers are of size 4096×4096 and 4096×1000, respectively. In both layers, 11 different rank values are included: $\{2, 3, \ldots\ldots, 12\}$. Figure 4 depicts all different solutions for the first layer. As we can see, there are 7759741 different solutions for this layer.

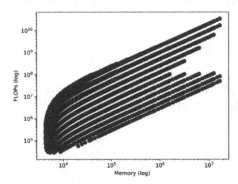

Fig. 4. All possible solutions based on T3F library for a layer of size 4096×4096 in the AlexNet model. Vertical axis shows the number of FLOPs (log scale) and horizontal axis shows the number of parameters (log scale)

3. Calculate the number of FLOPs and memory size for each solution: The mathematical expressions to calculate the required memory and FLOPs for each solution are given by Eqs. (3) and (4), respectively. More specifically, assuming a FC layer with shape *[X, Y]*, the memory size is given by the following formula:

$$Memory\_required = ((\sum_{i=1}^{L} \prod_{j=1}^{4} c_{i,j}) + Y) \times Type\_size \tag{3}$$

where L is amount of cores/length of combination, $c_{i,j}$ is j-th element in the i-th core, and Y is the length of bias vector. The LRF takes as input a 2D array and generates a number of 4D tensors (called also cores). To calculate the memory size required for a layer, we need first to calculate and sum up the number of parameters for each core. Then, the bias must be added to the calculated value. Finally, to find the required memory, the number of parameters is multiplied by the number of bytes for the used data type (e.g., 4 bytes for FP).

The number of FLOPs is given by the following formula:

$$FLOPs = (\sum_{i=L}^{1} (cl_i \times cr_i \times inr_i + (\prod_{j=1}^{4} c_{i,j} + inl_i \times inr_i))) + Y \tag{4}$$

where $inr_i = \prod_{j=1}^{L-1} x_j$, $inl_i = c_{i,2} \times c_{i,4}$, $cr_i = c_{i,2} \times c_{i,4}$, $cl_i = c_{i,1} \times c_{i,3}$ and x_j is j-th element in the input combination.

4. Discard inefficient solutions of each layer: As mentioned above, the design space is vast, therefore fine-tuning or calibrating the model for all possible solutions is not feasible. To address this, the whole design space (illustrated as a FLOPs vs. memory size pareto curve) is divide into four rectangles (see Fig. 5). The top-right part (red part in Fig. 5) is excluded for the remaining steps, since it contains solutions that require more memory and more FLOPs compared to the non-factorized (initial) solution. Note that the blue dot in the center of the graph corresponds to the memory/FLOPs of the initial layer. The top-left and bottom-right parts (yellow parts) are also excluded in the current version of our methodology. Although the latter two parts can contain acceptable solutions, we have excluded them as the solutions in these parts require more FLOPs (top left) or more memory (bottom right) compared to the initial model. The bottom left part (green part) includes solutions that exhibit less memory and less FLOPs with respect to the initial layer. As part of this work, we consider only the solutions in the green box i.e., these solutions will be forwarded to the remaining steps of our methodology. The solutions included in the two yellow boxes will be re-considered in a future version of this work.

5. Prune the design space: Till now, we considered each layer separately. As a next step, we take into consideration all the FC layers of the input DNN model in a unified way. In particular, in the current step, the 2D design space (green part in Fig. 5) of each layer is further broken down into smaller rectangles (tiles) of predefined size. In this paper, an 8 × 8 grid is considered i.e., each green rectangle in Fig. 5 is broken down into 64 tiles. Examining alternative configurations (e.g., 4 × 4 or 16 × 16 grids) is left for future work. The bottom-line idea is that the solutions residing into the same tile will exhibit a similar behavior. To safeguard the latter approach, multiple points (solutions) from each tile are extracted. More specifically, the four following solutions are considered from each tile:

- **Point 1:** min_FLOPs and min_memory
- **Point 2:** min_FLOPs and max_memory
- **Point 3:** max_FLOPs and min_memory
- **Point 4:** max_FLOPs and max_memory

The four solutions above include the best and worst solutions in terms of FLOPs and/or memory per tile; the solutions with highest FLOPs and memory (max_FLOPs, max_memory) are selected as it is more likely to provide higher prediction accuracy (after the re-calibration/training phase). Given that there are 64 tiles, a maximum number equal to 4×64 solutions are further processed for each layer and the rest are being discarded.

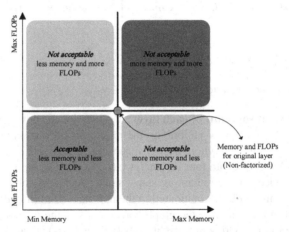

Fig. 5. The design space is illustrated as (FLOPs vs. memory) pareto curves and partitioned into rectangles. The red part and yellow parts are pruned (excluded) because they contain solutions with more memory and/or FLOPs compared to the original (non-factorized) layer (Color figure online)

After the design space is pruned at a layer level, the corresponding tiles of all layers are merged and the four points mentioned above are extracted. However, when multiple FC layers co-exist in the model (which is typically the case), the approach illustrated in Fig. 6 is followed. The main problem that we need to tackle at this point is that different layers might include tiles of different scales and consequently very diverse memory and FLOPs requirements. To address this in our methodology, each layer is organized as a separate grid in order to take into account the different scales (i.e., the size of each layer) as depicted in Fig. 6. Note that in the case of multiple FC layers, the corresponding grid cells must be selected for all layers. In the special case in which no solution exists in the corresponding grid tile (in one or more layers), the following two approaches are considered in our methodology: i) the nearest grid cell (to the empty cell) must be found and solutions from that cell are selected and ii) the grid cells that have at least one layer with no solution are skipped (excluded) and we only consider the grid cells where all layers contain at least one solution. This is illustrated in Fig. 6.

Let us give an example based on AlexNet model. Recall that in our methodology we consider two layers of AlexNet model with shapes 4096 × 4096 and 4096 × 1000 (shown in Fig. 6). It is clear that for each grid cell in the first layer (Fig. 6.a), there is an unique corresponding grid cell in the second layer (Fig. 6.b). By relying in the second grid cell selection policy (mentioned above) for the empty cells, many solutions will be further excluded and will not be considered in the following steps of the approach, further pruning the design space.

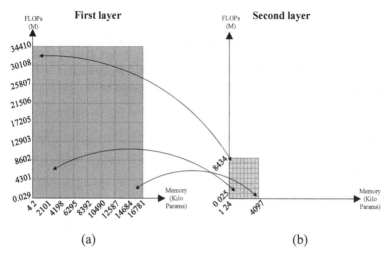

Fig. 6. An 8 × 8 grid corresponding to the AlexNet model. Two FC layers have been selected from the model for factorization. The left part of the figure (a) depicts the first layer with shape 4096 × 4096 (16781K parameters) and the right part (b) shows the second layer with shape 4096 × 1000 (4097K parameters). For each grid cell in the first layer (a), there is a unique grid cell in the second layer (c)

6. Fine-tune the remaining solutions: After selecting different points from each tile, the next step is to calibrate (i.e., re-train) the model for the extracted solutions and for a limited number of epochs (e.g., three to five epochs). The output of the latter step is to accommodate each extracted solution with the following points: FLOPs, memory, and accuracy loss.

7. Selection of suitable solutions: The next and final step is to go through the output solutions and produce the final output based on specific high-level criteria. This means that after step 6 is completed (calculation of loss and accuracy for the remaining solutions), we can enforce specific constrains (set by the user or the application) in terms of memory footprint reduction, FLOPs reduction, and/or accuracy loss. Note that our

Table 1. Number of solutions after each step. After step 7, solutions with accuracy degradation more than 1.5% are excluded

Method	Parameters (M)		Number of Solutions				Dataset
	Model	*FC (%)*	*Original*	*After step 4*	*After step 5*	*After step 7*	
LeNet5	0.062	0.059 (95.8%)	1528 M	157 M	156	150	MNIST
LeNet300	0.267	0.267 (100%)	1495 M	239 M	156	137	MNIST
VGG16	39.98	25.21 (63%)	7285832 G	1012815 G	144	43	CIFAR10
Alexet	25.73	21.94 (85.3%)	4327 G	2454 G	140	135	CIFAR10
Clock_Detection	0.96	0.912 (94.9%)	16 G	1708 M	256	215	Self-generated

approach is fully parameterized and any kind of high-level criteria can be employed (e.g., to exclude the solutions that have >1.5% accuracy drop). Table 1 shows in details the initial number of LRF solutions and the solutions that are pruned in each step of the proposed methodology for the five models that we consider in this work.

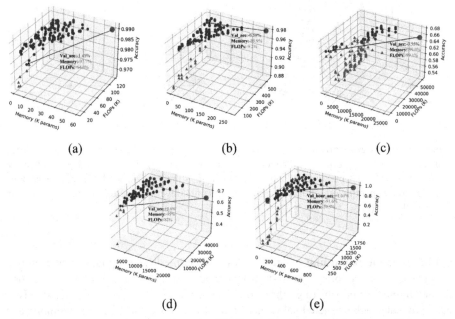

(a)   (b)   (c)

(d)   (e)

Fig. 7. 3D pareto curves (memory footprint, FLOPs, and accuracy) for the five studied models: (a) LeNet5, (b) LeNet300, (c) VGG16, (d) AlexNet, and (e) Clock_Detection. Green circles correspond to the non-factorized model; blue circles indicate the solutions with accuracy drop less than 1.5%; red triangles show the solutions with accuracy drop more than 1.5% (Color figure onlie)

4 Experimental Results

As noted our evaluation is based on multiple datasets and DNN models: LeNet300 and LeNet5 on MNIST dataset; AlexNet and VGG16 on CIFAR10 dataset; and Clock Detection model on self-generated data. In all cases, we compare our experimental results to the baseline (not factorized model). All experiments are initialized from reference models that we have developed from scratch and train for 100 epochs. For each compressed model, we report its validation accuracy, storage (number of parameters), and FLOPs. We calculate FLOPs based on the assumption that each multiplication or addition are considered as one FLOPs. For example, in a forward pass through a FC layer with weight matrix of m × n and bias of n × 1, the considered FLOPs are $2 \times m \times n + n$. We use an 8x8 grid for all cases and we exclude the solutions with > 1.5% accuracy drop compared to the initial model. The final results are shown in Fig. 7 as 3D pareto curve (memory, FLOPs, and accuracy) for each evaluated model.

In each graph in Fig. 7, the green circles correspond to the non-factorized model, the blue circles are referred to the solutions with accuracy drop less than 1.5% with respect to the initial model, and the red triangles are referred to the solutions with accuracy drop more than 1.5%. In addition, the extracted solution with the lowest memory footprint is annotated with the black arrow in all cases. Our experimental results on MNIST dataset show that we managed to achieve a 97.7% memory reduction in the LeNet5 model (Fig. 7.a) and 89.9% memory reduction in the LeNet300 model (Fig. 7.b) with only 1.45% and 0.59% accuracy drop, respectively. Similar results can be seen in the other models as well.

Table 2. Example solutions extracted from our methodology (numbers with green colors represent a reduction in memory footprint or number of flops or an increase in model accuracy; number with red colors correspond to accuracy drop). All numbers are normalized to the corresponding parameters of the initial model

Models (initial parameters)	Memory reduction	FLOPs reduction	Accuracy	Example Solutions
LeNet5 (Acc.=0.99, Mem.=58284, FLOPs=116364)	40.6%	11.3%	0.2%	*highest accuracy*
	97.7%	64.4%	−1.45%	*lowest memory*
	90.4%	86.2%	−0.4%	*lowest FLOPs*
LeNet300 (Acc.=0.979, Mem.=265600, FLOPs=530800)	84%	10.7%	0.1%	*highest accuracy*
	89.9%	9.2%	−0.59%	*lowest memory*
	88.5%	84.6%	−1.3%	*lowest FLOPs*
VGG 16 (Acc.=0.653, Mem.=33562624, FLOPs=50339840)	62.5%	25%	3.33%	*highest accuracy*
	99.9%	99.1%	−0.55%	*lowest memory*
	99.9%	99.1%	−0.55%	*lowest FLOPs*
AlexNet (Acc.=0.6408, Mem.=20878312, FLOPs=41751528)	62%	13%	13%	*highest accuracy*
	95%	82%	0.6%	*lowest memory*
	87%	83.9%	8.9%	*lowest FLOPs*
Clock_Detection (Acc.=0.97, Mem.=907400, FLOPs=1814600)	74.5%	61.5%	2.88%	*highest accuracy*
	91.6%	59.5%	1.64%	*lowest memory*
	91.5%	87%	−1.14%	*lowest FLOPs*

For clarity reasons, Table 2 present three specific example cases for all the models considered in this work. The three cases correspond to the solutions with: highest reported accuracy, lowest memory, and lowest FLOPs. As Table 2 indicates, our methodology is able to extract solutions exhibiting a reduction in memory footprint from 40.6% (in LeNet5) up to 99.9% (in VGG16) and a reduction in number of FLOPs from 9.2% (in LeNet300) up to 99.1% (in VGG16). Finally, it is important to note, that in many cases, our approach manages not only to reduce the memory footprint and the number of FLOPs, but also to increase the prediction accuracy of the specific models. More specifically, an increase in the accuracy is reported in eight out the 15 cases (up to 13% increase in AlexNet) as shown in Table 2.

5 Conclusion

In this paper, we presented a practical methodology that formulates the compression problem in DNN models using LRF as a DSE problem. The proposed methodology is able to extract a suitable set of solutions in a reasonable time. We evaluated our methodology on five different DNN models. Our experimental findings revealed that the proposed approach can offer a wide range of solutions that are able to compress the DNN models up to 97.7% with minimal impact in accuracy. Part of our future work includes the investigation of the additional techniques to further prune the design space. In addition, we plan to employ our methodology to different types of NN layers such as convolution layers. Finally, we also plan to extent and customize our methodology to NN belonging to different application areas, such as object detection, image segmentation, text and video processing.

Acknowledgements. This research has been supported by the H2020 Framework Program of the European Union through the Affordable5G Project (Grant Agreement 957317) and by a sponsored research agreement between Applied Materials, Inc. and Aristotle University of Thessaloniki, Greece (Grant Agreement 72714).

References

1. Hussain, F., Hussain, R., Hassan, S.A., Hossain, E.: Machine learning in IoT security: current solutions and future challenges. Commun. Surv. Tutor. (2020)
2. Saraswat, S., Gupta, H.P., Dutta, T.: A writing activities monitoring system for preschoolers using a layered computing infrastructure. Sens. J. (2019)
3. Mishra, A., et al.: Accelerating sparse deep neural networks. arXiv preprint arXiv:2104.08378 (2021)
4. Akmandor, A.O., Hongxu, Y.I.N., Jha, N.K.: Smart, secure, yet energy-efficient, internet-of-things sensors. Trans. Multi-scale Comput. Syst. (2018)
5. Long, X., Ben, Z., Liu, Y.: A survey of related research on compression and acceleration of deep neural networks. J. Phys. Conf. Ser. (2019)
6. Cheng, Y., Wang, D., Zhou, P., Zhang, T.: A survey of model compression and acceleration for deep neural networks. arXiv preprint arXiv:1710.09282 (2017)
7. Pasandi, M.M., Hajabdollahi, M., Karimi, N., Samavi, S.: Modeling of pruning techniques for deep neural networks simplification. arXiv preprint arXiv:2001.04062 (2020)

8. Song, Z., et al.: Dynamic region-based quantization for deep neural network acceleration. In: International Symposium on Computer Architecture (2020)
9. Huang, F., Zhang, L., Yang, Y., Zhou, X.: Probability weighted compact feature for domain adaptive retrieval. International Conference on Computer Vision and Pattern Recognition (2020)
10. Blakeney, C., Li, X., Yan, Y., Zong, Z.: Parallel blockwise knowledge distillation for deep neural network compression. IEEE Trans. Parallel Distrib. Syst. (2020)
11. Phan, A.-H., et al.: Stable low-rank tensor decomposition for compression of convolutional neural network. In: Vedaldi, A., Bischof, H., Brox, T., Frahm, J.-M. (eds.) ECCV 2020. LNCS, vol. 12374, pp. 522–539. Springer, Cham (2020). https://doi.org/10.1007/978-3-030-58526-6_31
12. He, Y., Kang, G., Dong, X., Fu, Y., Yang, Y.: Soft filter pruning for accelerating deep convolutional neural networks. arXiv preprint arXiv:1808.06866 (2018)
13. He, Y., Zhang, X., Sun, J.: Channel pruning for accelerating very deep neural networks. In: International Conference on Computer Vision (2017)
14. Han, S., Pool, J., Tran, J., Dally, W.J.: Learning both weights and connections for efficient neural networks. arXiv preprint arXiv:1506.02626 (2015)
15. Gou, J., Yu, B., Maybank, S.J., Tao, D.: Knowledge distillation: a survey. J. Comput. Vision (2021)
16. Novikov, A., Izmailov, P., Khrulkov, V., Figurnov, M., Oseledets, I.V.: Tensor train decomposition on TensorFlow (T3F). J. Mach. Learn. (2020)
17. Abadi, M., et al.: Tensorflow: a system for large-scale machine learning. USENIX Symposium on Operating Systems Design and Implementation (2016)
18. Sainath, T.N., Kingsbury, B., Sindhwani, V., Arisoy, E., Ramabhadran, B.: Low-rank matrix factorization for deep neural network training with high-dimensional output targets. In: International Conference on Acoustics, Speech and Signal Processing (2013)
19. Zhang, J., Lei, Q., Dhillon, I.: Stabilizing gradients for deep neural networks via efficient SVD parameterization. In: International Conference on Machine Learning (2018)
20. Bejani, M.M., Ghatee, M.: Theory of adaptive SVD regularization for deep neural networks. J. Neural Netw. (2020)
21. Swaminathan, S., Garg, D., Kannan, R., Andres, F.: Sparse low rank factorization for deep neural network compression. J. Neurocomput. (2020)
22. Chorti, A., Picard, D.: Rate analysis and deep neural network detectors for SEFDM FTN systems. arXiv preprint arXiv:2103.02306 (2021)
23. Ganev, I., Walters, R.: The QR decomposition for radial neural networks. arXiv preprint arXiv:2107.02550 (2021)
24. Chee, J., Renz, M., Damle, A., De Sa, C.: Pruning neural networks with interpolative decompositions. arXiv preprint arXiv:2108.00065 (2021)
25. Chan, T.K., Chin, C.S., Li, Y.: Non-negative matrix factorization-convolutional neural network (NMF-CNN) for sound event detection. arXiv preprint arXiv:2001.07874 (2020)
26. Li, D., Wang, X., Kong, D.: Deeprebirth: accelerating deep neural network execution on mobile devices. Conference on Artificial Intelligence (2018)
27. Bai, Z., Li, Y., Woźniak, M., Zhou, M., Li, D.: DecomVQANet: decomposing visual question answering deep network via tensor decomposition and regression. J. Pattern Recogn. (2021)
28. Gaetan, F., Gabriel, M., Olga, F.: Canonical polyadic decomposition and deep learning for machine fault detection. arXiv preprint arXiv:2107.09519 (2021)
29. Ma, R., Lou, J., Li, P., Gao, J.: Reconstruction of generative adversarial networks in cross modal image generation with canonical polyadic decomposition. In: Wireless Communications and Mobile Computing Conference (2021)
30. Kolda, T.G., Bader, B.W.: Tensor decompositions and applications. J. SIAM Rev. (2009)

31. Idelbayev, Y., Carreira-Perpinán, M.A.: Low-rank compression of neural nets: learning the rank of each layer. In: Conference on Computer Vision and Pattern Recognition (2020)
32. Oseledets, I.V.: Tensor-train decomposition. SIAM J. Sci. Comput. (2011)
33. Novikov, A., Podoprikhin, D., Osokin, A., Vetrov, D.: Tensorizing neural networks. arXiv preprint arXiv:1509.06569 (2015)
34. Pollock, D., Stephen, G.: Multidimensional arrays, indices and Kronecker products. J. Econometrics (2021)
35. Golub, G.H., Van Loan, C.F.: Matrix Computations. Johns Hopkins University Press, Baltimore (2013)
36. Hawkins, C., Liu, X., Zhang, Z.: Towards compact neural networks via end-to-end training: a Bayesian tensor approach with automatic rank determination. arXiv preprint arXiv:2010.08689 (2020)
37. Cheng, Z., Li, B., Fan, Y., Bao, Y.: A novel rank selection scheme in tensor ring decomposition based on reinforcement learning for deep neural networks. In: International Conference on Acoustics, Speech and Signal Processing (2020)
38. Kim, T., Lee, J., Choe, Y.: Bayesian optimization-based global optimal rank selection for compression of convolutional neural networks. IEEE Access (2020)
39. LeCun, Y.: LeNet-5, convolutional neural networks (2015). http://yann.lecun.com/exdb/lenet/
40. Krizhevsky, A., Sutskever, I., Hinton, G.E.: ImageNet classification with deep convolutional neural networks. Commun. ACM (2017)

Study of DNN-Based Ragweed Detection from Drones

Martin Lechner[✉][iD], Lukas Steindl, and Axel Jantsch[iD]

Christian Doppler Laboratory for Embedded Machine Learning, Institute of
Computer Technology, TU Wien, 1040 Vienna, Austria
martin.lechner@tuwien.ac.at

Abstract. Ambrosia artemisiifolia, also known as ragweed, is an invasive weed species that aggressively spreads across Europe. 4–5% of the
population suffers from strong allergic reactions to its pollen. This work
studies the use of aerial drones equipped with highly compressed deep
neural networks (DNNs) to scan large areas of vegetation for ragweed
with high speed and precision. Compared to the manual approaches with
an estimated survey cost of roughly 860 EUR/km^2, the proposed technique can cut the cost of ragweed detection and monitoring by orders of
magnitudes. Aerial drones are heavily limited by their battery capacity
and thus require an efficient computation platform. As such, it is not possible to use standard DNN models due to memory and computational
constraints. Offloading the workload into data centers introduces new
issues as the drones may operate in rural areas with poor network connectivity. To overcome these challenges, we train state-of-the-art object
detection and segmentation models on a ragweed dataset. The best
performing segmentation models were compressed using shunt connections, fine-tuned with knowledge distillation, and further optimized with
Nvidias TensorRT library for deployment on an Nvidia Jetson TX2. The
highest accuracy models still achieve between 200 ms and 400 ms inference latency, enabling real-time ragweed survey and potentially allowing
more advanced autonomous eradication use cases.

Keywords: Machine learning · DNN · Autonomous machines · Drones

1 Introduction

Over the last 20 years, the rise of Ambrosia Artemisiifolia extended the hayfever
season for millions of sensitized people in Europe from early summer to late
autumn. The plant originally native to North America came to our continent due
to upcoming global trade in the 19th century. Initially not spreading too much,
several factors such as industrialized agriculture and climate change speeded up
the infestation in Europe [7]. Figure 1 shows the rapid distribution of this alien
species across Europe.

This work was supported in part by the Austrian Federal Ministry for Digital and
Economic Affairs, in part by the National Foundation for Research, Technology and
Development, and in part by the Christian Doppler Research Association.

A. Orailoglu et al. (Eds.): SAMOS 2022, LNCS 13511, pp. 187–199, 2022.
https://doi.org/10.1007/978-3-031-15074-6_12

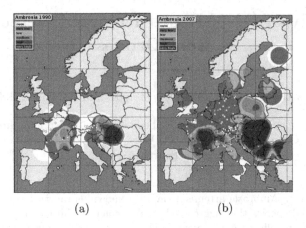

(a)   (b)

Fig. 1. Ragweed pollen concentration 1990 (a) and 2007 (b). Favored by climate change Ambrosia Artemisiifolia expands roughly 25 km from east to west every year. Data provided by the European Aeroallergen Network [2].

Richter et al. [16] simulated the dispersion of ragweed in Austria and Bavaria for different climate scenarios and found that taking no counteractions would raise the mean annual allergy-related cost from 133 Mio. EUR in 2005 to 422 Mio. EUR in 2050. For the same region, they calculated that investments of 15 Mio. EUR/year in traditional weed management would reduce the mean allergy-related cost by 82 Mio. EUR per year.

The effort for removing ragweed splits into the cost for detection (10%) and subsequent eradication (90%) and is estimated to be 8570 EUR per km^2 in total. Since eradication costs increase for larger plants, a survey should cover large areas in a short time. However, a person requires 25 h to monitor a single km^2 once. One way to lower the detection cost is to crowd-source the task. People are asked to take pictures of ragweed with their mobile phones and send them to the authorities for verification and removal coordination. The disadvantage of such an unstructured approach is that large areas might not be covered. In an interdisciplinary project, a ResNet50-Image-Classifier was trained to show that deep neural networks (DNNs) can distinguish ragweed from similar-looking plants in close-up images from mobile phones.

This work extends the idea of automated detection and proposes a novel method that uses highly optimized DNNs deployed to embedded devices to scan vegetation images collected with aerial drones. Compared to the traditional manual approach the proposed automated technique has the potential to cut the survey costs (860 EUR/km^2) by 80% and the survey time by 90%.

One challenge that comes with this approach is that offloading large datasets to the cloud may not be possible due to poor network connectivity in rural areas. Another challenge is that DNN Models with millions of parameters like ResNet50 cannot be deployed efficiently to embedded systems due to the lack of available memory and computation resources. Furthermore, the DNN cannot utilize the embedded platform entirely since image pre-processing (cropping, scaling) and data post-processing need additional resources.

We identify state-of-the-art DNNs to recognize ragweeds in images collected with drones, study methods to compress and optimize the DNNs, and map them on suitable embedded hardware. An optimized system can provide a cost-effective solution to support the combat against the spread of Ambrosia Artemisiifolia and to alleviate the medical conditions experienced by millions of people. This paper makes the following main contribution:

A case study of ragweed detection from drones based on standard DNNs, and specifically,

- study and comparison of segmentation and object detection DNNs,
- optimization and customization of the used DNNs,
- a method to find the optimal operating parameters for survey drones.

The rest of the paper is organized as follows: Sect. 3 describes our approach for drone-based ragweed detection, with our experimental results in Sect. 4 and a conclusion drawn in Sect. 5.

2   Related Work

2.1   Weed Detection and Eradication

Plascak et al. [14] use helicopters and drones at high altitudes to collect RGB and NGB pictures. To interpret the images, they created orthographic maps and manually engineered features such as tone, color, texture, pattern, form, size, height/altitude, and location. They highlight that the spatial distribution of ragweed can be estimated well by the strong green leaf color in early summer. Budda et al. [6] suggested a combination of robotic sprayer and drone systems to eradicate different kinds of weeds automatically. They trained an object detector to recognize certain weed types in an early plant stage to apply small amounts of pesticides. They emphasize the importance of flying drones at high altitudes to improve efficiency. Increasing the distance between camera and surface reduces the number of pixels per plant and degrades recognition quality. To mitigate this problem, they propose to upsample images using generative adversarial networks (GANs) and pass the output of the GAN as input to an object detector. The authors reported a 93.8% classification accuracy for the detected instances of the three weed classes they consider in their model. However, 50 out of 170 Ragweed examples were not detected by the Fast R-CNN Object Detector. Their solution also requires offloading the workload to the cloud, limiting the application to areas with sufficient network connectivity and bandwidth.

In 2019 the Laser Zentrum Hanover [3] proposed an eradication solution using drones and robots equipped with lasers to remove unwelcome plants. Mathiassen et al. suggest that laser treatment can indeed reduce the relative survival rate of certain weed species and demonstrated that laser treatment is an effective technique for weed control. Depending on infestation and plant development, a

Table 1. The optimal ragweed eradication method depends on the level of infestation and the size of the plant.

		Manual or piloted drone (chemical / mechanical)	Tractor-supported (chemical / mechanical)
Plant Stage	**Late**		
	Early	Autonomous drone (laser)	Autonomous robot (laser)
		Weak	**Strong**
		Infestation	

different removal technique might be optimal. Table 1 shows a classification of weed management strategies. In case of heavily infested vegetation with plants in the late stage, tractors and sprayers are likely the optimal eradication method. If the plants are still in an early stage, one could consider ground-based robots equipped with lasers as a viable solution [1,4].

2.2 Deep Learning and Model Compression

Deep neural networks have been proven to outperform classical approaches in various domains like object detection [5,12] and semantic segmentation [8], and applications like autonomous driving [9] and plant identification [13]. Object detection networks can be grouped into two approaches, two-stage detectors like Faster-RCNN [15] and single-stage detectors like YoloV4 [5] and singe-shot-detection (SSD) [12]. While two-stage detectors typically reach a higher accuracy, they are slower and require more resources than single-stage detectors. While object detectors predict bounding boxes for each found object in an image, the task of semantic segmentation is to assign a class to every pixel. DeeplabV3+ [8] is one of the latest methods for semantic segmentation, which can be combined with different sized backbones depending on the required accuracy and latency.

However, all state-of-the-art networks still need a lot of resources and require further optimization to run on embedded platforms and meet latency targets. Methods to compress deep neural networks include pruning, quantization, knowledge distillation [11], and shunt-connections [10]. Pruning is a technique to reduce the number of weights in a neural network and can be challenging in architectures containing residual blocks as found in ResNet or MobileNet variants. In knowledge distillation, one trains a smaller neural network with the output distribution of a larger DNN to achieve a comparable accuracy with a reduced number of parameters. On the other hand, Shunt-connections replace computationally expensive blocks of a DNN with much smaller ones.

3   System Architecture

3.1   Ground Sampling Distance

The ground sampling distance (GSD) describes the spatial density of image discretization. It gives the number of units of measurement on the ground that are represented by a single pixel in the observed image. A ground sampling distance of 1 cm/pixel means that 1 pixel in the image represents $1cm$ of ground distance in the real world. The ground-sampling distance is the relation between the width of the camera footprint on the ground g_w in cm and the sensor resolution sr_w in pixel.

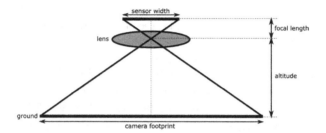

Fig. 2. The ground sampling distance is the relation between the width of the camera footprint on the ground g_w and the sensor width s_w

$$GSD = \frac{g_w}{sr_w} \qquad PS = \frac{s_w}{sr_w} \qquad (1)$$

For our considerations, we use the standard pinhole camera model to calculate the flight altitude for a given GSD and a given pixel size PS:

$$a = \frac{f \cdot g_w}{s_w} = f \cdot \frac{GSD}{PS} \qquad (2)$$

where a is the altitude, f is the focal length, g_w is the width on the ground, and s_w is the sensor width.

A more expensive camera with a higher resolution sensor could outperform cheaper models that require the drone platform to fly at lower altitudes for the same GSD. We derive a model based on equation (Eq. 2) to decide which drone-camera-combination is the most efficient for a specific GSD. Next, we need to find the limits of the GSD necessary for detecting ragweed. When creating a training dataset, image annotation is an important task typically performed by humans. We found that annotators require at least 100×100 pixels to identify a ragweed plant in an image.

Large ragweed plants often cover 1 m of the ground surface. To obtain 100×100 pixels the GSD should be 1 cm/pixel. Plants in an early stage cover a surface area of ≈ 10 cm. Detecting smaller objects requires a lower GSD of 0.1 cm/pixel. One could argue that it is cheaper to detect ragweed when the plant is larger.

Although the detection cost goes down for larger plants, the eradication cost is much higher when detected later, and laser-based removal techniques may no longer be viable.

3.2 Flight Parameter Model

A drone platform provides a maximal flight duration t and a maximal speed v. The cost of a flight is assumed to be c EUR. The mounted camera provides an image resolution of $h \times w$ pixels. The sensor height, width and focal length is given as s_h, s_w and f. For a certain GSD in cm/pixel, the ground area covered by an image is $g_w \times g_h \text{m}^2$ with

Table 2. Five final layers of the network for the original (Cityscapes) and the reduced (Ragweed) segmentation head.

Layer	Cityscapes	Ragweed
	Out shape (params)	Out shape (params)
decoder_decoder_conv0	271, 481, 19 (2451)	271, 481, 2 (258)
decoder_feature_project0	271, 481, 19 (1691)	271, 481, 2 (178)
add_3	271, 481, 19 (0)	271, 481, 2 (0)
resize_3	2161, 3841, 19 (0)	2161, 3841, 2 (0)
activation_87	2161, 3841, 19 (0)	2161, 3841, 2 (0)

$$g_w = \frac{w \cdot GSD}{100} \text{ and } g_h = \frac{h \cdot GSD}{100}. \tag{3}$$

The number of flights f_c required to scan $1 \, \text{km}^2$ *can be calculated as*:

$$f_c = \frac{10^6}{d \times g_w} \tag{4}$$

where d is the distance, a drone can travel during one flight.

Finally, we can calculate the total cost of scanning $1 \, \text{km}^2$ of vegetation at a given GSD by

$$\text{Total Cost per km}^2 = \frac{10^8 \cdot c}{t \cdot v \cdot w \cdot GSD} \tag{5}$$

This expression can be interpreted intuitively. The total costs decrease if a drone can fly longer (flight time t) and faster (speed v) with a higher sensor resolution. Ceteris paribus, a larger ground sampling distance allows the drone to fly at higher altitudes increasing the observed ground surface and reducing the overall data collection cost per km^2. Increasing the sensor resolution w also increases g_w resulting in the same effect.

The model also allows the calculation of the optimal flight parameters. Equation (2) gives the ideal altitude. Ignoring motion blur, the optimal speed is equal to the maximal speed of the drone. The number of pictures taken during a flight is and the required framerate to fully cover the ground are given by:

$$\text{images per flight} = \frac{d}{g_h} \qquad \text{required framerate} = \frac{t}{p} \qquad (6)$$

3.3 Dataset

In September 2020, we recorded roughly 130 min of video data and 200 high-resolution images of ragweed-infested dense vegetation in the eastern part of Austria at heights of 2.5 and 4 m. We used multiple configurations of camera systems and perspectives to obtain image data with the desired level of quality.

Inspired by the work of Buddha et al. [6] we annotated an object-detection dataset where we chopped the original 4k videos into eight non-overlapping video tiles. The final dataset consists of 971 image tiles with a resolution of 960×1080 pixels, of which 481 tiles show at least one region of interest. We split the images into 80% training samples and 20% test samples. We also created a segmentation dataset consisting of 139 images.

3.4 Object Detection Network

We used an SSDResNet50FPN as included in the TensorFlow Object Detection API for object detection, which is pre-trained on the MS CoCo 2017 dataset. We used a cosine decay learning rate with a base learning rate factor of 0.04 and a 2000 step warm-up phase with a warm-up learning rate of 0.013333. In total, we executed the training for 25000 steps.

3.5 Semantic Segmentation Network

Our model for semantic segmentation is based on the DeeplabV3+ architecture with a MobileNetV3 backbone and pre-trained on the Cityscapes dataset. In the next step, we trained, compressed, and fine-tuned our model using the Shunt-Connector-Framework from Haas et al. [10]. This includes modifying the segmentation head for our dataset. The cityscapes dataset is annotated on 19 output classes, whereas our ragweed dataset has only two classes (ragweed, background). However, the modifications have to be done in-place in order to load the pre-trained weights. Table 2 shows all modified layers. For training the shunt-inserted model, we used a constant learning rate of 0.05 and executed the training for 200 epochs.

4 Results

In the following sections, we first compare different drones for small and large ragweed detection in terms of cost-efficiency. Then, we describe our experimental setup and compare the results of object detection and segmentation on our ragweed dataset. Finally, we show the required optimization steps for embedded hardware deployment.

4.1   Drone Selection

As an example, we compare three off-the-shelf drones, a DJI Phantom 4 Pro 2 with a built-in camera, a DJI Matrice 300 RTK with a Zenmuse P1 (50 mm) camera, and a WingtraOne with a Sony QX1. For simplicity, we assume the operating costs to be the same for each drone and only use the deprecation costs set to $1/100 \times list\_price$ as costs per flight. We consider two scenarios. Scenario S1 aims to detect small ragweed plants that are 10 cm in size. A *GSD* of 0.1 cm/pixel will be assumed to achieve this goal. In Scenario S2, the drone should detect large ragweed (1 m in size). To obtain 100 × 100 pixels the *GSD* will be 1 cm/pixel.

Table 3. Overview of all required UAV parameters to decide which platform-sensor combination is most efficient and to compute the optimal flight parameters.

	DJI Phantom	DJI Matrice	WingtraOne
Flight duration [s]	1800	3300	3540
Cost per flight [EUR]	30	110	45
Speed [m/s]	20	23	16
Flight distance [km]	36	75.9	56.640
Camera	Built in	Zenmuse P1	Sony QX1
Resolution [px]	5472 × 3648	8192 × 5460	5456 × 3532
Sensor size [mm]	13.2 × 8	35.9 × 24	23.2 × 15.4
Focal length [mm]	8.8	50	20

With the parameters from Table 3, the ground dimensions mapped to a single image can be calculated using Eq. (3). Considering the real-world surface dimensions of a single image, we can derive the total observed ground surface of one flight. Table 4 summarizes the results. Note that the price per km^2 decreases by a factor of 10 when the GSD increases by a factor of 10.

Although the Matrice is about three times as expensive as the Phantom, it is still more cost-efficient in collecting images with the desired GSD. The optimal flight altitude can be calculated with Eq. (2).

Another metric is the minimal interval of images required to cover the entire ground surface during a flyover without overlaps. The Phantom-V4 in scenario S1 has to take $36000/3.65 = 9869$ pictures during an 1800 s long flight resulting in a framerate of 0.18 images per second. This sets a strict time limit for real-time onboard ragweed detectors. Due to the higher spatial resolution of the DJI-Matrice, the drone can fly higher and take fewer images relative to the Phantom for the same distance. However, it still takes more pictures as it can fly longer and faster. Table 4 shows the optimal flight parameters and time limits for both scenarios.

In conclusion, the relative drone efficiency does not depend on the scenario, as changing the GSD affects all drones equally. Ignoring the constant values in

Eq. (5) it is optimal to pick the drone-camera combination with the lowest ratio of drone *cost* to maximal-airtime ×velocity × resolution.

4.2 Experimental Setup

For our experiments, we used an Nvidia Jetson TX2 as it is the sweet spot between power, performance, and weight for a drone application. All networks are converted to Nvidia's neural network inference framework Tensor RT (TRT). It can quantize models with FP16 and INT8 operations while preserving the models' accuracy and supports layer-fusing, kernel-auto-tuning, and other optimizations. This allows us to run our networks at the highest possible efficiency.

Table 4. Efficiency metrics and optimal flight parameters of three UAV models for small and large ragweed detection. The costs per *km* scales linearly with the required GSD.

Scenario		S1			S2	
Drone	DJI Phantom	DJI Matrice	Wingtra One	DJI Phantom	DJI Matrice	Wingtra One
Efficiency Metrics						
Groundwidth [m/img]	5.47	8.19	5.46	54.72	81.92	54.56
Groundlength [m/img]	3.65	5.46	3.63	36.48	54.60	36.32
Ground area [km²/flight]	0.2	0.62	0.31	1.97	6.22	3.09
Flights per km²	5.08	1.61	3.24	0.51	0.16	0.32
Time [h/km²]	**2.54**	**1.48**	**3.19**	**0.26**	**0.15**	**0.31**
Costs [EUR/km²]	**152.3**	**176.9**	**145.6**	**15.2**	**17.7**	**14.6**
Optimal Flight Parameters						
Altitude [m]	3.65	11.41	4.7	36.48	114.09	47.03
Speed [m/s]	20	23	16	20	23	16
Images per flight	9,869	13,902	15,595	987	1,391	1,560
Framerate [images/s]	5.48	4.21	4.41	0.55	0.42	0.44

Table 5. Semantic segmentation *mIoU* results. *IoU reported on the training server.

Resolution	mIoU			
	dlv3*	dlv3s	dlv3trt	dlv3trts
961 × 541	0.588	0.625	0.574	0.625
1921 × 1081	0.670	0.695	0.634	0.695

Object Detection. On the ragweed testset, we achieved an Average Precision (AP) of 0.525 for an Intersection over Union (IoU) of 0.5 and a mean AP of 0.229 for IoU scores in the range of 0.5 to 0.95. Figure 3 shows that while the

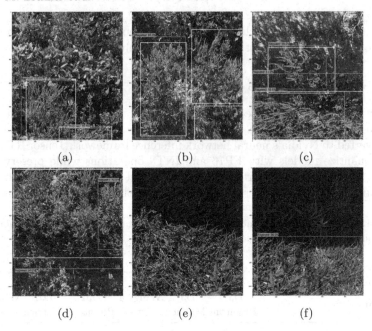

(a)   (b)   (c)

(d)   (e)   (f)

Fig. 3. The model predicts reasonable (green) bounding boxes if the plant is well separated from the rest of the vegetation. However, it sometimes fails (see (b) and (f)). Especially when vegetation is dense the (red) ground truth boxes overlap with the non-ragweed background. (Color figure online)

object detector can detect individual plants, it struggles in areas with dense vegetation. Thus, object detection is a valid approach in spring or early summer when vegetation is still sparse. After running optimizations with TensorRT, we obtained a latency of 95 ms at floating point 16 (FP16) and 124 ms at FP32. In FP16 mode, the AP@0.5IoU dropped slightly to 0.523, and the mean AP dropped to 0.227.

Semantic Segmentation. In our experiments, we compare the latency and the IoU of the original model with TensorRT optimizations and the shunt-inserted model with and without TensorRT optimizations. However, for the original model, we could not run it on a TX2 due to memory constraints. Thus we provide the IoU achieved on our training machine. Table 5 shows the $mIoU$ of the original model (dlv3), the shunt-inserted model (dlv3s), the TensorRT optimized model (dlv3trt), and the TensorRT optimized shunt-inserted model on two different resolutions (1/4 and 1/8 of the original 4k images). As a general trend, inserting the shunt connections followed by fine-tuning increases the $mIoU$. Also, the TensorRT-based optimizations have no impact on the $mIoU$ for the shunt-inserted model. In addition to the $mIoU$, Fig. 4a also shows the mean latency for all models on the Jetson TX2. Platform-specific optimizations clearly boost the latency, while shunt connections do not make a huge difference in terms of latency. However, due to the increased $mIoU$, the optimized, shunt-inserted models represent the Pareto optimum. The TensorRT optimized, shunt-inserted model (dv3trts) with a resolution of 1921 × 1081 has a mean latency of 200 ms which meets most of the framerate requirements from Table 4. In case of a DJI Phantom in scenario S1, only the lower resolution model with a mean latency of 45 ms is fast enough. Figure 4b shows the impact of the batch size during training together with the achievable $mIoU$ for three different resolutions on the training server. As expected, the highest resolution model achieves the best $mIoU$ scores. However, these models do not fit our target hardware or latency constraints. Figure 5 shows the predictions of the segmentation model together with the ground-truth labels for two sample images. In both scenarios, the predictions and the labeled ground-truth overlap to a large extent.

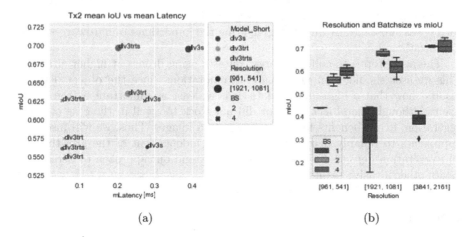

(a)   (b)

Fig. 4. Left: The Pareto-optima on the TX2 are the shunt-inserted deeplabv3+ models optimized with TensorRT (dv3trts). Shunt-optimization has little effect on a TRT-optimized models latency but significantly boosts its accuracy. The size of the points denotes the image size and the shape (dot, cross) the training batch size (BS). The test-batch size is always 1. **Right**: Higher resolution and larger training batch size improve the quality of the segmentation model.

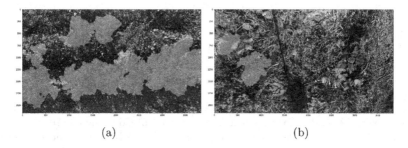

(a)   (b)

Fig. 5. Predictions of the segmentation model (yellow) and ground-truth (purple). (Color figure online)

5   Conclusion and Future Work

In this work, we presented a case study of ragweed detection from drones. The experiments show that the current state of the art in computer vision and model compression techniques is sufficient to detect ragweed with a high level of accuracy when the model runs on a resource constraint embedded system. Based on the given assumptions (860 EUR/km^2, 25 h/km^2), we can conclude that using drones to detect ragweed plants (15–180 EUR/km^2, 0.15–3.2 h/km^2) is between five and fifty times more cost-efficient and eight to a hundred times more time-efficient depending on the plant size.

Shunt connections and knowledge distillation allowed us to train much smaller models to a similar or even higher accuracy as the original models with a significantly reduced latency. However, the latency improvement due to TensorRT was substantially larger, highlighting the importance of hardware-specific optimizations.

The next step is to collect a larger dataset using drones at higher altitudes. This dataset should then needs careful annotations since the object detector results show that a high-quality dataset is at least as important as the model itself. Although the object detector did not work too well in the case of dense vegetation, it has benefits for sparse vegetation images. Thus, we will fuse both approaches to reliably detect ragweed plants independent of the growth state and vegetation density. Further, we plan to extend our approach to detect and locate other invasive plants.

References

1. Corteva leverages mobile robots to walk row crops. https://www.futurefarming. com/tech-in-focus/field-robots/corteva-leverages-mobile-robots-to-walk-row-crops/. Accessed 17 Dec 2021
2. European aeroallergen network. https://ean.polleninfo.eu/Ean/. Accessed Dec 2021
3. Laser zentrum hannover (lzh) presents anti-weed laser system at agritechnica. https://optics.org/news/10/11/12. Accessed 17 Dec 2021
4. Welaser project refines laser-based weed control. https://optics.org/news/12/3/52. Accessed 17 Dec 2021
5. Bochkovskiy, A., Wang, C., Liao, H.M.: Yolov4: optimal speed and accuracy of object detection. CoRR abs/2004.10934 (2020)
6. Buddha, K., Nelson, H.J., Zermas, D., Papanikolopoulos, N.: Weed detection and classification in high altitude aerial images for robot-based precision agriculture. In: 2019 27th MED, pp. 280–285. IEEE, July 2019
7. Buttenschøn, R., Waldispühl, S., Bohren, C.: Guidelines for management of common ragweed, Ambrosia artemisiifolia. University of Copenhagen (2010)
8. Chen, L., Zhu, Y., Papandreou, G., Schroff, F., Adam, H.: Encoder-decoder with atrous separable convolution for semantic image segmentation. CoRR abs/1802.02611 (2018)
9. Grigorescu, S.M., Trasnea, B., Cocias, T.T., Macesanu, G.: A survey of deep learning techniques for autonomous driving. CoRR abs/1910.07738 (2019)

10. Haas, B., Wendt, A., Jantsch, A., Wess, M.: Neural network compression through shunt connections and knowledge distillation for semantic segmentation problems. In: Maglogiannis, I., Macintyre, J., Iliadis, L. (eds.) AIAI 2021. IAICT, vol. 627, pp. 349–361. Springer, Cham (2021). https://doi.org/10.1007/978-3-030-79150-6_28
11. Hinton, G., Dean, J., Vinyals, O.: Distilling the knowledge in a neural network, pp. 1–9, March 2014
12. Lu, X., Kang, X., Nishide, S., Ren, F.: Object detection based on SSD-ResNet. In: 2019 IEEE 6th CCIS, pp. 89–92 (2019)
13. Mehdipour Ghazi, M., Yanikoglu, B., Aptoula, E.: Plant identification using deep neural networks via optimization of transfer learning parameters. Neurocomputing **235**, 228–235 (2017)
14. Plaščak, I., Barač, Z.: Remote detection of ragweed (ambrosia artemisiifolia l.). Tehnički glasnik (2018)
15. Ren, S., He, K., Girshick, R.B., Sun, J.: Faster R-CNN: towards real-time object detection with region proposal networks. CoRR abs/1506.01497 (2015)
16. Richter, R., et al.: Spread of invasive ragweed: climate change, management and how to reduce allergy costs. J. Appl. Ecol. **50**(6), 1422–1430 (2013)

PULP-TrainLib: Enabling On-Device Training for RISC-V Multi-core MCUs Through Performance-Driven Autotuning

Davide Nadalini[1,2(✉)] [iD], Manuele Rusci[2(✉)] [iD], Giuseppe Tagliavini[3(✉)] [iD], Leonardo Ravaglia[2], Luca Benini[2,4(✉)] [iD], and Francesco Conti[2(✉)] [iD]

[1] DAUIN, Politecnico di Torino, 10129 Turin, Italy
davide.nadalini@polito.it
[2] DEI, University of Bologna, 40136 Bologna, Italy
{d.nadalini,manuele.rusci,luca.benini,f.conti}@unibo.it
[3] DISI, University of Bologna, 40134 Bologna, Italy
giuseppe.tagliavini@unibo.it
[4] IIS, ETH Zurich, 8092 Zurich, Switzerland
lbenini@iis.ee.ethz.ch

Abstract. An open challenge in making Internet-of-Things sensor nodes "smart" and self-adaptive is to enable on-chip Deep Neural Network (DNN) training on Ultra-Low-Power (ULP) microcontroller units (MCUs). To this aim, we present a framework, based on *PULP-TrainLib*, to deploy DNN training tasks on RISC-V-based Parallel-ULP (PULP) MCUs. *PULP-TrainLib* is a library of parallel software DNN primitives enabling the execution of forward and backward steps on PULP MCUs. To optimize *PULP-TrainLib*'s kernels, we propose a strategy to automatically select and configure (autotune) the fastest among a set of tiling options and optimized floating-point matrix multiplication kernels, according to the tensor shapes of every DNN layer. Results on an 8-core RISC-V MCU show that our auto-tuned primitives improve MAC/clk by up to 2.4× compared to "one-size-fits-all" matrix multiplication, achieving up to 4.39 MAC/clk - 36.6× better than a commercial STM32L4 MCU executing the same DNN layer training workload. Furthermore, our strategy proves to be 30.7× faster than AIfES, a state-of-the-art training library for MCUs, while training a complete TinyML model.

Keywords: Deep learning · On-device training · Multi-core MCUs · Autotuning

1 Introduction

Deep Neural Network (DNN) inference on *ultra-low-power* devices has been the target of an extensive body of research and development in recent years [9,19,28, 29]. This disruptive paradigm has provided a critical mass for strong innovation in the architecture, programming models, and development stacks available for MicroController (MCU) devices, targeting edge sensors and smart devices.

A. Orailoglu et al. (Eds.): SAMOS 2022, LNCS 13511, pp. 200–216, 2022.
https://doi.org/10.1007/978-3-031-15074-6_13

In this context, the emerging open challenge concerns how to enable *on-device learning* and model adaptation directly on this class of devices. The present design flow of DNN models for deployment on edge devices is extremely static. DNN training is performed with a *train-once-deploy-everywhere* approach, using GPU-based servers featuring massive computation and memory resources. Only after training, the DNN model is deployed on edge platforms for inference-only execution. This static *train-once-deploy-everywhere* approach prevents adapting DNN inference models to changing conditions in the deployment environment, which may impact the statistical distribution of data and lead to significant in-field accuracy degradation and unreliable predictions [1].

Recently proposed methodologies based on Transfer Learning [21], Continual Learning [22], or Incremental Learning [16] aim at softening the risks of the *train-once-deploy-everywhere* design flow by taking a trained DNN model and enhancing or adapting it to data collected in-the-field. All of these methods perform DNN training tasks starting from the trained model and make use of backpropagation and stochastic gradient descent (SGD) algorithms. The deployment of these DNN training algorithms on MCU platforms results in a three-fold challenge. First, each layer of the DNN has to be computed both in forward and in backward propagation, differently from inference tasks, which require only the forward computation. Second, SGD demands floating-point operations, significantly more expensive than heavily quantized ones (8 bits or less) largely used for edge inference. Third, SGD often needs many iterations (100 or more) to achieve convergence instead of a single pass for inference - and contrarily to server training, it typically has to work on a single element, with little chance to employ batching to boost the training kernels' parallelism.

This paper addresses these challenges by introducing a framework for the efficient deployment of DNN training tasks on energy-efficient MCU devices. In particular, we rely on recent architectural advancements, which make multi-iteration backprop-based training more feasible on MCU-class devices [2, 26]. Among these, Parallel Ultra-Low-Power (PULP) devices [14] are multi-core MCUs exploiting architectural parallelism and near-threshold execution to enable high-performance and low-power processing at the edge. Our work introduces *PULP-TrainLib*, the first DNN training software library for RISC-V-based multi-core PULP devices. Our library consists of latency-optimized and tunable forward and backward training primitives of DNN layers, with multiple alternative configurations available for each training primitive tuned to better suit a given tensor shape in the forward and backward passes. Furthermore, to empower our framework for on-device DNN-training and optimize performance, we couple *PULP-Trainlib* with *AutoTuner*, an automated tool to select the fastest configuration and tile partitioning for every DNN layer.

In detail, our work includes the following novel contributions:

– *PULP-TrainLib*, the first open-source training library for RISC-V-based multi-core MCUs, including a set of performance-tunable DNN layer primitives to enable DNN training on ultra-low-power devices;
– *AutoTuner*, an automated tool exploiting an HW-in-the-loop strategy to opportunistically select the layer primitive that leads to the lowest latency, given the DNN structure and the memory constraints of the target device;

– A detailed analysis of *PULP-TrainLib* and the AutoTuner targeting an 8-Core RISC-V-based PULP platform, and a comparison with state-of-the-art results achievable on commercial STM32 MCUs.

Our approach demonstrates that training techniques such as Incremental and Continual Learning are achievable with realistic latencies (< 1 ms to train a tinyMLPerf's AutoEncoder[1] on a new input) on a device consuming an MCU-class active power budget (<100 mW), without sacrificing full programmability. The forward and backward primitives of *PULP-TrainLib* show an almost linear parallel speed-up on a multi-core RISC-V platform. Benchmarking over individual PointWise, DepthWise Convolution, and Linear layers, the AutoTuner optimizes the throughput by up to, respectively, $18.3\times$, $8\times$, and $11\times$ compared to a naïve implementation. This descends from the selection of the fastest matrix multiplication kernel for each set of tensor shapes, with a top performance of 4.39 Multiply-Accumulate operations per clock cycle (MAC/clk) to execute a single training step. Our optimized solution outperforms the execution on an STM32L476RG commercial MCU by $36.6\times$. Additionally, we benchmark our methodology on two TinyMLPerf benchmarks, a DS-CNN for Keyword Spotting (KWS) and a Deep Autoencoder for Anomaly Detection. Results on an 8-core PULP Platform show that the latency of a complete DNN training step is reduced to a minimum of 0.39 million clock cycles on the Deep Autoencoder (i.e., < 1 ms @400 MHz), applying the AutoTuner, $30.7\times$ faster than AIfES, the current state-of-the-art training library for MCUs. To foster future research on extreme-edge DNN training, we release PULP-Trainlib as open-source software[2].

2   Related Work

While edge DNN inference has been widely explored, on-device training is still an open problem due to the strict constraints of embedded platforms. To accelerate backprop-based training, Federated Learning [11,17,18] distributes the training process between several agents. TinyTL [5] proposes a lightweight (transfer) learning technique by limiting back-propagation to biases only, which also prevents the storage of the intermediate tensors required for weight gradient back-propagation. Compared with these works, we focus on accelerating the computational primitives of SGD, which can be adopted in the future to bring these approaches to low-power MCUs.

A limited set of works have already addressed the problem of model adaptation on MCUs. In TinyOL [25], the authors propose to use an Arduino Nano equipped with a 64MHz ARM Cortex-M4 for Transfer Learning, using a single trainable layer on top of a frozen and quantized inference model. Targeting the same platform, TinyFedTL [12] extends the concepts of TinyOL with a Federated approach, aiming at retraining the last layer in a distributed way. Ravaglia et al.

---

[1] TinyML Perf Models: https://github.com/mlcommons/tiny/tree/master/benchmark.

[2] PULP-TrainLib: https://github.com/pulp-platform/pulp-trainlib.

[24] target for the first time Continual Learning [22] on MCUs. The proposed HW/SW platform learns the model coefficients of multiple DNN layers using backpropagation. Our work generalizes this approach into a training framework that can be used beyond Continual Learning use-cases only, e.g. in an Incremental or Transfer Learning setting. Moreover, we improve the performances of the key computational steps by up to 2.3× thanks to novel optimized SW kernels and the Autotuning functionality. Close to our work, AIfES[3] is the only other publicly-released training software framework for MCUs. More in detail, such a framework currently enables the training of DNN models composed of exclusively Fully-Connected (aka Dense or Linear) layers. The software primitives are optimized on ARM Cortex-M MCUs using kernels of the CMSIS-DSP library, in particular floating-point matrix multiplications. In contrast, PULP-TrainLib includes a wider set of DNN layers (like 2D and Depthwise Separable Convolutions) and features a higher optimization level by applying autotuned loop unrolling and parallelization, requiring 30.7× fewer clock cycles than AIfES to execute a complete DNN model.

Our work combines PULP-TrainLib's software with an autotuning tool, searching for the software configuration (MM kernel and tiling) that optimizes a cost function, i.e. minimal latency. Autotuning is a widespread approach in high-performance, parallel computing (readers may refer to [3,20]). Representative examples are FFTW [10] and ATLAS [30], which aim at optimizing FFT and Basic Linear Algebra Subroutines (BLAS), respectively, using a code-generator autotuner. They achieve a speed-up of up to 55% and 20%, respectively, compared to non-optimized algorithms. Halide [23] integrates an autotuner on top of a stencil pipeline, also leveraging stochastic search to speed up the execution to up 5×. Tensor Comprehensions [27] extends this concept for DNN inference, providing a Just-In-Time compiler that exploits operator fusion, delegated memory management, and an autotuner to find the fastest implementation among a vast search space. To bypass the complexity of hardware-in-the-loop autotuning, the TVM [6] compiler for DNN inference replaces an autotuner with a learnable cost model to predict the fastest solution starting from a trial-based approach. The same authors present an alternative method [7] that learns domain-specific cost models by exploring the solution space of the target task.

To the best of our knowledge, our work is the first one to target autotuned hardware-in-the-loop optimization of DNN training on an MCU platform. We adopt a trial-based approach like FFTW and ATLAS [10,30]. Compared with Ragan-Kelley et al. [23], which adopts stochastic search, we prefer an exhaustive hardware-in-the-loop approach, capable of finding the best optimization for the problem by direct performance profiling. MCU-oriented autotuning tools, like uTVM[4] and the work of Chen et al. [8], are currently limited to inference – and currently do not achieve a speed comparable to hand-tuned libraries, like CMSIS-NN [13] and TinyEngine [15].

---

[3] AIfES for Arduino: https://www.arduino.cc/reference/en/libraries/aifes-for-arduino/.

[4] Apache μTVM: https://tvm.apache.org/2020/06/04/tinyml-how-tvm-is-taming-tiny.

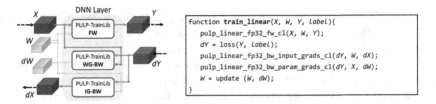

Fig. 1. SW primitives of *PULP-TrainLib* library (left) and corresponding pseudo-code showing how to train an individual linear layer (right). On the left, elements in blue show the path of the input tensor's data and gradient, while the red and green ones represent the weight and output, respectively. (Color figure online)

3 On-Device Training on PULP

3.1 The PULP Platform

PULP (parallel ultra-low power) is a computational platform for energy-efficient and scalable edge computing based on RISC-V cores [26]. In this work, we consider a PULP SoC instance that includes an MCU for control-related tasks and a multi-core cluster for parallel computation. The MCU features a single RISC-V core, a set of IO peripherals, and a 2 MB SRAM memory (L2) accessible by the cluster side through a DMA engine. The cluster includes 8 RISC-V cores sharing a 64 kB L1 memory, accessible in a single cycle. Each core implements a basic set of standard RISC-V extensions (RV32IMFC); additionally, a custom extension (Xpulp) provides DSP-like features to reduce overhead in highly uniform workloads, including post-increment load/store operations and 2-level nested hardware loops. Finally, each CPU is granted access to a private Floating Point Unit (FPU), capable of performing complex, single-cycle DSP instructions, like Fused Multiply-Add (FMA).

3.2 PULP-TrainLib Library

PULP-TrainLib is the first software library for DNN training on MCU-class RISC-V multi-core platforms. More in detail, we provide an optimized software design for the forward and backward propagation passes of multiple DNN layers, targeting the execution on the PULP Platform. Our library adopts floating-point data formats (fp32 and lower) for all the computations of the training steps.

Figure 1 (left) graphically represents the computational flow of the Forward and Backward training steps of a single DNN layer trained with the backpropagation algorithm. The *Forward* (FW) step receives the input tensor X and produces the output tensor Y based on the trainable weights W. This output propagates through the model's layers to compute the loss score with respect to the data label. Unlike inference, the intermediate tensors computed during the FW pass must be kept in memory for the *Backward* (BW) step. For every layer, the weight gradient dW is computed by the *Weight Gradient Backward* (WG-BW) function based on the stored activation feature map X and the gradient tensor

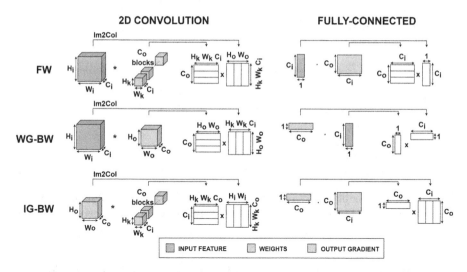

Fig. 2. DNN training matrix operations of FW and BW steps of a 2D Convolution (left) and a Fully-Connected layer (right). The tensor (and respective gradient) shapes involved in 2D Convolution have size $C_i \cdot H_i \cdot W_i$ for the input, $C_o \cdot C_i \cdot H_k \cdot W_k$ for the weights, $C_o \cdot H_o \cdot W_o$ for the outputs. In the case of a Fully-Connected, instead, their shape is C_i, $C_o \cdot C_i$, C_o, respectively. The Im2Col operator transforms the input feature map (FW, WG-BW) or the output gradient (IG-BW) to matrix form to exploit fast matrix computations.

dY, which is the derivative of the loss function with respect to the activation tensor. Such gradient signal then propagates to the previous layer by applying the *Input Gradient Backward* (IG-BW) step. This latter returns dX based on the transposed weight tensor W'. *PULP-TrainLib* provides a set of SW kernels that implement these training steps. For instance, Fig. 1 (right) illustrates the pseudo-code for training the coefficients of an individual fully-connected layer using *PULP-TrainLib*'s primitives.

Figure 2 shows the implementation details of the training steps in the case of a 2D Convolution and a Fully-Connected Layer. To leverage computationally efficient linear algebra kernels, the convolution operations are reshaped as Matrix Multiplications (MMs). To this aim, the data layout of the input X (or the output gradient dY) of a Conv2D layer is reshaped at runtime from a CHW tensor shape to a matrix form through an *im2col* transformation. This routine copies the input data within the receptive field of the filter into column contiguous arrays, stored into the L1 memory, to feed the MM kernel.

3.3   Accelerating SW Training Primitives

The workload of PULP-TrainLib primitives is dominated by MMs. The pseudo-assembly on a RISC-V core of a MM naïve kernel is reported in Fig. 3 (a). This baseline implementation makes use of three nested loops, which iterate over

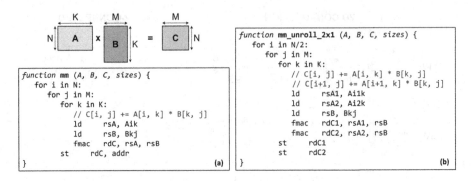

Fig. 3. Pseudo-assembly of the inner loops of (a) a naive MM and (b) of an optimized 2×1 unrolled MM. The matrix dimensions are highlighted on the top-left of the figure.

the matrix dimensions. The inner loop features 3 instructions: the 2 loads of the MM's operands and the floating-point FMA. Thus, in this case, the total number of instructions is $N \times M \times K \times 3$, where $N \times M$ is the size of the output matrix $C = A \cdot B$ and K is the size of the shared dimension.

The total number of instructions can be reduced by means of *loop unrolling*. This technique leads to a faster implementation by computing multiple outputs within the inner loop, hence exploiting data reuse. As a convention, we define the *unrolling factor* as $U \times V$, where U and V are, respectively, the number of rows and columns of the output matrix concurrently computed within the inner loop of the MM. In particular, Fig. 3 (b) represents a 2×1 loop unrolling, which features a 33% higher FMA/Load ratio with respect to the naïve baseline, therefore reducing the overall number of instructions.

Typically, the instruction count decreases with increasing unrolling factor $U \times V$. However, because of the limited size of the register file of the CPU, a spilling effect is observed with a 4×4 or larger unrolling. When this happens, the compiler generates code to spill accumulation registers that do not fit within the CPU's register file to the stack, resulting in a very significant reduction of efficiency and increased latency. Additionally, a slowdown effect can be observed if a dimension of the input matrices is not an integer multiple of the unrolling factor $U \times V$. The computation of the remaining elements that do not fit the MM's inner loop, which we call *leftover*, is handled by different sub-routines that employ less aggressive unrolling and incur in larger latency. In this case, a smaller unrolling factor can result in a faster solution. If the input tensors are smaller than the $U \times V$ unrolling size, the MM kernel turns into all-leftover computation, which greatly slows down the execution.

To address this performance issue, we provide multiple optimized MM functions (listed in Table 1), which can be used within the training primitives of the *PULP-TrainLib* to speed up the execution. In addition to unrolling, every MM kernel exploits data parallelism to efficiently run on the multi-core PULP cluster. Two parallelization strategies are proposed: each core can compute different

Table 1. PULP-TrainLib's optimized MM kernels

MM type	Unrolling factor	Parallelism	Description
mm	–	N or M	Naive MM
mm_uJ	$J = 2$	N or M	Unroll J inner products in K
mm_unroll_1xV	$U = 2, 4, 8$	N or M	Unroll U columns of C
mm_unroll_Ux1	$V = 2, 4, 8$	N or M	Unroll V rows of C
mm_unroll_UxV	$U, V = 2, 4$	N or M	Unroll U, V rows and columns of C

output rows (mm_unroll_UxV) by splitting the workload over the N dimension, or different output columns (mm_M_unroll_UxV), by chunking the M size. Simple unrolling over the K dimension is also provided (mm_uJ) to cover a set of corner cases in which the reduced sizes of N or M prevent the use of unrolling on both sizes (e.g., $N = 8$, $M = 1$, $K >> N$, with parallelization on N).

3.4   AutoTuner

As part of *PULP-TrainLib*, we propose an autotuning flow to optimally configure the DNN training primitives (e.g., which MM to use) based on *(i)* the DNN layer type and training step (e.g., PointWise FW) and *(ii)* the PULP platform settings (e.g., the number of cluster's cores and the L1 memory size). The AutoTuner is run offline, before the deployment to the MCU and the actual training - the best (fastest) software setting is identified, then deployed on the target device.

Because of the limited memory footprint, the DNN layer's input and output tensors may not entirely fit the on-chip memories, and in particular the L1 memory of the cluster. Therefore, a *tiling* process is required to partition the DNN layer's tensors into smaller sub-tensors, also referred to as *Tensor Tiles*. The tiles are transferred from L2 and L1 and processed in sequence. For each tensor tile requiring an *im2col*, this transformation is performed in L1, minimizing the impact on memory. Because the Tensor operand shapes highly impact the MM optimization, the AutoTuner aims at finding concurrently the optimal Tile shapes and the MM kernel, indicated as $TileShape^*$ and MM^*, that lead to the lowest latency.

Algorithm 1 details the procedure adopted by the AutoTuner to achieve this objective. To avoid complex and typically imprecise high-level modeling of the HW/SW platform, our AutoTuner exploits HW-in-the-loop to search for the optimal solution. In particular, we use GVSoC [4], a behavioural event-based MCU simulator capable of modeling any PULP-based device with less than 5% error on estimated cycles. For each training step, the tool measures the latency on the target HW of a pool of configurations identified by the tuple (MM, $TileShape$) and selects the one leading to the lowest latency.

Algorithm 1: AutoTuner for PULP-TrainLib

Input: PULP L1 Memory Size $L1MemSize$ and $\#cores$; DNN Training Layer;
      Tensors' Shapes: $TensorShape$; Table 1
Output: PULP-TrainLib config: MM^*, $TileShape^*$
Parameter: K_T: max tiling solutions to evaluate on HW

1 **Function** Tiler($L1MemSize$, T):
2 | TensorList $= \emptyset$
3 | **for** *each Tile of T* **do**
4 | | **if** Mem *(Tile)* $< L1MemSize$ **then**
5 | | | TensorList $+= (Tile,$ Mem $(Tile))$

6 | TensorList $=$ **sort** (TensorList);   // Decreasing Mem
7 | **return** Top-K_T(TensorList);   // K_T Entries

8

9 AutoTuner:
10 | **if** Mem *(TensorShape)* $< L1MemSize$ **then**
11 | | TensorList $= TensorShape$ // Single Entry
12 | **else**
13 | | TensorList $=$ Tiler ($L1MemSize$, $TensorShape$)
14 | **for** *each TensorShape in TensorList* **do**
15 | | **for** *each MM in Table 1* **do**
16 | | | Lat $=$ RunHW (DNN Train Layer, MM, $TensorShape$, $\#cores$)
17 | | | PerfLog $+= \{$ Lat, $TensorShape$, $MM \}$

18 | **return** MM^*, $TileShape^* =$ Top(PerfLog);   // Lowest Latency

---

The AutoTuner conducts a grid search to find the optimal tuple (MM^*, $TileShape^*$). Based on the layer type and the L1 memory size, a *Tiler* function computes all the possible tiling solutions and discards those exceeding the size constraint. The K_T feasible *TileShape* featuring the largest memory occupations are selected and coupled with the MM kernels of Table 1 to form the pool of configurations to be tested on HW. For example, in the case of $K_T = 5$, used in all our experiments, the autotuning of the PointWise FW kernel demands $5 \times 24 = 120$ simulations on GVSoC (one for each of the 24 optimized MM kernels), which can run in parallel. Our AutoTuner setup exploits an Intel Xeon-equipped node running up to 64 simulations in parallel and takes less than 15 min to return the optimal configuration for all three training steps of the mentioned kernel. We remark that this process needs to be performed only once before the deployment on the target. On the contrary, if the Tensor shape fits the L1 memory entirely, the Tiler module can be bypassed, and the AutoTuner directly measures on HW the fastest MM kernel.

Thanks to the AutoTuner tool, we can effectively deploy full DNN model training on the PULP platform using *PULP-TrainLib*'s primitives. After the autotuning, every forward and backward function of the pipeline invokes specific

	FW					WG-BW					IG-BW				
PointWise Convolution INPUT: 64x25x5 WEIGHTS: 64x1x1x16 OUTPUT: 16x25x5	Ideal: 7.37 MAC/clk					Ideal: 7.37 MAC/clk					Ideal: 7.37 MAC/clk				
	0,10	0,24	0,53	1,87	3,96	0,12	0,24	0,56	1,85	4,39	0,09	0,21	0,47	1,60	3,59
DepthWise Convolution INPUT: 16x27x3 WEIGHTS: 16x3x3 OUTPUT: 16x25x1	Ideal: 5.29 MAC/clk					Ideal: 5.29 MAC/clk					Ideal: 5.29 MAC/clk				
	0,04	0,06	0,07	0,38	0,39	0,04	0,06	0,07	0,40	0,42	0,02	0,04	0,05	0,29	0,32
Fully-Connected INPUT: 640 WEIGHTS: 640x16 OUTPUT: 16	Ideal: 3.88 MAC/clk					Ideal: 3.88 MAC/clk					Ideal: 3.88 MAC/clk				
	0,10	0,24	0,43	1,52	2,66	0,10	0,20	0,20	1,44	1,44	0,09	0,21	0,36	1,33	2,61
	STM32 NAIVE	PULP 1C NAIVE	PULP 1C OPT	PULP 8C NAIVE	PULP 8C OPT	STM32 NAIVE	PULP 1C NAIVE	PULP 1C OPT	PULP 8C NAIVE	PULP 8C OPT	STM32 NAIVE	PULP 1C NAIVE	PULP 1C OPT	PULP 8C NAIVE	PULP 8C OPT

Fig. 4. Execution of the DNN training steps for a PointWise Convolution Layer (upper), a DepthWise Convolution Layer (middle), and a Fully-Connected Layer (lower), using the primitives from *PULP-TrainLib* library. Experiments are performed on an STM32L476RG and on PULP GVSoC.

MM kernels to achieve a computation faster than a "one-size-fits-all" setting, in which all the primitives are using the same MM function.

4 Experimental Results

In this section, we evaluate the effectiveness of the training primitives of *PULP-TrainLib* and the autotuning flow. First, we benchmark the training kernels of single layers on both the PULP Platform and a commercial STM32 MCU. Second, we analyze the outcome of our AutoTuner given multiple DNN layer steps and shapes. Third, we demonstrate how our methodology enhances on-device adaptation, by benchmarking the training procedure on full TinyML DNN models. Last, we compare the performances of *PULP-TrainLib* with AIfES, a state-of-the-art SW library targeting on-device training on embedded devices.

4.1 Latency Optimization on PULP-TrainLib

We evaluate the proposed *PULP-TrainLib* library by running experiments on the GVSoC simulator. Figure 4 reports the latency, expressed as the ratio between MAC operations and clock cycles (MAC/clk), of the forward and backward passes of multiple DNN layers fitting into the L1 memory: PointWise Convolution, DepthWise Convolution, and Fully-Connected. We compare the baseline configuration, which uses a naive MM, with the functions tuned by the Auto-Tuner in the case of both 1 and 8 cores execution. The figure shows the best kernel configuration returned by the AutoTuner (indicated as OPT), i.e., the one with the highest MAC/clk. Additionally, we report the ideal latency, obtained by accounting for only the load, store, and MAC operations that would occur in case of unbounded memory and no stalls. For comparison purposes, we also profile the PULP-TrainLib primitives on an off-the-shelf STM32L476RG MCU, featuring a single-core ARM Cortex-M4 CPU with FPU support. All the experiments use the highest optimization level of the compiler (-O3).

The baseline PointWise and Fully-Connected kernels, when executed on a single core, achieve 0.24 MAC/clk during the forward step because they feature the same computational kernel (as shown in Fig. 2b). Also, the corresponding backward passes with naive MM show a similar performance level. On the contrary, the training steps of the DepthWise layers are > 4× slower than PointWise, mainly because of the overhead introduced by the *im2col* transformation and due to their inherently lower parallelism and possibility for data reuse.

When running on 8 cores, the parallel speedup of the baseline version is greater than 7.5 for all the training steps of a PointWise or a Fully-Connected Layer, thanks to the highly parallelizable nature of the MM kernel. Differently, the top speed-up for the training steps of the DepthWise Convolution is limited to 7 because of the *im2col* overhead. If compared with the STM32L476RG implementation, the execution of the baseline kernels on a single-core of PULP results to be up to 2.4 faster because of the low-latency FMA instructions, which take only 1 clock cycle to execute, 2× lower than the ARM-Cortex M4 implementation. Furthermore, the execution on PULP is accelerated thanks to PULP's Hardware Loops, which reduce the branching overhead of the inner loop.

By leveraging the optimized matrix multiplication kernel, the OPT solution speeds up the execution by up to 2.4× with respect to the baseline version, for both a single core and 8 parallel cores. In particular, the AutoTuner selects the 2 × 4 unrolled MM kernel for the training steps of the PointWise Layer in Fig. 4, mainly because the input matrices are significantly larger than the unrolling factor of the MM's inner loop. When combining the 8-core execution and the autotuned MM, the latency gain on PULP vs the STM32L476RG implementation grows up to 36.6×.

In the case of a Fully-Connected Layer, instead, the Autotuner selects the mm_unroll_1x4, mm or mm_M_unroll_1x8 for, respectively, the FW, the WG-BW, and IG-BW steps, with a performance of 2.66, 2.61, and 1.44 MAC/clk on 8 cores. Since a Fully-Connected Layer mainly relies on matrix-vector and vector-vector multiplications (as shown in Fig. 2), the most effective unrolling schemes feature a dimension of size 1 on the vector's sides.

Overall, if compared with the ideal scenario, the autotuned solution significantly increases FPU utilization, computed as the ratio between real and ideal MAC/clk performance, from 0.25 to 0.54 in the case of PointWise FW execution.

4.2   Effect of Tensor Shapes on AutoTuning

To better explore the output of the AutoTuner with respect to the tensor shapes, Fig. 5 shows the latency on 8 cores of two training primitives (PointWise FW and FC IG-BW) applied on multiple tensor *Shapes*. The tested shapes are detailed in the Figure and fit the L1 memory. Every plot reports the latency of the Top-5 fastest kernel configurations normalized and compared to the baseline performance.

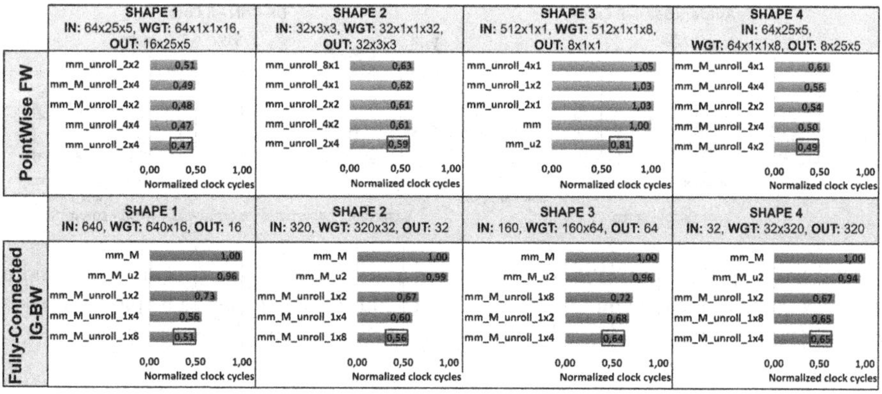

Fig. 5. Evaluation of the AutoTuner on a Pointwise Convolution Layer performing a Forward step (upper) and a Fully-Connected Layer performing an Input Gradient backpropagation step (lower) using multiple tensor Shapes (1–4). Every plot shows the latency measurements normalized with respect to the baseline, when using different optimized MM kernels.

In PointWise convolution, the top AutoTuner solution outperforms the baseline by 1.6–2.2×. The fastest solutions feature 2×4 or 4×2 unrolled MM kernels because the sizes of the involved matrices exceed both the number of cores and the maximum unrolling factors. An exception is represented by the *Shape 3* case: the presence of a tight input matrix, with shape $512 \times 1 \times 1$, leads to the computation of a high number of consecutive elements in the inner loop but a single iteration for each outer loop. For this reason, the only MM capable of accelerating the execution is **mm_u2**, which unrolls two successive products in K, reducing the data dependencies from adjacent FMA and LD which are present in the inner loop of the naïve implementation. On the other hand, the matrix-vector or vector-vector products featured by the Fully-Connected primitives result faster in the case of $1 \times V$ unrolling. As can be seen by comparing Shapes 1, 2 and 3, 4, Fully-Connected Layers with tighter input sizes privilege 1×4 unrolling, while wider ones benefit from 1×8 unrolling.

4.3   TinyML Benchmark Training

To assess the effectiveness of our approach on real DNN models, we deploy on PULP a forward and a backward pass of a Deep Autoencoder for Anomaly Detection and a DS-CNN for Keyword Spotting. Differently from previous experiments, the AutoTuner concurrently searches for both the fastest MM kernels and the layer-wise tile shapes. Figure 6 shows the latencies of a forward and a backward pass obtained by applying the AutoTuner over the two considered benchmarks (OPT bars). These solutions are compared with other implementations featuring the same tiling configuration but using fixed MM kernels, i.e., a "one-size-fits-all" approach.

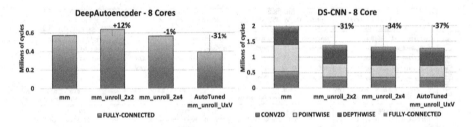

Fig. 6. Training time of two TinyML benchmarks - a Deep AutoEncoder (left) and a DS-CNN (right) - running on 8 cores and using 64 kB of L1 memory. The plot compares the autotuned vs"one-size-fits-all" solutions, agnostic to the DNN's structure.

Observing Fig. 6, the usage of a "one-size-fits-all" approach is particularly weak in the case of a Deep Autoencoder, which is composed of a sequence of Fully-Connected layers. In this case, the usage of 2×2 or 2×4 unrolling implies the presence of all-leftover computation, leading to a slow-down of 12% in the case of a fixed 2×2 optimization, and a very limited speed up of 1% in the case of a 2×4, when executing on 8 cores. Instead, the usage of autotuned kernels, which are mainly represented by 1×2, 1×4, and 1×8 unrolling, with both parallelism in N and M depending on the training step, introduces a high performance gain of 31% on 8 cores.

Concerning the DS-CNN, the large tensor sizes encourage the use of wide unrolling factors. However, 2×2 or 2×4 unrolling factors with parallelism in N are 6% and 3% slower than the autotuned execution. The use of 2×4 and 4×2 for Convolutions and of 1×4 and 1×8 for the last Fully-Connected classifier, each with both parallelism in N and M, produces a significant and uniform speed up.

Lastly, the introduction of autotuning on full DNN training steps of TinyML benchmarks enables real-time network updates, with a top performance of 0.4 million cycles for a Deep Autoencoder and 1.3 million cycles for a DS-CNN.

On a PULP-based device like Vega [26], running at 450 MHz, these performances result in 0.9 ms and 3 ms to execute a single training step. These latencies prove to be $15 \times$ and $108 \times$ faster, respectively, than the results available over the same models on a RISC-V MCU on MLCommons[5] which on the contrary performs a single inference step only, i.e. no backpropagation.

---

[5] TinyMLPerf results: https://mlcommons.org/en/inference-tiny-05/.

4.4   Comparison with the State of the Art

As a comparison with the current state-of-the-art, we profile the same-task performances of *PULP-TrainLib* and AIfES[6] Fraunhofer IMS's on-device learning software library. For this purpose, we configure AIfES to use the MM kernels provided by the optimized ARM CMSIS library. Since the current version of AIfES does not provide Convolutional Layers, we profile its performances over the Deep Autoencoder of Fig. 6, which is composed of Fully-Connected layers. The execution of AIfES kernels is measured, in clock cycles, on an ARM Cortex-M4-based STM32F407VGT6 MCU.

Figure 7 presents the results of a training step of the Deep Autoencoder with a batch size of 1 (i.e., the model forwards and backwards a single image at a time). With this setup, a complete model training with AIfES takes about 12 million clock cycles to execute (71.9 ms on an STM32F4 at 168 MHz), 3.3× higher than a non-optimized single-core training with *PULP-TrainLib*.

Compared to PULP-TrainLib, we notice a high slowdown in the execution of the IG-BW step. This is due to the vector-vector product on which this step relies, which induces an all-leftover computation on the CMSIS-NN unrolled kernels, requiring 19 instructions to execute each MM inner-loop iteration (2 ld, 1 fma, 2 add/sub, 1 branch, and 13 others to monitor the state of the computation and iterate over the outer loops). For this reason, this step suffers a 5.9× slowdown with respect to our baseline, single-core implementation, which is built to handle vector-vector and vector-matrix products with less overhead.

Furthermore, the vector-matrix products of the FW and IG-BW steps require roughly 2× the clock cycles of our single-core execution with AIfES. Even with unrolled CMSIS MM kernels, DNN kernels on the STM32F407 require 19 instructions to execute (8 ld, 4 fma, 6 add/sub, 1 branch). On the PULP RISC-V cores, the branching overhead can be avoided employing Hardware Loops.

Overall, we observe that the application of the AutoTuner leads to a 4.5× performance increase with respect to AIfES. On 8 parallel cores, we achieve an average parallel speedup of over 6.5× over each tile and layer of the DNN model, with respect to both our non-optimized and optimized single-core execution. Therefore, we verify that our AutoTuner is able to effectively achieve the same degree of optimization on both a single and a multicore training setup, for each tile and layer of the DNN model. This results in a 30.7× higher performance with respect to AIfES, on 8 parallel RISC-V cores.

---

[6] AIfES for Arduino: https://www.arduino.cc/reference/en/libraries/aifes-for-ardu ino/.

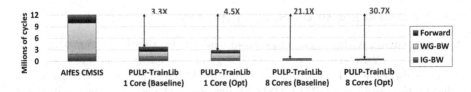

Fig. 7. Comparison of PULP-TrainLib with Fraunhofer IMS's AIfES training library for MCUs, using CMSIS as computational backend on a complete Deep Autoencoder model. AIfES' layer tiles are executed on an STM32F407VGT6 MCU.

5   Conclusion

In this paper, we presented *PULP-TrainLib*, the first software library for DNN on-device training on multi-core RISC-V-based MicroController Units (MCUs). Included into *PULP-TrainLib*, we introduced an *AutoTuner*, capable of jointly selecting the fastest matrix multiplication kernel optimization and tile size for a given DNN layer configuration. By applying the *AutoTuner* on the training primitives of *PULP-TrainLib*, we are able to run complete training steps of TinyML DNN models in almost real-time.

Acknowledgement. This work was supported in part by the EU Horizon 2020 Research and Innovation Project WiPLASH under Grant 863337 and in part by the ECSEL Horizon 2020 Project AI4DI under Grant 826060.

References

1. Amodei, D., Olah, C., Steinhardt, J., Christiano, P., Schulman, J., Mané, D.: Concrete problems in AI safety (2016)
2. Ankit, A., et al.: Panther: a programmable architecture for neural network training harnessing energy-efficient reram. IEEE Trans. Comput. **69**(8), 1128–1142 (2020)
3. Ashouri, A.H., Killian, W., Cavazos, J., Palermo, G., Silvano, C.: A survey on compiler autotuning using machine learning. ACM Comput. Surv. **51**(5), 1–42 (2018)
4. Bruschi, N., Haugou, G., Tagliavini, G., Conti, F., Benini, L., Rossi, D.: GVSoC: a highly configurable, fast and accurate full-platform simulator for RISC-V based IoT processors. In: 2021 IEEE 39th International Conference on Computer Design (ICCD), pp. 409–416 (2021)
5. Cai, H., Gan, C., Zhu, L., Han, S.: Tinytl: reduce activations, not trainable parameters for efficient on-device learning (2021)
6. Chen, T., et al.: TVM: an automated end-to-end optimizing compiler for deep learning. In: 13th USENIX Symposium on Operating Systems Design and Implementation (OSDI 2018), pp. 578–594. USENIX Association, Carlsbad, CA, October 2018
7. Chen, T., et al.: Learning to optimize tensor programs (2019)
8. Chen, Y.R., et al.: Experiments and optimizations for TVM on RISC-V architectures with p extension. In: 2020 International Symposium on VLSI Design, Automation and Test (VLSI-DAT), pp. 1–4 (2020)

9. David, R., et al.: Tensorflow lite micro: embedded machine learning on TinyML systems (2021)
10. Frigo, M., Johnson, S.: FFTW: an adaptive software architecture for the FFT. In: Proceedings of the 1998 IEEE International Conference on Acoustics, Speech and Signal Processing, ICASSP 1998 (Cat. No. 98CH36181), vol. 3, pp. 1381–1384 (1998)
11. Konečný, J., McMahan, H.B., Yu, F.X., Richtárik, P., Suresh, A.T., Bacon, D.: Federated learning: strategies for improving communication efficiency (2017)
12. Kopparapu, K., Lin, E.: TinyFedTL: federated transfer learning on tiny devices (2021)
13. Lai, L., Suda, N., Chandra, V.: CMSIS-NN: efficient neural network kernels for arm cortex-m cpus (2018)
14. Lee, S., Nirjon, S.: Neuro.zero: a zero-energy neural network accelerator for embedded sensing and inference systems. In: Proceedings of the 17th Conference on Embedded Networked Sensor Systems. SenSys 2019, New York, NY, USA, pp. 138–152. Association for Computing Machinery (2019)
15. Lin, J., Chen, W.M., Lin, Y., Cohn, J., Gan, C., Han, S.: Mcunet: tiny deep learning on IoT devices. Adv. Neural. Inf. Process. Syst. **33**, 11711–11722 (2020)
16. Losing, V., Hammer, B., Wersing, H.: Incremental on-line learning: a review and comparison of state of the art algorithms. Neurocomputing **275**, 1261–1274 (2018)
17. McMahan, B., Moore, E., Ramage, D., Hampson, S., Arcas, B.A.Y.: Communication-efficient learning of deep networks from decentralized data. In: Singh, A., Zhu, J. (eds.) Proceedings of the 20th International Conference on Artificial Intelligence and Statistics. Proceedings of Machine Learning Research, vol. 54, pp. 1273–1282. PMLR, 20–22 April 2017
18. Mills, J., Hu, J., Min, G.: Communication-efficient federated learning for wireless edge intelligence in IoT. IEEE IoT J. **7**(7), 5986–5994 (2020)
19. Murshed, M.G.S., Murphy, C., Hou, D., Khan, N., Ananthanarayanan, G., Hussain, F.: Machine learning at the network edge: a survey. ACM Comput. Surv. **54**(8), 1–37 (2022)
20. Mustafa, D.: A survey of performance tuning techniques and tools for parallel applications. IEEE Access **10**, 15036–15055 (2022)
21. Pan, S.J., Yang, Q.: A survey on transfer learning. IEEE Trans. Knowl. Data Eng. **22**(10), 1345–1359 (2010)
22. Pellegrini, L., Graffieti, G., Lomonaco, V., Maltoni, D.: Latent replay for real-time continual learning. In: 2020 IEEE/RSJ International Conference on Intelligent Robots and Systems (IROS), pp. 10203–10209 (2020)
23. Ragan-Kelley, J., Barnes, C., Adams, A., Paris, S., Durand, F., Amarasinghe, S.: Halide: a language and compiler for optimizing parallelism, locality, and recomputation in image processing pipelines. SIGPLAN Not. **48**(6), 519–530 (2013)
24. Ravaglia, L., et al.: A TinyML platform for on-device continual learning with quantized latent replays. IEEE J. Emerg. Sel. Topics Circ. Syst. **11**, 789–802 (2021)
25. Ren, H., Anicic, D., Runkler, T.: TinyOL: TinyML with online-learning on microcontrollers (2021)
26. Rossi, D., et al.: Vega: a ten-core SOC for IoT endnodes with DNN acceleration and cognitive wake-up from MRAM-based state-retentive sleep mode. IEEE J. Solid-State Circ. **57**, 127–139 (2021)
27. Vasilache, N., et al.: Tensor comprehensions: framework-agnostic high-performance machine learning abstractions (2018)
28. Wang, F., Zhang, M., Wang, X., Ma, X., Liu, J.: Deep learning for edge computing applications: a state-of-the-art survey. IEEE Access **8**, 58322–58336 (2020)

29. Wang, X., Magno, M., Cavigelli, L., Benini, L.: FANN-on-MCU: an open-source toolkit for energy-efficient neural network inference at the edge of the internet of things. IEEE IoT J. **7**(5), 4403–4417 (2020)
30. Whaley, R., Dongarra, J.: Automatically tuned linear algebra software. In: SC 1998: Proceedings of the 1998 ACM/IEEE Conference on Supercomputing, pp. 38–38 (1998)

Extra-Functional Property Estimation

The Impact of Dynamic Storage Allocation on CPython Execution Time, Memory Footprint and Energy Consumption: An Empirical Study

Christos P. Lamprakos[1,2(✉)] ⓘ, Lazaros Papadopoulos[1] ⓘ,
Francky Catthoor[2,3] ⓘ, and Dimitrios Soudris[1] ⓘ

[1] National Technical University of Athens, Iroon Polytechniou Street 9,
15780 Zografou, Greece
{cplamprakos,lpapadop,dsoudris}@microlab.ntua.gr
[2] Katholieke Universiteit Leuven, Oude Markt 13, 3000 Leuven, Belgium
[3] imec Science Park, Gaston Geenslaan 14, 3001 Leuven, Belgium
francky.catthoor@imec.be

Abstract. CPython is the reference implementation of the Python programming language. Tools like machine learning frameworks, web development interfaces and scientific computing libraries have been built on top of it. Meanwhile, single-board computers are now able to run GNU/Linux distributions. As a result CPython's influence today is not limited to commodity servers, but also includes edge and mobile devices. We should thus be concerned with the performance of CPython applications. In this spirit, we investigate the impact of dynamic storage allocation on the execution time, memory footprint and energy consumption of CPython programs. Our findings show that (i) CPython's default configuration is optimized for memory footprint, (ii) replacing this configuration can improve performance by more than $1.6x$ and (iii) application-specific characteristics define which allocator setup performs best at each case. Additionally, we contribute an open-source means for benchmarking the energy consumption of CPython applications. By employing a rigorous and reliable statistical analysis technique, we provide strong indicators that most of our conclusions are platform-independent.

Keywords: CPython · Dynamic storage allocation · Embedded systems · Energy efficiency · Benchmarking studies

1 Introduction

Today Python is one of the most popular high-level programming languages [1]. Its reference implementation is CPython [2]. Python source code is usually com-

This research work was partially supported by the Hellenic Foundation for Research and Innovation (HFRI) under the 3rd Call for HFRI PhD Fellowships (fellowship number: 61/512200), as well as by the European Union's Horizon 2020 research and innovation programme under grant agreement No. 101021274.

A. Orailoglu et al. (Eds.): SAMOS 2022, LNCS 13511, pp. 219–234, 2022.
https://doi.org/10.1007/978-3-031-15074-6_14

piled to bytecode and executed on the CPython virtual machine, which is implemented in C.

CPython is often criticized for its performance, which has previously been compared to that of other programming languages [18]. The results do indeed validate the criticism, but Python's extreme popularity cannot be ignored. Several Python libraries have dominated the programming landscape. SciPy [22] has democratized scientific computing, scikit-learn [16] has done the same for introductory machine learning projects, Pytorch [15] has almost monopolized deep learning pipelines in both academia and the industry.

CPython is not deployed just on servers or home computers, but is becoming all the more present on embedded systems [3,6]. This is largely owed to the availability of cheap single-board computers (SBCs) like the Raspberry Pi[1] and the BeagleBone[2], which are capable of running GNU/Linux.

We thus consider improving the execution time, memory footprint and energy consumption of CPython applications a worthwhile endeavor. We believe low-hanging fruit should be reaped before having to examine CPython's internals. Consequently, we focus on configurations exposed by the language runtime that cause observable, non-random effects on performance[3].

As regards the particular configuration under study, we picked dynamic storage allocation (DSA) for the following reasons: firstly, CPython does provide the option of configuring it. Secondly, DSA is a cornerstone operation used by most real-world programs and as a result demands attention. Finally, it is not well-understood [23], so treating it as a black box and benchmarking several versions of it may yield useful results.

1.1   Contributions

We conducted a reliable, statistically rigorous empirical study of DSA's impact on the execution time, memory footprint and energy consumption of CPython programs. Our first contribution is providing quantitative answers to the research questions: (**I**) to what extent can a CPython application's performance with respect to execution time, memory footprint and energy consumption be improved by modifying the runtime's DSA configuration? (**II**) how much do optimizations in the runtime itself affect the expected improvement? (**III**) are performance improvements sensitive to application-specific characteristics? By addressing these questions, we pave the way towards predicting the optimal DSA configuration for a given application without resorting to brute-force methods.

Our second contribution is an open-source modification of the `pyperformance` and `pyperf` packages, which enables the benchmarking of Python programs with

---

[1] https://www.raspberrypi.com/.

[2] https://beagleboard.org/bone.

[3] From this point onward, we will use the term "performance" to refer collectively to the set of execution time, memory footprint and energy consumption. See Sect. 3.1 for details.

respect to energy consumption. It can be used on all Linux-running machines featuring Intel's RAPL power capping interface [8,10]. All of our results and accompanying code are publicly available on GitHub[4].

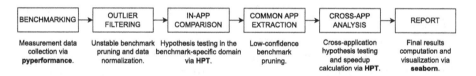

Fig. 1. The method followed to produce this paper's results.

2   Method

Figure 1 summarizes the general flow of our work. We used `pyperformance`[5] for data collection and the HPT method [7] for statistical performance analysis.

`pyperformance` is the official benchmark suite of the Python community. It contains a variety of real-world applications, which is a necessity when studying DSA (synthetic benchmarks have long been known to be unreliable in characterizing allocator performance [23]). `pyperformance` also offers utilities for the reproducibility and stability of results, like commands for system tuning and compiling isolated versions of CPython, test calibration and warmup, as well as automatic identification of unstable benchmarks. We used `pyperformance` to collect raw benchmark data, and filter unstable applications out (first and second boxes in Fig. 1).

HPT is a statistical analysis method for reliable performance comparison of systems. It is integrated in the PARSEC benchmark suite [5]. HPT employs hypothesis testing in order to answer questions of the form "X has better/worse performance than Y with a confidence of Z". It also computes quantitative, single-number speedup[6] comparisons (again, including the respective confidence)[7]. We used HPT to process the benchmark data recorded by `pyperformance` and derive fair, informed answers to the research questions stated in Sect. 1.1. This constitutes boxes 3–5 in Fig. 1.

Our method rests upon the fact that HPT allows *cross-application* deductions stemming from application-specific data[8]. The flow is repeated for each metric of interest (execution time, memory footprint, energy consumption):

---

[4] https://github.com/cappadokes/cpythondsa.

[5] https://github.com/python/pyperformance.

[6] The term "speedup" normally hints toward improvement in execution time. For this paper, we extend the term's semantics so as to include memory footprint and energy consumption as well. Thus a speedup of $1.2x$ should be interpreted as achieving 1.2 times less execution time, memory footprint, or energy consumption with respect to some baseline.

[7] According to the authors of HPT, merely relying on the geometric mean for summarizing computer performance is problematic [7].

[8] The curious reader is encouraged to consult [7] for a complete treatment of why this is feasible.

- **Benchmarking:** each application is calibrated and a warmup value is computed and discarded. 60 values per application are then measured. A suite consisting of B benchmarks thus produces $60 \cdot B$ values. All this work is conducted by `pyperformance`. This step is repeated for all the DSA configurations that we want to compare. A dataset corresponding to N configurations contains $60 \cdot B \cdot N$ values.
- **Outlier filtering:** `pyperformance` prints warnings for potentially unreliable benchmarks, if they include outlier values different than the mean by a multiple of the standard deviation. We discard such cases and normalize the remaining ones as speedups over a reference configuration. We propagate forward the greatest subset of benchmarks common across all configurations.
- **In-app comparison:** the qualitative aspect of HPT is employed for this step. Each candidate configuration C is compared to the reference configuration R over each benchmark T. The comparison tests the hypothesis "C has better performance than R on benchmark T". The result is summarized as a confidence value. If this confidence is lower than a predefined threshold (e.g. 95%) the comparison is discarded.
- **Common app extraction:** not all (C, R) pairs end up having identical sets of benchmarks with high-confidence comparisons. To mitigate this, we again identify the greatest subset of common benchmarks. We end up with a dataset that, for all configurations, (i) is stable and (ii) guarantees statistically significant comparisons.
- **Cross-app analysis:** in-app comparison is now conducted for the set of stable benchmarks. The result is used as input to a quantitative computation: each candidate configuration C is assigned a cross-application speedup S over the reference configuration R, along with a confidence value as usual. S has three possible types of values:
  - a **floating point** number denoting actual speedup, which states that C performs better than R across all benchmarks with high confidence. The speedup is a lower bound on the expected impact to an arbitrary application's performance[9].
  - an "**MI**" placeholder denoting Marginal Improvement. The candidate configuration C might improve an application's performance, but to a negligible degree. Cases may exist where C performs worse than the reference. No horizontal conclusion should be drawn.
  - a "**PD**" placeholder denoting Performance Degradation. This implies that C will cause worse performance for an arbitrary application compared to the reference configuration.

3   Experimental Setup

Figure 2 encapsulates our tools, experiment workflow and results generation process. In the next few paragraphs, we describe it in further detail. A comprehensive

---

[9] No speedup value stands on its own, but must be co-interpreted with the respective confidence value.

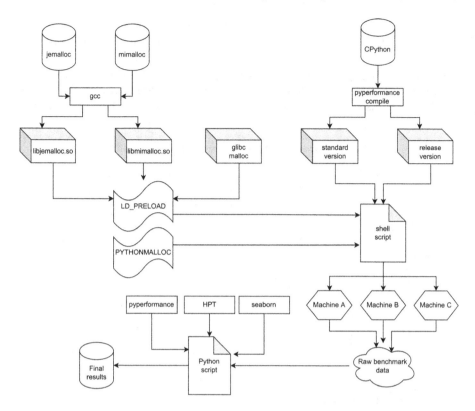

Fig. 2. Experimental setup summary. Note the different symbols for: trusted data (cylinders), software operations (rectangles), scripts, environment variables (flags), binary files (3D rectangles), raw data (cloud), machines (hexagons).

list of materials can be found at Table 1. With regard to the benchmarked applications, we mention $\sim \frac{1}{3}$ of them[10] in Table 2. Our main method, as described analytically in Sect. 2, is implemented by a Python script which processes the raw benchmarking data offline.

3.1 Rationale

We are interested in cross-application conclusions on the impact of DSA on CPython's performance. We define **conclusions** as answers to our research questions (Sect. 1.1). We define **performance** as the set of execution time, memory footprint and energy consumption (T, M, E). We used the default version of the **pyperformance run** command to measure execution time, and the -track-memory option for memory footprint. We modified **pyperformance** so as to report energy consumption readings in Linux machines which feature Intel's

---

[10] For the full catalogue, please consult https://pyperformance.readthedocs.io/bench marks.html.

RAPL [8] power-capping interface. E is the sum of core and DRAM energy consumption, E_C and E_M. According to RAPL's documentation, the core part includes caches and the MMU. Note that $E_C + E_M < E_T$ if E_T is the total energy consumption of the platform. We define **impact** as the speedup S achieved by configuration C against a reference measurement R. Formally, $S = \frac{R}{C}$. This is also the metric used by our main statistical analysis tool, the HPT method [7].

Table 1. Hardware and software used for the study.

Component	Machine A	Machine B	Machine C
Type	Server	Embedded SoC	PC
Processor	8x Intel Core i7-6700	4x ARMv8 Processor rev 1	12x Intel Core i7-8750H
Clock frequency	3.4 GHz	1.5 GHz	2.2 GHz
System memory	32 GiB	4 GiB	16 GiB
Operating system	Ubuntu 20.04.4 LTS	Ubuntu 16.04.7 LTS	Ubuntu 20.04.3 LTS
Linux kernel version	5.13.0-35-generic	4.4.38-tegra	5.13.0-37-generic
GNU glibc version	2.31	2.23	2.31
Energy interface	Intel RAPL [8,10]	N/A	Intel RAPL
CPython	3.10.2		
pyperformance	1.0.4 (modified)		
pyperf	2.3.1 (modified)		
mimalloc [14]	2.0.5		
jemalloc [9]	5.2.1		

3.2 PGO, LTO Sensitivity

Profile-guided and link-time optimizations (PGO, LTO) are available when compiling the CPython runtime. We want to investigate how these affect the performance impact caused by DSA–a sensitivity check between two extremes: a "standard" version which is the one built by default, and a "release" one that uses the `-enable-optimizations` and `-with-lto` options to enable PGO and LTO.

3.3 Configuration Points

CPython DSA may be configured with two degrees of freedom:

- enabling/disabling the use of CPython's internal allocator `pymalloc`. When enabled, it is invoked for request sizes up to 512 bytes. Controlled via the `PYTHONMALLOC` environment variable[11]. Enabled by default.
- selecting the `malloc` implementation which CPython invokes when requesting memory from the operating system. Controlled via the `LD_PRELOAD`[12] trick. The default one is the system's allocator, which is normally `glibc` in GNU/Linux-running machines.

---

[11] https://docs.python.org/3/c-api/memory.html
[12] https://man7.org/linux/man-pages/man8/ld.so.8.html

Table 2. Some of the benchmarked applications.

Name	Description
chameleon	HTML/XML template engine
django_template	High-level Python web framework
dulwich	Implementation of the Git file formats and protocols
fannkuch	From the Computer Language Benchmarks Game
float	Artificial, floating point-heavy benchmark originally used by Factor
genshi	Library for parsing, generating, and processing HTML, XML or other textual content
html5lib	Library for parsing HTML
json	API to convert in-memory Python objects to a serialized representation known as JavaScript Object Notation (JSON) and vice-versa
pathlib	Tests the performance of operations of the pathlib module of the standard library
pickle	Uses the cPickle module to pickle a variety of datasets
regex_compile	Stresses the performance of Python's regex compiler, rather than the regex execution speed
richards	The classic Python Richards benchmark. Based on a Java version
spectral_norm	MathWorld: "Hundred-Dollar, Hundred-Digit Challenge Problems", Challenge #3
telco	Benchmark for measuring the performance of decimal calculations. From the Computer Language Benchmarks Game
tornado_http	Web framework and asynchronous networking library, originally developed at FriendFeed

Thus N allocators produce $2 \cdot N$ candidate configuration points. In the case of this paper, $N = 3$ [malloc (glibc), mimalloc, jemalloc] and as a result we have 6 configuration points available. The aforementioned allocators were selected as popular representatives of the state of the art in DSA. Our process can be extended to other allocator libraries with minimal effort.

We refer to the pymalloc-enabled, malloc-linked configuration as reference, since it is the default setting.

3.4 Benchmarking Script

Batches of data are collected via a shell script which repeatedly executes pyperformance run commands[13], each time for a different configuration point. When available, pyperf system tune is used prior to data collection for ensuring more stable measurements. Raw benchmarking measurements are saved in compressed JSON format (the resulting files correspond to the arrow leaving the BENCHMARKING box in Fig. 1).

---

[13] https://pyperformance.readthedocs.io/usage.html.

3.5   Platform Independence

Our experiments are conducted on three platforms: a server-class workstation, an embedded system-on-chip (SoC) and a laptop PC. In each case, we follow the method described in Sect. 2 to compute the cross-application speedups of all configuration points on all performance metrics.

If (i) similar speedups are computed for the same configuration on different platforms and (ii) this holds true for both the standard and release versions (Sect. 3.2), we may consider our experiments platform-independent. This test relies on mere common sense and must not be taken for a formal method; its validity lies in the multiplicity of the tested machines and the reliability of our analysis method (Sect. 2).

4   Results

This section presents our study's findings. Before we proceed, however, we shall do our best to accustom the reader's intuition with our results' format. Let us thus map the research questions stated in Sect. 1.1 to suiting structures:

I. *To what extent can a CPython application's performance with respect to execution time, memory footprint and energy consumption be improved by modifying the runtime's DSA configuration?* We need to reason about an arbitrary application (not necessarily one included in the benchmark suite). As explained in Sect. 2, the HPT method computes cross-application speedups and the respective confidence values. We thus create a table of $(speedup, confidence)$ tuples with configurations as rows and performance metrics as columns, like Table 3.

II. *How much do optimizations in the runtime itself affect the expected improvement?* We create tables as the one described above for both the standard and release CPython builds (Tables 3, 4 and 5).

III. *Are performance improvements sensitive to application-specific characteristics?* We summarize a configuration's performance in a single benchmark as the geometric mean of all measured speedups. We attain visual answers to this question by printing the empirical cumulative distribution function (ECDF) of geometric mean speedups (Figs. 3, 4 and 5)[14]; if variability exists in the best-performing allocator setup per benchmark, the answer is positive.

4.1   Discussion

We now proceed with the findings extracted from the collected data. We shall refer to the non-optimized CPython build as "standard" and to the PGO-LTO one as "release". Although we display ECDF graphs for all three machines and

---

[14] A previous footnote mentions the inadequacy of performance summarization via the geometric mean. It refers, however, to cross-application results. In the present case, we are interested in application-specific speedups, which the geometric mean is normally used to summarize. Note that the harmonic mean could prove closer to the ground truth in special circumstances [11].

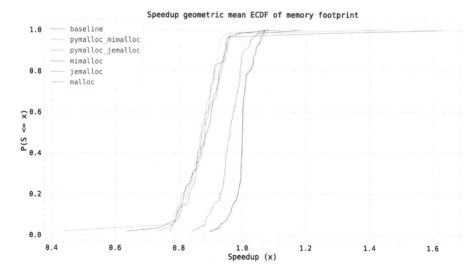

Fig. 3. ECDF of speedup over memory footprint (embedded SoC, release version). The baseline configuration outperforms all alternatives in almost all cases. This figure partly supports our first finding according to which CPython's default DSA is optimized for memory footprint. See Table 5 for details.

both types of CPython, not enough space exists for including everything. The complete code and data can be found at our accompanying repository[15]. For now, we limit ourselves to representative cases that partially support our findings and reveal the broadest possible area of our experiments' space.

Degree of Influence: modifying CPython's DSA has considerable impact when using the standard build (see "Standard" sections of Tables 3, 4 and 5 as well as Figs. 4 and 6). Particular gains can surpass 1.6x. To the contrary, performance is very hard to improve in the case of a release build–yet if constraints are tight, marginal improvements could be gained for specific applications (see for example Fig. 5).

External Allocator Optimality: in the standard case performance across all metrics of interest will be improved by disposing of `pymalloc` and using an external allocator for all request sizes (Tables 3 and 4, Figs. 4 and 6). This is possibly owed to the fact that a standard runtime introduces substantial overheads compared to native allocator code. An unresolved question here is why memory footprint is also better without `pymalloc`. We suspect but have not investigated a potential impact of PGO and LTO themselves on the runtime's final memory layout.

Footprint Optimality: if a release CPython is employed the default configuration (`pymalloc+glibc`) will achieve the best memory footprint with very high certainty (e.g. Fig. 3). If no other metrics are of interest, all alternatives should be avoided.

---

[15] https://github.com/cappadokes/cpythondsa.

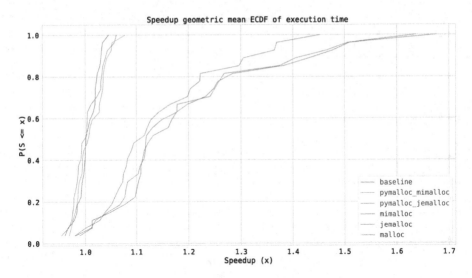

Fig. 4. ECDF of speedup over execution time (embedded SoC, standard version). All DSA configurations that make exclusive use of some external allocator outperform the ones employing CPython's `pymalloc`. This partly supports our finding that in builds without PGO and LTO, discarding `pymalloc` almost always improves performance. See Table 5 for details.

Platform Independence: execution time and memory footprint impacts for all configurations in both standard and release builds are very similar across all three tested machines, as shown in Tables 3, 5 and 4. We consider this a very strong indicator that conclusions involving these two metrics are *platform-independent*.

Energy Complexity: a weaker statement on platform independence can be made about DRAM energy consumption, since it is supported by two out of three machine datasets (Tables 3 and 4); the only outlier here is `pymalloc_jemalloc` in the release case. Core energy consumption on the other hand seems to be tied to each platform's microarchitecture (Tables 3 and 4, Fig. 6). Decisions involving it should always be driven by extensive profiling and careful study. Both DRAM and core energy are very difficult to improve in the release case[16].

5 Limitations

The allocators used for our study are not the only ones available–though they are popular enough to represent the state of the art. Options like Hoard [4], `supermalloc` [13] and others should be evaluated too for completeness.

---

[16] Recall that "core" energy includes cache memories and the MMU apart from the actual processor cores. Access to direct measurements from these subsystems would be very interesting for the scope of this paper, but the RAPL implementations we used did not expose such an option.

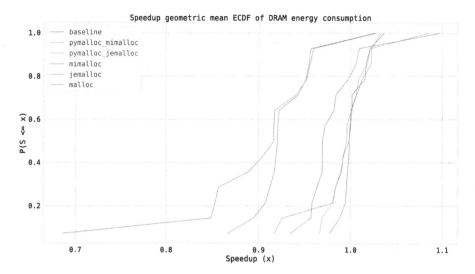

Fig. 5. ECDF of speedup over DRAM energy consumption (server-class workstation, release version). An horizontal solution is impossible to find. Impact against the baseline is marginal at best. This partly supports our finding that the energy consumption of a PGO-LTO optimized CPython runtime is very hard to improve upon, and is sensitive to application-specific characteristics. See Table 3 for details.

We use Intel's RAPL tool [8] for making energy measurements. RAPL does not report true energy consumption, but is rather a hardware model that has been shown to possess adequate accuracy [12]. There do exist methodologies for ensuring minimal error when using RAPL to measure the energy consumption of short code paths [10]; we did not implement them due to lack of time. As a result, the subsets of common stable benchmarks across configurations for core and DRAM energy were smaller than the ones for execution time and memory footprint. Future work should focus on producing more stable measurements across all metrics.

We showed in our findings that, particularly for release builds of CPython, performance improvements in some respects are possible yet marginal and sensitive to application-specific characteristics. Our work devotes no effort on actually defining these characteristics; an idea we did not manage to realize is to integrate analytical heap profiling to **pyperformance** and **pyperf**. Even if we had done this, however, more complex methods than HPT should be employed to analyze and categorize the collected profiles since heap behavior cannot be summarized with a single number. Static analysis methods are another idea. Future research must consider both of these routes.

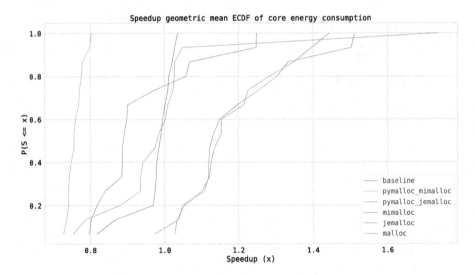

Fig. 6. ECDF of speedup over core energy consumption (laptop PC, standard version). The configurations featuring exclusive use of `jemalloc` and `malloc` yield significant improvements across most cases. This figure partially supports our finding that cross-application performance enhancement can be achieved in standard builds by discarding CPython's `pymalloc`. It also shows that core energy consumption can at times be extremely counterintuitive, as happens in the case of `pymalloc_jemalloc`. See Table 4 for details.

Table 3. Cross-application speedup and confidence values from the server experiment. MI stands for Marginal Improvement, PD for Performance Degradation. Note that MI results have the lowest confidence, which signifies to sensitivity application-specific characteristics. Also note that the reported speedups are lower bounds on the expected performance improvements. It is natural for cases like Fig. 6 to contain benchmark-specific speedups that are higher than their cross-application counterparts.

Configuration	Execution time	Memory footprint	Core energy	DRAM energy
Standard				
pymalloc_mimalloc	MI (58%)	PD (100%)	PD (100%)	MI (27%)
pymalloc_jemalloc	MI (48%)	PD (100%)	PD (100%)	MI (15%)
mimalloc	**1.125** (93.96%)	**1.035** (92.98%)	**1.135** (93.2%)	**1.115** (90.31%)
jemalloc	**1.105** (92.73%)	**1.075** (93.41%)	**1.09** (93.32%)	**1.1** (94.97%)
malloc	**1.115** (91.29%)	**1.11** (89.79%)	**1.12** (89.27%)	**1.1** (94.8%)
Release				
pymalloc_mimalloc	MI (35%)	**PD** (100%)	MI (45%)	MI (21%)
pymalloc_jemalloc	MI (21%)	**PD** (100%)	PD (99.58%)	PD (95.44%)
mimalloc	PD (99.99%)	**PD** (100%)	MI (11%)	PD (98.84%)
jemalloc	PD (100%)	**PD** (100%)	PD (99.95%)	PD (99.99%)
malloc	PD (100%)	**PD** (100%)	PD (99.99%)	PD (99.99%)

Table 4. Cross-application speedup and confidence values from the PC experiment. All comments on Table 3 apply here as well.

Configuration	Execution time	Memory footprint	Core energy	DRAM energy
Standard				
pymalloc_mimalloc	MI (82%)	PD (100%)	PD (99.95%)	MI (8%)
pymalloc_jemalloc	MI (7%)	PD (100%)	MI (18%)	MI (10%)
mimalloc	**1.125** (93.97%)	**1.03** (94.81%)	MI (10%)	**1.12** (93.55%)
jemalloc	**1.115** (99.3%)	**1.03** (89.65%)	**1.11** (94.21%)	**1.11** (93.55%)
malloc	**1.115** (91.39%)	**1.11** (90.96%)	**1.11** (94.21%)	**1.11** (93.55%)
Release				
pymalloc_mimalloc	MI (66%)	**PD** (100%)	MI (17%)	MI (30%)
pymalloc_jemalloc	MI (89%)	**PD** (100%)	**1.005** (83.71%)	MI-(56%)
mimalloc	PD (99.99%)	**PD** (100%)	MI (7%)	PD (99.76%)
jemalloc	PD (100%)	**PD** (100%)	MI (99.76%)	PD (99.98%)
malloc	PD (100%)	**PD** (100%)	PD (100%)	PD (99.99%)

Table 5. Cross-application speedup and confidence values from the embedded SoC. Energy measurements not available for this platform. The N/A entries denote corrupt data which we could not refine.

Configuration	Execution time	Memory footprint
Standard		
pymalloc_mimalloc	MI (84%)	N/A
pymalloc_jemalloc	MI (19%)	N/A
mimalloc	**1.12** (94.66%)	N/A
jemalloc	**1.11** (94.66%)	N/A
malloc	**1.095** (93.13%)	N/A
Release		
pymalloc_mimalloc	**1.01** (76.09%)	**PD** (100%)
pymalloc_jemalloc	MI (93%)	**PD** (100%)
mimalloc	PD (99.87%)	**PD** (100%)
jemalloc	PD (99.99%)	**PD** (100%)
malloc	PD (100%)	**PD** (100%)

6   Related Work

pyperformance is the official benchmark suite of the Python community. It contains a variety of real-world applications and also offers utilities for the reproducibility and stability of results, like commands for system tuning and compiling isolated versions of CPython, test calibration and warmup, as well as automatic identification of unstable benchmarks. HPT [7] is a statistical analysis method for reliable performance comparison of systems. It employs hypothesis testing in order to answer questions of the form "X has better/worse performance than Y with a confidence of Z". It also computes quantitative, single-number speedup comparisons. [19] and [17] benchmark the energy efficiency of programming languages. [21] evaluates multiple implementations of Python (CPython, PyPy, Jython etc.) against one another. To the best of our knowledge, no other study exists which quantifies the impact of DSA on CPython. With respect to memory allocation, [23] still remains the golden standard introduction to the field. `mimalloc` is presented in [14] and `jemalloc` in [9]. [20] is a Python interface utilizing Intel RAPL for energy measurements.

7   Conclusions

This work explored the impact of configuring CPython's dynamic storage allocation mechanism on execution time, memory footprint and energy consumption. It is motivated by Python's wide adoption in systems spanning from the edge to the server domain.

We used and extended the official benchmark suite of the language, `pyperformance`, to collect our measurements. We analyzed the data with HPT [7], a statistically rigorous method for making cross-application deductions.

According to our findings, the performance of standard CPython can be improved in all three performance aspects by exclusively using an external allocator (e.g. `jemalloc`) for all request sizes. Gains can surpass $1.6x$. Moreover, a runtime built with PGO and LTO provides optimal memory footprint out of the box. Energy consumption in the PGO-LTO case can only be improved marginally, and the suiting DSA configuration is sensitive to application-specific characteristics.

Our experiments took place in three different platforms. We show strong evidence that DSA's impact on execution time and memory footprint is platform-independent. Slightly weaker evidence for the independence of DRAM energy consumption is also provided. As regards core energy consumption (processor, caches, MMU) no similar statement can be made. To the best of our knowledge, this is the first rigorous study of the relationship between CPython and DSA.

Acknowledgement. We thank the anonymous reviewers of SAMOS for their feedback, and the conference's organizers for allowing us a place to present our work.

References

1. Stack Overflow Developer Survey 2020, February 2020. insights.stackoverflow.com/survey/2020/
2. CPython Repository, September 2021. github.com/python/cpython
3. Embedded python, February 2022. wiki.python.org/moin/EmbeddedPython
4. Berger, E.D., McKinley, K.S., Blumofe, R.D., Wilson, P.R.: Hoard: a scalable memory allocator for multithreaded applications. SIGPLAN Not. **35**(11), 117–128 (2000). https://doi.org/10.1145/356989.357000
5. Bienia, C., Kumar, S., Singh, J.P., Li, K.: The parsec benchmark suite: characterization and architectural implications. In: Proceedings of the 17th International

Conference on Parallel Architectures and Compilation Techniques, PACT 2008, pp. 72–81. Association for Computing Machinery, New York (2008). https://doi.org/10.1145/1454115.1454128

6. Cerfeda, L.F.: The rise of python for embedded systems, August 2021. www.zerynth.com/blog/the-rise-of-python-for-embedded-systems/

7. Chen, T., Guo, Q., Temam, O., Wu, Y., Bao, Y., Xu, Z., Chen, Y.: Statistical performance comparisons of computers. IEEE Trans. Comput. **64**(5), 1442–1455 (2015). https://doi.org/10.1109/TC.2014.2315614

8. David, H., Gorbatov, E., Hanebutte, U.R., Khanna, R., Le, C.: Rapl: memory power estimation and capping. In: 2010 ACM/IEEE International Symposium on Low-Power Electronics and Design (ISLPED), pp. 189–194 (2010). https://doi.org/10.1145/1840845.1840883

9. Evans, J.: A scalable concurrent malloc (3) implementation for FreeBSD. In: Proceedings of the BSDCan Conference. Ottawa, Canada, April 2006

10. Hähnel, M., Döbel, B., Völp, M., Härtig, H.: Measuring energy consumption for short code paths using rapl. SIGMETRICS Perform. Eval. Rev. **40**(3), 13–17 (2012)

11. Jacob, B., Mudge, T.N.: Notes on calculating computer performance. University of Michigan, Computer Science and Engineering Division (1995)

12. Khan, K.N., Hirki, M., Niemi, T., Nurminen, J.K., Ou, Z.: Rapl in action: experiences in using rapl for power measurements. ACM Trans. Model. Perform. Eval. Comput. Syst. **3**(2), March 2018. https://doi.org/10.1145/3177754

13. Kuszmaul, B.C.: Supermalloc: a super fast multithreaded malloc for 64-bit machines. SIGPLAN Not. **50**(11), 41–55 (2015). https://doi.org/10.1145/2887746.2754178

14. Leijen, D., Zorn, B., de Moura, L.: Mimalloc: free list sharding in action. In: Lin, A.W. (ed.) APLAS 2019. LNCS, vol. 11893, pp. 244–265. Springer, Cham (2019). https://doi.org/10.1007/978-3-030-34175-6_13

15. Paszke, A., Gross, S., Massa, F., Lerer, A., Bradbury, J., Chanan, G., Killeen, T., Lin, Z., Gimelshein, N., Antiga, L., et al.: Pytorch: an imperative style, high-performance deep learning library. Adv. Neural. Inf. Process. Syst. **32**, 8026–8037 (2019)

16. Pedregosa, F., et al.: Scikit-learn: machine learning in python. J. Mach. Learn. Res. **12**, 2825–2830 (2011)

17. Pereira, R., Couto, M., Ribeiro, F., Rua, R., Cunha, J., Fernandes, J.P., Saraiva, J.: Energy efficiency across programming languages: How do energy, time, and memory relate? In: Proceedings of the 10th ACM SIGPLAN International Conference on Software Language Engineering, pp. 256–267. SLE 2017. Association for Computing Machinery, New York (2017). https://doi.org/10.1145/3136014.3136031

18. Pereira, R., Couto, M., Ribeiro, F., Rua, R., Cunha, J., Fernandes, J.P., Saraiva, J.: Energy efficiency across programming languages: how do energy, time, and memory relate? In: Proceedings of the 10th ACM SIGPLAN International Conference on Software Language Engineering, pp. 256–267 (2017)

19. Pereira, R., Couto, M., Ribeiro, F., Rua, R., Cunha, J., Fernandes, J.P., Saraiva, J.: Ranking programming languages by energy efficiency. Sci. Comput. Program. **205**, 102609 (2021)

20. PowerAPI: pyjoules - a python library to capture the energy consumption of code snippets. github.com/powerapi-ng/pyJoules

21. Redondo, J.M., Ortin, F.: A comprehensive evaluation of common python implementations. IEEE Softw. **32**(4), 76–84 (2015). https://doi.org/10.1109/MS.2014.104

22. Virtanen, P., et al.: Scipy 1.0: fundamental algorithms for scientific computing in python. Nature Methods **17**(3), 261–272 (2020)
23. Wilson, P.R., Johnstone, M.S., Neely, M., Boles, D.: Dynamic storage allocation: a survey and critical review. In: Baler, H.G. (ed.) IWMM 1995. LNCS, vol. 986, pp. 1–116. Springer, Heidelberg (1995). https://doi.org/10.1007/3-540-60368-9_19

Application Runtime Estimation for AURIX Embedded MCU Using Deep Learning

Florian Fricke[1]([✉]) [ID], Stefan Scharoba[1] [ID], Sebastian Rachuj[2] [ID],
Andreas Konopik[1,2,3], Florian Kluge[3] [ID], Georg Hofstetter[3],
and Marc Reichenbach[1] [ID]

[1] BTU Cottbus-Senftenberg, Cottbus, Germany
{fricke,stefan.scharoba,marc.reichenbach}@b-tu.de
[2] Friedrich-Alexander-Universität Erlangen-Nürnberg, Erlangen, Germany
sebastian.rachuj@fau.de
[3] Elektronische Fahrwerksysteme GmbH, Gaimersheim, Germany
{florian.kluge,georg.hofstetter}@efs-auto.com
https://www.b-tu.de/en/fg-technische-informatik/,
https://www.cs3.tf.fau.de

Abstract. Estimating execution time is a crucial task during the development of safety-critical embedded systems. Processor simulation or emulation tools on various abstraction levels offer a trade-off between accuracy and runtime. Typically, this requires detailed knowledge of the processor architecture and high manual effort to construct adequate models. In this paper, we explore how deep learning may be used as an alternative approach for building processor performance models. First, we describe how to obtain training data from recorded execution traces. Next, we evaluate various neural network architectures and hyperparameter values. The accuracy of the best network variants is finally compared to two simple baseline models and a mechanistic model based on the QEMU emulator. As an outcome of this evaluation, a model based on the Wavenet architecture is identified, which outperforms all other approaches by achieving a mean absolute percentage error of only 1.63%.

Keywords: Embedded processor · Performance estimation · Artificial neural networks

1 Introduction

Due to the increasing use of driver assistance systems, which make driving more pleasant and safer, considerably more computing power is needed to enable these systems. However, it is still necessary that all safety-critical algorithms are executed under hard real-time constraints in order to react appropriately to dynamic traffic situations. These real-time conditions must be taken into account in early development phases to ensure correct system behavior in the later product. In the following, different approaches are shown which can be used for performance modeling during development.

© The Author(s), under exclusive license to Springer Nature Switzerland AG 2022
A. Orailoglu et al. (Eds.): SAMOS 2022, LNCS 13511, pp. 235–249, 2022.
https://doi.org/10.1007/978-3-031-15074-6_15

1.1   Performance Modeling Approaches

Performance modeling of processors is an important tool in system development, since the development of hardware and software of a system is interlocked. Thus, the software, which defines the system behavior, has special requirements for the hardware and, conversely, all design decisions regarding the hardware have an effect on the design of the software. In addition to performance, non-functional properties such as energy requirements, fault tolerance and execution time also play a major role in system design, especially in the case of embedded systems. In order to be able to carry out analyses on the basis of functional and non-functional requirements already during the exploration of the design space, simulation programs are indispensable [22].

Simulation Tools. Such tools make it possible to evaluate the characteristics of programs for the target architecture without modification and, depending on the kind of simulator used, it is possible to get insights regarding performance bottlenecks. Simulation tools exist in different levels of detail, which range from simple functional models to cycle-accurate simulators to register-transfer-level models. In addition to the simulation of the target architecture, it is possible to evaluate the performance of programs using analytical models, mechanistic models, and empirical models, that do not need to simulate the processor to predict the program's performance on the target architecture.

Analytical Models. Analytical models are fast and dynamic performance models which leverage heuristics and mathematical models to define performance metrics on a high abstraction level. They can either follow the white-box approach to utilize basic knowledge about processor performance to build a performance model, or, they can follow the black-box approach, which means learning from empirical data to build a performance model. The white-box approach comprises mechanistic modelling and the black-box approach comprises empirical modelling.

Mechanistic Models. White-box approaches are usually called mechanistic models [7]. They incorporate knowledge about the internal details of a processor. This can mean e.g. that the cache or pipeline behavior is implemented in the model to correctly estimate the latency introduced by these components. Since such models can be very slow, or require high compute power for simulation if all details of an architecture are included in the model, generally only the essential properties are modeled or abstract models are created. These models can also be combined with empirical models to avoid simulating all the details of the hardware.

Empirical Models. The term empirical model describes a huge variety of possible models that share the characteristic that the model's behavior is based on observations or measurements, meaning i.e. a black-box approach. This category includes simple models, such as first-order approximations, but also models resulting from methods of statistical analysis or machine learning. Due to the fact that we have dealt with performance modeling based on Artificial Neural Networks (ANNs) in the context of this work, this approach is presented specifically in the next paragraph.

Performance Modeling Using Artificial Neural Networks. An approach for empirical performance modeling that became feasible during the last years because of increased compute performance available for the analysis, is the use of machine learning [4]. There have been basic approaches to use methods from the field of artificial intelligence for empirical modelling of the performance of microprocessors. For this purpose, measurable events in the hardware were used with multidimensional regression to obtain an estimate of the program runtime [25]. The application of techniques from the field of machine learning using highly optimized software libraries on high-performance computers allows the automatic extraction of features from only slightly adjusted raw data. Libraries such as TensorFlow abstract the complex mathematical methods required to train artificial neural networks and allow the rapid exploration of a wide range of network topologies [1]. Since using ANNs for performance modeling is not very widespread yet, but offers advantages, like the automatic configuration of a model, this paper aims to analyze the applicability of this methodology to embedded systems design.

1.2   Structure of the Paper

Within this work, we will primarily concentrate on analytical and mechanistic models to predict the runtime of software running on the TriCore CPU of an embedded Infineon AURIX MCU. This microarchitecture platform is especially well-suited for safety-critical systems, but exhibits only a comparably simple processor pipeline, making it easy to model. Thus, creating simple mechanistic baseline models based on a full system emulator is feasible and will be presented in this paper. Furthermore, empirical models based on artificial neural networks are created and finally, all evaluated models are compared.

2   Related Work

Determining non-functional properties (NFP) can be done using two major approaches. Either, the underlying hardware's internals are used to derive a model from it, or the hardware is used in form of a black box. Eeckhout calls these mechanistic modeling and empirical modelling [7] and mentions that there is usually no pure form of them, but usually a mixture of both with an overhead for one side.

A typical example for a model that is more mechanistic is the interval simulation [10] that is also used as the basis of the Sniper simulator [2]. The authors of this simulator postulate an error of only 7% for an ARM-based out-of-order processor and 15% of an ARM-based in-order processor.

There are also mechanistic models that are only applicable on certain workloads. An example is the Execution Cache Memory (ECM) model that is meant for creating an analytical model of the runtime for stencil-like execution kernels [14]. For this, an average relative error of only 5% was measured on the investigated workloads.

Models like these, with their focus on mechanistic behavior, require much knowledge by the creator of the model. Especially for new architectures, a detailed analysis of the internals is needed to be able to offer a good estimation. Thus, statistical models that offer automatically derivable empirical data from the hardware could be reasonable. For speeding up simulations, these approaches were already realized, for example with the work of Nussbaum et al. [23]. This is a typical representative that uses the results from benchmark programs to generate a simplified processor model that is faster and maintains a high accuracy for the prediction of programs similar to the used benchmarks. Based on the SimpleScalar simulation model [5] as a reference, they achieve an average error of 8% with a very simplified model.

In recent years, a new approach for empirically predicting NFP was introduced. Ithemal is a prominent example of deep learning finding its way into the prediction of NFP [21]. It is meant as a replacement for static analyzers like the Intel Architecture Code Analyzer (IACA) and its authors argue that Ithemal reduces the error by half while maintaining the same speed as IACA.

In the field of embedded computing as focused in our work, there were also investigations about using deep learning. Hönig et al. determined a mean error of 1.8% in energy-demand of embedded devices in comparison to real measurements of an ARM Cortex-M4 platform with their work [15]. Their approach divides the software in its basic blocks. The training took place on automatically generated basic blocks, whose energy requirements were measured on the real hardware to gain the reference values. For an executed software, the final neural network creates an estimation for each basic block so that the overall energy requirement can be given.

In this paper, the approach of using artificial neural networks for predicting the runtime of a software for an embedded automotive architecture is presented. In comparison to previous work, a processor architecture was investigated, that has not been analyzed before. Furthermore, the hyperparameters of possible neural networks are examined in detail, allowing better design decisions in the future in comparison to related works.

3   Methodology

In order to assess the quality of the methodology used, it is necessary to compare it with existing approaches. No other approaches targeting the same hardware (an Infineon TriCore) were available so far. Therefore, the baseline was determined using two simple models. The simplest way to estimate the runtime of a program based on the executed operations is to use the average execution time of an instruction. A further method that takes context into account, at least to a small extent, is the first-order conditional estimator, which considers the order as well as the number of instructions. Both methods provide usable estimates and are therefore suitable as baselines for AI-based methodology. The results obtained using these estimators are shown in Table 1. Later in this section, possible realizations of the deep learning networks are introduced.

Table 1. Artificial dataset baseline model accuracy

Dataset	Baseline model	Train MAPE	Test MAPE
Artificial_code_no_loops	Mean Estimator	31.12	31.36
	Conditional Estimator	8.92	8.82
Artificial_code	Mean Estimator	28.51	29.59
	Conditional Estimator	17.06	17.08

3.1 Mechanistic Model, Based on QEMU

As it is possible to gather a lot of performance relevant data from the technical and the instruction set manual of the AURIX processor and the complexity of the performance model is lower than it would be for general-purpose processors, like e.g., current x86 models, it was decided to create a mechanistic performance model as a useful extension to the above-mentioned baseline. Starting from scratch would not have been possible, so it was decided to extend the existing processor model in QEMU [3]. In the first step, information about the operations have to be transformed to the QEMU-specific file format. These are mainly latencies, repeat rates and parameters. Furthermore, it is necessary to write some callback functions within the simulation that are called on execution of an instruction to drive the model. This is a commonly used approach to extend QEMU with more detailed performance modelling methods [18,20,26,27]. These callbacks contain the functionality to, e.g., calculate memory latencies, based on the addresses accessed. Using this model, the execution time could be determined with an error of 11% without considering and 7% with consideration of pipelining.

As the runtime was always over-estimated, the results can also offer a first reference point for safety-critical applications, but the proposed methodology is not able to replace the Worst-Case-Execution-Time (WCET) analysis. It could be shown, that working mechanistic models can be created using publicly available information, but the effort for creation and maintenance of these kinds of solutions is high, mainly because it requires a lot of manual work and changing to another processor type makes it necessary to recompile the emulator.

3.2 Using Artificial Neural Networks for Performance Estimation

The following discussion is based on the assumption that artificial neural networks for analyzing sequences are also suitable for runtime estimation of instruction sequences. That denotes a variation of the problem of predicting a temporal sequence, which is heavily used in e.g. NLP applications. Thus, the essential difference is that it is not the following element of the sequence that is to be determined as the result, but the runtime. Many other characteristics are very similar for both problems, for example, the complex dependencies between the elements of the sequence and the consideration of the order of elements.

A family of neural networks that are commonly used to process sequential data are recurrent neural networks (RNNs) [12]. Unlike typical feedforward networks, where the dataflow passes each processing layer only once, RNNs may contain feedback loops and store internal states. The current state of a layer depends on previously processed input data and affects the layer's output for future inputs. By this, the context of an element in the overall input sequence is respected.

The recurrent behavior of RNNs can be organized in several forms. In simple recurrent networks (SRNs) outputs may be influenced by arbitrarily long dependencies [9]. This may cause various problems during training, such as vanishing or exploding gradients.

Long Short-Term Memory networks (LSTMs) are a class of recurrent neural networks that solve this problem [13]. They extend the activation functions of SRNs with components that allow the influence of the input, the output and the current state on the output to be controlled. This makes this type of network far more complex and increases the effort required for training, but networks of this type are particularly well suited for sequences in which the elements influence each other in both the short and long term. Gated recurrent units (GRUs) are similar to LSTMs, but have fewer trainable parameters due to the lack of an output gate [6]. Another option to adopt LSTMs is the introduction of so called peephole-connections between the cell state and the gates, which makes this class of networks (later referred to as PLSTMs) more suitable for tasks that require to learn to measure the size of time intervals [11].

While the last paragraph was mainly concerned with the cells that make up the ANNs, this paragraph will present different possibilities for the global structure of the network. Bidirectional recurrent neural networks contain two recurrent layers, where one layer processes the input data in a given order and the other layer processes it in reverse order [28]. Therefore, these networks are able to consider not only past values, but also "future" values. Merging the outputs of the two layers can be done in different ways and is part of the hyperparameters of this type of network. Hierarchical Recurrent Neural Network [8] (H-LSTM) divide the sequences at certain points, for example, certain layers of the network can be optimized for the recognition of words, others for the interpretation of sentences. It is then distinguished whether a new token begins, processing is within a token, or the end has been reached. Based on this information, the context memory of the LSTM cells is controlled. Since this type of hierarchical structures can also occur in process traces (function calls, basic blocks, ...), an evaluation in the context of this work is reasonable.

As an alternative, Wavenets are also ANNs that are suitable for analyzing sequences [24]. In contrast to the other types presented, these do not belong to the RNNs but are a special form of Convolutional Neural Networks (CNNs). One-dimensional convolutional kernels are used, and the networks reduce the number of nodes per layer by a factor of two in each case. This property allows deep Wavenets to analyze very long sequences while retaining the advantage of efficient training of CNNs in contrast to RNNs.

Usually, none of these networks offers a good performance without the right input data. Thus, the next section describes how program traces can be arranged to make them suitable for the use in deep learning.

4   Training Data

Gathering high-quality input data is important for the training of deep neural networks. This section shows what kind of data is used in this paper, how it is processed, and what quality can be expected.

4.1   Preprocessing of the Training Data

As already mentioned in the introduction, the artificial neural network is to be trained with program traces of the real system. These can be recorded using a trace module integrated into the Infineon AURIX microcontroller and TriCore CPU and are then available for training. We employed a Lauterbach serial trace device to record traces over longer periods of time [19]. Timestamps in the traces have an accuracy of 2 CPU clock cylces.

In the following, the processing of the recorded training data is explained. This is necessary because the traces are available in the form of ASCII files after recording, which cannot be processed directly by a neural network.

The ASCII files contain the assembler instructions and their parameters, as well as time stamps, which can be used to calculate the execution time of the instructions. In order to convert these into a representation that is suitable for processing by an artificial neural network, the instructions must be represented as numbers. Since an instruction consists of the mnemonic and up to three parameters, a representation as a vector of four numbers is suitable.

If the ASCII representation was to be transformed into such a representation without further modification, it would be very difficult for the network to generalize. All addresses and immediate values used in the instructions would become individual tokens. Therefore, in an intermediate step, all immediate values and all direct and indirect addresses were replaced by a uniform token, respectively. This significantly reduces the number of tokens used, as now only the opcodes and the registers need to be coded. Since information about the execution times is only available at certain points in the trace, the instructions must be combined into sequences with known execution times. To make this possible, despite the different number of instructions per sequence, a placeholder instruction was created with which the sequences can be padded to achieve a constant length. The data set thus consists of sequences of instructions of a fixed length and their execution times.

In addition to the rather naïve processing of the training data described above, another variant was realized, which is based on Natural Language Processing (NLP) techniques. The main difference to the implementation described above is that no placeholders are used, instead two additional tokens were introduced. The "ARGS" token marks the beginning of the arguments of the respective instruction. Therefore, it is not necessary to use placeholders if less than three parameters are used. The "IET" token marks the end of an instruction and thus the point in a sequence where it may be split. Since it can happen during processing, that a sequence is interrupted at a point where no timestamp is available, a small inaccuracy can arise. The advantage, however, is that this type of representation has a positive effect on performance during training and on use with network structures optimized for NLP, such as the H-LSTMs.

In the following, the variant described above without delimiter is called Naive Data Representation, the other one will be called NLP Data Representation.

4.2   Analysis of the Training Data

In addition to the purely formal preparation of the data, it makes sense to analyze the data in order to get a basic impression of possible correlations. This makes it easier to classify problems that arise later, but can also be helpful in deciding on some hyperparameters for the neural networks to be created. For example, if there is only a small influence between commands with large distances in the command sequence, a network can be used that processes shorter sequences without having a significant impact on the quality of the output.

Since the microcontroller used in this paper is a model for safety-critical real-time applications and therefore many features such as out-of-order execution are not used, there are only minor deviations in the execution time, which are caused by the instruction order. Nevertheless, an analysis is useful to determine which effects can be detected and to what extent an artificial neural network is suitable for modelling. For this purpose, the trace files created for the training were examined with regard to the dependency of the execution time of a frequent instruction (add.f), taking into account the directly preceding instruction. Only those instructions were regarded that occur at least 500 times as predecessors, as otherwise no representative results would have been available due to the irregularly distributed time stamps. The analysis showed that the average execution time of the add.f instruction is between 7.2 ns and 8.8 ns depending on the preceding instruction, which corresponds to a deviation of about one third of a processor cycle at a processor clock of 200 MHz on the AURIX TC277 MCU. The analysis thus shows a clear dependence of the execution time on the instruction sequence, which is negligibly small for individual instructions, but must be taken into account in total. A deeper analysis of the instructions, which would have potentially revealed further dependencies based on the microarchitecture of the processor, was not carried out within the scope of this work. However, the findings from the analysis show that the selected neural networks are fundamentally suitable for the task.

The data sets used in this work are based on artificial code, including a command mix, which is representative for automotive applications. All datasets contain traces recorded with real processors. The first one is called `artificial_-code_no_loops`, the other one `artificial_code`. The first dataset contains code without loops, which results in fewer repetitions in the trace, as loops are unrolled on execution. The fact that raw traces, which have not been augmented by code orchestration tools, were used here is due to the fact that tools that make this possible are not always available for embedded platforms and an approach that is as generic as possible should be evaluated.

The corresponding applications were running and were addressed with real, external signals. Further technical details regarding tracing are not relevant for the following explanations and can be found in the technical documentation of the processor and trace module [16,17].

5   Evaluation

The next step, after preparing the training data, is to find a well-performing neural network. For this, a hyperparameter search was carried out first on a theoretical processor architecture. Following this, the findings were applied to the real architecture with the use of program traces.

5.1   Hyperparameter Search

As presented in Subsect. 3.2, various neural networks can be used for the task of runtime estimation. Furthermore, every possible network architecture has hyperparameters that need to be selected according to the task. Even with a small number of ANNs, the evaluation of different architectures and hyperparameter-sets requires the training of many networks, which is not feasible with the datasets presented above. A reason is especially that more than one network has to be trained per set of parameters, because there is a stochastic component in the training process. Therefore, artificial data sets were created based on a highly simplified processor architecture (so-called toy architecture) that offers only four instructions requiring different execution times. The simplified processor model has two pipelines (IP, LS) that can process either arithmetic or memory instructions because both processors considered have multiple pipelines, and the possibility of parallel processing affects the performance model. The details are shown in Table 2.

Based on these instructions, sequences were generated, whose total execution time also depends on the order of the sequence. Using a small training data set, various neural networks with different hyperparameters were then tested for their basic suitability in relation to the problem.

Table 2. Toy CPU architecture instruction timings

Instruction	Pipeline	Latency (cycles)
add	IP	2
div	IP	5
ld	LS	3
st	LS	3

For the practical evaluation, four different network types have been selected: SRN, GRU, LSTM and PLSTM. These networks have been trained using Stochastic Gradient Descent (SGD), Adaptive Moment Estimation (ADAM) and Root Mean Square Propagation (RMSProp) as optimizers. As loss functions, we evaluated Mean Squared Error (MSE), Mean Absolute Error (MAE) and Mean Average Percentage Error (MAPE). For the other hyperparameters we used the following parameters: training epochs (10; 50), batch size (1; 4; 16) and learning rates (0,01; 0,001). The overall rating of the resulting network's quality with respect to the given task has been done using MAPE. The results are shown in Fig. 1.

It can be observed, that the RMSProp optimizer shows the best overall performance, because it was able to fit the models for all used loss functions. Furthermore, the resulting models had the lowest performance spread. Clear outliers are the models with SGD optimizer and MAPE loss function, as well as the ADAM optimized networks using MSE. In both cases, the models had a big spread in the performance and the learning effect was too low.

One method to improve the overall performance is the introduction of an embedding layer in the networks, which has been done for all network types. This kind of layer is used to map indices with similar properties close to each other in the n-dimensional space. It is beneficial for NLP applications, e.g., for words with a similar meaning, but can also be helpful in this case, e.g., for instructions that have the same latency. The results are shown in Fig. 2.

The overall performance improvement in comparison to Fig. 1 can directly be seen. For the RMSProp optimizer, the differences are small, in nearly all other cases, the training process profits from the pre-structured data. The only exception is the SGD optimizer with MAPE loss-function, which did not improve in comparison to the version without embedding layer. In addition to the neural network's regressional loss, the average time that was required to train the networks has been evaluated and is shown in Table 3.

Without embedding layers, the LSTM has the lowest training duration as well as the best MAPE. It can be observed that the networks with embedding layer generally have a lower MAPE and that the LSTM and the PLSTM perform equally good. The long training duration of the PLSTM in comparison to the LSTM makes the LSTM the more reasonable choice.

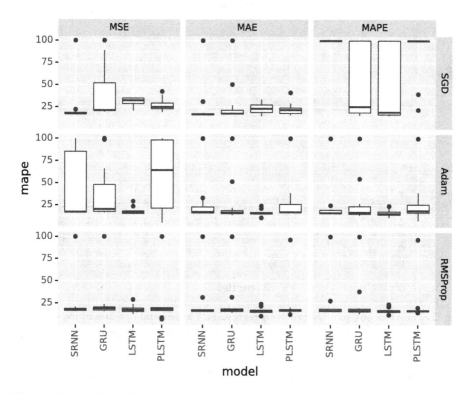

Fig. 1. Facetted box plot overview on regressional losses and optimizers for different types of RNN on the toy dataset

Table 3. Toy dataset sample mean MAPE and training duration for all models

Model	MAPE	Training duration
SRNN	35.21	9.53 s
GRU	31.99	10.55 s
LSTM	22.88	8.28 s
PLSTM	35.94	35.48 s
Emb-SRNN	25.06	8.26 s
Emb-GRU	19.03	12.32 s
Emb-LSTM	17.57	9.25 s
Emb-PLSTM	17.19	80.28 s

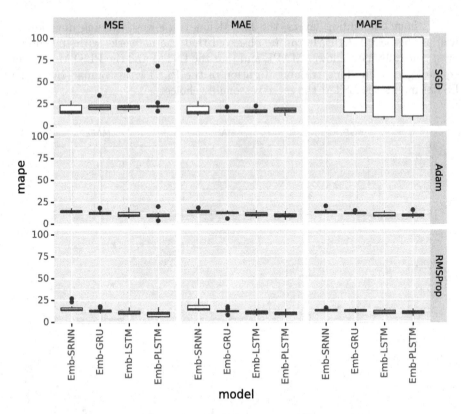

Fig. 2. Facetted box plot overview on regressional losses and optimizers for different types of RNN with an underlying embedding layer on the toy dataset

5.2 Architectures Chosen for the Evaluation with Program Traces

Since the analyses using the toy data set clearly showed the advantages of the LSTM architecture, this architecture was used for the further evaluations with the data from real program traces. The architectures we selected for further evaluation are the Bidirectional LSTM (BLSTM), the Bidirectional Peephole LSTM (BPLSTM), the Hierarchical LSTM (H-LSTM), the Bidirectional hierarchical LSTM (BH-LSTM), the Hierarchical Peephole LSTM (H-PLSTM) and the Wavenet. In all cases, the RMSProp optimizer and the MAPE loss function have been used. The selected batch size was 4 in all cases, and the learning rate was set to 0.01. All ANN architectures mentioned above have been trained using the `artificial_code_no_loops` and the `artificial_code` dataset. The required training and evaluation time as well as the respective MAPE values are shown in Table 4 for the `no_loops` dataset and in Table 5 for the dataset with loops.

The results show that the Wavenet model achieved the best accuracy and at the same time required the shortest training duration. With a MAPE of 1.63%

Table 4. `Artificial_code_no_loops` dataset training and evaluation

Model	Train MAPE	Train duration	Eval MAPE	Eval duration
BLSTM	13.72	1365.28 s	13.23	0.74 s
BPLSTM	18.07	3310.02 s	21.76	0.97 s
H-LSTM	3.61	3228.59 s	3.61	1.38 s
BH-LSTM	3.35	3699.42 s	2.76	1.44 s
H-PLSTM	2.26	3962.64 s	2.45	1.39 s
Wavenet	1.62	49.01 s	1.63	0.24 s

Table 5. `Artificial_code` dataset training and evaluation

Model	Train MAPE	Train duration	Eval MAPE	Eval duration
BLSTM	10.13	17 205.13 s	9.48	7.94 s
BPLSTM	8.10	50 315.80 s	8.24	7.15 s
H-LSTM	6.32	58 991.48 s	6.41	25.61 s
BH-LSTM	8.08	41 484.28 s	8.49	15.80 s
H-PLSTM	5.55	74 384.49 s	5.52	26.79 s
Wavenet	5.27	734.83 s	5.49	1.98 s

and 5.49%, respectively, it outperforms both baseline models and the mechanistic approach described in Subsect. 3.1. Some recurrent networks, particularly the H-PLSTM variant, produced similarly accurate results, but with training durations that were about two orders of magnitude longer. An analysis of the individual learning curves suggests, that the accuracy of the BLSTM and the BH-LSTM model could have been increased with more training epochs, while the other architectures already converged in 30 epochs. Overall, our evaluations lead to the conclusion that neural networks are a suitable approach for estimating program runtimes, since they provide sufficiently accurate results but require much less manual effort compared to mechanistic models.

6   Conclusion and Outlook

This paper presented a comparison of different methods for estimating the execution time of embedded processors. The TriCore processor of the Infineon AURIX MCU was used as an example.

Starting with two simple baseline models, a mean estimator and a first-order conditional estimator, a MAPE between 32% and 9% was achieved. As the conditional model, which takes the context of individual instructions into account, showed a better performance, it was expected that more complex models would be able to predict the runtime with even higher accuracy. Two distinct approaches have therefore been tested: a mechanistic model, based on QEMU, and several empirical models, based on ANNs.

The mechanistic model was able to reach a MAPE between 7% and 11%. However, as all characteristics of the processor have to be modeled manually, this approach demands a high development and evaluation effort on every change of the processor. In contrast, ANNs have the advantage that, once a workflow for data preparation and model training is defined, the adoption of a model to new data requires mostly compute power, but only little manual effort. As the design space for ANNs is huge, within this work, various network architectures and other hyperparameters have been explored. We identified Wavenets and H-LSTM networks as the best candidates in our evaluation, with MAPEs of 1.63% and 2.45%, respectively. Thus, it could be shown that artificial neural networks are in principle suitable for building processor performance models.

In future work, we aim to validate these findings on measured program traces of real automotive applications. In particular, the difference in accuracy when evaluating the data set with or without loops needs further investigation. Real data sets will inevitably contain a lot of code from loop bodies, since active waiting is often required in real-time applications with hard real-time conditions. Thus, further research must show whether unmodified datasets from real-world applications are suitable for building AI models, and how well they generalize.

Acknowledgement. We would like to express our gratitude to Elektronische Fahrwerksysteme GmbH for supporting this work. Furthermore, we are grateful to Lauterbach GmbH for their loan of an Off-chip Serial Trace device. This project would not have been feasible without such a device.

References

1. Abadi, M., et al.: Tensorflow: a system for large-scale machine learning. In: 12th USENIX symposium on operating systems design and implementation (OSDI 16), pp. 265–283 (2016)
2. Adileh, A., González-Álvarez, C., Ruiz, J.M.D.H., Eeckhout, L.: Racing to hardware-validated simulation. In: 2019 IEEE International Symposium on Performance Analysis of Systems and Software (ISPASS), pp. 58–67. IEEE (2019)
3. Bellard, F.: QEMU, a fast and portable dynamic translator. In: USENIX Annual Technical Conference, FREENIX Track, vol. 41, p. 46. California, USA (2005)
4. Buber, E., Diri, B.: Performance analysis and cpu vs gpu comparison for deep learning. In: 2018 6th International Conference on Control Engineering Information Technology (CEIT), pp. 1–6 (2018). https://doi.org/10.1109/CEIT.2018.8751930
5. Burger, D., Austin, T.M.: The simplescalar tool set, version 2.0. ACM SIGARCH computer architecture news 25(3), 13–25 (1997)
6. Chung, J., Gulcehre, C., Cho, K., Bengio, Y.: Empirical evaluation of gated recurrent neural networks on sequence modeling. arXiv preprint arXiv:1412.3555 (2014)
7. Eeckhout, L.: Computer architecture performance evaluation methods. Synthesis Lectures Comput. Architecture 5(1), 1–145 (2010)
8. El Hihi, S., Bengio, Y.: Hierarchical recurrent neural networks for long-term dependencies. In: Advances in Neural Information Processing Systems, pp. 493–499 (1996)
9. Elman, J.L.: Finding structure in time. Cogn. Sci. 14(2), 179–211 (1990)

10. Eyerman, S., Eeckhout, L., Karkhanis, T., Smith, J.E.: A mechanistic performance model for superscalar out-of-order processors. ACM Trans. Comput. Syst. (TOCS) **27**(2), 1–37 (2009)
11. Gers, F.A., Schmidhuber, J.: Recurrent nets that time and count. In: Proceedings of the IEEE-INNS-ENNS International Joint Conference on Neural Networks. IJCNN 2000. Neural Computing: New Challenges and Perspectives for the New Millennium, vol. 3, pp. 189–194. IEEE (2000)
12. Goodfellow, I., Bengio, Y., Courville, A.: Deep Learning. MIT Press (2016). http://www.deeplearningbook.orgwww.deeplearningbook.org
13. Hochreiter, S., Schmidhuber, J.: Long short-term memory. Neural Comput. **9**(8), 1735–1780 (1997)
14. Hofmann, J., Alappat, C.L., Hager, G., Fey, D., Wellein, G.: Bridging the architecture gap: abstracting performance-relevant properties of modern server processors. arXiv preprint arXiv:1907.00048 (2019)
15. Hönig, T., Herzog, B., Schröder-Preikschat, W.: Energy-demand estimation of embedded devices using deep artificial neural networks. In: Proceedings of the 34th ACM/SIGAPP Symposium on Applied Computing. SAC '19 (2019). https://doi.org/10.1145/3297280.3297338
16. Infineon Technologies AG: AURIX TC27x D-Step User's Manual, December 2014
17. Infineon Technologies AG: AURIX TC3xx User's Manual, February 2021
18. Kang, S., Yoo, D., Ha, S.: TQSIM: a fast cycle-approximate processor simulator based on QEMU. J. Syst. Architect. **66–67**, 33–47 (2016). https://doi.org/10.1016/j.sysarc.2016.04.012
19. Lauterbach GmbH: TriCore Debugger and Trace (2021)
20. Luo, Y., Li, Y., Yuan, X., Yin, R.: QSim: framework for cycle-accurate simulation on out-of-order processors based on QEMU. In: 2012 Second International Conference on Instrumentation, Measurement, Computer, Communication and Control, pp. 1010–1015 (2012). https://doi.org/10.1109/IMCCC.2012.397
21. Mendis, C., Renda, A., Amarasinghe, D., Carbin, M.: Ithemal: accurate, portable and fast basic block throughput estimation using deep neural networks. In: Proceedings of the 36th International Conference on Machine Learning (2019)
22. Nicolescu, G., Mosterman, P.J.: Model-based design for embedded systems. Crc Press (2018)
23. Nussbaum, S., Smith, J.E.: Modeling superscalar processors via statistical simulation. In: Proceedings 2001 International Conference on Parallel Architectures and Compilation Techniques, pp. 15–24. IEEE (2001)
24. Oord, A.v.d., et al.: Wavenet: a generative model for raw audio. arXiv preprint arXiv:1609.03499 (2016)
25. Powell, D.C., Franke, B.: Using continuous statistical machine learning to enable high-speed performance prediction in hybrid instruction-/cycle-accurate instruction set simulators. In: Proceedings of the 7th IEEE/ACM International Conference on Hardware/Software Codesign and System Synthesis, pp. 315–324 (2009)
26. Rachuj, S., Fey, D., Reichenbach, M.: Impact of performance estimation on fast processor simulators. In: Song, H., Jiang, D. (eds.) SIMUtools 2020. LNICST, vol. 370, pp. 79–93. Springer, Cham (2021). https://doi.org/10.1007/978-3-030-72795-6_7
27. Reichenbach, M., Knödtel, J., Rachuj, S., Fey, D.: RISC-V3: a RISC-V compatible CPU with a data path based on redundant number systems. IEEE Access **9**, 43684–43700 (2021). https://doi.org/10.1109/ACCESS.2021.3063238
28. Schuster, M., Paliwal, K.K.: Bidirectional recurrent neural networks. IEEE Trans. Signal Process. **45**(11), 2673–2681 (1997)

A Hybrid Performance Prediction Approach for Fully-Connected Artificial Neural Networks on Multi-core Platforms

Quentin Dariol[1,2]($\boxtimes$), Sebastien Le Nours[1], Sebastien Pillement[1],
Ralf Stemmer[2], Domenik Helms[2], and Kim Grüttner[2]

[1] Nantes Université, IETR UMR CNRS 6164, Nantes, France
`quentin.dariol@etu.univ-nantes.fr`
[2] German Aerospace Center (DLR-SE), Cologne, Germany

Abstract. Predicting the performance of Artificial Neural Networks (ANNs) on embedded multi-core platforms is tedious. Concurrent accesses to shared resources are hard to model due to congestion effects on the shared communication medium, which affect the performance of the application. Most approaches focus therefore on evaluation through systematic implementation and testing or through the building of analytical models, which tend to lack of accuracy when targeting a wide range of architectures of varying complexity. In this paper we present a hybrid modeling environment to enable fast yet accurate timing prediction for fully-connected ANNs deployed on multi-core platforms. The modeling flow is based on the integration of an analytical computation time model with a communication time model which are both calibrated through measurement inside a system level simulation using SystemC. The ANN is described using the Synchronous DataFlow (SDF) Model of Computation (MoC), which offers a strict separation of communications and computations and thus enables the building of separated computation and communication time models. The proposed flow enables the prediction of the end-to-end latency for different mappings of several fully-connected ANNs with an average of 99.5% accuracy between the created models and real implementation.

Keywords: Performance prediction · Multi-processor systems · SystemC simulation models · Artificial neural networks

1 Introduction

The Internet-of-Things (IoT) market is continuing to grow, as the number of connected devices is expected to reach 27 billion by 2025 (an increase of more than 200% compared to 2020) [5]. Along with this increase, the need for smart

This work has been funded by the WISE consortium, France (pSSim4AI project) and by the Federal Ministry of Education and Research (BMBF, Germany) in the project Scale4Edge (16ME0465).

embedded devices is emerging and efficient execution of AI algorithms such as Artificial Neural Networks (ANNs) has become thus a key challenge. To avoid the loss in throughput and energy caused by data transmissions when executing AI algorithms on distant servers, the focus is nowadays on their deployment on edge devices. Among edge devices, multi-core platforms are widely used due to the versatility they offer. However, ANNs are computation-intensive applications that require important amount of resources while embedded platforms are limited in memory and computing capacity and bear strict energy constraints. In this context, an intensive evaluation of ANN implementations on multi-core platforms is needed early in the design process to optimize solutions that meet performance constraints.

Several approaches have already been proposed to allow fast evaluation of ANN deployment on embedded platforms. Some approaches focus on the implementation and performance measurement on real target. The disadvantage of this process is that it represents a time consuming and error prone process as the ANN must be trained and then deployed on the real platform to evaluate the achieved performance. Because of long development cycle, the coverage of the design space is limited while using this evaluation technique. Other approaches focus on building analytical models to predict the achieved performance and possible influence of captured design parameters. These models tend however to be inaccurate when targeting architectures with complex effects due to shared resources usage. In the context of our work, execution of highly parallel applications such as ANNs on multi-core platforms may cause concurrent accesses from processing elements to shared memories which lead to performance loss. Modeling and predicting the impact of communications on the execution time of the application is a key element to enable accurate performance prediction for a large scale of multi-core architectures.

In this paper we propose a hybrid performance prediction workflow for fully-connected ANN deployment on multi-core platforms. This modeling approach enables the estimation of the end-to-end latency of the application while predicting the importance and impact of communications. The proposed models can be used at several levels of granularity to describe the ANN in combination with different mappings on the target platform. This offers the ability to compare configurations and thus explore the design space to find solutions that optimize timing. In our experiments, we observed that the prediction accuracy of the created models when compared with measurements performed on a real platform is more than 99.5% on average for 21 different scenarios. The proposed flow is tested with three different fully-connected ANNs, for which several partitionings and mappings are considered on architectures containing up to 7 cores. The platform used to measure real execution times is implemented on two different FPGAs.

The paper is organized as follows: Sect. 2 presents related work and how the work presented in this paper extends our previous workflow for performance prediction of ANNs. Section 3 presents the features of the proposed workflow.

Section 4 presents the experimental setup and results. Section 5 summarizes what is presented in the paper and presents our future work directions.

2   Related Work

Several approaches have been carried out to tackle the challenge of performance prediction for ANNs on embedded platforms. The approach in [3] focuses on performing Neural Architecture Search on embedded GPU platforms under accuracy, timing and energy constraints. Another notable approach is [18], which proposes a latency and energy evaluation flow to find optimized mappings of neural networks on edge devices. These approaches focus on the evaluation of the neural network through implementation and testing on real prototype. Such evaluation approaches require to systematically train and execute considered ANNs on the platform. To alleviate the development effort, models of performance are needed.

[1,4,6] focus on proposing performance models for the exploration of parameters of ANN topology such as the number of layers and the number of neurons. Their models allow predicting the impact of reduction techniques on ANN's latency. These approaches aim however at optimizing the inference of ANNs on single processor systems and do not enable prediction of timing for parallel execution of ANNs. Other approaches propose analytical modeling techniques to explore and optimize performance for highly parallel architectures [2,8,13,16]. In these approaches, the emphasis is put on the exploration of architectural alternatives used to implement an hardware accelerator for ANN inference. Because these architectures are equipped with dedicated high-speed communication channels between functions, the part of communications is irrelevant in overall inference time, and is not considered in the proposed models of performance. Multi-core platform's architectures are conceived to bear a high versatility in the regard that they can execute several different types of applications. They rely for this reason on more general purpose communication bus which bear a higher part in the application's latency and energy, and must be modeled. In our work we aim at enabling performance prediction for multi-core processing platforms by proposing an innovative modeling approach that combines simulation, analytical models and partial characterization through measurement.

The workflow presented in this paper is based on previous work presented in [17]. The previous workflow was based on a probabilistic simulation model and demonstrated to deliver fast yet accurate analysis on video processing applications. This paper presents the following contributions: (1) an hybrid analytical computation time model for fully-connected ANNs on processing cores. This model only need to be calibrated once and can then predict accurately the execution time of any partitioning of fully-connected ANNs, (2) the integration of this analytical computation time model in a simulation model with a communication time model to predict the execution of the application executed on several processing cores, (3) the validation of the modeling approach by comparing the predicted execution time with real duration measured on an execution platform.

3   Proposed Modeling Approach

A schematic of the proposed workflow is given in Fig. 1. This figure highlights the steps to build performance models used to predict execution time of fully-connected ANNs deployed on multi-core platforms. The first activity in the proposed flow is captured in orange on the figure. It focuses on the capture of the ANN in a model of computation and its mapping on the target platform (discussed in Sects. 3.1, 3.2 and 3.3). The next activity (highlighted in purple) focuses on the simulation and prediction of performance using the developed SystemC models (Sects. 3.4 and 3.5). The third activity (highlighted in green) focuses on the measurement of execution time in order to characterize the timing models proposed in this flow (Sect. 4.1). The fourth activity (highlighted in yellow) and final activity (highlighted in grey) focus respectively on the validation of the proposed models by comparing the predictions to the measured execution times and the exploration of several grains and mappings to optimize latency using the proposed models (Sects. 4.2 and 4.3).

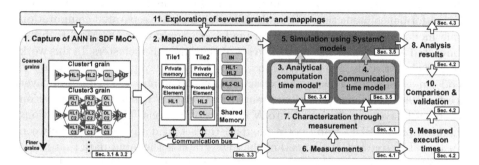

Fig. 1. Schematic of the modeling flow. This flow aims at enabling performance prediction for fully-connected ANNs on multi-core platforms. The processes marked with the * symbol are novel features to our flow.

3.1   Target Application: Fully-Connected ANNs

ANNs are applications often used to address data classification problems. Among neural networks, several algorithms are available. The most classical neural network algorithm is the fully-connected network, also called Multi-Layer Perceptron (MLP) [15]. The MLP consists of a set of neurons organized in layers (input layer, hidden layers and output layer). In such a fully-connected network each neuron is connected to every neurons of the previous layer. The operations required to compute the output of a neuron are presented in Eq. (1) from [14]. In this equation, φ is the activation function of the neuron. n is the number of inputs of the neuron and thus the number of neurons from the previous layer due to the MLP definition. The x_i and w_i are respectively the inputs and the weights of the neuron. B is the bias of the neuron. Because neurons of a same fully-connected layer are independent from one another, it is possible to parallelize their execution.

$$output = \varphi \left(\sum_{i=1}^{n} w_i x_i + B \right) \tag{1}$$

Our approach focuses solely on the optimization of the execution of the ANN on a embedded platform. The training of the ANN is not considered in the scope of this work.

3.2   Modeling ANNs with SDF

To ease the analysis and exploration of studied ANN implementations on the target platform, Synchronous Data Flow (SDF) Model of Computation (MoC) [10] is used. SDF is used to describe the data flow between actors via communication channels. It offers a strict separation of computation and communication (read, write) phases of actors. Computation and communication separation eases the performance prediction process by allowing building separated computation time model and communication time model. To apply the SDF MoC to fully-connected ANNs, we define as actors a set of neurons, called clusters. In this work we call cluster a given set of neurons from the same layer, which execution is modeled as an actor. The number of actors (i.e. the number of clusters) by layer is established based on the desired granularity. *ClusterN* denotes an organization where each layer is partitioned into N clusters of neurons. The communications channels of the SDF graph correspond to the set of data exchanged between clusters. The source (IN channel) of the SDF graph is the input data that needs to be classified by the ANN. The sink (OUT channel) of the SDF graph is the output result of the ANN. An example of how an ANN is described in a SDF graph is given in Fig. 2. In this case the actors of the SDF graph are the layers of the ANN and the channels between actors are the outputs of the layers.

Exploring the partitioning of ANNs using various grains is necessary. In this work, the level of granularity of a SDF graph is defined by the number of clusters. Coarser grains inhibit the acceleration that can be exploited from the parallelism of ANNs, whereas finer grains invoke numerous communication channels, which overload the communication bus of the considered platform. [11] presented a way of capturing ANN in SDF using several levels of granularity. In the example presented in Fig. 2 the ANN is described using the *Cluster1* grain, which is the more coarse level of granularity considered. Using this level of granularity, the actors considered in the SDF graph are the layers of the ANN. The finest granularity considered is the neuron grain, where the actors considered in the SDF graph are the neurons of the ANN. Intermediate grains are considered, which separates each layer into sets of actors. The number of actors (i.e. the number of clusters) by layer is established based on the desired granularity. The partitioning of layers into clusters is done in such a way that each actor contains nearly the same number of neurons. This allows for an equitable distribution of workload between actors. In Fig. 1, *Cluster1* and *Cluster3* graphs obtained from the same ANN are presented. Each layer of the ANN forms 1 actor in the *Cluster1* graph and 3 actors in the *Cluster3*. The *Cluster1* graph includes 3 actors and 4 communications channels, whereas the *Cluster3* graph includes 9 actors and 24 communication channels.

3.3 Mapping on the Targeted Architecture

The considered model of architecture is composed of a set of tiles where a tile is one single-core processor with private data and instruction memories. Executing instructions from this private memory causes no interference with other tiles. Data exchanges between different tiles are performed via a shared memory. The accesses to the shared memory are done using a communication bus. A schematic of the considered platform is given in Fig. 2. In this work, tiles are assumed to be identical except for private memory sizes. The target platform is thereby assumed to be homogeneous.

In the mapping step, the actors of the identified SDF graph are mapped on the tiles available on the platform. The communication channels between actors are mapped on the shared memory. The tiles will read (*ReadTokens()* statement) and write (*WriteTokens()* statement) the data necessary for the execution of the actors using the communication channels. During the execution of actors, the processing elements cannot be interrupted. The application is self-scheduled: the scheduling is established based on the dependency between actors. For a given SDF graph, several mappings of the application are possible. An example of mapping for a given ANN captured in SDF is shown in Fig. 2. In this example, the *HiddenLayer1* of the SDF graph is mapped on one tile while the *HiddenLayer2* and *OutputLayer* actors are mapped on a second tile. Comparing levels of granularity and mappings of the application allows finding solutions that jointly optimize timing properties and number of tiles.

3.4 Computation Time Model

We propose an analytical computation time model to predict the execution time of clusters of neurons from the same layers of the ANN. The analytical model is established based on the computations performed in order to set the output of a fully connected layer of an ANN (Eq. (1)). According to this equation, the execution time of a neuron from a fully-connected layer depends linearly on the number of inputs it has. From this information we can deduce the theoretical delay D_{neuron} required to compute the output of an artificial neuron. This delay is given in Eq. (2). In this equation n is the number of inputs of the neuron, D_Σ is the delay needed to compute the multiplication $w_i x_i$ and perform the associated sum, and D_φ corresponds to the delay needed to add the bias and compute the activation function of the neuron.

$$D_{neuron}(n) = nD_\Sigma + D_\varphi \tag{2}$$

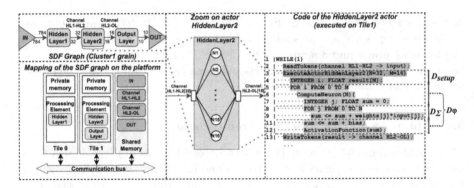

Fig. 2. Illustration of a coarse grain SDF graph (*Cluster1* as introduced in Sect. 3.2) mapped on the platform (introduced in Sect. 3.3). The content of the HiddenLayer2 actor and the computations performed inside it are detailed. The delays needed to perform the operations inside the actor are predicted using the highlighted analytical formula which is presented in details in Sect. 3.4.

Because neurons from a same layer are independent, the execution time of a cluster of neurons depends linearly on the number of neurons it contains. As presented in the code of actor *HiddenLayer2* in Fig. 2, the operations to compute neurons are repeated m times, where m is the number of neurons contained in the considered actor. The delay to compute these operations is therefore $m.D_{neuron}$. In addition to this delay, the initialization of the variables and the call and return procedures of functions provoke a delay named D_{setup}. Equation (3) presents the formula of the delay needed to compute a cluster of neurons.

$$D_{cluster}(n, m) = mD_{neuron}(n) + D_{setup} = nmD_{\Sigma} + mD_{\varphi} + D_{setup} \quad (3)$$

The D_{Σ}, D_{φ} and D_{setup} unitary delays can be characterized based on measured execution time of neurons. These delays only need to be characterized once for any given processing element, as the sum and multiplication operations and the activation functions considered in this work present insignificant execution time variability on the target platform. Once the unitary delays characterized, the proposed computation time model can therefore predict accurately performance for any considered level of granularity used to describe ANN applications.

3.5 Simulation Using SystemC Models

Our performance models were created with the SystemC language with the same organization as in [17]. In order to predict the performance of a given mapped SDF graph (SDFG) on the considered platform, both the computation time model presented in Sect. 3.4 and the message level communication time model presented in [19] are used. These two models are integrated in a behavioral description of each tile which describes the sequence of the mapped computation and communication statements. When an actor is being executed in simulation, the analytical computation time model is called to compute the corresponding delay. During communications through channels, the communication time model is called to compute the delays of communications on the platform even in the case of contentions at shared resources. The proposed model of performance is by construction composable: the number of tiles do not modify the nature of the model. It is therefore scalable regarding the mappings and the level of granularity used to describe the ANN. Different mappings are simulated and the obtained results are compared with measurements.

4 Experiments

4.1 Testing Configuration

To characterize our models of performance and to validate their prediction we implemented a hardware platform that followed the hypothesis of the proposed model of architecture, as presented in Sect. 3.3. The platform is implemented on both Xilinx Zynq-7000 and UltraScale MPSoC+ FPGA boards to test the portability of the modeling flow to several FPGAs. The observed variation in execution time was lesser than 0.05% when comparing the durations measured on both platforms.

Each MicroBlaze is equipped with a Floating Point Unit (FPU) and a hardware multiplier. The platform is composed of 7 tiles connected via an AXI shared interconnect. The tiles communicate through a shared memory via the shared interconnect. This platform integrates a timing measurement infrastructure, used to measure the computation time and communication time for SDF graphs executed on the platform. The measurement infrastructure was introduced in previous work. It is composed of two parts: the communication time measurement part presented in [19], and the computation time measurement part. The computation time measurement part measures the computation time of the SDF actor with code instrumentation. When an SDF graph iteration is started, the system issues a start signal. When it ends, the system issues a stop signal. Based on the elapsed time between the start and stop signals, the execution time of the SDF graph is measured.

In order to calibrate the proposed analytical computation time model, the base delays identified in Eq. (3) have been measured on the experimental platforms by varying the number of inputs of neurons and the number of neurons in clusters. The results showed that for fully-connected ANNs executed on the platform tile, the execution time varies linearly based on the number of inputs of neurons, and based on the number of neurons executed inside the cluster. We set $D_{\Sigma} = 47$, $D_{\varphi} = 146$ (ReLU activation function), and $D_{setup} = 39$ processor cycles. In this work, the ANNs are implemented using the lightweight open source library LibFANN [12] which enables the training and execution of MLPs in C programming language. All the tested ANNs used the ReLU activation function and the $float32$ precision. To verify and validate our modeling approach, we considered three fully-connected ANNs with different topologies. Two ANNs were developed and trained to perform digit recognition using the MNIST data set introduced in [9]. The first algorithm is a 3 layers fully connected ANN with a input layer of size 784 (28 × 28 grey scale pictures), a hidden layer containing 10 neurons and a output layer containing 10 neurons. This ANN reached 85% prediction accuracy. This algorithm is reffered as *MNIST 784-10-10* in the rest of the paper. The second algorithm is a 4 layers fully connected ANN with a input layer of size 784, a first hidden layer containing 32 neurons, a second hidden layer containing 16 neurons and an output layer containing 10 neurons. It is referred as *MNIST 784-32-16-10* in the rest of the paper. This ANN was trained and reached 89% prediction accuracy. We also considered a third ANN trained using the German Traffic Sign Recognition Benchmark (GTSRB) [7]. Different filters are applied to the images from the GTSRB data-set to render the building, training and deployment of the ANN on the considered platform possible. These filters include a max pooling and a grayscale filters to reduce the size of the input images to 576 pixels (24 × 24 × 1) and thus reduce the memory usage. This ANN is composed of a input layer of size 576, two hidden layers both containing 30 neurons and a output layer of 43 outputs. It is referred as *GTSRB 576-30-30-43*. Do to the simplification/optimization to allow the implementation of this application, this ANN reached less than 20% prediction accuracy. In order to test the accuracy of the proposed models for several grains, a set of SDF graphs which express different levels of granularity were used. Several mappings were also considered for each of these levels of granularity.

4.2   Experiment Results

In Table 1 the predicted end-to-end latencies by the proposed simulable model are compared with the end-to-end latencies measured on the real platform for several scenarios. The considered scenarios allow stressing the performance models to test and highlight three levels of scalability: (1) ANN topologies and level of granularity: several clusterings (from *Cluster1* to *Cluster7*) for the considered ANN topologies are tested to verify the accuracy of the proposed computation time model for coarse and fine grains, (2) amount of communications: the communication time model is tested and stressed when running multiple tiles simulations, as concurrent accesses to shared memories occur, (3) mapping and number of processing elements: several mappings are tested for each considered grains, with various number of processing elements. Mappings using up to 7 tiles and relying both on parallel and pipeline execution are tested.

For each considered partitionings, a 1-tile scenario is tested, in which all actors are implemented on only 1 tile. For the *Cluster2*, *Cluster3*, *Cluster4*, *Cluster6* and *Cluster7* mapped respectively on 2, 3, 4, 6 and 7 tiles, the actors issued from the partitioning of layers are mapped in order to enable a parallel execution of the application. For the *Cluster1* on 2/3 tiles scenario, each actor of the graph is mapped on a separate tile, to enable a streaming execution of the application. The other scenarios enable both a parallel and streaming execution of the application. E.g. in the *Cluster3* on 7 tiles scenario for the *MNIST 784-10-10* topology, each actor is mapped on a separate tile, to enable a parallel and

Table 1. Comparison of the measured and predicted end-to-end latency for different partitionings and mappings of fully-connected ANNs.

Experiment				End-to-end latency in thousands of processor cycles					
ANN topology	Grain	Nb. of actors/comm. channels	Tiles used	Measured	Comp. time model only		Simulation model		Comm. %
MNIST 784 −10 −10	Cluster1	2/3	1	393	376	−4.35%	394	+0.22%	5%
			2	387	370	−4.32%	387	+0.21%	52%
	Cluster3	7/16	1	430	376	−12.4%	431	+0.31%	13%
			3	170	151	−11.6%	170	−0.01%	26%
			7	191	148	−22.5%	187	−2.28%	89%
	Cluster7	15/64	1	502	377	−25.0%	506	+0.63%	26%
			7	120	75	−37.4%	121	+0.75%	64%
MNIST 784 −32 −16 −10	Cluster1	3/4	1	1238	1219	−1.51%	1239	+0.07%	2%
			3	1201	1184	−1.51%	1203	+0.18%	67%
	Cluster3	9/25	1	1281	1220	−4.83%	1279	−0.15%	5%
			3	443	421	−5.14%	442	−0.24%	8%
			7	443	407	−8.03%	440	−0.57%	70%
	Cluster7	21/113	1	1368	1220	−10.8%	1363	−0.33%	11%
			7	241	192	−20.4	241	+0.01%	28%
GTSRB 576 −30 −30 −43	Cluster2	6/13	1	967	930	−3.79%	964	+0.32%	3%
			2	486	466	−4.04%	483	+0.49%	4%
			7	433	408	−5.80%	437	−0.92%	57%
	Cluster4	12/41	1	1002	931	−7.12%	996	+0.55%	7%
			4	301	279	−7.12%	302	−0.42%	16%
	Cluster6	18/85	1	1039	931	−10.4%	1030	+0.80%	10%
			6	193	156	−18.8%	193	−0.39%	20%

streaming execution of the application. In the same scenario for the *MNIST 784-32-16-10*, the *HiddenLayer2* clusters actors and *OutputLayer* clusters actors were mapped to a same tile due to the target platform only having 7 tiles available. The column *Comm. %* shows the average predicted amount of time spent in polling and executing memory accesses on the shared memory for every tile according to the simulable model.

The predicted end-to-end latencies with associated prediction error are presented for the analytical computation time model used alone (*Comp. time model only* column). The predictions of the computation time model only are too optimistic and bear 10.8% error on average for the presented scenarios. The prediction error of the computation time model rises with the amount of communications in the considered scenario. When considering multiple tiles execution and SDF graphs of fine grains with numerous communication channels such as *Cluster7*, the computation time model error goes up to 37.4%. In order to predict the execution time of ANNs on multi-core platforms, a computation time model alone is not sufficient and the modeling of communications is necessary.

The simulable model bears an average accuracy of 99.5% for all the considered scenarios. The highest prediction error is reached for the *MNIST 784-10-10*, with granularity level *Cluster3* on 7 tiles scenarios: 2.89%. In this scenarios the average time spent in communication per tile over the overall execution time of the application is also the highest: 89%. For all the other scenarios, the error of the simulable model is less than 1%.

The high accuracy of our hybrid modeling flow is rendered possible by the following work hypothesis: (1) The strict separation of the computation and communication using SDF and the model of architecture, which enables the building of separated computation and communication time models. (2) The negligible effect of data dependant paths on latency when executing MLPs on the targeted platform. We have validated this hypothesis by performing measurements on the implementation platform while providing different input images to the ANNs, and observed that the impact of data dependency on the execution time is marginal. This is rendered possible by the type of ANN considered and by the use of FPUs and hardware multipliers on tiles, which normalize the execution of multiplication.

In our experiments, we only tested our modeling flow for ANNs using the ReLU activation function and *float32* precision. Extending the proposed modeling flow to other precisions (e.g. *float16* and fixed point precisions) and other activation functions would simply require a re-calibration of the proposed models. The current time measurement infrastructure used to calibrate and validate our models is built for architectures based on the AXI communication protocol. The effort to port our modeling flow to architectures featuring this protocol is thus minimal, while the effort to port it to other architectures is more significant.

4.3   Exploration of Partitionings and Mappings

The validated model of performance can be used to explore partitionings and mappings of fully-connected ANNs on multi-core platforms. This exploration allows evaluating deployments of ANNs on the considered platforms with no further prototyping effort on real platform. The results of the exploration of several partitionings and mappings for the two ANNs trained on MNIST are presented in Fig. 3. The displayed graphs give the predicted end-to-end latency of the application based on the number of tiles used for several levels of granularity and mappings. For each number of tiles the solution that optimize timing is highlighted in red on the graph, and the associated level of granularity (Cluster) as well as the average communication rate per tile are displayed. The other scenarios are depicted in blue.

The first graph (Fig. 3a) displays the exploration of end-to-end latency for the *MNIST 784-10-10* application. The end-to-end latency decreases when the number of tiles used increases until 5 tiles, as the parallel execution of the actors of the application allows to accelerate its execution time. The scenario that optimize the end-to-end latency for this topology is the *Cluster5* (C5) SDF graph executed on 5 tiles with a latency of 109 thousands of processor cycles. For configurations relying on more than 5 tiles, an increase of the overall end-to-end latency with the number of tiles used is observed, due to the raise of the communication time. For the 7 tiles execution, the scenario that optimize the timing is the *Cluster5* SDF graph with a latency of 114 thousands of processor cycles. The *Cluster7* execution on 7 tiles is 6% longer with a latency of 121 thousands of cycles. The average time spent in communications per tile is 89% for the *Cluster7* scenario (as displayed in Table 1) and 39% for the *Cluster5* scenario.

The second graph (Fig. 3b) displays the exploration of end-to-end latency for the *MNIST 784-32-16-10* application. In this case the overall end-to-end latency decreases with the number of tiles used up to 7 tiles. The computations account for a bigger part of the overall execution time. Therefore unlike the *MNIST 784-10-10*, the time spent in communications do not produce a significant overhead when using a platform containing up to 7 tiles. The optimal scenario is the *Cluster7* (C7) executed on 7 tiles with a predicted latency of 241 thousands of processor cycles and average communication rate per tile of 28%.

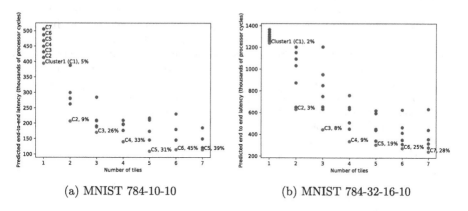

(a) MNIST 784-10-10   (b) MNIST 784-32-16-10

Fig. 3. Evolution of the end-to-end latency in thousands of processor cycles based on the number of tiles used for several partitionings and mappings of the considered applications. (Color figure online)

5   Conclusion

In this paper, we propose a hybrid performance prediction approach for fully-connected ANNs on multi-core platforms. This approach is based on SystemC simulation, which integrates an analytical computation time model and a communication time model calibrated through measurement to predict execution time. The proposed workflow achieves overall 99.5% accuracy for estimating the end-to-end latency of three fully-connected ANNs, with the highest prediction error on tested scenarios of 2.28%. This high accuracy is made possible by the separation of computation and communication using the SDF MoC and by the negligible effect of data dependant paths on the execution time. In future work we will expand our modeling flow to other ANN types such as convolutional neural networks, and we will consider adding power prediction to our modeling flow to enable the exploration of candidate solutions under both timing and power constraints.

References

1. Banbury, C., et al.: Micronets: neural network architectures for deploying tinyml applications on commodity microcontrollers. In: Proceedings of Machine Learning and Systems (2021)
2. Chen, Y.H., Emer, J., Sze, V.: Using dataflow to optimize energy efficiency of deep neural network accelerators. IEEE Micro (2017)
3. Galanis, I., Anagnostopoulos, I., Nguyen, C., Bares, G., Burkard, D.: Inference and energy efficient design of deep neural networks for embedded devices. In: IEEE Computer Society Annual Symposium on VLSI (ISVLSI) (2020)
4. Garbay, T., et al.: CNN inference costs estimation on microcontrollers: the est primitive-based model. In: 2021 28th IEEE International Conference on Electronics, Circuits, and Systems (ICECS) (2021)
5. Hasan, M.: State of iot 2022: Number of connected iot devices growing 18% to 14.4 billion globally, May 2022. https://iot-analytics.com/number-connected-iot-devices/, accessed: 07.06.2022
6. Heim, L., Biri, A., Qu, Z., Thiele, L.: Measuring what really matters: optimizing neural networks for tinyml (2021). https://arxiv.org/abs/2104.10645
7. Houben, S., Stallkamp, J., Salmen, J., Schlipsing, M., Igel, C.: Detection of traffic signs in real-world images: the German Traffic Sign Detection Benchmark. In: International Joint Conference on Neural Networks (2013)
8. Ke, L., He, X., Zhang, X.: Nnest: early-stage design space exploration tool for neural network inference accelerators. In: Proceedings of the International Symposium on Low Power Electronics and Design (2018)
9. Lecun, Y., Bottou, L., Bengio, Y., Haffner, P.: Gradient-based learning applied to document recognition. Proceedings of the IEEE (1998)
10. Lee, E., Messerschmitt, D.: Synchronous data flow. Proceedings of the IEEE (1987)
11. Luenemann, D., Fakih, M., Gruettner, K.: Capturing neural-networks as synchronous dataflow graphs. In: MBMV 2020 - Methods and Description Languages for Modelling and Verification of Circuits and Systems; GMM/ITG/GI-Workshop (2020)

12. Nissen, S.: Implementation of a fast artificial neural network library (fann) (2003). https://github.com/libfann/fann
13. Parashar, A., et al.: Timeloop: a systematic approach to dnn accelerator evaluation. In: IEEE International Symposium on Performance Analysis of Systems and Software (ISPASS) (2019)
14. Rosenblatt, F.: The perceptron: a probabilistic model for information storage and organization in the brain. Psychological review (1958)
15. Rumelhart, D., Hinton, G., Williams, R.: Learning representations by back-propagating errors. Nature **323**, 533–536 (1986)
16. Sombatsiri, S., Yu, J., Hashimoto, M., Takeuchi, Y.: A design space exploration method of SOC architecture for CNN-based AI platform. In: Workshop on Synthesis And System Integration of Mixed Information technologies (SASIMI) (2019)
17. Stemmer, R., Vu, H.D., Le Nours, S., Grüttner, K., Pillement, S., Nebel, W.: A measurement-based message-level timing prediction approach for data-dependent sdfgs on tile-based heterogeneous mpsocs. Appl. Sci. **11**, 6649 (2021)
18. Tsimpourlas, F., Papadopoulos, L., Bartsokas, A., Soudris, D.: A design space exploration framework for convolutional neural networks implemented on edge devices. IEEE Trans. Comput.-Aided Design Integrated Circuits Syst. **37**, 2212–2221 (2018)
19. Vu, H.D., Nours, S.L., Pillement, S., Stemmer, R., Grüttner, K.: A fast yet accurate message-level communication bus model for timing prediction of sdfgs on mpsoc. In: 2021 26th Asia and South Pacific Design Automation Conference (ASP-DAC) (2021)

Deep Learning Optimization II

A Smart HW-Accelerator
for Non-uniform Linear Interpolation
of ML-Activation Functions

Sebastian Prebeck[1,2]([✉]), Wafic Lawand[3], Mounika Vaddeboina[1,2],
and Wolfgang Ecker[1,2]

[1] Technical University of Munich, Arcisstraße 21, 80333 Munich, Germany
[2] Infineon Technologies AG, Am Campeon 1-15, 85579 Neubiberg, Germany
sebastian.prebeck@infineon.com
[3] Beirut Arab University, 11-5020 Riad El Solh, 11072809 Beirut, Lebanon

Abstract. The compulsive nonlinearity in neural networks (NN) is introduced by well-known nonlinear functions called activation functions. Performing AI-inferences on edge devices calls for efficient approximation of those complex functions on highly restrictive hardware (HW) platforms. When designing such systems, balancing area, footprint and power consumption at an application appropriate latency is key. To address those challenges, we propose a HW-based interpolation component capable of approximating arbitrary mathematical functions. A combinatorial search-based optimization algorithm is employed to find the optimal set of interpolation points for a set of functions while also considering non-uniform distributions. The proposed solution is accompanied by a Python-based HW generator, that facilitates the process of deploying software-computed search results on HW and provides room for generating different flavors of application-optimized HW. In an effort to reduce area footprint and delay, the proposed approach exploits symmetry and biased symmetry properties of functions and applies bit width optimizations to reduce the size of the utilized computational units. Additionally, property-aware reprogrammable solutions for multifunctional use cases are incorporated into our design. Experimental analyses show that our proposed method permits achieving better area utilization and deviation error results than state-of-the-art implementations.

Keywords: Linear interpolation · Activation function · Neural networks · Hardware generation · Minimum search · Nonuniform distribution

1 Introduction

Second-generation artificial intelligence is meant to extend the first generation by data privacy, offline capabilities, and latency/bandwidth reductions. Therefore, neural network (NN) inference computations of different applications migrate

A. Orailoglu et al. (Eds.): SAMOS 2022, LNCS 13511, pp. 267–282, 2022.
https://doi.org/10.1007/978-3-031-15074-6_17

from the cloud to low-power edge devices. From this perspective, previously developed high-performance neural network processing units (NPU) must be replaced with efficient, cheap, and optimized solutions that cater to the extensive computational demands of various new applications.

NNs commonly require nonlinearity between their layers, which calls for the adoption of activation functions to prevent the occurrence of folding. The computational complexity of such functions heavily varies among them. For some applications, plain functions (e.g. ReLU) which are inexpensive to implement by clamping are sufficient to reach the desired network accuracy. Other recent nets rely on more complex functions instead, such as Sigmoid [7] or Tanh [4]. The nonlinearity of those functions introduces additional computation complexity in extension to the common dot-product operation at edge devices. NPUs that come along with a CPU can dispatch the complex nonlinear computations to slow but area-efficient software routines. Alternatively, a floating-point unit (FPU) or a specialized hardware component can take over the task within a more reasonable latency, either as part of the NPU itself or as a custom extension to any CPU. For edge devices, the last two approaches are challenging due to the strict area and power constraints that those devices impose.

In this paper, we propose a dedicated HW component tailored to approximate complex mathematical functions with requirements conforming to the demands of edge devices. Memory components and multipliers are identified as the main contributors to area and power consumption. Thus, the amount of stored interpolation data along with their bit widths must be carefully chosen to attain the desired accuracy level, while staying within the resource and timing limits imposed by edge devices.

Our approach adapts and optimizes interpolation-HW for specific applications in an automated manner. It covers highly optimized static as well as fully dynamic run-time re-programmable solutions and multiple intermediate shades. To meet the requirements of a particular application, several implementation flavors with different features can be adopted.

Our contributions are summarized as follows:

- Adopting a SW search-based optimization algorithm for nonuniform interpolation
- Generating property-aware optimized interpolation HW
- Utilizing FP slopes with highly dynamic ranges for efficient interpolation lookups
- Generating property-aware HW with various levels of reconfigurability in an automated manner

This paper is structured as follows. In Sect. 2, related work for function approximation in hardware is presented. The contribution of this paper is elaborated in Sect. 3, which focuses on the key HW design features, SW-based preprocessing, and function mapping. Additionally, it describes an optimization method applied to slope multiplication that fully exploits the elaborated advantages. Section 4 elaborates on the results obtained for various activation functions with different features and compares the proposed work to other implementations in the literature. Section 5 concludes this paper and is followed by Sect. 6, which gives an outlook on future work.

2   Related Work

State-of-the-art approaches used for mapping functions to hardware can be classified into lookup table-based, piecewise linear or nonlinear interpolation, and Coordinate Rotational Digital Computer (CORDIC). Their advantages and disadvantages are discussed in this section.

2.1   Lookup Table Approximation

In [13,14], a lookup table (LUT) is utilized to represent any desired function with a fixed number of points. The chosen points must have a uniform distribution throughout the whole input domain to enable efficient mapping between input x-values and LUT addresses. Throughout the literature, there have been different implementation flavors for this kind of approach. In [14], a conventional ROM is used to store a limited number of y-values to approximate the Tanh function. This method has the shortest critical path delay, but its area increases exponentially with higher degrees of accuracy as mentioned in [13]. Conventional LUTs have been replaced with range addressable LUTs (RALUT) to further optimize the area. RALUT uses a special type of LUTs and adopts a slightly different address decoding system which is based on range matching instead of exact matching [12]. In [13], A.H.Namin et al. used an RALUT to approximate the Tanh function. The RALUT offers additional area optimizations for functions that attain saturation after a certain x-value, but share the same area limitations with conventional LUTs for functions that do not exhibit this property. Functions like Sigmoid and Tanh, shown in (1), bear this property and attain saturation in certain x-domains.

$$Sigmoid(x) = \frac{1}{1+e^{-x}} \qquad Tanh(x) = \frac{e^x - e^{-x}}{e^x + e^{-x}} \tag{1}$$

2.2   Piecewise Linear Approximation (PWL)

With the approach proposed in [11], complex functions are approximated by partitioning them into linear segments of polynomial order one. This linear representation is shown in (2), where j is set to 1, c_1 is the slope of the line, x is the input and c_0 is the y-intercept. As the number of segments increases and the interval size decreases, the approximated signal comes close to resembling the actual one. In [2], H. Amin et al. adopted this method to approximate a Sigmoid function. The significant enhancement offered by their work is the transformations that they applied to replace multipliers with shifters and thus save additional HW resources. Nevertheless, relying on shifters instead of conventional multipliers heavily restricts the accuracy of the function approximation due to the limitation of having at least one of the multiplicands set to a power of two. In [10], Z. Li et al. adopted a PWL-based curvature analysis technique for finding the optimal position of interpolation points to approximate a Sigmoid function. In their work, five multipliers, nine adders, and other comparison and multiplexing logic were utilized to achieve a maximum deviation error of 0.00784. Although the achieved deviation error is considered to be significantly low, the proposed architecture is resource-intensive.

2.3   Piecewise Nonlinear Approximation (PWNL)

An analogous method to PWL is PWNL which approximates functions by factoring in higher-order polynomials [19]. Equation (2) shows the general formulation of a nonlinear segment where j represents the desired polynomial order and c_i represents the distinct constants. The main drawback of this approach is the intensive use of multipliers to compute higher-order terms. In [17], I. Tsmots et al. approximated the Sigmoid function and its derivative using both PWL and PWNL methods. The PWNL method proved to be more effective when approximating the derivative of the Sigmoid function, achieving a maximum error of 0.04388 in comparison to the PWL method that achieved a maximum error of 0.07088. Another nonlinear approach that is based on the cubic Catmull ROM spline interpolation technique was proposed in [3] to approximate the Tanh function. In their approach, two LUTs along with a MAC unit were utilized to carry out the cubic spline interpolation of the Tanh function. For that purpose, a dot product operation is performed between two vectors that hold the control points and interpolation factors.

$$f(x) = \sum_{i=0}^{j} c_i x^i \tag{2}$$

2.4   CORDIC

CORDIC [18], originally proposed by J. E. Volder is an iterative approach that is commonly used in the literature to approximate complex nonlinear functions. This technique applies plane coordinate rotations to transform rectangular coordinates to polar coordinates. J. E. Volder proposes a minimalistic arithmetic unit that comprises shift registers, adders, and subtractors to perform the aforementioned transformations. With this technique, most of the functions can be approximated with high degrees of accuracy. In [15], Raut et al. used CORDIC to implement an activation function component that can be configured to compute Sigmoid and Tanh functions. Another similar work proposed by P. A. Kumar [9] employed the same technique to implement most of the trigonometric functions in HW. The main drawback of this approach is the amount of clock cycles needed to reach the desired level of accuracy. According to [5], 50 clock cycles were required to reach a maximum deviation of 0.005 for the Sigmoid function.

3 Proposed Approach

3.1 Overview

In this paper, we propose a hybrid method that partially considers previous work and adds further optimizations on top to fully harness their potential. This method is considered hybrid because it combines variations of the RALUT and PWL methods. Our proposed approach segments the desired function into intervals of nonuniform sizes and performs interpolation computations in HW. The segmentation in a nonuniform manner allows for dividing the function into high precision and low precision regions. High precision regions constitute nonlinear portions of the function that require several interpolation segments to allow accurate reconstruction of the original signal. In contrast, low precision regions cover mostly linear portions of the function that can be represented with a limited number of interpolation segments. Figure 1 displays an example of non-uniform segmentation for the sine function. The number of interpolation points in Fig. 1 is 12 in total and they are split as follows: 10 points are allocated for high precision regions and 2 points are allocated for low precision regions. By adopting this segmentation technique, resources are allocated efficiently to attain higher degrees of accuracy in comparison with the uniform segmentation technique.

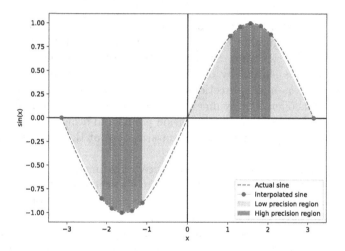

Fig. 1. Nonuniformly interpolated sine function

3.2 HW Generator

The proposed approach is implemented using a Python-based HW generator framework [6]. Its model-driven nature provides a highly configurable HW generation development platform, allowing the integration of intensive optimization searches with HW designs. Back-boned by Python, the generator provides a smart all-in-one solution, taking recourse to common Python libraries.

3.3   Integrated Features

Inspired by the work of [16] and by exploiting the flexibility offered through the HW generator, symmetry is integrated as one of the reconfigurable features that can optionally be selected during design time. For functions that exhibit symmetry properties, our component can be configured to either support origin symmetry or y-axis symmetry. This feature is disabled for non-symmetric functions. A function is considered to be symmetric with respect to the origin if it satisfies (3), and symmetric with respect to the y-axis if it satisfies (4). Accordingly, the HW generator is smart enough to populate and port map the corresponding HW components for the chosen type of symmetry. The utilization of this feature allows accounting for a reduced domain of the function. In that way, the number of interpolation points to be considered is halved. Additionally, the proposed approach accounts for input values that exceed the domain bounds of the chosen interpolation points by applying saturation. Detecting out-of-bounds values does not require additional logic. Instead, a saturation domain can be compressed to be represented with one point only. Holistically, these methods play a major role in reducing the utilization of HW resources.

$$Origin\ Symmetry : f(-x) = -f(x) \tag{3}$$

$$Y - Axis\ Symmetry : f(-x) = f(x) \tag{4}$$

With an eye toward further optimizing the datapath, x- and y-offsets are introduced as reconfigurable features. Some functions exhibit symmetry around a shifted origin. For instance, the Sigmoid function is symmetric with respect to an origin that is shifted by 0.5 in the positive y-direction. In this regard, offsetting in both x- and y-directions is in some functions essential to preserve the optimizations offered by symmetry. Additionally, x-offset is used to displace the x-values of the considered interpolation points and bring them closer to zero. This results in having smaller comparator sizes, but at the same time incurs an additional subtractor.

In some NN architectures, the chosen activation function varies among layers and in some cases among neurons [1]. To cater to the demands of different NN architectures, we added static and dynamic support for the slope, y-intercept, and x-values of the chosen interpolation segments. Each of those values can be selected to be set to a constant during design time, or reprogrammable during run-time. Unlike the static mode, the dynamic mode enables alternating between different activation functions during run-time. The dynamic option incurs additional HW resources and requires a setup routine to load new interpolation data whenever the function is interchanged, but at the same time offers utmost flexibility. Regardless of the chosen mode, symmetry and offset features are selectable in both.

3.4   Software Preprocessing

Before HW implementation, SW preprocessing is carried out using Python. A combinatorial search-based optimization algorithm that iterates over different combinations of interpolation points in high precision areas is employed to retrieve the domains and parameters of linear segments that achieve the least deviation error with respect to the actual function. To decrease the search space and accelerate the search process, we exclude domains that achieve saturation at the $y - axis$. Each function with its unique set of interpolation points is assessed separately based on a comparison performed between the interpolated function denoted by $\bar{f}(x_i)$ and the analytic function denoted by $f(x_i)$. The considered error estimation metrics are maximum absolute error denoted by ε_{max} and average absolute error denoted by $\varepsilon_{average}$, and are calculated as follows:

$$\varepsilon_{average} = \frac{\sum_{i=0}^{N-1} |\bar{f}(x_i) - f(x_i)|}{N} \tag{5}$$

$$\varepsilon_{max} = max(|\bar{f}(x_i) - f(x_i)|) \tag{6}$$

where N is the number of all considered points in the interval (x_{min}, x_{max}). After estimating the accuracy of approximation for all examined interpolations, the best fitting slope and y-intercept values that achieve the desired accuracy level are extracted for HW generation.

Neurons in neural networks usually perform arithmetic operations on real numbers which can be represented in a fixed or a FP format [17]. Dealing with FP formats in HW is costly from a timing, area, and power perspective. According to [8], adopting FP representations has a marginal benefit on the accuracy in comparison to quantized reduced precision formats represented in fixed point. To restrain from burdening the system with complex components like an FPU, real values are converted to integer values. The domain of the converted integer values grows by a factor of 10 for every considered decimal point. This factor is multiplied by all FP y-intercept and interpolation x-values that result from the search-based optimization algorithm. Thus, the designated x-domain determines the accuracy level aimed for. In our implementation, a maximum error of 0.02 is achieved with an x-domain that ranges from -10^4 to 10^4 and with a scaling factor of 10^3.

3.5   Proposed Architecture

The deployment of the HW generator in our approach gives room for designing an adaptable architecture. It enables generating a highly optimized static HW for supporting exactly one specific function as well as fully dynamic run-time reprogrammable solutions and multiple intermediate shades. The HW generation process is based on a set of reconfigurable architectural parameters including the number of interpolation points, offset support, symmetry support, input size, and the degree of reprogrammability for interpolation points. Those parameters define the desired function's properties deployed in the respective interpolation HW. The block diagram of the proposed architecture is displayed in Fig. 2.

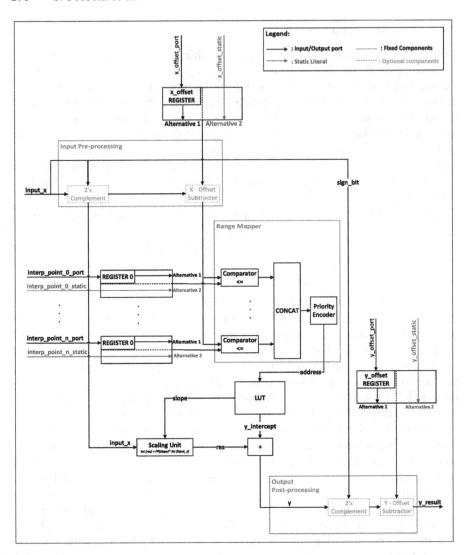

Fig. 2. Block diagram of the linear interpolation component

Pre/Post-Processing. The input preprocessing and output postprocessing components are feature-based components that depend on the function's properties. They include other subcomponents which get activated when certain features are enabled. For symmetry, a 2's complement component is needed to account for negative x-values that are not included in the set of chosen interpolation points but comprise the negative domain of the function. Specifically, origin symmetry requires this component from the input side to compute the absolute value of all incoming xs and another one from the output side to compute the negative y-value results. On the contrary, the y-symmetry feature requires only one 2's complement component from the input side since in this particular case, all y-values in the positive and negative domains are identical. In the same manner, the offset feature demands a subtractor from either the input side if the offset is in the x-direction, or from the output side if it's in the y-direction, or from both sides if it's in the x- and y-directions.

Range-Decoding. Owing to the adopted nonuniform segmentation scheme, range mapping logic is integrated into our component to determine the range that every input x belongs to. Each range represents a distinct interpolation segment correlated with a unique slope and y-intercept value. The range mapper component incorporates a set of comparators that are responsible for comparing input x-values with the xs considered for interpolation. For dynamic interpolation x-values, the input x is compared to an interface consisting of reprogrammable registers. As for the static mode, the input x is compared to a static literal value that is set during design time. In our approach, we position those comparators in an increasing order to obtain a standardized output sequence used to extract slope and y-intercept values from the LUT. This is accomplished with the help of a priority encoder (PE) that takes as input the concatenated results of all comparators and outputs the index of the most significant input bit. The result of the PE constitutes the read address of the LUT.

Lookup and Compute. A LUT with a configurable size is utilized to store the precomputed y-intercept and slope values. Each LUT entry holds the aforementioned datasets and represents a distinct linear segment. The bit width of each dataset is a configurable parameter that can be set to any size that matches the maximum size of the specified LUT's entry. The y-intercept and slope values associated with the chosen interpolation points are stored at the LUT and chosen based on the address determined by the PE. For static y-intercept and slope values, a static LUT with a read-only interface is generated. Contrarily, if those values are set to be dynamic, a reprogrammable register file with a read and write interface is generated. After extracting the correct datasets from the LUT, the interpolated y is computed by multiplying the input x with the slope value and adding the multiplication result to the extracted y-intercept value. The multiplication operation is carried out by a scaling unit (SU). The internal architecture of the SU is elaborated on in the following section.

3.6   Multiplier Optimizations

Multiplication is identified as one of the main drivers for area in PWL and PWNL interpolation-HW. Although the impact of the slope's decimal point precision on the interpolation results is minor, its magnitude is of high severity. The slope represented in a fixed point format doesn't exploit this property, resulting in a costly full-precision integer multiplier. A representation of the slope in a customized FP format on the other hand allows exploiting these properties. While reserving an appropriate amount of exponent-bits to represent the domain range, a low number of mantissa bits is sufficient for achieving reasonable interpolation accuracies.

We propose a hybrid multiplier named SU, which multiplies a FP slope with an integer input x for a specified precision, delivering an integer value as output. Its structure breaks down into pre-shift, mantissa multiplication, and post-shift logic. The purpose of the pre-shift is the realignment of the input integer to provide only the significant bits to the mantissa multiplication. Thereby, the precision capabilities of the mantissa multiplier, which is an integer multiplier with reduced width, are fully exploited. Its exact width depends on the specified precision. The post-shift compensates for the pre-shift and sets the proper slope's exponent. We optionally provide a feature for detecting overflows caused by exceeding the range of representable integers.

The maximum FP error produced by the SU is evaluated based on the number of bits discarded from either the mantissa or exponent fields. Each linear portion shares a common LUT entry to store the slope and y-intercept values. This stipulates allocating enough bits to represent the maximum y-intercept value. For an implementation instance, which supports a domain range of $(\pm 10^4)$ and utilizes 32-bit LUTs, the 15 least significant bits of the mantissa are discarded to reserve enough space for the maximum y-intercept value. In such implementations, the maximum FP error is estimated to be around 0.4% when compared to the full precision FP value.

4   Experimental Results

4.1   Optimized Search for Interpolation Points

To study the impact of adopting a minimum search optimization algorithm for finding an optimized distribution of a set of interpolation points, we investigate uniform and nonuniform segmentation schemes. Figure 3 illustrates the effect of each segmentation technique on the maximum absolute error for both Sigmoid and Tanh functions. It is evident from Fig. 3 that the maximum error for the nonuniform technique is dropping at a much higher rate than for the uniform technique. For instance, the uniform method for the Tanh function attains a maximum error of 0.766 with 2 interpolation points and drops to 0.02963 with 17 points compared to the nonuniform method which achieves a maximum error of 0.02438 with 5 points only. Similar behavior is observed with the Sigmoid function, where the uniform method attains a maximum error of 0.3028 with 2 interpolation points and drops to 0.01630 with 9 points compared to the nonuniform method which achieves a maximum error of 0.0131 with only 4 points. The presented results lay out the robustness of the nonuniform segmentation technique, portraying the significance of the adopted search-based optimization algorithm.

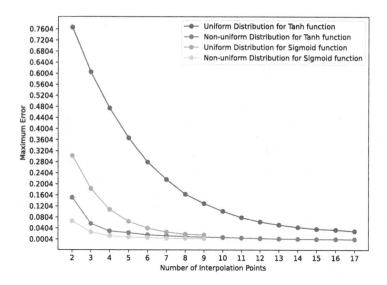

Fig. 3. Maximum absolute error of the Tanh and Sigmoid functions with uniformly and nonuniformly distributed interpolation points

4.2   Optimized Generated Hardware

We generate the interpolation hardware for various activation functions, utilizing different features and accuracy requirements for ASIC on $40nm$ technology. In the following paragraphs, the area results measured in gate equivalents (GE) along with their driving forces are discussed.

Function type and Features. As discussed in Sect. 4.1, each function requires a specific number of interpolation points to achieve the desired accuracy level. The maximum absolute deviation drops below 0.02 with 4 and 6 interpolation points for Sigmoid and Tanh respectively. It can be inferred from Fig. 4 that the area footprint of the Tanh function is 20% greater than that of the Sigmoid function for similar accuracy thresholds. This increase is explained by the fact that the linear segments of the Tanh function have steeper slopes and larger y-intercept

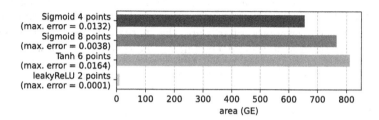

Fig. 4. Area results of static activation function implementations for different amount of interpolation points in the domain of $\pm 10^4$ without SU

values than those of the Sigmoid function, thus utilizing more HW resources to accommodate for larger lookups. The impact of utilizing the symmetry feature for the Sigmoid function is demonstrated in Fig. 4, where an area decrease of 24% is recorded for the implementation that has 4 interpolation points in comparison to the one with 8 points. Additionally, incorporating an x-offset with implementations that exhibit large interpolation x-values plays a role in reducing their size, thus leading to smaller comparator sizes. This comes at the cost of having an additional subtractor that compensates for the displacement enforced by the offset. For an x domain that ranges from -10^5 to 10^5, introducing an offset causes a reduction of the total area footprint by 3%, 7%, and 6% with respect to the baseline implementations for Sigmoid with 8 points, Tanh with 4 points, and Tanh with 11 points respectively as shown in Fig. 5. Contrarily, introducing an offset for an x domain that ranges from -10^4 to 10^4 has proven to be disadvantageous since it led to a slight increase in area footprint. This stems from the fact that for small interpolation values, the impact of adding a subtractor counterbalances the effect that the offset has on comparator sizes.

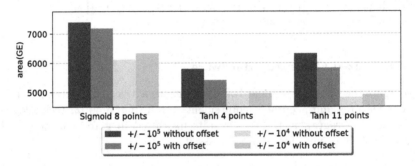

Fig. 5. Area results for Sigmoid and Tanh implementations with and without offset including SU

Domain Range and Bit Width. Area results for the generated hardware in the $\pm 10^4$ and $\pm 10^5$ domains are shown in Fig. 6. By moving from lower to higher domain ranges, the bit widths of the ports increased accordingly from 15 to 18 bits. The impact of this change manifests itself with a 4% increase across all implementations with different levels of reprogrammability excluding the SU. For the SU, this change causes an area scale up by 18%. Considering the SU together with the interpolation hardware, the share of the SU is found between 70% to 90% of the overall area, depending on the specific application.

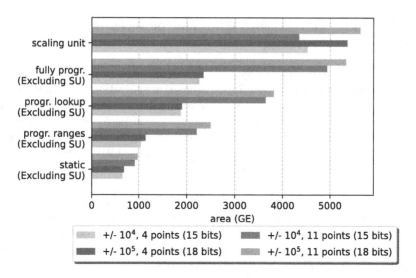

Fig. 6. Area results for different levels of reprogrammability for an instance of a Tanh function interpolated with 4 and 11 points across different x-domain ranges

Interpolation Points and Reprogrammability. Figure 6 shows the area results for an interpolated Tanh function. We interpolated the same function with 4 and 11 points and analyzed the behavior of the area based on various reprogrammability levels. The figure shows four levels of reprogrammability. The smallest footprint of $650\,GE$ is achieved by a fully optimized static hardware with 4 interpolation points. Increasing the number of interpolations to 11 increases the area by 39%, while the impact on accuracy is minimal as shown in Fig. 3. Figure 6 further shows the area occupied by every level of reprogrammability. Having a set of reprogrammable interpolation ranges results in a smaller footprint than having a reprogrammable lookup for dynamic y-intercept and slope values. The bit width reserved for reprogrammable ranges and the sizes of range comparators are proportional to the width of the input data, whereas the allocated size of the slope and y-intercept lookup table do not depend on it. Thus, increasing the bit width of the input-x negatively affects the area consumed by the reprogrammable interfaces allocated for interpolation x-values. In general, the more precise the definition of the use case and the specifications for the interpolation HW, the smaller the achievable area results of the approximation hardware. Thus, a large amount of interpolation points is expensive especially for applications requiring reprogrammability.

4.3 Comparison with Similar Works

Our work focuses on ASIC implementations and therefore relies on GEs as a measure to assess area. However, in the related literature, results are frequently presented in LUT counts, which are specific to FPGA environments. To be able to study the implications of our work and compare it to other proposed approaches in the literature, various instances of our function implementations are synthesized on a *Artix-7 XC7A35T-L1CSG324I* FPGA. Hardware implementation and accuracy results of different Sigmoid and Tanh implementations are summarized in Table 1 and Table 2 respectively.

Table 1 shows, that our adopted search-based optimization algorithm achieves the best error deviation results with the least number of segments. From an area perspective, our proposed Sigmoid implementation outperforms the PWL implementation proposed in [10], and the multiplier-based PWNL approach proposed in [17], but falls short when compared to the shifter-based PWL method proposed in [17]. However, the latter shows an increased mean and maximum deviation error.

As for the Tanh function, our 4 and 11 segment implementations achieve the best mean deviation error and utilizes significantly less resources than the Catmull ROM spline method proposed in [3]. However, the latter achieves the least maximum deviation error. With additional segments, our proposed method allows to achieve similar or lower deviation errors.

Table 1. Area and deviation results for the Sigmoid function

Implementation	Number of segments	Mean deviation	Max deviation	Platform	LUT	FF	DSP	Latency (ns)
Ref [17] PWL	4	0.01412	0.01850	Cyclone 3 EP3C16F484C6	246	–	–	–
Proposed Sigmoid	**4**	**0.0078**	**0.0131**	**Xilinx XC7A35T**	**294**	**9**	**2**	**4.915**
Ref [17] PWNL	-	0.00426	0.0178	Cyclone 3 EP3C16F484C6	368	–	–	–
Ref [10] PWL	9	0.0016	0.00784	Xilinx XC7V2000	493	32	0	9.6
Proposed Sigmoid	**5**	**0.0045**	**0.00489**	**Xilinx XC7A35T**	**313**	**15**	**2**	**5.07**

Table 2. Area and deviation results for the Tanh function

Implementation	Number of segments	Mean deviation	Max deviation	Platform	GE
Ref [13] Tanh RALUT method	–	0.0121	0.0181	TSMC 18μm	–
Ref [3] Catmull ROM spline method	–	–	0.000152	–	5840
Proposed Tanh	**4**	**0.00845**	**0.0302**	**TSMC 40 nm**	**4663**
Proposed Tanh	**11**	**0.000868**	**0.00542**	**TSMC 40 nm**	**5026**

5 Conclusion

Our work addresses the challenges imposed by computing activation functions on restrictive edge devices meant for performing NN inference. The proposed hybrid solution reuses concepts of PWL and RALUT to facilitate linearly interpolating those functions. The proposed smart HW accelerator is backboned by a SW preprocessing framework and a hardware generator, delivering optimized hardware for various use cases. The intensive exploitation of function properties, and the search for nonuniformly distributed while highly significant interpolation points, reduces lookup area and achieves desirable accuracies with the least number of interpolation points. By reducing the number of interpolation points from 11 to 4 for the Sigmoid function, we are able to achieve an area reduction of 39%. Additionally, exploiting offset and symmetry features further decreases the area with respect to baseline implementations by 7% and 24% respectively. The slope multiplication is performed with a hybrid float-x-integer SU, which allows the selection of the required precision depending on the application. Due to the slope's properties, treating the multiplication in a hybrid manner emerges to be more efficient than preserving the standard fixed-point operation mode.

6 Future Work

The exploration time in the adopted search-based optimization algorithm grows exponentially for more complex non-monotonic functions that require more interpolation points than the elaborated activation functions. For this reason, a variety of alternative optimization algorithms for detecting the optimal positions of linear interpolation points are going to be evaluated to reduce the search space and accelerate the search process. Moreover, a hybrid optimized reprogrammable, as well as static solution addressing various activation functions simultaneously, is within the scope of our future work.

Acknowledgements. Part of the work has been funded by the German Federal Ministry of Education and Research (BMBF) as part of the research project Scale4Edge (16ME0122K).

References

1. Agostinelli, F., Hoffman, M., Sadowski, P., Baldi, P.: Learning activation functions to improve deep neural networks. arXiv preprint arXiv:1412.6830 (2014)
2. Amin, H., Curtis, K., Hayes-Gill, B.: Piecewise linear approximation applied to nonlinear function of a neural network. IEEE Proc. Circuits Dev. Syst. **144**(6), 313 (1997). https://doi.org/10.1049/ip-cds:19971587
3. Chandra, M.: Hardware implementation of hyperbolic tangent function using catmull-rom spline interpolation. arXiv preprint arXiv:2007.13516 (2020)
4. Ciregan, D., Meier, U., Schmidhuber, J.: Multi-column deep neural networks for image classification. In: 2012 IEEE Conference on Computer Vision and Pattern Recognition, pp. 3642–3649. IEEE (2012)
5. Duren, R., Marks, R., Reynolds, P., Trumbo, M.: Real-time neural network inversion on the SRC-6e reconfigurable computer. IEEE Trans. Neural Networks **18**(3), 889–901 (2007). https://doi.org/10.1109/tnn.2007.891679
6. Ecker, W., Schreiner, J.: Introducing model-of-things (mot) and model-of-design (mod) for simpler and more efficient hardware generators. In: 2016 IFIP/IEEE International Conference on Very Large Scale Integration (VLSI-SoC), pp. 1–6 (2016). https://doi.org/10.1109/VLSI-SoC.2016.7753576
7. Hu, J., Shen, L., Albanie, S., Sun, G., Wu, E.: Squeeze-and-excitation networks, September 2017
8. Hubara, I., Courbariaux, M., Soudry, D., El-Yaniv, R., Bengio, Y.: Quantized neural networks: training neural networks with low precision weights and activations. J. Mach. Learn. Res. **18**(1), 6869–6898 (2017)

9. Kumar, P.A.: FPGA implementation of the trigonometric functions using the CORDIC algorithm. In: 2019 5th International Conference on Advanced Computing & Communication Systems (ICACCS). IEEE, March 2019. https://doi.org/10.1109/icaccs.2019.8728315

10. Li, Z., Zhang, Y., Sui, B., Xing, Z., Wang, Q.: Fpga implementation for the sigmoid with piecewise linear fitting method based on curvature analysis. Electronics **11**(9), 1365 (2022)

11. Lin, M.H., Carlsson, J.G., Ge, D., Shi, J., Tsai, J.F.: A review of piecewise linearization methods. Math. Probl. Eng. **2013**, 1–8 (2013). https://doi.org/10.1155/2013/101376

12. Muscedere, R., Dimitrov, V., Jullien, G., Miller, W.: Efficient techniques for binary-to-multidigit multidimensional logarithmic number system conversion using range-addressable look-up tables. IEEE Trans. Comput. **54**(3), 257–271 (2005). https://doi.org/10.1109/tc.2005.48

13. Namin, A.H., Leboeuf, K., Muscedere, R., Wu, H., Ahmadi, M.: Efficient hardware implementation of the hyperbolic tangent sigmoid function. In: 2009 IEEE International Symposium on Circuits and Systems. IEEE, May 2009. https://doi.org/10.1109/iscas.2009.5118213

14. Piazza, F., Uncini, A., Zenobi, M.: Neural networks with digital LUT activation functions. In: Proceedings of 1993 International Conference on Neural Networks (IJCNN-93-Nagoya, Japan). IEEE (1993). https://doi.org/10.1109/ijcnn.1993.716806

15. Raut, G., Rai, S., Vishvakarma, S.K., Kumar, A.: A CORDIC based configurable activation function for ANN applications. In: 2020 IEEE Computer Society Annual Symposium on VLSI (ISVLSI). IEEE, July 2020. https://doi.org/10.1109/isvlsi49217.2020.00024

16. Tommiska, M.: Efficient digital implementation of the sigmoid function for reprogrammable logic. IET Proc. Comput. Digital Tech. **150**(6), 403 (2003). https://doi.org/10.1049/ip-cdt:20030965

17. Tsmots, I., Skorokhoda, O., Rabyk, V.: Hardware implementation of sigmoid activation functions using FPGA. In: 2019 IEEE 15th International Conference on the Experience of Designing and Application of CAD Systems (CADSM). IEEE, February 2019. https://doi.org/10.1109/cadsm.2019.8779253

18. Volder, J.E.: The CORDIC trigonometric computing technique. IRE Trans. Electron. Comput. **EC-8**(3), 330–334 (1959). https://doi.org/10.1109/tec.1959.5222693

19. Zhang, M., Vassiliadis, S., Delgado-Frias, J.: Sigmoid generators for neural computing using piecewise approximations. IEEE Trans. Comput. **45**(9), 1045–1049 (1996). https://doi.org/10.1109/12.537127

Hardware-Aware Evolutionary Filter Pruning

Christian Heidorn[1][✉], Nicolai Meyerhöfer[1,2], Christian Schinabeck[2],
Frank Hannig[1], and Jürgen Teich[1]

[1] Friedrich-Alexander-Universität Erlangen-Nürnberg (FAU),
91058 Erlangen, Germany
{christian.heidorn,nicolai.meyerhoefer,frank.hannig,juergen.teich}@fau.de
[2] Fraunhofer Institute for Integrated Circuits IIS, 91058 Erlangen, Germany
christian.schinabeck@iis.fraunhofer.de

Abstract. Compression techniques for Convolutional Neural Networks (CNNs) are key to performance. One common technique is filter pruning, which can effectively reduce the memory footprint, number of arithmetic operations, and consequently inference time. Recently, several approaches have been presented for automatic CNN compression using filter pruning, where the number of pruned filters is optimized by nature-inspired metaheuristics (e.g., artificial bee colony algorithms). However, these approaches focus on finding an optimal pruned network structure without considering the targeted device for CNN deployment. In this work, we show that the typical objective of reducing the number of operations does not necessarily lead to a maximum reduction in inference time, which is usually the main goal for compressing CNNs besides reducing the memory footprint. We then propose a hardware-aware multi-objective Design Space Exploration (DSE) technique for filter pruning that involves the targeted device (i.e., Graphics Processing Units (GPUs)). For each layer, the number of filters to be pruned is optimized with the objectives of minimizing the inference time and the error rate of the CNN. Experimental results show that our approach can further speed up inference time by 1.24× and 1.09× for VGG-16 on the CIFAR-10 dataset and ResNet-101 on the ILSVRC-2012 dataset, respectively, compared to the state-of-the-art ABCPruner.

1 Introduction

Filter pruning has become one of the most important techniques to reduce inference time, memory footprint, and energy consumption of Convolutional Neural Networks (CNNs), in order to extend their usability in embedded devices, e.g., smartphones and other wearable devices [1]. However, determining the individual number of filters to be pruned in each layer is a challenging problem because CNNs may consist of dozens to hundreds of convolutional layers exhibiting up to 1,000 filters per layer, resulting in a vast design space [2]. Moreover, evaluating each pruned CNN configuration may take a considerable amount of time.

A. Orailoglu et al. (Eds.): SAMOS 2022, LNCS 13511, pp. 283–299, 2022.
https://doi.org/10.1007/978-3-031-15074-6_18

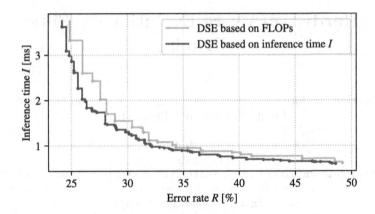

Fig. 1. Efficient sets obtained by a DSE with the objective of minimizing the number of floating-point operations (FLOPs) (red front) and of minimizing the inference time (blue front) on the Nvidia RTX 2080 Ti GPU, respectively. Each point represents a non-dominated pruned CNN configuration of the VGG-11 baseline model, trained on the CIFAR-10 dataset. (Color figure online)

Recent publications address this problem by presenting approaches to shrinking the design space while applying exploration-based optimization strategies such as evolutionary algorithms [2–4]. This can significantly reduce the number of operations required for inference of the CNN. The reduction is thereby achieved by different means, e.g., by setting bounds for preserved filters or defining a small set of fixed pruning rates applied to all layers [3]. Yet unfortunately, all approaches above ignore to incorporate also hardware knowledge of the target device, i.e., the GPU on which the CNN is deployed.

In this paper, we propose two approaches to reduce the design space by introducing (1) a *hardware-dependent pruning step size S* and (2) a *step size vector $\vec{S}$*, to lower the possible candidate set of filter pruning configurations. In Sect. 4.1, we explain how the step size S shall be determined for a given GPU target architecture.

Furthermore, the general objective of state-of-the-art filter pruning DSE methods found in literature is to minimize the number of floating-point operations (FLOPs), i.e., multiply-accumulate operations (MACs), required to compute the convolutional layers of a CNN. Although this objective may indirectly reduce the inference time on the target device, we show that focusing solely on MAC minimization does not always lead to performance-optimal configurations. Instead, we rather propose to incorporate the objective of inference time directly by performing hardware measurements on the target device.

As a motivating example, consider Fig. 1. Shown are two efficient sets[1] consisting of pruned CNN configurations (represented by each dot) obtained after

---

[1] Efficient sets are approximations of Pareto sets. As an evolutionary multi-objective algorithm typically cannot guarantee to find truly Pareto-optimal points, shown is the efficient set of non-dominated points after a DSE run.

performing a DSE, using the multi-objective evolutionary algorithm (MOEA) NSGA-II [5] (see Sect. 5 for the detailed settings) to find optimal pruning configurations for the VGG-11 benchmark [6] on the CIFAR-10 dataset [7]. One efficient set originates from a DSE performed with the objective of minimizing inference time (blue front) on an Nvidia RTX 2080 Ti GPU, the other one from a DSE performed with the objective of minimizing the number of FLOPs (red front). Minimizing the error rate is in both variants the second objective. Each DSE was run for 12 h, and the inference time of the resulting pruned CNN configurations optimized for FLOPs was then measured on the Nvidia RTX 2080 Ti for comparison. When visually inspecting the two fronts, it can be clearly seen that the minimization of FLOPs does not adequately minimize the inference times. But in order to compensate for the extra effort for the deployment and inference time measurements on a target platform, we present different approaches to reducing the design space, including separating the convolutional layers into groups and reducing the dataset size required for retraining during the DSE (see Sect. 4). Our contributions can be summarized as follows:

- Introduction of a hardware-aware DSE for systematically exploring the vast design space of filter pruning options of a given CNN. More specifically, we propose two approaches for reducing the design space by introducing a global step size S and a step size vector $\vec{S}$, that take into account artifacts influencing the inference time on the target architecture, in our case GPUs.
- MOEA-based DSE minimizing both the error rate R and inference time I of a given CNN rather than just FLOP counts and thus contrary to other state-of-the-art approaches. The DSE produces a so-called efficient set containing a large number of non-dominated configurations having a high diversity among the contradicting objectives.
- Evaluation: We demonstrate the powerfulness of our hardware-aware DSE for filter pruning on an Nvidia RTX 2080 Ti GPU for four different CNN benchmarks. Compared to the unpruned baseline and to the best pruned CNN configurations found by ABCPruner [3], we find solutions providing a speedup of the inference time I with similar error rates R.

2   Related Work

In CNN filter pruning or channel pruning (filter pruning "in reverse direction" [8]), entire filters are removed, which leads to (1) a reduction of the memory footprint, as the pruned filters do not have to be stored, and (2) a reduction of the inference time, as the arithmetic operations for the pruned filters are omitted. It appears that CNNs are typically over-parametrized and that the individual filters of each layer differ in importance, such that removing the less important filters has (almost) no impact on the overall error rate of the CNN [9]. The main question here is how to measure the importance of the filters. One area of research in filter pruning is therefore the introduction of different criteria for measuring the importance of filters. Here, the most common criteria are the ℓ^1 norm (importance of a filter corresponds to its absolute weight sum), geometric median, Taylor expansion loss, or Average Percentage of Zero activations (APoZ) [9–11]. Furthermore, ThiNet [12] reduces the number of filters of a convolutional layer i based on the preserved channels in the subsequent convolutional layer $i+1$. Here, based on a given compression rate (how many channels of layer $i+1$ are preserved) the reconstruction error of the resulting feature maps of layer $i+1$ is minimized by a greedy search algorithm.

Radu et al. [13] extensively study the effect of pruning different numbers of filters on the actual inference time on embedded hardware devices. Their findings show that filter pruning does not always lead to a speedup when deployed on the target platform, confirming our experimental findings (see Sect. 5.2). Li et al. [14] take into account the actual latency when executing the pruned CNN. Here, the latency is estimated with a heuristic model. However, the model may not be sufficiently accurate when being executed on a different platform or when a different version of a compiler (e.g., TensorRT) is used. Similarly, HALP [15] uses a look-up table acquired from pre-measurements, which may also impair accuracy. Another remaining question is how many measurements are required to get an accurate latency estimation for the vast design space.

However, what all approaches above have in common is that the pruning rates of filters have to be set manually for each layer, so that automatic compression of CNNs is not possible. Several recent works use Evolutionary Algorithms (EAs) for automatic filter pruning of CNNs to optimize for two conflicting objectives: the number of pruned filters and the overall error rate of CNNs [2,4]. KGEA [4] proposes a genetic algorithm to find the so-called *knee solution* in the resulting Pareto front, which gives a trade-off between the total number of filters of the CNN and the error rate. KGEA avoids using heuristic criteria and ranks the filters with the genetic algorithm (here NSGA-II). A problem appears for deeper CNNs, having more filters (e.g., ResNet-101), which lead to a significant increase of the design space. Moreover, the found knee solution for this approach only gives the optimal trade-off between the overall number of filters and the error rate of the CNN, while the real inference time is not evaluated on the hardware, and specific mappings of each convolutional layer on the hardware are not considered. Similar to this approach, ABCPruner [3] ranks the filters with an artificial bee colony algorithm to automatically find the least important filters for each layer. To reduce the design space and evaluate deeper CNNs, a parameter α is introduced, which represents a lower bound for the number of preserved filters in each layer: For $\alpha = 0.8$, 80% of the filters in each layer are preserved, and thus the design space for each layer is also reduced by 80%. The optimal solution corresponds to the trade-off between the number of FLOPs and the error rate of the CNN. However, α does not relate to the underlying hardware, and the user has to know which value fits best. α is set globally for all layers of the CNN, whereas in our approach, setting step sizes, i.e., for a group of layers, is much more fine-granular and takes into account the different importance of layers. IEEpruner [2] uses the NSGA-II algorithm to optimize the pruning criteria (i.e., ℓ^1 norm, geometric mean, APoZ) that measure the importance of filters. Each convolutional layer i is pruned considering the pruning criteria with the highest reduction of filters that still maintains the accuracy of the CNN. But this does not take into account the underlying hardware and the ultimate goal of minimizing the inference time is not considered by the MOEA. Furthermore, in our approach, also other criteria than the ℓ^1 norm may be used and integrated to measure filter importance, but this is not part of this work. The approach closest to ours is AACP [16], which also uses the ℓ^1 norm to determine the importance of filters and introduces a step size vector to reduce the size of the design space. An improved differential evolutionary algorithm (IDE) is used for optimization. However, it does also not incorporate information about the target hardware platform to define the step sizes for a group of layers. Another drawback is that no retraining is performed after each pruning step to maintain the accuracy of a pruned CNN [17]. Moreover, during DSE, some Pareto-optimal pruned CNN configurations found are no longer Pareto-optimal after applying retraining (see Sect. 5.3).

Finally, another deficiency of the approaches mentioned before is that minimizing the number of floating-point operations, number of filters, or memory space in some cases, does not necessarily lead to solutions minimal in the inference time. As our introductory example in Fig. 1 has shown, the selected mapping on the device highly impacts the inference time, which will be analyzed in detail in our experiment section (see Sect. 5). Rather, we are proposing a hardware-aware DSE for filter-pruning to directly minimize the inference time on a target device. Also, in contrast to previous approaches, we introduce techniques for design space reduction with respect to execution properties of the convolutional layers on the target hardware (GPUs in our case), which is explained in more detail in the next chapter.

3 Fundamentals

In the following, we briefly describe the idea of filter pruning of the convolutional layers (see Sect. 3.1). Afterwards, in Sect. 3.2, we investigate how the number of pruned filters affects the inference time of a convolutional layer when executed on a GPU.

3.1 Filter Pruning of CNNs

In CNNs, a convolutional layer i transforms so-called input feature maps, using a 3-dimensional tensor of shape $R_i \times C_i \times N_i$, into a 3-dimensional tensor of shape $R_{i+1} \times C_{i+1} \times M_i$, called output feature maps. Herein, R_i and C_i denote the number of rows and columns of one input feature map. N_i represents the number of input feature maps. Likewise, R_{i+1}, C_{i+1}, and M_i represent the number of rows, columns, and output feature maps. The transformation applies M_i 3-dimensional convolutional filters of shape $K_i \times K_i \times N_i$ on the input feature maps. In this context, K_i denotes the kernel size of the ith layer. The number of floating-point operations (FLOPs) to compute a convolutional layer i is obtained as $FLOPs_i = R_{i+1} \cdot C_{i+1} \cdot M_i \cdot N_i \cdot K_i^2$ [18].

Filter pruning aims to reduce the number of filters M_i. This involves ranking the filters M_i of a convolutional layer i. Best-known methods include the calculation of the ℓ^1 norm, the geometric median, or the Average Percentage of Zero activations (APoZ) [10]. In this work, the ℓ^1 norm is used. For each filter within a considered layer i, all weights are summed up, followed by ranking all filter sums. Then, the filters with the lowest sums are pruned. Filter pruning reduces the number of floating-point operations by a factor of $\frac{M_i}{m_i}$, where $1 \leq m_i \leq M_i$ is the number of preserved filters of convolutional layer i, resulting in a correspondingly reduced number of floating-point operations $FLOPs_i^{\text{pruned}} = R_{i+1} \cdot C_{i+1} \cdot m_i \cdot N_i \cdot K_i^2$ required for convolutional layer i. Since the number of output feature maps M_i of convolutional layer i is equal to the number of input feature maps of the subsequent convolutional layer $i+1$, $N_{i+1} = M_i$, the number of floating-point operations of layer $i+1$ is reduced by the same factor, i.e., $FLOPs_{i+1}^{\text{pruned}} = R_{i+2} \cdot C_{i+2} \cdot m_{i+1} \cdot m_i \cdot K_{i+1}^2$. In a nutshell, filter pruning may indirectly affect the performance (inference time) of a CNN by reducing the number of floating-point operations to be performed. On the other hand, the error rate R generally increases the more filters are pruned.

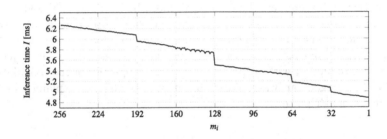

Fig. 2. Inference time for the entire VGG-16 model measured on an RTX 2080 Ti GPU upon reducing the number of filters m_i of the sixth convolutional layer, with $1 \leq m_i \leq M_i$. $m_i = M_i = 256$ denotes the unpruned case.

3.2   Inference Time Analysis of Convolutional Layers on GPUs

GPUs are a vital target to accelerate CNNs thanks to their provided massive hardware parallelism capable of performing trillions of FLOPs per second [19]. To study how the number of filters affects the inference time, we analyzed how the inference time of VGG-16 is influenced by the number of filters in the sixth convolutional layer on the RTX 2080 Ti GPU manufactured by Nvidia. In this experiment, the number of computed filters m_i ($1 \leq m_i \leq M_i = 256$) is gradually reduced from $m_i = 256$ to $m_i = 1$, the resulting model is compiled with Nvidia TensorRT [20], version 7.2.3, and the inference time I is measured on the Nvidia RTX 2080 Ti, here for a batch size $B = 128$. The corresponding results are visualized in Fig. 2. As expected, the inference time decreases with the number $M_i - m_i$ of pruned filters. However, one can see distinct steps at multiples of 64 and when the number of filters is 32. In addition, small dips (local minima) are visible, e.g., between 160 and 128. A similar step-wise decrease of the inference time with the number of pruned filters can also be observed when examining all other convolutional layers of VGG-16. The shown staircase steps are due to Nvidia's specific GPU architecture and the memory hierarchy [21]. As a result, one has to investigate for each combination of CNN, dataset, and GPU, individually how many filters can be pruned to obtain optimal inference time and accuracy trade-off solutions for the device on which the CNN is deployed. To systematically study the pruning vs. error rate trade-off for different CNNs, deployed on a concrete target platform (GPUs in this study), we present an automated design space exploration in the following.

4   Design Space Exploration

The contradicting objectives analyzed by our Design Space Exploration (DSE) are the inference time I as well as the error rate R, both to be minimized for a given CNN consisting of a set V of convolutional layers [18]. For each convolutional layer i, consisting of M_i filters in the unpruned case, the number of unpruned filters m_i, with $1 \leq m_i \leq M_i$, is optimized. With introducing a two-objective cost function f to be minimized and making use of a variable x_i per layer (i.e., $0 \leq i < |V|$), the optimization problem can be formulated as follows:

$$\min \quad f : \mathbb{N}^{|V|} \to \mathbb{R}^2$$
$$\mathbf{x} \mapsto (R(\mathbf{x}), I(\mathbf{x})) \tag{1}$$
$$s.t. \quad 1 \leq x_i \leq M_i, \, x_i \in \mathbb{N} \text{ for all } 0 \leq i < |V|.$$

The vector $\mathbf{x}$ is denoted as *pruned configuration* or *design point*. Here, the entries x_i denote the number of filters pruned for a convolutional layer i of the CNN, such that for each convolutional layer i the number of remaining filters is obtained as $m_i = M_i - x_i$. The size of the design space Ω of all possible filter pruning combinations is thus $|\Omega| = \prod_{i=0}^{|V|-1} M_i$. However, for many CNNs, this design space is prohibitively large, such that it would take a considerably large amount of time to explore and evaluate all design points. In the case of ResNet-18, including $|V| = 17$ convolutional layers, where the number of filters ranges from $M_i = 64$ to 512, the number of possible pruned configurations is $|\Omega| = 10^{38}$. To evaluate the error rate of each pruned configuration, compiling it using TensorRT [20] followed by measuring the inference time on the target hardware amounts to approximately 160 s for ResNet-18; this would result in more than 10^{32} years to explore the entire design space, which is not feasible. The evaluation time may even increase further if retraining is performed for each pruned configuration, which might be necessary to maintain the error rate of a pruned CNN. Therefore, we present two approaches to reduce the design space Ω, considering GPUs as target devices (see Sect. 4.1). Furthermore, we explain how to decrease the time for retraining of a pruned configuration during the DSE by reducing the size of the dataset, in Sect. 5.3.

4.1   Search Strategies

We propose to reduce the design space by (a) grouping the convolutional layers and by (b) introducing a global step size S and a step size vector $\vec{S}$, respectively, for the groups of convolutional layers. The motivation for (a) arises from the insight that layers with an equal number of filters have similar pruning rates in inference time optimal solutions, as could be seen for the VGG-16 layers in ABCPruner [3]. The motivation for (b) arises from the findings in Fig. 2, where steps in the inference time I are clearly visible as a function of the number of filters m_i with a spacing of 32 and 64 and small dips at a spacing of four filters.

We now introduce two approaches, the *grouped fixed step size* (GFS) approach, where a global step size S is fixed for all groups of convolutional layers, and the more fine-granular *grouped variable step size* (GVS) approach, where an individual step size can be set for each group, resulting in a step size vector $\vec{S}$. Figure 3 illustrates the grouping of the convolutional layers and the introduction of step sizes for the two approaches using the example of VGG-16, including $|V| = 13$ convolutional layers. The resulting size of the design space Ω is shown at the bottom of the Figure. First, the grouping of convolutional layers is performed, where all convolutional layers i are partitioned into disjoint groups $G_j \in G$. The layers in one group always have the same number of filters. In the example, the number of groups is chosen as $|G| = 4$, and the layers with the same number of filters M_i are grouped together. The number $|G|$ of groups of convolutional layers is adjustable and influences both the exploration time and the quality of the results obtained by the DSE, which is further investigated in Sect. 5.1.

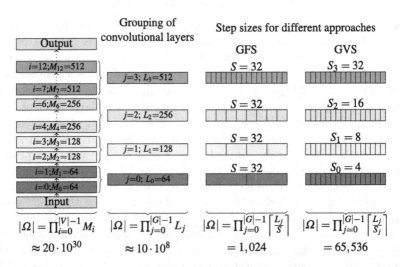

Fig. 3. Schematic of the GFS and GVS approaches for VGG-16. First, VGG-16's 13 convolutional layers i ($0 \leq i < 13$) are divided into $|G| = 4$ groups, visualized by the different colors. Secondly, in the case of the GFS approach, a global step size, e.g., $S = 32$, is set, and in the case of the GVS approach, different step sizes are assigned to the individual groups, here $\vec{S} = (4, 8, 16, 32)$, which leads to a finer granularity for the layers along with a smaller number of filters.

Grouped Fixed Step Size (GFS). In the case of the GFS approach, a global step size S is set (see e.g., $S = 32$ in Fig. 3) and the step size S is the same for all groups of convolutional layers. S can be set to $1 \leq S \leq L_j$, where L_j is the number of filters of the grouped convolutional layers G_j. The size of the resulting design space $|\Omega|$ is obtained as $|\Omega| = \prod_{j=0}^{|G|-1} \left\lceil \frac{L_j}{S} \right\rceil$. For the GFS approach, the optimization problem introduced in Eq. (1) therefore refines to

$$
\begin{aligned}
\min \quad & f : \mathbb{N}^{|V|} \to \mathbb{R}^2 \\
& \mathbf{x^{GFS}} \mapsto (R(\mathbf{x^{GFS}}), I(\mathbf{x^{GFS}})) \\
s.t. \quad & 1 \leq x_j^{GFS} \leq \left\lceil \frac{L_j}{S} \right\rceil, \ x_j^{GFS} \in \mathbb{N} \text{ for all } 0 \leq j < |G|.
\end{aligned}
\tag{2}
$$

Grouped Variable Step Size (GVS). In the case of the GVS approach, an individual step size S_j is defined for each group G_j of convolutional layers, resulting in a vector $\vec{S}$ whose elements are the individual step sizes S_j for each group of convolutional layers. In the VGG-16 example (see Fig. 3), a step size vector $\vec{S}$, with $\vec{S} = (4, 8, 16, 32)$, is chosen such that each group of layers contributes in equal proportion to the design space Ω. These step sizes S_j can be chosen according to $1 \leq S_j \leq L_j$. The resulting size of the reduced the design space is therefore $|\Omega| = \prod_{j=0}^{|G|-1} \left\lceil \frac{L_j}{S_j} \right\rceil$. For the GVS approach, the optimization problem introduced in Eq. (1) thus refines to

$$
\begin{aligned}
\min \quad & f : \mathbb{N}^{|V|} \to \mathbb{R}^2 \\
& \mathbf{x^{GVS}} \mapsto (R(\mathbf{x^{GVS}}), I(\mathbf{x^{GVS}})) \\
s.t. \quad & 1 \leq x_j^{GVS} \leq \left\lceil \frac{L_j}{S_j} \right\rceil, \ x_j^{GVS} \in \mathbb{N} \text{ for all } 0 \leq j < |G|.
\end{aligned}
\tag{3}
$$

5 Experiments

The following experiments were conducted for the VGG-11 and VGG-16 benchmarks [6] on the CIFAR-10 dataset [7], and the ResNet-18 and ResNet-101 benchmarks [22] on the ILSVRC-2012 dataset [23]. The optimization problems for the proposed GFS (see Eq. (2)) and GVS (see Eq. (3)) approaches were solved using the NSGA-II [5] multi-objective evolutionary algorithm (MOEA), embedded in the Opt4J framework [24]. The MOEA was configured with a population size of 100, 25 parents per generation, an offspring of 25 per generation, and a crossover rate of 0.95, and the DSE was performed over 1,000 generations. During the DSE, for each design point $\mathbf{x}$ (pruned CNN configuration), retraining for one epoch is applied, and the resulting error rate $R(\mathbf{x})$ is determined. After compilation with TensorRT [20], version 7.2.3, the resulting inference time $I(\mathbf{x})$ equals the computed average over 1,000 runs on an Nvidia RTX 2080 Ti GPU, a member of the Turing architecture family, which contains 11 GB GDDR6 RAM.

In the following, we evaluate the influence of the number of groups $|G|$ (see Sect. 5.1) and the effect of retraining with a reduced dataset on the error rate (see Sect. 5.3) of a design point in more detail. Subsequently, the GVS and GFS approaches are evaluated for four different benchmark CNNs (see Sects. 5.2 and 5.4).

5.1   Influence of Number of Groups $|G|$

The number of groups of convolutional layers $|G|$ is adjustable. Consequently, it influences the quality of the explored efficient sets after an equal number of evaluations, as can be seen in Fig. 4. Here, the *hypervolume indicator* [25] is used as a quality indicator to compare the evolution over time of the found efficient sets for the GFS approach, for a fixed step size of $S = 32$, with a varying number of groups of convolutional layers $|G|$, with $|G| = 4$, $|G| = 8$, and $|G| = 13$, respectively. As reference point, the unpruned configuration of VGG-16 is chosen. For each evaluation, the inference time I and error rate R of the found design point are normalized by the reference point's respective values, and the decrease in inference time and error rate (in percent) are added to the hypervolume. It can be seen that for the low number of groups, $|G| = 4$, the hypervolume increases faster. Moreover, for $|G| = 4$, the entire design space could be explored exhaustively, requiring only 1,024 evaluations of configurations. Comparing the hypervolume of the EA (orange) and the grid search (red), it can also be seen that the EA finds better configurations after the same number of evaluations and converges faster. The more groups $|G|$ of convolutional layers a CNN has, the more evaluations are typically required until the hypervolume exceeds the hypervolume with a relatively small number of groups. When comparing $|G| = 8$ and $|G| = 13$, it can also be observed that the curves converge to about the same hypervolume, which is higher than the hypervolume for only $|G| = 4$ groups.

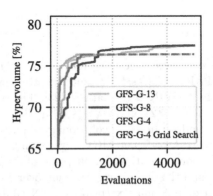

Fig. 4. Hypervolume of GFS with $|G| = 4$, $|G| = 8$, and $|G| = 13$ for a fixed global step size of $S = 32$ for VGG-16 trained on CIFAR-10 dataset, consisting of $|V| = 13$ convolutional layers. For $|G| = 4$ we added an optimization with grid search to evaluate the performance of the MOEA. (Color figure online)

This finding indicates that increasing the number of groups to the maximum is typically not necessary to maximize the hypervolume.

5.2 VGG-11 and VGG-16 on CIFAR-10

First, the GFS and GVS approaches were applied on VGG-11 and VGG-16. The entire CIFAR-10 dataset is used for retraining each explored design point during the DSE, which takes on average about 12 s, as the majority of time is spent for the compilation of the pruned configurations of VGG-16, which takes about 22.3 s on average. The batch size for retraining and inference time measurement is set to $B = 128$. For each DSE, 5,000 evaluations of pruned configurations were performed until the hypervolume converged (see Fig. 5(b)). For each pruned configuration in the resulting efficient set, retraining for 150 epochs was performed, which is the same number of epochs as used by ABCPruner. We applied the GFS approach, dividing the convolutional layers of VGG-11 and VGG-16, respectively, into $|G| = 8$ groups. The global step size is set to $S = 32$, because the inference time on the RTX 2080 Ti is significantly reduced if the filter number is a multiple of 32 and 64 (see Fig. 2). The size of the design space for the GFS approach is $|\Omega| = 16,384$. For VGG-11, we found a configuration achieving a speedup of 2.48× compared to the unpruned baseline with a slight decrease in accuracy of 1.89% (see Table 1). To show the effectiveness of our approach, we introduce the relative speedup metric, which is the ratio of the actual speedup if executed on the device and the expected speedup by FLOPs. For VGG-11, the found configuration achieves a relative speedup of 91.18% on the RTX 2080 Ti.

For VGG-16, the resulting efficient set is shown in Fig. 5(a), containing 18 configurations, more than found by ABCPruner (up to 10 configurations) or IEEpruner (only one pruned configuration). This allows the user to select the desired pruned configurations that meet his or her requirements, i.e., that are within a certain inference time corridor. The design point highlighted by the star in light blue in Fig. 5(a) achieves a slightly better top1-accuracy than the ABCPruner-80% configuration [3]. Although requiring more FLOPs, we achieve a speedup of 1.12× compared with the ABC-Pruner-80% configuration and a speedup of 2.67× compared to the VGG-16 unpruned model (see Table 1). This also confirms our findings from Fig. 1 that minimizing FLOPs does not necessarily lead to the lowest inference times. On the RTX 2080 Ti, our approach achieves a relative speedup of 84.49%, compared to the 62.90% achieved by ABC-Pruner-80%. Compared to the other filter pruning approaches such as ThiNet [12], KGEA [4], and IEEpruner [2], which also do not perform hardware-aware filter pruning, we already achieve a higher reduction of FLOPs (see the rightmost column in Table 1).

For the GVS approach on VGG-16, the convolutional layers were partitioned into $|G| = 8$ groups, and a step size vector with $\vec{S} = (8, 8, 8, 8, 16, 16, 16, 16)$ is chosen to have more possible combinations and a finer granularity for all groups $|G|$ of layers. The resulting size of the design space is $|\Omega| = 1,048,576$. In Table 1, we added a pruned configuration (VGG-16 GVS(a), purple star in Fig. 5(a)), which has a slight decrease in the top-1 accuracy of 0.10% compared to ABCPruner-80%; however, it also drastically decreases the inference time I and achieves an impressive speedup of 1.24× and 2.96× compared to ABCPruner-80% and the VGG-16 baseline, respectively. A second found pruned configuration (VGG-16 GVS(b)) has a 0.41% higher top-1 accuracy and still achieves a slightly higher speedup compared to ABCPruner-80%. Compared to the GFS approach we even achieve a higher relative speedup of 87.06% (VGG-16 GVS(a)) and 88.36% (VGG-16 GVS(b)).

In Fig. 5(b), the hypervolume of the DSE for the GFS and GVS approach for the VGG-16 benchmark are compared. It can be seen that the hypervolume of the GFS approach increases faster, meaning that better-pruned configurations with lower error rates and inference times compared to the unpruned baseline are found. The hypervolume for the GVS approach exceeds the hypervolume of the GFS approach after about 3,300 evaluations, as pruned configurations with a lower error rate R and inference time I are found which are not part of the design space of the GFS approach. This shows that the results can be improved with the more fine-granular GVS approach. However, here the tradeoff has to be made with respect to the overall time for the DSE.

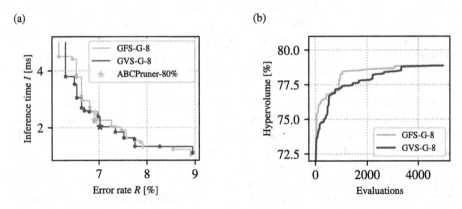

Fig. 5. Efficient set for VGG-16 on CIFAR-10 dataset determined by DSE using the GFS (light blue) and GVS (purple) approach, with $|G| = 8$, targeting the RTX 2080 Ti GPU, after 5,000 evaluations until the hypervolumes converged. In (a), the resulting efficient sets for the respective approach after retraining for 150 epochs are shown. The pruned configurations of our approaches (VGG16-GFS and VGG16-GVS(a)) and the configuration found by ABCPruner (ABCPruner-80%) which are used for the comparison in Table 1 are indicated by stars. In (b), the hypervolumes for the DSEs obtained by the GVS and GFS approaches are depicted. (Color figure online)

Table 1. Top1-accuracy ($= 100\% - R$), speedup compared to the unpruned baseline, FLOPs, expected speedup by the FLOPs compared to the unpruned baseline, the relative speedup, and the number of parameters for VGG-11 and VGG-16 on CIFAR-10 dataset, ResNet-18 and ResNet-101 on ILSVRC2012, respectively. The accuracy, inference time I, and FLOPs of the GVS and GFS approaches are compared with the state-of-the-art, including ABCPruner [3] (ABCP), ThiNet [12], KGEA [4], and IEEpruner [2]. For ABCPruner, we compiled the found configurations with TensorRT and measured the inference time on the RTX 2080 Ti. To show the effectiveness of our approach, we introduce the metric for the relative speedup, which is the ratio of the actual speedup if executed on the device and the expected speedup by FLOPs. For ThiNet, KGEA, and IEEpruner, no pruned CNN configuration was available to measure the inference time on the RTX 2080 Ti.

Pruner	Top1-accuracy	Speedup	FLOPs	Speedup expec. by FLOPs	Relative speedup	No. of parameters
VGG11						
Baseline	88.93%	1.00×	132.87M	1.00×	–	9.2M
GFS	87.04%	2.48×	48.68M	2.72×	**91.18%**	2.6M
VGG16						
Baseline	93.65%	1.00×	314.59M	1.00×	–	14.73M
GFS	93.09%	**2.67×**	99.58M	3.16×	**84.49%**	2.19M
GVS(a)	92.98%	**2.96×**	92.59M	3.40×	**87.06%**	1.42M
GVS(b)	93.50%	**2.43×**	114.20M	2.75×	**88.36%**	2.10M
ABCPruner-80%	93.08%	2.39×	82.81M	3.80×	62.90%	1.67M
ThiNet	93.31%	–	181.05M	–	–	5.25M
KGEA	93.45%	–	140.28M	–	–	4.07M
IEEPruner	93.83%	–	124.39M	–	–	2.29M
ResNet-18						
Baseline	69.66%	1.00×	1824.52M	1.00×	–	11.69M
GFS	65.32%	**1.58×**	1037.92M	1.76×	**89.77%**	9.20M
GVS	64.87%	**1.59×**	925.25M	1.97×	**80.71%**	7.40M
ABCPruner-70%	67.28%	1.44×	1005.71M	1.81×	79.56%	6.60M
ResNet-101						
Baseline	77.38%	1.00×	7868.40M	1.00×	–	44.55M
GFS	75.35%	**1.45×**	3734.09M	2.10×	**69.05%**	18.86M
GVS	75.47%	**1.41×**	3921.03M	2.01×	**70.15%**	22.50M
ABCPruner-80%	75.82%	1.33×	3164.91M	2.49×	53.41%	17.72M
ThiNet	75.30%	–	4476.33M	–	–	29.36M
KGEA	75.03%	–	4706.09M	–	–	24.31M
IEEPruner	78.21%	–	3672.18M	–	–	22.67M

5.3   Retraining with Reduced Data Set During DSE

Retraining can be pretty time-consuming, especially for large datasets, such as the ILSVRC-2012 dataset, which includes about one million images. Our experiments have shown that the Pareto-optimal configurations obtained without retraining during the DSE cannot be efficiently retrained after the DSE as important filters have gotten lost. In order to discard such ill configurations already during the DSE, we retrain each design point for one epoch on a very small subset of the dataset. We evaluated a DSE with 1,400 evaluations for the GFS approach (see Sect. 4.1) for ResNet-18 on the ILSVRC-2012 dataset, with

$|G| = 8$ and $S = 32$, where retraining for one epoch with 100% and 1% of the dataset is performed during the DSE. Even with a reduced dataset of 1%, the majority of pruned configurations (three quarters) can be found in the efficient set compared to retraining with the entire dataset (100%). In contrast, only one quarter of the pruned configurations could be found without retraining. For ResNet-18, the time to retrain a configuration using 100% of the dataset, which amounts to 2,862 s, decreases to 171 s when using only 1% of the dataset. Finally, using only 1% of the dataset, 16 more configurations can be evaluated within the same amount of time as when using the entire dataset.

5.4   ResNet-18 and ResNet-101 on ILSVRC-2012

Considering ResNet-18 and ResNet-101, we use 1% of the dataset for retraining each design point for one epoch during the DSE. However, as explained in Sect. 5.3, the solutions still include most of the Pareto-optimal design points. Again, the batch size is set to $B = 128$ for retraining. The inference time for ResNet-18 was determined for a batch size of $B = 128$, whereas for ResNet-101, the batch size for the inference time measurement was $B = 1$. On the resulting efficient sets, retraining of 90 epochs with the entire dataset is applied, which is the same number as used by ABCPruner.

For the GFS approach, the convolutional layers are divided into $|G| = 8$ groups, and the global step size S equals 32. For ResNet-18 on ILSVRC-2012, a selected configuration achieves a speedup of 1.58× compared to 1.44x provided by ABCPruner-70%, but with a 1.96% lower top1-accuracy (see Table 1). For ResNet-101 on ILSVRC-2012, the configuration found by the GFS approach achieves a 1.09× higher speedup than the ABCPruner-80% configuration, with a 0.47% lower top1-accuracy. The achieved relative speedup on the RTX 2080 Ti with the GFS approach for the respective benchmarks is 89.77% and 69.05% for ResNet-18 and ResNet-101, respectively, which is a significant improvement over the configurations found by ABCPruner.

For the GVS approach for ResNet-18 and ResNet-101, we choose a step size vector of $\vec{S} = (4, 4, 8, 8, 16, 16, 32, 32)$ to provide a finer granularity for the first convolutional layers, containing a lower amount of filters. On ResNet-101, the GVS approach found a sample configuration exhibiting a speedup of 1.41× with respect to the unpruned baseline (1.33× for ABCPruner-80%) as well as a decrease of 0.35% in top1-accuracy compared to the ABCPruner configuration.

In summary, we see a slight decrease of the top1-accuracy for the found pruned configuration for the ResNet-18 benchmark compared to the found ABCPruner configuration. This might be due to the smaller design space compared to ABCPruner, such that we do not explore sufficient pruned configurations. To achieve a better top1-accuracy, the design space has to be enlarged either by increasing the number of groups or decreasing the step size for each layer. For VGG-16 and ResNet-101, our approach finds better configurations that significantly reduce the inference time. In all cases our approach was able to increase the relative speedup significantly compared to ABCPruner.

6   Conclusion

We have presented a novel hardware-aware design space exploration (DSE) method for automatic filter pruning of CNNs. More specifically, we introduced two approaches for significantly reducing the huge design space of pruning options. These approaches provide knobs to adjust the DSE's granularity and consider execution properties of the convolutional layers on the target hardware (GPUs in our case). The resulting efficient set of non-dominated configurations provides a great diversity in terms of the two objectives inference time I and error rate R. Overall, our presented GVS approach can a achieve a speedup compared to the state-of-the-art ABCPruner by 1.24× for VGG-16 on the CIFAR-10 dataset and 1.09× for ResNet-101 on the ILSVRC-2012 dataset when deployed on an Nvidia RTX 2080 Ti device with similar error rates. Remarkably, for the investigated benchmarks, the actual speedup on the RTX 2080 Ti which is achieved by the majority of found configurations amounts to more than 80% of the expected speedup by FLOPs, e.g., 88.36% for VGG-16.

In the future, we intend to apply the proposed approach also to other accelerator architectures, such as FPGAs [26] and custom-tailored architectures for highly parallel CNN acceleration [27,28]. Another way to extend our approach is to integrate algorithms from the explainable AI domain, e.g., DeepLIFT [29], to determine the importance of single neurons or filters on the resulting output, i.e., the output feature maps. A recent work [30,31] showed how to extend DeepLIFT and use its importance measures to globally prune the filters of a CNN in order to minimize the number of FLOPs, which we intend to incorporate into our DSE.

Acknowledgment. This work was partially funded by the Deutsche Forschungsgemeinschaft (DFG, German Research Foundation)—Project Number 146371743—TRR 89 Invasive Computing and the German Federal Ministry for Education and Research (BMBF) within project KISS (01IS19070). Finally, we thank Joachim Keinert and Matthias Ziegler for their valuable review and inspiring discussions.

References

1. Hoefler, T., Alistarh, D., Ben-Nun, T., Dryden, N., Peste, A.: Sparsity in deep learning: pruning and growth for efficient inference and training in neural networks. J. Mach. Learn. Res. **22**, 241:1–241:124 (2021)
2. Zhang, Y., Zhen, Y., He, Z., Yen, G.G.: Improvement of efficiency in evolutionary pruning. In: Proceedings of the International Joint Conference on Neural Networks (IJCNN), pp. 1–8. IEEE (2021). https://doi.org/10.1109/IJCNN52387.2021.9534055
3. Lin, M., Ji, R., Zhang, Y., Zhang, B., Wu, Y., Tian, Y.: Channel pruning via automatic structure search. In: Proceedings of the Twenty-Ninth International Joint Conference on Artificial Intelligence (IJCAI), pp. 673–679 (2020). https://doi.org/10.24963/ijcai.2020/94
4. Zhou, Y., Yen, G.G., Yi, Z.: A knee-guided evolutionary algorithm for compressing deep neural networks. IEEE Trans. Cybern. **51**(3), 1626–1638 (2021). https://doi.org/10.1109/TCYB.2019.2928174

5. Deb, K., Pratap, A., Agarwal, S., Meyarivan, T.: A fast and elitist multiobjective genetic algorithm: NSGA-II. IEEE Trans. Evol. Comput. **6**(2), 182–197 (2002). https://doi.org/10.1109/4235.996017

6. Simonyan, K., Zisserman, A.: Very deep convolutional networks for large-scale image recognition. In: Proceedings of the 3rd International Conference on Learning Representations (ICLR) (2015)

7. Krizhevsky, A.: Learning Multiple Layers of Features from Tiny Images. University of Toronto (2012)

8. Ma, X., et al.: Non-structured DNN weight pruning - is it beneficial in any platform? The Computing Research Repository (CoRR) (2020). arXiv:1907.02124 [cs.LG]

9. Li, H., Kadav, A., Durdanovic, I., Samet, H., Graf, H.P.: Pruning filters for efficient ConvNets. In: Proceedings of the 5th International Conference on Learning Representations (ICLR) (2017)

10. Molchanov, P., Tyree, S., Karras, T., Aila, T., Kautz, J.: Pruning convolutional neural networks for resource efficient inference. In: Proceedings of the 5th International Conference on Learning Representations (ICLR) (2017)

11. Hu, H., Peng, R., Tai, Y.-W., Tang, C.-K.: Network trimming: a data-driven neuron pruning approach towards efficient deep architectures. The Computing Research Repository (CoRR) (2016). arXiv:1607.03250 [cs.NE]

12. Luo, J.-H., Zhang, H., Zhou, H.-Y., Xie, C.-W., Jianxin, W., Lin, W.: ThiNet: pruning CNN filters for a thinner net. IEEE Trans. Pattern Anal. Mach. Intell. **41**(10), 2525–2538 (2019). https://doi.org/10.1109/TPAMI.2018.2858232

13. Radu, V., et al.: Performance aware convolutional neural network channel pruning for embedded GPUs. In: Proceedings of the IEEE International Symposium on Workload Characterization (IISWC), pp. 24–34. IEEE (2019). https://doi.org/10.1109/IISWC47752.2019.9042000

14. Li, X., Zhou, Y., Pan, Z., Feng, J.: Partial order pruning: for best speed/accuracy trade-off in neural architecture search. In: Proceedings of the IEEE Conference on Computer Vision and Pattern Recognition (CVPR), pp. 9145–9153. IEEE (2019). https://doi.org/10.1109/CVPR.2019.00936

15. Shen, M., Yin, H., Molchanov, P., Mao, L., Liu, J., Alvarez, J.M.: HALP: hardware-aware latency pruning. The Computing Research Repository (CoRR) (2021). arXiv:2110.10811 [cs.CV]

16. Lin, L., Yang, Y., Guo, Z.: AACP: model compression by accurate and automatic channel pruning. The Computing Research Repository (CoRR) (2021). arXiv:2102.00390 [cs.CV]

17. Han, S., Pool, J., Tran, J., Dally, W.J.: Learning both weights and connections for efficient neural network. In: Proceedings of the Annual Conference on Neural Information Processing Systems, pp. 1135–1143 (2015)

18. Schuster, A., Heidorn, C., Brand, M., Keszöcze, O., Teich, J.: Design space exploration of time, energy, and error rate trade-offs for CNNs using accuracy-programmable instruction set processors. In: Kamp, M., et al. (eds.) ECML PKDD 2021. CCIS, vol. 1524, pp. 375–389. Springer, Cham (2021). https://doi.org/10.1007/978-3-030-93736-2_29

19. Baischer, L., Wess, M., Taherinejad, N.: Learning on hardware: a tutorial on neural network accelerators and co-processors. The Computing Research Repository (CoRR) (2021). arXiv:2104.09252 [cs.LG]

20. Nvidia Corp. Nvidia TensorRT Documentation (2021). https://docs.nvidia.com/deeplearning/tensorrt/developer-guide/index.html

21. Nvidia Corp. Nvidia Deep Learning Performance Documentation of the Behavior due to GPU Execution Model and Hierarchy (2021). https://docs.nvidia.com/deeplearning/performance/dl-performance-gpu-background/index.html
22. He, K., Zhang, X., Ren, S., Sun, J.: Deep residual learning for image recognition. In: Proceedings of the IEEE Conference on Computer Vision and Pattern Recognition (CVPR), pp. 770–778. IEEE (2016). https://doi.org/10.1109/CVPR.2016.90
23. Russakovsky, O., et al.: ImageNet large scale visual recognition challenge. The Computing Research Repository (CoRR) (2014). arXiv:1409.0575 [cs.CV]
24. Lukasiewycz, M., Glaß, M., Reimann, F., Teich, J.: Opt4J - a modular framework for meta-heuristic optimization. In: Proceedings of the Genetic and Evolutionary Computing Conference (GECCO), pp. 1723–1730. ACM (2011). https://doi.org/10.1145/2001576.2001808
25. Zitzler, E., Thiele, L.: Multiobjective evolutionary algorithms: a comparative case study and the strength Pareto approach. IEEE Trans. Evol. Comput. 3(4), 257–271 (1999). https://doi.org/10.1109/4235.797969
26. Plagwitz, P., Hannig, F., Ströbel, M., Strohmeyer, C., Teich, J.: A safari through FPGA-based neural network compilation and design automation flows. In: Proceedings of the 29th IEEE International Symposium on Field-Programmable Custom Computing Machines (FCCM), 9–12 May 2021, pp. 10–19. IEEE (2021). https://doi.org/10.1109/FCCM51124.2021.00010. ISBN 978-1-6654-3555-0
27. Heidorn, C., Witterauf, M., Hannig, F., Teich, J.: Efficient mapping of CNNs onto tightly coupled processor arrays. J. Comput. 14(8), 541–556 (2019). https://doi.org/10.17706/jcp.14.8.541-556. ISSN 1796-203X
28. Heidorn, C., Hannig, F., Teich, J.: Design space exploration for layer-parallel execution of convolutional neural networks on CGRAs. In: Proceedings of the 23rd International Workshop on Software and Compilers for Embedded Systems (SCOPES), pp. 26–31. ACM (2020). https://doi.org/10.1145/3378678.3391878
29. Shrikumar, A., Greenside, P., Kundaje, A.: Learning important features through propagating activation differences. In: Proceedings of the 34th International Conference on Machine Learning (ICML), vol. 70, pp. 3145–3153 (2017)
30. Sabih, M., Hannig, F., Teich, J.: Utilizing explainable AI for quantization and pruning of deep neural networks. The Computing Research Repository (CoRR) (2020). arXiv:2008.09072 [cs.CV]
31. Sabih, M., Hannig, F., Teich, J.: DyFiP: explainable AI-based dynamic filter pruning of convolutional neural networks. In: Proceedings of the 2nd European Workshop on Machine Learning and Systems (EuroMLSys), pp. 109–115. ACM (2022). https://doi.org/10.1145/3517207.3526982

Innovative Architectures and Tools for Security

Obfuscating the Hierarchy of a Digital IP

Giorgi Basiashvili⬤, Zain Ul Abideen$^{(\boxtimes)}$⬤, and Samuel Pagliarini⬤

Centre for Hardware Security, Tallinn University of Technology (TalTech),
Tallinn, Estonia
{gibasi,zain.abideen,samuel.pagliarini}@taltech.ee

Abstract. Numerous security threats are emerging from untrusted players in the integrated circuit (IC) ecosystem. Among them, reverse engineering practices with the intent to counterfeit, overproduce, or modify an IC are worrying. In recent years, various techniques have been proposed to mitigate the aforementioned threats but no technique seems to be adequate to hide the hierarchy of a design. Such ability to obfuscate the hierarchy is particularly important for designs that contain repeated modules. In this paper, we propose a novel way to obfuscate such designs by leveraging conventional logic synthesis. We exploit multiple optimizations that are available in the synthesis tool to create design diversity. Our security analysis, performed by using the DANA reverse engineering tool, confirms the significant impact of these optimizations on obfuscation. Among the many considered obfuscated design instances, users can find options that incur very small overheads while still confusing the work of a reverse engineer.

Keywords: Obfuscation · Hardware intellectual property · ASIC · Logic synthesis

1 Introduction

Security has emerged as a prime design criterion for modern integrated circuits (ICs). Alongside the continuous miniaturization trend that ICs have benefited from for decades, new security threats have emerged and are now frequently studied. Among them, the theft of intellectual property (IP) has been the target of many studies [4,5,7,9–12].

The range of studied threats that ICs are susceptible to is quite large. Even before ICs undergo fabrication, the chips (or byproducts of the IC design process, e.g., netlists) can be maliciously modified, a threat that is usually termed a hardware backdoor or a hardware trojan [2]. During fabrication, an adversary located at an *untrusted* foundry may proceed to analyze the IC or its components in order to gain reverse engineering knowledge [7]. Thus, this adversary would be able to reproduce the IP for his/her own malicious purposes. This threat can take the form of a simple IP theft or IC overproduction, i.e., when the entire IC is produced beyond the contracted amount. To a large extent, the security

The original version of this chapter was revised: an error in the name of the corresponding author was corrected. The correction to this chapter is available at
https://doi.org/10.1007/978-3-031-15074-6_28

A. Orailoglu et al. (Eds.): SAMOS 2022, LNCS 13511, pp. 303–314, 2022.
https://doi.org/10.1007/978-3-031-15074-6_19

threats herein described are due to the globalized nature of the IC supply chain; in some cases, the end-user is also considered untrusted and is assumed to be adversarial.

Many attempts have been made to counter the reverse engineering capabilities of adversaries. Approaches anchored on partial trusted fabrication have been proposed [9] but have not been adopted by the industry. Logic locking [10] studies have received a fair amount of attention and many derivatives of the original concept have emerged [12]. However, powerful attacks against logic locking are continuously proposed. SATisfiability-based attacks [11], in particular, have been very effective at breaking security assumptions of logic locking schemes.

In this paper, however, we perform a study on how to obfuscate the hierarchy of a system as not to give hints to an adversary about the intent of the system. The ability of 'hiding' the hierarchy is particularly important for systems that instantiate the same module repeated times.

2   Proposed Approach

2.1   Motivation and Background

There are multiple examples of designs that repeatedly instantiate the same module. For instance, in the hardware implementation of neural networks, neurons that contain multiply-and-accumulate type of functions are instantiated hundreds to thousands of times [3]. This common design style is also seen in cryptographic hardware accelerators that are round-based, such as the AES [6]. A generic representation of such type of system is shown in Fig. 1 (top panel), where a notion of a shared bus that connects all the repeated elements is also introduced.

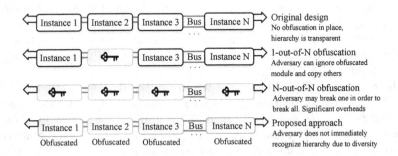

Fig. 1. Approaches to obfuscate a hierarchical design, from locking to design diversity.

Next, assuming the system is an IP that is worth protecting against reverse engineering threats, one could take a state-of-the-art locking approach [5] and apply it to a single module (second panel). While this approach seems interesting at first – it would withstand known attacks such as SAT – a capable adversary would bypass the problem entirely by replacing the obfuscated module with one of the transparent ones. It follows then that all instances have to be obfuscated under a key-based approach (third panel). However, even if the approach appears to have merit, once a single module is broken, they may all be broken. It is also important to notice that logic locking approaches are not overhead-free, the cost to obfuscate all N modules can be rather large [4].

Generally speaking, the complete reverse engineering process is quite hard and time consuming. The process is specially hard if the adversary only has access to a finalized chip and proceeds to delaminate it, take 'pictures' in steps of units of micrometers, and finally stitch them together to make sense of the design. The process is also known to be imperfect, suffering from misalignment and resolution issues. This process requires a skilled person, automation, equipment, and time. However, as said earlier, for designs that consist of N number of repeated modules, the vulnerability is higher. A small part/module of the design could leak information which prompts as a full exposure of the design to the adversary. Even if one of the submodules is poorly processed and has alignment issues, the adversary would still successfully recover a correct netlist by simply matching subnetlists of the same chip.

The illustrative example depicted in Fig. 1 is an attempt to demonstrate that current obfuscation practices have not sufficiently tried to hide the design hierarchy. In the next subsection, we introduce a synthesis-based approach to achieve slightly modified designs in a way that would make it harder from an adversary to notice the repeated instances. The different colors on the bottom panel of the image try to convey this concept of design **diversity**.

2.2   Hierarchical Obfuscation

The implementation part of the ASIC design flow can be divided into two phases: logic synthesis and physical synthesis. In this work, we propose to obfuscate the hierarchy of a design during logic synthesis. In other words, we will introduce obfuscation during the process of translating an RTL description into a mapped netlist of standard cells.

To this end, we make use of Cadence Genus. It is well know that the constraints applied during synthesis, as well as the composition of the standard cell library, play a vital role in the synthesis process. But there are many other 'knobs' of the synthesis process that selectively enable certain optimization strategies. We exploit these optimization strategies to create design diversity, thus eliminating obvious regularity in a design. Furthermore, the RTL of the original design remains unchanged; users are not required to redesign their logic to make it look different.

There are many parameters and options to define/select when performing logic synthesis, so it ought to be studied if the chosen options indeed generate different netlists. Based on the findings of [8], we apply the following optimization techniques:

1. Clock gating
2. Ungrouping
3. Datapath analytical

4. Bubble pushing
5. Tighten max transition
6. Retiming for delay
7. Retiming for area
8. Clock gating + retiming for delay
9. Bubble pushing + retiming for area

The optimization techniques are not enabled by default, they are enabled with different attributes[1]. Most optimizations are enabled with a true/false setting. Exceptions are optimization 3 (it has multiple levels, from basic to extreme) and optimization 5 (it takes a time interval in picoseconds).

Even if these are classic circuit optimization techniques, we offer a short explanation for each as follows. **Clock gating** reduces the dynamic power of the design. It determines non-enabled behavior of the registers and prevents clock from propagating to them. Therefore, these registers are clock gated using an enable signal. This technique incurs a small increase in area due to the gating logic. Synthesis tools are responsible to infer enable signals automatically. **Ungrouping** allows the synthesis tool to flatten the design hierarchy and consider optimizations that traverse boundaries. This optimization typically saves area and improves timing. *Datapath analytical* performs aggressive datapath optimization that compromises area for timing. When **bubble sort** is enabled, it pushes the inverters between in/out pins of flip-flops. This technique is also referred to as an inversion of sequential (output) cells. **Tighten max transition** is related with the transition time, it is a longest time required to change the logic state. Tightening max transition results in buffers being placed on the signals with slow transitions, even for paths where this phenomenon would cause no timing violation. Max transition (clock or data) is the maximum slew, it comes either from the library or the designer manually can target in the constrained file. This helps to achieve the timing closure. **Retiming** repositions combinational cells with respect to flip-flops, from one stage to another stage. It is typically targeted for delay. It can also be issued to target area but never at the cost of delay, that is, delay remains the primary optimization target.

In most experiments reported later on, one and only one optimization is enabled at a time. For optimizations 8 and 9, two optimizations are exploited concurrently, thus we utilize a plus sign and label them "opt_A + opt_B.". For all experiments, the synthesis effort was kept medium for fairness.

Figure 2 illustrates our methodology that exploits the aforementioned techniques during the logic synthesis to evaluate the obfuscation of the design's hierarchy. The complete process is fully automated and scripted to enable a push-button analysis. We provide RTL description (i.e., Verilog or VHDL), timing constraint and standard cell library of the targeted technology. We use the Nangate 15nm library of standard cells throughout the evaluation.

---

[1] For Cadence Genus, these attributes are *lp_insert_clock_gating*, *auto_ungroup*, *dp_analytical_opt*, *br_seq_in_out_phase_opto*, *max_transition* and *retime -min_delay*, *retime -min_area*.

Once the input files are provided to the commercial synthesis tool, then it generates the gate-level netlists. More precisely, the logic synthesis internally does a bit more, it synthesizes, optimizes and maps the netlist. The gate-level netlist is the mapped one exported from the synthesis tool. This process is straightforward and the Tcl script helps to achieve the automation. During the synthesis process, a part of optimization is targeted with a custom parameter as highlighted in the center of Fig. 2. The working principle of utilized optimization techniques and their corresponding parameters are reported in the previous section. We enable one optimization at a time (opt_A) and then we combine another technique (opt_A + opt_B) in the synthesis tool.

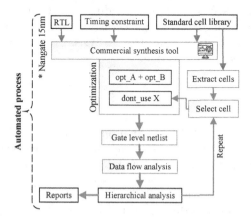

Fig. 2. The methodology to evaluate the hierarchy of design in the context of reverse engineering.

Besides this, we exploit another technique that also transforms the structure of the design. We force the synthesis tool, with the help of *set_dont_use* command, to avoid a given cell. Hence, the composition of the standard cell library is changed. Concerning the *set_dont_use* command, we highlight that the Nangate library contains 67 cells. One by one, we force the synthesis not to use a single cell, synthesize the design, and export a netlist. For instance, in the first run, we prevent the $AND2\_X1$ (2-input AND with a driving strength of 1) cell from being used. In simple words, the synthesis tool will explore other available cells from the library to make a functionally equivalent $AND2\_X1$. The use of standard cells with different drive strengths or completely different cells will lead to changes in area, power, and possibly timing of the design. We repeat this process for all the cells, available in the library. By using this technique, every design will be functionally equivalent but marginally different (or distinct) from the previous one. First, this process was done without any optimizations, then it was repeated for the previously mentioned optimizations and their combinations. Next, we use the *set_dont_use* technique to explore the synthesis space of the design. The complete process generates 603 netlists which we calculate with the number of cells multiplied by optimization techniques (67×9).

However, in some cases, this difference might not be enough to alter the design significantly enough. Accordingly, we have to check every design and verify its characteristics, such as area, power and delay of the critical path to eliminate the duplicate designs. This is achieved with a custom script that shrinks the netlist and keeps only unique instances.

In the next step, we exploit an open-source tool named DANA to analyze the design [1]. DANA stands for Dataflow Analysis for Gate-Level Netlist Reverse Engineering. DANA is a fully automated, technology-agnostic data flow methodology for gate-level netlists. It analyses the individual FFs and groups them into high-level registers. It provides an easily readable summary, such that the user of tool can make sense of a netlist that *a priori* looks like a sea of gates. We perform data flow analysis for each individual netlist and export a report. We repeated this process for all the unique netlists to conclude the analysis. For collecting final results and statistics of this analysis, we use another custom script which we present in the next section.

3   Results

This section reports the results of our proposed methodology. Recalling again, the objective was to develop a key-less and structural obfuscation methodology that will apply to circuits that have modules instantiated multiple times.

To evaluate our methodology, we have selected a representative design that displays such pattern. We have selected a Global Positioning System (GPS) correlator, which is one of the integral parts of a GPS-capable hardware. A correlator attempts to identify to which satellite of the GPS constellation it is talking too. A system with multiple correlators executes this tasks in parallel, yielding in faster signal acquisition and therefore short sync time.

We used the RTL description of the GPS correlator and generated the results for the a single design. We did not change the RTL of the design throughout the analysis for fairness. We note the number of unique netlists that are generated by optimization techniques. A total of 509 unique designs were generated. With *set_dont_use cell*, it was able to generate 55 designs. Clock gating, datapath analytical and bubble pushing generates 50, 56 and 53 designs each. Most of the unique designs were generated by tightening max transition (62), retiming for the delay (61), and its combination with clock gating (62). However, it should be noted that ungrouping was not able to generate a single unique design. Retiming for area and its combination with bubble pushing generates 53 and 57 designs. Nevertheless, the number of duplicate designs varies depending on the optimization strategy.

3.1   Power-Performance-Area Evaluations

Our proposed obfuscation is key-less and infers almost a little overhead or almost zero. The performance does not impact the optimization techniques. But, the area and power vary therefore it should be investigated. We have used a very relaxed clock frequency in order to allow the synthesis tool to make less constrained decisions. Table 1 shows the minimum and maximum values for the area and power trade-offs with respect to changes in the applied optimization technique. The first column list the applied optimization technique, columns two to three for the minimum and maximum values of the area, columns four to five for the minimum and maximum values of the leakage power and the last two columns list the values for the dynamic power.

Table 1. Minimum and Maximum values of area, number of cells, leakage and dynamic power of the generated designs

Optimization technique	Area (μm^2)		Cells		Leakage power (mW)		Dynamic power (mW)	
	Min	Max	Min	Max	Min	Max	Min	Max
Baseline	432.9	461.6	762	845	0.012	0.013	2.368	2.414
Clock Gating	432.7	462.2	750	810	0.012	0.013	0.600	0.935
Ungrouping	432.9	461.6	762	845	0.012	0.013	2.368	2.414
Datapath Analytical	433.2	458.8	750	821	0.012	0.013	2.368	2.431
Bubble Pushing	437.1	459.1	758	840	0.012	0.013	2.293	2.469
Tightening max transition	598.8	990.3	1168	1644	0.022	0.062	0.706	2.091
Retiming for Delay	440.9	600.9	737	1047	0.012	0.018	2.944	4.398
Retiming for Area	434.7	458.8	767	840	0.012	0.013	2.399	2.460
Clock Gating + Retiming for Delay	425.2	560.9	711	966	0.012	0.018	1.084	1.562
Bubble Pushing + Retiming for Area	440.0	460.3	755	842	0.012	0.013	2.350	2.537

Figure 3 illustrates the probability distribution function (PDF) for the unique netlist. Panels (a), (b), (c) and (d) highlight the PDFs for the area, number of cells, leakage power and dynamic power, respectively. The red dot represents the location of the baseline design, and gives us an idea about the overall results. The data of the distinct netlists shows the perfect fit for the normal distribution curves. The distribution of the leakage power is a little bit different but still faces variance. Thus, we have a wide range of variety which indicates that there are significantly different designs from one another. Concerning panel (a), the baseline design is approximately closer to the mean value. Almost half of the designs have less area as compared to the baseline design. The same case is for the number of cells as seen in panel (b). Similarly, the leakage power of the baseline design is closer to the mean value. More than half of the designs consume more leakage power as compared to the baseline design. Regarding the dynamic power, the baseline design is far from the mean value and a large number of designs consume higher power as compared to the baseline design. It is noteworthy, that we observe the change in the hierarchy of the structure and the effect of the variation is reflected in the area, number of cells, leakage power and dynamic power.

Next, we are going to observe the percentage increase and decrease of the area, number of cells, leakage power and dynamic power. Table 2 lists the analysis of different overheads for their corresponding techniques. The first column list the optimization technique, the second column shows the percentage increase/decrease in the area, the third column shows the percentage

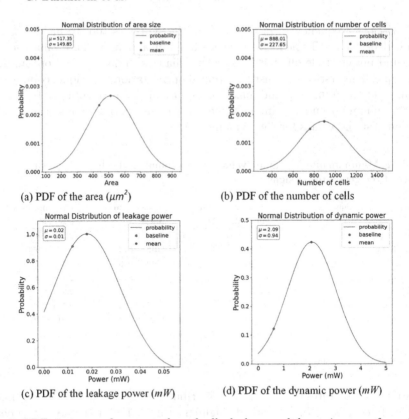

(a) PDF of the area (μm^2)

(b) PDF of the number of cells

(c) PDF of the leakage power (mW)

(d) PDF of the dynamic power (mW)

Fig. 3. PDFs in terms of area, number of cells, leakage and dynamic power for unique designs.

increase/decrease in the number of cells, last two column represents the leakage and dynamic power.

We note that clock gating offers a significant decrease in the dynamic power. Datapath analytical lowers area, cells and dynamic power between 1–3%. The same is happening for the bubble pushing. Tighten max transition has a significant impact on area, cells and leakage power. But it shows a remarkable decrease in the dynamic power (84.3%). We should note that a large number of distinct designs were generated from this technique. The retiming for delay also has a similar behavior for area and cells (20.18% and 12.71% increase) but it also shows an increase in the leakage and dynamic power. The combination of clock gating and retiming for delay shows an increase in every parameter except dynamic power, analogous to tighten max transition. The combination of bubble pushing and retiming for the area also shows a little increase/decrease in the parameters. In a nutshell, all the techniques have little impact on the area, cells and power consumption except tighten max transition, retiming for delay and a combination of clock gating & retiming for delay.

Table 2. Percent increase/decrease in the baseline design and a variants generated with the corresponding optimization technique

Optimization technique	Area (%)	Cells (%)	Dynamic power (%)	Leakage power
Clock gating	−0.3	−0.7	−119.4	0
Ungrouping	0	0	0	0
Datapath analytical	−1.4	−2.9	−0.4	0
Bubble pushing	−0.5	−0.7	−2.7	0
Tighten max transition	+69.8	+60.1	−84.3	+131.4
Retiming for delay	+20.1	+12.7	+51.3	+28.5
Retiming for area	−0.5	−0.3	+0.7	0
Clock gating + Retiming for delay	+18.9	+13.6	−66.5	+34.4
Bubble pushing + Retiming for area	+0.4	−2.1	+4.5	0

3.2 Security Analysis

This section details the security analysis with DANA. The tool analyses the dataflow between flip-flops to structure the registers. From the abstraction level, the entire design contains flip-flops, connections to their respective sequential successors and predecessors. The constructed relationship between flip-flops helps the adversary to accomplish his/hers reverse engineering goals. DANA offers two modes: (a) Normal Mode and (b) Steered Mode. In Normal Mode, DANA autonomously analyzes the given netlist, without any prioritization. Using the Steered Mode, the analyst can alternatively take care of extra information to virtually "steer" the algorithms. This includes prioritizing DANA for the specific register sizes, i.e., a reverse engineer learns different information from datasheets. Furthermore, If the reverse engineer already has a clue that the design under analysis is, for instance, a 16-bit CPU, he would hope to observe multiple 16-bit register and thus steer DANA towards said size.

Evaluation Method. To accomplish the patterns for the reverse engineering, we first executed DANA in a normal model and then in the steered mode. We run DANA on a machine equipped with 32 processors (Intel(R) Xeon(R) Platinum 8356H CPU @ 3.90 GHz). After running DANA twice, we compare the results with the baseline design to analyze how the hierarchy is varying with respect to the applied technique. Figure 4 shows the register groups for the baseline and various optimization techniques. The figure in panel (a) shows the baseline design that includes different sizes of registers. Blue bubbles show the registers, straight lines are connections between different registers, and circular lines are connections from a register to itself. Concerning the size of registers, the larger the bubble is, the larger the size of the register. From the graph, it is clear that it shows two 10-bit registers and other sizes of registers. This hierarchy shows the internal register size and connectivity of the registers. This is straight forward clue for the adversary to restructure the registers and its connected circuitry.

Now, we investigate how optimization changes the characteristics of the design. The figure in panel (b) shows the synthesized design where we enabled clock gating optimization in commercial synthesis tool. We can see different 10-bit registers. A large number of register are diminished and we only see few

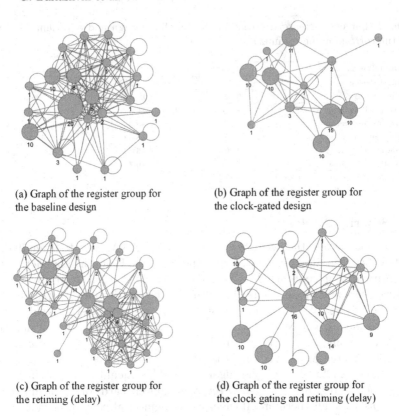

(a) Graph of the register group for the baseline design

(b) Graph of the register group for the clock-gated design

(c) Graph of the register group for the retiming (delay)

(d) Graph of the register group for the clock gating and retiming (delay)

Fig. 4. Graphs of the register group for various optimization techniques).

registers with a variety of sizes. It allows us to clearly see distinctions between different groupings. In these unrolled designs, the sizes of register does not correspond to the correct sizes declared in the RTL code. Panel (c) of Fig. 4 shows the graph for the synthesized design with retiming for delay. Here, we can analyze that complete graph consists of a large number of register and we still can see a 10-bit register. This also offers a unique structure of the design and DANA is unable to map it in the same way. In the next example, shown in panel (d), we exploit two different optimizations (clock-gating and retiming for delay) at the same time. Again, we obtain a distinct graph. To summarize these results, we can confidently state that a design composed of many instances of the same module but each instance is synthesized differently, will present itself as a **challenge to a reverse engineering adversary**.

All these experiments presented so far were executed in the normal mode of DANA. Now, we exploit the steer mode of DANA with the register size of 10-bits as shown in Fig. 5. It is a fair assumption that from non-steered mode, and adversary might reach the conclusion that 10-bit registers are present. We can see that the structure of the design is explicitly different from the previ-

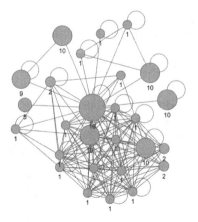

Fig. 5. Graph of the register group for the clock-gating and retiming (delay) with steered mode (Register size 10).

ous ones. DANA still is unable to highlights clues even in steering mode. This implied the high level of obfuscation for the design. The adversary make use of the different reverse engineering tools along with high skills but still it requires an additional effort to correctly identify the design. Our applied optimization techniques perfectly modifies the structure of the design. This places barriers for DANA's clustering algorithm which incorrectly identifies the register group. This is the case for every optimization technique.

Remarks. The optimizations techniques are contributing towards obfuscation, to confuse the adversary to understand the architecture of design. It is noteworthy that the combination of two different optimizations has a large impact on the hierarchy of the design (see Fig. 4, panels (c) and (d)). On the other hand, if the design goal is keep the overheads under control, then tighten max transition and retiming for delay are excluded for the list. However, many other optimizations still remain attractive solutions.

4   Conclusion

Numerous designs consist of repeated modules or multiple copies for a specific part of the design. These designs are highly vulnerable to reverse engineering. In this paper, we have presented a unique obfuscation by leveraging the logic synthesis and different optimizations techniques. Our methodology specifically targets these types of designs. Our proposed flow is beneficial as the crucial initial step for security analysis. Our flow for the obfuscation is completely automated and does not incur high overheads, nor RTL changes. Our extensive analysis of a large number of designs reveals that optimization techniques partially or completely modify the structural representation of the design, thus creating a challenge for reverse engineering.

Acknowledgements. This work has been partially conducted in the project "ICT programme" which was supported by the European Union through the ESF.

References

1. Albartus, N., Hoffmann, M., Temme, S., Azriel, L., Paar, C.: Dana universal dataflow analysis for gate-level netlist reverse engineering. IACR Trans. Cryptographic Hardware Embedded Syst. **2020**(4), 309–336 (2020). https://doi.org/10.13154/tches.v2020.i4.309-336. https://tches.iacr.org/index.php/TCHES/article/view/8685

2. Becker, G.T., Regazzoni, F., Paar, C., Burleson, W.P.: Stealthy dopant-level hardware trojans. In: Bertoni, G., Coron, J.-S. (eds.) CHES 2013. LNCS, vol. 8086, pp. 197–214. Springer, Heidelberg (2013). https://doi.org/10.1007/978-3-642-40349-1_12

3. Duarte, J., et al.: Fast inference of deep neural networks in FPGAs for particle physics. J. Instrum. **13**(07), P07027 (2018)

4. Dupuis, S., Flottes, M.L.: Logic locking: a survey of proposed methods and evaluation metrics. J. Electron. Testing **35**(3), 273–291 (2019). https://doi.org/10.1007/s10836-019-05800-4. https://hal-lirmm.ccsd.cnrs.fr/lirmm-02128826

5. Han, Z., Yasin, M., Rajendran, J.J.: Does logic locking work with EDA tools? In: 30th USENIX Security Symposium (USENIX Security 21), pp. 1055–1072. USENIX Association, August 2021. https://www.usenix.org/conference/usenixsecurity21/presentation/han-zhaokun

6. Hsing, H.: Aes-128 (2013). https://opencores.org/projects/tiny_aes

7. Meade, T., Zhang, S., Jin, Y.: Netlist reverse engineering for high-level functionality reconstruction. In: 2016 21st Asia and South Pacific Design Automation Conference (ASP-DAC), pp. 655–660 (2016). https://doi.org/10.1109/ASPDAC.2016.7428086

8. Pagliarini, S., Benites, L., Martins, M., Rech, P., Kastensmidt, F.: Evaluating architectural, redundancy, and implementation strategies for radiation hardening of finfet integrated circuits. IEEE Trans. Nucl. Sci. **68**(5), 1045–1053 (2021). https://doi.org/10.1109/TNS.2021.3070643

9. Rajendran, J., Sinanoglu, O., Karri, R.: Is split manufacturing secure? In: 2013 Design, Automation Test in Europe Conference Exhibition (DATE), pp. 1259–1264 (2013). https://doi.org/10.7873/DATE.2013.261

10. Roy, J.A., Koushanfar, F., Markov, I.L.: Epic: Ending piracy of integrated circuits. In: 2008 Design, Automation and Test in Europe, pp. 1069–1074 (2008). https://doi.org/10.1109/DATE.2008.4484823

11. Subramanyan, P., Ray, S., Malik, S.: Evaluating the security of logic encryption algorithms. In: 2015 IEEE International Symposium on Hardware Oriented Security and Trust (HOST), pp. 137–143 (2015). https://doi.org/10.1109/HST.2015.7140252

12. Sweeney, J., Mohammed Zackriya, V., Pagliarini, S., Pileggi, L.: Latch-based logic locking. In: 2020 IEEE International Symposium on Hardware Oriented Security and Trust (HOST), pp. 132–141 (2020). https://doi.org/10.1109/HOST45689.2020.9300256

On the Effectiveness of True Random Number Generators Implemented on FPGAs

Davide Galli, Andrea Galimberti$^{(\boxtimes)}$ [ID], William Fornaciari [ID], and Davide Zoni [ID]

Politecnico di Milano, P.zza L. Da Vinci, 20133 Milan, Italy
davide11.galli@mail.polimi.it,
{andrea.galimberti,william.fornaciari,davide.zoni}@polimi.it

Abstract. Randomness is at the core of many cryptographic implementations. True random number generators provide unpredictable sequences of numbers by exploiting physical phenomena. This work compares multiple literature proposals of true random number generators targeting FPGAs. The considered TRNGs are obtained as the combinations of three digital noise sources, namely, NLFIRO, PLL-TRNG, and ES-TRNG, and three post-processing techniques, namely, XOR, Von Neumann, and LFSR. The resulting combinations of such components are evaluated in terms of security, throughput, and resource utilization. The experimental results, which were collected on Xilinx Artix-7 FPGAs, highlight the importance of the post-processing stage for security purposes and reveal NLFIRO as the best digital noise source and LFSR as the best post-processing technique, having the highest throughput with excellent security performance without compromising area and power consumption.

Keywords: Field programmable gate arrays · True random number generators · Hardware-based security primitives · Side-channel attacks

1 Introduction

Modern embedded systems at the edge are pervasively deployed in our living environment and they are increasingly in charge of performing critical tasks or managing sensitive data, thus calling for new and stringent privacy and security requirements in addition to the more traditional energy-efficiency ones.

The use of efficient cryptographic primitives represents the de-facto solution to guaranteeing the privacy and security of the exchanged and processed data. However, the security strength of the cryptographic system is directly connected to the quality of the used random numbers, thus highlighting true random

Supported by the EU Horizon 2020 "TEXTAROSSA" project (Grant No. 956831).

A. Orailoglu et al. (Eds.): SAMOS 2022, LNCS 13511, pp. 315–326, 2022.
https://doi.org/10.1007/978-3-031-15074-6_20

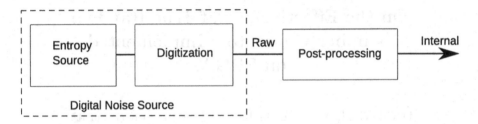

Fig. 1. Baseline architecture of a TRNG.

number generators (TRNGs) as essential components in the security infrastructure [8]. The correct implementation of TRNGs is indeed paramount to ensuring the effective security of the wide array of cryptographic primitives where they are employed, such as traditional [7] and post-quantum [10,12,19,20] key exchange mechanisms, digital signature schemes [5,11,15], and countermeasures to side-channel attacks [3,21]. A TRNG must therefore produce a sequence of numbers such that the generated values are statistically independent, uniformly distributed, and unpredictable.

The architecture of a generic TRNG is depicted in Fig. 1, and it can be split into three main components. They are, respectively, entropy source, digitization, and post-processing, with the latter also referred to as conditioning.

The entropy source is the only component in the architecture that generates true randomness by exploiting some physical phenomenon, while the other components are purely deterministic. Whenever the entropy source generates analog signals, a digitization module is required to transform them into digital form. The combination of an entropy source and a digitization module is also referred to as a digital noise source, which is notably often indicated in the literature as the TRNG itself due to its role in producing the actual entropy underlying the random number generation. The digital noise source outputs the *raw random numbers*, so-called since they are frequently vulnerable to statistical flaws.

Therefore, a post-processing module is used to improve the statistical and security properties of the TRNG. The post-processed output, with increased entropy, is also referred to as *internal random numbers*. Notably, applying conditioning methods is not mandatory for the design of a TRNG, and it can instead be avoided if the entropy produced by the digital noise source is already sufficient for the target application of the TRNG.

Contributions - This manuscript presents an exploration of the state-of-the-art TRNGs targeting FPGAs, evaluated according to resource utilization, throughput, and security. The goal is to identify the best-performing combinations of digital noise sources and conditioning methods that optimize the three aforementioned quality metrics. The experimental results highlight the combination of an NLFIRO digital noise source and an LFSR post-processing method as the best-performing solution with respect to the throughput and security metrics At the same time, ES-TRNG might be an effective solution in tightly resource-constrained scenarios, albeit with a drastic reduction in the throughput.

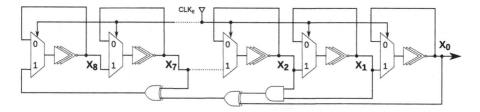

Fig. 2. Architecture of a NLFIRO TRNG.

2 Methodology

This section describes the architectures of the considered TRNGs, detailing separately the three digital noise sources and the three post-processing methods. In particular, the evaluated digital noise sources are the NLFIRO, PLL-based, and edge-sampling TRNGs, while the considered post-processing methods are XOR, Von Neumann, and LFSR conditioning techniques. Notably, all of them are suitable for an FPGA implementation, albeit exploiting different physical phenomena and working principles.

2.1 Digital Noise Sources

NLFIRO TRNG. Non-linear feedback ring oscillators (NLFRO) [16] enhance the design of ring oscillators by incorporating a non-linear feedback function. NLFRO-based TRNGs harvest their high entropy from different sources, namely, noise and variation in delay cells, unpredictable behavior in astable logic elements, and non-linear feedback loops.

Each stage of the ring oscillator presents a multiplexer driven by a clock signal CLK_E, making it possible to reconfigure the ring oscillator between a local loop and an open loop. When the clock is low, the local loop is closed and the signal runs in a ring oscillator composed by an inverter chain. When the clock is high, the loop is open and the entire feedback starts working. CLK_E must have the same frequency and duty cycle of the sampling clock, while a phase shift of $-90°$ is required to leave a sufficient margin for the toggling of the global feedback.

We implement the Fibonacci configuration of the NLFRO with nine stages and three NOT gates as inverter chain, which is referred to as NLFIRO [16]. Figure 2 depicts the architecture of the implemented NLFIRO, whose feedback function is shown in Eq. (1).

$$f(x) = x^7 \oplus (x^2 \cdot x^1) \oplus x^0 \tag{1}$$

For each TRNG, two NLFIROs are XORed together after being sampled in two D-FFs, and the result of the XOR is registered in another D-FF.

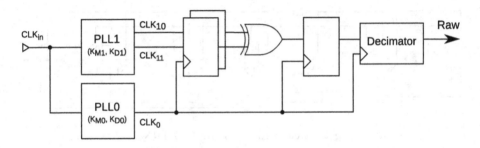

Fig. 3. Architecture of a PLL-based TRNG.

PLL-Based TRNG. A PLL-based TRNG [2,9] exploits the coherent sampling principle. As shown in Fig. 3, which depicts its architecture, a reference clock clk_0 is used to sample two other clock signals clk_{10} and clk_{11}, where clk_{10} is delayed of 90° respect to clk_{11}, in two corresponding D flip-flops (D-FFs). The outputs of such D-FFs are then XORed together and registered in another D-FF. Since the output bits of the latter suffer of a period pattern, they are then decimated by XORing K_D consecutive bits to destroy such pattern and obtain a stream of raw bits.

The reference and sampled frequencies are mutually related according to Eq. (2), where K_{M1}, K_{M0}, K_{D0}, and K_{D1} are the frequency multiplication and division factors.

$$f_1 = f_0 \frac{K_{M1}K_{D0}}{K_{M0}K_{D1}} = f_0 \frac{K_M}{K_D} \tag{2}$$

The output signal of the last D-FF features a pseudo-random pattern with a period $T_Q = K_D/f_0 = K_M/f_1$, which is however removed by the decimator. The output bit-rate R of the generator and its sensitivity S to jitter are defined according to Eq. (3) and Eq. (4), respectively.

$$R = T_Q^{-1} = \frac{f_0}{K_D} \tag{3}$$

$$S = f_1 K_D = f_0 K_M \tag{4}$$

Consequently, R and S are maximized by increasing f_0 and K_M and decreasing K_D. The algorithm proposed in [1] is exploited to find the best parameters for all the PLLs, allowing to obtain a sufficient entropy and bit rate while fulfilling the hardware requirements of the PLL instances.

Edge-Sampling TRNG. The edge-sampling TRNG (ES-TRNG) [18] is characterized by a low resource utilization, with the core TRNG module occupying only 5 LUTs and 6 FFs, as shown by its architectural representation depicted in Fig. 4. Two components devoted to resynchronization and control logic are however also required, in addition to such TRNG core logic.

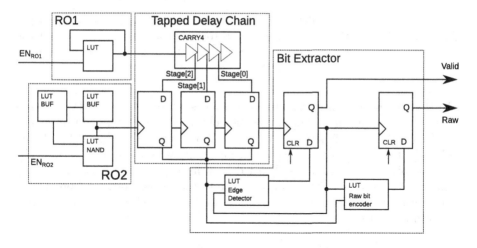

Fig. 4. Architecture of an edge-sampling TRNG.

The ES-TRNG digital noise source exploits the entropy produced by the timing phase jitter of a free-running ring oscillator. The architecture of a ES-TRNG consists of a small ring oscillator RO1 with an enable signal. The output of RO1 is then digitalized through a tapped delay chain which slows down the signal and allows saving three different values in three FFs (Stage[2:0]). The latter FFs are driven by a larger ring oscillator RO2. As the final processing step, a bit extractor module is tasked with extracting a high-entropy bit from the sampled stages Stage[2:0].

The core idea of ES-TRNG is to repeat the sampling at high frequency thanks to RO2 and focus only on the region around the edges of the RO1 signal, where the bits have higher entropy.

RO1 must be reset after generating a new raw bit and be enabled for a period T_A before starting RO2. The accumulation time T_A is used by RO1 to increase the entropy. The designer shall find a trade-off between the required entropy value and the desired throughput.

2.2   Post-processing Methods

XOR Post-processing. XOR post-processing [6] processes n bits of the raw input stream at a time. In particular, such n bits are XORed together, which reduces the throughput by a factor of n. Taking the parity of n independent bits reduces the internal bias ϵ to $\epsilon_{internal} = 2^{n-1}\epsilon_{raw}^n$, resulting into a higher entropy. For the purposes of this work, n was set to 2 for NLFIRO, while XOR post-processing was not applied to PLL-TRNG and ES-TRNG sources.

Von Neumann Post-processing. The Von Neumann conditioning method [13] splits the input bits into non-overlapping pairs and, for pairs whose first and second bits are different, it outputs the first bit, while nothing is output if the two bits hold the same value. The throughput is not constant, but it can never exceed 1/4 of the raw throughput, i.e., the throughput of the digital noise source.

LFSR Post-processing. A linear-feedback shift register (LFSR) is a shift register whose input bit is a linear function of its previous state, and it is defined by a characteristic polynomial. The bit positions that affect the next state are called the taps. The taps are XORed sequentially with the output bit and the new raw bit, and the result is then fed back into the leftmost bit. LFSRs are employed for post-processing purposes due to their good statistical properties. In this work, the raw bits are processed by a LFSR [17] whose feedback function is shown in Eq. (5).

$$f(x) = x^{32} \oplus x^{30} \oplus x^{24} \oplus x^{21} \oplus x^{20} \oplus x^{9}$$
$$\oplus \, x^{8} \oplus x^{7} \oplus x^{6} \oplus x^{2} \oplus x^{0} \tag{5}$$

3 Experimental Evaluation

The considered TRNG designs were evaluated according to a set of three quality metrics: area, performance and security. Area expresses the number of LUTs and FFs occupied by the design, performance indicates how many random bits per second are produced by each batch of TRNGs and it is expressed in megabits per second, and security measures how many tests of the NIST suite are passed, as a ratio of the total number of tests. The NIST SP800-22 suite [4] consists of 15 algorithmic tests and 188 subtests, which allow evaluating the unpredictability of the output of a TRNG and therefore its suitability for cryptography applications. Performing the NIST tests required collecting 33 million random bits, split into 33 individual sequences of 1 million bits each. The NIST SP800-22 tests were carried out by employing the C implementation publicly available on the NIST website [14].

3.1 Setup

NLFIRO was evaluated with each of the three post-processing methods as well as without any conditioning, considering bit widths of 1, 8, 32, 64, and 128 bits. PLL-based TRNG was tested without any conditioning, since the raw output of the digital noise source already provided the highest security according to NIST tests, while the bit width was limited to 1 and 4 bits due to the scarce availability of PLL components on the target FPGAs. Finally, ES-TRNG was implemented both without post-processing and with LSFR, since the latter conditioning method showed the best overall metrics of the three discussed ones, with the same bit widths employed as NLFIRO.

All the implemented TRNG designs were instantiated on chips from the Xilinx Artix-7 FPGA family, in particular on the Artix-7 35 (xc7a35tcpg236-1) and 100 (xc7a100tcsg324-1) chips, targeting a clock frequency of 50 MHz.

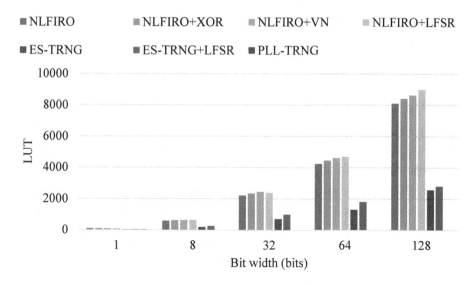

Fig. 5. Resource utilization, expressed as the number of LUTs, of TRNGs combining different digital noise sources and post-processing methods at various bit widths.

Synthesis, implementation, and generation of area reports were all carried out through Xilinx Vivado 2020.2. All designs were automatically placed and routed, without any specific constraints.

3.2 Resource Utilization

Figure 5 shows how the number of LUTs grows circa linearly with respect to the bit width for all three considered digital noise sources. NLFIRO is the TRNG which occupies the largest amount of LUTs. ES-TRNG requires a significantly smaller amount of LUTs, with a maximum of 2806 for a 128-bit LFSR post-processing configuration, but it requires instead the most FF resources, as highlighted by Fig. 6. This high amount of FF is due to the resynchronization circuit of ES-TRNG together with its control circuit, which is not necessary instead for NLFIRO. PLL-based TRNGs require the smallest amount of LUTs and FFs, requiring 21 of both resources with a 1-bit bit width. Even though PLL-based TRNGs consume minimal amounts of LUT and FF resources, it must be noted that PLLs are a very limited resource on FPGAs, and they might also be required in other components of the design.

Focusing on the post-processing methods, LFSR results in the most resource-hungry one, while XOR is the smallest conditioning architecture.

3.3 Throughput

Figure 7 shows the throughput for the considered TRNG designs. NLFIRO is the best performing digital noise sources, providing a raw random bit every clock

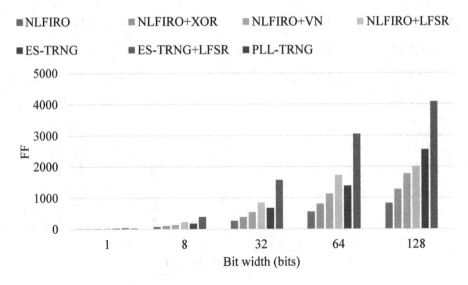

Fig. 6. Resource utilization, expressed as the number of FFs, of TRNGs combining different digital noise sources and post-processing methods at various bit widths.

cycle, eclipsing every other design, with a maximum of 6.4 Gb/s in its best configuration. On the other hand, ES-TRNGs are around 30 times slower than NLFIRO. PLL-based TRNGs have the lowest throughput, moreover their bit width is limited to 4 due to the limited amount of PLLs available on the target FPGAs.

While LFSR produces the maximum overall throughput, with no reduction compared to not applying any post-processing, the XOR and Von Neumann conditioning methods reduce instead the throughput. In particular, Von Neumann post-processing is the slowest one.

With respect to the bit width, the throughput increases linearly for all TRNGs.

3.4 Security

Figure 8 reports the experimental results related to the security metric. The bar chart expresses the number of passed NIST tests out of 15. PLL-based TRNGs ended up as the best digital noise sources from the viewpoint of the security metric, being able to pass every test even without any post-processing stage. Such good performance is due to the careful selection of PLL parameters that guarantee a high entropy sensitivity. NLFIRO manages to pass most of the tests, however not being secure enough in absence of post-processing. Finally, the raw entropy of ES-TRNG is excessively weak, with only one NIST test passed if no conditioning is applied.

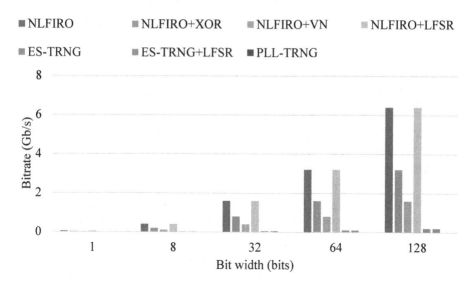

Fig. 7. Throughput, expressed as bit rate in Mb/s, of TRNGs combining different digital noise sources and post-processing methods at various bit widths.

The experimental results highlighted the critical role of the post-processing stage, which is more obvious in the ES-TRNG case. LFSR always allows all the TRNGs to pass 15/15 NIST tests and 188/188 subtests for every bit-width up to 64, while all the other conditioning method always fail at least one subtest in some configuration.

Concerning bit width, the experimental results highlighted a significant drop in security when moving from 64- to 128-bit bit width, with all the TRNGs with the larger bit width failing the majority of the NIST tests and being therefore unsuitable to cryptography applications.

3.5   Overall Results

NLFIRO-based TRNGs provide the best throughput and a high security, albeit at the cost of the largest resource utilization in terms of LUTs and FFs. ES-TRNG-based solutions occupy a smaller area, although producing a significantly smaller throughput and a reduced security, when not applying any post-processing method. PLL-based TRNGs provide the highest security without needing any conditioning, but their bit width, and therefore their throughput, is strongly limited by the amount of PLLs available on the target FPGA chip.

Concerning post-processing methods, LFSR provides the best improvement in security without any reduction in the TRNG throughput, producing however the largest resource utilization. Nevertheless, the difference in LUT and FF resources occupied compared to the other two post-processing methods or to not applying any conditioning is minimal, particularly with respect to the total

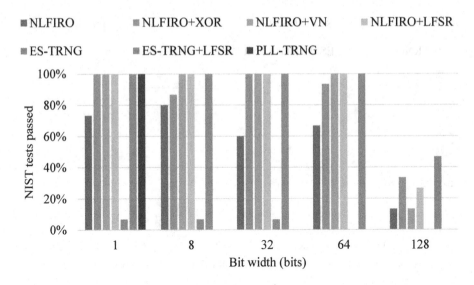

Fig. 8. Security, expressed as the percentage of NIST tests passed, of TRNGs combining different digital noise sources and post-processing methods at various bit widths.

resources available on the target chip and to the area occupied by the other components of the TRNG and of the overall design. On the contrary, applying the XOR and Von Neumann post-processing methods results in a steep reduction in the throughput metric, while not applying any conditioning provides a low security, except for PLL-TRNGs.

Finally, regarding bit-width, the experimental results highlighted a critical drop in security for bit widths larger than 64, i.e., equal to 128, which makes such TRNGs, albeit faster than those with smaller bit widths, not suitable for cryptography applications.

4   Conclusions

This work evaluated different combinations of digital noise sources and post-processing techniques to identify optimal TRNGs that are suitable for cryptographic applications on FPGA targets. In particular, we considered the NLFIRO, PLL-based TRNG and ES-TRNG digital noise sources and the XOR, Von Neumann, and LFSR post-processing methods, while also analyzing the impact of varying the clock frequency and the bit width of the TRNG.

The experimental evaluation was carried out according to three quality metrics, encompassing functional and non-functional requirements. Functional quality metrics included the security and the throughput of the TRNG, while the non-functional metric studied in this work was the resource utilization.

On the one hand, the experimental results highlighted the combination of an NLFIRO digital noise source and an LFSR post-processing method as the best-performing solution with respect to the throughput and security metrics. On the other hand, ES-TRNG-based solutions were shown to be effective choices in tightly resource-constrained scenarios, albeit with a drastic reduction in the throughput. In addition, the results validated the strong positive impact of conditioning methods on the security of the TRNG, while emphasizing the need to limit the TRNG bit width up to 64 bits to avoid a critical drop in the generated entropy.

References

1. Allini, E.N., Petura, O., Fischer, V., Bernard, F.: Optimization of the PLL configuration in a PLL-based TRNG design. In: 2018 Design, Automation Test in Europe Conference Exhibition (DATE), pp. 1265–1270 (2018). https://doi.org/10.23919/DATE.2018.8342209
2. Balasch, J., et al.: Design and testing methodologies for true random number generators towards industry certification. In: 2018 IEEE 23rd European Test Symposium (ETS), pp. 1–10 (2018). https://doi.org/10.1109/ETS.2018.8400697
3. Barenghi, A., Fornaciari, W., Pelosi, G., Zoni, D.: Scramble suit: a profile differentiation countermeasure to prevent template attacks. IEEE Trans. Comput. Aided Des. Integr. Circuits Syst. **39**(9), 1778–1791 (2020). https://doi.org/10.1109/TCAD.2019.2926389
4. Bassham, L.E., et al.: SP 800-22 rev. 1a. A statistical test suite for random and pseudorandom number generators for cryptographic applications. Technical report, NIST, Gaithersburg, MD, USA (2010)
5. Bernstein, D.J., Duif, N., Lange, T., Schwabe, P., Yang, B.Y.: High-speed high-security signatures. J. Cryptogr. Eng. **2**(2), 77–89 (2012). https://doi.org/10.1007/s13389-012-0027-1
6. Davies, R.B.: Exclusive OR (XOR) and hardware random number generators (2002). http://www.robertnz.net/pdf/xor2.pdf
7. Diffie, W., Hellman, M.: New directions in cryptography. IEEE Trans. Inf. Theory **22**(6), 644–654 (1976). https://doi.org/10.1109/TIT.1976.1055638
8. Eastlake, D.E., Crocker, S., Schiller, J.I.: Randomness requirements for security. RFC 4086 (2005). https://doi.org/10.17487/RFC4086. https://www.rfc-editor.org/info/rfc4086
9. Fischer, V., Drutarovský, M.: True random number generator embedded in reconfigurable hardware. In: Kaliski, B.S., Koç, K., Paar, C. (eds.) CHES 2002. LNCS, vol. 2523, pp. 415–430. Springer, Heidelberg (2003). https://doi.org/10.1007/3-540-36400-5_30
10. Galimberti, A., Montanaro, G., Zoni, D.: Efficient and scalable FPGA design of GF(2m) inversion for post-quantum cryptosystems. IEEE Trans. Comput. 1 (2022). https://doi.org/10.1109/TC.2022.3149422
11. Johnson, D., Menezes, A., Vanstone, S.: The elliptic curve digital signature algorithm (ECDSA). Int. J. Inf. Secur. **1**(1), 36–63 (2001). https://doi.org/10.1007/s102070100002
12. McEliece, R.J.: A public-key cryptosystem based on algebraic coding theory. DSN Progress Report, pp. 114–116 (1978)
13. von Neumann, J.: Various techniques used in connection with random digits. In: Householder, A.S., Forsythe, G.E., Germond, H.H. (eds.) Monte Carlo Method, National Bureau of Standards Applied Mathematics Series, vol. 12, chap. 13, pp. 36–38. US Government Printing Office, Washington, DC (1951)

14. NIST: NIST SP 800-22: download documentation and software. https://csrc.nist.gov/projects/random-bit-generation/documentation-and-software

15. Rivest, R.L., Shamir, A., Adleman, L.: A method for obtaining digital signatures and public-key cryptosystems. Commun. ACM **21**(2), 120–126 (1978). https://doi.org/10.1145/359340.359342

16. Tao, S., Yu, Y., Dubrova, E.: FPGA based true random number generators using non-linear feedback ring oscillators. In: 2018 16th IEEE International New Circuits and Systems Conference (NEWCAS), pp. 213–216 (2018). https://doi.org/10.1109/NEWCAS.2018.8585569

17. Wu, X., Ma, Y., Chen, T., Lv, N.: A distinguisher for RNGs with LFSR postprocessing. In: Wu, Y., Yung, M. (eds.) Inscrypt 2020. LNCS, vol. 12612, pp. 328–343. Springer, Cham (2021). https://doi.org/10.1007/978-3-030-71852-7_22

18. Yang, B., Rožic, V., Grujic, M., Mentens, N., Verbauwhede, I.: ES-TRNG: a high-throughput, low-area true random number generator based on edge sampling. IACR Trans. Cryptogr. Hardw. Embed. Syst. **2018**(3), 267–292 (2018). https://doi.org/10.13154/tches.v2018.i3.267-292. https://tches.iacr.org/index.php/TCHES/article/view/7276

19. Zoni, D., Galimberti, A., Fornaciari, W.: Efficient and scalable FPGA-oriented design of QC-LDPC bit-flipping decoders for post-quantum cryptography. IEEE Access **8**, 163419–163433 (2020). https://doi.org/10.1109/ACCESS.2020.3020262

20. Zoni, D., Galimberti, A., Fornaciari, W.: Flexible and scalable FPGA-oriented design of multipliers for large binary polynomials. IEEE Access **8**, 75809–75821 (2020). https://doi.org/10.1109/ACCESS.2020.2989423

21. Zoni, D., Barenghi, A., Pelosi, G., Fornaciari, W.: A comprehensive side-channel information leakage analysis of an in-order RISC CPU microarchitecture. ACM Trans. Des. Autom. Electron. Syst. **23**(5) (2018). https://doi.org/10.1145/3212719

Power and Energy

SIDAM: A Design Space Exploration Framework for Multi-sensor Embedded Systems Powered by Energy Harvesting

Pierre-Louis Sixdenier$^{(\boxtimes)}$, Stefan Wildermann, Daniel Ziegler, and Jürgen Teich

Friedrich-Alexander-Universität Erlangen-Nürnberg (FAU), Erlangen, Germany
{pierre-louis.e.sixdenier,stefan.wildermann,daniel.ziegler, juergen.teich}@fau.de

Abstract. Multi-sensor embedded systems often consist of a central unit being responsible to manage a heterogeneous set of attached sensors. Particularly when such systems are deployed in areas without access to a static power supply, they have to be powered using energy harvesting to operate autonomously. Objectives such as availability and data loss rate depend on the set of attached sensors, the system configuration (e.g., used photovoltaic (PV) module, batteries, and data storage), as well as environmental factors such as the location of the deployed system. Moreover, also the employed energy management strategy and its parametrization severely influence the system characteristics. In fact, different strategies can lead to different tradeoffs in terms of the above objectives. In this paper we propose a design methodology to automatically explore the design space of configurations of multi-sensor embedded systems and to determine and configure the best energy management strategy for a given sensor configuration and location. Our methodology includes a real-time analysis and a simulation-based DSE to explore the design space. We investigate a case study from a biomonitoring project and demonstrate the benefits of the proposed design methodology: A system—including its configuration and energy management strategy— has to be tailored to the characteristics of the set of attached sensors and the location it operates. Else designs exhibit suboptimal characteristics when operating at sites or for sensor sets for which they were not optimized.

Keywords: Design space exploration · Energy harvesting · Energy management · Embedded systems

1 Introduction

Internet of Things (IoT) devices typically perceive their environment via sensors and exchange the perceived information with each other. One typical IoT architecture revolves around multiple sensors being connected to a central node that

A. Orailoglu et al. (Eds.): SAMOS 2022, LNCS 13511, pp. 329–345, 2022.
https://doi.org/10.1007/978-3-031-15074-6_21

acts as a gateway to the outside world. There exist multiple application domains to such multi-sensor systems like predictive maintenance [12], civil infrastructure monitoring [1], etc.

Our work is motivated by a bio-monitoring project [13], in which such a multi-sensor system is deployed in a remote environment to monitor the wildlife biodiversity. This system is also composed of multiple heterogeneous sensors (including stereo cameras, phenocams, microphone arrays, and radars for capturing data about insects, birds, and mammals) and a central system for collecting, processing, storing, and transmitting this data to a backend. The system is powered by at least one solar panel. The system must provide an energy management that carefully controls the overall power consumption and sensor data streams according to available energy. As animals are active at different hours of the day and night and during different seasons of the year, so do the sensors.

There exist several works on energy management techniques for energy-harvested embedded systems with varying workloads under uncertain solar energy supply. However, important objectives such as the availability and data loss of a multi-sensor system strongly depend on many factors which are fixed in the early design phase, and particularly before deploying such systems, e.g., the peak power of the PV plant, the battery capacity, and/or the type of and capacity of storage. Moreover, the selection and parametrization of the energy management technique also has to be part of the design process. Finally, environmental conditions that influence the system depend on the location of operating the system, e.g. the amount of energy harvested by the solar panels will be determined by the yearly sunlight, which is not the same everywhere on earth. Altogether, these parameters and configurations span a vast design space of options which should be carefully explored in order to identify and then select Pareto-optimal settings.

In this paper, we propose for the first time such a design methodology to automatically explore and determine the best PV plant configuration, battery, data storage, and transmission parameters (hardware) as well as select and configure the best energy management strategy (software) for a given set of sensors and a location before an on-site deployment. Our hardware/software co-design methodology involves a real-time analysis of the system workload as well as a multi-objective evolutionary algorithm (MOEA) that performs design space exploration (DSE) while using a fast simulation-based evaluation of objectives in-the-loop for each design point.

The paper is organized as follows: Sect. 2 summarizes the related work. Section 3 presents a formal model of multi-sensor embedded systems covered by our work. Section 4 describes the proposed design methodology. We then introduce three distinct energy management strategies (Sect. 5) and evaluate our methodology in Sect. 6.

2   Related Work

Several strategies for energy management (EM) on energy-harvesting embedded systems have been proposed, e.g., [4,6,9,15], also covering aspects of systems investigated in this paper, like scheduling of mandatory and optional functions [15], considering workload with time-varying utility [4], and predicting the future energy supply [6]. However, none of them focuses on automatic exploration of tradeoffs caused by different configurations of such an embedded system.

Only for wireless sensor networks and resource-constrained IoT networks, DSE approaches exist [5,14]. However, their main focus lies on the exploration of the network topology, particularly not considering energy-harvesting nodes with varying energy supply and their design parameters. A simulation model for energy-harvesting sensor nodes is proposed in [3] and including a case study on finding optimized design points wrt. battery capacity and solar panel size. But different to our approach presented in this paper, this work does not provide any techniques for automatic optimization and DSE. Moreoever, the authors only cover systems with lightweight nodes and thus cannot handle multiple heterogeneous sensors with varying activity profiles as our approach. In fact, the authors from [11] have recently "identified a vacancy in DSE methods for IoT nodes." They provide a method to decide which tasks to execute on the IoT node and which in the cloud. Exploited are also tasks that perform additional preprocessing on the IoT node as this may reduce the amount of data to be transmitted. A proposed DSE explores the tradeoff between energy consumption for on-node processing and transmission. Our proposed approach is able to explore this tradeoff by introducing the concept of *optional tasks*. Still, [11] does not cover many additional aspects of our methodology such as the consideration of uncertain energy supplies, etc.

3 Formal Model

3.1 System Model

Figure 1 illustrates our formal system model. The energy supply (green) is provided by solar power with a battery energy storage. A set S of sensors (yellow) is connected to the system. The system (blue) consists of a multi-core processing unit for sensor data processing, and finally a transmission unit for data transmission. Both units have access to a shared storage system, where write requests of the processing unit have higher priority than read requests by the transmission unit. An energy manager (EM) manages the overall system including sensor, harvesting, transmission and storage subsystems.

Sensor events are typically not uniformly distributed over time but might have sensor-specific variations, e.g., over the span of a day or a year, as Fig. 2 illustrates. Let $W(t) \subseteq S$ *specify the working set of sensors active* at time t.

Data of a sensor $s \in S$ is processed by a set of tasks $T_s = T_s^m \cup T_s^o$, where T_s^m will be called *mandatory tasks* (e.g., fetching and encoding data) and T_s^o *optional tasks* (e.g., segmentation and compression). The set of all tasks is denoted by $\mathcal{T}$. Each task $\pi_i \in \mathcal{T}$ is specified as a tuple $\pi_i = (\omega_i, p_i, \gamma_i, m_i)$ where ω_i denotes the *worst-case execution time*, p_i the *period* (e.g., sampling rate of the sensor), γ_i the *compression ratio* (specifying how the data can be reduced by the task processing it), and m_i specifies the *mapping* of the task (i.e., the processing core executing the task).

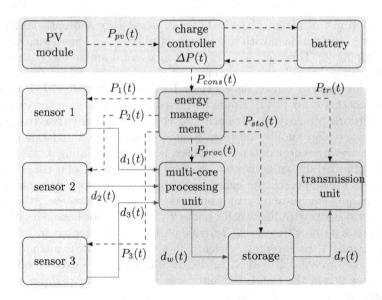

Fig. 1. Exemplified model of an embedded multi-sensor systems using energy harvesting as considered in this paper. The dashed lines indicate how power is distributed in the system. The solid red lines illustrate the flow of data from sensors to the transmission unit. (Color figure online)

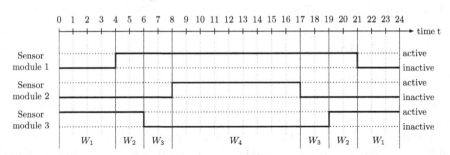

Fig. 2. Illustration of the concept of workload scenarios W_k based on combinations of activity profiles of the sensor modules over one day.

3.2   Energy Management Control Knobs

As mentioned in the beginning, we also want to model, explore and evaluate the behaviour of the energy management (EM) system during a DSE. To identify relevant control knobs over time, and explore such settings is particularly important for systems with an unpredictable power supply. In the following, we characterize such settings.

First, the system can be *up* or *down*. When down, the power supply to all sensors, the storage as well as the processing and transmission units are turned off so that no power is drained. In this case, the power $P_{cons}(t)$ consumed by the system (see Fig. 1) is zero.

Second, the EM can decide to serve (control) only a subset $S^a(t)$ of the working set of sensors $W(t)$ at time t. In the following, $S^a(t)$ is called the set of *active sensors* at time t, i.e., $S^a(t) \subseteq W(t)$.

Third, let set $T_{run}(t)$ denote the set of tasks which are actually executed at time t and which can also be adapted over time. $T_{run}(t)$ should contain all mandatory tasks of active sensors $s \in S^a(t)$ and it may contain a subset of their optional tasks. Obviously, the set of executed tasks influences the power consumption of the processing system $P_{proc}(t)$ as well as the storage system $P_{sto}(t)$.

Finally, the EM can adapt the *transmission rate* $\beta \in [0, 1]$. It specifies how much of the maximal transmission data rate $\overline{d_{tr}}$ to use for transferring locally stored data to the backend, and thus affects the transmission $P_{tr}(t)$ and storage $P_{sto}(t)$ power consumption.

Note that additional sophisticated techniques could be modeled and applied like adapting the sampling rates of sensors (rate control) and with that also periods of tasks, or dynamic voltage frequency scaling of processors. These are, however, not considered in this paper.

3.3   Data Flow

An active sensor $s \in S^a$ generates data with a specific data rate $\overline{d_s}$. Tasks running on the processing unit may process this data (e.g., segmentation, compression) and reduce it according to compression ratio γ_i. The actual rate $d_s(t)$ of data from sensor s to be stored and transmitted therefore depends on the tasks $T_{run}(t)$ executed at time t and their compression ratio. It is computed as

$$d_s(t) = \overline{d_s} - \sum_{\pi_i \in T_{run}(t) \cap T_s} (1 - \frac{1}{\gamma_i}) \cdot \overline{d_s}. \tag{1}$$

Finally, overall data rate is the sum over all active sensors:

$$d_{proc}(t) = \sum_{s \in S^a(t)} d_s(t). \tag{2}$$

As illustrated in Fig. 1, the data is assumed to be buffered in the local storage before it is read again and transmitted. The *data rate* $d_w(t)$ of writing to the local storage depends on $d_{proc}(t)$ and the *maximum write rate* $\overline{d_w}$ of the storage (e.g., flash, SSD, etc.)[1]. The rate $d_r(t)$ of data read from the storage device and transmitted depends on the chosen transmission rate $\beta(t)$, the *maximum read rate* $\overline{d_r}$, and the available memory bandwidth not occupied by data writes[2]. The data stored on disk at time $t + \Delta t$ is then:

$$D_{sto}(t + \Delta t) = \min\{D_{sto}(t) + \Delta t \cdot (d_w(t) - d_r(t)), \overline{D_{sto}}\} \tag{3}$$

depending on the write and read data rate. When the data on the storage approaches its *maximal capacity* $\overline{D_{sto}}$, data is lost.

---

[1] When statically designing such systems (see Sect. 4), we can layout the system that $d_w(t)$ is never higher than the storage's maximum write rate.

[2] We give data writes higher priority to avoid data loss.

3.4   Power and Energy Model

According to our system model, the overall power consumption is obtained as

$$P_{cons}(t) = P_{sense}(t) + P_{proc}(t) + P_{sto}(t) + P_{tr}(t). \tag{4}$$

The power drained by the active sensors is denoted by

$$P_{sense}(t) = \sum_{s \in S^a(t)} P_s. \tag{5}$$

Processing power $P_{proc}(t)$ depends on the tasks executed on the processing unit, which is a (multi-core) processor with a set C of cores. The utilization of a core $c \in C$ at time t is given as

$$\alpha(c,t) = \sum_{\pi_i \in T_{run}(t) \wedge m_i = c} \frac{\omega_i}{p_i}. \tag{6}$$

Now, the overall power consumption of data processing depends on how often the cores are idle (and require idle power $P_{idle,c}$) and how often they are active (and require active power $P_{active,c}$), i.e.:

$$P_{proc}(t) = \sum_{c \in C} P_{idle,c} \cdot (1 - \alpha(c,t)) + P_{active,c} \cdot \alpha(c,t). \tag{7}$$

The power consumption of accessing the storage depends on the data write and read rates, with read power P_r, write power P_w, and idle power $P_{idle,sto}$:

$$P_{sto}(t) = \frac{d_r(t)}{\overline{d_r}} \cdot P_r + \frac{d_w(t)}{\overline{d_w}} \cdot P_w + \left(1 - \frac{d_r(t)}{\overline{d_r}} - \frac{d_w(t)}{\overline{d_w}}\right) \cdot P_{idle,sto}. \tag{8}$$

Finally, the power for data transmission depends on the amount of data transmitted:

$$P_{tr}(t) = \left(1 - \frac{d_{tr}(t)}{\overline{d_{tr}}}\right) \cdot P_{idle,tr} + \frac{d_{tr}(t)}{\overline{d_{tr}}} \cdot P_{active,tr} \tag{9}$$

All idle power consumptions can only be avoided when turning of the components, i.e., the system is down (see Sect. 3.2).

According to Fig. 1, we assume energy is supplied via photovoltaic and a battery. Whether the battery is loaded or discharged depends on the difference between the power $P_{pv}(t)$ provided by photovoltaic and the overall consumed power $P_{cons}(t)$, i.e.,

$$\Delta P(t) = \begin{cases} (P_{pv}(t) - P_{cons}(t)) \cdot \rho_{char}, & \text{if } P_{pv}(t) \geq P_{cons}(t) \\ P_{pv}(t) - P_{cons}(t), & \text{else} \end{cases} \tag{10}$$

where ρ_{char} is the battery charging efficiency. The energy stored in the battery at time step $t + \Delta t$ is thus

$$E_{bat}(t + \Delta t) = \min\left\{E_{bat}(t) + \Delta t \cdot \Delta P(t), \overline{E_{bat}}\right\} \tag{11}$$

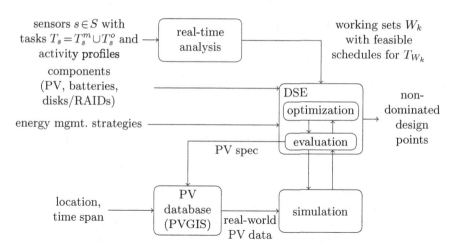

Fig. 3. Overview of the SIDAM design methodology for embedded multi-sensor systems powered by energy harvesting.

and limited by the maximal capacity $\overline{E_{bat}}$. We assume that the battery does not discharge itself and no power is lost during discharging.

Finally, the EM has to ensure that the battery does never fully discharge, e.g., by turning off all components (see Sect. 5).

4   Design Methodology

How efficient a system is working under uncertain energy supply over time depends on environmental but also several design parameters. Now, we propose our design flow (see Fig. 3) that consists of (a) a real-time analysis to verify a feasible schedule of all tasks executed per working set, (b) Evolutionary Algorithm (MOEA) based on a Multi-Objective Evolutionary Algorithm (MOEA) to explore the parameter design space, and (c) a fast simulation in-the-loop for evaluation of each explored design point.

4.1   Real-Time Analysis

In this step, all working sets $W_k \subseteq S$ are determined based on the sensors' activity profiles (cf. Fig. 2). The set of tasks T_{W_k} of one working set W_k can be divided into mandatory tasks $T_{W_k}^m = \bigcup\limits_{s \in W_k} T_s^m$ and optional tasks $T_{W_k}^o = \bigcup\limits_{s \in W_k} T_s^o$. The task of the block of real-time analysis in Fig. 2 is threefold: (a) to determe a subset $T' \subseteq T_{W_k}^o$ of the optional tasks which could be executed together with the mandatory ones in case sufficient energy is available. Further, (b) for each task $\pi_i \in T_{W_k}^m \cup T'$, determine a mapping m_i to a processor $c \in C$ of the multi-core processor system. And finally, (c) verifying that *the worst-case response time* (WCRT) of each task $\pi_i \in T^m_{W_k} \cup T'$ does not exceed its period p_i. The computation of the WCRT depends on the chosen scheduling strategy as well as the mapping of all tasks.[3]

According to a) to c), the block real-time analysis in Fig. 2 involves to solve the following two-objective optimization problem:

$$\text{maximize } |T'| \tag{12}$$

$$\text{minimize} \sum_{\pi_i \in T^m_{W_k} \cup T'} \max \left\{ \text{WCRT}(\pi_i, m_i, T^m_{W_k} \cup T') - p_i, 0 \right\} \tag{13}$$

(12) tries to schedule as much optional tasks as possible, while (13) corresponds to minimizing deadline misses, i.e., the amount of tasks finishing after their period in the worst case. We solve this optimization problem with a MOEA. When no solution without deadline misses can be determined (i.e., (13) is > 0 for all solutions), the designer has to adapt the working set or the multi-core system. Else, we select a zero deadline violating solution which maximizes (12) to build $T_{W_k} = T^m_{W_k} \cup T'$. In this case, the set $T_{run}(t)$ of tasks executed in the system will always be a subset or equal to $T_{W(t)}$.

4.2 Design Space Exploration

Important objectives of embedded multi-sensor systems powered via energy harvesting are their costs, and other non-functional characteristics including availability, loss of sensor data, and maintenance efforts (e.g., manually replacing full disks in the field). These objectives are influenced by the selection of (i) the PV plant, (ii) the battery (iii) the storage system, (iv) an transmission unit, and finally the selection and configuration of (v) an energy management strategy.

Our design methodology contains a library with available components and their characteristics influencing the system's data flow and energy (see Sect. 3). The selection of these options defines the following search space:

(i) Set X_{pv} of PV modules, each $x \in X_{pv}$ associated with its costs $c(x)$, peak power and internal loss (required for obtaining $P_{pv}(t)$ as described in Sect. 4.3).

(ii) Set X_{bat} of batteries, each $x \in X_{bat}$ has costs $c(x)$, a capacity $\overline{E_{bat}}(x)$ and charging efficiency $\rho_{char}(x)$ (see (10), (11)).

(iii) Set X_{sto} of disks and/or RAIDs, each $x \in X_{sto}$ has costs $c(x)$, a capacity $\overline{D_{sto}}(x)$, read and write speeds $(\overline{d_r}(x), \overline{d_w}(x))$, as well as power consumption $(P_{idle,sto}(x), P_r(x), P_w(x))$ (see (3), (8)).

(iv) Set X_{tr} of transmission modules, each $x \in X_{tr}$ has costs $c(x)$, a maximal transmission rate $\overline{d_{tr}}(x)$ and power consumptions $(P_{idle,tr}(x), P_{active,tr}(x))$ (see (9)).

---

[3] For the results presented in this paper, we assume a round-robin scheduler and a corresponding WCRT analysis based on [8,10] without loss of generality as our approach is also compatible with any other scheduling strategy and WCRT analysis.

Our DSE explores the design space by allocating components (i-iv) from the library as well as selecting and configuring an EM strategy (v), where E defines the set of all possible energy management strategies. We will introduce distinct configurable strategies with their decision variables in Sect. 5. For a given set S of sensors, working sets W_k, and geographic location L, the goal of DSE can be formally specified as follows.

$$\text{minimize} \begin{pmatrix} \text{cost}(x) = \sum_{x \in \mathbf{x}} c(x) \\ \text{availability}(\mathbf{x}, e, S, W_k, L) \\ \text{maintenance\_events}(\mathbf{x}, e, S, W_k, L) \end{pmatrix} \tag{14}$$

$$\text{subj. to} \quad \mathbf{x} \in X_{pv} \times X_{bat} \times X_{sto} \times X_{tr}, \ e \in E \tag{15}$$

As we are dealing with multiple, conflicting objectives, we also apply a MOEA [2] here to explore $\mathbf{x}$ and e. SIDAM uses the publicly available optimization framework Opt4J [7] using NSGA-II as MOEA.

While the evaluation of the financial costs $cost(x)$ of a design x solely depends on the (static) hardware configuration, the other objectives depend on dynamic aspects of autonomous operation under uncertain energy supply. Therefore, for the evaluation of these objectives, SIDAM performs for each explored design point a simulation of the behavior of the system over the duration of one or multiple years to capture seasonal variations. As the MOEA is an optimization technique performing thousands of evaluations, a fast simulation model is required to perform a DSE in a reasonable amount of time.

4.3 Simulation

Evaluation of a system design is performed based on a fast system dynamics simulation. For this, we directly evaluate the data flow and energy models from Sect. 3 with a step size of Δt. The data flow and the power consumption depend on the set of sensors active at time step t, which is based on the activity profiles of sensors (cf. Fig. 2). In our experiments, we assume that activity profiles and $W(t)$ have an hourly resolution.

Moreover, the models depend on the solar power $P_{pv}(t)$ provided by the PV modules. The power itself depends on the location of the station as well as the characteristics of the PV modules with which the system design is configured. The EU Commission's open access PVGIS platform[4] offers comprehensive solar radiation data and tools for calculating the yield of solar cells. The time series data of the PV power used for the simulation are automatically downloaded from PVGIS via its web-based API. We assume crystalline silicon cells and that they are optimally oriented for the specified location. Retrieved data is cached locally to accelerate simulation of subsequent designs with the same PV module characteristics. The time series have an hourly resolution. We perform

---

[4] https://ec.europa.eu/jrc/en/pvgis.

a linear interpolation between two data points for being able to simulate more fine grained Δt.

Finally, EM controls the behavior of the overall system and is thus also simulated. Section 5 presents case studies of such energy management strategies.

Simulation is then performed to simulate a given time span, which ideally includes at least one year to capture seasonal aspects. PVGIS contains historical data, so for example years with extreme weather conditions can be chosen to evaluate corner cases. During simulation, the time steps in which the station is down are counted to calculate the *availability*, as well as the time steps in which sensors were turned off by EM (*sensor downtime*). Furthermore, as soon as $D_{sto}(t)$ exceeds a given threshold, we count this as a *maintenance event*, as a team would have to visit the site to manually replace disks to avoid data loss.

5   Energy Management Strategies

The performance of an embedded multi-sensor system strongly depends on the applied EM. As we will also show in the experiments, different EM strategies may have different tradeoffs regarding the objectives. We therefore do not focus on a single strategy. Rather, we present three distinct strategies ranging from a simple static strategy to a sophisticated approach relying on prediction techniques. All strategies themselves are parameterized. These parameters are also explored as decision variables by the DSE. Table 1 illustrates the encoding of this search space, including the selection of one of the three EM strategies, as well as their parameters and possible value ranges.

All strategies have in common, that they switch between three basic states depending on the battery level E_{bat} (see Fig. 4). In normal state q_n, only the control decisions of the respective EM strategy apply. In critical state q_c, all sensors are turned off (i.e., set of active sensors $S^a(t) = \emptyset$). In state q_d, the system is down to avoid a deep discharge of the battery. Threshold b_d is fixed and b_c can be statically set or be automatically determined by the DSE. To avoid any oscillation between two states, the state machine implements a hysteresis with b_Δ. The three EM strategies are described next.

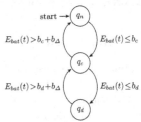

Fig. 4. States for normal, critical operation, and turning the base station off.

Static EM uses a static transmission rate β and either statically schedules all optional tasks or none. The transmission rate and whether optional tasks are scheduled or not are decision variables set by the DSE for a design point that uses static EM.

Adaptive transmission EM decides depending on a configurable *threshold* θ_{tr} on battery level $E_{bat}(t)$ whether to transmit data (with $\beta = 1$) or not. Like with static EM, scheduling of optional tasks is statically configured. If optional tasks are configured to be executed, they are only scheduled when the battery level is above the threshold. Threshold and the decision on considering optional tasks or not are decision variables set by DSE for a design point that uses this strategy.

Table 1. Encoding of the search space for selecting an EM strategy and configuring its parameters. The encoding of strategies is 0 for *static EM*, 1 for *adaptive transmission EM*, and 2 for *predictive EM*. Here, $\pi(X)$ specifies the set of all possible permutations of set X.

EM selection		
	Parameter	*Value range*
	Energy management	$\{0, 1, 2\}$
EM configuration		
Strategy	*Parameter*	*Value range*
0:	Transmission rate β	$[0, 1]$
	Run optional tasks	$\{$true, false$\}$
1:	Threshold θ_{tr}	$[0, 1]$
	Run optional tasks	$\{$true, false$\}$
2:	Forecast horizon	$[1, 24]$
	Threshold θ_{bat}	$[0, 1]$
	Task priority	$\pi\{T_s^o \cup \{\pi_{tr}\}\}$

Predictive EM is the most sophisticated strategy in our case study. It predicts the future battery level E_{bat} over a configurable *forecast horizon* with hourly resolution. For this, the PV power over this horizon is predicted including the current hour. Furthermore, the base energy consumption of the station is calculated based on the working set when executing all mandatory tasks over this horizon. The strategy aims at executing as many optional tasks and transmit as much data as possible within the next hour *without the future battery level falling below a configurable threshold θ_{bat} within the forecast horizon*. The strategy uses a configurable priority of optional tasks. For the optional tasks, a decision is made according to these priorities in an iterative process whether they will be executed or not, but only as long as they do not violate the above criterion on the future battery level. Also, data transmission gets a priority within this process. If transmission is selected to be executed for the next hour, the transmission rate β is set such that it does not violate the criterion. Forecast horizon, threshold, and priorities of a design are decision variables set by the DSE. In our experiments, we assume a perfect prediction by consulting the PVGIS time series data.

6   Experimental Evaluation

In this section, we demonstrate the benefits of the proposed design methodology SIDAM by showing that (a) the location of an energy-harvesting system is important to be considered during the DSE, (b) totally different EM strategies may lead to different tradeoffs in terms of availability and cost.

We define a site configuration $C = (S, L)$, with S being the set of sensor modules deployed on the site and L the site's location. For the following experiments, S is a subset of 4 sensors of the set $\hat{S}$ containing 6 sensors as specified according to Table 2. Furthermore, two possible values for L are considered:

Table 2. The characteristics of the considered sensors S_a

	Camera	Smellscapes	Bioacoustic	Weather station	Malaisetraps
Daily activity	Daylight	24 h	24 h	24 h	Daylight
Working period	All year	Summer	All year	All year	Summer
$P_{working}$ (W)	7	9	5	2.88	2
P_{idle} (W)	1	0	0	2	2
Data rate (KB/s)	400	150	300	5	5

L_C: Connemara located in Ireland, which has a yearly photovoltaic power output (PVOUT) of 859.3 kWh.
L_{DV}: Death Valley located in California with a yearly PVOUT of 1,845.4 kWh.

For our evaluations, we defined a library containing (i) photovoltaic modules with peak powers in the range of $[50; 50, 000]$ W with a step of 50 W , (ii) batteries with capacities in the range of $[50; 50, 000]$ Wh with a step of 25 Wh, (iii) six different disk/RAID components, (iv) two transmission unit instances, and (v) the presented EM strategies. All costs were set to the current market prices. Overall, the search space has a cardinality of $\approx 2 \cdot 10^{25}$ different designs.

In the following experiments, we investigated the impact of the value of C_i on their designs D_i obtained by DSE. Every optimization with a population size of 150 each converged after 200 generations. Each design point was simulated for the time span of a year (i.e., $24 \cdot 365 = 8, 760$ iterations of the model in Sect. 3 with a resolution of $\Delta t = 1$ h). Every DSE finished after less than 40 s using 4 threads on an Intel(R) Core(TM) i7-4770 CPU @ 3.40 GHz with 32 GB of RAM.

Using the simulator, we evaluated how the design optimized for one location would perform when deployed at the other location. It means simulating D_C in the context of C_{DV} and vice-versa, with $C_C = (S_N, L_C)$ and $C_{DV} = (S_N, L_{DV})$. Here, the set S_N of sensors operated at both locations contains a camera, a smellscapes sensor and a malaisetrap sensor; while the locations differ. The results are shown in Fig. 5. Each scatter plot represents the set of non-dominated designs after each DSE terminated after 200 generations. The left column represents the set of designs D_C, while the right column represents D_{DV}. The top row designs have been tested with the configuration C_C at location L_C, while the bottom ones have been tested with C_{DV} at location L_{DV}. It can be seen that operating an energy-harvesting system with an availability of 1 in L_{DV} is cheaper than in L_C, as less expensive components are required due to a higher PVOUT. Many of the designs that have been optimized for the less favorable conditions in Connemara operate quite well (availability of 1) for the advantageous conditions in Death Valley (bottom left), but at a generally higher cost than their counterparts D_{DV} (bottom right). Another observation is that, although the configuration choice has an impact on the objectives of design points found by the DSE, it is more impactful on the diversity of these designs. We can see in the figure that the designs cost range goes from 500 to 750 for the Death Valley-optimized designs, whereas it goes from 500 to 1350 for Connemara-optimized designs while this cost range contains designs valuable for this location.

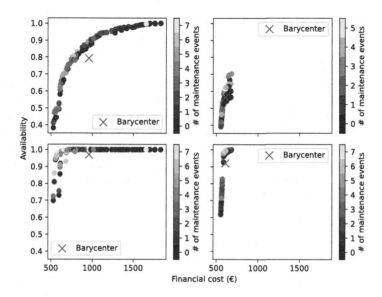

Fig. 5. Availability vs. costs vs. number of maintenance events for C_C (top row) and C_{DV} (bottom row) with D_C (left column) and D_{DV} (right column). Shown are the non-dominated design points and their barycenter.

In addition, we evaluated two configuration C_A and C_B, with $C_A = (S_A, L_C)$ and $C_B = (S_B, L_C)$ where both operate at the same location L_C, but S_A is composed of a camera, a bioacoustic sensor and a smellscapes sensor, whereas S_B is composed of a bioacoustic sensor, a malaisetrap sensor and a weather station. Again, we compared the objective values when operating the non-dominated designs D_A and D_B with the intended and with the other configuration. The results are shown in Fig. 6 (C_A (top row) and C_B (bottom row); D_A (left column) and D_B (right column)). We can see here that the designs D_A optimized for sensors S_A also perform well when operating with sensors S_B. The same holds for designs D_B. We can conclude that the impact of different sets of sensors on the objectives is lower relative to the impact of different locations.

The proposed DSE also explores which EM strategy to choose for each design point. Figure 7 shows the set of non-dominated design points after the DSE runs for the 4 configurations C resulting of all combinations of $\{S_A, S_B\}$ and $\{L_C, L_{DV}\}$ (all defined in the previous experiments). The radii of the plotted points indicate the amount of maintenance events (bigger radius is more events). Out of the three power management policies, at least two are part of each front of non-dominated points. *Predictive EM* has the highest share in all fronts of non-dominated points, with the best cost vs. availability tradeoffs. However, *static EM* and *adaptive transmission EM* obtain design points with better cost vs. amounts of maintenance event tradeoffs. This means that there is no single EM strategy that dominates all the others, and thus the selection and configuration of EM should be part of DSE for energy-harvesting IoT nodes when all objectives matter.

In a further experiment, we evaluated the advantage of our automated solution over a manual approach. To manually find optimized designs, we defined financial budgets and manually select the components for the design while staying within the defined budget. We show in Fig. 8 the performances of a set of three designs obtained for three different budgets (low: 500€, medium: 1,400€, and high: 2,600€) across different configurations compared to the respective designs automatically optimized by our presented methodology. We see in these results that the designs produced manually are less cost-efficient than the designs produced by our optimizing framework. We furthermore see that we would have to fine-tune designs for each configuration, as the obtained objectives signigicantly between the different configurations. Noteworthy, DSE runs faster than the time it took us to carefully design the system manually.

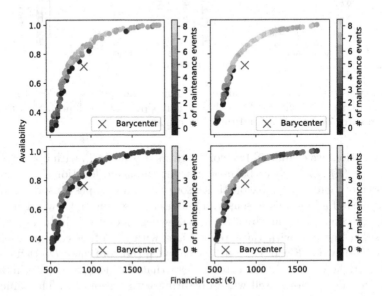

Fig. 6. Availability vs. costs vs. number of maintenance events for C_A (top) and C_B (bottom) with D_A (left) and D_B (right). Shown are the non-dominated design points and their barycenter.

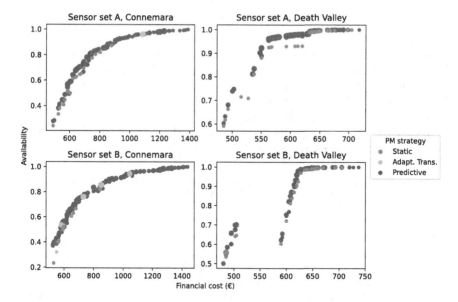

Fig. 7. Non-dominated sets after DSE, each color corresponding to one of the 3 EM strategies. The size of the dots represent the number of maintenance events that were triggered during a simulation run. (Color figure online)

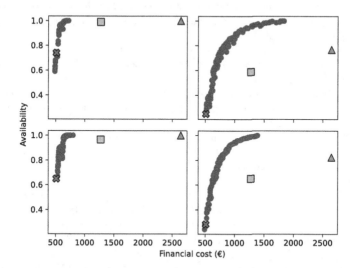

Fig. 8. Explored tradeoff curves between availablility and cost, each subplot corresponding to a different configuration. Blue points denote automatically explored design points. The three design points marked by other colours are the 3 manually constructed designs kept the same across configurations. (Color figure online)

7 Conclusion

Few papers deal with DSE for IoT devices which are powered by energy harvesting. We have proposed a design flow that addresses this pent-up demand. We have shown that determining a system design with high availability and low maintenance efforts depends on the proper dimensioning of hardware like the PV plant and the battery, but also environmental factors of the location where the system is deployed and, importantly, also the EM strategy implemented on the system. A holistic design flow as proposed in this paper is thus indispensable for making critical decisions in the early design phase.

Acknowledgment. This work was supported by the German Federal Ministry of Education and Research (development of AMMODs).

References

1. Birken, R., Zhang, J., Schirner, G.: System Level Design of a Roaming Multi-Modal Multi-Sensor System, chap. 23. Woodhead Publishing (2014)
2. Blickle, T., Teich, J., Thiele, L.: System-level synthesis using evolutionary algorithms. Des. Autom. Embedded Syst. **3**(1), 23–58 (1998). https://doi.org/10.1023/A:1008899229802
3. Castagnetti, A., Pegatoquet, A., Belleudy, C., Auguin, M.: A framework for modeling and simulating energy harvesting WSN nodes with efficient power management policies. EURASIP J. Embedded Syst. **2012**, 1–20 (2012)
4. Geissdoerfer, K., Jurdak, R., Kusy, B., Zimmerling, M.: Getting more out of energy-harvesting systems: energy management under time-varying utility with preact. In: IPSN, pp. 109–120 (2019)
5. Iovanovici, A., Topirceanu, A., Udrescu, M., Vladutiu, M.: Design space exploration for optimizing wireless sensor networks using social network analysis. In: ICSTCC, pp. 815–820. Sinaia, Romania, October 2014
6. Liu, Q., Mak, T., Zhang, T., Niu, X., Luk, W., Yakovlev, A.: Power-adaptive computing system design for solar-energy-powered embedded systems. IEEE VLSI **23**(8), 1402–1414 (2015)
7. Lukasiewycz, M., Glaß, M., Reimann, F., Teich, J.: Opt4j: a modular framework for meta-heuristic optimization. GECCO 2011, New York, NY, USA, pp. 1723–1730. Association for Computing Machinery (2011). https://doi.org/10.1145/2001576.2001808
8. Migge, J., Jean-Marie, A., Navet, N.: Timing analysis of compound scheduling policies: application to posix1003.1b. J. Sched. **6**(5), 457–482 (2003)
9. Moser, C., Chen, J.J., Thiele, L.: An energy management framework for energy harvesting embedded systems. J. Emerg. Technol. Comput. Syst. **6**(2), 1–21 (2008)
10. Racu, R., Li, L., Henia, R., Hamann, A., Ernst, R.: Improved response time analysis of tasks scheduled under preemptive round-robin, pp. 179–184. ACM (2007). https://doi.org/10.1145/1289816.1289861
11. Shallari, I., Leal, I.S., Krug, S., Jantsch, A., O'Nils, M.: Design space exploration for an IoT node: trade-offs in processing and communication. IEEE Access **9**, 65078–65090 (2021)

12. Tiwari, A., Ballal, P., Lewis, F.L.: Energy-efficient wireless sensor network design and implementation for condition-based maintenance. ACM Trans. Sen. Netw. **3**(1), 1 (2007)
13. Wägele, W., et al.: Towards a multisensor station for automated biodiversity monitoring. Basic Appl. Ecol. **59**, 105–138 (2022)
14. Zhao, Z., Barijough, K.M., Gerstlauer, A.: Network-level design space exploration of resource-constrained networks-of-systems. ACM Trans. Embed. Comput. Syst. **19**(4), 1–26 (2020)
15. Zhou, J., Yan, J., Wei, T., Chen, M., Hu, X.S.: Energy-adaptive scheduling of imprecise computation tasks for QoS optimization in real-time MPSoC systems. In: DATE, pp. 1402–1407 (2017)

A Data-Driven Approach to Lightweight DVFS-Aware Counter-Based Power Modeling for Heterogeneous Platforms

Sergio Mazzola[1]($\boxtimes$)(iD), Thomas Benz[1](iD), Björn Forsberg[1], and Luca Benini[1,2](iD)

[1] Integrated Systems Laboratory (IIS), ETH Zürich, Zürich, Switzerland
{smazzola,tbenz,bjoernf,lbenini}@iis.ee.ethz.ch
[2] DEI, University of Bologna, Bologna, Italy

Abstract. Computing systems have shifted towards highly parallel and heterogeneous architectures to tackle the challenges imposed by limited power budgets. These architectures must be supported by novel power management paradigms addressing the increasing design size, parallelism, and heterogeneity while ensuring high accuracy and low overhead. In this work, we propose a systematic, automated, and architecture-agnostic approach to accurate and lightweight DVFS-aware statistical power modeling of the CPU and GPU sub-systems of a heterogeneous platform, driven by the sub-systems' local performance monitoring counters (PMCs). Counter selection is guided by a generally applicable statistical method that identifies the minimal subsets of counters robustly correlating to power dissipation. Based on the selected counters, we train a set of lightweight, linear models characterizing each sub-system over a range of frequencies. Such models compose a lookup-table-based system-level model that efficiently captures the non-linearity of power consumption, showing desirable responsiveness and decomposability. We validate the system-level model on real hardware by measuring the total energy consumption of an NVIDIA Jetson AGX Xavier platform over a set of benchmarks. The resulting average estimation error is 1.3%, with a maximum of 3.1%. Furthermore, the model shows a maximum evaluation runtime of 500 ns, thus implying a negligible impact on system utilization and applicability to online dynamic power management (DPM).

Keywords: Power modeling · Energy estimation · Performance counters · Heterogeneous systems · Linear models

1 Introduction

Power concerns are shaping general-purpose computing in the post-Dennard scaling era, imposing a transistor utilization wall determined by the increasingly high power density of chips. The *dark silicon* challenge triggered the shift from general-purpose processing units to highly parallel and specialized accelerators, able to achieve higher performance and energy efficiency at the price of increased architectural heterogeneity [20].

© The Author(s), under exclusive license to Springer Nature Switzerland AG 2022
A. Orailoglu et al. (Eds.): SAMOS 2022, LNCS 13511, pp. 346–361, 2022.
https://doi.org/10.1007/978-3-031-15074-6_22

Power management paradigms addressing such architectures are a priority: today, dynamic hardware adaptations are extensively exploited to meet power and thermal constraints. Dynamic voltage and frequency scaling (DVFS) and clock gating are two common examples of the DPM techniques that allow tuning energy consumption to the application demand. For power management to be possible, online power measurement is a requirement. Several off-the-shelf Several off-the-shelf systems-on-chip (SoCs) come equipped with built-in power sensors; however, such a solution is often problematic due to its final deployment costs, poor scalability, the coarse granularity of measurements, and low speed [11]. A robust DPM control loop, on the other hand, requires fast and accurate measurements, in addition to resource-level introspection for fine-grained power tuning.

It is well-known that performance monitoring counters (PMCs) activity correlates with the power consumption of diverse hardware components [5,8,22]. As part of the digital domain, their usage is cheap, and their readings are fast and reliable, thus paving the way for accurate and efficient power models for DPM policies. PMCs also provide a high degree of introspection for the power consumption of individual components [10], which empowers PMC-based models with desirable responsiveness and decomposability [6].

Modern computer architectures expose hundreds of countable performance events [3,15]. Hence, the parameter selection for a robust statistical power model often requires considerable knowledge of the underlying hardware, compromising the generality of this approach while increasing its complexity and deployment time. Growing parallelism and heterogeneity, together with the frequent lack of open documentation, further hinder this challenge. A careful choice of the model parameters is necessary for several additional factors: first, PMCs can simultaneously track only a limited number of performance counters. Also, the amount of model predictors directly impacts its evaluation overhead, which is required to be small for practical DPM strategies and minimal interference with regular system operation. DVFS determines an additional layer of modeling complexity, as hardware behavior at varying frequencies has to be considered.

In this work, we develop a data-driven statistical approach to PMC-based power modeling of modern, DVFS-enabled heterogeneous computing systems. While targeting the multi-core CPU and the GPU of a heterogeneous platform, our methodology can be extended to include any additional sub-system, like memories and accelerators. With respect to the extensive research carried out in the field of statistical PMC-based power modeling, the distinctive trait of our approach is the *combination* of general applicability, automated model construction, lightweight model evaluation, and high accuracy. In detail, our main contributions are:

- a data-driven, automatic, and architecture-independent framework to select the PMCs best representing the power consumption of the CPU and the GPU sub-systems of a generic target platform;
- the development of a system-level power model based on a lookup table (LUT), composed of a set of lightweight, linear power models, one for each

DVFS frequency of each sub-system; this approach addresses the platform parallelism and heterogeneity while modeling DVFS non-linearities with simple, low-overhead computation and limited modeling complexity;
- the training and the validation of the mentioned power models against real hardware: an off-the-shelf modern heterogeneous system, the NVIDIA Jetson AGX Xavier [15] board.

The rest of the paper is organized as follows: in Sect. 2 we depict the state of the art (SoA) to place our work into perspective; Sect. 3 details our methodology and its background, while Sect. 4 describes its implementation on an off-the-shelf heterogeneous modern platform. Finally, in Sect. 5 we evaluate the results of our models' implementation, drawing conclusions in Sect. 6.

2   Related Work

In the last 20 years, PMC-based statistical power modeling aimed to online usage has been explored from several points of view [1,11]. Bertran et al. [7] identify two families of models, based on their construction: *bottom-up* and *top-down*. In this section, we adhere to this taxonomy to present the SoA and compare it to our proposal, with particular reference to Table 1.

Bottom-up approaches rely on extensive knowledge of the underlying architecture to estimate the power consumption of individual hardware sub-units. Isci et al. [10] pioneers this field by breaking down the consumption of a single-core Pentium 4 CPU into PMC-based power models for 22 of its main sub-units. Bertran et al.'s more systematic approach [6] refines this idea by extending it to a DVFS-enabled multi-core CPU. Sub-units models are *composed* to obtain accurate and *responsive* higher-level models. However, such a complex model building requires heavy manual intervention and architectural awareness, jeopardizing model generality. The reported mean absolute percentage error (MAPE) for power estimations is 6%, but their results highlight the strict dependency between bottom-up models' accuracy and architectural knowledge of the platform.

Top-down approaches target simple, low-overhead, and generally applicable models. They commonly assume a linear correlation between generic activity metrics and power consumption. Among the first attempts in the field, Bellosa [5] models the power consumption of a Pentium II processor with a few manually selected PMCs. Subsequent works [18,19] refine the idea with a more elaborate procedure for PMC selection and multi-core support. Bircher and John [8] are the first to go towards a thorough system-level power model, tackling the issue from a top-down perspective for each sub-system. To the best of our knowledge, no past research studies a combination of accurate and lightweight models addressing DVFS without requiring expert architectural knowledge.

More recent works have targeted CPU power modeling in mobile and embedded platforms. Walker et al. [21] employ a systematic and statistically rigorous technique for PMC selection and train power models for ARM A7 and A15

Table 1. Comparison of our work with the SoA in statistical power modeling

	Bertran et al. (2012) [6]	Walker et al. (2016) [21]	Wang et al. (2019) [22]	Mammeri et al. (2019) [13]	Our work
Heterogeneity	CPU only	CPU only	iGPU only	✓	✓
Generality	low	ARM cores	no	mobile	✓
Automation	low	✓	no	low	✓
Architecture-agnostic	no	no, ARM	no	average	✓
Lightweight model	no	✓	✓	no	✓
DVFS support	✓	✓	no	no	✓
Decomposability	✓	no	no	no	✓
Accuracy (MAPE)	power 6%–20%	power 3%–4%	power 3%	power 4.5%	power 7.5% energy 1.3%

embedded processors. However, only one trained weight is used to predict the power consumption at any DVFS state, which can be prone to overfitting. In contrast to their work, we target a broad range of platforms with more straightforward statistical methodologies and models, nevertheless carefully dealing with DVFS and reaching comparable accuracy numbers.

Top-down power modeling approaches have also been applied to GPUs. Wang et al. [22] analyze the power consumption of an AMD integrated GPU (iGPU), carefully studying its architecture and selecting the best PMCs to build a linear power model. Redundant counters are discarded to reduce the model overhead, with power MAPE below 3%. However, the generated model is not generally applicable and requires expert knowledge. Recent works resort to deep learning for creating accurate black-box power models: Mammeri et al. [13] train an artificial neural network (ANN) with several manually chosen CPU and GPU PMCs. With an average power estimation error of 4.5%, they report power estimates 3× more accurate than a corresponding linear model; however, the overhead of evaluating a neural network at runtime is not negligible, as it requires a number of multiply–accumulates (MACs) two orders of magnitude higher than for a linear model. Potentially long training time, complex manual selection of the neural network topology, and lack of decomposability are additional drawbacks of this approach.

Our model shares its decomposability and responsiveness with bottom-up approaches but resorts to top-down modeling for individual sub-systems: we trade a lower per-component introspection for a systematic modeling procedure requiring very little architectural knowledge and minimal human intervention, targeting broad applicability. We indeed refine the approaches in [8,17,18] to allow the selection of a minimal set of best PMCs for accurate and lightweight power models. Our LUT-based approach addresses the platform heterogeneity and its DVFS capabilities while employing lightweight linear models. To the best of our knowledge, no previous work thoroughly combines all the mentioned features. In this paper, we focus on power modeling for the CPU and GPU sub-systems of a heterogeneous platform, but our methodology can be extended

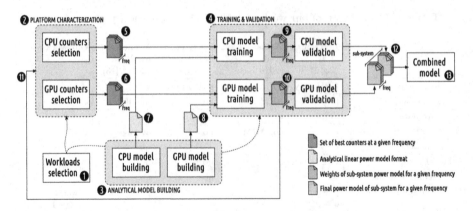

Fig. 1. Scheme of the proposed data-driven, automatic power modeling approach for DVFS-enabled heterogeneous platforms

to any additional sub-system, either considering its local counters, if available, or its related CPU counters as in [8].

3   Methodology

The main focus of our work is DVFS-aware power consumption estimation of heterogeneous systems based on individual sub-systems modeling. To achieve this, we develop a LUT-based statistical power model of our target platform (Fig. 1, **⑫**). Two parameters index the LUT: the sub-system d to be modeled and its current operational frequency f_d, corresponding to d's DVFS state. Each entry of the LUT is a linear power model P_d. The model is driven by X_{d,f_d}, the set of d's PMCs tracked when operating at f_d, weighted by the set of trained weights W_{d,f_d}:

$$LUT[d][f_d] = P_d(X_{d,f_d}, W_{d,f_d}), \quad d \in D^* \text{ and } f_d \in F_d^* \tag{1}$$

We refer to the process of defining X_{d,f_d} for each d at each f_d as *platform characterization* (Fig. 1, **②**). It is architecture-agnostic and performed one time per target system. We refer to the set of all sub-systems of the platform as D. For each $d \in D$, its available DVFS states are denoted by the set F_d. Our methodology targets a subset of sub-systems $D^* \subseteq D$, and, for each $d \in D^*$, a subset of frequencies $F_d^* \subseteq F_d$. Both D^* and F_d^* are user-defined parameters. For our methodology, we consider $D^* = \{CPU, GPU\}$. However, the described approach can be extended to any $D^* \subseteq D$. The choice of F_d^* is discussed in Sect. 4.3.

The power models P_d for the two sub-systems are built independently (Fig. 1, **③** and **④**); their composition results in an accurate and decomposable system-level power model (Fig. 1, **⑬**), developed with minimal effort. For the whole procedure, we operate a careful choice in terms of workloads for a representative dataset (Fig. 1, **①**). With reference to Fig. 1, we describe the several steps in the following.

3.1 Analytical Model Building

For each sub-system d, we individually develop an analytical power model (Fig. 1, ❸). As the frequency f_d is factored out by the LUT, the individual P_d (Fig. 1, ❼ and ❽) are linear models; however, their LUT composition is still able to capture the non-linearities of DVFS state variations. The analytical formats of P_{CPU} and P_{GPU} are discussed in the following.

CPU Sub-system Power Model. Our analytical CPU power model is based on the classical complementary metal–oxide–semiconductor (CMOS) power model, and assumes per-cluster DVFS: $P_{CPU} = P_{leak} + P_{dyn} = P_{leak} + \alpha C V^2 f$. For the sake of model simplicity, we consider the static power to be equal to the leakage P_{leak}. To account for possibly hardware-managed power gating, we include it in our model by defining the metric g_i, i.e., the percentage of time the core i is not power-gated. The dynamic power P_{dyn} of the whole CPU can then be defined as the summation of each core i's contribution $P_{dyn,i}$ over all cores as

$$P_{dyn} = \sum_{i=1}^{\#cores} \left[(1 - g_i) \cdot \left(P_{gate,i} - P_{leak,i} \right) + \alpha_i C_i V^2 f \right] \tag{2}$$

where $P_{gate,i} - P_{leak,i} < 0$ and accounts for the leakage power saved when core i is gated, while $\alpha_i C_i V^2 f$ represents its activity when non-gated. $P_{gate,i}$ and $P_{leak,i}$ are respectively the gated power and the leakage power of core i. The term g_i is computed using each core's cycle counter, while we resort to the CPU performance counters $x_{ij} \in X_{CPU,f}$ coming from the platform characterization to model the switching activity α_i. Factoring out of the summation P_{gate}, which represents the power dissipated when all cores are power-gated, we can highlight the contribution of each core i and each PMC x_{ij} to P_{CPU} rewriting it as

$$P_{CPU} = P_{gate} + \sum_{i=1}^{\#cores} \left[g_i \cdot \left(P_{leak,i} - P_{gate,i} \right) + \sum_{j=1}^{\#PMCs} x_{ij} C_i V^2 f \right] \tag{3}$$

The core parasitic capacitance C_i is a constant of the platform; additionally, as $d = CPU$ and $f_d = f$ index the LUT from Eq. 1, V and f are also constant: consequently, we lump them into model weights. We do the same for $P_{leak,i} - P_{gate,i}$, which is now positive. The resulting analytical expression, in Eq. 4, can be trained with a linear regression.

$$P_{CPU} = L + \sum_{i=1}^{\#cores} \left(g_i \cdot G_i + \sum_{j=i}^{\#PMCs} x_{ij} \cdot A_{ij} \right) \tag{4}$$

L, G_i and A_{ij} are the parameters of the model, from the $W_{CPU,f}$ set. g_i and x_{ij} are the input independent variables, or the *predictors*.

GPU Sub-system Power Model. Like for the CPU, the GPU power model (Fig. 1, ❽) also considers leakage and dynamic power. The same considerations of the CPU model hold as the LUT approach fixes the DVFS state for P_{GPU}. However, due to commonly stricter limitations of GPU's PMUs (cf. Section 3.2), it would not be general enough to always assume the availability of a clock cycle counter. Consequently, the model P_{GPU} is simply driven by the PMCs $x_j \in X_{GPU,f}$ coming from the platform characterization.

$$P_{GPU} = K + \sum_{j=i}^{\#PMCs} x_j \cdot B_j \tag{5}$$

The model parameters in Eq. 5 are K, modeling the constant leakage power, and B_j, weighting the dynamic activity. Before feeding the model, the counters x_j are normalized to the sampling period: as no other measures of time are present in P_{GPU}, this is required for robustness to sampling jitter.

3.2 Platform Characterization

Independently for each sub-system d and frequency f_d, we perform a one-time correlation analysis between all of its local PMCs and the sub-system power consumption, looking for the optimal X_{d,f_d} set in terms of model accuracy, low overhead and compliance with PMU limitations (Fig. 1, ❺ and ❻). We refer to this procedure as *platform characterization*. Our characterization is meant as an automatic, architecture-agnostic, and data-driven alternative to manual intervention when it comes to PMC selection. Given the sub-system d, its characterization involves the following steps:

1. for each DVFS state $f_d \in F_d^*$, profile *all* performance events exposed by d while tracing d's power; to track all events despite the PMU limitations, we make use of *multiple passes* [2,16] and avoid *counter multiplexing* [14][1];
2. normalize the PMC samples with respect to the sampling periods to work around sampling jitter;
3. compute a linear least squares (LLS) regression of each PMC's activity trace over its related power measurements, for each f_d; events with a p-value above 0.05 are discarded as not reliable for a linear correlation;
4. individually for each f_d, sort the remaining events by their Pearson correlation coefficient (PCC) and select the best ones that can be profiled simultaneously (i.e., compose X_{d,f_d} for all $f_d \in F_d^*$).

The generated X_{d,f_d} counter sets (Fig. 1, ❺ and ❻) are directly employed to build the linear models for each d and f_d in the LUT (Eq. 1). While multiple

---

[1] With *counter multiplexing* the PMCs are time-multiplexed in a round-robin fashion; this increases overhead and decreases accuracy. To avoid it when profiling *all* available events, we perform *multiple passes*: given a set of performance events that cannot be thoroughly profiled simultaneously, we replay the same workload (i.e., we induce the same power consumption profile) until all events have been tracked.

passes are used to profile all available events during the offline platform characterization, with an online deployment in mind for our models, we require X_{d,f_d} to only contain events that can be tracked simultaneously by the PMU. To this end it is usually enough to select, for each frequency f_d, the desired number of best counters, up to the PMU limit. To find the optimal number of performance counters with respect to model accuracy, results from model evaluation can be employed (Fig. 1, arrow ⑪).

On the other hand, some platforms [2,14,16] might have stricter PMU constraints. Not only PMCs are limited in number, but some of them are mutually exclusive: *compatibility* must also be considered. As documentation about performance events compatibility is not usually available, we tackle this issue with a PMU-aware iterative algorithm based on the profiling application programming interface (API) provided by the vendor. Given the sub-system d, its frequency f_d and the list of PMCs, the algorithm heuristically tries to group the PMCs with highest PCC one by one, adding to X_{d,f_d} only events that, basing on the provided API, can be counted in a single pass.

3.3   Train, Validate, Combine

With the sets of counters X_{d,f_d} from platform characterization we compose the LUT from 1 by individually training a linear power model P_d for each sub-system $d \in D^*$ at each $f_d \in F_d^*$ (Fig. 1, ④). The output of each training is a set of weights W_{d,f_d} (Fig. 1, ⑨ and ⑩). We then validate each individual $P_d(X_{d,f_d}, W_{d,f_d})$. The final result of this process is the complete LUT to model the power of all the components in the heterogeneous system (Fig. 1, ⑫).

For this step, we build a dataset with the characteristics discussed in Sect. 3.4 by extracting traces of workloads activity and power consumption. We acquire data points in a continuous, periodical sampling mode to collect information at a fine grain such that the desired responsiveness, necessary for DPM, can be achieved by the resulting model [6]. To train each individual $P_d(X_{d,f_d}, W_{d,f_d})$, we perform a non-negative least squares (NNLS) linear regression of the PMCs values over the power measurements, obtaining the set of non-negative weights W_{d,f_d}. Compared to unconstrained LLS, non-negative weights are physically meaningful, and prove to be robust to multicollinearity, which makes them less prone to overfitting.

After individual training and validation, we combine the CPU and GPU models into a system-level power model (Fig. 1, ⑬) defined as $P_{SYS} = \sum_{d \in D^*} P_d(X_{d,f_d}, W_{d,f_d})$. In other words, the system-level power model is the *reduction sum* of the LUT in Eq. 1 along the sub-systems dimension d. Modeling the sub-systems individually until this step allows us to avoid profiling all possible pairs of $\langle f_{CPU}, f_{GPU} \rangle$ for training, which is simpler, faster, and more robust to overfitting. The final model is decomposable, accurate, and computationally lightweight. We validate the combined model with a dataset built by concurrently profiling activity and power consumption of CPU and GPU.

3.4   Workloads Selection

The platform characterization, training, and validation steps are based on the careful choice of a representative set of workloads for the heterogeneous platform. Our workloads selection (Fig. 1, ❶) is mainly driven by the following parameters: firstly, complete coverage of all targeted sub-systems is required to fully address the heterogeneity of the platform. Secondly, for each sub-system, the workload should be able to induce a broad range of different behaviors for a workload-independent result.

Our reference for this is Rodinia 3.1 [9], a benchmark suite designed for heterogeneous and parallel systems supporting OpenMP, OpenCL, and CUDA. For the CPU characterization and modeling, we employ Rodinia's OpenMP benchmarks; for the GPU, we use the CUDA benchmarks. For the composition of the Rodinia suite, Che et al. follow Berkeley's dwarf taxonomy [4], which fulfills the variety of behaviors we require. Furthermore, we increase such variety by developing additional synthetic benchmarks targeting generic CPU sub-units to minimize the possibility of biasing the model towards the training set [6,7]. Such insights have not been reported for GPU power models.

4   Experimental Setup

For the implementation of our methodology, we target a modern DVFS-enabled heterogeneous system, the NVIDIA Jetson AGX Xavier. In this section, we describe our measurement environment and data acquisition setup, putting everything together for the implementation and practical demonstration.

4.1   Target Platform Description

The target platform for our experiments is an NVIDIA Jetson AGX Xavier, powered by the Xavier SoC [15]. It is a highly parallel and heterogeneous SoC provided with an 8-core 64-bit ARMv8.2 CPU, a 512-core NVIDIA Volta GPU and several additional accelerators for deep-learning, computer vision, and video encoding/decoding. With several DVFS *power profiles* available for its sub-systems, this platform represents a fruitful target to explore the issues tackled by this paper. In particular, the CPU complex can be clocked at 29 different discrete frequencies between 115 MHz and 2266 MHz, while the GPU has 14 available DVFS states between 115 MHz and 1377 MHz.

4.2   Data Acquisition

Power Measurements. The NVIDIA board features two 3-channel INA3221 power monitors whose information can be read using Inter Integrated Circuit (I2C) sysfs nodes. In particular, they can measure the power consumption of the CPU and GPU power domains independently.

As mentioned in Sect. 1, on-board power monitors are not robust tools for DPM mainly due to their speed, in this case limited by the I2C protocol, coarse time granularity, due to their analog nature, and low resolution, which for the Xavier is limited to approximately 200 mW due to the board configuration. However, their usage does not require external equipment, and they can be programmatically and reliably driven. Hence, they are still helpful for building datasets to achieve higher introspection, time granularity, and responsiveness enabled by PMCs-based power models.

Activity Measurements. Based on an ARMv8 instruction set architecture (ISA), the NVIDIA Carmel CPU Complex exposes 84 performance events per core [3]. The PMU of each core implements three 32-bit hardware performance counters, which can track any of the available events; an additional 64-bit counter dedicated to clock cycles is also present. This particularly suits the CPU power model of Eq. 4. To keep a low profiler overhead, we avoid higher-level tools such as perf. Instead, we directly access the PMU counters by reading their memory-mapped registers via assembly instructions.

The NVIDIA Volta GPU of the Xavier SoC features eight 64-core streaming multiprocessors (SMs). Its PMU exposes a total of 61 performance events: 41 of them are instantiated in each of the eight SMs, while the remaining 20 are related to the L2 cache and have four instances each. The maximum number of events that the PMU can track in parallel is not fixed and depends on their compatibility to be counted simultaneously. NVIDIA provides developers with several tools to retrieve GPU PMC information [17]; we employ CUDA Performance Tools Interface (CUPTI) [16], which features the lowest reading overhead.

4.3   Methodology Implementation

With reference to the notation of Sect. 3, we implement our methodology on an NVIDIA Jetson AGX Xavier platform targeting a sub-system set $D^* = \{CPU, GPU\}$ and the following DVFS states sets:

- $F^*_{CPU} = \{730, 1190, 2266\}$;
- $F^*_{GPU} = F_{GPU} = \{$all 14 frequencies from 115 to 1377$\}$.

All f_d frequencies are expressed in MHz^2. Note that, at lower CPU operating frequencies, operating system (OS) interference becomes predominant, affecting our measurements. Consequently, we limit our study to a subset of the most generally useful frequencies for the host CPU.

Profiling a workload on the target platform is necessary during several steps of our methodology. To this end, we developed a profiler that entirely runs on the Xavier board, tracing the PMC of each sub-system while collecting power measures, as outlined in Sect. 4.2. Samples are acquired in a continuous mode with a sampling period of 100 ms. Higher sampling periods turn our not to gain additional information due to the electrical inertia of the on-board analog power monitors. The profiler samples PMCs and power values in the same sampling period, to grant the time correlation [12] needed for an effective correlation analysis and training (cf. Section 3.2 and Sect. 3.3).

---

^{2} We round decimal frequency values to integers for readability.

Table 2. The ten best CPU counters from platform characterization at each frequency, with their PCC. The counters selected for the model are reported in green.

Performance	Frequency [MHz]		
event	730	1190	2266
Cycles counter	**0.56**	**0.57**	**0.60**
Exception taken	0.51	0.54	**0.57**
Instr. retired	**0.52**	**0.57**	0.55
FP activity	**0.54**	**0.56**	**0.59**
SIMD activity	0.50	0.52	0.52
Speculative branch	0.49	0.52	0.53
Speculative load	0.52	0.53	0.54
Speculative L/S	0.51	0.53	0.53
L1 I$ access	**0.53**	**0.54**	**0.56**
L1 D$ access	n/d	0.54	n/d
Data memory access (read)	0.52	0.53	0.54

Table 3. The ten GPU PMCs selected by our PMU-aware algorithm at each frequency based on platform characterization; their PCC with GPU power consumption is reported. The finally selected counters are reported in green.

Performance event		Frequency [MHz]		
#	Description	115	829	1377
1	CTAs launched	n/d.	n/d.	0.45
2	Cycles active warp (SM)	**0.77**	**0.67**	**0.65**
3	Acc. warps/cycle (SM)	**0.74**	**0.65**	**0.57**
9	Cycles w/ active warps	**0.58**	0.48	0.46
10	Acc. warps per cycle	**0.55**	0.47	n/d.
19	Cycles w/o issued instr.	**0.55**	n/d.	**0.55**
20	Cycles w/ 1 issued instr.	0.54	**0.53**	**0.55**
21	Instr. executed per warp	0.54	**0.54**	**0.55**
22	Active threads instr.	0.53	n/d.	n/d.
23	Active and not pred. off threads instr.	n/d.	**0.55**	**0.55**
29	LDG instr. executed	n/d.	**0.54**	n/d.
45	Reads T$ to L2, slice 0	**0.72**	**0.76**	**0.76**
53	Reads T$ to L2, slice 1	**0.72**	**0.76**	**0.75**

In terms of selected CPU workloads, we employ 17 different OpenMP benchmarks from the Rodinia suite in several multi-thread configurations and five additional synthetic benchmarks. For the GPU, we employ ten different CUDA benchmarks from Rodinia. To average out possible interference in our measurements, like unpredictable OS activity on the CPU, each workload is always profiled three times.

5   Results

This section reports the result of our methodology applied to the NVIDIA Jetson AGX Xavier; we first go through the results of the PMC selection, subsequently discussing the individual power models. We then show how the composed system-level power model achieves the objectives discussed in Sect. 1.

5.1   Platform Characterization

CPU PMC Selection. For the CPU characterization, we profile the workloads reported in Sect. 4.3. Table 2 shows the main results for the CPU counter selection[3]. For readability, only the ten best counters are shown, and the ones

---

[3] Due to space limitations we abbreviate PMC names in the tables; for a thorough description see their related documentation [3,16].

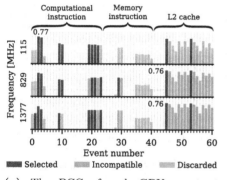

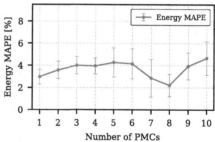

(a) The PCC of each GPU event at three frequencies, computed during platform characterization. The highest PCC is annotated for each frequency. The different colors identify the result of our PMU-aware selection algorithm.

(b) GPU power model energy estimation error as a function of the number of model predictors. The energy is accounted for the whole execution of the validation set, and its error is averaged over the estimations at all 14 frequencies.

Fig. 2. Results from the analysis for GPU PMC selection.

selected to model the power at each f_d are highlighted. The PCC of the clock cycle counter is also reported.

Overall, the power consumption of the cores is highly correlated with the number of cycles of activity, the number of retired instructions, the floating-point activity, and various cache-related events. As no events compatibility issues emerged for the CPU, according to the PMU capabilities, we consider the three best counters at each frequency and the additional PMU register dedicated to the cycle counter. As the eight Carmel cores in the SoC are identical and only per-cluster DVFS is supported by the platform, we choose to use the same PMC configuration for all cores.

GPU PMC Selection. The results for the GPU characterization, obtained profiling the workloads discussed in Sect. 4.3, are shown in Fig. 2a; for readability, only three of the 14 explored frequencies are reported. The histograms report the PCC of all 61 GPU events over the DVFS states. As it turns out, Volta GPU's PMU presents PMC compatibility constraints (cf. Sect. 3.2); three event categories hence result from the execution of our PMU-aware algorithm: *selected*, the ones selected to drive the power model; *incompatible*, the PMCs with a high enough PCC but discarded due incompatibility with better PMCs; *discarded*, all the remaining counters after the selection is completed.

Our correlation analysis shows that the utilization rate of the L2 cache, a 512 KB memory pool shared among all the GPU SMs, is generally a good proxy for GPU power consumption, with most high-PCC counters belonging to its domain. Nevertheless, from Fig. 2a it is clear how our selection algorithm grants enough PMCs heterogeneity such that a broad range of GPU behaviors

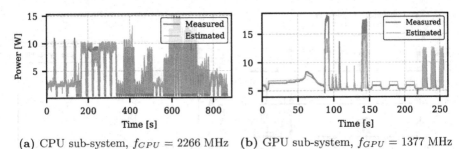

(a) CPU sub-system, $f_{CPU} = 2266$ MHz   **(b)** GPU sub-system, $f_{GPU} = 1377$ MHz

Fig. 3. Example results from individual CPU and GPU power models validation (instantaneous power model estimates and power measures from INA3221)

is captured: since a limited number of events can be usually tracked for the same domain (e.g., computational resources, L2 cache), the algorithm intrinsically selects non-redundant PMCs, covering all GPU components and decreasing *multicollinearity* among model predictors.

Moreover, the PMU-aware algorithm proves to be able to select at most ten performance events to be counted simultaneously, reported in Table 3[3]; the table uses the same event numbering of Fig. 2a. Among those, we pick the optimal configuration by analyzing the energy estimation accuracy of the GPU power model as a function of the number of counters driving it (Fig. 2b). We opt for eight input variables: this implements the feedback from model evaluation discussed in Sect. 3.2.

5.2 Sub-system Models Evaluation

CPU Power Model. For the CPU, we train the linear model from Eq. 4 with a NNLS regression for each frequency with a total of four independent variables per core. With the dataset discussed in Sect. 5.1, we use the initial 70% for training and the remaining 30% for validation.

In terms of instantaneous power accuracy, the model achieves a MAPE between 3% and 4.4% based on the frequency, with a standard deviation of approximately 5%.

As can be seen in Fig. 3a, our model tracks the measured instantaneous power consumption of the CPU over time. The instantaneous behavior of the estimated power consumption is more volatile than the measured one. As a matter of fact, PMCs are much more closely coupled to the workload and more responsive when compared to the INA3221 power monitors, which present the limitation discussed in Sect. 4.2. Our focus is on minimizing the error when integrating power over time, that is, calculating energy quantities. With a maximum energy estimation error of 4%, which drops below 3% at 1190 MHz, our model delivers an accuracy competing with SoA or even superior.

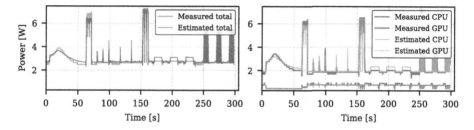

Fig. 4. Instantaneous power estimate for the system-level power model and its power breakdown with $f_{CPU} = 1190\,\mathrm{MHz}$, $f_{GPU} = 829\,\mathrm{MHz}$

GPU Power Model. For the GPU, we likewise train the linear model of Eq. 5 for each of the 14 GPU frequencies with a NNLS linear regression. The workload comprises the benchmarks discussed in Sect. 5.1; its initial 60% is used as the training set, while the remaining 40% is the validation set.

As for the CPU case, we can effectively track the actual instantaneous power measured by the INA3221 monitors while obtaining higher time granularity (Fig. 3b), achieving a power MAPE between 6% and 8% (based on the frequency) in the instantaneous measurements. The standard deviation over all frequencies is approximately 8%. When employed to estimate the energy over the full validation set, our model achieves a maximum error of 5.5% over all frequencies, with an average of 2.2%.

5.3   Combined Model Evaluation

After building, training, and validating both CPU and GPU power models individually, we put them together to obtain a system-level power model for every possible combination of f_{CPU} and f_{GPU}. For the validation of the final, combined model, we employ the CUDA benchmark suite from Rodinia 3.1, as it proved to induce valuable activity in both of our sub-systems of interest.

An example of the instantaneous power estimate is shown in Fig. 4; the achieved instantaneous power MAPE has an average of 8.6% over all CPU and GPU frequency combinations. In terms of energy, it reaches an average estimation error of 2.5%. A sub-sample of frequency combinations is reported in Table 4 as an overview. However, our results highlight how the energy estimation error of the combined model is generally higher when f_{CPU} and f_{GPU} diverge from each other. In particular, when f_{GPU} is very low compared to f_{CPU}, stalls and speculative behaviors may occur in the host CPU, which are hardly grasped by our model and jeopardize CPU's power estimation accuracy. As such configurations are generally not used in practice due to their sub-optimal efficiency, we focus on frequencies $f_{GPU} > 600\,\mathrm{MHz}$. With these considerations, we report an instantaneous power MAPE of 7.5% and energy estimation error of 1.3%, with a maximum of approximately 3.1%. To estimate the evaluation overhead of our system-level model, we implement it as a binary for the Carmel CPU and measure its runtime. Based on the frequency of the core, running between 730 MHz

Table 4. Energy estimation error of the system-level power model at different frequencies over the full validation set

Freq	CPU	730			1190			2266		
[MHz]	GPU	319	829	1377	319	829	1377	319	829	1377
	Error	5.7%	1.8%	1.4%	1.8%	1.5%	0.7%	6.6%	1%	0.6%

and 2266 MHz, we report an execution time between 500 ns and 150 ns, which confirms its negligible impact on system performance.

6 Conclusions

In this work, we described a systematic, data-driven approach to DVFS-aware statistical power modeling of the CPU and GPU sub-systems of a DVFS-enabled heterogeneous platform using their respective PMCs. Our proposed methodology achieves an unprecedented combination of general applicability, automated model construction, lightweight model evaluation, and high accuracy. We tackled the mentioned challenges with a data-driven statistical methodology for the model parameters selection, a LUT-based nature for the system-level model, and the linearity of the individual per-sub-system and per-frequency power models. The validation of our power models on the NVIDIA Jetson AGX Xavier reported an energy estimation accuracy aligned or superior to the SoA while achieving desirable responsiveness and decomposability, complemented by a low model evaluation runtime. These results pave the way for further work to assess the benefits of our models to online power monitoring and DPM policies based on online power estimates. Further investigations will also include the application of our approach to different target platforms for the quantification of its general applicability.

Acknowledgements. Supported in part by the European Union's Horizon 2020 research and innovation program, in the context of the AMPERE (#871669) and Fractal (#877056) projects.

References

1. Ahmad, R.W., et al.: A survey on energy estimation and power modeling schemes for smartphone applications. Int. J. Commun Syst **30**(11), e3234 (2017)
2. AMD GPUOpen: GPUPerfAPI v3.10 user guide (2021). https://gpuperfapi. readthedocs.io/en/latest/index.html
3. ARM Holdings: ARM Cortex-A57 MPCore processor technical reference manual, February 2016. https://developer.arm.com/documentation/ddi0488
4. Asanovic, K., et al.: The landscape of parallel computing research: a view from Berkeley (2006)
5. Bellosa, F.: The benefits of event: driven energy accounting in power-sensitive systems. In: Proceedings of the 9th Workshop on ACM SIGOPS European Workshop: Beyond the PC: New Challenges for the operating System, pp. 37–42 (2000)

6. Bertran, R., Gonzalez, M., Martorell, X., Navarro, N., Ayguade, E.: A systematic methodology to generate decomposable and responsive power models for CMPs. IEEE Trans. Comput. **62**(7), 1289–1302 (2012)

7. Bertran, R., Gonzalez, M., Martorell, X., Navarro, N., Ayguadé, E.: Counter-based power modeling methods: top-down vs. bottom-up. Comput. J. **56**(2), 198–213 (2013)

8. Bircher, W.L., John, L.K.: Complete system power estimation using processor performance events. IEEE Trans. Comput. **61**(4), 563–577 (2011)

9. Che, S., et al.: Rodinia: a benchmark suite for heterogeneous computing. In: 2009 IEEE International Symposium on Workload Characterization (IISWC), pp. 44–54. IEEE (2009)

10. Isci, C., Martonosi, M.: Runtime power monitoring in high-end processors: methodology and empirical data. In: Proceedings. 36th Annual IEEE/ACM International Symposium on Microarchitecture, 2003. MICRO-36, pp. 93–104. IEEE (2003)

11. Lin, W., et al.: A taxonomy and survey of power models and power modeling for cloud servers. ACM Comput. Surv. (CSUR) **53**(5), 1–41 (2020)

12. Malony, A.D., et al.: Parallel performance measurement of heterogeneous parallel systems with GPUs. In: 2011 International Conference on Parallel Processing, pp. 176–185. IEEE (2011)

13. Mammeri, N., Neu, M., Lal, S., Juurlink, B.: Performance counters based power modeling of mobile GPUs using deep learning. In: 2019 International Conference on High Performance Computing & Simulation (HPCS), pp. 193–200. IEEE (2019)

14. May, J.M.: MPX: Software for multiplexing hardware performance counters in multithreaded programs. In: Proceedings 15th International Parallel and Distributed Processing Symposium. IPDPS 2001, pp. 8-pp. IEEE (2001)

15. NVIDIA Corporation: Jetson AGX Xavier developer kit (2018). https://developer.nvidia.com/embedded/jetson-agx-xavier-developer-kit

16. NVIDIA Corporation: CUPTI v11.6 user guide (2021). https://docs.nvidia.com/cupti

17. Pi Puig, M., De Giusti, L.C., Naiouf, M., De Giusti, A.E.: A study of hardware performance counters selection for cross architectural GPU power modeling. In: XXV Congreso Argentino de Ciencias de la Computación (CACIC)(Universidad Nacional de Río Cuarto, Córdoba, 14 al 18 de octubre de 2019) (2019)

18. Pusukuri, K.K., Vengerov, D., Fedorova, A.: A methodology for developing simple and robust power models using performance monitoring events. In: Proceedings of WIOSCA, vol. 9 (2009)

19. Singh, K., Bhadauria, M., McKee, S.A.: Real time power estimation and thread scheduling via performance counters. ACM SIGARCH Comput. Archit. News **37**(2), 46–55 (2009)

20. Taylor, M.B.: Is dark silicon useful? harnessing the four horsemen of the coming dark silicon apocalypse. In: DAC Design Automation Conference 2012. pp. 1131–1136. IEEE (2012)

21. Walker, M.J., et al.: Accurate and stable run-time power modeling for mobile and embedded CPUs. IEEE Trans. Comput. Aided Des. Integr. Circuits Syst. **36**(1), 106–119 (2016)

22. Wang, Q., Li, N., Shen, L., Wang, Z.: A statistic approach for power analysis of integrated GPU. Soft. Comput. **23**(3), 827–836 (2017). https://doi.org/10.1007/s00500-017-2786-1

A Critical Assessment of DRAM-PIM Architectures - Trends, Challenges and Solutions

Chirag Sudarshan$^{(\boxtimes)}$, Mohammad Hassani Sadi, Lukas Steiner, Christian Weis, and Norbert Wehn

Microelectronic Systems Design Research Group, TU Kaiserslautern, Kaiserslautern, Germany
{sudarshan,sadi,lsteiner,weis,wehn}@eit.uni-kl.de

Abstract. Recently, we are witnessing a surge in DRAM-based Processing in Memory (PIM) publications from academia and industry. The architectures and design techniques proposed in these publications vary largely, ranging from integration of computation units in the DRAM IO region (i.e., without modifying DRAM core circuits) to modifying the highly optimized DRAM sub-arrays inside the banks for computation operations. Additionally, the underlying memory type, e.g., DDR4, LPDDR4, GDDR6 and HBM2, for DRAM-PIM is also different. This paper presents the assessment of DRAM-PIM architectural design decisions adapted in all DRAM-PIM publications. Our study presents an in-depth analysis of computation unit placement location, i.e., from the chip-level down to DRAM sub-array-level, and discusses the implementation challenges for a computation unit in various regions of commodity DRAM architectures. We also elaborate on the architectural bottlenecks associated with the scalability of DRAM-PIM performance and energy gains, and present architectural approaches to address the issues. Finally, our assessment covers other important design dimensions, such as computation data formats and DRAM-PIM memory controller design.

Keywords: Processing-in-Memory · PIM · DRAM · CNN · DNN

1 Introduction

Emerging applications, such as Deep Neural Networks (DNN), are data-driven and memory intensive. The computation of these applications on compute-centric standard processing systems results in performance and energy efficiency saturation due to memory-bound issues like high data-access energy, long latencies and limited bandwidth [1]. One of the trending approaches to address the memory-bound issues and achieve high energy efficiency is Processing-in-Memory (PIM). PIM places computation logic inside the memory to exploit minimum data movement and massive internal data parallelism. PIM architectures are proposed for various memories such as SRAM, DRAM, RRAM, and

A. Orailoglu et al. (Eds.): SAMOS 2022, LNCS 13511, pp. 362–379, 2022.
https://doi.org/10.1007/978-3-031-15074-6_23

FeFETS. In this work, we focus on DRAM-based PIM as the data accesses from the main memory DRAM devices is the key throughput and energy efficiency bottleneck in many compute-centric accelerator platforms [1]. DRAM-PIM is an active research topic in academia and industry, with increasing number of publications in recent times. Furthermore, the major memory vendors like Samsung and SK Hynix have fabricated and published their respective first engineering samples of DRAM-PIM in [2] (FIMDRAM) and [3] (Hynix-AiM). DRAM-PIM accelerator chips from start-ups like UPMEM are now commercially available [4].

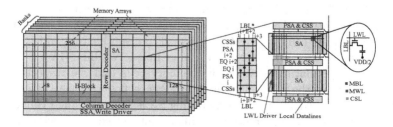

Fig. 1. DRAM device architecture with open bitline sub-array design.

The state-of-the-art DRAM-PIM publications have proposed various distinct architectures with unique design decisions. These architectures are largely varied, ranging from integration of computation units near the DRAM bank periphery or IO region to modifying the DRAM-core design or intricate Sub-Array (SA) design for computation operations. Furthermore, the choice of the underlying commodity DRAM architecture (e.g., DDR5, GDDR6, LPDDR5, HBM2E), computation data format, support for bank-to-bank communication, and techniques for external control of DRAM-PIM is also very distinct in each of the prior works. In summary, the prior works have proposed several point solutions to demonstrate a specific architectural approach and design techniques to implement a DRAM-PIM. However, there exists no publication that presents a global view on the design space of DRAM-PIM and a critical assessment of the various design dimensions. In contrast to other PIM candidates, one of the most appealing features for DRAM-PIM is to function both as a high density main memory and as an energy efficient accelerator. Hence, it is also important to assess the compatibility of various DRAM-PIM design approaches with the existing commodity DRAM architecture and its technology.

In this work, we present a detailed analysis of the DRAM-PIM design space, elaborate on the implementation challenges of incorporating new PIM units into the commodity DRAM architecture, identify the throughput and energy efficiency bottlenecks, and finally present novel architectural approaches to address the challenges. Our DRAM-PIM design space analysis covers the following design dimensions: 1) computation unit placement location, 2) computation data format, and 3) DRAM-PIM programming, external control techniques and memory controller modifications. Our paper provides new insights on the constraints of commodity DRAM architectures from PIM perspective and presents new architectural directions and approaches for the next generation DRAM-PIM research work, especially for the scientific community.

2   Background

This section reviews the basics of commodity DRAM. A DRAM device is organized as a set of banks that include memory arrays, as shown in Fig. 1. Each bank consists of row and column decoders, Master Wordline Drivers (MWLD), and Secondary Sense Amplifiers (SSAs). The memory array is designed as a hierarchical structure of SAs (e.g., 1024×1024 cells). To access the data from DRAM, an activate command (ACT) is issued to a specific row, which activates the associated Master Wordline (MWL) and Local Wordline (LWL). This initiates the charge sharing between the memory cells and the respective Local Bitlines (LBLs) in the SA. The voltage difference between the LBLs of a SA and the reference LBLs from the neighboring SA is sensed by the Primary Sense Amplifiers (PSAs) (i.e., differential amplifiers) integrated near each of the SAs. The concurrently sensed data by the PSAs of all the SA in a row of SA (referred to as H-Block) creates an illusion of a large row buffer or a page (e.g., page size = 2KB). After row activation, read (RD) or write (WR) commands are issued to specific columns of this logical row buffer, using Column Select Lines (CSLs) to access the data via Master Bitlines (MBLs) by the SSAs. Reading or writing the data from/to the PSAs of an H-block (or page) to SSAs is performed in a fixed granularity of *IO data width* $\times$ *bursts length* (e.g., $16 \times 8 = 128$ bit in DDR4). In order to activate a new row in the same bank, a precharge (PRE) command has to be issued first to equalize the bitlines and to prepare the bank for a new activation.

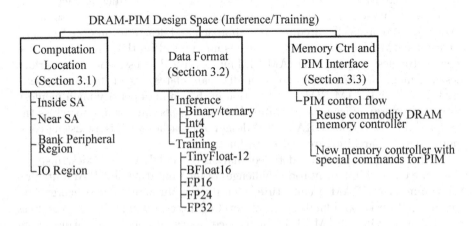

Fig. 2. Three main Dimensions of DRAM-PIM design space.

3   Design Space Assessment

In this section, we present a detailed analysis of the DRAM-PIM design space, which is one of the main contributions of this paper. We elaborate on the implementation challenges and throughput/energy gains of various architectural decisions. As mentioned in the introduction section, we consider DRAM-PIM to function as both a main memory device and a high throughput, energy-efficient accelerator. Hence, it is important for DRAM-PIM architectures to be compatible with the commodity DRAM architecture and to maintain its high density. This is inline with the goal of industrial DRAM-PIM architectures like Samsung's FIMDRAM [2]. Figure 2 shows the design space of DRAM-PIM and in the following subsections we discuss each of the three design dimensions in detail. To the best of our knowledge, we investigated all the available DRAM-PIM publications [2–17] with the emphasis on DNN for our design space assessment.

3.1   Design Dimension 1: Computation Unit Location

The four key locations to integrate the computation units in a DRAM device are 1) Inside SA, 2) Near SA or in PSA region, 3) Bank peripheral region and 4) IO region. Each of these regions within a DRAM has extremely different data access energy, available number of parallel data bits, computation unit integration challenges, and amount of modifications required to the DRAM-core.

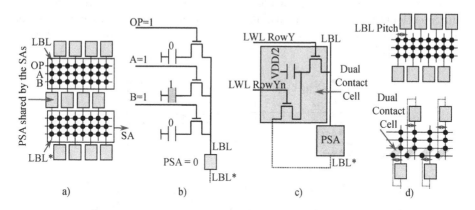

Fig. 3. Ambit implementation. a) Basic operation principle of Ambit, b) Dual Contact Cell (DCC) proposed by Ambit to implement NOT operation, c) Commodity DRAM unit cell physical device structure, d) Comparison of commodity DRAM SA vs. modifications required to SA for connecting LBL* to the DCC.

Inside SA Computation: One of the main advantages of "Inside SA" or "Near SA" approaches is that the highest possible data parallelism within a DRAM is available in these regions. For example, the amount of data available for

computation at SA level is as high as 1024 bits/SA (or 2KB per H-Block), while
the data per cycle at a bank peripheral region or IO region is reduced to 128 or
256 bits. Additionally, SA level also comes with the lowest data movement energy.
Ambit [7] was one of the first DRAM-PIM publications to propose inside the
SA computation for bulk logic operations like AND, OR and NOT. Ambit was
further adapted by publications like DrACC [9], LACC [11], DRISA [8], and Max-
PIM [17] to implement DRAM-PIM architectures for DNN inference. The basic
operation principle of Ambit is to simultaneously activate three rows within a SA
to implement a majority function and perform bulk AND or OR operation during
the DRAM activation process. Figure 3b shows the example for AND operation.
For functional completeness, Ambit also proposes NOT operation using a special
row with Dual Contact cells (DCC). Figure 3c shows the cell structure of DCC.
DrACC and LACC further proposed to include multiple special rows to perform
XOR, NOT and shift operations within a SA. This leads to the modification of
the DRAM SA, which is highly optimized for area, density, and yield. Figure 3d
shows one of the example modifications to the SA, i.e., LBL spacing has to be
doubled to route the LBL* from PSA to DC cell without violating the minimum
pitch. DRISA, on the other hand, proposed to integrate logic gates for NOT
operation in the PSA region rather than modifying the SA. The drawback of
modifying the DRAM SA is that this IP block is designed with specialized buried
gate RCAT or SRCAT transistors for extremely low leakage, the LBL pitch is
precisely adjusted for minimal crosstalk, and a $6F^2$ layout with shared LBL cell
contact by the neighboring cell transistors is employed for high density. The
inclusion of new special rows for computation operation is likely to impact the
aforementioned factors and in turn affect the memory operation. Hence, we aim
to explore the design approaches that strictly do not modify the DRAM SA.

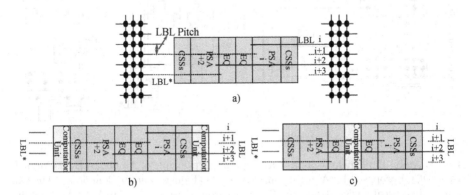

Fig. 4. PSA floorplan of conventional vs. with computation unit for PIM. a) Conventional PSA region, b/c) example computation unit integration in the PSA region,
where metal tracks have to be reserved in the computation unit for LBL and LBL* to
be connected to respective PSA.

Near SA Computation: The "Near SA" approach integrates computation units at the output of the PSA without modifying the SA design. Unlike SA, the PSA region's physical design is similar to logic design with conventional planar transistors. This enables the integration of CMOS-based logic gates in this region, but with certain restrictions that are outlined in this paragraph. The "Near SA" approach is employed in the following publications [10,12–14], where the DNN computations are split into primary and secondary stages that are placed near PSA and bank peripheral region, respectively. The integration of new computation units near the SA is highly challenging due to the Open Bit-Line (OBL) array architecture employed in almost all recent commodity DRAM architectures, which offers high density. This array architecture uses the bitlines from the vertically neighboring SA as reference bitlines for the PSAs to access the data from any given SA. Figure 4 compares the example floorplans of the conventional PSA region in Fig. 4a (i.e., including the column select block (CSS) and equalizer block (EQ)) and the PIM architecture PSA region in Fig. 4b and c. The new computation units integrated near the SA have to reserve the metal lines to allow the wires that connect LBLs and respective PSAs to pass through them (refer to Fig. 4b and c). This makes the routing within the new computation logic challenging, especially considering the fact that the DRAM process has a very limited number of metal lines (e.g., three or four). It also increases the length of the wires that connect LBLs and PSAs, which impacts the data sensing operation if the height of the computation unit is beyond the design considerations of the PSA. Hence, this imposes a height restriction to the new computation units in order to avoid the redesign of the PSA. Additionally, the new computation unit has to ensure that the wire load capacitance at the PSA inputs is balanced, as a PSA is a differential amplifier. Therefore, the computation units have to be integrated in one of the two possible ways shown in Fig. 4b and c. Overall, these restrictions constrain the integration of area-intensive units like multipliers and adders (i.e. >8-bit) in the PSA region, which are the basic operations in DNNs. Please note, the floorplan shown in Fig. 4 is for an example scenario where a PSA's width is equal to four LBL pitch. All the aforementioned constraints of the PSA region for the computation units persist even for a layout design where a PSA's width is equal to two LBL pitch.

Challenge 1: Integration of computation units like multipliers and adders (i.e. >8-bit) in the PSA region.

Bank Peripheral Region Computation: In this approach, the computation units are integrated at the output of a bank without modifying the core design of DRAM banks. The DRAM-PIM architectures such as Samsung's McDRAM [18,19] and FIMDRAM [2], Hynix's Newton [6] and AiM [3], and UPMEM-PIM [4] place computation units in the bank peripheral region. The main advantage of the bank peripheral region is its low physical restriction compared to the PSA and SA regions, which enables the integration of area-intensive units. However, the available data bits per cycle at the bank output (i.e., prefetch) are reduced to a maximum of 256 bits (i.e., number of MBLs or

#MBLs) compared to 2 KB at the PSA region of an H-Block. This limits the number of parallel computation units integrated at the output of the bank to a value defined by the ratio $\#MBLs/DataWordSize$ and the peak throughput per bank to $(\#MBLs/DataWordSize) \cdot Freq$. Increasing the #MBLs per bank in an area-optimized commodity DRAM bank design is difficult as all the wires including the power lines are tightly packed due to limited number of metal layers. Additionally, the data prefetch size per bank is predefined by the JEDEC specification for a given DRAM type. Increasing these values for the sake of higher throughput violates the JEDEC specification in the memory-mode operation of DRAM-PIM and the DRAM bank has to be redesigned to support different prefetch sizes for computation and memory mode.

The peak computation throughput is also alternatively increased by increasing the number of parallel operating banks or by reducing the data access latency within the bank. Increasing the number of banks integrated with large computation units in the bank peripheral region results in the reduction of memory density. Samsung's FIMDRAM with 16 banks reduces the density per die to half of the commodity counterpart (i.e., HBM2) due to the area overhead of computation units. This area overhead is expected to increase for future DRAM-PIMs, as the computational capability and functionalities are increased to support a wide sector of applications. Hence, this compromises the density and capability to operate as a main memory.

The data access latency within the bank (i.e., PSA to SSA) defines the peak operating frequency of computation units, which mainly depends on the bank height, wire capacitance/resistance, operating voltage, and technology node. For example, LPDDR4-based McDRAM operated the computation units at 250 MHz due a data access latency of 4 ns, although by design it was capable of operating at up to 1 GHz. Hynix-AiM shows that the data access latency is as low as 1 ns for smaller bank heights (like in GDDR6) and operates computation units at 1GHz. One of the major factors that impact the data access latency is the DRAM bank height that varies for different DRAM types. Table 1 compares the bank height of various recent DRAM types, which is proportional to data access latency between the types, as the DRAM vendor publications do not disclose the

Table 1. Bank height comparison for various DRAM types

DRAM type	Technology	Die capacity (in Gb)	Die dimention $W \times H$ (in mm)	Bank height[a] (in mm)
DDR4 [21]	1Y ($\approx 17\,nm$)	8	8.08 × 4.19	1.83
DDR5 [22]	1Y	16	9.2 × 8.2	1.92
LPDDR4 [21]	1Y	8	4.28 × 8.03	3.55
LPDDR5 [23]	10 nm 2nd Gen	12	4.4 × 12.44	2.65
LPDDR5 [24]	10 nm 2nd Gen	16	5.609 × 10.86	3.122
HBM2 [25]	20 nm	8	12 × 8	0.762
HBM2E [26]	10 nm 2nd Gen	16	11 × 10	0.904
FIMDRAM [2,5] (HBM2)	20 nm	4	10.28 × 8.2	**0.49**
AiM [3] (GDDR6)	1Y($\approx$17 nm)	4	8.4 × 4	**0.532**

[a] Bank height is proportional to data access latency within the bank

internal latencies. Additionally, the reduced bank height also reduces the energy consumption for accessing data within the bank as compared to other DRAM types with large bank heights but a similar technology node. As we can see in the table, the choice of DRAM type by FIMDRAM and Hynix-AiM is associated with a low bank height. Achieving a similar throughput and energy efficiency in other DRAM types like LPDDR5, DDR5, etc. with large bank height is challenging. As per Samsung, the LPDDR5 and DDR5 are the target DRAM types for DRAM-PIMs in edge applications [20].

Challenge 2: Increasing the computation throughput without decreasing the density or violating JEDEC specifications.

Challenge 3: Achieving low data access energy within the bank, especially for DRAM types with large bank heights.

IO Region Computation: This approach integrates all or a portion of the computation units in the IO region of the DRAM, as it has the fewest physical restrictions. Figure 5a compares the data access energies of the different regions of a commodity 20 nm HBM2 DRAM. The energy required to transfer the data between the bank and IO region is 3× higher than the energy within a bank. Hence, architectures like Hynix-AiM proposed to place only the large shared global buffers in this region, due to the area advantage of this region and to reduce the area overhead of computation units near the banks. Figure 5b shows 256 bits of data (i.e., one of the operands for the Multiply-Accumulate (MAC) operation) received per cycle by computation units in all the banks from the shared buffer. This transfer of data consumes a major portion of energy per computation operation. Alternatively, receiving the data from a neighboring bank (Fig. 5c) results in disabling half of the computation units and reduced throughput. The shared buffer is also used to transfer data between the banks, which is vital for DNNs such as convolution neural networks, where one input

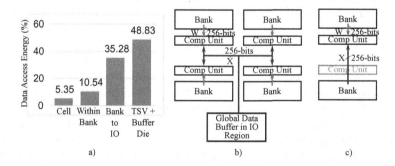

Fig. 5. High energy consumption for transferring data to and from IO region. a) Energy breakdown of read operation in 20 nm standard HBM2 device [5], b) Hynix-AiM distributing input feature map data to all banks from a global buffer in IO region and weights from the bank: High energy consumption, c) Hynix-AIM fetching both input feature map data and weight from the bank: throughput reduction by half [3].

feature map is convoluted with various kernels. This results in a high energy consumption for the exchange of data between banks. On the contrary, architectures like FIMDRAM do not support bank-to-bank communication.

Challenge 4: Enabling low energy data exchange between the banks and between banks and buffers.

3.2   Design Dimension 2: Computation Unit Data Format

Recently, DNN accelerator publications are exploring a range of low bit-width computation (i.e., < 8 bit) for inference and training (refer to Fig. 6). The low bit computation in standard accelerators reduces the area and power consumption per MAC unit and increases the overall throughput. Figure 6 shows various data formats employed in DNN accelerators and their respective accuracy degradation compared to 32-bit floating point format. DRAM-PIMs have also explored different data formats such as binary/ternary [8–10], Int8 [11–14] and floating point [2,3,6] for weights and/or activations quantization. Reducing the data width results in higher throughput due to an increase in data words fetched per data access within the bank (i.e., increase of ratio $\#MBLs/DataWordSize$). It also reduces the overall data access energy within the bank as fewer data accesses are required to fetch the given number of data words. Hence, the authors of [15] presented a 12-bit floating point data format (1-bit sign, 7-bit exponent, 4-bit mantissa) called TinyFloat to quantize the weights, gradient and activations for reduced data width DNN training in DRAM-PIM as compared to 16-bit in FIM-DRAM and Hynix-AiM. For a $\#MBL$ size of 128 bits, this 12-bit format reduced the data access energy by 20% and increased the throughput by 25% compared to 16-bit formats. Similarly, calculating the data access energy reduction and throughput increase for an 8-bit data format could result in 50% and 100%, respectively. The reduction of the data format can also potentially enable the integration of computation units in the PSA region of DRAM-PIMs designed for training (i.e., Challenge 1). Hence, it is very important to explore the low bit-width training for DRAM-PIMs. Recently, IBM presented an 8-bit data format for weights and activations of DNN training called Hybrid Floating Point format (HFP8). However, their work proposed to employ two different 8-bit formats for the forward and backward path (refer to Fig. 6), which results in two different MAC unit designs. Additionally, operations like gradient computation are proposed to be computed in a 16-bit floating point format, which results in three different types of computation. As a result, this technique does not have area gains over the DRAM-PIM architectures with a 16-bit data format like FIMDRAM and Hynix-AiM. Hence, in Sect. 4.2, we propose a new technique to adapt an 8-bit data format for DNN training that operates all DNN training computation with quantized 8-bit data.

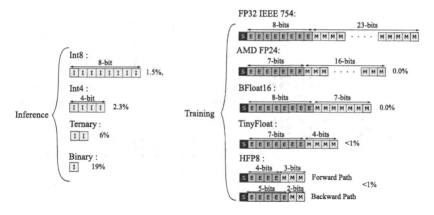

Fig. 6. Data formats employed in state-of-the-art standard DNN accelerators for inference and training and their accuracy degradation compared to FP32. Accuracy degradation values are extracted from [27–30] for inference, and [15,31,32] for training.

3.3   Design Dimension 3: Memory Controller

In this section, we assess the techniques for external control of a DRAM-PIM, for offloading of computation tasks to the DRAM-PIM, and the required modifications to memory controller designs proposed in prior DRAM-PIM publications. One of the main aims of FIMDRAM and UPMEM-PIM is to be a drop-in replacement for JEDEC-compliant commodity DRAM without modifying the host processor, memory controller or DRAM interface. These approaches offload the computation instructions as regular data to the DRAM-PIM device. The DRAM-PIM device is then switched from memory mode to computation mode after the desired program is loaded. The change to computation mode is done either by activating a reserved row (in FIMDRAM) or by sending a special sequence of commands (e.g., sequence of ACTs) to the DRAM (in UPMEM-PIM) to start the computation. After finishing the execution, the DRAM-PIM is switched back to memory mode to access the computation result and load new computation data. One of the major drawbacks of this approach is the disabling of data accesses until the entire computation program is finished. This stalls the host processor data requests when the same DRAM-PIM device is used for both host main memory storage and acceleration (e.g., edge domain). On the other hand, Hynix-AiM introduced new commands like ADD, MUL, etc. for PIM operations and proposed to modify the memory controller accordingly to support these new commands. This enables the interleaved access of data using conventional commands and perform computation operations using PIM commands, provided that the specified timing dependencies between the commands are satisfied. Hence, simultaneously operating both in memory mode and computation mode. However, the command bus width of DRAM-PIM has to be increased if the future generation DRAM-PIMs increase the computation capability and its associated commands. On the contrary, newer generation commodity DRAM

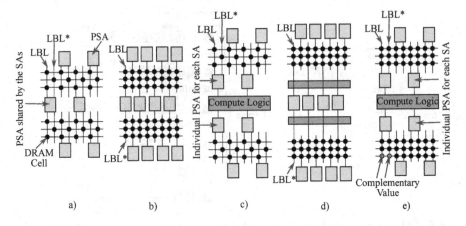

Fig. 7. Comparing DRAM BitLine array architectures from PIM perspective: a) Conventional Folded BitLine b) Conventional Open BitLine c) Folded BitLine with new compute logic d) Open BitLine with new compute logic e) Quasi BitLine (QBL) with new compute logic. QBL elimination the PSA sharing and enabling integration of large computation unit in the PSA region.

devices like LPDDR4 are targeting a low command/address bus width (e.g., 6 bits in LPDDR4).

Challenge 5: Designing a control flow to enable simultaneous operation of memory mode and compute mode that does not require modifications of the command bus width in each new generation of DRAM-PIM.

To understand the feasibility of memory controller modifications, we refer to the trends in commodity DRAM protocols and timing changes across different DRAM types and generations. E.g., the switch from DDR3 to DDR4 required the memory controller to support new timings for bank groups. DDR5 and LPDDR4 increase the data burst length from 8 to 16 compared to their previous generations. Additionally, the support for higher interface frequencies in each generation required design updates to the analog drivers in the physical layer (PHY). Hence, the modification of memory controllers was inevitable for every new generation of DRAM. However, this did not impact the host processor or its interface with the memory controller. As a result, the modification of the memory controller for a DRAM-PIM without disturbing the host processor or the underlying DRAM interface is considered acceptable.

4 Architectural Approaches

In this section, we identify the future research directions from the architectural perspective to tackle the aforementioned challenges. These new architectural approaches/directions that are commodity DRAM compliant can be adapted by future DRAM-PIM research to achieve the desired design goals.

4.1   Design Dimension 1 Solutions: Computation Unit Location

Near SA Computation Solution: Our first architectural approach referred to as Quasi Open Bitline (QBL) addresses Challenge 1 by enabling seamless integration of computation units without any modification of the DRAM SA or PSA design. We first compare various commodity DRAM bitline array architectures such as Folded BitLine (FBL) and Open BitLine (OBL) (Fig. 7a–d) from the PIM perspective. Figure 7a and 7b show the legacy FBL and OBL array architectures. The key advantage of the OBL array architecture over FBL is its high memory density. As a result, almost all recent commodity DRAM bank architectures are constructed using OBL. However, FBL offers a distinct advantage to PIM by duplicating the shared PSAs between the vertically neighboring SAs into individual sets of PSAs for each SA (refer to Fig. 7c) and making space between the SAs for the new computation logic with low physical restrictions. Additionally, the computation unit height neither impacts the LBL length nor requires any design/layout modifications to the existing PSA. Although OBL is not favorable for computation, it is widely used in all recent DRAM architectures and is highly recommended from the memory density perspective if the DRAM-PIM has to function as main memory as well. Hence, to reuse the existing OBL-based SA design for PIM and to achieve the FBL-like advantages with OBL, we present a new QBL array architecture for DRAM-PIM. Figure 7 shows the QBL array architecture that emulates the FBL structure using OBL arrays and its PSA design. It is important to note that QBL does not require any major modifications to the SA or PSA design of OBL, but only requires a minor interconnection modification, i.e., LBL to PSA. In QBL, two consecutive LBLs of a given SA are connected to the same PSA, where one of them is the reference line. This eliminates the dependency on the vertically neighboring SA and makes space for the new computation logic without major physical restrictions. However, QBL reduces the storage capacity of each SA by half, as two

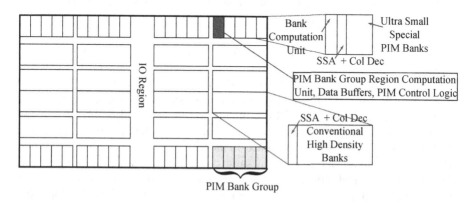

PIM Bank Group

Fig. 8. Proposed device-level DRAM-PIM architecture that satisfies the JEDEC standard of the underlying DRAM to support main memory functionality and high energy efficiency + high throughput accelerator functionality.

consecutive cells are employed to store a single binary value. The circuit-level analysis of QBL is presented in [33], but their work only compared QBL with OBL for LBL noise analysis. Our work is the first to present the benefits of QBL for a DRAM-PIM architecture.

Bank Peripheral and IO Region Solution: To address the density reduction of QBL and Challenge 2, we propose a DRAM-PIM device composed of two types of banks, i.e., conventional banks and PIM banks. As shown in Fig. 8, the commodity DRAM bank design is employed for conventional data storage purpose, while the PIM bank is optimized for energy efficient computations. Hence, this satisfies the JEDEC specification and high density requirements without compromising on the computation unit design decisions. Furthermore, the high throughput demand of Challenge 2 and low data access of Challenge 3 is addressed by using smaller size banks (e.g., 32 Mb or 16 Mb) for computation banks (compared to 1 Gb in LPDDR5 for example). This enables the integration of a high number of banks (i.e., >=32) in the given area (i.e., increased bank parallelism for computation), and the small bank height results in low data access energy, similar to GDDR6, irrespective of the DRAM type. Please note that the computation banks can be constructed with or without the QBL array architecture. Furthermore, to reduce the area overhead of the computation banks, only basic computation units like MAC are placed in each bank, while the other substantial computation logic like activation function, PIM control unit, and instruction and data buffers are placed at the output of the bank group (refer to the green block in Fig. 8). The placement of a computation unit at the output of a bank group is also proposed in GradPIM [16], but this architecture placed all the computation unit in the bank group region without exploiting the bank parallelism within the bank group. Please note, the bank group region accesses the data from the banks sequentially due to a single shared data bus for all the banks in a bank group. This results in only one bank transferring the data per cycle to the computation units, which reduces the peak throughput. Hence, our architecture approach aims to attain a good trade-off between area overhead and throughput.

The high energy consumption of bank-to-bank communication (Challenge 4) is due to the worst case consideration of data exchange between the extreme corner banks. Hence, Hynix-AiM proposed to place a global buffer in the IO region. On the contrary, our device-level architecture shown in Fig. 8 proposes to integrate the buffers in each PIM bank group to enable reduced bank-to-bank communication within the bank group. The separate buffers per bank group also enable each PIM bank group to operate on individual data as compared to Hynix-AiM where all banks operate with the same data. This increases the computation flexibility and efficient utilization of the available computation resources. Additionally, this flexibility increases the data reusability within the bank group and reduces the frequent exchange of data through the IO region.

4.2   Design Dimension 2 Solutions: Computation Unit Data Format

In this section, we propose an 8-bit floating point data format to compute DNN training with quantized weights, gradient and activation values. Typically, the IEEE floating point number system is represented as $(-1)^{sign} \cdot (2^{Exponent} - Bias) \cdot 1.Mantissa$ and bias is set to $2^{NumberOfExponentBits-1} - 1$. Instead of modifying the number of mantissa bits and exponent bits to achieve the desired range and precision for each DNN path, we propose to alter the bias to achieve the desired range and lowest representable number. Figure 9 shows the range modification of an 8-bit floating point format (FP8 = 1-bit Sign, 5-bit Exponent and 2-bit Mantissa) with the bias set to 29 compared to a typical bias of 15. Increasing the bias also reduces the quantization step size near the lowest number. This increases the precision when we shift the lowest representable number to the lower values. Hence, by adjusting the lowest representable number, we also confine the high precision near that number or for a desired zone. To evaluate the accuracy results, we use PyTorch library with ADAM optimizer, cross entropy loss function and weights initiated from Glorot coefficient. After 50 epochs of training, the resulting accuracy reduction in most cases is less than 1% for our proposed FP8. Table 2 shows the DNN training accuracy of the proposed FP8 for various networks and datasets, with a bias of 28 for forward path and 29 for backward path. Quantization of weights, gradient and activation values with the proposed FP8 format doubles the number of data words per data access and reduces the total number of data access by half as compared to FP16 format used in FIMDRAM or Hynix-AiM. Additionally, designing a MAC unit with bias as one of the inputs allows reusing the same computation unit for forward, backward and gradient operation contrary to [31].

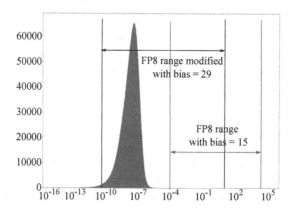

Fig. 9. Histogram of DNN training for gradient computation. FP8 range and lowest representable number adjusted using exponent's bias as 29 instead of 15.

Table 2. Data format vs. Top-1 Accuracy. The networks are trained with TinyImageNet [34] (TIN) and CIFAR100 [35] (C100) datasets

Format	VGG16 (TIN)	Resnet18 (TIN)	VGG16 (C100)	Resnet18 (C100)
FP32	52.10%	45%	68.6%	71.6%
FP16	45.4%	35%	24%	41%
BFloat16	52%	45%	67.7%	71.5%
TinyFloat	52%	45%	67.6%	71.1%
Proposed FP8	51%	44.6%	61%	68.6%

4.3   Design Dimension 3 Solutions: Memory Controller

This section proposes a new external control flow of DRAM-PIM for simultaneous processing of data and computation commands. Our control flow does not require the modification of the DRAM interface when new computation commands are introduced in the further generations of DRAM-PIM. We propose to introduce a single new computation command for DRAM-PIM that is common to all computations. Similar to conventional DRAM commands, this new computation command also has address (ADDR), bank (BA), bank group (BG) and data (DQ) fields. The address and data field are used to pack a set of instructions to be executed by the specified bank or bank group of DRAM-PIM. Depending on the type of instructions sent to a given bank in the special compute command, the memory controller waits for a specified time to access the data or perform the next set of compute operation from the same bank or bank group. This is similar to commodity DRAM where a read command has to wait until the activate operation is completed for a given bank or a new activate cannot start until the precharge operation is finished for that bank. During this wait, the memory controller can send commands to other banks similar to conventional DRAMs. This approach does not require any modification to the DRAM interface for supporting new compute instructions in the further generations of DRAM-PIM. The proposed control flow, protocol and timings are all similar to the JEDEC-compliant commodity DRAMs. From the host processor, the compute request can be sent to the memory controller as a regular read/write request but to a dedicated address where the data from the host for this request corresponds to compute instructions. The memory controller buffers the incoming data and compute requests, differentiates between data and compute requests, calculates the latency for each request, packs compute requests into a special compute command, and ensures that the desired timing latency for the packed set of commands is respected after the compute command has been sent.

5   Conclusion

In this paper, we presented the detailed assessment of DRAM-PIM design space to elaborate the challenges of incorporating PIM computation units in a commodity DRAM architecture. Our assessment covered the three key design dimensions of DRAM-PIM, i.e., 1) computation unit placement location, 2) computation data format and 3) DRAM-PIM memory controller. We discussed a total of five challenges in various design dimensions and identified architectural approaches to address these challenges. Our solutions included 1) QBL array architecture to enable computation unit integration near PSA, 2) a device-level DRAM-PIM architecture for high throughput and high density, 3) an 8-bit floating-point format to reuse the same MAC unit for various ranges, and 4) a new control flow that modifies the memory controller, but does not require the change of the command bus width for every new generation of DRAM-PIM devices. In the future, we will employ the proposed architectural approaches to design an extremely energy-efficient DRAM-PIM architecture for DNN inference and training, which operates as high density main memory as well.

Acknowledgment. This work was partly funded by the German ministry of education and research (BMBF) under grant 16KISK004 (Open6GHuB), Carl Zeiss foundation under grant "Sustainable Embedded AI" and EC under grant 952091 (ALMA).

References

1. Jouppi, N.P., et al.: In-datacenter performance analysis of a tensor processing unit. In: Proceedings of the 44th Annual International Symposium on Computer Architecture, ISCA 2017, pp. 1–12. ACM, New York (2017)
2. Kwon, Y.-C., et al.: 25.4 A 20 nm 6 GB function-in-memory DRAM, based on HBM2 with a 1.2TFLOPS programmable computing unit using bank-level parallelism, for machine learning applications. In: 2021 IEEE International Solid- State Circuits Conference (ISSCC), vol. 64, pp. 350–352 (2021)
3. Lee, S., et al.: A 1 ynm 1.25 V 8 Gb, 16 Gb/s/pin GDDR6-based accelerator-in-memory supporting 1TFLOPS MAC operation and various activation functions for deep-learning applications. In: 2022 IEEE International Solid- State Circuits Conference (ISSCC), vol. 65, pp. 1–3 (2022)
4. Devaux, F.: The true processing in memory accelerator. In: 2019 IEEE Hot Chips 31 Symposium (HCS), pp. 1–24 (2019)
5. Lee, S., et al.: Hardware architecture and software stack for PIM based on commercial DRAM technology: industrial product. In: 2021 ACM/IEEE 48th Annual International Symposium on Computer Architecture (ISCA) (2021)
6. He, M., et al.: Newton: a DRAM-maker's accelerator-in-memory (AiM) architecture for machine learning. In: 2020 53rd Annual IEEE/ACM International Symposium on Microarchitecture (MICRO), pp. 372–385 (2020)
7. Seshadri, V., et al.: Ambit: in-memory accelerator for bulk bitwise operations using commodity DRAM technology. In: Proceedings of the 50th Annual IEEE/ACM International Symposium on Microarchitecture, MICRO-50 2017, pp. 273–287. ACM, New York (2017)
8. Li, S., et al.: DRISA: a DRAM-based reconfigurable in-situ accelerator. In: Proceedings of the 50th Annual IEEE/ACM International Symposium on Microarchitecture, MICRO-50 2017, pp. 288–301. ACM, New York (2017)
9. Deng, Q., et al.: DrAcc: a DRAM based accelerator for accurate CNN inference. In: Proceedings of the 55th Annual Design Automation Conference, DAC 2018, pp. 168:1–168:6. ACM, New York (2018)

10. Sudarshan, C., et al.: An In-DRAM neural network processing engine. In: 2019 IEEE International Symposium on Circuits and Systems (ISCAS), pp. 1–5 (2019)
11. Deng, Q., et al.: LAcc: exploiting lookup table-based fast and accurate vector multiplication in DRAM-based CNN accelerator. In: 2019 56th ACM/IEEE Design Automation Conference (DAC), pp. 1–6 (2019)
12. Li, S., et al.: SCOPE: a stochastic computing engine for DRAM-based in-situ accelerator. In: 2018 51st Annual IEEE/ACM International Symposium on Microarchitecture (MICRO), pp. 696–709 (2018)
13. Ghaffar, M.M., et al.: A low power in-DRAM architecture for quantized CNNs using fast winograd convolutions. In: The International Symposium on Memory Systems, MEMSYS 2020, pp. 158–168. Association for Computing Machinery, New York (2020)
14. Sudarshan, C., et al.: A novel DRAM-based process-in-memory architecture and its implementation for CNNs. In: Proceedings of the 26th Asia and South Pacific Design Automation Conference, ASPDAC 2021, pp. 35–42. Association for Computing Machinery, New York (2021)
15. Sudarshan, C., et al.: Optimization of DRAM based PIM architecture for energy-efficient deep neural network training (Accepted for Publication). In: 2022 IEEE International Symposium on Circuits and Systems (ISCAS), pp. 1–5 (2022)
16. Kim, H., et al.: GradPIM: a practical processing-in-DRAM architecture for gradient descent. In: 2021 IEEE International Symposium on High-Performance Computer Architecture (HPCA), pp. 249–262 (2021)
17. Zhang, F., et al.: Max-PIM: fast and efficient max/min searching in DRAM. In: 2021 58th ACM/IEEE Design Automation Conference (DAC), pp. 211–216 (2021)
18. Shin, H., et al.: McDRAM: low latency and energy-efficient matrix computations in DRAM. IEEE Trans. Comput.-Aided Des. Integr. Circ. Syst. **37**(11), 2613–2622 (2018)
19. Cho, S., et al.: McDRAM v2: in-dynamic random access memory systolic array accelerator to address the large model problem in deep neural networks on the edge. IEEE Access **8**, 135223–135243 (2020)
20. Kim, J.K., et al.: Aquabolt-XL: samsung HBM2-PIM with in-memory processing for ML accelerators and beyond. In: 2021 IEEE Hot Chips 33 Symposium (HCS), pp. 1–26 (2021)
21. TechInsights. 1Y DRAM Analysis Product Brief (2019)
22. Kim, D., et al.: 23.2 A 1.1V 1ynm 6.4 Gb/s/pin 16 Gb DDR5 SDRAM with a phase-rotator-based DLL, high-speed SerDes and RX/TX equalization scheme. In: 2019 IEEE International Solid- State Circuits Conference - (ISSCC), pp. 380–382 (2019)
23. Chi, H.-J., et al.: 22.2 An 8.5 Gb/s/pin 12 Gb-LPDDR5 SDRAM with a hybrid-bank architecture using skew-tolerant, low-power and speed-boosting techniques in a 2nd generation 10 nm DRAM process. In: 2020 IEEE International Solid- State Circuits Conference - (ISSCC), pp. 382–384 (2020)
24. Kim, Y.H., et al.: 25.2 A 16 Gb Sub-1V 7.14 Gb/s/pin LPDDR5 SDRAM applying a mosaic architecture with a short-feedback 1-Tap DFE, an FSS bus with low-level swing and an adaptively controlled body biasing in a 3rd-generation 10 nm DRAM. In: 2021 IEEE International Solid- State Circuits Conference (ISSCC), vol. 64, pp. 346–348 (2021)
25. Sohn, K., et al.: A 1.2 V 20 nm 307 GB/s HBM DRAM with at-speed wafer-level IO test scheme and adaptive refresh considering temperature distribution. IEEE J. Solid-State Circ. **52**(1), 250–260 (2017)

26. Oh, C.S., et al.: 22.1 A 1.1V 16 GB 640 GB/s HBM2E DRAM with a data-bus window-extension technique and a synergetic on-die ECC scheme. In: 2020 IEEE International Solid- State Circuits Conference - (ISSCC), pp. 330–332 (2020)

27. Jacob, B., et al.: Quantization and training of neural networks for efficient integer-arithmetic-only inference. In: Proceedings of the IEEE Conference on Computer Vision and Pattern Recognition (CVPR) (2018)

28. Banner, R., et al.: Post training 4-bit quantization of convolutional networks for rapid-deployment. In: Wallach, H., et al. (eds.) Advances in Neural Information Processing Systems, vol. 32. Curran Associates Inc. (2019)

29. Zhu, C., et al.: Trained Ternary Quantization (2016)

30. Hubara, I., et al.: Binarized neural networks. In: Lee, D., et al. (eds.) Advances in Neural Information Processing Systems, vol. 29. Curran Associates Inc. (2016)

31. Lee, S.K., et al.: A 7-nm four-core mixed-precision AI chip with 26.2-TFLOPS hybrid-FP8 training, 104.9-TOPS INT4 inference, and workload-aware throttling. IEEE J. Solid-State Circ. **57**(1), 182–197 (2022)

32. Kalamkar, D., et al.: A study of BFLOAT16 for deep learning training (2019)

33. Takahashi, T., et al.: A multigigabit DRAM technology with 6F/sup 2/ open-bitline cell, distributed overdriven sensing, and stacked-flash fuse. IEEE J. Solid-State Circ. **36**(11), 1721–1727 (2001)

34. Le, Y., et al.: Tiny ImageNet visual recognition challenge (2015)

35. Krizhevsky, A.: Learning multiple layers of features from tiny images (2009)

European Research Projects on Digital Systems, Services, and Platforms

SafeDX: Standalone Modules Providing Diverse Redundancy for Safety-Critical Applications

Ramon Canal[1,2]([⊠]) [iD], Francisco Bas[1,2], Sergi Alcaide[1] [iD], Guillem Cabo[1] [iD],
Pedro Benedicte[1] [iD], Francisco Fuentes[1], Feng Chang[1] [iD], Ilham Lasfar[1] [iD],
and Jaume Abella[1] [iD]

[1] Barcelona Supercomputing Center (BSC), Barcelona, Spain
ramon.canal@bsc.es
[2] Universitat Politècnica de Catalunya (UPC), Barcelona, Spain

Abstract. RISC-V Instruction Set Architecture (ISA) is gaining significant popularity in Europe as the main driver for developing open source hardware. Commercial products and academic prototypes based on RISC-V become increasingly available, including cores, components and full systems-on-chip (SoCs). While those RISC-V IPs are suitable for many markets, those with safety requirements (e.g., automotive, space, avionics, health, railway) need specific support rarely available in RISC-V developments. Such support relates to observability and controllability features to ease verification, validation and the implementation of safety measures. Among those requirements, SoCs targeting the most stringent safety levels must provide some form of diverse redundancy to avoid the so-called Common Cause Failures (CCFs).

This work presents and compares some technologies providing diverse redundancy for cores that lack appropriate native support (e.g., dual-core lockstep – DCLS). In particular, we introduce the SafeDX group of components, which include two components enforcing diverse redundancy across cores, either by hardware means (SafeDE) or software-only means (SafeSoftDR), as well as one component measuring the diversity across two cores executing redundant tasks (SafeDM). We show the different tradeoffs in terms of software constraints, hardware intrusiveness, and compatibility with existing SoCs that make each of the three SafeDX components best suited for alternative deployment scenarios.

1 Introduction

The democratization of hardware design along with the European desire for technological sovereignty have converged into strong support for the RISC-V

This work has received funding from the European Union's Horizon 2020 research and innovation programme under grant agreement no. 871467. This work has also been partially supported by the Spanish Ministry of Science and Innovation under grant PID2019-107255GB-C21 funded by MCIN/AEI/10.13039/501100011033.

A. Orailoglu et al. (Eds.): SAMOS 2022, LNCS 13511, pp. 383–393, 2022.
https://doi.org/10.1007/978-3-031-15074-6_24

Instruction Set Architecture (ISA) [18], whose popularity growth is comparable to that of experienced by Linux on the software side in the past. Nowadays, developing full Systems on Chip (SoCs) or independent components has become affordable even for research institutions and small/medium enterprises, which can build upon the RISC-V ISA for their developments to avoid ISA licensing costs, and to operate without specific export restrictions.

The number of cores and SoCs based on RISC-V currently available is large and rapidly increasing, being a fraction of them, open-source. More that 100 SoCs and cores can already be found in the RISC-V International web portal [18], with a wide range of providers including SiFive, Semidynamics, ETH Zurich/U. Bologna, UC Berkeley, Codasip, Syntacore, Microchip, and Andes, to name a few. Some popular SoCs and cores include those based on SiFive/UC Berkeley's Rocket core, LowRISC's Ibex core, and PULPino and Ariane belonging to ETH Zurich/U. Bologna.

While those cores and SoCs are suitable for a wide variety of markets, products for safety-critical systems must provide specific support for verification, validation, and realization of safety measures, which most existing RISC-V products lack. In particular, SoCs for safety-critical systems must provide appropriate observability and controllability features, as well as specific support to mitigate faults and manage errors. To our knowledge, in the context of RISC-V, only products from two providers adhere to the needs of safety-critical systems. Those include CAES Gaisler's NOEL-V core and SoC [7] targeting the space domain, and NSI-TEXE's NS31A and other CPUs [17] targeting the automotive domain. In the case of NOEL-V IP, a large number of components are provided as open-source through CAES Gaisler GRLIB [6]. However, open-source components do not include safety and reliability support, which are, instead, only available under commercial license. In the case of NSI-TEXE's IP, it is not open source. Therefore, while few RISC-V products provide support for safety-critical systems, the relevant features are not open source.

In this context, the Computer Architecture and Operating Systems interface (CAOS) group at the Barcelona Supercomputing Center (BSC) has started the development of a set of open-source RISC-V based IPs with permissive licenses to pave the way towards reaching safety-critical markets with RISC-V open-source products. Those components provide observability, controllability, and support for safety measures, and include multicore interference-aware statistics units (SafeSU) [4,5], programmable traffic injectors (SafeTI) [21], and several hardware and software components to mitigate Common Cause Failures (CCFs), namely SafeDE [2], SafeSoftDR [16], and SafeDM [3].

CCFs include those faults that, despite implementing redundancy, can lead the system to failure due to producing identical errors in the redundant components. For instance, radiation effects affecting clock signals or voltage droops can make two cores experience identical external disturbance and, if their internal state is identical, experience identical errors, which would escape detection by comparing cores' outputs. CCFs are typically addressed by implementing some sort of diverse redundancy, as explicitly requested in functional safety standards (e.g., ISO26262 [14] in the automotive domain). Diverse redundancy is often achieved by means of coding for data storage and communications (e.g., error correction codes) and by means of Dual Core LockStep (DCLS) for computation. DCLS is implemented efficiently building on staggering (i.e., time-shifting the execution in redundant cores) so that, despite two identical cores executing identical software, they do it with few cycles of delay of the trail core with respect to the head core, so that their internal *electrical* state (i.e., current flow) at any point in time differs, and hence, any fault affecting both cores will never lead to identical errors. Examples of commercial cores providing DCLS include the Infineon AURIX family based on the TriCore ISA [13], and some STMicroelectronics controllers based on the PowerPC ISA [24], and the aforementioned NSI-TEXE's products based on RISC-V. However, DCLS needs explicit modifications in the cores and makes redundant cores not visible at the user level.

This paper presents and compares alternative technology developed by the CAOS group at BSC to achieve diverse redundancy for cores. Those components, namely SafeDE, SafeSoftDR, and SafeDM, provide diverse redundancy without introducing modifications in existing cores, hence easing their adoption. However, each component brings its own set of pros and cons, which we review and compare in this work. All of them allow using cores independently or in lockstep mode, but need redundant tasks being created at the software level as opposed to DCLS. The main characteristics of each solution are as follows:

- **SafeDE** [2]. It provides hardware support to enforce time staggering across two cores. The hardware cost is tiny, and the staggering imposed is very low, but hardware modifications are needed, and constraints are posed on the execution path followed by redundant tasks, which must not diverge.
- **SafeSoftDR** [16]. It is the software-only counterpart of SafeDE. Hence, no hardware support is needed, but staggering imposed is non-negligible to manage the monitor loop at software level. The same SafeDE constraints on path divergence hold.
- **SafeDM** [3]. It monitors diversity across cores executing redundant tasks. The hardware cost is tiny, no specific staggering is imposed, and no constraint is posed on the execution paths followed by redundant tasks. On the other hand, since diversity is assessed rather than enforced, software support is needed to manage scenarios where existing diversity is insufficient.

Overall, those components provide interesting alternatives to classic DCLS, and they do it in the context of RISC-V and open source hardware, with some of them already being offered as open source at https://bsccaos.github. io/. Moreover, they have already been integrated in highly mature SoC prototypes by CAES Gaisler developed in the context of two European projects: H2020 SELENE [22] and H2020 ECSEL FRACTAL [11].

The rest of this paper is organized as follows. Section 2 presents some background on the development process of safety-relevant systems, and on diverse redundancy. Section 3 describes and compares SafeDE, SafeSoftDR, and SafeDM. Finally, some conclusions are provided in Sect. 4.

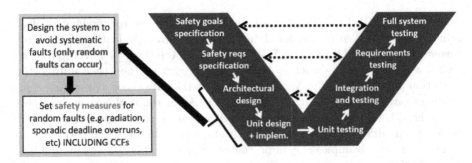

Fig. 1. V-model of the development process of a safety-relevant system.

2   Background

2.1   Development Process of a Safety-Relevant System

Safety-critical systems must be designed, verified, and validated following the development process described in the corresponding domain-specific safety standards. For instance, ISO26262 [14] and ISO/PAS 21448 [23] (aka SOTIF) in the automotive domain, EN50126/8/9 [8–10] in the railway domain, and DO254 [20] and DO178C [19] in the avionics domain are the most relevant standards in those domains. The development process is often represented in the form of a V-model, as the one depicted in Fig. 1. The development starts by describing the safety goals of the system, from which specific and unambiguous safety requirements are obtained. Then, the system architecture is designed and safety requirements mapped so that such architecture implements all such requirements.

The system is designed so that the risk of having systematic hardware faults or software faults can be regarded as residual. However, random hardware faults are unavoidable, and hence, appropriate safety measures need to be included in the system architectural design to mitigate those faults and manage potential errors to make the failure probabilities residual. The design must then be properly verified to prove that it is safe by construction and later validated once implemented and after each integration step to collect testing evidence confirming that the system behaves according to its specifications in front of relevant use scenarios.

The highest integrity systems, such as for instance ASIL-D[1] in automotive, must implement diverse redundancy as safety measure. Diverse redundancy is a safety measure intended to avoid CCFs, as explained before, by guaranteeing that, upon a fault, if the multiple redundant items reach an erroneous state, such state differs across them so that errors can be detected by comparison.

---

[1] ASIL stands for Automotive Safety Integrity Level. There are 4 ASIL levels being ASIL-A, the lowest integrity – yet safety-related – category, and ASIL-D, the highest. Non-safety-related items are allocated QM (Quality Managed) level.

2.2   Diverse Redundancy Realizations

Diverse redundancy can be efficiently implemented for data storage and communication by means of coding. Error correction codes such as Single Error Correction Double Error Detection (SECDED) codes are often used for data storage (e.g., in DRAM and cache memories) and Cyclic Redundancy Check (CRC) codes for data communication. However, diverse redundancy is often achieved by means of full redundancy in the case of computation, being DCLS the preferred solution. DCLS has the advantage of being fully transparent for the user since only one core is visible at the user level, and hardware manages redundancy, staggering, and comparison of off-core activity. Unfortunately, there is no way to use DCLS cores as independent cores for less critical tasks, as it occurs for the Infineon [13] and STMicroelectronics [24] DCLS processors introduced before.

To provide increased flexibility, some works have introduced the concept of diverse redundancy on non-lockstep cores [1], where redundant processes are created at the user level, and either hardware support or software libraries provide means to guarantee diversity. Such diversity can be achieved by different means, as we present later in this paper, but in all cases, there are some pros and cons with respect to classic DCLS. In particular, the main advantage relates to the ability to use the cores for diverse and redundant execution or for non-redundant execution, hence providing much more flexibility and increased performance than DCLS for non-critical and lowly-critical tasks. The main drawback relates to the fact that, since execution is fully duplicated at the software level, such solution cannot be applied to those parts of the software interacting with I/O devices, which could lead to system misbehavior (e.g., by triggering an actuator twice), and there is a monitor executing periodically that needs to be protected. Hence, native DCLS is needed at least for one pair of cores to manage I/O activities and, if the monitor is a software process, to run the monitor periodically.

The following section introduces the different incarnations of the diverse redundancy on non-lockstep cores.

3   SafeDX Components

Diverse redundancy on non-lockstep cores has been realized with three different incarnations so far:

- **SafeDE** [2]. SafeDE is a hardware module enforcing staggered execution across two independent cores to achieve diversity analogously to DCLS.
- **SafeSoftDR** [16]. SafeSoftDR is a software library providing comparable functionality to SafeDE, but with software-only means.
- **SafeDM** [3]. SafeDM is a hardware module measuring diversity across two cores running a task redundantly building on the fact that having two cores fully synchronized is extremely unlikely to occur.

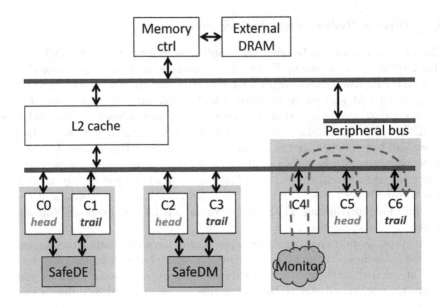

Fig. 2. Example of safety-critical microprocessor with SafeDX solutions integrated.

In the remaining of this section, we briefly introduce the three solutions. Figure 2 shows a simplified diagram of the integration of the solutions in a RISC-V SoC. This platform has been developed through the H2020 De-RISC [25], H2020 SELENE [12] and H2020 FRACTAL [15] projects.

3.1 SafeDE Hardware Diversity Enforcement Module

SafeDE is a hardware module enforcing staggered execution across two cores intended to run a task redundantly. For the sake of commodity, we refer to the core running the task replica ahead of the other as *head core* or only *head*, and the core running the task replica behind the other as *trail core* or only *trail*. SafeDE needs the following interface signals with the cores:

- (INPUT) Instruction count from both the head (I_{head}) and the trail cores (I_{trail}).
- (OUTPUT) Signals to reset the instruction counts of both the head and trail cores.
- (OUTPUT) Signal to stall the execution of the trail core only. However, since any of the two cores could take the role of trail core, the stall signal of both cores needs to be controlled by SafeDE.

The operation of SafeDE is as follows:

1. The staggering threshold (TH_{stag}) describing the minimum number of instructions that the head must be ahead of the tail must be initialized. This value relates to the number of instructions that the trail core can execute

before being effectively stalled once the stall signal is raised. For instance, if the stall signal stalls the fetch stage of the trail core, then TH_{stag} must be at least larger than the number of instructions that can be in-flight in the pipeline of a core, since those many instructions could be committed despite the fetch stage is stalled and hence, with a lower staggering the trail core could catch up with the head core despite being stalled. Typically, TH_{stag} is just some tens of instructions.

2. The cores enter into the redundantly executed region. This is indicated by writing a specific memory-mapped register (*active*) of SafeDE. The first core setting its *active* register, is regarded as the head core and the other one as the trail one.

3. Whenever one core sets its *active* register, SafeDE resets its instruction count.

4. Whenever the two cores have set their *active* registers, SafeDE reads I_{head} and I_{trail} continuously, computes the difference ($Diff = I_{head} - I_{trail}$), and compares it against TH_{stag}. If $Diff > TH_{stag}$, the stall signal of the trail core is unset, and it is set otherwise, hence stalling the trail core if it is only a few instructions behind the head one and there is risk of the trail catching up with the head.

5. Eventually, the head core completes the execution of the redundant code region and resets its *active* register. At that point, since only one *active* signal is up, the reset signal of the trail core is unset until it also resets its *active* register.

6. The user has to take care of comparing the outcome of redundant executions to detect errors.

Hence, SafeDE preserves staggered execution while both cores are in the protected code region. Note that SafeDE is only effective if both cores execute the same instruction stream. Otherwise, if cores execute different instruction streams, then their instruction counts are no longer enough to avoid synchronization, and staggering could be lost. Different instruction streams could be had if, for instance, an *if* condition depends on a random value that may differ across redundant processes or a physical address of some process-local data, which necessarily will differ across processes. Hence, in those where instruction streams may diverge, SafeDE must not be used and, instead, native DCLS execution is needed.

3.2   SafeSoftDR Software Diversity Enforcement Library

SafeSoftDR is a library providing analogous functionality to SafeDE but without any specific hardware support. Instruction counts from both head and trail cores, namely I_{head} and I_{trail} are reset and read by a software process which we refer to as *monitor* (see Fig. 2, core C4). The trail core execution is stalled and resumed using software signals (e.g., SIG_STOP and SIG_CONT) whenever needed. Overall, SafeSoftDR interface is as follows:

– (INPUT) Instruction count from both the head (I_{head}) and the trail cores (I_{trail}) accessed by software.

- (OUTPUT) API calls to reset the instruction counts of both the head and trail cores.
- (OUTPUT) Software signals to stall/resume the execution of the trail core only (e.g., SIG_STOP/SIG_CONT).

The operation of SafeSoftDR is as follows:

1. The end-user calls the monitor passing the function to be executed with diverse redundancy and its parameters as the monitor parameters.
2. The monitor replicates input and output data for the trail process.
3. The monitor resets I_{head} in the head core and spawns the head process on that core.
4. The monitor resets I_{trail} in the trail core, spawns the trail process on that core, and stalls it with SIG_STOP immediately.
5. The monitor reads with the appropriate API both I_{head} and I_{trail} from the head and trail cores, respectively, and proceeds analogously to SafeDE: computes the difference ($Diff = I_{head} - I_{trail}$), and compares it against TH_{stag}. If $Diff > TH_{stag}$, a SIG_CONT signal is sent to the trail core if it is stopped. Else, if $Diff \leq TH_{stag}$, a SIG_STOP signal is sent to the trail core if it is not stopped. This step periodically repeats every T_{check} cycles.
6. Eventually, the head process completes the execution. At that point, the monitor sends a SIG_CONT signal to the trail core if it is stopped and lets it execute until completion.
7. Whenever both processes complete their execution, the monitor compares their outcomes and returns whether the execution was faulty or fault-free.

Note that SafeSoftDR has two critical and related parameters: TH_{stag} and T_{check}. The latter defines the overhead incurred due to monitoring overheads. Such monitoring task, in the case of SafeDE, is not performed in any core since a specific module performs it. However, in the case of SafeSoftDR, the monitor runs on a core, hence using computing resources. Therefore, the larger T_{check}, the lower the overheads. However, TH_{stag} – the number of instructions used as staggering threshold – must be large enough so that the monitor can retrieve I_{head} and I_{trail} from the head and trail cores, compare them, and stall the trail core if needed, plus wait for T_{check} cycles until the next monitoring round. Hence, TH_{stag} is set to the maximum number of instructions that could be executed in that period, so the larger T_{check}, the larger TH_{stag}, and hence, the later the trail process will finish. Hence, from a staggering point of view, we want T_{check} to be as low as possible. Overall, as shown in [1], T_{check} values of around $100\mu s$ are convenient, although the particular value to use is completely architecture-dependent and must be tuned for the particular system at hand.

3.3   SafeDM Hardware Diversity Monitor

SafeDM, differently from SafeDE and SafeSoftDR, does not enforce diversity. It builds on the observation that powerful multicores running complex applications on top of sophisticated operating systems are very likely to provide naturally staggering across redundant tasks. Moreover, the fact that redundant processes are created at the software level makes them have different data addresses, which already brings diversity. Hence, diversity is very likely to exist. However, evidence is needed of such diversity to build the safety concept, and SafeDM provides such evidence. In particular, the safety concept can be built assuming that there is diversity as long as SafeDM does not report otherwise, and whenever a lack of diversity is reported, then corrective actions are taken at the system level.

Since random hardware faults have electrical effects impacting current flows at the circuit level, diversity needs to exist at the electrical level. Therefore, even if two cores are fully synchronized, executing the same instructions in the same pipeline stages, diversity may still exist if values being operated or carried out across stages differ (e.g., physical memory addresses). Therefore, SafeDM computes a signature for redundant cores building on the contents of the data pipeline registers and the current instructions at each stage, which determines the electrical activity occurring in the core. SafeDM computes a signature summarizing such information for each core (e.g., using XOR gates) and compares the signatures of both cores. If they differ, then diversity is guaranteed to exist. If they do not differ, either there is a lack of diversity, or such diversity exists but is not reflected in the signature due to different reasons, such as the following ones:

- Generating signatures can cause some aliasing so that diverse input data is mapped into identical signatures.
- Diversity may exist in non-monitored parts of the core (e.g., internal logic of complex functional units) but not in those registers used to compute the signature.

Hence, whenever a lack of diversity is reported, false positives may occur. In general, as shown in [3], those false positives are very unlikely to occur. A way to mitigate them is setting a threshold for the lack of diversity tolerated so that, for instance, if lack of diversity occurs less than 0.01% of the time during a given period (e.g., less of 100 cycles every 1,000,000 cycles), it is assumed that execution is diverse enough considering that it is extremely unlikely to have a CCF affecting only cycles with lack of diversity.

In any case, SafeDM counts the cycles with a lack of diversity, and it is up to the safety designer to determine when those values need to be read and reset.

Note that, differently from SafeDE and SafeSoftDR, SafeDM works independently of whether redundant cores follow divergent execution paths, hence posing fewer constraints on the software that can be run redundantly in the cores.

3.4 Comparison

Table 1 provides a comparison across the different solutions against the main features and limitations of the different solutions to achieve diverse redundancy. As shown, no solution is superior to the others on all fronts, and hence, the most convenient solution may vary across SoCs and across systems.

Table 1. Comparison across the different mechanisms for diverse redundancy.

Criteria	DCLS	SafeDE	SafeSoftDR	SafeDM
Diverse redundancy guaranteed	√	√	√	×
All cores are user visible	×	√	√	√
Low staggering	√	√	×	N/A
Non-intrusive execution	N/A	×	×	√
Supports divergent paths	N/A	×	×	√

4 Summary

Diverse redundancy is a mandatory safety measure for the most stringent integrity levels in safety-critical systems (e.g., ASIL-D in automotive according to ISO26262) since it allows preventing CCFs. Classic solutions build on DCLS that, while highly effective and efficient, make half of the cores not user-visible and hence, not usable by low-criticality or non-critical tasks. Software redundancy has been proposed as a way to alleviate DCLS disadvantages, but support for diversity is needed to adhere to the corresponding safety requirements.

This paper presents and compares alternative solutions to achieve diversity on top of software redundancy. In particular, it shows that SafeDE enforces diversity at the hardware level with low cost, yet potentially stalling the trail core. SafeSoftDR performs analogous functionality to SafeDE, but without hardware support, yet imposing non-negligible staggering between the head and trail core. Finally, SafeDM, while not enforcing diversity explicitly, is non-intrusive with the execution of the tasks and poses no constraints on whether redundant tasks can take divergent paths.

References

1. Alcaide, S., Kosmidis, L., Hernandez, C., Abella, J.: Software-only based diverse redundancy for ASIL-D automotive applications on embedded HPC platforms. In: 2020 IEEE International Symposium on Defect and Fault Tolerance in VLSI and Nanotechnology Systems (DFT), pp. 1–4 (2020). https://doi.org/10.1109/DFT50435.2020.9250750
2. Bas, F., et al.: SafeDE: a flexible diversity enforcement hardware module for light-lockstepping. In: IEEE International Symposium on On-Line Testing and Robust System Design (IOLTS), pp. 1–7 (2021). https://doi.org/10.1109/IOLTS52814.2021.9486715
3. Bas, F., Benedicte, P., Alcaide, S., Cabo, G., Mazzocchetti, F., Abella, J.: SafeDM: a hardware diversity monitor for redundant execution on non-lockstepped cores. In: IEEE Design, Automation and Test in Europe Conference (DATE), pp. 1–6 (2022)
4. Cabo, G., et al.: SafeSU-2: safe statistics unit for space MPSoCs. In: IEEE Design, Automation and Test in Europe Conference (DATE) (2022)

5. Cabo, G., et al.: SafeSU: an extended statistics unit for multicore timing interference. In: IEEE European Test Symposium (ETS) (2021)
6. CAES Gaisler: GRLIB IP Library. https://gaisler.com/index.php/products/ipcores/soclibrary
7. CAES Gaisler: NOEL-V Processor. https://gaisler.com/index.php/products/processors/noel-v
8. EN50129 - railway applications. communication, signalling and processing systems. Safety related electronic systems for signalling (2003)
9. EN50128 - railway applications: Communication, signalling and processing systems - software for railway control and protection systems (2011)
10. EN50126 - railway applications: The specification and demonstration of dependability, reliability, availability, maintainability and safety (rams). Generic RAMs process (2017)
11. FRACTAL Consortium: FRACTAL website (2021). https://www.fractal-project.eu/. Accessed May 2022
12. Hernàndez, C., et al.: Selene: self-monitored dependable platform for high-performance safety-critical systems. In: 2020 23rd Euromicro Conference on Digital System Design (DSD), pp. 370–377 (2020). https://doi.org/10.1109/DSD51259.2020.00066
13. Infineon: AURIX Multicore 32-bit microcontroller family to meet safety and powertrain requirements of upcoming vehicle generations. http://www.infineon.com/cms/en/about-infineon/press/press-releases/2012/INFATV201205-040.html
14. International Standards Organization: ISO/DIS 26262. Road Vehicles - Functional Safety (2009)
15. Lojo, A., et al.: The ECSEL fractal project: a cognitive fractal and secure edge based on a unique open-safe-reliable-low power hardware platform. In: 2020 23rd Euromicro Conference on Digital System Design (DSD), pp. 393–400 (2020). https://doi.org/10.1109/DSD51259.2020.00069
16. Mazzocchetti, F., et al.: SafeSoftDR: a library to enable software-based diverse redundancy for safety-critical tasks. In: FORECAST: Functional Properties and Dependability in Cyber-Physical Systems Workshop (held with HiPEAC conference) (2022)
17. NSI-TEXE: NS31A : RISC-V 32bit CPU which supports ISO26262 ASIL D. https://www.nsitexe.com/en/ip-solutions/ns-series/ns31a/
18. RISC-V International: RISC-V International website. https://riscv.org/
19. RTCA and EUROCAE: DO-178B/ED-12B, Software Considerations in Airborne Systems and Equipment Certification (1992)
20. RTCA and EUROCAE: DO-254/ED-80, Design Assurance Guidance for Airborne Electronic Hardware (2000)
21. Sala, O., et al.: SafeTI: a hardware traffic injector for MPSOC functional and timing validation. In: IEEE International Symposium on On-Line Testing and Robust System Design (IOLTS), pp. 1–7 (2021). https://doi.org/10.1109/IOLTS52814.2021.9486689
22. SELENE Consortium: SELENE website (2021). https://www.selene-project.eu/. Accessed May 2022
23. ISO/PAS 21448 road vehicles - safety of the intended functionality (2019)
24. STMicroelectronics: 32-bit Power Architecture microcontroller for automotive SIL3/ASILD chassis and safety applications (2014)
25. Wessman, N.J., et al.: De-RISC: the first RISC-V space-grade platform for safety-critical systems. In: 2021 IEEE Space Computing Conference (SCC), pp. 17–26 (2021). https://doi.org/10.1109/SCC49971.2021.00010

HW/SW Acceleration of Multiple Workloads Within the SERRANO's Computing Continuum

Invited Paper

Argyris Kokkinis[✉], Aggelos Ferikoglou, Ioannis Oroutzoglou,
Dimitrios Danopoulos, Dimosthenis Masouros, and Kostas Siozios

Aristotle University of Thessaloniki, Thessaloniki, Greece
{akokkino,aferikog,ioroutzo,ddanopou,dmasoura,ksiop}@physics.auth.gr

Abstract. Nowadays, we witness emerging cloud technologies and a growth of cloud computing services that are used for numerous applications with diverse requirements. Although the technological innovations in the field of cloud computing; a power-efficient and automatic deployment of different applications in a multi-cloud environment is still a major challenge. SERRANO aims to take important steps in providing a transparent way of deploying applications in the Edge-Cloud-HPC computing continuum, by providing an abstraction layer that automates the process of application deployment across the various computing platforms and realizing an intent-based paradigm of operating federated infrastructures. In this paper, the acceleration process of different algorithms in the edge and cloud infrastructure of the SERRANO's platform is described. Specifically, we showcase the benefits of HW and SW acceleration in four different algorithms from three use-case scenarios. The achieved results show that an increase at the application's performance ranging from 7x and 6.6x up to 229x and 113.14x for the cloud and edge devices respectively, can be achieved when the evaluated workloads are executed in the SERRANO's infrastructure.

Keywords: Edge computing · Cloud continuum · Hardware accelerators · GPU · FPGA · Heterogeneous computing · SERRANO

1 Introduction

Nowadays, the ever-increasing demands for high performance computations and low power designs have fundamentally changed the human perspective on developing and executing applications on both the edge and the cloud [1]. Next-generation analytics, Machine Learning (ML) algorithms and workloads that require high-performance are deployed on heterogeneous computing ecosystems with diverse computational capabilities and power requirements [2]. Edge computing is typically hindered by power consumption, area footprint and cost [3], while high-performance computations in data centers require secure and high-speed data transfer from the local platforms to the processing infrastructures [4].

© The Author(s), under exclusive license to Springer Nature Switzerland AG 2022
A. Orailoglu et al. (Eds.): SAMOS 2022, LNCS 13511, pp. 394–405, 2022.
https://doi.org/10.1007/978-3-031-15074-6_25

To meet the user requirements for energy-efficiency, high throughput and security in the new computing paradigm, adaptive computing has been introduced [5]. Acceleration platforms such as Graphics Processing Units (GPUs) and Field-Programmable Gate Arrays (FPGAs) can achieve higher performance than most of the typical processing systems without compromising the user requirements for energy-efficiency and security [6]. A solution for achieving energy-efficient and high-performance execution is to utilize HW and SW accelerators at the entire computing ecosystem, from the edge to the cloud, leveraging the low power consumption of the edge devices and the processing power of the data centers [7].

In this paper, we present the process of accelerating algorithms in the SERRANO's [8] infrastructure, towards generating a library of SW and HW IP[1] kernels that will showcase the capabilities of the SERRANO platform. The rest of this manuscript is structured as follows: Sect. 2 provides background information on GPU and FPGA acceleration. In Sect. 3 the SERRANO platform described and the accelerated algorithms that compose the library of accelerators is analyzed. In Sect. 4, the platform's future goals are discussed. Finally, Sect. 5 concludes this paper.

2 Background

Designing hardware for FPGAs can be performed at varying levels of abstraction with the commonly used being the register-transfer level (RTL) and the algorithmic level. These methodologies differ; RTL (i.e., VHDL, Verilog) is used for circuit-level programming while algorithmic level methodologies such as High-Level Synthesis (HLS) are used for describing designs in a more abstract way. Although the traditional FPGA design flow is able to deliver performance and power optimized solutions, the increasing demands for a small time to market window has led to the adoption of the latter designing methods for generating efficient hardware accelerators [9].

Xilinx Inc. [10], one of the main FPGA vendors on the market, has put significant effort into providing a user-friendly toolset for employing HLS for FPGA design. In this context, Xilinx introduced Vitis, a framework which provides a unified OpenCL interface for programming edge and cloud Xilinx FPGAs. Vitis aims to simplify the designing process and as a result let developers focus on the Design Space Exploration (DSE) phase, which targets the performance optimizations with respect to the architecture and resources of the available devices.

In HLS context directives are added in the C/C++ kernel code, to instruct the compiler on how to synthesise the bitstream (the representation that is used for programming the device). There is a wide range of different directives (also referred to as pragmas) that a developer can use. Pragmas are mainly divided in two categories: a) those that affect kernel performance and b) those that aim to provide helpful information to the compiler for the synthesis process (e.g., define the minimum and maximum iterations of a for loop, define false dependencies).

---

[1] Intellectual Property.

Similarly to the FPGAs, GPUs are widely used in the recent years for accelerating computationally intensive applications. Over the last few years, GPUs have already become a fundamental component in most of the world's fastest supercomputers, considered among the most mature and widely-used type of hardware accelerators. Additionally, while their programmability is significantly improved over the years with high level languages (such as CUDA and OpenCL) GPU programming is more and more becoming mainstream in the scientific community.

CUDA, the most popular GPU programming model, stands for Compute Unified Device Architecture and is a parallel programming paradigm supporting only NVIDIA GPUs, which was released in 2007 by NVIDIA [11]. On the other hand, OpenCL (Open Computing Language) was launched by Apple and the Khronos group as a way to provide a benchmark for heterogeneous computing that was not restricted to only NVIDIA GPU's. It offers a portable language for GPU programming that can run on CPUs, GPUs, Digital Signal Processors and other types of processors. Additionally, the CUDA programming model enables developers to scale software, increasing the number of GPU processor cores as needed, while we can use CUDA language abstractions to program applications and divide programs into small independent problems.

3   The SERRANO Platform

SERRANO's[2] target is to introduce an ecosystem of technologies that will allow the seamless and transparent execution of various workloads on cloud and edge resources. Those new technologies will range from specialized hardware resources and SW/HW co-design methodologies up to software toolsets that will customize the workloads' execution based on their performance, energy efficiency and QoS[3] requirements. Therefore, through the SERRANO platform, performance demanding and security-critical applications will be executed on the cloud, edge and fog computing devices that will be able to dynamically satisfy the user-defined requirements. Besides, edge and cloud resources, SERRANO will also incorporate HPC[4] processing nodes in its infrastructure, having a plethora of heterogeneous computing resources.

The SERRANO platform will allow the transformation of cloud, distributed edge and HPC resources into a single infrastructure. The workloads' execution in the computing continuum will be controlled by an automated cognitive and resource-aware orchestrator. The SERRANO platform aims to introduce novel concepts and approaches that target to close existing technology gaps, towards the realization of a unified cloud-to-edge infrastructure. Technologies and mechanisms related to security and privacy in distributed computing and storage systems will be developed as well as hardware and software acceleration on cloud and edge. Finally, technological approaches and methodologies that aim

---

[2] https://ict-serrano.eu/.

[3] Quality-of-Service.

[4] High-Performance Computing.

Table 1. Accelerates algorithms per use-case scenario

Use-case	Algorithm	Description
Secure storage	AES	Encryption/decryption
FinTech	Kalman Filter	Time-series smoothing
FinTech	Savitzky-Golay Filter	Time-series smoothing
Anomaly detection	DBSCAN	Clustering algorithm

to improve the domains of cloud secure storage, dynamic data movement among cloud to edge devices and energy efficient execution of workloads at different computing nodes will compose the SERRANO platform.

The realization of the SERRANO platform will be evaluated on three use-cases from the industry: (i) a use-case from the field of security and distributed data storage, (ii) a use-case on machine anomaly detection in manufacturing environments and (iii) a use-case from the fintech domain on market prediction and portfolio analysis.

The SERRANO infrastructure:

The cloud infrastructure is coupled with both programmable FPGA accelerators and GPU devices. These FPGA and GPU accelerators are used not only to increase the performance of servers but also to increase the power efficiency. These devices are connected in the server though PCI, specifically PCI Express 3.0 x16, an interface standard for connecting high-speed components. Then they will be selected in a seamless and common mechanism for deployment based on the application, requirements. The cloud FPGA and GPU devices that are attached in the SERRANO's cloud side are: (i) one Xilinx Alveo U200 acceleration card, (ii) one Xilinx Alveo U50 acceleration card and (iii) two NVIDIA Tesla T4 GPUs. In addition to the above, NVIDIA BlueField-2 Data Processing Units (DPUs) are also provided.

In the edge infrastructure. System on a Chip (SoC) devices are deployed. Those devices include chips that are either FPGA or GPU and processor which is usually an ARM embedded CPU (Cortex A53 or Cortex A9), DDR memories and the peripherals. The edge FPGA and GPU devices of the SERRANO's infrastructure are: (i) one Xilinx MPSoC ZCU102 device, (ii) one Xilinx MPSoC ZCU104 device, (iii) one NVIDIA Xavier AGX and (iv) one NVIDIA Xavier NX. Furthermore. the SmartBox device which is an industry-ready box for data gathering at the edge with a 60GB disk size is also employed at the SERRANO's edge side.

Among the multiple **HPC** [12] resources that are provided in the SERRANO platform, the HPE Apollo 9000 Hawk is one of them. This is an HPC unit with 5,632 compute nodes with a peak performance of 26 PetaFLOPS.

3.1 SERRANO's Architecture

The architecture of the SERRANO platform will follow an hierarchical model for orchestrating the workloads' execution in the heterogeneous infrastructure.

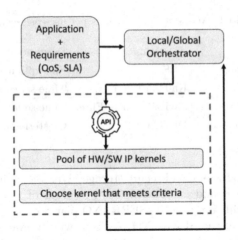

Fig. 1. The orchestration process of enabling the most suitable accelerated version

Specifically, SERRANO will employ three distinct mechanisms based on Machine-Learning (ML) models:

(i) the central resource orchestrator: This is the central resource-aware orchestration component that decides the computing ecosystem (i.e. cloud, fog, edge) that is suitable for the execution of the provided workload.

(ii) a set of local orchestastors: Those components are aware of the availability of the underlying nodes at the corresponding computing ecosystem and direct the execution of workload towards the node that is available and can optimally deliver the user requirements for energy efficiency and performance.

(iii) the telemetry framework: This mechanism part of the SERRANO platform collects and analyses data across the SERRANO infrastructure and dynamically communicates with the SERRANO's central resource orchestrator. As a result, the workloads' execution can be dynamically re-directed to different computing nodes across the SERRANO ecosystem and optimized on the fly based on the user-defined requirements.

3.2 SERRANO's Library of Accelerators

In order to evaluate the SERRANO platform on the three use-cases a library that consists of accelerated applications from the three use-case scenarios for the cloud, edge and HPC computing nodes is developed. Each accelerated version of the corresponding algorithms will exhibit different performance, energy efficiency and QoS behavior allowing the central and the local orchestrators to select the version of the accelerator and the computing node that best fits the current criteria. This flow is depicted in the Fig. 1.

Table 1 shows the algorithms that have been accelerated per use-case scenario.

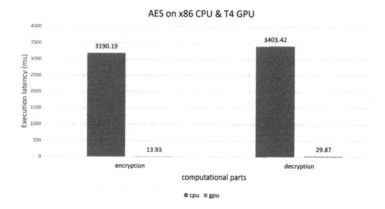

Fig. 2. Acceleration of AES tasks on cloud NVIDA T4 GPU

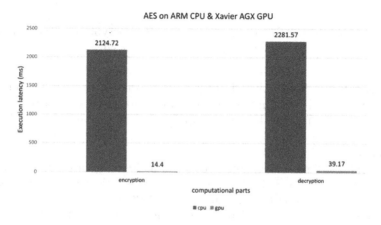

Fig. 3. Acceleration of AES tasks on edge NVIDIA Xavier AGX GPU

AES:

AES-GCM (Advanced Encryption Standard with Galois Counter Mode) [13] is a block cipher mode of operation that provides high speed of authenticated encryption and data integrity and is suitable to be employed in communication or electronic applications. It consists of two main functions, block cipher encryption and multiplication and it can either encrypt or decrypt with 128-bit, 192-bit or 256- bit of cipher key. For the SERRANO use case, an AES-GCM algorithm of 256-bits is implemented.

The AES encryption and decryption tasks were accelerated on the cloud and edge GPU devices of the SERRANO infrastructure, a NVIDIA T4 and a Xavier AGX. Two CUDA kernels of 1024 threads were developed for the two parts of the AES algorithm. The accelerated versions were evaluated for encrypting and decrypting 32 MB data. The Figs. 2 and 3 show the latency of the two accelerated tasks compared to the baseline CPU execution. Specifically, a speedup of 229x

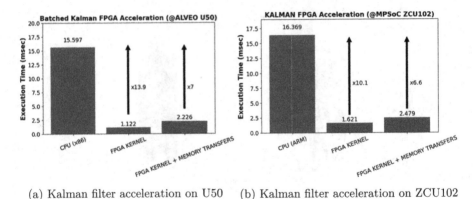

(a) Kalman filter acceleration on U50   (b) Kalman filter acceleration on ZCU102

Fig. 4. Acceleration of Kalman filter on Alveo U50 and MPSoC ZCU102

and 113.14x is achieved for the encryption and the decryption tasks at the cloud GPU device while the execution time speedup for the edge device is 147.55x and 58.14x respectively.

Kalman Filter: The Kalman filter [14], also referred to as linear quadratic estimation, is used to estimate unknown variables based on a series of noisy measurements. It has a wide range of applications in guidance, navigation and finance. Kalman filtering is based on a linear dynamical system discretized in the time domain.

The Kalman filter was approximately parallelized and accelerated on cloud and edge FPGAs of the SERRANO infrastructure, specifically on the Alveo U50 acceleration card and on the ZCU102 MPSoC FPGA.

To accelerate a sequential application (such as Kalman filter) the original code should be restructured in a way that parts of the execution flow can be parallelized. In the Kalman filter's case, we split the initial signal into multiple batches and perform filtering in parallel to each of these sub-signals. Although this parallelization strategy breaks the dependency, it is evident that it approximates the original algorithm's output.

At first, the way the described parallelization strategy affects the algorithm's output is investigated. The batch size is the most important parameter in this approach as the more batches we use the higher parallelization we can achieve. To further investigate this parameter, batched Kalman filters are executed for different batch sizes and measure the score (i.e. the number of output values that are equal to the original). As the input signal consists of floating-point values, we consider that two numbers are equal when their absolute difference is below 0.001. The results of the experiment are depicted in the Fig. 5. This Figure shows that as the batch size increases, and hence less batches are used, the algorithm's output becomes more like the original. The acceleration of the Kalman filter was evaluated for smoothing a time-series of 200 KB.

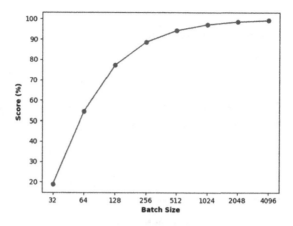

Fig. 5. Batched Kalman Filter's score for different batch sizes

Based on Fig. 4a 7x decrease at the algorithm's execution time is achieved when the acceleration card is employed. Similarly, based on Fig. 4 the speedup at the edge device is 6.6x. In both cases the time that is required for transferring data to and from the FPGA accelerator are measured.

Savitzky-Golay Filter: The Savitzky-Golay filter [15] is a digital filter that is frequently used for smoothing time series data by fitting adjacent data points with low-degree polynomials. The smoothing process is performed by applying discrete convolution between the signal's coefficients and adjacent data points.

In order to accelerate the Savitzky-Golay filter on FPGAs a dataflow architecture was designed. This architecture is composed of three distinct sub-units, namely the **read, convolve** and **write**. Those units were designed in order to perform the memory read, write and the convolution computations in a pipelined manner. The designed architecture is illustrated in the Fig. 6. The operation of the read, compute and write components is described below.

read: The purpose of this module is to perform memory read transactions through the interface port and store the input's signal values in a First-In-First-Out (FIFO) stream. The FIFO stream has a depth of two and buffers the input elements, allowing the convolve module to perform operations continuously without stalling its operation for reading data from the memory.

compute: This sub-component performs the convolution task and begins its operation once the first window[5] input values have been stored in an array in the local memory. The convolution is performed in pipelined loops with each loop executing a number of window multiplications between the input signal and the filter's coefficients in parallel. Moreover, a shifting mechanism is used for accessing the next available input data. Specifically, when all the window input values that are stored locally have been convolved, then the elements of

---

[5] i.e. a filter's parameter that is defined by the designer [15].

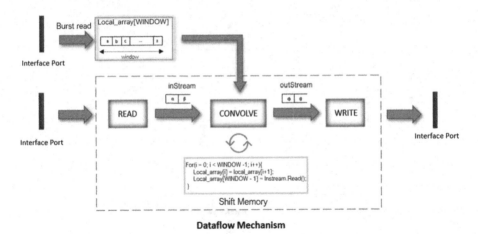

Dataflow Mechanism

Fig. 6. Designed acceleration architecture

this array are shifted, and the first element of the FIFO stream is moved in the last address of the local array. This process is repeated until all the input data elements have been moved in the local memory array and have been convolved. The output of each convolution is stored in a FIFO stream that is connected to the write module.

write: This module performs the memory write transactions by writing the output data elements that are stored in the FIFO stream, provided by the convolve unit, to the global memory.

The acceleration of the Savitzky-Golay filter was evaluated on a time-series of 200 KB and the proposed accelerators were deployed on Alveo U50 acceleration card and on the ZCU102 MPSoC FPGA. Based on Fig. 7 a speedup of 17.5x is achieved for the filter's execution on the U50 card, similarly the speedup at the edge device is 17.8x.

DBSCAN: Density-based spatial clustering of applications with noise (DBS CAN) is a data clustering algorithm proposed by Martin Ester, Hans-Peter Kriegel, Jörg Sander and Xiaowei Xu in 1996 [16]. It is a density-based clustering non-parametric algorithm, meaning that given a set of points in some space, it groups together points that are closely packed together, marking as outlier points that lie alone in low-density regions. DBSCAN is one of the most common clustering algorithms and also most cited in scientific literature. The density of instances is a key concept in the DBSCAN algorithm. The intuition is that the most common patterns will be close to each other, whereas the anomalous ones will be far from the nominal ones. By computing the pairwise distance measures of the instances, the areas that fulfil some criteria are identified and the instances are grouped. These criteria are specified by two parameters that define when two instances are considered close as well as the minimum quantity of close instances needed to consider an independent cluster. There is also the possibility for DBSCAN to not classify cer-

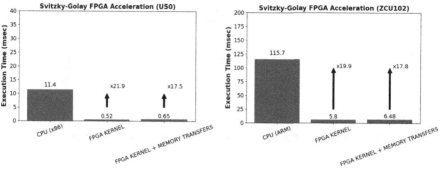

(a) Savitzky-Golay filter acceleration on U50

(b) Savitzky-Golay filter acceleration on. ZCU102

Fig. 7. Acceleration of Svitzky-Golay filter on Alveo U50 and MPSoC ZCU102

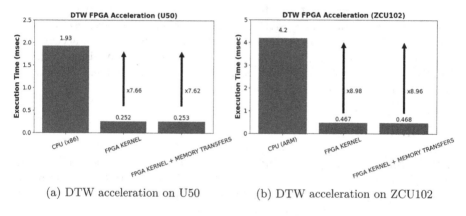

(a) DTW acceleration on U50

(b) DTW acceleration on ZCU102

Fig. 8. Acceleration of DTW on Alveo U50 and MPSoC ZCU102

tain instances in a particular cluster, if they are too far from the others. Dynamic time warping (DTW) is an algorithm for measuring similarity between two temporal sequences. This algorithm (i.e. DTW) is the computational kernel of the DBSCAN algorithm. Therefore, the DTW is accelerated in the cloud and edge FPGAs of the SERRANOs infrastructure.

The acceleration strategy of the DTW algorithm that was followed is based on the instantiation of multiple IP circuits on the FPGA device and their parallel execution for different chunks of the input data. In addition, all of the algorithm's loops were pipelined using the corresponding HLS directive. The target initiation interval (II) was set to one (II = 1). Finally, custom data types were used to further decrease the available resources and create a more efficient design. The accelerated algorithms were evaluated on 200 KB input data targeting the Alveo U50 acceleration card and the ZCU102 MPSoC FPGA. Furthermore, 6 IPs are executed in parallel in the U50 card while only two in the edge ZCU102 device. Based on Fig. 8 a speedup of 7.62x is achieved for the filter's execution on the U50 card and the speedup at the ZCU102 FPGA is 8.96x.

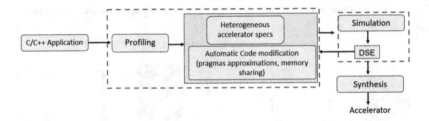

Fig. 9. Semi-automated flow for creating a library of accelerators

4   Future Work

The next step of the SERRANO project is the development of tools that will facilitate the designer to develop accelerators for edge and cloud GPU and FPGA devices. Based on those tools the acceleration process will be semi-automated, minimizing the design time and increasing the accelerators' performance and energy efficiency. Based on those tools, the library of accelerators will be enriched, allowing the SERRANO's orchestration mechanisms to choose the optimal accelerators for execution for every user requirement. This semi-automated designing flow is illustrated in Fig. 9.

5   Conclusions

In this manuscript we present the process of accelerating various algorithms on cloud and edge devices within the SERRANO's computing continuum and towards the direction of creating a library of multiple accelerators. Also we manage to provide acceleration techniques for edge and cloud infrastructures. We describe various programming models that enables us to accelerate the use-cases and we further examine a set of optimization techniques. Finally, we apply and evaluate our accelerators on hardware and software devices, showing that we achieve up to x229 performance speedup compared to baseline CPU execution.

Acknowledgments. This work has been supported by the E.C. funded program SER-RANO under H2020 Grant Agreement No: 101017168.

References

1. Firouzi, F., Farahani, B., Marinšek, A.: The convergence and interplay of edge, fog, and cloud in the AI-driven internet of things (IoT). Inf. Syst. **107**, 101840 (2022)
2. Massari, G., Pupykina, A., Agosta, G., Fornaciari, W.: Predictive resource management for next-generation high-performance computing heterogeneous platforms. In: Pnevmatikatos, D.N., Pelcat, M., Jung, M. (eds.) SAMOS 2019. LNCS, vol. 11733, pp. 470–483. Springer, Cham (2019). https://doi.org/10.1007/978-3-030-27562-4_34

3. Shi, W., Cao, J., Zhang, Q., Li, Y., Xu, L.: Edge computing: vision and challenges. IEEE Internet Things J. **3**(5), 637–646 (2016)
4. Ungerer, T., Carpenter, P. Eurolab-4-HPC long-term vision on high-performance computing, arXiv:1807.04521 (2018)
5. Xilinx, Accelerate Your AI-Enabled Edge Solution with Adaptive Computing, Introducing Adaptive System-on-Modules, e-book
6. Wu, Q., Ha, Y., Kumar, A., Luo, S., Li, A., Mohamed, S.: A heterogeneous platform with GPU and FPGA for power efficient high performance computing. In: 2014 International Symposium on Integrated Circuits (ISIC), pp. 220–223. IEEE, December 2014
7. Kokkinis, A., Ferikoglou, A., Danopoulos, D., Masouros, D., Siozios, K.: Leveraging HW approximation for exploiting performance-energy trade-offs within the edge-cloud computing continuum. In: Jagode, H., Anzt, H., Ltaief, H., Luszczek, P. (eds.) ISC High Performance 2021. LNCS, vol. 12761, pp. 406–415. Springer, Cham (2021). https://doi.org/10.1007/978-3-030-90539-2_27
8. Ferikoglou, A., et al.: Towards efficient HW acceleration in edge-cloud infrastructures: the SERRANO approach. In: Orailoglu, A., Jung, M., Reichenbach, M. (eds.) SAMOS 2021. LNCS, vol. 13227, pp. 354–367. Springer, Cham (2022). https://doi.org/10.1007/978-3-031-04580-6_24
9. Numan, M.W., Phillips, B.J., Puddy, G.S., Falkner, K.: Towards automatic high-level code deployment on reconfigurable platforms: a survey of high-level synthesis tools and toolchains. IEEE Access **8**, 174692–174722 (2020)
10. Xilinx (2022). https://www.xilinx.com
11. Sanders, J., Kandrot, E.: CUDA by Example: An Introduction to General-Purpose GPU Programming. Addison-Wesley Professional, Boston (2010)
12. HLRS, Systems - HLRS High Performance Computing Center Stuttgart 2016–2020. https://www.hlrs.de/systems/
13. Käsper, E., Schwabe, P.: Faster and timing-attack resistant AES-GCM. In: Clavier, C., Gaj, K. (eds.) CHES 2009. LNCS, vol. 5747, pp. 1–17. Springer, Heidelberg (2009). https://doi.org/10.1007/978-3-642-04138-9_1
14. Welch, G., Bishop, G.: An introduction to the Kalman filter (1995)
15. Press, W.H., Teukolsky, S.A.: Savitzky-Golay smoothing filters. Comput. Phys. **4**(6), 669–672 (1990)
16. Ester, M., Kriegel, H.P., Sander, J., Xu, X.: A density-based algorithm for discovering clusters in large spatial databases with noise. In: KDD, vol. 96, no. 34, pp. 226–231, August 1996

LSTM Acceleration with FPGA and GPU Devices for Edge Computing Applications in B5G MEC

Dimitrios Danopoulos[1]([envelope]), Ioannis Stamoulias[1,2], George Lentaris[1], Dimosthenis Masouros[1], Ioannis Kanaropoulos[1], Andreas Kosmas Kakolyris[1], and Dimitrios Soudris[1]

[1] National Technical University of Athens, Athens, Greece
{dimdano,glentaris,dsoudris}@microlab.ntua.gr
[2] National and Kapodistrian University of Athens, Athens, Greece

Abstract. The advent of AI/ML in B5G and Multi-Access Edge Computing will rely on the acceleration of neural networks. The current work focuses on the acceleration of Long Short-Term Memory (LSTM) kernels playing a key role in numerous applications. We assume various LSTM sizes while targeting FPGA and GPU hardware for both embedded and server MEC purposes. Systematically, we perform a design space exploration to determine the most efficient acceleration approach and most suitable configuration for each device. We use High-Level-Synthesis to implement our proposed circuit architectures on Xilinx FPGAs, while we use high level tools for NVIDIA GPUs such as PyTorch's JIT compiler or ONNX runtime. Our exploration shows that the full parallelization of an LSTM array multiplication quickly overutilizes the FPGA, while on GPUs LSTM models can be deployed more easily. Instead, the best approach for FPGAs is to find a balance between parallelizing LSTM gates and vector multiplications. Our comparative study shows that FPGAs prevail in light LSTM models, whereas GPUs prevail in larger model topologies. Moreover, we show that far- and near-edge FPGAs achieve similar latency, however, near-edge GPUs can achieve one order of magnitude faster execution than far-edge GPUs. The best results range in 0.3–5 ms latency per execution with acceleration factors in 12×–174×.

Keywords: 5G · Forecasting · Anomaly detection · LSTM · FPGA · GPU

1 Introduction

Emerging applications in the edge computing era require efficient AI/ML and high performance computing systems to process huge amounts of data at remote locations. Especially in the upcoming B5G/6G networks, AI/ML is expected to play a key role in the MEC domain, both for user applications and for infrastructure zero-touch management. Everyday scenarios, such as autonomous vehicles and smart city/factory operations, will rely on processing & decisions made closer to the location of data generation due to extremely low-latency requirements. Real-time analytics and forecasting will force the adoption of hardware accelerators across the entire edge–cloud computing continuum with small and large devices, and especially GPUs and FPGAs.

The LSTM type of artificial neural network has achieved state-of-the-art classification accuracy in multiple useful tasks for MEC applications, such as the aforementioned forecasting, network intrusion detection, and anomaly detection [6]. Anomaly detection algorithms identify data/observations deviating from normal behavior in a dataset. Similarly, forecasting algorithms estimate what will happen in the future by using historical data. The LSTM provide solutions at the cost of increased compute and memory requirements, which makes their deployment challenging, especially for resource-constrained platforms, such as embedded FPGAs and GPUs. Furthermore, the internal mechanisms of LSTM networks make it more challenging to parallelize the computations in an acceleration platform as they require state-keeping in between processing steps. This creates data dependencies and often limits the parallelization degrees.

Recently, the research community has started deploying hardware accelerators of LSTM networks to increase the performance and energy efficiency of such computationally intensive tasks for data prediction on the aforementioned scenarios. Also, depending on the scenario, throughput or latency optimized systems need to be developed. Thus, it is important to embrace the heterogeneity paradigm in order to provide high performance systems, such as FPGAs and GPUs, which can cover a plethora of acceleration schemes and offload the general purpose CPUs when needed.

To study the computational aspects and the benefits of accelerating LSTMs in a practical fashion, the current paper presents our exploration of implementing LSTM kernels on FPGA and GPU devices for both far- and near-edge computing scenarios. The main contributions are:

1. Examine various LSTM structures from an acceleration point of view, i.e., assess parallelization and overhead benefits/costs for certain types of HW.
2. We extend our study for multiple LSTM kernels and devices, i.e., anomaly detection and timeseries forecasting, on multiple small and large FPGA/GPUs of distinct underlying architecture and CPU-to-device interfaces.
3. We perform a design space exploration (DSE) to determine the most efficient acceleration approach based on certain performance trade-offs and Quality of Service (QoS) preferences.

2   Background and Related Work

2.1   AI@EDGE with Acceleration for MEC

The H2020 project *AI@EDGE* [7] aims to develop a "connect-compute" platform that efficiently creates and manages end-to-end network slices. This decentralized HW & SW platform will be placed inside broader MEC domain(s) to support a diverse range of AI-enabled applications and provide security/privacy, flexibility, and acceleration. In particular, *AI@EDGE* key underlying technologies include HW virtualization, multi-tier orchestration, serverless computing, programmable pipelines to create and use trustworthy AI/ML models upon request, multi-connectivity disaggregated radio access, as well as multiple forms of programmable HW acceleration. The final AI/ML capabilities of the platform will serve both the closed-loop automation for the infrastructure/network (e.g., monitoring, zero-touch management) and also the applications at user level (e.g., download and execute certain AI functions upon user request).

Towards achieving the aforementioned goals, which combine acceleration with virtualization and easy-to-use (even serverless) computing, the selected approach was to exploit ubiquitous SW frameworks and diverse HW devices from dominant GPU and FPGA vendors. That is to say, e.g., instead of low-level FPGA programming with VHDL, we opted for high-level synthesis and TensorFlow-based end-to-end toolflows. Such an approach facilitates quick development and flexible function deployment via Docker containers, i.e., makes the platform attractive to users and facilitates the integration of multiple HW accelerators to an already complex distributed system. Representative devices in the "connect-compute" platform include Xilinx U280 FPGA [16] and NVIDIA V100 [12] for near-edge nodes (server-class computing), as well as Xilinx Zynq MPSoC [19] and NVIDIA Jetson AGX Xavier [10] for far-edge nodes (embedded computing). Representative toolflows include Xilinx Vitis AI and Vitis HLS for FPGAs [17,18], as well as NVIDIA CUDA-X and ONNX for GPUs [1,11].

2.2 LSTMs for Time Series Prediction

LSTM networks are a type of Recurrent Neural Network (RNN) that uses more sophisticated units in addition to standard units. The LSTM cell adds long-term memory with its special gates inside in order to solve problems that require learning long-term temporal dependencies. More specifically, a number of "gates" is used to control the information inside the memory, keeping, forgetting or ignoring it when needed. This very important in order to learn the long-term dependencies in sequences which have a long-term trend. Designing an optimal LSTM for Time Series Prediction can be challenging and it requires extensive hyperparameter tuning. For example, the number of LSTM cells used to represent the sequence can be crucial in achieving high accuracy.

Besides predicting future sequences in time-series, LSTMs can successfully detect anomalies in data. Constructed as autoencoders [2], the goal is to minimize reconstruction error based on a loss function, such as the mean squared error. Autoencoders are self-supervised learning models that can learn a compressed representation of input data. When coupled with LSTM layers in a Encoder-Decoder LSTM topology, it allows the model to be used to encode, decode and recreate the input sequence. LSTM autoencoder networks are widely used in many applications for real-time anomaly detection such as manufacturing, network intrusion detection systems and others [9,14].

2.3   Related Work

To optimize the performance or power efficiency of LSTM networks, which cover a wide range of applications, a plethora of hardware accelerators has been proposed from the academia. These applications span from anomaly detection systems [5] such as network intrusion or timeseries forecasting. The following related work involves designs for similar accelerator platforms for relatively similar problems that cover our domain problem.

A plethora of FPGA implementations have been investigated such as [3] in which the authors accelerated an LSTM model on a Xilinx FPGA achieving 21× speed-up from the ARM Cortex-A9 CPU of the embedded SoC. Also, Chang et al. [4] presented three hardware accelerators for RNN on Xilinx's Zynq SoC FPGA for character level language model achieving up to 23× better performance per power than a Tegra X1 board. Additionally, in FINN-L [15] the authors presented a library extension for accelerating Bidirectional Long Short-Term Memory (BiLSTM) neural networks on FPGA. They performed a thorough DSE in terms of power, performance and accuracy and showed the throughput scalability on a Pynq and MPSoC FPGA board, although no latency metrics were presented. Last, Fowers et al. [8] presented the Brainwave NPU which achieved more than an order of magnitude improvement in latency and throughput over state-of-the-art GPUs on large RNNs at a batch size of 1. Concerning GPU implementations, there is fewer related work as they usually pose a smaller research problem as FPGA implementations. However, there are quiet a few implementations [20, 21] which focus on LSTM training on GPU platforms in order to reduce energy footprint and accelerate the training algorithm.

3   Methodology

Our primary purpose is to assess the complexity and efficiency of accelerating LSTM-based networks on GPU and FPGA devices in the context of a decreased/viable time-to-market cost (c.f. Sect. 2.1). To this end, we devise an evaluation methodology combining a certain degree of optimization and exploration goals, which we summarize in the following steps:

1. Define a representative set of LSTM-based network structures based on numerous real-world applications and spanning a considerable range of computational demands (e.g., input size, units, layers).
2. Define a representative set of tools and devices, i.e., FPGA, GPU, and CPU, which provide today indicative acceleration results in major AI applications and cover a wide range of processing nodes in the edge–cloud continuum.
3. Propose and explore parallelization techniques as well as high level tools for end-to-end AI model deployment.
4. Prune the search space and implement the proposed designs to derive actual results regarding execution time, power and accuracy.
5. Compare the results and define the most promising implementation approach per LSTM and device, as well as assess the overall acceleration potential for LSTMs in this heterogeneous infrastructure.

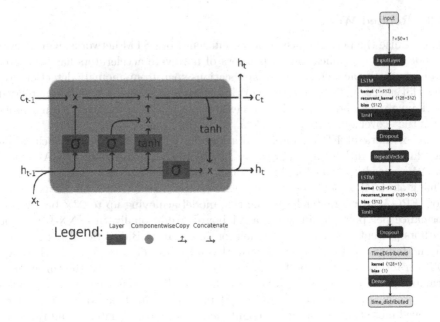

Fig. 1. LSTM illustration. Left: LSTM cell, Right: an LSTM topology used in the experiments

3.1 Representative LSTM Networks

As a first step of our methodology, we consider a wide range of LSTM topologies as part of our DSE analysis. Each LSTM, depending on its parameters can have different acceleration potential on a particular hardware device. Several of the models used were built as an encoder-decoder structure targeting network intrusion detection systems. The main parameters of the encoder and decoder layers are the number of *units*, that can differ between the layers of the same LSTM, the number of the input and output *features*, and the number of *timesteps*, which is the same for all the layers of a LSTM. Both encoder and decoder layers have the same core logic usually coupled with a bias vector and an activation function afterwards. Each layer iterates $\times timestep$ times and cannot be parallelized due to data dependencies as the results of each time step are used in the next iteration and are also stored for the next layer. Along with the encoder-decoder LSTMs we investigated the use of encoder-decoder LSTMs with dense (or fully connected) layer at the end and also with single-cell LSTM models (targeting stock or temperature prediction applications). In Fig. 1, at the left side we illustrate the core functions inside a typical LSTM cell. On the right of the figure, we show the architecture of one of the LSTMs used in the evaluation. Last, we summarize each LSTM and its characteristics in Table 1. All models were developed with Tensorflow Deep Learning library.

Table 1. LSTM characteristics

Model	LSTM characteristics				Model characteristics	
	Layers	Timesteps	Features	Type	Params	Flops
LSTM-Autoenc-1	4	2	60	Autoencoder	0.07M	0.3M
LSTM-Autoenc-2	4	2	80	Autoencoder	0.1M	0.54M
LSTM-Autoenc-3	4	2	159	Autoencoder	0.5M	2.10M
LSTM-Autoenc-4	4	2	230	Autoencoder	1.1M	4.4M
LSTM-Autoenc-5	2	50	1	Autoencoder	0.2M	20M
LSTM-Dense	2	30	1	LSTM+Dense	0.2M	12.3M
LSTM-cell	2	50	5	LSTM-cell	0.9M	62.7M

3.2 Acceleration Devices and Programming

We leveraged an heterogeneous hardware architecture as the range of applications especially in the cloud and edge domains is diverse and each device behaves differently depending on the scenario and application. AI@EDGE will employ a development model for AI accelerators based on High Level Synthesis for FPGAs (using Xilinx Vitis) and CUDA programming model for GPUs. It's worth mentioning that the acceleration flow for GPUs was done through ONNX format for model serialization (wherever supported). A similar tool from Xilinx, called Vitis AI, was also tested but the support for LSTMs is limited. FPGAs and GPUs as hardware platforms will be attached directly in servers or shared over the network in edge workloads. In Table 2 we list several popular devices from FPGA and GPU domains both for edge (top) and cloud (bottom) domains but we selected only some representatives from each domain that can cover the spectrum of deployment scenarios.

Table 2. List of FPGA and GPU devices in edge (top) and cloud (bottom)

Device	Device specifications					
	Type	Memory	DSP	LUT	BRAM	CUDA cores
MPSOC ZCU102	FPGA	4 Gb	2520	600K	32Mb	-
MPSOC ZCU104 [✓]	FPGA	2 Gb	1728	504K	38 Mb	-
Jetson Nano [✓]	GPU	4 Gb	-	-	-	128
Jetson Xavier NX [✓]	GPU	8 Gb	-	-	-	384
Jetson Xavier AGX [✓]	GPU	32 Gb	-	-	-	512
Alveo U50	FPGA	8 Gb	6840	1182K	47Mb	-
Alveo U200	FPGA	64 Gb	5952	872K	35Mb	-
Alveo U280 [✓]	FPGA	32 Gb+8 Gb	9024	1304K	72 Mb	-
Nvidia P40 [✓]	GPU	24 Gb	-	-	-	3840
Nvidia A30 [✓]	GPU	24 Gb	-	-	-	3584
Nvidia V100 [✓]	GPU	32 Gb	-	-	-	5120

4   Proposed Designs

4.1   FPGA Acceleration

Our design space exploration, for accelerating a LSTM using FPGAs, started with decreasing the latency of the LSTM kernel for a single input execution. Then, we used multiple kernels to achieve higher throughput. The first decisions during our exploration were based on three characteristics of the LSTM algorithm. Those characteristics are the recursion and the increased number of multiply-accumulate operations required inside each layer (lstm cell) and the way the data are exchanged between the layers of a LSTM. The computationally intensive parts of the LSTM algorithm, in terms of required processing time and number of operations (determined by the number of units and features of the lstm cell), are the calculations of the four activation vectors. Parallelization at those calculations is necessary, especially for a low latency implementation. Next, we present a summary of the considered acceleration techniques.

1. Parallelization at the layer level, where multiple layers would process data in parallel. This parallelization technique could achieve a speed up of maximum the number of layers, but the number of layers of a LSTM is significantly lower than the number of units/features. Disadvantages in this implementation include increased resources, underutilized hardware and extra logic for synchronizing and buffering, thus it was not an ideal choice for acceleration.
2. Parallelization inside each lstm cell at the iteration level, where multiple time steps, for different input data, could be processed in parallel using a systolic array architecture. Some of the disadvantages using this technique were increased resources, less scalable architecture, and an implementation that does not reduces the latency.
3. Parallelization inside each lstm cell at the calculation of the activation vectors. Considering the resources of the targeted FPGA, the developer can choose to process in parallel one or more of the activation vectors and also parallelize each calculation internally.
4. For further decreasing the latency, a fixed-point instead of floating-point architecture can be used. This change reduces the required resources of the kernel, reduce latency and memory transfer overhead.

For our basic architecture (Fig. 2) we implemented four parallel engines, one for each activation vector $(i_t, f_t, \tilde{c}_t, o_t)$ and inside each of those engines we parallelized the multiply-accumulate operations for each row of the matrix with the active vector. To achieve the desirable parallelization the active vector and the weight matrices were partitioned in their entirety and second dimension, respectively. The code at Fig. 3 presents the high level description for parallelizing the multiply-accumulate operations. Each time step is calculated sequentially inside the lstm cell. To create the required layers of the LSTM system we execute sequentially the same lstm cell with the necessary changes in the weight and bias values. Last, the weights and biases are read from the DDR memories at the beginning of a new layer execution, before the first iteration, using wide memory interfaces.

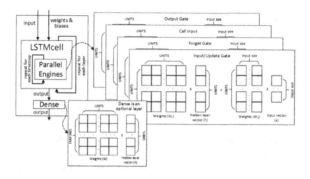

Fig. 2. Proposed LSTM architecture

```
dtype row_vector_mul(const dtype w[MX_COL],dtype h_x[MX_COL],dtype b){
    dtype2 res, first, temp;
    LOOP_MATRIX:for(int j=0; j<MX_COL; j++) {
        #pragma HLS LOOP_TRIPCOUNT min=mn_col max=mx_col
        #pragma HLS PIPELINE II = 1
        first = (j==0) ? (dtype2)b : res;
        temp = (dtype2)w[j] * (dtype2)h_x[j];
        res = first + temp;
    }
    return res;
}
void gate(dtype W[MX_UNITS][MX_COL],dtype b[MX_UNITS],
          dtype h_x[MX_COL],dtype out[MX_UNITS],int type){
    #pragma HLS ARRAY_PARTITION variable=W dim=2 complete
    #pragma HLS ARRAY_PARTITION variable=b complete
    #pragma HLS ARRAY_PARTITION variable=h_x complete
    dtype2 act_fun[MX_UNITS];
    LOOP_ROW:for(int i=0; i<MX_UNITS; ++i) {
        #pragma HLS LOOP_TRIPCOUNT min=mn_un max=mx_un
        #pragma HLS PIPELINE II = 1
        act_fun[i]=row_vector_mul(W[i],h_x,b[i]);
        if(type==0) out[i] = sigmoid(act_fun[i]);
        else        out[i] = tanh(act_fun[i]);
    }
}
```

Fig. 3. Parallelization of the activation vector

4.2   GPU Acceleration

In the case of GPUs, we follow a more straightforward approach. We employ
the PyTorch [13] open source machine learning framework, as the backbone
for developing our DNN models. To leverage the GPU capabilities, we utilize
PyTorch's optimized, built-in libraries that allow the effortless execution over
the accelerator. Moreover, we utilize PyTorch's Just-In-Time (JIT) compiler and
ONNX format for model serialization (wherever possible). With these runtimes
on Nvidia GPUs we ensured a more optimal way to deploy our LSTM models
into the GPU architecture which provided a significant increase in the speed of
the network inference compared with the default Pytorch implementation.

5   Evaluation

5.1   Resources and Accuracy

In general, we focused on resource re-use techniques for the FPGA design where we could do fine grain optimizations. For example, we are re-using the same LSTM cell for each subsequent layer of each LSTM model. During the first call of the kernel all the weights and biases are transmitted to the DDR memories of the FPGA device and are read from the kernel whenever is necessary.

Table 3 presents the resource utilization percentages and latency considering implementations on the Alveo U280 device, for the network intrusion detection system. The floating-point (FP) implementation requires 39.07% of the LUTs, 26.66% of the registers and more than half of the DSP blocks (57.55%) and can process a single input in 3.38 ms. Utilizing the same kernel with a floating-point interface but moving to an internal 16 bit fixed-point arithmetic we can achieve a reduction of 28% in LUTs, 22% in registers and 45% in DSP blocks and reduce the execution time to 2.14 ms. Simply by changing the interface to fixed-point we can further reduce the execution time to 1.20 ms, with almost the same resource utilization. Moving to 8, 6, and 4 fractional bits the accuracy drops to 95.17%, 94.19%, and 86.41% respectively. Thus, 16 bit arithmetic provides a good trade off between accuracy, resources and performance. Also, 512-bit memory interface was used between kernels and DDR memory, allowing us to reduce even further the latency of the LSTM kernels. Last, towards our DSE we utilized multiple engines (row 4) for the LSTM kernel parallelizing further the process and multiple LSTMs (rows 5–7) for increasing throughput.

Table 3. Resource utilization and latency for LSTM-Autoenc-5 model on U280 FPGA

	LUT	LUT Mem	REG	BRAM	DSP	Time
U280 resources	1304K	590K	2607K	2016	9024	
FP	39.07%	25.25%	26.66%	2.26%	57.55%	3.38 ms
16 bit fixed(float I/O)	10.63%	11.88%	4.36%	1.10%	12.18%	2.14 ms
16 bit fixed (fixed I/O, 512 bit interface)	15.05%	6.38%	6.49%	2.26%	16.44%	0.72 ms
16 bit fixed (fixed I/O, 512 bit interface, x2 engines)	21.47%	6.43%	9.08%	2.43%	28.60%	0.66 ms
16 bit fixed(fixed I/O, 512 bit interface, 32 batch input, 4x LSTMs)	35.49%	24.66%	12.74%	3.58%	52.99%	7.31/32 = 0.23 ms
16 bit fixed(fixed I/O, 512 bit interface, 64 batch input, 4x LSTMs)	35.49%	24.66%	12.74%	3.58%	52.99%	14.04/64 = 0.22 ms
16 bit fixed(fixed I/O, 512 bit interface, 128 batch input, 4x LSTMs)	35.49%	24.66%	12.74%	3.58%	52.99%	27.37/128 = 0.21 ms

Next, Table 4 presents the resource utilization percentages and the execution times considering implementations for the embedded ZCU104 FPGA device.

This is a smaller device from the cloud Alveo U280 in terms of resources, hence the parallelization factor is diminished and the design space is a bit narrower. Due to the decreased parallelization the floating point kernel required 443.61 ms for processing one input. However, the fixed-point implementations could fit in the device with the same parallelization we had for the alveo U280 board.

Table 4. Resource utilization and latency for LSTM-Autoenc-5 model on MPSoC ZCU104 FPGA device

	LUT	LUT Mem	REG	BRAM	DSP	Time
ZCU104 resources	230K	102K	460K	624	1728	
FP (parallelization/8)	73.26%	70.49%	35.20%	18.97%	28.47%	443.61 ms
16 bit fixed (float I/O)	37.50%	36.57%	14.63%	17.67%	63.60%	1.41 ms
16 bit fixed (fixed I/O)	56.21%	69.03%	22.71%	17.67%	63.60%	1.18 ms

Our second case study is a group of LSTMs for anomaly detection targeting LSTM-Autoenc-1 through LSTM-Autoenc-4. The LSTMs for the anomaly detection use a 4-layer model with two encoders and two decoders. All models require 2 time steps to complete the process as also presented in Table 1. Table 5 presents the resource utilization percentages and the execution times considering floating-point and fixed-point implementations for the LSTM kernels 1, 2, 3 and 4, targeting the U280 Alveo FPGA device. As expected, the resources and the achievable execution times are increasing moving from models with lower number of units and features to model with higher number of units and features. Moving to a 16 bit fixed-point implementation we can see again a significant drop in the resource requirements across all kernels and in latency.

Table 5. Resource utilization and latency for LSTM autoencoders on U280 device

	LUT	LUT Mem	REG	BRAM	DSP	Time
U280 resources	1304K	590K	2607K	2016	9024	
FP LSTM-Autoenc-1	15.20%	4.66%	11.10%	2.09%	24.92%	0.44 ms
FP LSTM-Autoenc-2	19.55%	6.16%	14.34%	2.09%	32.90%	0.55 ms
FP LSTM-Autoenc-3	40.81%	21.31%	26.03%	0.28%	64.39%	2.31 ms
FP LSTM-Autoenc-4*	40.23%	52.21%	9.86%	46.42%	12.47%	4.35 ms
16 bit fixed LSTM-Autoenc-1	3.89%	2.08%	1.55%	1.10%	5.35%	0.37 ms
16 bit fixed LSTM-Autoenc-2	5.31%	2.70%	2.21%	2.09%	6.95%	0.51 ms
16 bit fixed LSTM-Autoenc-3	9.74%	9.68%	1.99%	0.28%	13.12%	1.20 ms
16 bit fixed LSTM-Autoenc-4	17.69%	18.38%	2.60%	0.28%	18.79%	2.40 ms

Table 6 presents the resource utilization percentages and the execution time considering a floating- and a fixed-point implementation of LSTM-Autoenc-1, targeting the MPSoC ZCU104 FPGA device. As we can see even in a device that can be in a far-edge node we can have the same expected execution times as for those in a near-edge node.

Table 6. Resource utilization and latency for LSTM Autoencoder on ZCU104 FPGA

	LUT	LUT Mem	REG	BRAM	DSP	Time
ZCU104 resources	230K	102K	460K	624	1728	
FP LSTM-Autoenc-1	60.28%	24.76%	35.10%	16.38%	68.23%	0.61 ms
Fixed LSTM-Autoenc-1	20.30%	12.04%	7.41%	7.41%	27.95%	0.44 ms

5.2   Inference Performance on Edge and Cloud GPUs

We evaluate the inference time of a single-element batch with respect to the examined LSTM models defined in Table 1 and the various GPU accelerators considered, as presented in Table 2. Table 7 shows the respective results, which also reveal three major insights.

Table 7. Inference time for various LSTM models in each GPU device

Model	GPU Devices					
	Nano	NX	AGX	V100	P40	A30
LSTM-Autoenc-1	1.16 ms	0.74 ms	0.80 ms	0.22 ms	0.48 ms	0.25 ms
LSTM-Autoenc-2	1.18 ms	0.69 ms	0.80 ms	0.23 ms	0.49 ms	0.26 ms
LSTM-Autoenc-3	1.20 ms	0.72 ms	0.92 ms	0.27 ms	0.49 ms	0.29 ms
LSTM-Autoenc-4	1.21 ms	0.75 ms	0.93 ms	0.31 ms	0.49 ms	0.33 ms
LSTM-Autoenc-5	8.30 ms	2.61 ms	3.16 ms	0.84 ms	1.59 ms	1.04 ms
LSTM-Dense	5.42 ms	1.69 ms	1.89 ms	0.57 ms	1.05 ms	0.64 ms
LSTM-Cell	8.37 ms	2.42 ms	2.41 ms	0.88 ms	1.62 ms	0.98 ms

First, we observe that scaling the number of input features has minimal impact on performance. Indeed, in the case of the first four (LSTM-Autoenc-1–LSTM-Autoenc-4) examined models, where the number of features scale from 60 up to 230, we notice a negligible degradation in performance, both for Edge and Cloud devices. Second, we see that the number of timesteps is the major performance bottleneck of LSTM-based models. This observation was expected, since as shown in Table 1, models with higher amount of timesteps also reveal a total higher number of FLOPs. However, the imposed performance degradation is not proportional over all the devices. We observe that for less powerful devices, i.e., Jetson Nano and Xavier NX the overhead of adding more timesteps is greater, reaching up to 8× and 4× slower execution respecitvely (LSTM-Autoenc-5 vs

LSTM-Autoenc-4). On the other hand, AGX and Cloud devices are less affected, with an average slowdown of 3×. Last, as expected, there is a significant performance boost between edge and cloud devices, with up to 10× speed-up in certain cases (LSTM-Autoenc-5). This showcases the potential of model offloading from the edge to the cloud for faster execution.

5.3   Acceleration Performance

Towards evaluating the aforementioned LSTM models across several FPGA and GPU devices we summarize the potential of each device in this paragraph. Depending on the scenario of the application and the LSTM model topology the most efficient accelerated kernels will be placed inside broader MEC domain(s) of the "connect-compute" platform of *AI@EDGE*. For example, for the LSTM-Autoencoder-5 the latency on the cloud V100 GPU (0.84 ms) is close to the cloud U280 FPGA (0.66 ms without batch). The latency in a typical server CPU, specifically Intel Silver 4210, it is 18.8 ms thus the achievable acceleration is 22.4×–28.5×. For a larger model (LSTM-Autoencoder-4) the typical latency in this server CPU is 54 ms thus the acceleration becomes 12.4×–174× with the upper value coming from the V100 device. In the same scenarios but for the edge domain, we have the NX GPU and ZCU104 FPGA compared with a typical embedded CPU such as the ARM Cortex-A53. The first aforementioned model has a latency of 30 ms while the second larger model has a latency of 100 ms in ARM A53. The acceleration from the edge hardware platforms becomes 11.5×–25.4× for the first model, with the upper limit achieved from the ZCU104 FPGA, while in the second model we achieved a speed-up 15×–133×. Overall, in small model architectures the FPGA implementation seems more promising while, usually in larger models, GPUs become more efficient.

6   Conclusion

In this work we investigated the acceleration of various LSTM models on multiple hardware platforms. The LSTM models represented real world applications such as network intrusion detection, anomaly detection, stock prediction or temperature forecasting. We covered a wide range of devices spanning from the edge to cloud assuming a flexible deployment method that will become part of the "connect-compute" platform of *AI@EDGE*. Through diverse experimentation and tuning of possible design space tradeoffs we showed that mid- to large-size LSTMs can benefit greatly from HW acceleration, especially at the far-edge deployment (embedded devices). The best results range in 0.3–5 ms latency per execution with acceleration factors in 12×–174×.

Acknowledgements. Work partially supported by H2020 project "AI@EDGE" (g.a. 101015922). The authors would like to thank Stefano Secci et al., from CNAM Paris, for providing LSTM example kernels for anomaly detection apps.

References

1. Bai, J., Lu, F., Zhang, K., et al.: Onnx: open neural network exchange (2019). https://github.com/onnx/onnx
2. Bank, D., Koenigstein, N., Giryes, R.: Autoencoders. CoRR **abs/2003.05991** (2020). https://arxiv.org/abs/2003.05991
3. Chang, A., Martini, B., Culurciello, E.: Recurrent neural networks hardware implementation on FPGA, November 2015
4. Chang, A.X.M., Culurciello, E.: Hardware accelerators for recurrent neural networks on FPGA. In: 2017 IEEE International Symposium on Circuits and Systems (ISCAS), pp. 1–4 (2017). https://doi.org/10.1109/ISCAS.2017.8050816
5. Diamanti, A., Vilchez, J.M.S., Secci, S.: LSTM-based radiography for anomaly detection in softwarized infrastructures. In: 2020 32nd International Teletraffic Congress (ITC 32), pp. 28–36 (2020). https://doi.org/10.1109/ITC3249928.2020.00012
6. Ergen, T., Kozat, S.S.: Unsupervised anomaly detection with LSTM neural networks. IEEE Trans. Neural Netw. Learn. Syst. **31**(8), 3127–3141 (2020). https://doi.org/10.1109/TNNLS.2019.2935975
7. EU: H2020 project AI@EDGE (2022). https://aiatedge.eu/
8. Fowers, J., et al.: A configurable cloud-scale DNN processor for real-time AI. In: 2018 ACM/IEEE 45th Annual International Symposium on Computer Architecture (ISCA), pp. 1–14 (2018). https://doi.org/10.1109/ISCA.2018.00012
9. Homayouni, H., Ghosh, S., Ray, I., Gondalia, S., Duggan, J., Kahn, M.: An autocorrelation-based LSTM-autoencoder for anomaly detection on time-series data, pp. 5068–5077, December 2020. https://doi.org/10.1109/BigData50022.2020.9378192
10. Nvidia: Jetson AGX Xavier Developer Kit (2022). https://developer.nvidia.com/embedded/jetson-agx-xavier-developer-kit
11. Nvidia: NVIDIA CUDA-X (2022)
12. Nvidia: NVIDIA V100 TENSOR CORE GPU (2022). https://www.nvidia.com/en-us/data-center/v100/
13. Paszke, A., et al.: Pytorch: an imperative style, high-performance deep learning library. In: Advances in Neural Information Processing Systems, vol. 32 (2019)
14. Provotar, A., Linder, Y., Veres, M.: Unsupervised anomaly detection in time series using LSTM-based autoencoders, pp. 513–517, December 2019. https://doi.org/10.1109/ATIT49449.2019.9030505
15. Rybalkin, V., Pappalardo, A., Ghaffar, M., Gambardella, G., Wehn, N., Blott, M.: Finn-l: library extensions and design trade-off analysis for variable precision LSTM networks on FPGAs, pp. 89–897, August 2018. https://doi.org/10.1109/FPL.2018.00024
16. Xilinx: Alveo U280 Data Center Accelerator Card (2022). https://www.xilinx.com/products/boards-and-kits/alveo/u280.html
17. Xilinx: Vitis (2022). https://www.xilinx.com/products/design-tools/vitis/vitis-platform.html
18. Xilinx: Vitis AI (2022). https://www.xilinx.com/developer/products/vitis-ai.html
19. Xilinx: Zynq UltraScale+ MPSoC ZCU104 Evaluation Kit (2022). https://www.xilinx.com/products/boards-and-kits/zcu104.html

20. Zhang, X., et al.: H-LSTM: co-designing highly-efficient large LSTM training via exploiting memory-saving and architectural design opportunities. In: 2021 ACM/IEEE 48th Annual International Symposium on Computer Architecture (ISCA), pp. 567–580 (2021)

21. Zheng, B., Vijaykumar, N., Pekhimenko, G.: Echo: compiler-based GPU memory footprint reduction for LSTM RNN training. In: 2020 ACM/IEEE 47th Annual International Symposium on Computer Architecture (ISCA), pp. 1089–1102 (2020)

The TEXTAROSSA Approach to Thermal Control of Future HPC Systems

William Fornaciari[1]([⊠])[iD], Federico Terraneo[1][iD], Giovanni Agosta[1][iD],
Zummo Giuseppe[2], Luca Saraceno[2], Giorgia Lancione[2], Daniele Gregori[3][iD],
and Massimo Celino[4][iD]

[1] Politecnico di Milano, Milan, Italy
{william.fornaciari,federico.terraneo,giovanni.agosta}@polimi.it
[2] In Quattro srl, Roma, Italy
{giuseppe.zummo,luca.saraceno,giorgia.lancione}@in-quattro.com
[3] E4 Computer Engineering SpA, Scandiano, Italy
daniele.gregori@e4company.com
[4] Agenzia nazionale per le nuove tecnologie, l'energia e lo sviluppo economico
sostenibile (ENEA), Roma, Italy
massimo.celino@enea.it
https://heaplab.deib.polimi.it, https://www.in-quattro.com,
https://www.e4company.com/, https://www.enea.it

Abstract. Thermal control is a key aspect of large-scale HPC centers, where a large number of computing elements is employed. Temperature is directly related to both reliability, as excessing heating of components leads to a shorter lifespan and increased fault probability, and power efficiency, since a large fragment of power is used in the cooling system itself. In this paper, we introduce the TEXTAROSSA approach to thermal control, which couples innovative two-phase cooling with multi-level thermal control strategies able to address thermal issues at system and node level.

Keywords: High Performance Computing · 2-phase cooling · Thermal modeling and control

1 Introduction

High Performance Computing is a strategic asset for countries and large companies alike. Such infrastructures are of key importance to support a variety of applications in domains such as oil & gas, finance, and weather forecasting. Recently, emerging domains have been gaining traction, such as bioinformatics, medicine, security and surveillance. These newer applications tend to fall in

This work is supported in part by the EuroHPC JU and the Italian Ministry for Economic Development (MiSE) under GA 956831 "TEXTAROSSA".

the classes of High Performance Data Analytics (HPDA) and High Performance Computing for Artificial Intelligence (HPC-AI). The trend in the design of such infrastructures is more and more exploiting heterogeneous hardware architectures to cope with the request of peak performance and to meet the need of achieving a "Green HPC". This paths have prompted Europe to align its research priorities in HPC along a Strategic Research Agenda (SRA[1]) resulting from wide consultations within the European Technology Platform for HPC (ETP4HPC), the PRACE initiative[2], and the PlanetHPC[3] initiative.

The need to achieve high efficiency while remaining within reasonable power and energy bounds, is extensively discussed in the SRA, focusing also on the main technology challenges posed by these objectives. Such challenging goal can only be addressed with an holistic approach that takes into account multiple factors across the HPC hardware/software stack, including the use of application-specific, extremely efficient hardware accelerators, efficient software management of resources, data and applications, and efficient cooling systems. Together, these components can provide the desired computational power while keeping under control the power consumption of the supercomputer.

1.1 Strategic Goals

TEXTAROSSA aims at contributing to the strategic goals of the EuroHPC Strategic Research and Innovation Agenda [11] and the ETP4HPC Strategic Research Agenda 4 [16], remaining aligned with other European and national initiatives in the context of HPC and computing architectures, including in particular the European Processor Initiative (EPI) and the EuroHPC Pilot projects [4].

Thermal control is a key goal of TEXTAROSSA, together with energy efficiency, performance, and ease of integration of new accelerators based on reconfigurable fabrics. Thermal control is achieved via innovative two-phase cooling technology at node and rack level, fully integrated in an optimized multi-level runtime resource management driven by power, energy, and thermal models fed by on-board sensor data. The aspects related to the development of new IPs, including mixed-precision computing, data compression, security, scheduling and power monitoring go beyond the scope of this work, as they address a wide range of different contributions at software and hardware level, including the integration of electronic design automation tools. We note here that these technologies will be key to opening new usage domains, including High Performance Data Analytics (HPDA) and High Performance Artificial Intelligence (HPC-AI) [3].

Two architecturally different, heterogeneous Integrated Development Vehicles (IDVs) will be developed: IDV-A by ATOS, X86/64 and GPUs, and IDV-E by E4, featuring ARM and FPGA. These IDVs will be used as testbed and workhorse by TEXTAROSSA's developers. The IDVs will be a single-node platform, easy to configure and reconfigure, extensible in terms of components,

---

[1] https://www.etp4hpc.eu/sra.html (last accessed June 2022).

[2] https://prace-ri.eu (last accessed June 2022).

[3] https://cordis.europa.eu/project/id/248749 (last accessed June 2022).

devices, peripherals, flexible in terms of supported SW (OS, utilities, drivers, run-time libraries), instrumented with thermal sensors, electric probes, thermally-induced mechanical stress sensors.

The developers will use the IDVs to test their codes, algorithms, drivers without having the constraints of a large system and having the advantage to be able to test their developments on different components through a very quick reconfiguration process.

1.2   Thermal Control in TEXTAROSSA

Since the advent of dark silicon, computing architecture needs both optimized heat dissipation solutions and run-time thermal control policies to operate reliably and efficiently despite the steady increase in power density and related issues such as hot spots [12]. Thermal control policies in the state of the art include: Linear Quadratic Regulators (LQR) [21]; Model Predictive Control (MPC) [20]; and Event-based control solutions [15].

Through detailed system modeling [17] and a multilevel thermal control strategy TEXTAROSSA aims to overcome the complexity of controlling an HPC platform from node to system level with minimal overhead. As the fastest temperature gradients occur at the silicon active layer, we will use fast event-based control loops [15] acting on DVFS [23] to limit the maximum operating temperature of compute elements. A key differentiating feature of the TEXTAROSSA approach to thermal control is that the inner control loop will in turn interact with higher level control loops operating the two phase cooling infrastructure of the node, which is comparatively slower and has higher overheads but has the capability to increase the heat transfer coefficient on-demand, thus allowing to relieve the need to reduce frequency using DVFS, in turn improving performance. A further supervisory control layer will allow to set the desired temperatures at the rack level based on reliability metrics. Multilevel control allows thus to partition the system level control problem into multiple interacting control loops, each optimized for the specific thermal dynamics to control.

1.3   The TEXTAROSSA Consortium

TEXTAROSSA started in April 2021, and will last for three years. It is supported by joint funding from the European High Performance Computing (EuroHPC) Joint Undertaking and the national governments of Italy, France, Poland, and Spain. The project is led by the Italian national agency for new technologies, energy and the sustainable economic development (ENEA) with technical leadership provided by CINI, an Italian consortium grouping together three leading universities, Politecnico di Milano, Università degli studi di Torino, and Università di Pisa. The three Italian universities are part of the lab of CINI[4], created in 2021, that is grouping together the main academic and research entities

---

[4] https://www.consorzio-cini.it/index.php/it/laboratori-nazionali/hpc-key-technologies-and-tools (last accessed March 2022).

working in the field of high-performance and Exascale computing in Italy. In Quattro, an Italian startup company, provides the innovative 2-phase cooling system described in this paper, while E4 Computer Engineering is in charge of the Integrated Development Vehicle. Fraunhofer (Germany), INRIA (France), ATOS (France), BSC (Spain), PSNC (Poland), INFN (Italy), CNR (Italy), Université de Bordeaux (France), CINECA (Italy) and Universitat Politècnica de Catalunya (UPC) complete the consortium, providing contributions on software, hardware, development platforms, and applications that are outside the scope of this paper. More information on the activities carried out during the execution of TEXTAROSSA can be found in the project website[5].

2   The TEXTAROSSA Platform

TEXTAROSSA leverages an Innovative Integrated Development Vehicles (IDV-E) platform developed by E4 Computer Engineering according to an open architecture model and exploiting a heterogeneous architecture (nodes using ARM64 plus FPGA solutions). The IDV-E platform will implement a multi-node HPC platform, and will allow prototyping and benchmarking all innovations addressed in the following points:

1. *New integrated heterogeneous architecture at node level:* extending the experience of core partners in the European Processor Initiative (development of processor and accelerators IPs, and integrated heterogeneous HPC platforms exploiting both ARM64 and RISC-V cores) to boost the EuroHPC roadmap in terms of energy-efficiency, high-performance and secure HPC services.
2. *High-efficiency cooling system at node and system levels:* innovative and high-efficiency cooling mechanism (based on a two-phase cooling technology) for HPC platforms at node and system levels and power monitoring and controller IP exploiting new models of the thermal behavior and of a multi-level control strategy. The data collected in this project as well as the know-how developed by the partners with respect to the two-phase cooling technology will be representative of the working environment of the EPI-based nodes.
3. *Innovative tools for seamless integration of reconfigurable accelerators:* such tools, targeting the AI/DNN computing paradigm, include compilers, memory hierarchy optimization and runtime systems, scaling over multiple interconnected reconfigurable devices, and SW header-only based on Fast Flow and memory hierarchy optimization in an EPI-like HPC architecture, compiler tools for mixed-precision, all in heterogeneous HPC platform and in future EPI tool chain. Automatic instrumentation of the accelerators with energy/power models to enhance a global (fine grain) power monitoring and control [8,22].

The node designed by E4 will apply the two-phase thermal management solution developed by InQuattro to the most thermal critical components, i.e. the CPUs.

---

[5] https://textarossa.eu (last accessed March 2022).

During the first year of the project the opportunity to apply these components to the accelerators (FPGA) has been evaluated within a co-design approach, and the decision to apply the cooling system also to the FPGA device was made. It was considered that the cooling of the accelerator does not constitute a substantial increase in complexity in terms of mechanical complication such as increase in the number of pipes, increase in heat exchangers, increase of the delivery liquid cooling flow rate.

After a careful evaluation of the possible commercial platforms based on ARM technology, the choice of the system to which to apply the two-phase cooling system fell on the Ampere Mt.Collins 2U system with Ampere Altra Max processor; the main reasons are: (i) it supports a number of PCIe slots providing the possibility of adding FPGA boards (up to 3) and/or other boards if needed, (ii) it has the physical space for adding the cooling system, (iii) it presents a good match between the amount of heat to be removed and the design point of the cooling system developed in the project, (iv) it has an architecture (ARM) compatible with that of the EPI project, (v) the possibility of receiving the system in times compatible with the project (an aspect not taken for granted given the current state of shortage worldwide).

As for the FPGA, the choice fell on the U280 Xilinx Passive Model, it is able to provide significant computing power and the flexibility of memory access via HBM2 or DDR protocol with a maximum consumption of 225W. This device also guarantees the use of the VITIS software stack, widely used in research by the various TEXTAROSSA partners.

The Mt.Collins system integrated in E4 laboratory is shown in Fig. 1. It is a dual socket configuration in a 2U form-factor with Ampere Altra Max Processors, is an excellent fit for Android in the Cloud, AI/ML and HPC usages.

The Ampere Altra Max processor-based Mt.Collins dual socket rack servers provide high performance with industry leading power efficiency per core.

The versatile platform offers 160 PCIe Gen4 lanes for flexible I/O connectivity via PCIe slots and another 16 PCIe Gen4 lanes for OCP 3.0 networking. Mt.Collins supports thirty-two DDR4 3200 MT/s DIMMS with a maximum memory capacity of 8 TB.

It also supports OCP NIC 3.0 connector with multi-host support to capitalize on the mechanical, thermal, manageability, and security benefits.

In addition, Mt. Collins includes one internal M.2 NVMe storage interface for ultra-fast reads/writes, eliminating PCIe switch adapters.

Mt. Collins includes MegaRAC®, BMC, and Aptio®V BIOS support. Key features include dynamic fan control, temperature monitoring, and TPM 2.0 for security. The platform includes two redundant power supplies providing the reliability required for datacenters. BMC includes support for IPMI and Redfish protocols for remote management.

The dimensions are: 33.36 in. (L) x 17.63 in. (W) x 3.425 (H).

Ampere Altra Max processor (based on ARMv.8.2+) offers up to 128 cores operating at a maximum of 3.0 GHz. Each core is single threaded by design with its own 64 kB L1 I-cache, 64 kB L1 D-cache, and a huge 1 MB L2 cache,

Fig. 1. Mt.Collins System from the top, on the left the space for the disks (covered by the metal plate of the case), in the center you can see the two sockets with the memories around, on the right at the top the two power supplies of the system, on the left center a black container for one of the possible accelerator boards.

delivering predictable performance 100% of the time by eliminating the noisy neighbor challenge within each core.

The processor technology is 7 nm FinFET with a TDP of 250 W.

The Ampere Altra Max processor offers high bandwidth and memory capacity of up to 4 TB per socket.

With 128 lanes of PCIe Gen4 per socket with support for 192 PCIe Gen4 lanes in 2P configuration that can be bifurcated down to x4, Ampere Altra Max provides maximum flexibility to interface with off-chip devices, including networking cards up to 200 GbE or more, and storage/NVMe devices.

Ampere Altra Max supports cache coherent connectivity to off-chip accelerators; 64 of the 128 PCIe Gen 4 lanes support Cache Coherent Interconnect for Accelerators (CCIX), that could be used for networking, storage, or accelerator connectivity.

The Ampere Altra Max processor provides extensive enterprise server-class RAS capabilities. Data in memory is protected with advanced ECC in addition to standard DDR4 RAS features. End-to-end data poisoning ensures corrupted data is tagged and any attempt to use it is flagged as an error. The SLC is also ECC protected, and the processor supports background scrubbing of the SLC cache and DRAM to locate and correct single-bit errors.

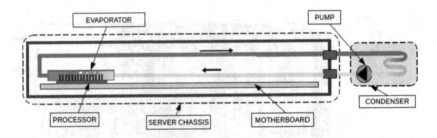

Fig. 2. Two-phase schematic loop in a server configuration.

Currently the system is available at the E4 laboratory ready to be coupled to the two-phase cooling system.

The potential problem we expect is related to the removal of the fans (even partially). The attention point consists in the system checks that may be performed at the BIOS level that could activate safety mechanisms if the checks detect the lack of fans. These mechanisms could interrupt the system startup process.

To overcome this problem, if it occurs, several strategies are possible, i.e. (i) request a BIOS change from the vendor, (ii) replace the fans with resistors, in this case consumption would be constant and it would be possible to subtract them from the total value.

While the possible problem with the BIOS is something that should be taken into account, for the time being we do not envision any roadblock for the development of the implementation of the cooling circuitry.

3   Innovative 2-Phase Cooling

3.1   Technology Description

Thermal control with two-phase cooling is a new technology for the sector of electronics cooling. This technology has been extensively studied and developed for cooling the most critical components in fusion power reactors [6]. Recently, two-phase cooling has been miniaturized matching the small dimensions of electronic components. Compared to classical cooling systems like heat pipes and liquid cooling (single phase forced convection), the new technology is able to remove higher heat fluxes, at lower pumping energy, lower mass of the entire loop, and to maintain the target surface of the electronic component isothermal.

The concept of a two-phase cooling system is quite simple, as shown in Fig. 2.

The technology uses a cold plate, (aluminum or copper), that serves as a heat sink, a direct on chip evaporative heat exchanger. The cold plate is a multi-micro-channels evaporator: a metal plate with micro fins machined on it. The evaporator is placed in direct contact with the processor (CPU or GPU) case whit the aid of a thermal paste in order to obtain stable and low thermal contact resistance. The coolant flows through micro-channels in the evaporator to capture heat from the processor by evaporation processes, and then flows on to a condenser, in which heat is dissipated to the surrounding environment via water or air. The coolant coming out of the condenser travels back through the pump, and the cycle repeats itself. The loop is a hermetically sealed closed system, so the processors and all electronic components are not in direct contact with the fluid. Other important features for two-phase cooling technology are the use of dielectric liquids that eliminates the risk of electric damages caused by an accidental leakage of the coolant, and a virtually zero maintenance that eliminates the requirement of skilled personnel. The mentioned dielectric fluids are non-flammable, non-toxic, perfectly compatible with the environment with extremely low GWP (Global Warming Potential) and Ozone Depletion Potential (ODP).

In Quattro is developing the two-phase cooling system and will integrate it at rack level for data center with liquid thermal transport infrastructure installed, as shown in Fig. 3. The two-phase cooling system will be designed for high density CPU and GPU configurations up to 5 kW per server. All the server cooling systems will be integrated at rack level with a CDU (Coolant Distributor Unit) that will transfer heat to the data center liquid thermal transport infrastructure. Each rack will be able to remove up to 90 kW using water in the liquid transport infrastructure as hot as 45 °C, eliminating the need for expensive and inefficient chillers or cooling towers.

3.2 Advantages and Innovation

Two-phase cooling can be seen as an evolution of the liquid cooling system. Therefore, the main advantages of liquid cooling compared to traditional air cooling are extended to two-phase cooling systems: higher energy efficiency, smaller footprint, lower cooling system total cost of ownership, enhanced server reliability, lower noise, etc. The main difference lies in the use of latent heat (vaporization and condensation) instead of sensible heat, depending on heat capacity, in removing thermal loads from processors. Latent heat is many times higher than thermal capacity of liquids. This allows evaporative cooling technologies to remove heat more efficiently with lower flow rates, and allows the processors to work continuously at top clock speed by removing higher thermal power densities. In particular, lower mass flow rate results in lower electrical energy spent for pumping the fluid in the cooling system with interesting economic and technical advantages.

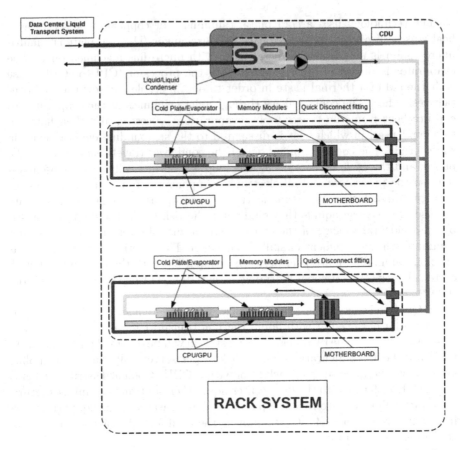

Fig. 3. Two-phase schematic loop in a rack configuration with liquid-to-liquid condensing unit.

4   Thermal Modeling

The use of evaporative cooling systems in HPC environment promises significant compelling advantages, including the possibility to improve computing systems performance thanks to the reduced need for frequency throttling, as well as improved PUE resulting in increased profitability and sustainability through improved energy efficiency. However, evaporative cooling solutions are also significantly more complex to design, and require dedicated control policies for optimal performance.

As a result, thermal simulation has a prominent role for efficient and effective cooling systems [13] and control policy [14] design. The thermal simulation of evaporative cooling systems is also significantly more complex compared to traditional cooling systems, such as air and water cooling, due to the inherent nonlinear phenomena related to evaporation.

Efficient and accurate thermal simulation of evaporative HPC cooling systems is currently an open research challenge that TEXTAROSSA aims to overcome, as well as the integration of evaporative thermal models with state-of-the-art integrated circuit thermal simulators.

4.1   Simulation Approach

The thermal design power (TDP) of HPC computing architectures is steadily increasing, and computer architectures are becoming increasingly heterogeneous. At the same time, a shift to heterogeneous solutions is being observed also in heat dissipation solutions. Traditional air cooling is progressively being replaced with liquid cooling in the server and high end desktop market, and more innovative solutions such as the evaporative cooling we are proposing in TEXTAROSSA are expected to soon become a necessity.

To effectively handle the simulation of heterogeneous heat dissipation solutions, a paradigm shift in the construction of thermal simulators for computer architectures is required. Most existing thermal simulators are in fact monolithic, in that they essentially hardcode the equations describing the physics of the problem and only provided very limited configurability, only in terms of model parameters.

The TEXTAROSSA simulation approach is instead based on co-simulation with domain-specific languages for the modeling and simulation of systems expressed in terms of differential equations. This approach, that we introduced with the design of the 3D-ICE 3.0 thermal simulator [18] also suits the need for efficient co-simulation of chip thermal models, which can be reasonably modeled using only linear differential equations, together with evaporative heat sink models, that conversely require nonlinear differential equations to be modeled.

The transient differential equation solver of 3D-ICE 3.0, unlike monolithic thermal simulators, only simulates the integrated circuit and heat spreader, and provides a co-simulation interface to a seaprate heat sink model, thus allowing arbitrary heat sinks to be simulated without the need to modify and revalidate the core of the thermal simulator. The 3D-ICE 3.0 co-simulation interface adheres to the FMI [1] standard, thus providing access to a vast set of languages and tools [2] for the modeling of heat dissipation solutions.

In TEXTAROSSA, we chose to rely on the Modelica [9] object-oriented modeling language for modeling evaporative cooling loops, and in particular the OpenModelica open source implementation [10]. Work is currently underway in extending the ExternalMedia Modelica library [7] to support co-simulation with 3D-ICE. This library provides access from Modelica models to the CoolProp [5] library for computing the thermodynamic properties of refrigerant fluids used in evaporative cooling systems. After this task is completed, a dedicated library will be developed for the simulation HPC cooling based on evaporative technologies.

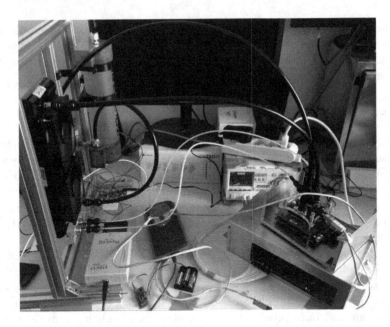

Fig. 4. Experimental setup for the characterization of the prototype evaporative cooling cycle. Thermal test chip platform fitted with evaporator (right), radiator, tank and pump completing the cooling loop (left).

4.2   Experimental Validation

Accurately modeling physical phenomena such as evaporative thermal dissipation calls for experimental data. Some of the thermal phenomena related to evaporation rely on empirical correlations, thus experiments are needed to fine tune correct parameter values.

The availability of high quality experimental data allows to perform validation not only of entire thermal models, but also of individual components that can be later rearranged to simulate a far wider range of heat dissipation solutions than can be reasonably realized for experimentation.

In TEXTAROSSA, we performed thermal experiments with a prototype evaporative cooling loop, collecting data that will be used for model validation. For performing these experiments, we relied on a Thermal Test Chip platform [19] developed at Politecnico di Milano. TTCs are a key part of the TEXTAROSSA stategy for the validation of thermal models, as the direct use of MPSoCs such as processors or GPUs to perform thermal experiments is made extremely difficult by the uncertainty in the power spatial distribution across the silicon die during computational workloads in modern processors, as well as due to the insufficient number of temperature sensors to fully reconstruct the temperature spatial distribution.

The TTC platform that we developed [19], provides a total of 16 heating elements and 16 temperature sensors, arranged as a 4×4 grid, coupled with a

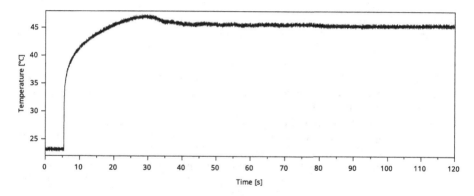

Fig. 5. Temperature of the TTC active silicon layer subject to a 30 W power step. Note the temperature decrease after the initial overshoot when evaporation starts (temperature data averaged from the 4 center temperature sensors).

fast sensing and actuation chain allowing to measure temperatures with a 0.1 °C resolution at up to 1 kHz sample rate, as well as to produce spatial (hot spots) as well as temporal temperature gradients.

Characterization experiments have already been performed with a prototype evaporative cooling cycle developed by INQUATTRO as part of TEXTAROSSA, using the setup of Fig. 4. The prototype cooling cycle uses an air radiator, that will be replaced with a water heat exchanger in a subsequent design iteration. Figure 5 shows a sample of the collected data, a transient test consisting in a 30W uniform power step applied to the TTC, reporting the active silicon temperature averaged from the four center temperature sensors. The figure clearly shows a temperature reduction after the initial transient, indicating the transition from single to two phase cooling.

5   Conclusion

In this paper, we presented the approach towards thermal control adopted in the EuroHPC TEXTAROSSA project. The approach is based on an innovative two-phase cooling system, coupled with thermal monitoring, modeling, and control policies. Initial experiments, performed on a TTC coupled with a prototype two-phase cooling system, show how the temperature can be effectively controlled, leading to a reduction of the working temperature. Future works include larger-scale experimentation on E4's integrated development vehicle, employing more advanced versions of the two-phase cooling system.

References

1. The Functional Mock-up Interface (FMI) standard. https://fmi-standard.org/
2. Tools supporting the Functional Mock-up Interface (FMI) standard. https://fmi-standard.org/tools/

3. Agosta, G., et al.: TEXTAROSSA: Towards EXtreme scale Technologies and Accelerators for euROhpc hw/Sw Supercomputing Applications for exascale. In: 2021 24th Euromicro Conference on Digital System Design (DSD), pp. 286–294. IEEE (2021)

4. Aldinucci, M., et al.: The Italian research on hpc key technologies across eurohpc. In: Proceedings of the 18th ACM International Conference on Computing Frontiers, pp. 178–184 (2021)

5. Bell, I.H., Wronski, J., Quoilin, S., Lemort, V.: Pure and pseudo-pure fluid thermophysical property evaluation and the open-source thermophysical property library coolprop. Ind. Eng. Chem. Res. **53**(6), 2498–2508 (2014)

6. Boyd, R.: Subcooled Flow Boiling Critical Heat Flux (CHF) and Its Application to Fusion Energy Components-Part I. A Review of Fundamentals of CHF and related Data Base. Fusion Technol. **7**, 7–31 (1985)

7. Casella, F., Richter, C.: ExternalMedia: A Library for Easy Re-Use of External Fluid Property Code in Modelica. In: Modelica, March 3rd-4th, 2008

8. Cremona, L., Fornaciari, W., Zoni, D.: Automatic identification and hardware implementation of a resource-constrained power model for embedded systems. Sustain. Comput. Informatics Syst. **29**(Part), 100467 (2021). https://doi.org/10.1016/j.suscom.2020.100467

9. Fritzson, P.: Principles of Object-Oriented Modeling and Simulation with Modelica 2.1. John Wiley & Sons, London, UK (2004)

10. Fritzson, P., et al.: The OpenModelica integrated environment for modeling, simulation, and model-based development. MIC—Model. Identif. Control **41**(4), 241–295 (2020). https://doi.org/10.4173/mic.2020.4.1

11. Group, E.R.I.A.: Strategic research and innovation agenda 2019. Technical report (2019)

12. Hankin, A., et al.: HotGauge: a methodology for characterizing advanced hotspots in modern and next generation processors. In: 2021 IEEE International Symposium on Workload Characterization (IISWC), pp. 163–175 (2021)

13. Iranfar, A., et al.: Thermal characterization of next-generation workloads on heterogeneous MPSoCs. In: Proceedings of 2017 SAMOS, vol. 2018, pp. 286–291, January 2018

14. Leva, A., et al.: Event-based power/performance-aware thermal management for high-density microprocessors. IEEE Trans. Control Syst. Technol. **26**(2), 535–550 (2018)

15. Leva, A., et al.: Event-based power/performance-aware thermal management for high-density microprocessors. IEEE Trans. Control Syst. Technol. **26**(2), 535–550 (2018). https://doi.org/10.1109/TCST.2017.2675841

16. Malms, M., et al.: Etp4hpc's strategic research agenda for high-performance computing in europe 4. Technical report (2020)

17. Papadopoulos, A., et al

18. Terraneo, F., et al.: 3d-ice 3.0: Efficient nonlinear mpsoc thermal simulation with pluggable heat sink models. IEEE Trans. Comput.-Aided Design Integrated Circuits Syst. **41**(4), 1062–1075 (2022). https://doi.org/10.1109/TCAD.2021.3074613

19. Terraneo, F., Leva, A., Fornaciari, W.: An open-hardware platform for MPSoC thermal modeling. In: Embedded Computer Systems: Architectures, Modeling, and Simulation, pp. 184–196 (2019)

20. Zanini, F., Atienza, D., Benini, L., De Micheli, G.: Thermal-aware system-level modeling and management for multi-processor systems-on-chip. In: 2011 IEEE International Symposium of Circuits and Systems (ISCAS), pp. 2481–2484 (2011)

21. Zanini, F., Atienza, D., De Micheli, G.: A control theory approach for thermal balancing of mpsoc. In: Proceedings of 2009 ASP-DAC, pp. 37–42. IEEE Press (2009)
22. Zoni, D., Cremona, L., Fornaciari, W.: Design of side-channel-resistant power monitors. IEEE Trans. Comput. Aided Des. Integr. Circuits Syst. **41**(5), 1249–1263 (2022). https://doi.org/10.1109/TCAD.2021.3088781
23. Zoni, D., Fornaciari, W.: Modeling DVFS and power-gating actuators for cycle-accurate noc-based simulators. ACM J. Emerg. Technol. Comput. Syst. **12**(3), 27:1–27:24 (2015). https://doi.org/10.1145/2751561

Correction to: Obfuscating the Hierarchy of a Digital IP

Giorgi Basiashvili⬥, Zain Ul Abideen$^{(\boxtimes)}$⬥,
and Samuel Pagliarini⬥

Correction to:
Chapter "Obfuscating the Hierarchy of a Digital IP"
in: A. Orailoglu et al. (Eds.): *Embedded Computer Systems:*
Architectures, Modeling, and Simulation, **LNCS 13511,**
https://doi.org/10.1007/978-3-031-15074-6_19

In an older version of this paper, there was a spelling error in the name of the corresponding author. It was incorrectly written as "Zail Ul Abideen". This has been corrected to "Zain Ul Abideen".

The updated version of this chapter can be found at
https://doi.org/10.1007/978-3-031-15074-6_19

A. Orailoglu et al. (Eds.): SAMOS 2022, LNCS 13511, p. C1, 2022.
https://doi.org/10.1007/978-3-031-15074-6_28

Author Index

Printed in the United States
by Baker & Taylor Publisher Services